The Political Thought
of Max Weber

The political thought of Max Weber

In quest of statesmanship

Ilse Dronberger

JOHANNES GUTENBERG–UNIVERSITAT MAINZ
Auslands- und Dolmetscherinstitut

APPLETON - CENTURY - CROFTS
EDUCATIONAL DIVISION
MEREDITH CORPORATION   New York

To my children

PETER, KLAUS, and INGE

PREFACE

This book attempts to understand and analyze the political thought of Max Weber; to isolate and discuss the principal motives which can be discerned, and to explore certain German social, economic, and political trends between 1885 and 1920 which sustained these motives.

Considering the monumental content of Weber's work and the conceptual method of its approach, it is not possible to deal authoritatively with the entire range of his thought. In fact, writing on Max Weber's scholarly achievements reminds one of "shooting at a moving target." Meanwhile, a whole new literature about him has arisen and is constantly increasing. For these reasons Weber's work can no longer be considered only in terms of meeting him on his own ground during his own life-time. Instead, a reconsideration seems required of Weberian formulations in the light of all that is new, especially in political thought, since the demise of the Weimar Republic and the rise and fall of the Third Reich. This book will concentrate on the practical aspects of Max Weber's political philosophy. Therefore it should be noted again that this study examines only a segment of Weber's work, and yet it has proved necessary, because of the volume of Weber's own writings and the publications inspired by them, to re-evaluate continually one's own thoughts about his work and its influence.

It is, of course, understood that an inquiry into Weber's contribution to an understanding of the socio-political and economic aspects of human existence cannot be made unless some attention is also paid to his philosophy of history as well as to his sociology of religion.

I have incurred many debts in completing this work. I have been grateful for the generous assistance of the Department of Political Science of the University of Chicago and the Rockefeller Foundation.

Their fellowships and grants made it possible for me to begin work on this study several years ago, and to visit Max Weber's widow, Marianne Weber, in her home in Heidelberg. I should also like to acknowledge my debt to the late Professor Herman Finer for his guidance and criticism of the manuscript.

I am also indebted to the Harper Library at the University of Chicago, the Library of Congress, the British Museum and the Library at the London School of Economics and Political Science for their co-operation in providing some of the more fugitive references.

I especially appreciated the assistance and guidance offered by the *Bundesarchiv* in Koblenz and the *Max Weber Institut* of the Ludwig-Maximilians-Universitaet in Munich. I wish to record here my indebtedness and profound gratitude to the director of the *Max Weber Institut*, Professor Johannes Winckelmann, at whose invitation this author was able to visit the *Institut*.

Above all, my thanks go to Robert Presthus of York University for a close reading of several drafts of the manuscript for which the final responsibility is mine. It is difficult for me to express the true measure of my appreciation for his helpfulness and understanding and for having been godfather to this book from the beginning. Whatever acknowledgement I record here is only too inadequate a recognition for the counsel he has so generously provided.

I am grateful to all those who have helped in various ways. They are not, however, responsible for the opinions expressed or for any errors of form or content.

To Joy D. Griffith I owe thanks for a loyal performance; her connection with this book far exceeds the typing of the several drafts of the manuscript. She helped with much of the organization of widely scattered material both in the United States and in Germany.

Finally I want to thank my husband, Warren Dronberger, for his infinite patience during the years the book was in process. His knowledge of German has helped me with many translation problems and his constructive criticism and suggestions concerning bibliographical source material were indispensable.

                                                                                    I.D.

Ingelheim/Rhein

FOREWORD

The masterful scholarly achievements of Max Weber, German lawyer-economist-sociologist (1864–1920), have been widely reported in America. His analysis of social class, the symbiotic relation between protestantism and capitalism, and the pervasive rationalization of capitalism which culminated in modern bureaucracy and widespread personal disenchantment have had a decisive impact upon our scholarship. Among American thinkers, perhaps only Thorstein Veblen conducted his inquiries on an equally grand scale of analysis. Weber's contributions included a re-definition of social class which provided a conceptual alternative to a vulgarized Marxism. While he defined class in essentially economic terms, his concept of status groups helped explain the persistence of other bases of social propinquity, including style of life, honor, and *noblesse oblige*. This resistance to the claims of property as the basis for social rank Weber found to have existed since Hellenic times, as well as among exotic societies such as India and China.

A similarly broad compass informed Weber's analysis of the influence of such protestant religious values as personal responsibility and hard work upon the development of capitalism. Here, in perhaps the most influential of his writings, he reached down through history and out into space, including America, to arm his hypothesis. Witnessing a baptismal ritual in the Midwest, he inquired as to why a certain individual was submitting to the rite. The reply became part of *The Protestant Ethic and the Spirit of Capitalism:* "Because he wants to open a bank . . . once being baptised he will get the patronage of the whole region and he will outcompete everybody."

Weber's work on bureaucracy has been perhaps the most significant influence upon the study of large-scale organizations in the United

States. In tracing the historical development of bureaucracy, Weber revealed the evolution of social thought which inspired this "most efficient" of all instruments for handling huge undertakings. The transformation of authority from its earliest "patriarchal" and "feudal" forms to its modern legitimation by "legal-rational" norms was a central theme. It seems that Weber regarded Western European history as a process unfolding from such earlier stages to the later, bureaucratic, era in which the rationalization of means inspired by industrial capitalism resulted in a common apparatus for organizing collective effort. Meanwhile, Weber made a useful methodological contribution, his "ideal type" bureaucratic model, an analytical fiction which provided a benchmark against which organizations in the real world might be set and better understood.

Although contemporary scholarship has moved beyond them, such contributions remain impregnable. It is with certain other aspects of Weber's life and work, largely neglected in North America, that Ilse Dronberger's careful study deals. These concern the nature and consequences of Weber's political philosophy and his political career, which included a vital role as sometime self-appointed adviser and critic of Kaiser Wilhelm, his ministers and his generals, member of the German delegation at Versailles, and codesigner of the Weimar Constitution. Her analysis goes beyond Weber's economic and sociological contributions to the somewhat less happy subject of his political orientations, both theoretical and pragmatic. This is the context in which her work must be judged and in which it makes its contribution. Enriched by not sufficiently explored or unused German sources and extended personal interviews with Marianne Weber, as well as the author's intimate knowledge of the country, the book adds a new dimension to our knowledge and understanding of the work of a great social scientist.

It is of course a truism that intellectual formulations are in the deepest sense shaped by the historical context in which they occur. Yet appreciations of Max Weber's work have sometimes seemed to regard his thought as surmounting time and space. Moreover, as often occurs with men of such compelling genius, there has been an understandable tendency to idealize his personal values, to neglect any untoward consequences of his intellectual and political philosophy. Indeed, Weber's biographers have sometimes portrayed him as a democrat and "liberal," in the twentieth-century meaning of that elusive characterization.* Perhaps this judgment reflects the fact that previous analyses

---

* Among others, H. H. Gerth and C. W. Mills, *From Max Weber: Essays in Sociology*, (New York: Oxford University Press, 1946); Reinhard Bendix, *Max Weber: An Intellectual Portrait*, (Garden City, New York: Doubleday and Co., 1960); Karl Loewenstein, *Max Weber's Staatspolitische Auffassungen in der Sicht unserer Zeit* (Frankfort and Bonn: Atheneum, 1965). As F. S. Hughes says in a review of Bendix's work, "At his hands Weber's nationalism and his emphasis on

While judgments such as these cannot and should not be permitted to impair Weber's vast scholarly contribution, perhaps they are a necessary counterpoise to previous works which sometimes tend to neglect the historical context and the authoritarian cast of his political philosophy, as well as the undemocratic implications of some of his policies. Professor Dronberger does not, however, nor should anyone, leap to the unwarranted conclusion that Weber was in any way responsible for the Nazi cataclysm. In a work of impressive scholarship, she has enlarged the terms of reference within which the life and thought and influence of a great scholar can be understood.

Robert Presthus

CONTENTS

The Political Thought
of Max Weber

"... *for we that must be thought the causers of all events, good or bad, have reason also to take some leisure in part to foresee them.*"

Thucydides, *The Peloponnesian War.*

I

Max Weber:
A political biography

Max Weber began his career as a jurist and historian and became a sociologist in the course of his encounter with "the ghost of Karl Marx." In his monumental work, *Wirtschaft und Gesellschaft* (Economy and Society),[1] he reexamined Marx's thesis. Never suggesting the exclusive prevalence of spiritual forces as opposed to the material conditions of existence, Weber maintained that modern capitalism arose from specific historical circumstances rather than from inexorable historical necessity. Allowing for the existence of potential freedom in the spheres of human activity, Weber noted that opportunities for taking advantage of this freedom may present themselves at certain transitional periods in history, when institutional values and beliefs may be in question. Weber's conception of this idea of freedom in history envisaged the realization of the capacity of men to mold their own destiny. His *Wissenschaftslehre* was designed to define its contents in a manner which strengthened the formal quality of theoretical results. In Weber's essay, "Die Objektivitaet Sozialwissenschaftlicher und Sozialpolitischer Erkenntnis" (1904), not "the material relations between things, but the intellectual connection between problems" is the criterion by which the fields of the sciences are defined.[2] According to Weber's definition, the function of social science is to provide "concepts and judgments which are not empirical reality, nor pictures of it; but which allows us to arrange it intellectually in a valid manner."[3]

As a sociologist and historian Max Weber's interest focused upon the question of the survival of human freedom and responsibility in confrontation with the irreversible trend toward rationalization in Western civilization. Weber advanced the thesis of potential counter-forces arising from "charisma" which may destroy decadent institutions, replacing them with those more attuned to current needs. Charisma, a

1

revolutionary force itself, becomes when confronted with nationalism, another dynamic historical force, engaged in a dialectical process. Rationalism, based upon the pragmatic and scientific intelligence of man, encounters the spontaneous rise of irrational charisma; whether constructive or destructive, charismatic leaders may effect changes in historical development during given periods of crisis in history.[4] The crux of the historical process is to be found in the permanent interaction between institutional behavior and charisma. His conviction of the fundamental significance of the "capitalist spirit"; of the rational technological development combined with the rational economic ethos of society existing under a system of industrial capitalism; and his concern that the modern rational "professional" fails to see meaning in his work, provided the impetus for Weber's studies in the sociology of religion.[5] He was particularly concerned with the religious origins of the modern work ethos and the attendant pressures of secularization and nullification of meaning inherent in that ethos. The modern "professional," accordingly, fails to perceive meaning in his work; the levelling effect of the commonplace in everyday life causes modern man to remain oblivious to the confusion implicit in the coexistence of antagonistic, mutually exclusive values; above all, he does not want to become aware of his own evasiveness in response to the challenge, compelling him to choose between these colliding values.[6]

In comparing the political qualities typical of German citizens of his time with those characterizing their forebears living in medieval times, Weber found the former blessed with no more political acumen than their Athenian counterparts possessed in comparison with those who fought the battle of Marathon.[7]

Recording the fate of the Athenians, Thucydides had written:

. . . as the power of Hellas grew, and the acquisition of wealth became more an object, the revenue of the states increasing, tyrannies were by their means established almost everywhere. . . . Wars by land there were none, none at least by which power was acquired; we have the usual border contests, but of distant expeditions with conquest for object we hear nothing among the Hellenes. There was no union of subject cities round a great state. . . . But at last a time came when the tyrants of Athens and the far older tyrannies of the rest of Hellas were, with the exception of those in Sicily, once and for all put down by Lacedaemon. Not many years after the deposition of the tyrants, the battle of Marathon was fought between the Medes and the Athenians. Ten years afterwards, the barbarian returned with the armada for the subjugation of Hellas. In the face of this great danger, the command of the confederate Hellenes was assumed by the Lacedaemonians in virtue of their superior power; and the Athenians, having made up their minds to abandon their city, broke up their homes, threw themselves into their ships, and became a naval people. . . .[8]

Explaining the impact of the war upon the Athenians, Thucydides continues:

> The Median War, the greatest achievement of past times, yet found a speedy decision in two actions by sea and two by land. The Peloponnesian War was prolonged to an immense length, and, long as it was, it was short without parallel for the misfortunes that it brought upon Hellas. Never had so many cities been taken and laid desolate, here by the barbarians, here by the parties contending (the old inhabitants being sometimes removed to make room for others): never was there so much banishing and blood-shedding. . . .
>
> All this came upon them with the late war, which was begun by the Athenians by the dissolution of the thirty years' truce made after the conquest of Euboea. . . . The real cause I consider to be the one which was formally most kept out of sight. The growth of the power of Athens, and the alarm which this inspired in Lacedaemon, made war inevitable.[9]

Similarly, the growth of German power and the alarm this inspired in the rest of Europe, foreshadowed an inevitable conflict: Max Weber foresaw the coming of the Great War, fearing it to be inevitable but hoping it could be avoided. His historical investigations, guided by a strong interest in the potential directions in which currently new personality types might be developed in contemporary Germany, led him to examine the historical conditions of ancient and medieval autonomy of the cities and the freedom of the citizens. Unless the interests of the patrician families were found to collide seriously with those of the citizens, the former "monopolizing the council seats could everywhere maintain . . . closure easily. . . . But once such conflicts emerged, or once the self-esteem of the outs, based on growing wealth and education, and their economic dispensability for administrative work had risen to a point where they could no longer tolerate the idea of being excluded from power, the makings of new revolutions were at hand. Their agents were once again sworn burgher unions. . . ."[10]

As a political analyst Weber was constantly engaged in applying his extraordinary perceptiveness and knowledge of history to the interpretation of contemporary German politics. Thus Weber, who spent the major part of his teaching career at the Universities of Heidelberg and Munich, must be viewed in the light of two distinct considerations. The first derives from his creative insight as a scholar and from the stimulus to further research which his work provides. The other is based upon the dynamism of recent history, which demands renewed investigation of the meaning and significance of his political thought for contemporary politics.

Although American scholars have analyzed Weber's sociological writings extensively, systematic treatment of his political thought has been relatively neglected. "Systematic" is intended to include the attempt to translate into a consistent framework the whole of reality, attitudes, values, and ultimate goals within the realm of human experience. Perhaps the revival of interest following World War II among German scholars in Weber's political writings is due to the fact that both his work and his personality seem to offer a partial explanation for some of the events in recent German history. As Arnold Hauser states, "The past is the product of the present, because for one, each new historical situation is the outcome of a different line of development and so has its own preconditions, and for another because the various effects bring to light different features and different aspects of the same historic events." [11]

Max Weber's life and thought were dominated, to a far greater extent than commonly assumed, by his interest in German politics. He was born on April 21, in Erfurt, Thuringia, 1864, sixteen years after the defeat of liberal nationalism in the revolution of 1848, and six years before the unification of Germany under Bismarck and Prussia, auspices quite different from those the liberals of 1848 had envisaged. By the time Max Weber, the oldest son of a well-to-do-German family, became interested in German politics, there were few in the academic world who did not embrace the nationalistic and imperialistic objectives framed by the ruling circles of the newly founded German Empire at the conclusion of the Franco-Prussian War in 1871.

Many students of political science and sociology have become familiar with Max Weber, the scholar, but have had less acquaintance with either his political writings or with his political activities. Lack of familiarity with Weber's political writings, as well as with the political context of Weber's time in Germany, renders his image frequently as a timeless genius who stands above and outside the mainstream of history. Max Weber was too towering a figure to be classified as a typical representative of a so-called typically German culture, but he was nevertheless deeply affected by prior and contemporary German intellectual and political currents. Bismarck drew considerable support for his *Realpolitik* from German intellectuals who defended his foreign policy as well as the more pronounced imperialism of his successors. Max Weber's own writings reflect a new vitality and depth of analysis; yet, basing his views on the results of his scholarly research, Weber struggled heroically

to keep in double harness objective, i.e., value-free, acts of cognition and acts of will inspired by value judgments. High among Weber's values—not in spite of, but because of, his profound humanism—was the power of the state: 'Of what use is the best social policy if the Cossacks are coming?' Nationalism and an expansionist foreign policy, moreover, were to serve as the ideals to revive the German bourgeoisie who, in Weber's opinion, were in a spiritual decline and therefore incapable of the national leadership only they could supply.[12]

At the domestic level, Weber perceived "the coils of bureaucracy" as the main threat, and he therefore explored all possible avenues offering opportunities for securing "freedom of action for charismatic leaders." [13]

Germany's political history provided much of the context of his academic work, in which frequently his political philosophy was fused with the practical aspects of German politics. The nation's fate under Kaiser Wilhelm II during and after Bismarck's chancellorship; the inadequate leadership qualifications of Bismarck's successors; the events leading up to the World War I; the war itself; the provisions of the peace treaty; and finally the birth of the Weimar Republic—all became part of his daily existence.

Weber always worked toward a scientific understanding of economic, political, cultural, and social institutions in a specific historical context, from which future trends of development might be derived. As a political theorist, he sought to comprehend political reality by bringing propositions of general validity to bear upon it. Yet, the heart of Weber's concern remained the political life and future of his own country. His largely self-imposed abstention from political office did not weaken his intense political passion.

. . . Max Weber perceived the fatal weakness of an empire whose policy-makers were appointed officials rather than statesmen with the gift of leadership—for leaders emerge only from political struggle, which was non-existent. Weber deplored the frightening superiority of Western statesmen over the German bureaucrats. The system was to blame.[14]

The contemporary thrust of his political writings necessarily confronted him with two limitations: one was to be found in his German origin as it conditioned, at least in part, his perspective; the other oriented him toward a given public by whom he wanted to be heard. Despite this "personal equation," Weber never yielded to the temptation of sacrificing his moral commitment as a scholar to truth as he saw it, exchanging it for public office. Instead, he remained faithful to the task he had set for himself, to interpret historical processes and political events to his countrymen, telling them, the authorities as well as the man in the street, the unpopular truths as he saw them.

Considering the emasculation of German liberalism by Bismarck, the fall of Bismarck, and the fateful compromise between the anachronistically overpowerful landed interests and heavy industry, Max Weber's political writings were inevitably disturbing because they deliberately punctured his contemporaries' neat assumptions concerning the true state of the nation in Wilhelmine Germany with which he was so profoundly dissatisfied. The tenor of his analysis did not provide them with the reassurance that might have been comfortingly echoed in governmental circles or within the leadership and the rank and file of the political parties. It would be misleading to employ his writings as partial evidence to explain the speed and ease with which national socialism captured the imagination of many Germans; nevertheless, they demonstrate some of the afflictions that beset Germany in Weber's lifetime such as Pan-Germanism, the greed of eastern landowners, the pervasive economic disequilibrium, and the social stresses and strains in a state that had outgrown its political framework. Through Weber's journalistic contributions and his private correspondence especially, familiarity may be gained with the militarist and anti-militarist tendencies within the German nation and its political parties. The great merit of his publicistic writings rests in his successful merging of the events leading up to and during World War I with a profoundly exhaustive analysis of German political institutions of his time—all by means of an account of historical events and the roles played by the Kaiser, the chancellor, other influential public figures, the military, the bureaucracy, groups with vested interests, and political parties. How far Weber was handicapped during and immediately after the war by the fact that in the former period, the German government had not released all available information and in the latter that some particularly relevant documents might still have remained confiscated either by the German government or retained in foreign custody is difficult to determine. However, it is certain that he would have benefited from certain sources unknown to him at the time, such as the papers of Count Westarp who played a leading role in Parliament in 1918 as the almost undisputed leader of the conservative faction in Parliament and a fanatic opponent of social democracy. Kurt Riezler's memoirs might have been of prime import for Weber in his evaluation of the role of Chancellor Bethmann-Hollweg during the fateful period of prewar diplomacy and World War I, when he served as secretary to the chancellor.

Weber recognized that much of social life rests on foundations of essentially nonrational moral or religious qualities: "It was also Weber who predicted that there will be a reaction to the rationalism of the nineteenth century." [15] Frequently he spoke out as if from a great distance and as the political mentor of his nation; yet his journalistic contributions reveal the depth of his involvement; in his scholarly political writings it is this tension between attempted detachment and partisan involvement that caught Weber, the scholar and political analyst, in an irreducible dilemma.

Still, Max Weber effectively exercised his capacity for smashing idols as a merciless critic of trite phraseology and, above all, as a foe of mediocrity. The architectonic sweep of his political philosophy reflects his struggle against the destructive forces of political emotionalism. He opposed the creative spirit of responsible human rationality to the destructive forces and the dehumanizing process of rationalization and mechanization. He regarded the political sphere as subject to the same principle as all other aspects of Western civilization, namely the derivation of human freedom from the self-determination of human reason.[16]

His position as a political writer was that of a German liberal who combined in himself strong nationalism, individual freedom, and a faith in private property which sought to establish a common ground with social democracy. His closest political associate was Friedrich Naumann, whose political bent of mind also bore certain characteristics typical of the turn of the century. They differed, however, in both content and method, in several respects: "Where Weber was an acutely analytical rationalist seeking to make room for the irrational forces necessary in public life without giving way to them, Naumann was a popularizing, idealistic, emotional preacher seeking to reconcile social irreconcilables by a sheer effort of will. This attitude is best epitomized in the title of his book *Democracy and Empire,* in which he tried, in the age of William II, to bring home to the emperor the social tradition and responsibility of his dynasty, and to the workers the necessity, in their own interest, of espousing the cause of nationalism." [17]

Still, avoiding both the Scylla of utopian idealism and the Charybdis of nihilist realism, Naumann tried to be a realistic liberal. He failed in this attempt partly because of the very nature of his aspiration. Since political realism demands that politics must deal with facts, it also requires that it should not fight power relationships and processes from the standpoint of idealism. Naumann, while lacking in political realism, sought to evolve a higher synthesis by positing a "social empire" which "nevertheless represents . . . the biggest single step ever taken in the name of German Protestantism away from its traditionally condescending attitude toward the working class. Naumann was determined not merely to alleviate their material situation but to admit them as full members of society—partly because of his genuine sympathy with them, partly because he was conscious of the failure of the most recent attempt, that of Adolf Stoecker, to propagate 'conservative socialism' in the name of Christianity." [18] Naumann's type of "Christian socialism" was consonant with German political developments because in Germany "executive power was never weakened as much as in the United States, and in Germany important features of welfare were part of the picture as early as the 1880's." [19] Adolph Stoecker, an anti-Semitic Protestant pastor at court and Adolph Wagner, professor of political economy at the University of Berlin, had founded the "Christian Social Workmen's

Party," which was antagonistic to both bourgeois liberalism and proletarian Marxism, both of which they viewed as "inspired and dominated
by Jews." [20]

Four years Max Weber's senior (1860–1919), born in Stoermthal,
Saxony, Naumann was a Protestant theologian and a publicist. In practical politics he had had little success; the experiment of his *National-
Sozialer Verein*, founded in 1896, miscarried in 1903. His *Democracy
and Empire*, published in 1900, and both his periodical magazines,
Die Hilfe and *Die Zeit*, espoused a combination of monarchical, national
and imperialistic thought with liberal, parliamentary, and social concerns. He served as a member of the Reichstag from 1907 to 1912 and
1913 to 1918. He was as critical as Weber of William II; his patriotism
and imperialism as well as Weber's influence upon his views were
strongly reflected in his well-circulated book, *Mitteleuropa*, published
in 1915. Here he exhorted Germany to assume a role of leadership
appropriate to its status as a great Central European empire. Prior to
his death in 1919, he was among the founders of the Democratic party
which Weber was to join; he also was a member of the Weimar National
Assembly. Naumann's prewar National Socialist party stood for

national socialism and democracy on the one side, army and navy enthusiasm
on the other. Eugen Richter made fun of his socialistic imperialism, but it
made no difference to them. . . . At the end of 1907 he finally reached the
Reichstag. His hour had come at last, so it seemed. Now he could get busy
in great style, and the nation, the world of culture would listen to his words
. . . slowly a glass wall was built around him. The 'slave uprising' began. He
might talk all he pleased on party days, he could let himself be applauded
by enthusiastic audiences elsewhere, but in the Reichstag he was frozen out.
Here reigned *minores dii arteriosclerosis*—and new blood was not desired.[21]

The social and political climate of Naumann's and Weber's time and
their own situation are perhaps made more intelligible by the following
illustration:

One can . . . understand why Social Democrats were excluded from the
officer's corps, for their party was dedicated to a republican form of government. . . . Only a Conservative was considered really *kaisertreu*. . . . Catholic
officers were acceptable even though they generally considered themselves
Centrists; and a National Liberal scion of a Rhenish industrial or mercantile
family could at least expect toleration. But a Progressive was beyond the
pale. This was true of reserve officers as of those on active service. The
Hamburg attorney, Carl Petersen, was a member of one of the most respectable student corporations, his family had once provided Hamburg with a
mayor, and he was later to be mayor himself. Nevertheless, on two separate
occasions Petersen was called before the local military commandant and
required to justify the fact that he had sheltered Friedrich Naumann in his
house.[22]

Another illustration may serve as a catalyst explaining Weber's reputed leftist sympathies within the context of the age in which he lived and the associations he had with persons significant to him, such as Naumann. Thus when another mayor of Hamburg introduced his son-in-law to the emperor, referred to him also as a member of the Reichstag, the Kaiser inquired about the son-in-law's party affiliation. Upon being told that he was a National Liberal, the Kaiser's retort was: "Well, that's acceptable—but only just." [23]

Actually, the post-Bismarckian, semi-absolutist government continued Bismarck's line of thinking, a line to which Max Weber also subscribed, namely, that the desirable goal was the conduct of a "well-reasoned, unified, and steady policy beyond the reach of party prejudices and party fluctuations, a policy needed by a country located in the center of Europe and surrounded by many dangers." [24] In reality, however, as Weber brilliantly demonstrated, "William II's ideas were forever vacillating, and the various agencies of the German government, the foreign office, the navy department, and the army, conducted contradictory foreign policies. Each of these policies, though in varying degrees, rested on flimsy premises, since none of them took into consideration the over-all potentialities of German foreign policy." [25] Nevertheless, with the exception of the Social Democratic party, which in 1912 obtained 35 percent of the vote, the vast majority of the German people underwrote Germany's foreign policy, although class differences accounted for variations in the degree of popularity with which the population viewed the various measures. However, when the shift away from Bismarck's "continental" politics to *Weltpolitik* occurred, the German bourgeoisie eagerly endorsed it: "The large and prosperous German middle classes from the big industrialist to the storekeeper and from the high bureaucrat to the university professor and school teacher were the chief believers in this new version of German *Realpolitik,* so completely bare of the realism of Bismarck, whom they worshipped, and so empty of European *Kultur,* of which the German middle classes claimed to be the true guardians." [26]

Thus Max Weber's outlook was largely shaped by the milieu into which he was born. Although he was highly critical of the fact that the political and social system had been eminently unproductive of political leadership from the ranks of the bourgeoisie, he also felt the working classes were not yet adequate to the task of ruling the country. Weber strongly urged the enactment of legislation to bring about social reform and greater social justice. He joined the *Kathedersozialisten* (Academic Socialists), a group of economists who advocated state-sponsored social reform. They sought to continue Bismarck's work of augmenting the power of the state, thereby retaining the political *status quo.* Transcending his thinking, however, they injected the prin-

ciple of economic nationalism into their own program. Their political
influence was considerable, partly because of the scholarly reputation
of the group. Under the leadership of Gustav Schmoller the Academic
Socialists in 1873 founded the *Verein fuer Sozialpolitik*. Most of the
members of the *Verein* were nationalists, monarchists, and protectionists,
adhering to the historical school of economic thought, which looked
to the state as the protector of the national welfare. Gustav Schmoller
(1838–1917), professor of economics in Halle, Strassburg, and Berlin,
was generally regarded as the leader of the "younger" generation
historical school. This group abandoned the preoccupation with theory
to which the older school subscribed in favor of the practical aspects
of economics. Economics now became only a part of the study of
society, with economic motivations being only one of many forces
impinging upon human action. Schmoller charged that the older historical school, including Wilhelm Roscher (1817–1894) and Karl Knies
(1821–1898), both professors whose lectures Max Weber attended, had
been guilty of developing theories on the basis of insufficient historical
evidence. Schmoller himself favored state socialism, opposing it to
both economic liberalism and social democracy as he defended the
concept of a social monarchy. Schmoller did not question the existence
of the class struggle, and in fact, acknowledged its inevitability. Schmoller, moreover accepted Marx's dictum that legal institutions set up by
the upper classes tended to favor their interests, a fact which in itself
caused both class abuse and the domination by one class of other
classes within the state. The state's role was therefore one of arbitration
between classes, protecting the weaker from the stronger, a function
reserved for every state in its own interest. The state and its bureaucracy were to maintain a neutral attitude toward class struggle and party
strife and were to be backed in this endeavor by an informed public
opinion. Schmoller viewed the state as "the finest ethical institution for
the education of the human race," and in his presidential address to the
association, exhorted the emperor and the bureaucracy to recognize
their role as "the most natural representatives of the state idea, the
only neutral elements in the social class war," who should inaugurate a
sweeping legislative program of social reform.[27]

The similarities of interpretation between the historical school and the
Marxists were striking, and the *Kathedersozialisten,* 'Socialists of the Chair,'
as the members of the *Verein* were called, took great pains to differentiate
themselves by denouncing both Marx's theory of surplus value (the theory
of the exploitation of labour which was so crucial in giving to Marxism its
revolutionary character) and working-class internationalism. Yet certain like-
nesses persisted: Schmoller even agreed with Marx as to the inevitability of
socialism, though he saw its triumph as a consequence of an alliance between

socialism and the German 'bureaucratic and military monarchy,' rather than by revolutionary action of an international proletariat.[28]

While Schmoller did not speak in defense of capitalism, he regarded it as a stage in historical evolution. Concerning the latter, Fritz Stern comments: "Stage schemes in economic history were devised mostly by members of the German historical school of economists who attempted to substitute, as it were, historical generalization for economic theory. Most scholars are now agreed that such an attempt failed even in the hands of Schmoller." [29] The efforts of the *Verein* were directed toward the achievement of evolution rather than revolution in anticipation of the succeeding historical stage to guard against the possibility of "foreign domination or military dictatorship which were inherent in revolution. Revolution Schmoller regarded as 'always the most precarious of all games of chance'." [30] Not least because he agreed with Schmoller's view of revolution, Max Weber became engaged in the study of agricultural workers which he conducted for the *Verein fuer Sozialpolitik* in 1892. Here he employed the national interest as the single most important criterion for making political judgments. The rise of socialism, the anti-socialist law introduced by Bismarck in 1878 having just been revoked in 1890, frightened the German middle classes. Weber's allegiance to his own class and his persuasion that the working class was not yet ready to take over the reins of government impelled him to speak out accordingly before his colleagues in the *Verein* without, however, succumbing to the proverbial fear characterizing the bourgeoisie in terms of its image of the proletariat. At the same time, Weber did not consider it inimical to his own class interests to challenge their lack of conciliatory efforts toward the working classes.

Joseph Schumpeter (1883–1950) wished he "could induce the reader to peruse the short history of that unique organization (the *Verein fuer Sozialpolitik*) that was so characteristic of what Imperial Germany really was. . . ." [31] The short history to which Schumpeter referred, written by the long-time secretary of the *Verein*, Franz Boese, (*Geschichte des Vereins fuer Sozialpolitik*, Berlin, 1933), describes the outlook of the "socialists of the chair" as follows:

Whatever we may think of the scientific achievements of the professors who organized themselves into the *Verein fuer Sozialpolitik* and whose work often lacked scientific refinement, they were aglow with a genuine ardor for social reform and entirely successful in spreading it. They resolutely faced bourgeois displeasure not only in framing individual measures of practical reform but also in propagandizing the spirit of reform. Like the Fabians, they deprecated class war and revolution. But, also like the Fabians, they knew where they were going—they knew and did not mind that socialism loomed at the end of their way. Of course, the state socialism they envisaged was national and conservative. But it was neither a fake nor utopian.[32]

Needless to say, Max Weber did not agree with the socialist inclinations of his colleagues, although he concurred with much of Schumpeter's analysis. Referring to the *Sozialistengesetz,* designed to forbid activities in which socialists may engage, Schumpeter says:

The fatal mistake was really Bismarck's. . . . Through an unfortunate combination of circumstances, it so happened that this vitiated the whole course of subsequent events. For the one thing those exile-shaped men could not stand was militarism and the ideology of military glory. And the one thing which the monarchy—otherwise in sympathy with a large part of what reasonable socialists considered as immediately practical aims—could not stand was sneers at the army and at the glories of 1870. More than anything else, this was for both what defined the enemy as distinguished from the mere opponent. Add Marxian phraseology—however obviously academic—at the party conventions on the one hand and the aforesaid blustering on the other and you have the picture." [33]

Max Weber's activities in the *Verein fuer Sozialpolitik* first afforded him an opportunity of combining his theoretical research with practical politics, and making contact with various leaders in both the academic and political spheres. His work for the *Verein* went far in spelling out the connection between his scholarship and his politics. Weber's whole life, in fact, was marked by a pervasive conflict between a thrust toward personal involvement in a career of a practical politician and a commitment to the life of the scholar. The dilemma presented by the necessity of this choice remained a very real one for him almost to the end of his life.

His work for the *Verein* first afforded him a thorough grasp of the social and political problems of his time. His awareness and criticism of certain aspects of Bismarck's legacy, of the German bourgeoisie's excessive deference to the Kaiser and the aristocracy, and of the political parties generally actually originated in this period. Weber had spent his early life under Bismarck's rule. His father, autocratic as a person, was politically a right-wing liberal. While still a student Weber absorbed much of the political atmosphere of his parental home, although he was later to break with his father's national liberalism. Having dispensed with his father's supportive attitude toward Bismarck's anti-socialist stand, Weber, however, adopted the latter's nationalist position. His inaugural lecture at the University of Freiburg in 1895 represented probably the clearest statement of his belief in both Bismarck's *Realpolitik* and in imperialism.

While Weber remained constant in his nationalism, it nevertheless became increasingly modified by a sympathetic understanding of the problems of the working classes and an increasing readiness to work with them politically; therefore, he was especially critical of Bismarck's social policies including insurance against sickness, accidents and old age, but withholding representation from able-bodied workers. Since the structure of the mass army was based upon the principle of comradeship, Weber felt the same rights and privileges should apply in civilian life. It is difficult to tell whether Weber's social conscience stemmed partly from the Christian and socially conscious outlook of his mother or whether the spirit of comradeship which he had cherished during his military training had left an imprint upon him, conditioning his social attitudes in favor of the common man.

Reconciling the depth of his capacity for intensely human compassion with the type of industrial practices upon which capitalism was based and which he underwrote as essential for the maintenance of the national power state presented him with some difficulty. His sociopolitical outlook was thus conditioned by two discrete conditions: the influence of early associations in his home with his father and his uncle, Hermann Baumgarten, the historian, as well as the age and country in which lived, led him to embrace nationalism and imperialism; the other condition, derived its influence from his mother, reflected in an increasing concern for social justice.

When Weber was only 29, he delivered his first address before the *Verein* in which he dealt with the conflict between German and Polish interests in East Prussia. He focused upon the conflict of nationalities in the Prussian provinces which until the eighteenth century had been part of Poland and which still had a high proportion of Polish-speaking residents. His research findings concerning the social conditions of farm laborers in the East Elbian parts of Germany, entitled "Die Verhaeltnisse der Landarbeiter im Ostelbischen Deutschland," and "Entwicklungstendenzen in der Lage der ostelbischen Landarbeiter"[34] were followed by other articles on the subject, all published between 1892–1895.[35]

The vital assumption upon which the *Verein fuer Sozialpolitik* rested was that contemporary social problems could be solved by cooperation among rationally oriented and progressive civil servants, scholars, and business and industrial leaders. Moral considerations could be infused sufficiently into economic policies to encourage a positive problem-solving approach, drawing upon the knowledge of experts in their respective fields, to whatever problems might arise out of conditions of modern industrial capitalism. The objective was to achieve consensus through compromise among various conflicting interests, thereby ameliorating class antagonisms. It was hoped that ideological contrasts and extremist views could thus be held to a minimum, although this was to prove illusory.

At the meetings of the *Verein,* Weber clashed with both the socialists over his interpretation of the workers' discontent in the rural areas of eastern Germany and with his more conservatively inclined colleagues. Weber first investigated the relations between Germans and Poles while the conciliatory policy of the Prussian administration towards its Polish subjects was in progress. During the latter part of his administration, Bismarck had begun to inaugurate a planned program of colonization involving German farmers of the eastern provinces, as well as closing the German border to migratory labor from Poland, a move which Weber endorsed. After 1890, however, Bismarck's policy was dropped by his successor. Weber considered this change in policy a betrayal of Germany's vital national interest in favŏr of preservation of the class interest of the Junkers. The latter in fact welcomed the influx of cheap labor from across the German-Polish border and ignored the consequences which, in Weber's judgment, involved jeopardizing the standard of living of indigenous German workers.

In Weber's view, the German farm workers were concerned more with upward mobility than with a change in labor relations or acquisition of land (which, to Weber, was a manifestation of their cultural superiority). Previously, whatever ambitions the workers might have had to raise their status had been restricted to employment based upon an annual contract, thus curbing their demands for greater economic advancement and social status. Pointing out the difference between the expectations of the Social Democrats and the East German agricultural workers, Weber stressed that in the latter case, the incidence of individual striving for success was evident, whereas urban labor, largely represented by the Social Democrats, was opting for "nominal collectivism." [36] Thus the chief concern of the farm workers was the creation of conditions conducive to individual success. Consequently, a rising level of expectations directed toward higher wages and improved working conditions became manifest among German farm labor. The contrast between their demands and the wage scale applicable to foreign labor essentially priced the German farm workers out of the labor market competition with the migratory workers from Poland and Russia.

Weber significantly regarded the individualism of the German workers as a psychologically based preference for freedom, thus relegating economic matters to a secondary level:

It is pointless to argue about such elementary movements, which give expression to the tremendous and purely psychological magic of 'freedom.' In good measure this is a grand illusion, but, after all, man and so also the farm laborers do not live 'by bread alone.' The efforts and aspirations of the farm laborers make just this evident to us, that the 'bread and butter question' is of secondary importance. [37]

These studies of agricultural labor (to be discussed later in more detail) were of the utmost importance because they marked Max

Weber's first public act as a politically engaged man who also remained prominent as a social scientist and a political analyst. His subsequent political writings derived their impetus from the above-mentioned research, serving as a foundation for his political interests and analyses from the 1890's until the end of his life. His profound analysis of the conditions of rural East Elbian labor, which he linked with a critical discussion of contemporary Germany, is still relevant to the present as it was to the meeting of the *Verein fuer Sozialpolitik* in 1893. Weber noted that although he was speaking to colleagues who were considerably older than he, his words seemed to suggest a certain resigned attitude. This attitude, he said, was based upon the realization that the generation to which he belonged would have to confront problems quite different from those which the older generation faced. Weber was profoundly conscious of the "heavy curse" with which the younger generation was saddled. Hence it could no longer afford the "activism" and "naive enthusiasm" that characterized the older generation. Alluding to the then current cleavages among German political parties, Weber stated that today appeals to a sense of national unity which obtained previously do not elicit the same response:

Tremendous illusions were necessary to create the German empire, but now that the honeymoon of unification is over these illusions are gone and we cannot re-create them artificially. . . . If today an enemy appeared at the eastern border and threatened us with military power, there is no doubt that the nation would rally to the colors to defend the frontiers of the country. But when we undertake the peaceful defense of German nationality on the eastern border we encounter several mutually conflicting interest groups. As we look around for allies, we find that this defense will run counter to the interests of the large landed proprietors. It must be undertaken against the instincts of large portions of the population who lean towards Manchester liberalism and free trade, and who see (in governmental measures to protect the East German peasantry) a dangerous precedent that may be extended to other fields. And as we finally consider the proletariat—well, the time is still far away when we can feel free to join the urban proletariat in the effort to solve social problems. . . .[38]

Weber's early writings in many respects reflect the temper of the age in which he lived. With monarchial, national, and even imperialistic thought championing the moral autonomy of the national power state went a concern for social and liberal aims. A successful foreign policy was predicated on progressive social policy at home. Joining subsequently with the rest of the nation in its enthusiasm in August 1914, he never doubted the fact of Germany's historical mission. On the contrary, to maintain and extend it must ever be the objective; that alone could vindicate the mission and the war itself. Protection of her national

security had to involve protection of Germany's borders adjoining
Eastern and Western countries, even if this threatened the national
sovereignty of the other states. To this dictum Weber adhered in his
discussion of "war aims" in 1915 in his correspondence with the editor
of the *Frankfurter Zeitung*. Opposing German annexationist aims,
Weber's own aims would have threatened the sovereignty of Belgium,
Poland, and Luxemburg at the very least. As J. P. Mayer correctly
notes:

. . . . it is worthwhile to examine this 'no annexation policy' a little more
closely: Weber is for Polish and Baltic 'autonomous' national States in the
east: 'with the right for us to build and garrison fortresses (north of Warsaw),
also to build strategic railways; the same conditions for Austria south of
Warsaw. Apart from that: customs' union with Poland, Lithuania, and Latvia,
otherwise full autonomy (sic'). No German settlement policy outside our
frontiers.' . . . With regard to the west, Max Weber proposes permanent
military occupation of Luxembourg; occupation for a period of twenty years
of Liège and Namur until Belgium fortifies and defends Ostend and her
southern frontier. 'Nothing else (in Europe). Only the military indispensable,
no 'annexations.' It is open to doubt whether Weber's war aims were *de
facto* much different as compared with the war aims of the *Alldeutsche*. More
subtle they certainly were. Weber still firmly believed in the conception of
the state as power-State, a conviction to which he adhered to his death.
Germany, the German people, is *his* supreme law? [39]

His above-mentioned address to the convention of the *Verein* had foreshadowed, as early as 1893, the subsequent articulation of these political
ideas, incorporated in his inaugural address at the University of Freiburg two years later which focused upon *raison d'état* rather than on
humanitarian or international ideals.[40]

Weber's political philosophy was thus dominated simultaneously
by both paradoxical and pessimistic views concerning the future: "Karl
Jaspers saw him as a new type of man who had the poise to hold
together in synthesis the tremendous tensions of his own self as well
as the contradictions of external public life without resorting to illusions.
Every day that Weber 'wasted for things political' instead of 'objectifying himself' seemed a pitiful loss to Jaspers. . . ."[41]

J. P. Mayer speaks rightly of the "tragic character of his moral
stature," [42] saying that Weber's paradox does not characterize him alone;
it also marked the fate and destiny of Germany. In his studies in
ancient Judaism, Weber himself was struck by certain similarities
characterizing both the history of ancient Jewry and contemporary
Germany. In his study of the prophets he was cognizant of their
"irregular and compulsive psychic states," identifying more especially
with Jeremiah.[43] It appears that ". . . this was perhaps the only way

Weber was capable of 'directly revealing himself' and in which he 'could communicate his own self-image. . . .'" In his portrayal of the "'prophets of disaster and doom,' Weber illuminated his own personal and public experiences." [44]

As noted earlier, Weber's social and political commentary on the reasons for the diminishing German population among the East Elbian farm workers, especially those living on the large estates, had stirred up a great deal of controversy among his fellow members of the *Verein*. To compensate for their losses, the big estate owners sought to employ migratory workers, mostly "Russian" Poles who were supposed to leave again for Russia at the end of the season; nevertheless, each year, many of them stayed in Germany. Finding cultural and living standards superior among Germans as compared to the Poles, Weber explained that the former were unable to compete successfully with the latter. As the large estates underwent industrialization, the German farm workers increasingly experienced proletarianization. On the other hand, traditional social and economic relations no longer existed between the owners and their workers because of the change from a patriarchical to a capitalistic system. German workers generally welcomed this change, in Weber's view, despite their less favorable economic status, because of the greater political freedom which favored their release from the soil until they felt free to leave the homestead altogether. As mentioned before, not only did the Junkers not discourage their departure, but on the contrary, were quite willing to encourage it. Having increasingly employed foreign labor, and finding it not only less costly but also easier to get along with, they were only too willing to continue this practice and to do without German labor altogether.

Such views stamped Weber as a left-wing sympathizer at the convention. Yet, Weber was not motivated by philanthropic ideas. He was primarily concerned with enrolling the working classes' support of German foreign policy. Thus domestic social policy must aim at giving the workers a greater share of self-determination and at educating them politically so that they might exercize political responsibility: Gustav Schmoller in his capacity as head of the *Verein* wrote Lujo Brentano a letter of thanks for having prevented Weber from drawing attention to the internal division within the *Verein* by publishing an article about the latter. What did get published, a rather general account of both Alfred's and Max Weber's charges against bureaucracy, caused considerable stir among the general public.[45]

That Weber should be regarded as politically "left" seems paradoxical. Perhaps this characterization reflects mainly his recognition that both social fabric and policy could strongly affect individual morale. In the main, however, Weber's views were "conservative," especially in an economic context. Throughout his life Weber engaged in a dialogue with the ghost of Karl Marx, and S. M. Miller's point is well taken when he says: "The Weberian stress on bureaucracy and its development in industrial society was partly an effort to show that alienation, the other side of rationalization, was not exclusively a product of capitalism but could be brought about in many different kinds of societies, including socialist ones." [46] Thus in 1909 at a meeting in Vienna, when someone suggested that municipal employees' remuneration might compare favorably with that granted by private enterprise, Alfred Weber took issue with the speaker by questioning the transfer of the means of transportation from the hands of private ownership as a socially desirable measure. Max Weber defended his brother's position by emphatically protesting against the growing trend toward public planning for state and municipal socialization. Reporting on the Vienna meeting of the *Verein* in 1909, Albert Salomon writes: "Because he saw that it was impossible to hold back the development of increased technical rationalization, he always felt it incumbent upon him to point out with warning the significance of every new step in the direction of further intensive organization of society." [47]

Weber stated his own position as follows: "This passion for bureaucratization . . . is a desperate one. . . . We are in the midst of a development in which the world will come to know of nothing further than such systematized individuals. The central problem, therefore, is not how we can more greatly further and hasten this process but rather what we have to set up against this machinery to keep a portion of humanity free from this parcelling of the soul and from this supremacy of ideals of bureaucratic life." [48]

The tensions issuing from this meeting in 1909 were to have consequences extending beyond the lifetime of the members of the *Verein*. The meeting initiated an airing of views on the social scientist's responsibility to both individuals and to society; the characteristics distinguishing the natural from the social sciences; and the social scientist's role in the sphere of values. Weber had first stated his own position on values most clearly in the first section of the statement on editorial policy of the *Archiv fuer Sozialwissenschaft und Sozialpolitik* in 1904. This statement is available in English translation, entitled: "Objectivity in Social Science and Social Policy." [49] The social sciences, in Weber's view, are "strictly empirical sciences," which are "the least fitted to presume to save the individual the difficulty of making a choice. . . . It can never be the task of an empirical science to provide binding norms and ideals from which directives for immediate practical activity can be derived." [50]

At a later meeting, not long before World War I, in Düsseldorf in January 1914, a dispute broke out over the apparently most controversial question at issue, namely the status of values in the social sciences. At Schmoller's request, no minutes of this meeting were recorded so as to protect the association, and perhaps even science itself, from criticism from the press and the general public. Since the proceedings of this meeting were not publicized, relatively few concrete facts are known. However, it is clear that the participants engaged in turbulent discussions. Earlier in 1905, Weber had caused quite a storm at a meeting of the *Verein;* in his view, all socio-political systems must be assessed in terms of the types of human beings they are likely to produce. Hence he criticized prewar political and social institutions for vitiating both the rise of political leaders and the chances for

free and autonomous individuals of independent opinions. His bitter struggle against a legal administration which protected strike-breakers was prompted not by economic motives or particular sympathies but by a belief that such decisions trampled upon the sense of honor of the workers and desecrated their human rights and feelings. A state which, in the case of its army, fostered the cultivation of the spirit of camaraderie and honor, would be unable to tolerate such a situation.[51]

Having spoken out in this vein on the subject of industrial relations as applied in large-scale enterprises, he then went on to enlarge upon the relationship between cartels and the state. In this address he spoke out against the blindness of the government which caused it to engage in a policy of suppression of the Social Democrats. Weber had consistently defended any efforts aimed at the social and cultural emancipation of the working classes:

He admired the proletarian movement so long as it possessed the strength to feel conscious of itself as a cultural movement. The way of radical opposition . . . he considered dangerous and foolish. . . . He considered the class of peasants, petty bourgeoisie, officials and every increasing number of administrative workers as a great bar to a proletarian revolution in Central Europe.[52]

Salomon lucidly explains the reasons for Weber's rejection of socialism which was based upon his scientific insight, which "showed him what would be the economic costs, in the sense of technical rationalization, of an ethically oriented socialism and how, therefore, the desired goals of higher standard of living and higher cultural levels might easily become converted into the opposite. Even these facts would perhaps not have prevented him from becoming a socialist had he only recognized the binding character of its ideals. This, however, he found impossible." [53]

Weber's liberal views as he expressed them before his colleagues in the *Verein* reveal the extraordinary degree of his civic courage as well as the depth of his understanding of the social implications inherent in a rapidly industrializing society; he wished to utilize his own scientific insights, combining his scholarly activities with any practical contributions he might make, by applying his findings to the promulgation of public policies. However, he grew impatient with his colleagues in the academic world who were either extremely conservative or else willing to subordinate themselves to the authorities for reasons best known to them. The authorities did not heed his challenge and he felt himself increasingly a voice in the wilderness. In keeping with his not infrequently demonstrated capacity for impatience, he threw caution to the winds at some of the *Verein* meetings. Addressing such a meeting, he granted that there are competent men in the upper echelons of the civil service; Weber recoiled, however, at the thought that

. . . the world could one day be filled with nothing but those little cogs, little men clinging to little jobs and striving towards bigger ones—a state of affairs which is to be seen . . . playing an ever-increasing part in the spirit of our present administrative system, and specially of its offspring, the students. This passion for bureaucracy, as we have heard it expressed here, is enough to drive one to despair. It is as if in politics the spectre of timidity —which has in any case always been rather a good standby for the German— were to stand alone at the helm; as if we were deliberately to become men who need 'order' and nothing but order, who become nervous and cowardly if for one moment this order wavers, and they are torn away from their total incorporation in it. . . .[54]

Weber saw the reason for this situation in the generally prevailing authoritarian predisposition shared by many Germans. Opposing the extension of public ownership, Weber said:

Gentlemen, I could not but shake my head at the illusion which seems to have possessed all of you here that, when the private employer has been replaced to the fullest possible extent by the state or municipal official, the result will be anything other than the administration of state authority from the employer's point of view. . . .[55]

Weber criticized the prospect of a growing concentration of power at the local and state levels over more and more workers. He disputed the benefit to be derived from increasing concentration of power in the hands of civil servants at the state and local levels. Weber, inquiring from his audience whether this would furnish a more propitious foundation for social politics, was equally emphatic about the impropriety of introducing the notion of nationalization:

The principle of ever-widening nationalization and communalization has found varying degrees of expression in the *Verein fuer Sozialpolitik* since the beginning of its history. . . . An essential factor in the predilection for bureaucracy which exists among us in varying degrees, is a purely moral sentiment: namely, the belief in the unshakability of the undoubtedly high moral standard of German officialdom. Here, however, the 'ethical' aspect of the machine today plays a decidedly minor part.[56]

Weber's reasons for initiating debate on the role played by values in the social sciences at these meetings are not altogether obvious. It appears that the issue was raised less for reasons of substance and methodology in terms of a confrontation between facts and values than on what might be termed circumstantial grounds. The opposition he provoked as he championed the rights of the working classes against the aristocracy and industrialists, as well as the indignation he caused by his attack upon the bureaucracy, led Weber to recognize that the *Zeitgeist* was stronger than his challenge. He had probably not expected to run into so much opposition. When faced with a majority of opponents among his colleagues, he charged that value judgments had been operative where factual accounting was required. As indicated previously, the avowed aims of the *Verein* had been to study social problems scientifically and on the basis of academic findings to make sound judgments which were necessarily normative. Hence, it would seem that Weber's charge was not altogether fair. In fact, he modified some of his earlier arguments in comments during a subsequent discussion on another occasion in which he himself recalled the traditional aims of the *Verein*.

Nevertheless, the spirits he had summoned could not be so easily dismissed. Originally having intended to divert attention from what had become a political quarrel by a discourse concerning the relevance of values to academic inquiry, he had, in fact, achieved a shift of attention from politics to a discussion of "ethical neutrality." Weber did not subscribe to the isolation of the "philosopher-kings." Instead, because of his passionate interest in the affairs of his country, he wished to make a contribution of his own in practical terms to practical problems. His challenge to his colleagues having met with a negative response, especially in matters of social policy, he injected *Wertfreiheit* (freedom from value judgment), as a secondary challenge—almost as if out of despair.

In his inaugural address of 1895 in Freiburg, "Der Nationalstaat und die Volkswirtschaftspolitik," [57] Weber had significantly referred to "Nationaloekonomie" as a "political science." In his judgment, the heart of its subject matter was the "power-political interests" of the nation. The challenge Weber addressed to the German nation consisted in the demand that its level of political performance be raised to heights

worthy of a politically mature state. The lack of political education of
the German people constituted his own ultimate political concern. Many
of the influences contributing to Weber's definition of the term "political"
and his assessments of concrete political situations are to be sought in
his reactions to the coming of the war in 1914. His death in 1920 spared
him the vicissitudes which confronted Germany in the immediate postwar period.

Today we cannot know whether Weber would in time have modified his perspective. Certainly his conception of what is "political" contains a dynamic element reflecting vital power relationships based upon
the ultimate standard of Germany's requirements as a great nation;
the validity of this dictum he was never to question. Nor did his Freiburg address include the idea of the *polis* or *politeia*.[58] What this
address repeatedly illustrated was his own relationship to history in its
manifestation of the "political" sphere as it stood revealed in the historical process. For Weber it is *within* history that the highest source of
authority and ultimate judgment concerning human action resides, both
of which he considered binding; the infusion of this value Weber also
never denied. Patriotic considerations, in turn, however, also led to a
clear acknowledgment of the state's obligation, based upon an inexorable historical process, to include as part of its political mission conditions of social justice necessary for the maintenance of a given
political order.

As he stressed again and again, Weber was especially convinced
that the reordering of relations at the domestic level was an indispensable prerequisite for a successful foreign policy. For example, despite
his greatness, the events which form the historical background of Bismarck's tragedy derived partly from ideological antagonisms. The unresolved class struggle would remain a source of trouble, since without
a domestic solution and considering the lack of adequate national
leadership, all efforts towards enhancing Germany's power-political
position abroad would remain unsuccessful. Essentially it was Bismarck's
statesmanship which gave birth to the Reich, to which he gave unity.
Slowly but irrevocably the nation's economic structure changed, a circumstance which demanded a different political order. Economically
dying, the aristocracy had lost its justification to govern the nation
politically. Yet no class had yet demonstrated the necessary qualifications
to assume the responsibility of exercising political authority in the
interest of the power-political concerns of the nation in an age characterized by global international politics. The aristocracy's role was played
out, but neither the bourgeoisie nor the proletariat could measure up
to the challenge.

Weber never yielded to the temptation of meeting such realities
with political fantasies or of neglecting present problems for the sake

of vague future expectations. Pondering historical events, Weber could not help searching and hoping for new leaders who might inspire a new trend in the political imagination of the German nation, thereby offering other great powers, and especially Russia, a dialogue on a new level. Weber advocated the resolution of political issues by a rational evaluation of a given situation, especially those issues which could not be evaded by either the German nation or its eastern neighbors.

Weber's very pathos is reflected in his hope for and faith in the creation of an atmosphere within Germany which would ultimately justify his view of Germany's "calling as a nation." Whatever conflict Weber might have experienced as a realist whose judgment was determined principally by political and economic points of view, he was apparently able to resolve. By making use of all the most cogent political, economic, legal, and ethical arguments to settle the still unanswered question of the political education of the nation, Weber aspired to the realization of his political hopes for Germany: "For ourselves we can envisage only one thing: what must be accomplished is an enormous task of political education. There can be no duty for us more serious than for everyone in his own circle to be conscious of this task: to cooperate in the achievement of the political education of our nation, which must remain the ultimate aim especially of our own science. Economic developments during transitional periods threaten to distintegrate natural political instincts; it would be a misfortune if the science of economics would aspire to the same goal . . ." [59]

What Weber proposed as an historical alternative was nothing short of a new political stratum capable of wielding authority. Again, one moves in an atmosphere in which historical verdicts have authority, in this case that of the meaningful interpretation of contemporary social and political developments. Weber was thus led to the conclusion that to guard against the retention of the sources of political misjudgment or neglect, the entire German nation must be mentally prepared for political action so that its future leaders would find themselves supported as they responded to the challenge of given political situations. Max Weber, more than any other German scholar, offered the German people a clearer picture of the goals and challenges involved: to remove ignorance of or hostility to national goals was his objective for political education. If the politician's scope of action were thereby broadened, it nonetheless would remain his responsibility to make the best use of it within the realm of objective possibilities.

Characteristically, Weber's judgment is historically based:

It has been the attainment of *economic power* which at all times inspired a class to realize its claim to *political leadership*. What is dangerous and in the final analysis irreconcilable with the national interest is when an economically declining class retains political authority. But still more dangerous is when classes which exert economic power, enabling them to compete for positions of leadership lack political maturity for the exercise of governmental authority. Both endanger Germany today and this is really the key to the current dangers inherent in our situation.[60]

Weber's relationship to cumulative historical experience is again clear; he seeks to identify the "constant" factor, employing it in the context of past and future.

His political portrait would be unfairly drawn if consideration were not given to certain tensions and oscillations underlying his reflections upon necessary changes in the internal structure on one hand and the rational chances of their success on the other. Nor did he present all his thoughts on politics persuasively. It has been suggested that Weber's sometimes virulent nationalistic claims must be seen against his personal background. The long periods of his illness transformed and modified the aggressive symptoms of his nationalistic position. Although Weber never expressed himself on this subject specifically, his physical crises may have connoted for him crisis situations of a psychological nature.[61]

In several instances he found given circumstances considerably at odds with the objective policy guide-lines he suggested. Thus, regarding the question "whether it would not be wiser to conduct the current of German parliamentarization into the channels of the *Reich*," [62] Weber was referring to a broadening of the rights of the Reichstag as well as to the creation of a new type of Bundesrat (Federal Council) accessible to the parties within the *Laender* through the governments of the *Laender*. After the November 1918 revolution, however, important international political conditions brought a somewhat more temporizing attitude toward this question. Certain strains on the morale and discipline of the nation convinced him that the critical need, both inside and outside Germany, was an atmosphere in which, step by step, its ability to overcome the critical problems of the immediate future could be demonstrated. His inventory of the situation indicated that the technical problems of internal reorganization raised bitter struggles with regional pressure groups, and were therefore politically too risky to be faced lightly by any future government. Thus highly problematic means and limitations would not yet have to be faced during the revision of the Reich's internal structure. The problem was particularly serious in the economic sector of society, where a consistent, serious policy aimed at reform had been delayed for so long. Potentially weakening effects upon Germany's internal political structure and the fear that the economic system itself might be endangered engaged Weber's political imagination to his death. One may question some of his postulates, but there can be no doubt of the importance of his thesis and the persuasiveness of his analysis. As Johannes Winckelmann writes:

At the domestic level, the fundamental ideas contained in Max Weber's *Politische Schriften* are not outdated despite the passage of time. This applies especially to the exposition of the prerequisites for the structure and function of democracy. . . . In the area of international politics, his train of thought as expressed in his writings revolved repeatedly around the question of the nature and substance of a German foreign policy—one which must exclude the danger of an East-West coalition against Germany: Bismarck's *'Alptraum der Koalitionen'* (nightmare of coalitions). Again and again the author seeks to point up the decisive importance of Russia's position as a world power for the future of the West.[63]

Weber found sufficient reasons to advocate a democratic form of government for Germany, primarily because such a move would tie her to the West. In 1918 he urged cooperation with the majority Social Democrats, with whom he identified to the point of "non-distinguishability." He refused to participate in the "grave digger activity" currently undermining socialism, then underway in certain ideological circles in Berlin and Munich. Instead, the achievements of the revolution, thus far primarily negative in his view, should be consolidated "without any mental reservation or ambiguity" and expanded in the direction of "Planmaessige Sozialisierung" (planned socialization). [64] In outlining his conception of the new Germany, Weber demanded that the bourgeoisie unite unreservedly in "one great democratic-republican party." [65] The aims of "an honest, unreservedly peaceful and unreservedly radical bourgeois" democracy could fuse with those of the socialist democracy for several decades before any separation would occur.[66] Again and again he underscored the importance of the new political structure for Germany's future economy. While the importance of the purse was not underestimated, it was nevertheless not the only consideration in the assessment of the position of the bourgeois entrepreneur. Since Germany depended upon other countries, particularly on America, for raw materials and foreign credits, the bourgeoisie would have to stand behind the government. "A well-trained bourgeois organizer, even if he appeared with an empty purse—possibly as a well-paid agent of American capitalists—would enjoy a better chance of success than a dilettante or a socialist. . . ." [67] The exclusion of the bourgeoisie, on the other hand, would only result in a high price, which the proletariat would have to pay for decades to come "for the revolutionary carnival which a number of revolutionary agitators will and can conduct only until the collapse of the economic reserves occurs." [68]

The problem of the rational economic organization of the future Weber wanted to see solved by retaining as much as possible of the existing establishment. Ultimately this also became one of the guiding principles in his evaluation of the future of the German constitution. One of the most controversial issues presented itself in the question of opting either for a centralized or federal structure in the future German state. Weber favored as centralized an authority as possible, modelled after the Canadian and Australian states: ". . . any decentralized solution is not only more costly from the standpoint of expenditures but is generally uneconomical, particularly as it presents an obstacle to socialized planning." [69] As the most pressing needs of the immediate future, Weber saw the reduction of the Reich's public debt, proposals concerning the type of socialization of the economy to be introduced, and the manner in which it was to be financed.[70] Apart from this general framework, Weber was willing to modify his views, accept compromise solutions, and even to be satisfied with partial answers. Writing in December 1918, concerning financial problems and their solution, Weber admits: "We must resign ourselves to not knowing anything about this as yet. In all other sectors in which these fundamental problems are not so precarious, no revolutionary changes are really pressing." [71] A strictly socialist organization of the economy would warrant a centralized political organization. Conversely, private industry in a free economy was compatible with federalism. Standardization need occur only in the administration of justice, currency, trade policy, and taxation of industrial production.[72]

Weber's own position at the end of 1918 cannot be considered clear-cut. Even though he never seemed to tire of outlining constitutional details, he showed little inclination toward the development of a farsighted plan. While he was well informed about the history and structure of constitutions of other countries, he incorporated this knowledge merely as illustrations in his own writings. His lack of faith in the spirit of a constitution was nevertheless reflected in his own work.

As Karl Loewenstein argues, Weber shared the attitudes of many of his contemporaries toward a parliamentary form of government: "In the Germany of that period we knew next to nothing about genuine parliamentary government as it operates in the hands of party leaders who have advanced to responsible positions." [73] As a consequence, misconceptions about its substance continued to stir and confuse many minds. Certainly the limitations of an Imperial Germany, transformed almost overnight into a parliamentary democracy, were to be dramatized by subsequent events. Personally, Max Weber shared the distrust of the Weimar Republic of many who were essentially unsympathetic to demands for a new form of government. The condition in Germany was not one in which the spirit of democracy had penetrated politics. While the traditional political ideas were played out, many Germans, notably among the intelligentsia, still retained the premises of a bygone age.

Employing due caution, never compromising himself, Weber nevertheless did not allow his personal feelings to dictate his political thinking at this critical juncture for postwar Germany. While he placed little credence in the authenticity of the Revolution of November 1918, and most of its leaders, he accepted modern trends and was willing to shift his perspective when warranted. His support of the new system of government can perhaps be explained by the primacy he assigned to foreign policy over domestic issues. In any case, it was clear to him that no opportunity for making a choice between two potential forms of government existed. The Reich Bismarck had established was shattered. Failure to confront this "moment of truth" would only further impair Germany's international position.

Weber's aim at revision of Prussia's role and its bureaucracy as the core of the federal administrative machinery remained unchanged. Even after the November revolution he perceived the hoped-for effect to be the consistent removal of the "Greater Prussian constituent parts" of the Reich. Yet Weber was realist enough to know that no simple, Bismarckian panacea resolving such a major relationship was available now. Whatever followed, Weber cogently argued, the importance and tenacity of Prussia as a single administrative unit was a political fact which could hardly be forgotten or ignored. Recognizing Prussian fiscal power and the magnitude of the organization of its financial economy, he realized at the same time the danger of particularistic tendencies alien to the Republic among the East Elbian Junkers.[74] The transfer of the center of gravity of parliamentary development from Prussia to the Laender, which Weber now advocated in contrast to his earlier view in 1917, demanded a centralizing influence at the top. Filled with misgivings concerning events in Berlin, he also feared the potential effects of future centralist tendencies. Thus, to compensate for a decentralized regime, Weber demanded that the *Reichspraesident* be vested with considerable power to stabilize the unity of the Reich and to guard the constitution. The Weimar constitution substantially adopted Weber's proposals concerning the authority of the *Reichspraesident,* though not to the extent to which future holders of that office subsequently exercised it. As will be shown later, posterity has found this position of dominance quite expensive.[75]

The same type of merciless criticism which he once applied to Prussian officialdom in high political offices, Max Weber now in 1918 applied to the seemingly aimless revolutionary wing within the democratic ranks. Nevertheless, the initial revulsion with which Weber reacted to the seamy side of the revolution was gradually moderated, and indeed gave way to resignation. Never able to establish a close community of spirit with the Revolution, Weber became somewhat more sympathetic toward the difficulties facing a young and inexperienced democracy. However, he severely criticized the humiliating peace treaty which the government had accepted at Versailles. In his last two great speeches, *Politik als Beruf* (Politics as a Vocation), dealing with the nature and function of political parties and their penetration by bureaucracy from a highly realistic perspective,[76] and *Wissenschaft als Beruf* (Science as a Vocation).[77] It appears that two spheres which had been inextricably connected became clearly divorced. Political action is upgraded to where it becomes the object of theory. In *Wirtschaft und Gesellschaft* it has become integrated into historical theory. As an object of science it engages the scientist. Viewed from this new perspective, the professional politician becomes an object of study alongside the professional types of the bureaucrat and the entrepreneur. In "Wissenschaft als Beruf," Weber restated the ideal of the German university professor, who though he personally might represent the highest standards of scholarship, finds himself ethically bound not to engage in value judgments. Max Weber's own scholarly pursuits were to remain politically oriented, even though he refrained from expressing his personal views in the lecture hall. His political science reflected a firm grasp of the subject matter, the aim of which he held to be cognition and perception, culminating in insight rather than in political action itself.

Yet at the 1964 annual convention of the German Sociological Society in Heidelberg, commemorating the 100th anniversary of Weber's birth, Benjamin Nelson deplored the fact that his critics rarely, if ever, meet Max Weber on this latter ground. Nor, in his judgment, did they relate to him as an intellectual Titan engaged in a dialogue with other creative minds in "the anguished search for truth and responsible existence." The majority position of the American delegation to the convention was well represented by Benjamin Nelson's rejoinder to Herbert Marcuse:

A heavy price is paid when his perspective is sacrificed on the twin altars of politics and topicality. To tie him without remainder to Wilhelmine Germany and National Liberal politics, as unfriendly criticis are now doing, is in the end to rule out the import of his lifelong strivings for universal vision and ultimate relevance, to turn him into what he was not—a mere creature of his time, a spokesman for reactionary imperialistic interests, a quixotic mediocrity in the self-assumed role of a Machiavelli, an irresponsible adventurer ready to underwrite military dictatorship—indeed, a forerunner of 1933. Surely his own time knew him and the future will remember him under other guises than these.[78]

The concluding remarks in Juergen Habermas' discussion of Max

Weber further illuminate the distance between the American and German majority viewpoints in the area of political concern. Referring to Talcott Parsons, who credited Weber's work with having anticipated the end of ideology by having transcended historicism, utilitarianism, and Marxism,[79] Habermas took issue with his American colleagues. Indicating that he envied his American colleagues, whose own political traditions permitted such a generous appraisal of Max Weber, Habermas stated that the temptation to apply the American colleagues' yardstick is great but inadvisable. In Germany, Max Weber's political sociology had a different historical tradition. During World War I, Weber evoked the image of a Caesaristic *Fuehrerdemokratie* on the contemporary basis of the imperialism of the national state. While Habermas did not hold Weber accountable for the course of recent German history, he considered Carl Schmitt a "natural son" of Max Weber. He further denied the validity of Parsons' assertion that Weber had broken the spell of ideology.[80]

Reinhard Bendix countered by stating that while colleagues from other countries could appreciate the intellectual significance of the historical and ideological burden, it was rather extraordinary that in Germany Weber was mentioned in his capacity of a politician while in India several Indian colleagues had expressed admiration for Weber's sociological studies dealing with Indian religions. "Projecting this state of affairs into the future," said Bendix, "it could mean that in Germany Weber's contributions will be viewed from the political direction only (occasionally even now his scientific ideas are being set aside by virtue of the tendency to politicize) while the reception of his scientific work will be relinquished to foreign countries." [81]

Commenting on Nelson's and Bendix' discussions of his address, Herbert Marcuse refers to an enormous mistrust characterizing both their reports, which leads to a denunciation of conceptual reasoning as evidenced in: "*ressentiment,* a fear of any conceptualization transcending the present, not in terms of a transcendental world, but in terms of history, insofar as history anticipates the present." [82] Peter H. Merkl, a political scientist, likewise a native-born German, observes similarly that in the last analysis Thomas Mann's unpolitical bourgeoisie still remains to be accounted for.

Our interest here cannot be a search for culprits to be charged with anticipating the Nazi holocaust. Nevertheless, one might agree with Habermas and Merkl that influential men in the German universities generally, particularly considering the high esteem accorded the academic profession in Germany even today, cannot escape criticism of what in Germany from 1890 to 1914 seemed to be "two complementary and contradictory processes—a cultural revival and the beginnings of a *secession* of the intellectuals.' The tension between the two was to give a character of painful self-searching to German intellectual life in its most critical quarter-century."[83] Stuart Hughes points to Weber as being the one man whose intellectual detachment was adequate to the task of portraying and analyzing Germany's political situation. Perhaps Weber was more fortunate than some of his teaching colleagues since his academic career was largely interspersed with nonteaching periods during which he enjoyed a greater degree of freedom of expression.[84] Merkl's characterization appears applicable even to Weber when he compares German pride in an "inner freedom" with the philosophy of Spinoza, which, however, "is small compensation for the lack of interest in 'external freedom.' Instead of cultivating the public virtues of good citizenship, the German bourgeois cultivated his private virtues, his 'inner life' (*Innerlichkeit*) and 'beautiful soul,' and followed the doubtful precept that 'quiet and order are the first duties of a citizen' (*Ruhe ist die erste Buergerpflicht*)."[85]

Merkl identifies one of the most serious short circuits characterizing German youth, even today: "The failure to induct the new generations into the ways of civic participation is a typical example of the failure of emancipated man to take firm control of his new life."[86] Weber greatly admired the British model of the culturally active gentleman: "This was the model which Max Weber, in an echo of German national liberalism before World War I held up against the 'lacquered plebians' of Prussia who were not up to playing such a national role."[87]

Hughes succinctly portrays the catalyst in response to the war:

Despite his fears and his reservations about his country's war leadership, Weber could not help feeling that the conflict was "great and wonderful" in the devotion it called forth. Troeltsch and Meinecke, at least in the early years of the war, were equally caught up in the popular mood of quasi-religious inspiration. And they agreed wholeheartedly with Weber's formulation that the Germans bore a 'responsibility to history' to keep European civilization from an exclusive domination by Russian, Latin, and Anglo-Saxon values.[88]

In this respect, Hughes points out that the attitude of the intellectuals was not essentially different from that of the general public, the latter being typically and "tragically torn between patriotic enthusiasm and half-guilty forebodings."[89] Thus when Reinhard Bendix stresses his Indian colleagues' interest in Weber's writings on Indian religion, deploring the priority which his German colleagues at the convention of the German Sociological Society accorded to Weber's political writings, it must be remembered that the recent tragic past and its residues are still close to German experience.

Nor was it Weber's scholarly achievements and the respect in which these were held, even in the most diverse intellectual and ideological camps, which were at issue at the convention; hence it seems natural that they did not receive primary attention. His qualifications as political mentor of his nation are more problematic. It should not be surprising, therefore, that the German Sociological Society concerned itself precisely with this role—one which was so important to Weber himself. Equally notable, some German social scientists today are addressing themselves to the vital task of continuing political reappraisals on the basis of previous and subsequent events, especially after so many of them had remained aloof for so long. They have shown the courage to include the conclusions which Max Weber drew from his own brilliant analyses—just because of the breadth and depth marking his academic stature and the general and profound esteem in which he is held. As a political analyst he had few equals. Yet, Stuart Hughes says, "Weber's hankering after personal leadership—along with his ineradicable nationalism—is enough to make us question the whole basis of his political thinking." [90] In the *arena of practical politics* in which Weber regarded himself as both misunderstood and unappreciated by the authorities and the *demos,* some students of Weber's political writings would concur with Hughes when he describes Weber's guidance as "frequently dangerous." [91]

Hughes considers the greatest flaw in Weber's intellectual process to be in the field of psychology. He was too much given over to those things which were subject to rational explanation. Hughes further refers to Weber's choices as being characterized by a kind of desperation. Weber had an abiding faith in the value of human freedom, yet faced with its problematic aspects in a society caught up in the inevitable process of rationalization and bureaucratization, he sought to pursue the values of freedom *within* the confines of a rationalized society. Neither time nor progress nor the process of rationalization could be arrested. Intellectually, in fact, he endorsed the latter as a product of disciplined reasoning faculties. Moreover, the source of human freedom he had always considered to be found in human reason. Yet, Hughes says, "The vistas of the future that opened out before him were bleak in the extreme."

Alvin Gouldner similarly conceives the core of Weber's outlook to be based upon a dualism between rationality as exemplified in bureaucracy and science, and emotional forces on a more elemental level. The latter is encompassed by his concept of charisma: "He regards each of these forces as inimical to the other. He himself is ambivalent to each of them; he views each as both dangerous and necessary." [92] While fearing them both, he was yet unable to abandon either of them. Seeing no solution to their irreconcilablity, he adopted the strategy of segregation. Charismatic irrationality was to be excluded from certain institutions such as universities, yet he "admits it into and, indeed, exalts its manifestations in the inward personal life of individuals. He wanted certain of the role structures in modern society to be rational; but he also wanted the roleplayers to be passionate and willful." [93]

Since the claims of reason and faith are in constant competition with each other, the autonomy of each requires careful guarding. In the final analysis, only those values may be said to be authentic which, when set against the inner conscience, culminate in a sense of awareness of the commitment which derives from a conscious decision. Weber was concerned with the preservation of statesmanship and the prevention of its deterioration into meaningless routine. In this sphere he wanted to see only human beings of the highest caliber, capable of experiencing the depths of personal commitment. In this sphere also, he believed, there was still a safety valve for genuine greatness to come to the fore for those who dare to act, fully aware of all the demons evoked by the game of politics.

Weber's concern was thus directed at the preservation of high politics as an arena where human autonomy could operate, where pure value preferences could still find expression. Weber himself was always aware, however, that rationality's own survival might be threatened. He had repeatedly experienced himself as a man in whom much remained untamed, and this struggle was to debilitate his own nervous system. He was both afraid of and drawn to the Nietzschean *Herrenmensch,* the Dionysian element in man. His fear of these irrational forces, however, was not so great as to wish for their disappearance, even in an era which marks "the disenchantment of the universe." Vitality and power not only derive their energy from these forces, both are indispensable for human existence.

Thus from where Max Weber stood, all science and reason are assigned as tasks dedicated to the role of means; the ends, ultimately, are determined by the given values, which, however inscrutable, will be decisive in the final analysis. What this conception further involves is an effort to achieve a compromise between two Western traditions, namely reason and faith, by virtue of pursuing freedom from value judgment. Transcending this effort is Weber's supreme hope of salvaging in modern man the romantic component of his nature.

The realms of reason and faith, however, while separate, are yet not equal. While reason may both consult and cross-examine conscience, conscience has the last word; passion and reason ultimately account for the final deed.[94] His own sober realism and intellectual sophistication armed Weber against dogmatism and facile answers. Again and again he offered his countrymen meaningful courses of action without dictating what meanings they should create for themselves. The point he sought to drive home was recognition of the necessity to make responsible choices and to muster the necessary moral fortitude to stand by them.

In what follows I shall question some aspects of Weber's basic premises. The relative lack of research into his political writings suggests a need for a reappraisal of this essential part of his life and work. The role of the opposition in a democratic system of government is vital, and Weber himself represented the dissident *par excellence.* His political writings must neither be forgotten nor must their study be obscured by misinterpretation, which judged in retrospect always remains a possibility. While they present a challenge to the researcher, the validity of some of his thoughts on politics seems questionable in the perspective of our own time. Nevertheless, the multiplicity of his political concerns and the versatility of his scholarship continue to sustain our interest. Perhaps now more than ever the questions he asked and the issues he raised can offer both contemporary focus and historical perspective:

In Weber, a philosophy of struggle and power of Marxist and Nietzschean inspiration is combined with a vision of universal history leading to a disenchanted world and an enslaved humanity stripped of its highest virtues. For himself and perhaps for others, Max Weber placed above all else not so much success and power as a certain nobility, the courage to face the human condition as it appears to someone who denies himself any illusions, those of religion and those of political ideologies. All who believe themselves to be in possession of an absolute or total truth, all who want to reconcile the contradictory, Marxist-Hegelian, doctrinaire values of democracy or of natural law, continue—and rightly so—the controversy against a thinker who gives a dogmatic quality to the rejection of dogmatism, who lends a definitive truth to the contradiction of values, who in the last analysis knows nothing but partial science and purely arbitrary choice. . . . It is not sure that Weber's practice always corresponds to his theory. It is doubtful that Max Weber refrained from all value judgment, still more doubtful that value reference and value judgment are radically separable. Weber's sociology might be more scientific, but it would, I think be less fascinating if it were not the work of a man who was constantly asking himself the ultimate questions—the relation between knowledge and faith, science and action, the Church and prophecy, bureaucracy and the charismatic leader, rationalization and personal freedom —and who, thanks to an almost monstrous historic erudition, searched all civilizations for the answers to his own questions, at the risk of finding himself, at the end of his necessarily inconclusive explorations, alone and lacerated in the choice of his own destiny.[95]

The incongruities and tensions emerging from Max Weber's political biography appear to derive less from our attempts to consider his writings in retrospect rather than from the fact that he belonged to an era from which we are separated by half a century. The problem presents itself as a very real difference in perspective, for in the last part of the twentieth century the consequences of events that have occurred since Weber's time have become our legacy. Yet his political writings are permeated by an air of distinctive and exceptional quality because they reflect the essence of his own titanic intellectual stature and passionate devotion through which he succeeded in revealing to posterity the magnitude and complexities of his age. His deep personal commitment coupled with his seemingly paradoxical reactions to it, have inspired the vision of his life as the lava released from a volcano, representing the dawn of a revolutionary age.[96] Commenting on Weber's singular determination to remain "engaged," Benjamin Nelson correctly points to "the winding paths Weber took in his efforts to answer the questions which haunted him. . . ."[97] Any attempts "to make Weber appear wholly systematic" would make him "more mechanical than he ever was."[98] Weber's significance for future political history cannot yet be assessed. It will largely depend upon developments extending into the next half-century: on whether German and European statesmen will succeed in accomplishing European integration, on whether current attempts to arrive at a more or less permanent settlement with Eastern Europe will be given a chance, and on whether West Germany's leaders and people will be able, in Karl Jaspers' words, "to breathe democratic life" into "the formal democracy" which Max Weber helped establish. Weber's rather indifferent and sometimes negative attitude toward the spirit of democracy reflected the indifference of the majority of Germans.

The forty years intervening between the founding of the *Reich* and the outbreak of World War I have created for the historian a complex canvass of shifting cross-influences within "a none too healthy bourgeoisie." Liberals who had stressed their position in the traditional scheme of things, were not prepared to endorse more than a fractional or even marginal social change orientation. Consequently, as stated previously and as Peter Gay astutely demonstrated, most Germans, including the intellectuals, showed a marked reluctance in identifying themselves with Weimar culture.[99]

Writing after World War II, most social scientists agreed that the legacy of what Theodor Eschenburg has aptly called "improvised democracy" was one marked by an atmosphere of crisis, with which the Weimar government did not cope with adequate foresight and measured caution, especially in selecting those from whom it sought help. Significantly, however, until the middle of this century, it was the general consensus among social scientists that Communism and chaos would have been the only alternative. Yet, meanwhile evidence has established the fact that the alliance between what remained of the military establishment and the new republic, instead of saving democracy, merely succeeded in preserving the officer corps of the Imperial army, as Weber himself had hoped. Nor did the Social Democrats propose any plans for the establishment of a new democratic army. Paul Sethe, in fact, charged the Social Democrats with lack of respect for their own tradition to which they might have turned, accepting it as a legacy. Instead the Social Democratic Party has allowed itself to be maneuvered further to the right within its own ranks, presenting the left as "the big bogeyman." [100] In 1964, Karl Dietrich Bracher [101] suggested that the democratic impulses latent in the workers-and-soldiers-councils might have been credited with more respect, as Weber himself did on one occasion. In quest of statesmanship, he raised the question whether the great body of citizens could meet the challenge of cultivating a new political spirit. Unfortunately for Germany, the political socialization process remained incomplete. The Social Democrats and the Catholic Center party could not overcome the political liability of having been treated as enemies of the state until shortly before they took on the responsibilities of power. Their lack of parliamentary experience and the hiatus between them and the conservatively oriented civil servants complicated the work of the government further.

While some sincere democrats manifested considerable civic courage, the attitude of many judges who allowed political murderers either to go unpunished or to be let off easily, and the role of German intellectuals, steadily reduced the chances of success for the Weimar Republic. German university professors and school teachers, with few exceptions, failed to identify with the new constitution. Many continued in their loyalty to the previous regime and, as a consequence, were both unable and unwilling to familiarize German youth with democratic ideas, much less implant in them the desire to exercize their democratic rights and duties.

Unpolitical attitudes are not typical of German citizens alone, but in other countries democratic values and faith in political freedom, when tested, appear firmly rooted. Considering Germany's non-democratic political tradition, continued apathy may well result in what Professor Eschenburg called "a sleeping democracy." [102]

Theodor Heuss once referred to Weber's indomitable passion for wanting to master reality and seeking to combat the symptoms of "Epigonentum." It is rather meaningless today to label him as a conservative or liberal, monarchist or republican, right-wing or left-wing element within his own party. Apparently paradoxical aspects of his political thought must be weighed in the context of particular situations. Considered in this light, they manifest themselves as "legitimate and consistent positions" necessarily involving a process of revaluation and reorganization in response to existing cleavages within the nation and outer demands made upon German foreign policy.[103] Weber's criticism of the weakness in the German bourgeoisie stemming partly from its concern with material things, economic progress, self-satisfaction and political indifference to the challenge of competing political theories of social reconstruction, has a contemporary ring. The disparate elements in Weber's political thought cannot be welded into a self-consistent whole because the tensions of his own thought blend with the tensions of a forty-year period of turbulence. Still, fifty years after his death, his own political consciousness and perspective furnish an example to an enlightened minority; his essay, "Politics as a Vocation" reminds us that only through patient and persistent, genuinely political conduct based on a sense of proportion, and if given enough time by the voters, can such political leadership succeed. Self-criticism, loyalty to democratic principles, esprit de corps within the government and the development of parliamentary practices represent the best hope for modern Germany fifty years after Weber's death to acquire a more meaningful conception of democracy. Above all, Max Weber did not evade the modern era beginning for Germany when he saw its dawn; instead he sought to meet it on its own ground.

NOTES

[1] Max Weber, *Wirtschaft und Gesellschaft* (Tuebingen: J. C. B. Mohr, 1925); the latest edition was edited by Johannes Winckelmann (Tuebingen: J. C. B. Mohr, 1956).

[2] Max Weber, *Gesammelte Aufsaetze zur Wissenschaftslehre* (Tuebingen: J. C. B. Mohr, 1922), p. 166.

[3] *Ibid.*, p. 113.

[4] Cf. Karl Dietrich Erdmann, "Die Zukunft als Kategorie der Geschichte," *Historische Zeitschrift*, Vol. 198, 1964, p. 49.

[5] Cf. Max Weber, *Gesammelte Aufsaetze zur Religionssoziologie*, 3 vols. (Tuebingen: J. C. B. Mohr, 1920/21).

[6] Cf. Max Weber, *Gesammelte Aufsaetze zur Wissenschaftslehre*, edited by Johannes Winckelmann (Tuebingen: J. C. B. Mohr, 1951), pp. 493f.

[7] Max Weber, *Gesammelte Aufsaetze zur Sozial-und Wirtschaftsgeschichte* (Tuebingen: J. C. B. Mohr, 1924), p. 278.

[8] Robert Maynard Hutchins and Mortimer J. Adler, eds., "Thucydides: 'The History of the Peloponnesian War'," *Encyclopaedia Britannica* (Chicago: William Benton, 1955), pp. 352–354.

[9] *Ibid.*, pp. 354–355.

[10] Guenther Roth and Claus Wittich, eds., Max Weber, "The Patrician City in the Middle Ages and in Antiquity," in *Economy and Society: An outline of Interpretative Sociology* (New York: Bedminster Press, 1968), pp. 1281–1282. Copyright © Bedminster Press, New York. Reprinted by permission of the publisher.

[11] Arnold Hauser, *The Philosophy of Art History* (New York: Alfred A. Knopf, 1959), p. 245.

[12] W. M. Simon, *Germany: A Brief History* (New York: Random House, 1966), p. 243.

[13] *Ibid.*

[14] Karl Jaspers, *The Future of Germany* (Chicago: The University of Chicago Press, 1957), p. 32.

[15] Else Frenkel-Brunswick, "Environmental Controls and the Impoverishment of Thought: The Role of Psychology in the Study of Totalitarianism," in Harry

Eckstein and David E. Apter, eds., *Comparative Politics: A Reader* (New York: The Free Press, 1963), p. 494.

16 Johannes Winckelmann, ed., *Max Weber: Staatssoziologie: Soziologie der rationalen Staatsanstalt und der modernen politischen Parteien und Parlamente* (Berlin: Duncker & Humblot, 1966), p. 16.

17 W. M. Simon, *op. cit.*, p. 244.

18 *Ibid.*

19 A. F. K. Organski, *The Stages of Political Development* (New York: Alfred A. Knopf, 1965), p. 168.

20 Hans Kohn, *Nationalism: Its Meaning and History* (Princeton, N.J.: Van Nostrand, 1965), p. 77.

21 Eric Dombrowski, *German Leaders of Yesterday and Today* (Freeport, N.Y.: Books for Libraries Press, Inc. [first published 1920], reprinted 1967), pp. 74–77.

22 Erich Eyck, *A History of the Weimar Republic: From the Collapse of the Empire to Hindenburg's Election*, Vol. I (Cambridge, Mass.: Harvard University Press, 1962), p. 3. Reprinted by permission of the publisher.

23 Eugen Schiffer, *Ein Leben fuer den Liberalismus* (Berlin: Grunewald, 1951), p. 129, cited in *ibid.*, p. 3.

24 Hajo Holborn, *The Political Collapse of Europe* (New York: Alfred A. Knopf, 1966), p. 79.

25 *Ibid.*

26 *Ibid.*, pp. 80–81.

27 W. M. Simon, *op. cit.*, p. 225, cf. also Gustav Schmollere, *Grundriss der allgemeinen Volkswirtschaftslehre* (Munich, 1923), Vol. II, pp. 562–647.

28 Bernard Semmel, *Imperialism and Social Reform: English Social Imperial Thought 1895–1914* (Garden City, N.Y.: Doubleday, 1968), p. 197. See also Gustav Schmoller, *op. cit.*, pp. 562–647. Bernard Semmel, *Imperialism and Social Reform*, George Allen and Unwin Ltd. Reprinted by permission of the publisher.

29 Cf. Fritz Stern, ed., *The Varieties of History from Voltaire to the Present* (Cleveland: The World Book Company, 1956), p. 311.

30 Bernard Semmel, *op. cit.*, p. 197.

31 Joseph A. Schumpeter, *Capitalism, Socialism and Democracy* (New York: Harper, 1950), p. 342 fn. Reprinted by permission of the publisher.

32 *Ibid.*, pp. 341–342.

33 *Ibid.*, p. 343.

34 "Die Verhaeltnisse der Landarbeiter im ostelbischen Deutschland," Auf Grund der Erhebungen des Vereins fuer Sozialpolitik, *Schriften des Vereins fuer Sozialpolitik*, Vol. 55, part 3, Leipzig, 1892. "Entwicklungstendenzen in der Lage der ostelbischen Landarbeiter," *Archiv fuer soziale Gesetzgebung und Statistik*, Vol. 7, 1894, reprinted in *Gesammelte Aufsaetze zur Soziologie und Sozialpolitik* (Tuebingen: J. C. B. Mohr, 1924).

35 "Privatenquêten ueber die Lage der Landarbeiter," *Mitteilungen des evangelisch-sozialen Kongresses*, April, June, July, 1892. "Die Erhebung des evangelisch-sozialen Kongresses ueber die Verhaeltnisse der Landarbeiter Deutschlands," *Christliche Welt*, Vol. 7, 1893, pp. 534–40. "Die Erhebung des Vereins fuer Sozialpolitik ueber die Lage der Landarbeiter," *Das Land*, Vol. 1, 1893, pp. 8f., 24ff., 43ff., 58f., 129f., 147f.

36 Cf. Reinhard Bendix, *Max Weber: An Intellectual Portrait* (Garden City, N.Y.: Doubleday, 1962), p. 23. Copyright © 1960. Reprinted by permission of the publisher. Also by permission of Methuen & Co., Ltd., London.

37 "Verhaeltnisse der Landarbeiter," cited in Bendix, *ibid.*, pp. 22–23.

38 *Gesammelte Aufsaetze Zur Sozial-und Wirtschaftsgeschichte* (Tuebingen: J. C. B. Mohr, 1924), pp. 467–69, cited in Bendix, *op. cit.*, pp. 30–31.

39 J. P. Mayer, *Max Weber and German Politics: A Study in Political Sociology* (London: Faber and Faber, 1943), p. 57, cf. *Politische Schriften*, p. 459 cited by J. P. Mayer. Reprinted by permission of Faber and Faber Ltd. from *Max Weber and German Politics: A Study in Political Sociology* by J. P. Mayer.

40 Cf. Hans H. Gerth and C. Wright Mills, transl. and eds., *From Max Weber: Essays in Sociology* (New York: Oxford University Press, 1946), p. 35. Reprinted by permission of the publisher.

41 *Ibid.*, pp. 26–27.

42 Cf. J. P. Mayer, *op. cit.*, p. 89.

43 Cf. Gerth and Mills, *op. cit.*, p. 27.

44 *Ibid.*
45 Cf. Franz Boese, *Geschichte des Vereins fuer Sozialpolitik* (Berlin: Duncker & Humblot, 1939), pp. 108, 113, and 133–35.
46 S. M. Miller, *Max Weber* (New York: Thomas Y. Crowell, 1966), p. 7.
47 Albert Salomon, "Max Weber's Political Ideas," *Social Research: An International Quarterly*, Vol. II, No. III, 1935, p. 378. Reprinted by permission of the publisher.
48 *Gesammelte Aufsaetze zur Soziologie und Sozialpolitik* (Tuebingen: J. C. B. Mohr, 1924), p. 414, cited in Albert Salomon, *op. cit.*, p. 378.
49 Edward A. Shils and Henry A Finch, *Max Weber on the Methodology of the Social Sciences* (Glencoe, Ill.: The Free Press, 1949), pp. 49–112.
50 *Ibid.*, p. 19.
51 Albert Salomon, *op. cit.*, p. 372.
52 *Ibid.*, pp. 377–78.
53 *Ibid.*, p. 378.
54 J. P. Mayer, *op. cit.*, pp. 96–97, "Max Weber on Bureaucratization in 1909," Appendix I.
55 *Ibid.*, p. 97.
56 *Ibid.*, p. 98.
57 Max Weber, *Gesammelte Politische Schriften*, pp. 7–30; in the second edition, edited by Johannes Winckelmann (Tuebingen: J. C. B. Mohr, 1956), pp. 1–25. Reprinted by permission of Johannes Winckelmann. Quoted hereafter as *P.S.*, 1st. ed., or *P.S.*, 2nd. ed.
58 Cf. Gerhard Schulz, "Geschichtliche Theorie und Politisches Denken bei Max Weber," *Vierteljahrshefte fuer Zeitgeschichte*, Vol. XII, No. 4, 1964, p. 334.
59 *P.S.*, 2nd. ed., p. 24.
60 *Ibid.*, p. 19.
61 Gerhard Schulz, *op. cit.*, p. 336.
62 *P.S.*, 2nd. ed., "Bismarck's Erbe in der Reichsverfassung" (Review of an article bearing the same title by Erich Kaufmann, October, 1917), p. 232. Cf. also an essay Weber wrote on "Bayern und die Parlamentarisierung im Reich," *ibid.*, pp. 221–228, which appeared also in October 1917.
63 Johannes Winckelmann, "Vorwort zur Zweiten Auflage," *P.S.*, 2nd. ed., p. XXXIII.
64 *P.S.*, 2nd. ed., p. 472; report in the *Frankfurter Zeitung* of December 2, 1918, on a political speech delivered by Max Weber on December 1, 1918.
65 *Ibid.*, p. 475.
66 *Ibid.*
67 *Ibid.*, pp. 473–74.
68 *Ibid.*, pp. 474–75.
69 "Deutschlands kuenftige Staatsform," *P.S.*, 2nd. ed., p. 464.
70 *Ibid.*, p. 468.
71 *Ibid.*
72 *Ibid.*, p. 445.
73 Karl Loewenstein, *Beitraege zur Staatssoziologie* (Tuebingen, 1961), p. 326.
74 Prussia had represented an administrative monstrosity when the German Federation was founded in 1871 since the Land (State) of Prussia comprised two-thirds of the territory of the empire. Bismarck's statecraft accomplished the fusion of the machineries of the federal and Prussian authorities, making the two practically identical. The absurd federal structure which contained a Prussia larger in size and population than all the other states combined was ultimately essentially retained under the Weimar Constitution.
75 See *P.S.*, 2nd. ed., p. 470, where Weber argues in favor of the creation of a plebiscitary *Reichspraesident* as head of the executive entitling him to cast the suspensive veto. The referendum would be his recourse if between the *Bundesrat* (Federal Council) on one hand and the parliament and its trusted agents, the ministers, on the other hand no agreement was reached on a given issue. The referendum would be employed as the means of settling constitutional conflicts between the federal and central authorities. Cf. also "Der Reichspräsident" in *ibid.*, pp. 486–489, where Weber in February 1919 carefully elaborated his previously stated views.
76 *P.S.*, 2nd. ed., pp. 493–548. Cf. Weber's address "Politik als Beruf," delivered before a student audience in Munich, which appeared in print in October 1919.

77 Cf. *Gesammelte Aufsaetze zur Wissenschaftslehre*, pp. 524–555.
78 Benjamin Nelson, "Diskussion ueber 'Industrialisierung und Kapitalismus'," in Otto Stammer, ed., *Max Weber und die Soziologie Heute: Verhandlungen des 15. Deutschen Soziologentages* (Tuebingen: J. C. B. Mohr [Paul Siebeck], 1965), p. 197. Cf. Herbert Marcuse, "Industrialisierung und Kapitalismus," in Otto Stammer, *op. cit.*, pp. 161–180. Reprinted by permission of the publisher.
79 Talcott Parsons, "Wertgebundenheit und Objektivitaet in den Sozialwissenschaften: Eine Interpretation der Beitraege Max Webers," in Otto Stammer, *op. cit.*, pp. 60–64.
80 Juergen Habermas, "Diskussion ueber 'Wertfreiheit und Objektivitaet'," in Otto Stammer, *op. cit.*, p. 81.
81 Reinhard Bendix, "Diskussion ueber 'Industrialisierung und Kapitalismus'," in Otto Stammer, *op. cit.*, p. 187.
82 Herbert Marcuse, "Schlusswort," in Otto Stammer, *op. cit.*, p. 217.
83 H. Stuart Hughes, *Consciousness and Society: The Reconstruction of European Social Thought 1890–1930* (New York: Alfred A. Knopf, Inc., 1958), p. 51. Reprinted by permission of the publisher.
84 *Ibid.*, p. 50.
85 Peter H. Merkl, *Germany: Yesterday and Tomorrow* (New York: Oxford University Press, 1965), p. 247.
86 *Ibid.*, p. 247.
87 C. Wright Mills, "The Complacent Young Men," in Louis Horowitz, ed., *Power, Politics and People: The Collected Essays of C. Wright Mills* (New York: Oxford University Press, 1963), p. 392.
88 H. Stuart Hughes, *op. cit.*, pp. 369–370.
89 Hughes, *op. cit.*, p. 370.
90 *Ibid.*, p. 333.
91 *Ibid.*, p. 333.
92 Alvin W. Gouldner, "Anti-Minotaur: The Myth of a Value-Free Sociology," in Louis Horowitz, ed., *The New Sociology; Essays in Social Science and Social Theory* (New York: Oxford University Press, 1964), p. 212.
93 *Ibid.*, p. 213.
94 *Ibid.*, p. 214.
95 Raymond Aron, *Main Currents in Sociological Thought*, Vol. II, Durkheim/Pareto/Weber (New York: Basic Books, 1967), pp. 251–252. Reprinted by permission of the publisher.
96 Cf. Hermann Rudolph, "Max Weber: Gestalt der Wende 50 Jahre nach seinem Tod," *Frankfurter Allgemeine Zeitung*, June 19, 1970, Nr. 138, p. 32.
97 Benjamin Nelson, Book Review, *The Sociology of Max Weber* by Julien Freund, New York: Pantheon Books, 1968, *American Sociological Review*, June 1970, vol. 35, No. 3, p. 550.
98 *Ibid.*
99 Peter Gay. *Weimar Culture—the outsider as insider.* London: Seder & Warburg, 1969. Cf. also Alex Natan, "Es ist nicht alles Gold. . . . Die Verklärung der Weimarer Zeit," Book Review of the above book by Peter Gay, *Die Zeit*, March 13, 1970, Nr. 11, p. 47. See also Sebastian Haffner, *Die verratene Revolution. Deutschland 1918/19.* Munich: Scherz, 1969, and Ernst Niekisch. *Die Legende von der Weimarer Republik.* Köln: Wissenschaft und Politik, 1968.
100 Cf. Barbara C. Beuys, "Angst vor der Roten Front: Eine junge Demokratie liefert sich selber ans Messer," *Die Zeit*, March 13, 1970, Nr. 11, p. 48. See also Lothar Gall. *Der Liberalismus als regierende Partei. Das Grossherzogtum Baden zwischen Restauration und Reichsgründung.* Veröffentlichungen des Instituts für Europäische Geschichte. Mainz: Franz Steiner, 1968.
101 Barbara C. Beuys, *op. cit.*, p. 48.
102 Theodor Eschenburg. *Der Beamte in Partei und Parlament.* Frankfurt: Alfred Metzner, 1952, p. 195.
103 Cf. Hermann Rudolph, *op. cit.* p. 32.

II

The political context
of Max Weber's thought

This chapter attempts to weave the political issues of Max Weber's time into a context in which his political philosophy appears as an integral part of its historical background. Demands of brevity militate against an exhaustive account of the political history covering even his own lifetime in their full controversial setting. The theme of this discussion is essentially to recall how Germany, in the nineteenth century, in her long-drawn-out search for unity and order found liberalism and nationalism to be incompatible and how one aim was ultimately abandoned to achieve the other, which was valued more highly. Actually, "France, Germany, and Spain were destined . . . to unify more or less completely even before a spontaneous political development of a nationalist character spread from one border to the other. The geographic unity of those areas was discovered in the great states of the Roman and later Carolingian empires; and, as Ratzel put it, these natural regions then strove to become political territories."[1]

Located at the heart of Europe,

. . . in the case of Germany, the geographical situation has a special meaning for the development of public institutions.

The main fact to be remembered is that Germany, with practically insuperable natural boundaries on the north and south, has had no fixed frontiers on the east or west for many centuries. International conflicts, wars, and an hereditary enemy complex resulted from this state of things. And, defying nature, the solution adopted has been one that has taken great rivers, which in their courses should unite the human effort of all those fortunate people through whose territories they flow, and has turned them into things to be cut into pieces and distributed like so many parcels of private property among as many different leaseholders. In the case of every big river in Central Europe—Rhine, Elbe, Danube, Oder, and Vistula—this policy has been adopted. But that is a question of international policy which does not concern this history. What matters is the importance which the undefined boundaries to the east and west of Germany have for German domestic policy. The conflict between 'Westerners' and 'Easterners,' so well known to all students of the World War, has, in a different sense of the words, been an ever recurring problem to German politicians, who have had to steer their way between the two currents of constitutional practice.[2]

Indeed, Germany has been the archetype of a country torn by divisions and antagonisms. Her political and social modernization has, as a consequence, been particularly intense and difficult. It seems necessary, at the outset, to trace in some detail the major outlines of this political experience, since it provides the framework within which Weber's thought was largely shaped.

Surveying Central European history from about 1500 on, one observes various attempts by the German people to construct a stronger state. The obstacles to such designs are apparent from a study of events at the various diets.[3] As Otto Hintze states:

. . . in Germany an enduring state developed only after the emergence of the petty principalities and the territorial states, which lasted until the foundation of the new empire. In fact, everywhere on the continent the small territorial states preceded the modern nation-states. . . . The moving forces of this process are not limited to natural and social factors such as population growth, development of communication and so on. Rather, they include above all a political drive to power, rivalries and conflicts between neighbors, and the constant pushing and shoving between states by which the European equilibrium reestablished itself in the face of a traditional preponderance of one power with universal tendencies.[4]

A review of comparative political institutions, moreover, reveals a fundamental difference between Germany and other major countries: the absence in Germany of a consistent political culture. Anglo-American countries, including Great Britain, the United States, Canada, Australia, and New Zealand share certain pluralist features and a common heritage of political culture and traditions. While each country has established political institutions considered most likely to serve its needs, the political culture characterizing each reflects a similarity of spirit which permeates their political life. A high level of consensus exists on both political framework and political procedures. In all these countries, moreover, political parties have long enjoyed the freedom to organize and to compete for power, and a vast number of pressure groups struggle to influence their decision making, their common system of values includes liberalism, individualism, and an essentially non-ideological orientation which leaves room for political compromise. Germany, in comparison, has never had this pragmatic ideological and institutional framework.

To retrace the contours of German history for the purpose of illustrating a supposedly unilinear movement in the direction of Germany's quest for internal unification and external supremacy, culminating in the Third Reich would be merely oversimplifying the contest between opposing forces. A country geographically in the center of Europe, repeatedly ripped asunder throughout her history, modernizing herself economically more rapidly than politically, and increasingly respected and feared by her neighbors, presents a fluctuating and enigmatic image.

German society, moreover, was marked by a high degree of proliferation in terms of

central elites, even if relatively traditional and autocratically oriented, epitomized in the personality of Bismarck. These elites established modern unified political frameworks and at the same time aimed at industrialization of their countries; but on their own terms. They wanted to intensify the process of industrialization and of continuous social mobilization; but within frameworks of conservative national state and political order. While granting basic political and social rights to the citizen, they attempted to minimize the autonomous social transformation of these groups, especially of the workers: and they did not legitimize their autonomous social and political organization and expansion, nor their incorporation into the central symbolic and institutional system as equal parties or participants.[5]

Protestantism in Germany may have been partly responsible for producing pressure for a national identity which would supercede religious and regional bases of identity and for politics to be organized along class lines. In Weber's words, "normally, Protestantism . . . absolutely legitimated the state as a divine institution and hence violence as a means. Protestantism, especially, legitimated the authoritarian state." [6] Traditionally, however, there has been considerable diversity within Germany, and Germans have demonstrated extreme individualism as illustrated in their decentralized culture, their particularism in politics, and their past disunity in confrontation with their enemies.

But the parties in Imperial Germany were remarkably stable with respect to both their programs and their constituency. Except for some minority splinter-groups, they were organized along class lines, reflecting definite ideological orientations. The German party system was nevertheless staid and definitely in need of some of the vitality which Max Weber hoped to pump into it. Some of the active social groups, although they shared certain features with other European secondary elites, still displayed unique characteristics reflecting the German social structure:

First, most of these groups and strata were weaker in their political articulation and effectiveness and in their ability to effect transformation of the central political institutions. Second, and closely connected with the former, they were less autonomous in their status aspiration and perception, being still strongly oriented to the more aristocratic or 'absolutistic' symbols of status. Hence they tended to maintain a greater extent of internal closeness, mutual divisiveness, and lack of internal flexibility—characteristics and orientations that they evinced also in the political field, especially in the ideologies and organization of the numerous political parties which developed throughout parties of the unsuccessful 1848 Revolution up to the later various democratic liberal and socialist parties of the Empire.[7]

Meanwhile, the Bismarckian political system tended to deny full and effective participation in the political process to these groups. Culture, institutions, and events worked against political maturation in Germany.

These tendencies were not changed by economic growth and associated changes in the latter part of the nineteenth century. Changes took place in the bureaucracy, but these were such as to make it even more the servant of the state.

Under such conditions, indeed, alliances tended to develop between the autocratic elite and the various relatively modernized and differentiated groups and strata; especially the larger industrialist and financial groups, on the one hand, and the more organized workers on the other. But these alliances were based mostly on purely accommodative considerations and contractual arrangements, and were not fully bolstered up by new common precontractual ones, by new common flexible political and cultural symbols. Hence the level of cleavages and unsolved conflicts tended to rise continuously.[8]

A number of important developments in Germany following the Franco-Prussian War of 1870–71 tended to accelerate the growth of the economy enormously. A casual observer of the economic scene might well have believed that the German bourgeoisie had a great deal to be complacent about. Certainly at the time it appeared that most of the major objectives of a Western society were being achieved. A significant acceleration in productivity having occurred in many areas of the economy, particularly in heavy industry and railway construction, Germany began to rank as a highly industrialized economy. This superb productive efficiency and the expansion in fiscal and monetary activities caused Germany to look increasingly beyond the domestic market. Certainly also Germany could not be said to suffer from a crisis of confidence as far as economic progress was concerned. Domestically, too, the creation of a favorable economic climate between 1870 and 1900 issued in a favorable psychological climate; "many towns more than doubled their population; Berlin grew from a city of 775,000 to one of 1,880,000 inhabitants. While in 1870 only thirty-six percent of the Germans lived in towns, by 1900 the percentage had increased to 54.4, with a corresponding increase of the numbers employed in industry and trade." [9] Yet, while the country as a whole increased in prosperity, many working-class families lived a life of poverty.

Bismarck, a Junker by birth, took pride in standing above parties. Both Bismarck and Weber believed that a political party might put its own interests ahead of patriotism when its own survival seemed at stake. Thus from 1867 until 1878, Bismarck allied himself with the National Liberals, making some concessions to liberal principles. So long as he believed that party to be sympathetic to his national aspirations by supporting his policy of militarism, free trade, and working toward greater centralization of government, he could afford to offer concessions. Bismarck foresaw correctly that by appearing as the champion of direct and universal manhood suffrage, he could gain the support of the German masses for his nationalistic policies, including his military plans. Thus even Bavaria and the South German states responded by heeding the call to arms against the French.

In 1879 Bismarck severed his connection with the National Liberal party when it opposed his plan to abandon his policy of laissez-faire. He then made common cause with the Conservatives, who were strongly committed to "throne and altar" and the army and extremely antagonistic toward any legislation threatening the rights of the aristocracy. While Bismack continued to place the nation above party, his own brand of nationalism was contained within realistic limits, always marked by flexibility and political realism. On the other hand, in both fields, foreign and domestic, his reasoning revolved almost exclusively around political rather than social or economic issues. He was preoccupied with the conduct of foreign wars in order to consolidate his work of unification, symbolized in the *Kulturkampf*, as well as in his efforts to create political alliances. Although he endorsed liberal laissez-faire economic policies, he underestimated the significance economic forces were to have for politics at both the domestic and foreign levels.

Meanwhile the rise of the Socialist movement began to make itself felt, the very effect which Bismarck had hoped to forestall. The trade union movement gained in size and momentum, as did the Social Democratic party itself after 1875. The "State Socialism" which Bismarck introduced in the eighties was designed to enlist support among Germans of all classes in the service of the national interest. Having passed the tariff legislation of 1879 to protect agrarian interests and to further the growth of heavy industry, he hoped that Germany's output would surpass Britain's by the turn of the century. Bismarck's new program increased wages and employment for the German working class. Nevertheless, growing social discontent fostered Social Democratic strength in the Reichstag. In 1878, Bismarck managed the passage of legislation outlawing the Social Democrats and banning the press. He hoped to counter socialism by a social program of his own, culminating in 1883 in the passage of the Sickness Insurance Law; in 1884 and 1885, in the Accident Insurance Laws; and in 1889 in an Old Age Insurance Law.

Bismarck's Reichstag in its own right was, in fact, a rather impotent body. This circumstance is closely linked to the failure of the German bourgeoisie to assume leadership as its counterparts were doing in other western European countries. Only a multicausal explanation can furnish a key to an understanding of this fact. Whereas in other European countries the bourgeoisie fought for its rights against feudalism, breaking down its rigid pattern of social stratification, and stressing individual liberty as well as free enterprise coupled with the rights of property and religious freedom, this development was stunted in Germany.

The collapse of the liberal ideal in 1848 and the unbroken exercise of power by reactionary forces precluded unification upon genuinely liberal national foundations. Bismarck's accomplishment of unification, gigantic as it was, resulted neither in liberty nor in unity. His real achievement rested in the mastery of the political art in combination with military organization. His work was affected by many interrelated factors; the lateness of Germany's unification; the speed and lateness of industrialization, the Thirty Years' War, which devastated the cities constructed by the bourgeoisie; and the collapse of the Habsburg monarchy, coupled with the ascendance of the House of Hohenzollern, symbolizing Prussian militarism. ". . . in France the liberalism of 1789 has proved the most lasting heritage. . . . It was only outside France that the essential Napoleonic traits were revived and then only after the nineteenth century, the age of the bourgeoisie and of nationalism, had ended in the German 'spirit of 1914' and in Lenin's revolution, both opposed to the principles of 1789." [10]

The Napoleonic wars had prepared the ground in Germany for two powerful ideas, those of liberalism and nationalism. Liberalism constituted the legacy of the Age of Enlightenment, and its implementation in France was encompassed by the slogan "Liberty, Equality, Fraternity." Nationalism drew its support mostly from animosity toward the French occupation of most of Europe. While the nineteenth century saw the rise of the liberal state in Britain, France, and the United States, Friedrich Nietzsche "forecast correctly the character of the new era that began in August, 1914, and ended in November, 1917, in which individual national life no longer formed the center of concern." [11] While the French Republic had been hailed in Europe "as the fulfillment of the hope of the ages, as a universal message destined for all peoples and guaranteeing the peace of mankind," it was to inaugurate, in fact, a tragic new era resulting from the revolutions of 1848:

(This) was not a world of harmony and fraternity but of conflict and violence. Soon the new nationalism stressed collective power and unity far above individual liberty: it tended to mean independence from outside rather than freedom within. None of the new nationalities could resist, as soon as the opportunity offered itself, the temptation to assert its rule over ethnically disputed territory and populations. Nationalism changed in the middle of the nineteenth century from liberal humanitarianism to aggressive exclusivism, from the emphasis on the dignity of the individual to that on the power of the nation, from limitation and distrust of government to its exaltation.[12]

This transformation in the "character of nationalism in the middle of the nineteenth century occurred not only among the Germans but among all the peoples of Central and Eastern Europe. The new spirit of violence, of glorification of heroic deeds, of the revival of a dim past and of its use as an inspirational source . . . was first noticeable in 1848. . . . After 1848, nationalism entered the age of what had become known by German words—for the Germans played the leading role in this transformation—as the age of *Machtpolitik* and *Realpolitik* based on power and self-interest . . ."[13]

On the other hand, Sigmund Neumann assesses the failure of the Revolution of 1848, stating:

The Revolution of 1848 had been 'no mere coup d'état.' Its aims were political in nature and it sought to establish a social basis; yet the weakness of this social basis was obvious. The German Constituent National Assembly of 1848 with its arguments over generalities, was symbolic of the state of mind in which the newly rising classes found themselves and because of which they were unable to exploit the 'revolutionary situation. . . .' Although the Frankfurt Assembly thus represented an impressive articulation of the liberal and national desires of the German middle class, it was not strong enough to force the Prussian Monarch and his princely confreres to accept the revolution. Political control soon passed into the experienced hands of the old masters.[14]

The alternatives consisted either in the acceptance of an autocratic regime or in working for a new and liberal society, shouldering all the responsibilities accompanying that endeavor. The nineteenth century had, indeed, seen the rise of liberalism and with it, the aspiration to the birth of a new Europe, once the feudal foundations of the old Europe had given way. Liberty, however does not lend itself to a mere empirical definition. Whereas institutions may embody aspects of liberty, the conditions under which liberty flourishes are in a continuous process of becoming. The consequences of Bismarck's reign included the pollution of the very idea of liberalism; the hope that Europe might yet adopt a spirit of liberal nationalism had to be abandoned for over half a century.

The only foundation upon which an international order might have had a chance of success, even after Bismarck's departure from the political arena, was to be found within the traditional balance of power framework. This balance had been expertly manipulated for twenty years under Bismarck's administration. Not long after his fall, however, this precarious type of international policy was destroyed, partly, at least, by the ineptitude of his successors and their imperialistic aspirations which ignored or scorned the risks resulting from them. The coming of World War I appeared inevitable. Occasionally, genuinely liberal voices insisted upon making themselves heard. But the widespread enthusiasm in support of the war in Germany when it came, even though it had not been desired by most people, only served to intensify the ardor of the illiberal forces who later silenced these liberal voices. In the end, with the Germans having inflicted the Treaty of Brest-Litovsk upon the Russians and having had the Treaty of Versailles imposed upon themselves, hopes for the revival of a spirit of European unity had to be set aside. What emerged immediately after the war were camps consisting of victors and vanquished, aggravated in turn by power-political alliances and internal political developments within the Soviet Union and Germany.

Reflecting upon what he calls "the revolutionary age" as one characterized by a "greater transformation than in the previous thousand years," Bernadotte Schmitt refers to the period between about 1775 and 1875 as the century of revolution, the underlying forces of which began to assert themselves mostly in Europe. Yet while they gained increasing momentum, ". . . they did not come into their own . . . and exercize preponderant influence until the generation or half century preceding the Great War." Designating the period following the revolutionary age as "fifty years of synthesis," Schmitt concludes that "the Great War reveals a fact obscured by the great material prosperity of the second period: the fact that the work of synthesis was not complete, that the constructive ideas of mid-nineteenth century had been kept in check in certain regions by conservative forces which rested on the support of tradition and military power. . . ." [15] In fact, the phenomenon of the French revolution, coupled with Napoleon I's example became the catalyst of momentous changes in Germany "Napoleon understood the dynamism of the French Revolution, this immense release of energy, this gateway to ceaseless activity and boundless ambition. His personality was admirably suited to his time. In a period which exalted the individual and his opportunities, Napoleon, as Friedrich Nietzsche so clearly sensed, was an extreme individualist, for whom

France and Europe, nation and mankind, were but instruments of his destiny." [16]

Although the structure of the old empire still obtained at the beginning of the new era, two large monarchies, Prussia and Austria, now began to consolidate their gains. Defeat in the war with France (1792–1795) had

so little disturbed social stability that, driven by their greed for booty and compensation, the governments themselves were able to introduce many of the essential principles of the Revolution. The bigger states devoured the smaller, the secular states the ecclesiastical. Unlike France, the lightning bolts of revolution in Germany were wielded by the sovereigns and did not strike at the ruling class as a whole, but only its weakest links. In the states of the Confederation of the Rhine, revolution from above was pursued most consistently and logically; here an absolutist will created uniform and (under Napoleon's protectorate) sovereign formations out of feudal variety and against silent resistance. But it was in Prussia that the revolution from above was most effective.[17]

Some Germans had been strongly sympathetic toward the French Revolution and subsequently did not offer more than token resistance to the Napoleonic forces. The most favorable response had occurred among some of the intellectuals and among people living near the French border.

The impact of both the Enlightenment and the French Revolution had been manifest particularly in the western parts of the country. Initial support, however, waned partly as a result of legal difficulties stemming from conflicting interests involving German and French territories around Alsace. Conversely, since Napoleon's image seemingly resembled that of Charlemagne, some German intellectuals entertained the hope that he had come to unify all of Central and Western Europe. Again the dream of unity was to be dispelled. On the other hand, the trend toward radicalism in France, the tales of woe told by members of both the nobility and the church hierarchy who had become refugees in the Rhineland, had had their impact, even though some of them were probably exaggerated. Frederick William II (1786–1797), the nephew of Frederick the Great and one of the most icompetent of the Hohenzollern dynasty, was indifferent toward the war with France. His interest was directed toward the East, where Prussian chances for territorial gain seemed to hold more promise. By 1794, the French Army had conquered all of Belgium. Germany and Austria both withdrew their forces across the Rhine. Thus the Treaty of Basel (March, 1795) included an exchange of western territories for eastern ones, a policy in keeping with Prussian tradition. This treaty was to inaugurate the ultimate collapse of the Holy Roman Empire during the following decade. It also demonstrated Prussia's preoccupation with her own power-political interests, which seemed to ignore the concerns of the Empire as a whole. The emergence of a nation-wide German nationalism had been postponed partly by virtue of a narrow parochialism, which gave rise to much infighting among the nobility. What emerged was the guiding principle of the balance of power concept based upon the self-interest of rulers.

The territorial revolution begins with the partition of Poland, 1772–1795, which excited considerable indignation at the time. It was in fact a body blow at the doctrine later described as historic right, and set a precedent which was promptly utilized by the French Directory to seize the Rhineland and the Netherlands and by Napoleon Bonaparte to reorganize Italy and Germany. These achievements are often looked upon as merely so many things to be undone by the Congress of Vienna. Actually they were revolutionary acts of the greatest moment. No doubt Napoleon's manipulations of the map were dictated by his own political necessities, but they also pointed the course of the future. His kingdom of Italy, incomplete though it was, provided patriots of the Peninsula with an ideal for the future; his reduction of the number of German states facilitated enormously the work of Bismarck, and his later oppressions aroused German national sentiment from the torpor of centuries. The diplomacy of Metternich might restore the old arrangements and prevail for a time, but the imponderables were against him and his successors. In the revolutions of 1848 the primary aim of the Italians was national unity; in the Frankfort Parliament, the principal topic of debate was the area to be included in a German national state, and the decision was revolutionary, for it was against the inclusion of Austria, which had been part of Germany for 800 years.[18]

The aims of the Revolution of 1848, however, were not realized by either the Germans or the Italians. But this very defeat of their aspirations for unification induced both countries to achieve these goals by other means. "The actual work of unification by Cavour and Bismarck, heroic as it was, was only the logical conclusion of the work begun in 1797 and 1803." [19] In 1809 the House of Habsburg made its final attempt to establish supremacy in Germany. The attempt ended in dismal failure for Austria-Hungary and the sacrificial marriage of the Emperor's daughter, Marie Louise, to Napoleon. From now on Germany's future was bound up with Prussia and the Hohenzollern dynasty because "the Dual Monarchy of Austria-Hungary was a much weaker state than the German Empire. It possessed no military laurels . . . its economic progress was much slower and uneven, and large parts of it were very poor and backward. Above all, only the political aspirations of the Hungarians were satisfied by the *Ausgleich* of 1867, while those of the many Slav nationalities remained unfulfilled. In the course of the nineteenth century the Czechs, the Poles, and the Slovenes acquired their own middle and educated classes, hence their demands for political concessions became louder. But such concessions would have threatened the position of the Germans who were the leading nationality in the Austrian half of the Dual Monarchy." [20]

Max Weber has sometimes been "misunderstood" in that his writings have been viewed apart from their relationship with these previous political experiences. Weber, of course, never experienced mid-twentieth century manifestations of internationalism. Believing in the traditional state system, he was primarily concerned with the interests of the German state at the level of rational analysis and action. As Franz Schnabel has shown: "The program and slogans of nationalism— natural living space, historical borders, assimilation and national will— which derived in part from the French Revolution and for the rest from German romanticism, were widespread among the liberals in the sixties and seventies, and were already being fully acted upon among the eastern European peoples." [21]

By the time Max Weber was born (1864) Bismarck had already deprived the liberals among the German bourgeoisie of any effective power. The middle classes were protected by the authorities from effective expressions of dissatisfaction of the working classes and commercial interests were encouraged to take advantage of economic expansion at home and abroad. However, political control of domestic affairs remained the exclusive prerogative of the conservative classes. Max Weber's political philosophy was to be moulded by his allegiance to the middle class into which he was born, by his encounter with the disservice Bismarck was to render this class's interests by withholding political power from it, and by his own support of Bismarck's power-political ideas.

The majority of liberals believed with Bismarck that there were no really significant tasks transcending the sphere of the state. There could not have been many who envisaged a higher world order. Franz Neumann recalls the issues in tracing the origins of the German National Liberal Party from its inception in 1867, on which it had always strongly supported all attempts to augment the power of the state. The party advocated an army and a navy program and a policy of expansion and colonialism. The struggle of Eugen Richter, leader of the left Liberals within the Party, against a military buildup did not elicit a favorable response, even in his own party. As Neumann states, as early as 1893, German liberalism ceased to fight against the enlargement of the military establishment. In fact, German liberalism actually initiated naval construction; its impetus came from the industrial bourgeoisie, rather than from the emperor, the bureaucracy, or even the conservatives.[22]

During the early years of the era, conflict and division flourished among the various political parties. Bismarck took advantage of the situation to weaken the political power of the middle class, which was never fully and effectively exerted. The industrial middle class was represented by the National Liberal Party, while commercial interests were to be found in the Progressive Party, which was to the left of the National Liberals. To the left of both of these was the People's Party, known for its advocacy of an ideal democratic freedom, including a classless society. Characterized as an enemy of the state, it soon subsided into political isolation.

The National Liberal Party, the strongest party during the first phase of the Second Reich, was founded on June 12, 1867. Geographically, its membership was by no means homogeneous since in southern Germany the Reich concept enjoyed considerable support, whereas in northern Germany opposition to conservatism proved useful in gaining votes. Politically, members ranged from extreme nationalists of Treitschke's brand to passionate defenders of the *Rechtsstaat* such as Rudolf von Gneist and Eduard Lasker, the latter heading the left wing within the party. The newly founded party accentuated the division of the moderate from the radical wing of the liberal movement in Germany. The Old Liberals, justifying the aims of the conservative government in the name of freedom, considered both bourgeoisie and intellectual liberalism bankrupt.

Hermann Baumgarten's views reflected the persuasions of the Old Liberals perhaps most accurately. To the student of Max Weber, his position is of considerable interest. Historian and lifelong friend of Max Weber's father, he was to have great influence upon Weber's own political development. The Weber and Baumgarten families were related. It was in Baumgarten's home that Weber's father met his future wife, Max Weber's mother. For Whitsuntide vacations in 1882, Otto Baumgarten invited his cousin for the first time to Strassburg. This visit became significant for Weber because with it began a close personal contact. He became the political confidante of Hermann Baumgarten, who found in Weber a good foil for his disappointment in the conduct of German politics during that time.[23]

Marianne Weber acknowledges that politically Weber was influenced by Hermann Baumgarten to view the affairs of the nation from a position closely resembling Baumgarten's own perspective.[24] Wolfgang Mommsen similarly notes the impact of Baumgarten's thought upon Max Weber.[25] For both men the training of political leaders and the necessity for political maturity became the central issue underlying the political process as it evolved in Germany. Both were concerned with the relationship between a political regime and the level of national political maturity.[26] In his analysis of the debacle of German liberalism, Baumgarten pointed to the permanent political importance of the bourgeoisie as being its main cause. Recognizing the bourgeoisie's economic significance as well as its industrial and academic ingenuity, he maintained that " 'all modern states . . . will have to grant an important influence to bourgeois forces'—(whose) interests and tendencies will have to be considered above all by every wise statesman.' (Yet,) 'for genuine political action the middle class is . . . little fitted' . . . 'The bourgeois is created for work and not for rule. The ablest forces of the bourgeoisie have worked themselves up from the bottom . . . Such a career . . . gives character, freedom, and purity of soul. But whoever has risen so is in a sense too good for politics.' " [27] Baumgarten called instead for men "for whom politics is their life's profession." These men should come from those members of the aristocracy who would be, nevertheless, liberally inclined toward the lower strata.

Max Weber was to occupy himself again and again with the problem of the political immaturity of the German people, the roots of which he found in the recent past, especially in the negative aspects of Bismarck's chancellorship. He especially deplored the naive worship bestowed upon Bismarck by the German bourgeoisie, coupled with the uncritical acceptance of the principle of *Realpolitik*, and the blind stereotyped hatred of Bismarck entertained by the opposition, which permitted its policies to be guided by that perspective.[28] His passionate debates with Baumgarten about Bismarck and the meaning of liberalism for Germany's future separated Weber increasingly from the National Liberalism of his father. In his attitude toward left-wing liberalism (*Freisinnigen*), however, he concurred with his father, condemning its "doctrinaire" opposition toward increasing the military budget.[29]

In Baumgarten's judgment, "intellectual liberalism was the unrealistic expression of the bourgeoisie's invalid claims to political power." Consequently, his renunciation of political liberalism was accompanied by the recommendation that liberals and middle classes alike give up their ambitions for political hegemony, accept the existing order of politics, and "learn to see in the state rather than in their own desires the source of their real blessings." [30] Weber, too, charged the middle classes with political naïveté and the absence of a will to power. He pointed to a *spezifische Obrigkeitsgesinnung* (a specific German attitude toward authority) derived from Lutheran religiosity as having been a contributing factor [31] to the fact that "nowhere in the world has a proud nation ever been induced by the unlimited admiration of the personality of a politician to sacrifice so unreservedly its factual convictions." [32]

Baumgarten's pessimistic assessment of the political impotence of liberalism led him to demand support for the Prussian government in both domestic and foreign policy areas, with the nobility providing the guide-lines.[33] Leonard Krieger concludes that "Baumgarten had formally transferred the liberal as well as the national function of his

political ethic into the charge of the established authorities." [34] This
statement is corroborated by Baumgarten's own conclusion:

As soon as German liberalism comes out for the great deeds which it now
acknowledges . . . there can be no doubt that the next decade will bring us
the German state which has become as pressing for our science, art, and
morality as for our political development and national power-position . . . I am
of the firm conviction that a satisfactory solution of our political problems
will come only when liberalism ceases to be primarily opposition.[35]

Weber did not share his father's and his uncle's hopes for a
more liberal domestic policy under a different monarch, nor did he
fully share the pessimism of Hermann Baumgarten. Marianne Weber
pointed to this period as the "awakening of social and socio-political
interests" in Weber, causing him to abandon the National Liberal
orientation of the older generation.[36] Writing to Baumgarten on April
30, 1888, Weber refers to the "undeniable fact" that liberalism as it
existed in the seventies had relegated the social objectives of the state
to an unjustifiable level of importance.[37] Essentially, however, Weber
was bourgeois in sentiment; he resisted forming a permanent allegiance
either to the right or to the Social Democrats. None of the existing
bourgeois parties met with his favor, neither the National Liberals with
whom he had bonds of kinship because of his father, nor the *Freisinn,*
with whom he agreed on liberal constitutional issues. Any definitive
commitment to a given political party was ruled out since his pessimistic diagnosis of the rational chances of success for liberalism under
existing conditions precluded any such loyalty.

The extreme complexity of events in Germany during Weber's
lifetime causes even informed students to disagree about some of his
interpretations. Perceiving something unreal about the climate of bourgeois social and political tranquility, he sought to penetrate beneath
the surface of German society. He was disturbed by its lack of depth
and the absence of a realistic sense of direction. There was, indeed,
something strangely empty and purely imitative in the pseudodiplomacy
in which some of Bismarck's successors engaged. In spite of its calm
surface, Weber saw the corrosions of life in a society whose main
standard-bearers, the German bourgeoisie, lacked a sense of civic
responsibility. He was cognizant of the powerful economic interest
groups who resisted what they considered the encroachment of irksome
restrictions, which in the national interest might be imposed upon their
economic liberties. Indeed, Weber's own perspective here was not far
removed from Bismarck's conception of the role of the state: "By
destiny and tendency Bismarck's profession became the modern political
system of reason of state and embattled interests. . . . He considered

that territorial compactness and the independence of modern great states, which recognize legal order among themselves only in the shape of alternating alliances, constituted not merely a valuable, but in fact a final achievement of civilization. In order to safeguard and to extend this system of state power, he promoted the welfare of the people, though wholly in the spirit of the old statecraft, and was convinced that only a power-state could guarantee happiness and prosperity." [38]

One question preoccupied many contemporary intellectuals: since German society had succeeded in producing impressive cultural achievements while raising the general standard of living through her advances in science and technology, why had German politics, especially in the area of foreign policy, been so starved for adequate talent through sheer lack of opportunity for the rise of competent leaders and a sound post-Bismarck diplomacy which would have enabled Germany to take her place among the other great nations? Weber especially deplored the absence of genuine political leadership and purposeful political action among organized labor. But the central problem remained the resistance of the entire German social structure to concerted public action in both domestic and foreign fields.

The half century preceding World War I was, in fact, marked by extraordinary accomplishments in the diplomatic, military, and economic sectors. Bismarck had united most of Germany under Prussian hegemony, proclaiming a German Empire with the King of Prussia as the new emperor whose first chancellor he became. He then proceeded to exploit both military and political victories, linking the libertarian sentiments of nationalism to his power-political purposes. Although he never fully accomplished his objective, he succeeded in rendering the German people ideologically impotent, regardless of whether they affirmed or rejected his actions. Thus, following his own value judgments and applying them to the realities of power, Bismarck made no secret of his intentions: prior to 1872, his aim was the extension of Prussian domination; after 1872, he generally strove to assure the political future of the German Reich. Determined to retain effective ultimate authority in his own hands, Bismarck's policy decisions were based upon power-oriented pragmatism aimed at the strengthening and security of the nation-state. After 1879, his personal style of action and his major efforts were directed at the protection of the German economy. Throughout this period, Bismarck's administration was able to maintain the domestic political status quo. The rise of socialism clearly appeared as the sword of Damocles to the industrialists, financiers, and agrarian interests. Partly as a result of this general condition, and partly because of a major effort directed toward the specific goal, it was possible for his administration to win sweeping legislative victories in the economic field. The distinctive feature of his domestic policy had been the maintenance of the existing social order. In an effort to break the potential power of the rising labor movement Bismarck had dubbed the Socialists as "enemies of the State." Thus the political successes of Bismarck carried a price. In 1878 he had attempted to destroy the Socialist movement. His hope of success had rested in the introduction of social reforms while outlawing the Social Democratic Party and the trade unions for a period of twelve years. Yet, Germany had passed the point where supporting the disadvantaged elements, assuring minimum standards of their well-being was the main problem. Subsequently, in 1907, Max Weber was to criticize the ruling classes for their serious mistake in refusing to grant universal suffrage to social democracy. He warned that continued commitment to this program could only widen the gulf between bourgeoisie and proletariat, thus alienating the masses from the nation-state. His view was predicated on the assumption that thus the revolutionary element would gain influence upon the movement at the expense of the party bureaucracy which had a vested interest in the status quo. In his political analysis, he pointed to the party as becoming a state within a state with more and more people having a personal stake in promotion and material benefits. The key to understanding for Weber lay in the changing mode of German political life. It was a change in which the rhetoric of the middle classes became largely irrelevant. He argued that certain elements among the Social Democrats had more cause for apprehension than the bourgeoisie, namely those among them who had an ideological commitment to revolutionary ideology. He contrasted the material interests of the professional politicians with the concerns of the revolutionary ideologues, seeking to demonstrate that if the former could be persuaded that their material interests would be protected, then they in turn would seek to protect themselves against those in their own ranks who would jeopardize their status rather than militate against the bourgeosie. Historical interest demanded that the mutual distrust and resentments of the past be overcome. The gulf between the classes could be bridged if Social Democrats could hold membership in veterans' associations and be offered posts in church administrations. Thus the party would experience disunity within its own ranks. Instead of social democracy scoring political victories by conquering city and state, the state would succeed in conquering social democracy.[39]

Thus Weber sought to offer what seemed to him a valid alternative policy because the accommodation of the various group interests in a pragmatic, empirically based effort to solve this specific problem became paramount for him. He perceived this opportunity to be based on an understanding of the relationship between the bureaucratization of the Social Democratic Party and the concomitant split within its ranks. Nevertheless: "even those who like Max Weber were convinced of the necessity for a reform of the Bismarckian constitution did not see how it could be achieved in view of the great power of the monarchy, which, in the midst of an unexampled prosperity, enjoyed the full support of upper and middle classes. This frustration generated political weariness and passivity among those who might have contributed to the conduct of politics or at least to political education." [40] Thus, in effect, the practical application of Bismarck's plan aimed at greater social justice was not to become the important lever in the hands of his administration for which he had hoped. Working-class demands were aimed at political power, not merely at social and economic gains. The tension between the traditional system of government and the presence of entirely new social forces in Imperial Germany, a result of the industrial revolution, was not solved in Imperial Germany, but instead contributed to its disintegration.

The repeal of the anti-socialist laws together with the enactment of the industrial code gave evidence that the Social Democrats and the existence of class conflicts could no longer be overlooked. Yet no adequate acknowledgment of this conflict, much less a reconstruction of the domestic policy, was forthcoming. It is true that after the repeal of Bismarck's anti-socialist legislation and the enactment of the industrial code, there followed the establishment, in 1890, of the "Generalkommission der Gewerkschaften," an organization representing a number of socialist labor unions. This was later to become, after World War I, the "Allgemeine Deutsche Gewerkschaftsbund," a central labor federation which might be compared with the Trades Union Congress in Britain or with the American Federation of Labor. As Franz Neumann states, during this period "the social power of the working-class movement and its fight against the state (which) eventually led to a situation in which the state, while no longer daring to attack the existence of the trade unions directly, sought to make their life and activity as difficult as possible by means of a whole series of special provisions, including the help of the penal code and the courts of law, and in particular the police force." [41]

Philip Lothmar, who had pioneered the German labor law, characterized this phase as follows: *"Die Gewerkschaft ist frei, aber sie ist vogelfrei."* ("The trade union is free, but it is as free as an outlaw.") [42] Examining the history of German organized labor during that period, Franz Neumann outlines it most succinctly in *Behemoth:*

The attempt to reconcile the working classes to the state was carried as far as the ruling forces dared; further efforts in this direction would have meant abandoning the very foundation on which the empire rested—the semi-absolutistic and bureaucratic principles of the regime. Only political concessions to the working classes could bring about a reconciliation. The ruling parties were unwilling, however, to abolish the Prussian three-class franchise system and to establish a responsible parliamentary government in the Reich itself and in the component states. With this recalcitrance, nothing remained for them but a war to the death against socialism as an organized political and industrial movement.[43]

Thus at a time when Europe was moving toward responsible government, such conditions vitiated the growth of a genuine parliamentary system in Germany. Yet from 1890 on, the socialist trade unions, having joined forces under Carl Legien, experienced considerable growth, while the democratic trade unions lagged. In the latter case, only the salaried employees' sector gained in importance. Official reaction to those who challenged the status quo took three forms:

1. the reorganization of the Prussian bureaucracy into a stronghold of semi-absolutism;
2. the establishment of the army as a bulwark of monarchical power; and
3. the welding together of the owning classes.[44]

To those accustomed to Western parliamentary processes, these are puzzling features in the German governmental system.

Foreign policy was conducted by the chancellor, who was responsible only to the monarch. Few chancellors were so fortunate as to be handed for so long a blank check to fill out as they pleased. The chancellor personally made all major decisions in the fields of foreign and military security policy, defending them in Parliament. Routinized institutional assignments were passed on to the state secretaries. While it is true that the German Imperial system lacked elements generally regarded as vital to the democratic process, however, it was not unresponsive to public opinion. Despite the sometimes questionable parliamentary tactics by which the government, in using its majority, achieved its victories in the legislature it also appears that it was not the pace of policy initiative and degree of competence of leading officials of the government which make this period a memorable one, but the over-all pattern of the Wilhelminian period must be derived from the multitude of attitudes and values, actions and inactions of many people. In fact, the Prussian aristocratic establishment had traditionally viewed the navy somewhat apprehensively because any acceleration in its construction program could only contribute to a curtailment of developmental plans for the army. Army and Prussian nobility were bound to each other by tradition. Moreover, officers in the army by virtue of inheritance and tradition had a more exclusive image of themselves, whereas the officers of the navy subscribed to a more bourgeois outlook. Thus the build-up of the fleet was actually deplored by high officials of the Foreign Office, especially by members of the landed aristocracy, who

looked with disfavor upon the financial sacrifices to be made for a
project which held no benefits for them. Thus neither the chancellor
nor the Foreign Office persisted in certain policies; on the contrary,
the navy measure was forced through by Admiral Tirpitz who
headed the Reich Naval Office; who in turn drew his support from
the Kaiser, nationalistic organizations, big business and heavy industry.
In this instance, the Foreign Office acquiesced primarily to allay
criticism. The quest for colonial enterprises derived support partly from
the growing strength of capitalistic interests rather than from the
Foreign Office alone; enthusiastic popular support combined with the
exhortation by certain groups to national "vigor and vitality" played a
decisive role in the imperialist designs contained in the subsequent
program of War Aims. Both the expansion program of the navy and
the colonial aspirations were supported by considerable segments of
public opinion which viewed both projects as tools for the promotion
of the national interest. In the army, also, especially in the higher ranks,
there were those who disavowed imperialist designs and colonial
experiments. Both in the Foreign Office and in the army there were
men who tended to favor specific, limited settlements of specific disputes. They would have preferred accommodation with England rather
than victory over her. Nevertheless, the Kaiser's personal style, the High
Command, the wave of imperialism, the naval construction program,
the organizational activities of some of the chauvinistic associations
make it possible now to identify a certain direction of movement which
gives to the Wilhelminian era a distinctive tone. These factors rather
than either the philosophical and moral convictions or the degree of
imagination and pace of policy initiative of Germany's statesmen
Bethmann, Michaelis, and Hertling, and Jagow, Zimmermann, and
Kuehlmann were historically decisive. Max Weber, it will be recalled,
repeatedly criticized the government, charging it with ineptitude. He
demanded a program subordinated to the necessities of power, one in
which risks, wherever possible, were to be avoided, in which unrealistic
aims and unwarranted enthusiasm should not dictate foreign policy.
Thus Weber called for innovating experimental policy directions strongly
opposing the policy made by dilettantes. While admitting that the
skilled administrator, the bureaucrat, has an important role to play in
government, crucial policy issues in German politics were, in fact,
initiated by bureaucratic officials. Weber was highly critical of bureaucrats among leading politicians. He argued that when the work of a
politician is viewed as essentially a matter of technical competence
rather than as the defense of controversial policies, when bureaucrats
are thus entrusted with policy formulation, this will result in the
encouragement of more bureaucrats to move into politics, a prospect
which Weber anticipated with considerable apprehension.

The scheme underlying the promise conceived by demagogues and made in 1917 by Zimmermann offering to Mexico, California, New Mexico, and Texas, was too far from realization to disturb the enemy, but the threatened intrusion into the sovereignty of another state, if nothing else, demonstrated that German politics needed regeneration. Certain tragic though coincidental factors vitiated efforts designed to achieve this purpose, however, Chancellor Bethmann-Hollweg received his dismissal from the Kaiser only three days after finally universal franchise was granted to Prussia, a measure he had vigorously championed, and five days before the anti-annexationist Peace Resolution was adopted. As Gerhard Ritter said ". . . he fell, ironically, at the moment when for the first time a Reichstag majority was forming which might have supported his policy of moderation. The panic of the delegates—more especially the Center Party—was in part responsible for his dismissal, but the primary agents were Ludendorff and Hindenburg, who forced the reluctant Kaiser's hand, and definitely established their political predominance . . ." [45]

In another instance, the Foreign Office had been able to uphold its position. Before the War when General Friedrich von Bernhardi, formerly a member of the General Staff but subsequently removed from it, published his book expressing regrets that Germany failed to take advantage in the Morocco crisis in 1911 by pressing her colonial demands, the Foreign Office sought to suppress publication of his book, and the Kaiser publicly rebuked him. Prospects of somewhat more responsible political behavior might yet have existed had Bethmann been retained.

A fair historical treatment must address itself to the multidimensional aspects of that period. There is no equivocation about the role played by the right-wing political parties and their press, the powerful interest groups and concomitant lobbying organizations. Secretiveness prevailed in the upper reaches of the military establishment concerning Germany's actual military situation. Politicians, press, and the population at large were inadequately informed of the threat of defeat even when it became a real possibility.

On the other side of the ledger, it can hardly be held that Max Weber and a few other notable social scientists merely submitted to pressure and propaganda. Sometimes his publicistic writings revealed a certain combination of pessimism and ambivalence, reflecting Weber's assumption that Germany could walk the narrow line between aggression and appeasement. He denounced the glaring faults of the conduct of Germany's politics; yet, he thought that if Germany was ever to become a national power-state it could not achieve this status except through the medium of a powerful executive, a formidable navy to protect her trade, and a disciplined people. Weber's lack of ideological commitment led him to recognize the irrelevance to the modern world of many of the old catch-phrases, but even he, the liberal, independent and penetrating political thinker stressed national power rather than civil liberties. For Weber the political and social unity of the state was a necessary prerequisite for Germany as an imperial power-state or else the founding of the Reich would have been meaningless. Whereas political thought in England and France had tended to stress the rights of the individual rather than the power of the state, essentially the attitude toward political authority, many Germans argue, must be different by virtue of Germany's own historical background and geographical location from that afforded by people in countries which have been favored more both historically and geographically. A country with open frontiers surrounded by unfriendly neighbors, it is said, has cause to view threats from other nations with more concern than civil liberties.

Both world wars have raised the compelling question concerning the origin of the seeds of these catastrophic events. When his project, the creation of a nation-state, was completed at the price of three wars, Bismarck had no wish to pursue imperialist aims but instead cooperated in the maintenance of peace in Europe which lasted for a generation. Neither condemnation nor eulogy of Bismarck will serve to broaden our historical perspective. He embodied the *Zeitgeist,* the spirit of his age. While England and France could afford to consolidate themselves into powerful national states at a slower pace, both Italy and Germany had to accomplish this feat within a short span of time.

Explanations of causes which ultimately precipitated World War I must lay bare the deeper roots of the *Zeitgeist* which involved the interplay between internal dynamics and external pressures, both nationally and internationally. The change from "continental" politics of Bismarck's age to "world" politics was enthusiastically endorsed by the German bourgeoisie. Men of property ranging from big industrialists to businessmen, from administrators to school teachers and university professors, welcomed this new type of *Realpolitik* which would have been alien to him whose example they professed to emulate. These sentiments Admiral Tirpitz exploited to obtain support for both the Navy Bill and for his expansionist aims which formed the core of the platform of the "Fatherland Party" which he had founded during the war. There is no single explanation for the enormous popular support of imperialist expansion which had its beginning toward the latter part of the nineteenth century. Colonies, of course, could supply valuable raw materials and military bases, serving strategic purposes in wartime. They also held out possibilities for adjustments to shifts in the balance of power. Economically, colonies were attractive because they offered protected markets for a nation's manufactured goods, and exclusive sources of raw materials, and a promise of successful capital investment. Nationalist feelings and interest in imperialist designs encouraged by the yellow press, however, did not capture the interest of the common man in Germany alone; both obtained in other countries, too. Germany, in fact, did not derive much more than national prestige satisfaction since her colonial imports and exports were minimal and her capital investment small.

The prime function of power at the national level is to serve the national interest, that is to preserve the state's territorial security and integrity by the maintenance of military, economic, and cultural strength. Concern and fear are most likely when a country feels its national interest threatened. Although trade rivalries and colonial competition soared, the tensions they created were not directly responsible for World War I. These conflicts were settled by means of diplomacy. The prospect of war became more imminent when Britain saw herself compelled to take sides against Germany, with German naval policy deciding the alignments. Both camps were fully prepared for war. Wars among the Balkan states could remain localized due to the smallness of these states. Localization of a conflict in which the great powers themselves were involved proved impossible, however.

Admittedly Germany's constitution and authority structure both before and more especially during the war constituted a fateful handicap. As will be noted later, it is however highly speculative to trace developments underlying the war to the disquieting aspects of the German Imperial system. It is true that the Kaiser's conduct was inconsistent, and that the various branches of the German government were lacking in consensus, thereby hindering consistency and continuity in foreign policy. As a result, consideration of the ultimate consequences of German foreign policy was thus neglected. The task of political analysis here is an extraordinarily difficult one. Part of the difficulty stems from the great uncertainty about the accurate reading of the direction and outcome of the course of events effected by pressures and counter-pressures. It is difficult to estimate whether a mood of moderation might have prevailed under certain conditions aimed at the prevention of the war or whether all efforts would have been doomed to failure by the elements of fear and pride. It has been argued that the magnitude of the general disillusionment with the German Empire felt by foreign governments stemmed from the image of inflexibility and anachronism which it presented to the world. Yet Czarist Russia, too, did not exemplify a modern political structure. Conversely, after the Revolution the term "imperialism" was cited as the domination of finance capital by Lenin. This equation did not prove accurate, however. Certainly the capitalistic aspirations to locate areas for profitable investment contributed to colonial expansion. But imperialism has more than one objective. Having engaged itself in the forcible occupation of Czechoslovakia, the Soviet Union did not behave in line with Marxist-Leninist theory; by invading an allied socialist country in which there was no revolt against the dominant role of the Communist Party or against the basic alignment of the state, the Soviets have shown themselves to be an intolerant imperialist power. Since capitalism has been eliminated imperialism too should have been eliminated. The fact is, however, that it survived capitalism in Russia.

What went frequently unrecognized in studies of German politics on the other side of the ledger, is that before Robert von Puttkammer, Conservative Prussian minister of the interior from 1881 to 1888, effected changes in both the spirit and the letter of German legislation and in the policies relating to the public service, "the earlier bureaucracy of the eighteenth and early nineteenth centuries was far from conservative and made common cause with the champions of the rising industrial capitalism against feudal privilege. The transformation of the bureaucracy set in when the nobility itself began to participate extensively in capitalist enterprise." [46] Even the liberals were dismissed by Puttkammer in a systematic purge. The Kaiser, meanwhile, issued an edict demanding that "civil servants to whom the execution of my government is entrusted and who, therefore, can be removed from office by disciplinary action," cast their votes for his candidates in elections.[47] The ingredients of the struggle included Puttkammer's dictum that in Prussia, "the special favorite of God," [48] religion was to be a part of bureaucratic life.

The second phase of the attack against liberalism and socialism culminated in the conversion of the army into an instrument of reaction. The officer's corps was composed of members of the aristocracy to whom inherent qualities of leadership were ascribed. Even foreign-born noblemen were considered more worthy of being included in the Prussian military caste than members of the bourgeoisie, who in the opinion of Frederick II of Prussia were only "canaille."

Another far-reaching measure subsequently accomplished an alliance between two former antagonists, the army and the bourgeoisie. In the last two decades of the nineteenth century, the liberals were confronted with a choice between their own national aspirations on the one hand and their dedication to constitutional liberties and an effective parliament, on the other. As mentioned, Bismarck's successful foreign policy, German victories on the battlefield, and the country's unification ultimately caused the majority of liberals to endorse his policies. However, a deeper reason underlies historical developments here. Leonard Krieger pinpoints it when he writes: "The liberal spirit did affect German institutions and these institutions penetrated through the facade of professional politics to effect real changes in the life of the nation. But the process was incomplete and unintegrated. Not only was the capstone of political rights wanting but spiritual and material liberties were never organized into a single system of rights, and consequently the half-finished structure crumbled under the strain of later social and international conflicts." [49]

This period, which had been preceded by one consisting of reaction to the events of 1848, also saw a transformation in the character of liberalism itself. Before 1848, it had been the proponent of idealized political principles which, however, remained unrealized. In the years after 1848, liberalism was marked by a weakening of this core of principles and a decline in its intellectual appeal and cohesion which ultimately diminished its potential for opposing the growth of the semi-absolutistic political system in Germany. The various older liberal groups came to depend more and more on the rising economic bourgeoisie for support. Ultimately, the middle-class interests predominated over the intellectual tradition.

German liberalism in fact has never been able to overcome the consequences of its initial self-betrayal. Its condition was partly revealed by the identification of many of Germany's foremost intellectuals with the National Liberal party, which envisaged the fusion of individual and collective liberty. This party was instrumental in linking important parts of the German bourgeoisie with the authoritarian state politically, while socially an alliance was formed with the landed aristocracy. The bourgeoisie, in effect, lent its support to the status quo in exchange for protection against social democracy. Instead of favoring political concessions to the working classes, the bourgeoisie entered into an alliance with its former enemy, the aristocracy.

The price which the German bourgeoisie would have to pay as it embarked upon its new course of conciliation and pacification promised to be high indeed. The resulting domestic tranquility became the cause of its protracted moral stagnation and a poverty of political imagination which prevented it from recognizing the larger issues involved in its failure to exercize the political power to which its economic position entitled it. Instead, a new type of "feudal bourgeois" arose from the politically immature ranks of the bourgeoisie, represented especially perhaps by the *Reserveoffizier* who despite his typical lower-middle-class status "had all the conceit of the old feudal lord, with few of his virtues, little of his regard for loyalty or culture. He represented a coalition of the army, the bureaucracy, and the owners of the large estates and factories for the joint exploitation of the states." [50] Meanwhile, the army had been undergoing an expansion program of such magnitude (also voted for by the National Liberals in parliament) that its strength increased from 1,200,000 in 1888 to 2,000,000 by 1902.[51]

Domestically, the bourgeoisie's image of the future was one of continued political and economic stability. In the area of foreign policy it envisaged continuity along previously established lines of expansion of Germany's economic power and a greater voice for her in the conduct of international politics. German civilians were unable to resist the temptation of transforming themselves into a society in which the freedom of political competition necessary for democracy was destroyed: "The structural and psychological mechanisms that characterized the army crept steadily into civilian life until they held it in a firm grip."[52] Thus while it could be said of France that the nineteenth century witnessed a fusion of the army into the bourgeoisie, in Germany this process was reversed, namely, "society was fused into the army." [53]

Another step supporting the suppression of liberalism and socialism was the establishment of a political alliance between agrarians and industrialists. No longer did the industrialists have to fear the opposition of the agrarians to their extensive naval program; the Prussian Conservative party, in return for the industrialists' vote in favor of protective tariffs, cast its ballots in support of the navy bill. The union between these two formidable forces against liberalism and socialism was cemented by Johannes von Miquel, who was responsible, initially in his capacity of leadership of the National Liberal party in 1884 and subsequently as Prussian minister of finance, for insuring the party's right-wing majority support of Bismarck's policies at home and abroad. This move resulted in his sinister *Sammlungspolitik*, collective effort launched by all 'true patriots' against the threat of Social Democracy.

Ralf Dahrendorf, who was appointed himself in 1969 parliamentary state secretary in the West German Foreign Ministry, in a realistic appraisal of future German social and political developments, emphasizes the far-reaching consequences of the attitude toward conflict emanating from Germany's political and social institutions. He posits four prerequisites without which liberal democratic government cannot function:

First, the effective realization of an equal status of citizenship for all participants in the political process; secondly, the presence of competing elites and interest groups none of which is capable of monopolizing the roads to power; thirdly, the prevalence of a set of values which, by contrast to the private virtues of withdrawal and non-participation, may be described as public virtues, and, finally, the acceptance of differences of opinion and conflicts of interest as an inevitable and indeed creative element of social life.[54]

Concentrating on the last factor, Dahrendorf inquires: "What is it in the ways in which conflict is dealt with in the institutions of German society that can help explain the apparent impossibility to establish successful and lasting democratic political institutions?" [55] Doubtful whether paternal authority in Imperial Germany really surpassed its counterparts in England or elsewhere, he takes issue with those who blame the authoritarian character of German society on the

German family. Much more pertinent is the question of how discussion and debate are handled in German society and the role played by the German educational system:

When Max Weber advanced his thesis of the desirability of a value-free approach to social science, and in particular his demand for a complete abstention from value judgments in academic teaching, one of his main points was that 'in the lecture-room where one sits in front of one's listeners, they have to be silent and the lecturer has to speak'. For this reason (so Weber argued) it would be irresponsible to exploit the situation by mixing values with facts. But may it not be that the educational situation envisaged by Weber is as dated (and placed) as, say, Freud's notion of the super-ego as the internalized father? Is it not conceivable that academic teaching could be conducted in such a way that the students do not 'have to be silent', and that the lecturer is exposed to questions, objections, debate and discussion? It would be rewarding to explore the implications of these—rhetorical—questions for the demand of a value-free social science. As far as attitudes to debate and conflict are concerned, they point to a conception of the educational situation which is characteristic of German society.[56]

Some concern has been expressed about the gap which exists in the Federal Republic between the ability of the educational system to train a new generation of teachers and educational needs. Pressures for restructuring the school system are strong and various ways for meeting them are in the process of being devised, especially in certain *Laender* noted for a progressive outlook on education, such as Hesse. Evidence of change exists; yet it is not easy to discern future trends. There are at present only hints about potential future patterns. Moreover, regarding officially nurtured institutions designed for orderly operation, respect for the democratic process demands the assimilation of political activism at a time when, for various reasons, accepted political and social values are being questioned. In both Eastern and Western countries student unrest is a widely experienced phenomenon. In practical politics there are certain lessons to be learned concerning the reconciliation of conflicting interests and values, which causes students seeking political self-expression to find it difficult to accept compromises which they feel to be outdated. Hence they incline, in Weber's terms, to adhere to an "ethic of conviction" stressing ultimate ends rather than to abide by any "ethic of responsibility." The most fundamental problem is the fact that such pressures might not occur and the government might not be held to account for its actions because the democratic process does not fulfil its political implications "except in the context of a society the institutions of which are everywhere based on the acceptance and rational canalization of conflict." [57] In Germany, however, a pervasive pattern of "conflict evasion" has traditionally marked the various spheres of social organization, including the educational and legal systems, the family and the church, as well as the relationship between labor and industry. In the latter sphere, as will be shown, both labor and management have long been accustomed to viewing the state as the final arbiter.

Both the constitution and the franchise were designed to furnish the conservative forces consisting of officialdom, the military establishment, and the landowners with a majority in both houses of the Prussian *Landtag*. In the *Reichstag* various interests were represented and organized in political parties, but it could not be regarded as a decision-making body, nor could it check the executive branch in its exercise of power. "Decisions were made elsewhere by authorities which looked upon themselves and were looked upon by others as impartial adjudicators of right and wrong ('the reality of the moral ideal') above the petty disputes and conflicts of the parties. In the structure of the executive, this notion of the State as the ultimate authority and source of law and morality was and is clearly expressed by the preferential position accorded to civil servants (and within the civil service to lawyers as the institutional interpreters of substantive morality)." [58] What is characteristic—and its significance will be more fully treated later— is that the traits ascribed to the Prussian 'civil service ethos' (the concepts of duty, incorruptibility, loyalty, and impartiality) are closely related to this moral image of the state.

From 1918 to 1933, various manifestations appeared of widespread disdain of 'party dissension,' 'lobbying by divergent interest groups,' and of the whole 'political bargaining process' through pressure groups. All were stigmatized as *Kuhhandel* (trading of cattle). Hence the antipathy toward the Weimar 'system,' which failed to transcend "the grime of civil society" in favor of "the splendour of the State." [59]

This belief in the ethical neutrality of the State and the suspicion of conflicting interests reflected the fact that: "In so far as parliamentary government was ever accepted in Weimar Germany, it was accepted as a second best solution, often indeed as a mere mechanism for finding the right man or men, i.e., him or those who know all the right answers. Thus for many, elections and parliamentary debates seemed acceptable as a procedure of personnel selection, but not as a method of government." [60] This concept of parliament as a training ground for leaders on which the political struggle between rising talents could be fought out also represents Max Weber's view.

In Imperial Germany, the chancellor was appointed by the emperor and was responsible to him rather than to parliament. Moreover, members of the *Bundesrat* (Federal Council), charged with the responsibility of functioning as the upper-chamber and main executive organ, could not sit in the *Reichstag*. Consequently, however talented and aspiring a politician might have been, membership in the *Reichstag* normally would not have provided him with potential access to ministerial posts. In fact, politicians were less frequently selected for such positions than civil servants, a practice Weber severely criticized. Franz Neumann asserts correctly that liberty is not jeopardized merely by the legislative activity of the administration; the real threat derives from a social structure which is prejudicial to the rise of contending political forces. A high level of debate among responsible political parties within a flexible social structure is far more conducive to liberty than "the monopolization of legislation by the legislature and the reduction of the administrative power into a law-enforcing agency." [61]

The *Reichstag* controlled expenditures and could enact or reject legislation. Bismarck, however, backed by the National Liberal Party, inaugurated a system whereby the military budget was voted on for a period of seven years, depriving the *Reichstag* of the privilege to investigate the activities of the military on an annual basis. Commenting upon Bismarck's political legacy, Weber deplored the fact that it included a nation "without any kind of political education," . . . "without any kind of political will" . . . "a completely powerless parliament," leaving the affairs of the state in the hands of professional civil servants instead of letting the state be governed by politicians.[62]

Commenting upon criticism of Germany's alleged inability to develop political talent and a properly functioning parliamentary system, Marriott and Robertson conclude:

It was not the lack of political talent in the German nation that was responsible for the degradation of politics. A nation that could produce political leaders such as Bennigsen, Windthorst, Lasker, Richter, Bebel, was not lacking in men of high political gifts. But political conditions which make a government irresponsible to representative institutions, which grant to political groups freedom of criticism, but exempt them from all responsibility for that criticism, which faced by parties that know that no matter how strong they may be, they will never have the sobering responsibility of office, nor gain the official experience that alone can turn politicians into statesmen, are bound to produce two pernicious results. Parties degenerate into groups, fighting simply for the material interests of the sections which have elected them, with the inevitable lowering and materialization of all political values. Secondly, ability will desert an arena bereft of all real power and influence, and flow to the quarters where real power and responsibility reward talent and ambition. . . . The constitution made the politician powerless, and because the politician was powerless political life adapted itself to his position. In short, the motor forces and brains that made German policy after 1890 are not to be found in the Reichstag, and an autocracy that expects the political health of representative self-government in an organism deprived of the free functioning of the vital processes asks for the impossible. A no less potent reason was the cold but living hand of Prussia, 'the Kingdom which dips one wing of the Eagle in the Niemen and the other in the Rhine.' The grip of the Prussian governing class on the Imperial Executive was the real *arcanum imperii*.[63]

Probing more deeply into German failures in various areas of conflict and the negative effect upon future popular political involvement, Dahrendorf cites the structural defects within a modern industrial society such as Germany which fail to bind the masses more closely to a pluralistic polity, enabling the select few or the chosen one to claim infallibility, a claim which has traditionally gained the confidence of so many. The course of political modernization in Germany raises questions about the form and organization of authority in societies in which industrialization has been highly accelerated. Certainly the German experience suggests that authoritarian forms of political organization can be extremely effective in the industrialization process. In fact, the primacy of highly centralized government in the modernizing process has been accepted as a fact of life by non-western developing countries. Does this initial stage of authoritarianism, however, commit the German polity to a long-term adherence to authoritarianism? Moreover, is a process of gradual transition from authoritarian to democratic forms of political behavior required for the emergence of a political system which is both modern and enduringly democratic? Thus Dahrendorf writes:

While the rapid expansion of industrial production in Imperial Germany has certainly resulted in profound changes, its more striking feature is how this process was incorporated in the earlier traditions of German society. Today, we tend to describe these traditions as 'pre-industrial.' But, in fact, the German case was the first to prove that the social relations characteristic of feudal conditions everywhere need not disappear either immediately or entirely as industrialization sets in. The authoritarian welfare state and the industrial feudal society may appear contradictions in terms, but in Germany they were not contradictions in reality (unless one wants to regard the very explosiveness of these combinations as one of the sources of the instability of German politics after 1871).[64]

Max Weber's examination of charismatic authority suggests the connection between the appearance of charismatic personalities and situations in which traditions are breaking down. Societies undergoing cultural change lend themselves ideally to the rise of such leaders; a society in which confusion over values has etched itself deeply into its members' consciousness is highly prone to project earlier political and economic crises upon future ones, thus becoming all the more receptive to a leader who conveys a sense of mission, making his God-sent role believable. A decade before the founding of the Weimar republic, opposing the "personal rule" of the Emperor following Bismarck's resignation, Max Weber wrote to Friedrich Naumann: "What is decisive is: . . . A dilettante has the threads of policy in his hands." The *Berliner Tageblatt* raised the inevitable question: "How is this possible? Here is a people of over 60 million, a nation that has reached the heights of its own power, a nation of the highest intelligence, and yet the fate of the chancellor and, on his fall, the choice of his successor are dependent upon the will of one single individual. Such a condition is unbearable for a self-respecting nation." [65]

Bismarck had been successful in deferring war with France, whose enmity he had incurred by the seizure of Alsace-Lorraine. This was due perhaps as much to the particular state of international relations during that period as to his own efforts to foil attempts at formation of hostile alliances. However, whereas Bismarck had exhibited a cautious finesse in his foreign policy, others subsequently disregarded the need for discretion all too frequently. Repeated diplomatic ineptitude was equalled only by designs to advance what was viewed as Germany's vital national interest. England's hostility was incurred by the construction of a powerful German navy, while Russia resented Germany's support of the Habsburg Empire in the latter's Slavic policies. The clash in 1906 between Chancellor Buelow and the Center Party on the colonial issue led him to seek support from a Conservative-Liberal Bloc. His efforts proved successful: "All the liberal groups followed Buelow's slogans in the hope that the government would grant concessions to the bourgeoisie and mitigate the excessive predominance of the Prussian nobility. Not only did the National Liberals support the government, but also all the Independent groups, whose resistance to imperialism had constantly diminished since the death of Eugen Richter." [66] Yet, the "quarrel over Southwest Africa, was," as Rosenberg states, not reflecting the "vital interest of the German masses." [67] Nevertheless, the election of 1907 proved advantageous for the government because the Social Democrats lost half of their seats and Buelow was able to form a majority, called the Buelow-bloc, of Conservatives and National Liberals. Thus ". . . an insignificant colonial conflict was enough to defeat the strongest socialist party in the world in an election. So slight was the power of attraction of peaceful and anti-imperialist ideas as soon as a question arose which, even slightly, went beyond the concerns of daily life. All the Liberals immediately went over to the government, millions of indifferent voters espoused the national cause, and the Social Democrats lost a series of their firmest strongholds." [68]

Maximilian Harden, a man of great talents and editor and publisher of *Die Zukunft*, was one of the outstanding figures who protested the Emperor's ineptitude. In connection with the *Daily Telegraph* incident, Harden correctly described both the public outcry against the

highhanded methods of the Emperor: "Personal government, absolutism, impulsive action, romantic politics, duty of responsible advisers,
all these old themes were heard once again; only this time the orchestra
was much larger and played it *fortissimo.*" [69] Harden actually was both
the

deadly enemy of the Emperor and of the Social Democrats. Although for
obvious reasons Harden never formally declared himself in favour of a German Republic, nevertheless his constant and amazingly successful discrediting
of the Emperor and his friends must have daily aroused republican feelings.
If the question be asked who did most during the reign of William II to
pave the way for the present German Republic, the answer must be returned
that it was Maximilian Harden. A long way behind him came Erzberger,
while Karl Liebknecht had no share in the task of preparation whatsoever.[70]

In analyzing the defects of the Kaiser's administration, Harden saw as
one of the main reasons the Kaiser's prerogative to make his own
decisions on vital issues; in addition, Harden pointed to what he
judged to be erosive influences exercised upon the monarch by some
of his most trusted friends and courtiers. The provocative implications
of Harden's views were to find ready acceptance when the contents
of the Kaiser's *Daily Telegraph* interview in 1908, in which he had made
some astoundingly indiscreet pronouncements on foreign policy, reached
the German public. Although the study of isolated personal acts does
not by any means lay bare the whole of the German political scene,
no real understanding can be achieved without some insight into
the political techniques of the Kaiser. The *Daily Telegraph* incident
entailed the Kaiser's consent to publication of an interview in which
he passionately avowed his friendship for England. William II claimed
that the purpose of the German naval construction program was not
to employ the fleet against Great Britain, but for potential use in the
Far East to safeguard German trade interests and colonial possessions.
In fact, during the Boer War,

when Russia and France had secretly inquired of Germany whether she would
make common cause with them against England, he had not only refused but
had revealed the whole plot in a letter to Queen Victoria; still more—at a
moment when the English army found itself in a critical situation in South
Africa he had, in collaboration with the German General Staff, drawn up a
plan of campaign indicating the way in which the Boers could best be
defeated which was dispatched to London, and which advised the employment of almost the same tactics as those by which Lord Roberts subsequently defeated the Boers; yet despite all this, he continued to be looked
upon as the enemy of England. Before the Emperor gave his own consent
to the publication of the article in the *Daily Telegraph*, he sent the text to
Prince Buelow with orders to read it through and to make such alterations or

omissions as he thought desirable. As Buelow subsequently admitted, he did not himself peruse the article, owing to the pressure of work, but he sent it instead to the Foreign Office with instructions to go through it carefully.[71]

Instead of making a careful study of the document, the Foreign Office merely suggested a few superficial changes, after which it placed its stamp of approval upon publication of the article.

Rosenberg shows that by not availing itself of the opportunity of either criticizing the article or taking exception to its intended publication, the Foreign Office must assume a considerable share of responsibility for its consequent publication on October 28. It had access to the original documents since they were in its own archives. One of these was entitled "'Twenty-two Aphorisms on the Conduct of the War in South Africa' from the pen of William II—completely harmless observations of a general nature from which the English generals could not have derived the slightest benefit. . . . Yet so great was the veneration in which an Imperial memorandum was held that not a single official dared to make any real alteration in its text." [72] Rosenberg assigns to the *Daily Telegraph* affair the role of a "classic example of the way in which Germany was governed throughout the reign of William II." [73] Buelow himself was seriously at fault for not having read the proposed release prior to its publication. As a consequence, he offered his resignation, the acceptance of which the Kaiser could not afford since Germany was deeply embroiled in the Bosnian crisis at the time and because of public opinion. Nevertheless, as Rosenberg shows, the *Daily Telegraph* affair caused the Kaiser to face the "gravest crisis that occurred in Germany until 1918. . . ." [74]

The debates in the *Reichstag* on November 10–11th confronted the Kaiser with the opposition of all the political parties. Following the first *Reichstag* debate, the Kaiser in his distress demanded to know from Valentini, the head of his Civil Secretariat, the meaning of all the furor. He even considered the possibility of abdicating in response to the

universal criticism which was being directed at him, criticism which extended to his whole reign and way of life. He realized he was regarded as a failure and even a menace but could not understand why. Convinced as he remained that the article would fulfill its purpose of improving Anglo-German relations, he could not realize that the objection of the German public was not to the circumstances of its publication but to the ability of their ruler to say such things, even in private.[75]

His resentment was directed primarily toward his chancellor, and not without just cause, for having let him down. Conversely, the Kaiser's leading critics such as

Harden, Naumann and Weber demanded that Buelow should exploit the incident by taking the reins of government out of the hands of the Emperor and putting them into the hands of the Chancellors and Ministers. . . . Only thus would it become possible to get away from the zig-zag course imparted to German policy by perpetual imperial interference with Ministerial activities. The difficulty about this theory was that, so long as the Chancellor and Ministers were chosen by, and depended for their tenure of office on the good pleasure of the Emperor, he could not easily be denied a voice, in their policy. If Ministers were not to be chosen by him, what other source was there except the *Reichstag,* which would inevitably have chosen party leaders.[76]

Even if Max Weber's dictum that only qualified politicians could counteract the Kaiser's political ineptitude was eminently sound, Balfour is correct when he asserts: "Whether a majority could have been found for such a change in 1908 is hard to say, while the question whether aristocracy, army, and bureaucracy would have accepted such a change without fighting is even harder to answer. What is certain is that Buelow, no matter what he may have said later, never thought of taking a step which conflicted with the whole theory on which Germany was run." [77] Even the liberal forces in Germany were hopeful that pursuit of imperial plans for Germany would bind the wounds struck by social cleavages and political immaturity. Actually, then, very few voices were raised in protest against Germany's aspirations to a colonial empire backed by a powerful navy. The question whether Germany was engaged in a struggle for power or whether such an assumption derives from a misunderstanding is still of interest today. Willy Schenk seeks to demonstrate that following the formation of the *Entente* and the debacle of the Algeciras Conference, the historical import of the path leading to a collision course with England upon which Germany had embarked should have been obvious to any astute observer.[78] Yet: "Now or never was the moment in which to carry through a reform of the Bismarckian Constitution." [79]

The Revolution of 1848 had been marked by a primary concern on the part of liberalism for German national unity. Helga Grebing suggests that the failure of the Revolution did not cause the German bourgeoisie any widespread, deeply felt political sense of disappointment; instead it concentrated most of its attention upon economic concerns. In fact, the German bourgeoisie as a whole did not experience a disenchantment at all, except for those who responded to the situation by emigrating; included in their number were approximately three to four thousand intellectuals. In Grebing's judgment, the majority of German citizens appeared to be well adjusted to authoritarian monarchical rule in a state which offered security, protection, and, in fact, freedom from having to engage in the political decision-making process. Excellence in the cultural and economic sectors became their major concern. Consequently in 1848, the German bourgeoisie irretrievably lost its chance for deliverance from authoritarian rule. When the political and social aspirations of the Revolution failed to materialize, the struggle for national unity and greatness offered a welcome substitute for the political and social debacle.[80] Moreover, these conditions not only continued to persist during the reign of William II (1890–1918), but became, in fact, intensified.

Germany was becoming one of the most powerful and most modern industrial states on earth, but the economically leading class hardly participated in the political process. In the age of imperialism, the Reich acquired colonies, conducted *Weltpolitik* and perhaps strove to 'seize World power,' but neither the mass of the population, the parties, nor parliament were able to influence foreign policy. The state having assumed new functions, became an intervening state. . . .[81]

Although constitutional patchwork disguised the alignment of forces, after 1890 the diversion and irresponsible handling of political power became increasingly apparent, heightened by the intrigue of men in high positions in whose charge the destiny of Germany was placed. However, Tormin asserts that, "the masses who were affected by this state intervention strove to obtain the might to engage in political co-determination as political interest grew (participation in *Reichstag* elections 1871 51 per cent, 1890 71.6 per cent, 1912 84.9 per cent), the most important decisions were not made by the elected bodies. All the parties strove to address themselves to the masses . . . although the parties (with the exception of the Left Liberals and the SPD) tried to neutralize the influence of the masses with auxiliary organizations and to retain the present structure of notables as long as possible . . ."[82]

The German citizen typically viewed the state as maintaining a neutrality of interest, thus ascribing to it an ethically superior status. The state was seen to tower above political parties and their struggle. In reality, of course, this very state was dominated by the Conservatives and served their interests. Tormin considers the political stagnation at the domestic level as largely responsible for the fact that the outbreak of World War I was welcomed by many as a "release and deliverance" because "finally a great common task lay ahead once again." [83] In view of this public sentiment and the *'Burgfrieden"* (party-truce) proclaimed by the Kaiser, the political parties in the early part of the war strove even less than before the war to extend their influence within the *Reichstag*. They were now content to abdicate their potential share in the formulation of public policy and to transfer their share of public responsibility for the conduct of German politics to the person of the Chancellor and the military establishment.

Before the war, both the *Daily Telegraph* interview by the Emperor in 1908 and the Zabern Affair late in 1913, involving the assumption of police powers over civilians by the military in Alsace, would have provided plentiful ammunition to Socialists and Progressives to press for constitutional reforms. These included abolition of the three-class system in Prussia, introduction of ministerial responsibility, and democratic control of foreign policy. The widespread dismay and consensus of opinion had created a more favorable climate than ever before for such peaceful constitutional reforms. Both the political parties and the press agreed in their protest against the Kaiser's personal style of government.

The Conservative and Center parties, however, articulated their views only by means of verbal protest, thus preventing the formation of a majority in the *Reichstag* which might have taken effective action. Similarly, the Zabern incident created a political storm but failed to result in change. The National Liberals and Centrists as well as the Progressives and Socialists united in protest against the usurpation of power by the military. On November 28, 1913, a Colonel von Reuter arrested 28 civilians in the streets of Zabern. Von Falkenhayn, Prussian minister of war, ruthlessly defended the action, in which he received the support of Chancellor von Bethmann-Hollweg. This backing of the officer corps further antagonized the *Reichstag* delegates, leading to a no-confidence vote, passed by a majority of 293 to 55, for the chancellor in connection with the Zabern affair. Only the Conservatives and the *Reichspartei* supported the government. William II, the Chancellor, and the military rallied to the defense of the army: "A court-martial in Strassburg on January 10, 1914 cleared Reuter completely, declaring that the civilian police had failed to keep order and his action was therefore justified. Reuter was even rewarded with an imperial decoration. Thus once more was seen the fragility of German parliamentary institutions, and the source of real power was again revealed to be where Bismarck had originally placed it—in the throne and in the army." [84]

When war broke out in 1914, few opposed it. Max Weber merely reflected public opinion when he wrote on October 15, 1914: "This war with all its ugliness is nevertheless great and wonderful. It is worth experiencing." [85] All parties arrived at a political truce, to last for the duration of the war, and the government was assured of a united war effort. The *Reichstag* thus transferred its own powers to the military establishment. Conflict evasion reigned supreme. The Social Democrats, having opposed military appropriations in the *Reichstag*, now voted in their favor. The generally favorable attitude of the SPD at the outbreak of the war toward war credits and its concomitant identification with the government and therewith its war aims has been widely criticized. Upon deeper inquiry, however, the decision to respond to the government's request by voting in favor of war credits is not altogether surprising. Although the Social Democrats were by no means fully integrated into German society, they had not remained unaffected by the widespread popular conviction that the war was not only inevitable but that it should be anticipated as a means of national consolidation and renewal. Whatever the real responsibilities, the great majority of Germans believed that their government had entered the war for a good cause in defense of the fatherland against malicious attack. Certainly the rank and file of the SPD respected widely held values such as the need for discipline, national pride and powerful central government theories; nor was *Spiessbuergertum* (Philistinism) unknown among Social Democrats. The Party had also been exposed to the ferment of patriotic ideas which had become manifest in August 1914. Moreover, the fact that Germany was engaged in a war with Russia, whose regime epitomized reaction, might serve as a partial explanation of the action of the SPD resulting on August 3, 1914 in a vote of 74 in favor and 14 against the granting of war credits.[86]

On the other hand, early in 1916, even Baron von Richthofen, a National Liberal, had spoken out in favor of parliamentary reform. Max Weber, Friedrich Meinecke, Friedrich Naumann, and Hans Delbrueck continuously demanded suffrage reforms in Prussia. Ultimately, however, it was less the appreciation that the man in the street, who had been considered qualified to wear a uniform should be permitted to participate in the political life of his country than the exigencies of military reversals, that induced the rightists to accept reforms in 1918. Demands for "democratization" accompanied the mobilization of Germany's last military resources. This "revolution from above" was to stem the tide of any attempts at a revolution from below, however, as well as to obtain a more advantageous bargaining position vis-à-vis the enemy.[87]

Following Hertling's resignation on September 30, 1918, and at the request of the High Command, Prince Max von Baden assumed the office of chancellor. A fairly liberal representative of the South German aristocracy, he favored a broader parliamentary base. His cabinet contained Socialists, Progressives and Centrists. The Chief of the General Staff of the Army, Field Marshal Ludendorff, was dismissed immediately and replaced with General Groener, while Field Marshal von Hindenburg's position remained untouched. The latter even now advocated the annexation of Longwy-Briey.[88] The fact that Erzberger and Stresemann, two important party leaders, were to enter the cabinet, gave this last imperial government a parliamentary appearance, the first such in German history. Prince Max wanted peace, but both he and his ministers protested against an immediate armistice, thinking it premature and

not in the best interest of the German people. Therefore he did not
want to rush into any premature negotiations with the Allies. The chancellor wanted to be able first to form a government. He was not given
the opportunity to carry out this plan since the High Command summoned leading parliamentarians to appraise them of the military establishment's pessimistic outlook on Germany's chances of winning the war.
The effect of the High Command's assessment hit like a bombshell on
the morning of October 2, when Vice-Chancellor von Payer had
assembled the leaders of all parties to hear Major von dem Dusche, a
representative of the High Command:

None of the deputies had realized the pass to which things had come and
the result was consternation. Even the Socialist, Ebert, went white as a sheet
and was unable to utter; Stresemann looked as though someone had struck
him; the Conservative, von Waldow, walked up and down saying that the
only course left was to put a bullet through one's head (which he did not,
however, proceed to do). Heydebrand—the man who had reacted so violently
to Lloyd George in 1911—summed up the situation in a phrase destined to
echo down the years, 'We have been deceived and betrayed' (Wir sind
belogen und betrogen). . . .[89]

Thus Germany's *military* rather than her civilian leaders first insisted
upon requesting an armistice, a move which Prince Max had hoped to
postpone. Upon further persistence in their demands, Prince Max indicated that he would not act upon them unless the High Command were
to put in writing its request that the government ask the Allies for an
armistice. In answer Paul von Hindenburg sent this letter on October
3, 1918:

The Supreme Command continues to hold to its demand expressed on
September 29 of this year that a request for an armistice should be sent to
our enemies immediately. As a result of the collapse on the Macedonian
front, the consequent weakening of the reserves on the western front, and
the impossibility of making good the very severe losses which we have
suffered in the last days, there is, as far as is humanly possible to judge, no
future chance of forcing a peace on the enemy. . . .[90]

Only then did Prince Max von Baden send his request to President
Wilson during the night of October 3. Following a few weeks of negotiations, on November 11 the German armistice delegation was compelled
to sign the armistice document.

    Yet Germany found it difficult, after World War I, to come to terms
with her recent past: "It is unquestionable that an increasingly large
percentage of Germans from the abdication and flight of the Emperor,
William II, accepted, fervently believed in, and worked for, this inter-

round the Nationalist party—the party of the old regime which included nearly all the notable people of Wilhelminian days from . . . Tirpitz to . . . Kapp—all those who took upon themselves to represent the 'national' cause, made themselves the centre of the opposition at once to the treaty and the regime . . ." [101]

Counterrevolutionary forces responsible for the Kapp Putsch, the Hitler *coup* in 1923, and the political murder of leading republican figures anticipated the events leading to the success of the National Socialists on January 30, 1933. Upon the death of the first president of the Republic, Friedrich Ebert, in 1925, the election of Field Marshal Paul von Hindenburg further underscored the growing significance of right-wing influence. His reelection in 1932 at the age of eighty-four confirmed it. While Hindenburg remained loyal to the constitution during the first years of his presidency, in his last years he tolerated undue influence from his son, from von Papen, and the landowning Junker class. Karl Dietrich Bracher, in tracing the main objectives which Hindenburg had outlined for himself, relates how he failed in all of them: to win World War I; to prevent Germany from becoming a republic; to defeat the enemies of the republic; and to curb Hitler, whom he misjudged. In spite of these failures, the Hindenburg myth continued to grow. [102]

Weber foresaw the advent of reaction in Germany. Golo Mann writes: "Since Max Weber in the nineties had spoken of the longing of the German middle classes . . . since the activities of the pan-Germans and the violence of the First World War, *one* current of German life had been flowing towards the morass of Nazism." [103] Weber also foresaw the ascendance of political leaders of the charismatic type. Here Weber seemed to focus mainly upon the functional attributes of charismatically endowed leaders. They are necessary to galvanize into action a politically inert and naive working class and a politically uncommitted bourgeoisie. They alone can escape the "castration of bureaucracy." He seemed less aware of the possible tragic consequences of Caesaristic political leadership. "Within this prospect, Weber found no radical contradiction: democracy and charismatic authority did not figure among his irreconcilables." [104]

German experience under the aegis of National Socialism has shown how rapidly bureaucracy, once is well under way, moves to its appointed end, as exemplified by the Fascist tendency not to tolerate any autonomous or semi-autonomous organs between the individual and the state. Franz Neumann, it will be recalled, defined Fascism as "the dictatorship of the Fascist (National Socialist) Party, the bureaucracy, the army and big business—dictatorship over the whole of the people, for the complete organization of the nation for imperialist war." [105]

While Weber could not and did not anticipate the excesses of

Fascism, he was concerned with the great difference between individual responsibility on the one hand and the demands of a highly industrialized state with its attending bureaucracy on the other. These two opposing principles he held to be of vital importance for the future. He realized that technological trends implied further bureaucratization and rationalization which in turn implied a pervasive diminution in individual initiative. Accordingly he emphasized such roles as the plebiscitary political leader with charismatic qualities. Charisma should, in the context of these technological trends, be able to keep members of society from becoming mediocrities in flight from themselves.

Weber, however, was exempt from one distortion from which he saw others suffering, namely the illusion of ending the domination of man over man. Instead, "Whether in business, politics, or military affairs, great leaders had to be created as an antidote to bureaucracy; only by keeping the charismatic principle alive could the world be saved from mediocrity. . . . However, not too long after he died the charismatic and bureaucratic principles were fused in his homeland into the most horrendous synthesis the world has ever known." [106]

Weber's essential concern was for the rational allocation of the immense reservoir of power characteristic of a *Machtstaat*, i.e., for the fund of prestige, experience, and skill which must be acquired by those charged with responsibility for the power state, especially in its relation with other states. Personally, he was always ambivalent about the extent to which he should play an active role. Moreover, as noted earlier, his intellectual detachment prevented him from making the analytical concessions required for political success. In any event, the call to political activism never came. Commenting in 1920 on Weber's role in the political life of his nation, Theodor Heuss stated: "German politics allowed this leading figure to slip by unused. Mediocrity was afraid of him for good reason, for he laughed at it bluntly and trampled on it in a sovereign manner." [107]

Wolfgang Mommsen also pointed to the tragedy for German liberalism at the beginning of the twentieth century of a man of such towering caliber, whose political analyses so frequently illumined German politics, renouncing active political involvement. At the same time, Mommsen regards Weber as having been in some ways ill-suited for an active political role. Too demanding in his volition, he was too far ahead of his own politically active contemporaries. This posture was aggravated by the passion of his temperament and the razor-edge sharpness of his critical appraisals. The inevitable guerilla warfare and the perennial compromises and tactical subterfuges of politics would have completely disenchanted him. "His volcanic temperament, in the long run, could never have stood the tactics of parties and factions, which he himself had portrayed so incisively." [108] Mommsen may be right in his assumption that the epitaph which Weber applied to Marx applied to him as well: "He wanted to attain power over the minds of men rather than to gain control of the masses." [109]

Weber's attitude toward the class struggle and the tactical imperatives of the Social Democratic Party, further disqualified him for political activism. Believing that the labor movement's future was tied to the capitalistic system and that its chances for survival could be found only within that system, he rejected the attitude toward the class struggle current among the Social Democrats of the period. He repeatedly mocked the German bourgeoisie's fear of the red spectre. The German Social Democrats he considered "infinitely" more harmless than they appeared to themselves. Following the convention of the Social Democratic Party in Mannheim in 1906, he wrote to Robert Michels that underneath all "the revolutionary dreams of the future" one could sense total impotence:

Bebel and Legien stressed ten times, at least, 'Our Weakness.' In addition, the utterly petty bourgeois apparel, the many stout inkeepers' faces, the inertia, and the *absence* of a willingness to draw the consequences in a right-wing direction, if the path toward the left is blocked or considered blocked— these gentlemen do not frighten anybody anymore.[110]

Mommsen rightly criticizes Weber for overlooking the fact that the party executive could not initiate a revisionist policy without alienating a considerable faction within the party, thereby jeopardizing its unity. It was characteristic of Weber's way of thinking and objectively unfair to conclude that the Party had lost all "enthusiasm" because it rejected radical action, while at the same time he complained that it could not bring itself to participate in positive action within the framework of currently existing social conditions.[111]

In 1907, Weber again conveyed to Michels his low opinion of the Social Democrats; he had "the feeling that every chance for cooperation with Social Democracy has *disappeared* for us, since one cannot do business with political catatonics for one thing; for another, while 'poison and gall' may be valuable substances, they are no surrogates for enthusiasm. . . ." [112] Similarly, at the Convention of the *Verein fuer Sozialpolitik* (Association for Social Policy) in Magdeburg in 1907, Weber portrayed the Social Democratic Party negatively. Stripped of all energizing faith, the Party could do no more than engage in "lame, phraseological, nagging, complaining debates and arguments." [113]

When Robert Michels rejected this critique of German Social Democracy, Weber's answer again reveals the sharp response characterizing his own thinking: Michels ought to regard his, Weber's, "enigmatic address simply as the speech of a 'class conscious bourgeois' addressed to the cowards of his own class." [114] Moreover, Weber considered "a hallucination the idea that a class party allegedly with class ideals could become anything else than a 'machine' in the American sense of the term." Consequently, he advised the Party, in characteristically provocative language: "You fools, social democracy, whether it be parliamentarian or syndicalistic will more and more become nothing 'worse' (from *your* standpoint) than a communal party machine." [115]

Later, however, Weber began to rethink his position on the Social Democratic Party. He came to regard it as the first of a completely new type of political party on the continent, fashioned in the image of existing parties in America, and to some extent in England, namely the bureaucratically organized mass party. Ostrogorski's work dealing with the organizational forms of parties in modern democratic societies impressed Weber.[116] Even at the convention of the *Verein fuer Sozialpolitik* in 1905, he saw that the German Social Democrats were headed in the direction of the American model, becoming a party of patronage. At that time, Weber still regarded these events negatively. Gradually, however, based upon Ostrogorski's interpretation of the bureaucratically organized, patronage party in the United States, he accepted the non-ideological party as the party of the future. German Social Democrats attracted his interest all the more because "in *contrast* to conditions in those parties, German Social Democracy still represents something like a 'Weltanschauung,' thereby not *merely* constituting a 'technical machine', as is true of the American parties." [117]

Despite his implied respect, Weber thought that parties characterized by a *Weltanschauung* represented an anachronism. He assessed the role of the German Social Democrats against the background of arrested progress in Germany's domestic politics. That he was largely correct cannot be questioned. He was on less safe ground when he asserted that the bureaucratic apparatus of party life and politics would *ipso facto* vitiate the future viability of ideologically charged parties. Even though bureaucratization inhibited if not terminated Social Democratic revolutionary aspirations, it has also become clear that a radical ideological slant may characterize thoroughly bureaucratized parties.

Life in Germany between 1933 and 1945 reflected the penetration of bureaucracy into practically all areas of human activity. With authority from the top down and obedience from the bottom up, ideological enforcement became the task of the Nazi hierarchy, namely the "monopolistic political 'party' and its subsidiaries."[118] Both Gerth and Burin found that Weber over-estimated the *political* importance of *technical* proficiency when he claimed that "the 'political master' finds himself in the position of the 'dilettante' who stands opposite the 'expert'. . . ." [119]

When Hitler arrogated to himself the determination of military strategy during the war, he made clear that he felt he could ignore the military experts. The expert, though more skilled, became subordinated to the ideologue. The cases of Himmler and Eichmann, for example, furnished illustrations of the coordination of technical skill and ideological fanaticism: [120]

> Weber's generalizations about bureaucratic tenacity must be modified at least to the extent that they fail to take into account . . . the impact on the 'rational-legal' type of bureaucracy of a political system of charismatic leadership, mass irrationality, and terrorism—and of the new irrational types of bureaucracy peculiar to such a system. When Weber formulated his statements he doubtless thought of the resilience of the bureaucracy in the face of political changes not incompatible with the rational bureaucratic ethos he so brilliantly analyzed. Whatever the validity of these statements for such cases as republican France, they cannot apply where that ethos itself is antithetic to the new system of political domination.[121]

The increasing bureaucratization of party organization and spirit, which Weber so brilliantly traced, was subsequently modified by him in the light of historical events. As Mommsen demonstrates, while Weber initially deplored the loss of idealistic convictions by the parties, he subsequently welcomed this process which might help overcome sterile political *Weltanschauungen,* a requirement which would better serve the national interest of Germany as a *Machtstaat.*[122]

Weber's political wisdom and the similarity of his position on the role of German parties to that of Karl Jaspers half a century later is illustrated by his conviction that should the Social Democrats attain administrative positions either in municipal or state government, in the final analysis the only dangers that might arise concerned revolutionary elements within the party: "In the long run, it will become evident that Social Democracy will conquer neither the municipalities nor the state. The situation is reversed inasmuch as the state will conquer the party. Politically responsible cooperation would liberate Social Democracy from the labyrinth of politically sterile ideologies in which they have become enmeshed." [123] This estimate of the Social Democratic Party is shared by many today who have witnessed the SPD superseding its past in the 1969 election with Willy Brandt to head the government as chancellor. Yet in Weber's time, only a small fraction of the German bourgeoisie would have viewed the situation in this way. Therefore, perhaps, Weber saw his task as defining political goals for those who are incapable of recognizing their own historic interest. The Godesberg Programme in 1959 was to transform the party of the working class into one with national appeal, although once again in 1970 efforts of the opposition partly are directed at a revival of the stigma which the SPD had suffered for so long.

The foregoing political experiences provided both the context and the inspiration for Max Weber's political thought. An understanding of his concerns and reactions to his country's tragic encounter with history during his lifetime seems to require such a review. We can now turn to an analysis of specific aspects of his political thought.

NOTES

1 Otto Hintze, "The State in Historical Perspective," in Reinhard Bendix et al., eds., *State and Society: A Reader in Comparative Political Sociology* (Boston: Little, Brown and Company, 1968), pp. 165–166.

2 Albrecht Mendelssohn-Bartholdy, *The War and German Society: The Testament of a Liberal* (New Haven: Yale University Press, 1937), p. 100.

3 Cf. Leopold von Rancke, *Deutsche Geschichte im Zeitalter der Reformation* (Leipzig: Duncker und Humblot, 1867), Vol. I, Chapter 1.

4 Otto Hintze, *op. cit.*, p. 166.

5 S. N. Eisenstadt, *Modernization: Protest and Change* (Englewood Cliffs, N.J.: Prentice Hall, 1966), p. 70.

6 H. H. Gerth and C. Wright Mills, transl. and eds., *From Max Weber: Essays in Sociology* (New York: Oxford University Press, 1946), p. 124.

7 S. N. Eisenstadt, *op. cit.*, p. 70.

8 *Ibid.*

9 F. L. Carsten, *The Rise of Fascism* (Berkeley and Los Angeles: University of California Press, 1967), p. 22.

10 Hans Kohn, *Reflections on Modern History: The Historian and Human Responsibility* (Princeton, N.J.: D. Van Nostrand, 1963), pp. 110–111.

11 *Ibid.*, p. 111.

12 Hans Kohn, *Nationalism: Its Meaning and History* (Princeton, N.J.: Van Nostrand, 1965), p. 50.

13 *Ibid.*, pp. 52–53.

14 Sigmund Neumann, "Germany," in Taylor Cole, ed., *European Political Systems* (New York: Alfred A. Knopf, 1961), p. 337.

15 Bernadotte E. Schmitt, *The Fashion and Future of History* (Cleveland: The Press of Western Reserve University, 1960), p. 79. Reprinted by permission of the publisher.

16 Hans Kohn, *Reflections on Modern History: The Historian and Human Responsibility* (Princeton, N.J.: D. Van Nostrand, 1963), p. 91.

17 Hans Rogger and Eugen Weber, *The European Right: A Historical Profile* (Berkeley and Los Angeles: University of California Press, 1965), p. 267. Reprinted by permission of the publisher.

18 Bernadotte E. Schmitt, *op. cit.*, p. 83.

19 *Ibid.*, p. 84.

20 F. L. Carsten, *op. cit.*, p. 32.

21 Franz Schnabel, "The Bismarck Problem," in *German History: Some New German Views*, edited by Hans Kohn (Boston: The Beacon Press, 1954), p. 83.

22 Franz Neumann, *Behemoth: The Structure and Practice of National Socialism 1933–1944* (New York: Octagon Books, Inc. [Copyright 1942, 1944, by Oxford University Press], 1963), p. 206. Also cf. Eckart Kehr, *Schlachtflottenbau and Parteipolitik 1894–1901* (Berlin, 1930).

23 Cf. Marianne Weber, *Max Weber: Ein Lebensbild* (Tuebingen: J. C. B. Mohr [Paul Siebeck], 1926), p. 85. Reprinted by permission of the publisher. Quoted hereafter as *Lebensbild*.

24 Cf. *Ibid.*

25 Cf. Wolfgang J. Mommsen, *Max Weber und die Deutsche Politik 1890–1920* (Tuebingen: J. C. B. Mohr [Paul Siebeck] 1959), p. 12. Reprinted by permission of the publisher.

26 Cf. *ibid.*, p. 12.
27 Hermann Baumgarten, "Der deutsche Liberalismus," in *Preussische Jahrbuecher*, VIII, p. 471–72, quoted in Leonard Krieger, *The German Idea of Freedom* (Boston: Beacon Press, 1957), p. 441. Reprinted by permission of Beacon Press, © 1957 by Leonard Krieger.
28 Cf. *Lebensbild*, pp. 125–126.
29 Cf. Letter to Baumgarten of 6–29–1887, *Jugendbriefe* (Tuebingen: J. C. B. Mohr, 1936), p. 249. Cited in W. Mommsen, *op. cit.*, p. 14.
30 Leonard Krieger, *op. cit.*, p. 441.
31 Cf. Max Weber, *Wirtschaft und Gesellschaft*, 4th Edition (Tuebingen: J. C. B. Mohr, 1956), p. 660: "Viewed politically the German was and is indeed the specific 'Untertan' (subject) in the innermost meaning of the word and therefore Lutheranism was the religiosity adequate to him (und war daher das Luthertum die ihm adequate Religiositaet.)"
32 *P.S.*, 2nd. ed., p. 299. Cf. also *Lebensbild*, p. 126.
33 Hermann Baumgarten, *op. cit.*, p. 625.
34 Leonard Krieger, *op. cit.*, p. 441.
35 Cf. *ibid.*, pp. 626–27.
36 *Lebensbild*, p. 132.
37 Cf. Eduard Baumgarten, *Max Weber: Werk und Person*, documents selected and commented on by Eduard Baumgarten (Tuebingen: J. C. B. Mohr [Paul Siebeck], 1964), p. 67.
38 Franz Schnabel, "The Bismarck Problem," *op. cit.*, p. 92.
39 Address to the *Verein fuer Sozialpolitik*, in *Schriften des Vereins fuer Sozialpolitik*, Vol. XXV, 1908, pp. 296–97.
40 Hajo Holborn, *A History of Modern Germany 1840–1945*, Vol. III (New York: Alfred A. Knopf, 1969), p. 411.
41 Franz Neumann, *European Trade Unionism and Politics*, edited by Carl Rauschenbusch with a Preface by Harold J. Laski (New York: League for Industrial Democracy, June, 1936), pp. 20–21.
42 *Ibid.*, p. 19.
43 Franz Neumann, *Behemoth*, p. 3.
44 *Ibid.*, p. 3.
45 Gerhard Ritter, *The German Problem: Basic Questions of German Political Life, Past and Present* (Columbus, Ohio: Ohio State University Press, 1965), p. 177.
46 Franz Neumann, *Behemoth*, p. 4.
47 Eckart Kehr, "Das soziale System der Reaktion in Preussen unter dem Ministerium Puttkammer," in *Die Gesellschaft*, Vol. II, 1929, pp. 253–74, see especially p. 269, cited in Franz Neumann, *Behemoth*, p. 6.
48 A statement made by Puttkammer to his father in May 1859, and cited by Eckart Kehr, *op. cit.*, p. 254.
49 Leonard Krieger, *op. cit.*, pp. 3–4.
50 Franz Neumann, *Behemoth*, p. 5.
51 *Ibid.*
52 Alfred Vagts, *A History of Militarism* (New York, 1937), p. 11.
53 Cf. Eckart Kehr, "Zur Genesis des Kgl. preussischen Reserveoffiziers," in *op. cit.*, p. 492, cited in Franz Neumann, *Behemoth*, p. 6.
54 Ralf Dahrendorf, "Conflict and Liberty: Some Remarks on the Social Structure of German Politics," originally published in "*The British Journal of Sociology*" (1963), in Ephraim H. Mizruchi, ed., *The Substance of Sociology: Codes, Conduct and Consequences* (New York: Appleton-Century-Crofts, 1967), p. 410. Reprinted by permission of the publishers.
55 *Ibid.*
56 *Ibid.*, p. 411.
57 *Ibid.*, pp. 417–418.
58 *Ibid.*, p. 416.
59 *Ibid.*
60 *Ibid.*
61 Franz Neumann, *The Democratic and the Authoritarian State: Essays in Political and Legal Theory*, edited by Herbert Marcuse (New York: The Free Press, 1964), p. 142.
62 *P.S.*, 2nd. ed., pp. 307–308. Cf. also Erich Eyck, *Das Persoenliche Regiment Wilhelms II* (Zuerich: Rentsch 1948).
63 J. A. R. Marriott and Charles J. Robertson, *The Evolution of Prussia: The Making of an Empire* (London: Oxford University Press, 1965), pp. 433–435.
64 Cf. Dahrendorf, *op. cit.*, p. 419.

65 Erich Eyck, op. cit., Rentsch, 2nd. ed. (New York: The Macmillan Co., 1966), p. 499 cited in Koppel S. Pinson, Modern Germany, pp. 287–288.

66 Arthur Rosenberg, Democracy and Socialism: A Contribution to the Political History of the Past 150 Years (Boston: Beacon Press, 1965), p. 320.

67 Ibid.

68 Ibid., p. 321.

69 Maximilian Harden, Die Zukunft, Vol. IXV, 1908, cited in Pinson, op. cit., p. 287.

70 Arthur Rosenberg, Imperial Germany: The Birth of the German Republic 1871–1918 (Boston: Beacon Press, 1964), p. 40. Reprinted by permission of the publisher. Also by permission of Oxford University Press, London, England.

71 Ibid., pp. 51–52.

72 Ibid., p. 52.

73 Ibid.

74 Ibid., pp. 52–53.

75 Michael Balfour, The Kaiser and His Times (Boston: Houghton Mifflin Company, 1964), p. 291. Reprinted by permission of the publisher.

76 Ibid., p. 292.

77 Ibid., pp. 292–293.

78 Cf. Willy Schenk, Die Deutsch-Englische Rivalitaet vor dem Ersten Weltkrieg In Der Sicht Deutscher Historiker: Missverstehen Oder Machtstreben? (Aarau: Keller Verlag, 1967).

79 Arthur Rosenberg, op. cit., p. 53.

80 Cf. Helga Grebing, Geschichte Der Deutschen Parteien (Wiesbaden: Franz Steiner Verlag, 1962), pp. 13–14.

81 Walter Tormin, Geschichte der deutschen Parteien seit 1848 (Stuttgart: W. Kohlhammer Verlag, 1968), p. 97.

82 Ibid.

83 Ibid., p. 98.

84 Pinson, op. cit., p. 289.

85 P.S.. 2nd. ed. (Letter to Ferdinand Toennies of October 15, 1914), p. 458.

86 Walter Tormin, op. cit., p. 123.

87 Fritz Fischer, Germany's Aims in the First World War (New York: W. W. Norton, 1967), p. 624. Reprinted with the permission of the publishers from Griff nach der Weltmacht by Fritz Fischer. Copyright 1961 by Droste Verlag and Druckerei GmbH, Duesseldorf. Translation Copyright © 1967 by W. W. Norton & Company, Inc., and Chatto and Windus, Ltd.

88 Ibid., p. 635.

89 Michael Balfour, op. cit., pp. 395–96.

90 Arthur Rosenberg, The Birth of the German Republic, 1871–1918, trans. Ian D. Morrow (New York: 1931), p. 245 cited in Pinson, op. cit., p. 343.

91 J. A. R. Marriott and Charles J. Robertson, op. cit., pp. 459–460.

92 Max Weber quoted by Golo Mann (no reference pertaining to Weber's statement cited). Golo Mann, The History of Germany Since 1879 (New York: Frederick A. Praeger, 1968), p. 336. Reprinted by permission of the publisher. Originally published by Chatto and Windus Ltd., London.

93 Albrecht Mendelsohn-Bartholdy, op. cit., p. 19.

94 Fourth Subcommittee of the National Assembly and the Reichstag, edited by Albrecht Philipp, Die Ursachen des deutschen Zusammenbruchs im Jahre 1918, 12 Vols. (Berlin, 1928), Vol. V, p. 95. Cited in Pinson, op. cit., p. 346.

95 Golo Mann, op. cit., p. 331.

96 Eric Dombrowski, German Leaders of Yesterday and Today (Freeport, N.Y.: Books for Libraries Press, Inc. [first published 1920], reprinted 1967), p. 90.

97 Golo Mann, op. cit., p. 365.

98 E. Jaeckh, War for Man's Soul (New York, 1943), pp. 3–4, cited in Pinson, op. cit., p. 434.

99 F. L. Carsten, op. cit., pp. 86–87.

100 Ibid., pp. 87–88.

101 R. T. Clark, The Fall of the German Republic (New York: Russell & Russell, 1964), p. 65.

102 Karl Dietrich Bracher, Die Aufloesung der Weimarer Republik (Stuttgart and Duesseldorf: Ring Verlag, 1955), p. 480.

103 Golo Mann, op. cit., p. 419.

104 H. Stuart Hughes, Consciousness and Society: The Reorientation of European Social Thought 1890–1930 (New York: Alfred A. Knopf, 1958), p. 333.

105 Franz Neumann, *European Trade Unionism and Politics, ibid.*, p. 35.
106 Irving M. Zeitlin, *Ideology and the Development of Sociological Theory* (Engle-wood Cliffs, N.J.: Prentice-Hall, 1968), p. 158. Reprinted by permission of the publisher.
107 Theodor Heuss, *Max Weber: in Deutsche Politik*, Vol. 5, 1920, cited in René Koenig and Johannes Winckelmann, *Max Weber zum Gedaechtnis: Materialien und Dokumente zur Bewertung von Werk und Persoenlichkeit* (Koeln und Opladen: Westdeutscher Verlag, 1963), p. 72.
108 W. J. Mommsen, *op. cit.*, p. 147.
109 *Ibid.*
110 Letter of October 8, 1906, cited in Mommsen, *ibid.*, p. 122.
111 *Ibid.*, pp. 122–123.
112 Letter to Michels, February 1, 1907, copy in the estate of Max Weber, cited in Mommsen, *ibid.*, p. 149.
113 Max Weber, *Gesammelte Aufsaetze zur Soziologie und Sozialpolitik* (Tuebingen: J. C. B. Mohr [Paul Siebeck], 1924), p. 410.
114 Letter of November 6, 1907, copy in Weber's estate and quoted in Mommsen, *op. cit.*, p. 123.
115 *Ibid.*
116 M. Ostrogorski, *La Democratie et l'organisation des parties politiques* (2 Vols., Paris, 1903).
117 Letter of March 26, 1906. Copy in the estate of Max Weber, quoted in Mommsen, *op. cit.*, p. 124.
118 Burin in "Bureaucracy and National Socialism: A Reconsideration of Weberian Theory," Robert K. Merton, *Reader in Bureaucracy* (New York: The Free Press, 1952), p. 37. Cf. also H. H. Gerth's analysis of the Nazi Party in terms of "charismatic and bureaucratic," H. H. Gerth, "The Nazi Party: Its Leadership and Composition," *American Journal of Sociology*, XLV, pp. 517–541.
119 H. H. Gerth and C. Wright Mills transl. and eds. (New York: Oxford University Press, 1946), p. 232.
120 Cf. E. Kohn-Bramstedt, *Dictatorship and Political Police* (London, 1945), pp. 241–47.
121 Frederic S. Burin, *op. cit.*, pp. 43–44.
122 W. J. Mommsen, *op. cit.*, p. 125.
123 Max Weber, *Gesammelte Aufsaetze zur Soziologie und Sozialpolitik*, p. 409, cited in *ibid.*, p. 126.

III

Max Weber and German Party Politics

In the course of his political analyses Max Weber made incisive criticisms of contemporary German party politics. Underlying his critique lay his conviction that "the choice of the object of investigation and the extent of depth to which this investigation attempts to penetrate into the infinite causal web, are determined by the evaluative ideas which dominate the investigator and his age."[1] There can be little disagreement with his central proposition that although a German political party system existed, it did not represent the true locus of power. Bismarck's political legacy included a nation altogether lacking in political education. Although nominally representative institutions had existed in Germany almost half a century before the Revolution of 1918, the very success of statesmen such as Bismarck encouraged most of Weber's countrymen to accept passively the direction of public affairs first by the chancellor, subsequently by an incompetent monarch, and finally, during the war, by a virtual military dictatorship. Neither the electorate nor members of parliament were granted an opportunity to participate decisively in the process of government.

As a result, Weber's central concern was how best to provide a training ground for political leadership and participation in the face of strong opposition to the emergence of potential leaders who, through personal experience and responsible engagement, might exercise political wisdom and the art of practical politics at the highest level. Weber handled this theme with care and sensitivity, offering a profound analysis of the complex interrelationships between nascent liberal and social movements, existing economic and social conditions, and the near-exclusion of the political parties from genuine responsibility. His scholarly work was impeccable, deriving from an encyclopedic knowledge of history combined with an apparently insatiable desire for knowledge and an unusual perceptive facility. While his research on the most theoretical aspects of political sociology is contained in a chapter of *Economy and Society*, namely his discussion of the ideal types of forms of domination and the differentiation of political regimes, a considerable part of his exegesis is polemical in style, suggesting certain conclusions, but all the more stimulating for that reason.

In his publicist role, Weber clearly evolved distinct views. He especially deplored the failure of the parties to close ranks, a condition which was as manifest before the Revolution following World War I as in the days of the Weimar Republic: "the worst feature of the existing (1896) condition of politics is the constant diminution of moderate elements."[2]

As mentioned previously, liberalism and democracy had been continuously under fire by Bismarck, who established the German Empire as a bulwark against democracy by not allowing the political parties any responsibility, an experience which alone could afford them the chance to make politics as meaningful as the politicians themselves care to make it. In the absence of such prerequisites, expediency and partisan identification rather than the good of the country became their preoccupation: "The Conservatives, and to a lesser extent the Free Conservatives, represented agrarian interests; the National-Liberals, 'big business;' the Left Liberals, the professions and those in commerce who were in favor of free trade; the Centre, the defence of Catholicism; the Social-Democrats, the interests of the working class. . . . Moreover, the divorce of the parties from the practical work of government helped to strengthen the grip of the Central Party Committees, consisting of the established leaders, over their followers since new talent for the task of administration was not required."[3]

Weber recognized the true character of Bismarck's system and its two crucial failings: the exercise of his enormous power was bought at a high political cost to the German people, and was contingent upon the continued goodwill of the Kaiser. Not every Kaiser might be as easy to manipulate as William I nor every statesman as skilled as Bismarck, a contingency which might well give both Germany and Europe nightmares. Weber also recognized as politically valid and humanly understandable, the spread of democratic ideas in both the *Reich* and in Prussia, and hence the increasing clamor for greater political justice issuing in the demand that the "very basis of Conservative power—the Three-Class suffrage in Prussia—with its gross inequalities should be assimilated to the system of manhood suffrage granted by Bismarck himself for elections to the *Reichstag*. No logical justification could be found for a system in which a Prussian citizen was, in Prussia, unable to secure fair representation for his views, whilst in the *Reich* he could do so."[4]

When both the right of franchise and the secret ballot were proclaimed in the newly founded Empire, Bismarck was confronted with the misgivings of the Conservatives, who assumed that Bismarck was toying with the idea of establishing a genuinely parliamentary form of government. The National-Liberals hoped, meanwhile, "through their powerful representation in the elected house to extend the slender powers granted to the *Reichstag* in the constitution." [5] This hope proved illusory because, in keeping with the interests of the Prussian Junkers, Bismarck was not about to preside over the liquidation of either the Kaiser or his own class. He merely required the "support of the wider movement for national unity represented by the National-Liberals in his task of unifying Germany, and, especially from 1866 to 1870, he was anxious to secure the support of the Liberals in the southern states. . . . He intended to stand himself, and to keep the monarchy, above all parties, including even the Conservative parties, and to use them all, except those which he regarded as fundamentally hostile to the state, for the state's purposes." [6] Thus Bismarck in planning his political strategy, had to draw heavily upon the support of the National-Liberals in both Prussia's *Landtag* (Landparliament) and in the *Reichstag*. But he refused to relent in his anti-Liberal stand and was, on the contrary, annoyed with the National Liberals because they did not appear to comprehend "the absolute necessity of a minimum of concession to Liberalism, in order to secure the unity of Germany without sacrificing the basic conservative-monarchical institutions of Prussia. . . ." [7]

Bismarck subsequently tried to lessen his dependence upon the National Liberals by splitting the party on the issue of protective tariffs. Thus in the winter of 1877–78, he received a majority in the *Reichstag* consisting of Conservatives, Center and some National-Liberals favoring the bill. In 1879 the protective tariff bill became law. Following two attempts on the Kaiser's life in 1878, which he blamed on the Social Democrats in demanding anti-Socialist legislation, Bismarck sought to work even more closely with the Conservatives and to drive a wedge between the Liberals. The Center, consisting of high-ranking Catholic clergy, the aristocracy, and industrialists, was mostly conservative, and consequently could be counted upon to support the government. A strong and clear right-oriented trend became an established fact: "By 1881, then, the essential features of German government at home had been worked out in practice and, thereafter, continued unchanged, except for a brief interval under Caprivi, until 1918 . . . Through the controlled press and at elections the whole influence of government was thrown against the parties of the Left, whilst the Socialists had to face the provisions of the anti-socialist law." [8]

Cooperation between bureaucracy and police further insured the success of the government's repressive tactics. The educational system, subservient to the government which controlled the teachers and their teachings, similarly reinforced the structure of the government's power. Given the backing of a combination of agrarians and industrialists whose offspring furnished a high proportion of the officers' corps, the upper echelons within the bureaucracy, and the industrial magnates, power was not likely to slip out of governmental hands. Bismarck did not need to remind these groups of the need for retaining the existing social framework within which they must operate. Thus their misgivings about developments in the direction of responsible parliamentary rule did not offer any real alternative to the liberal forces short of consolidating their strength within one national and democratic party. To insure the continued development of unity among Liberals such a party should transcend class barriers in the interest of properly informed democratic debate on the issues of the time. On the other hand, to challenge the feudal system in both agriculture and industry successfully, the German bourgeoisie would have had to ally itself with the Social Democrats, on whom they were afraid to depend. The son of a National-Liberal deputy, Max Weber initially adopted an attitude of uncompromising opposition toward left-wing Liberalism similar to that of his father's. His main concern was over the common front left-wing Liberalism had presented against the expansion of the military budget, as well as its opposition to the modest colonial policy of the eighties. This appreciation caused Weber to identify initially with the prevailing hostility of German political elites, which in fact intensified more or less permanently the tension between the socialists and the bourgeois liberals. He was subsequently to abandon this attitude.

While Weber wanted the parties to place all issues regarding the national power position of Germany above factionalism, he had great reservations about the wisdom of the "socialist law" (1878–1890), which stripped the SPD of all legitimacy. Disagreeing with his father and Baumgarten on this issue, Weber sought to demonstrate already in 1884 the primacy of equality before the law; indeed, "it would be preferable to muzzle everyone somewhat than to put some in chains entirely."[9] His characteristic sense of fairness recoiled from Bismarck's heavy-handed policy, which could only lead to further erosion of the foundations of liberalism.

Weber, moreover, astutely noted both changes in attitude as well as in personnel within the Social Democratic Party. Initially, the years of persecution and exile had resulted in the alienation of Social Democracy from parliamentary Liberalism. This factor, in turn, resulted in a gathering of radical Leftist forces under August Bebel and an unhealthy legacy of ambivalence and scepticism toward parliamentary government. The effectiveness of the extreme Left as a political force may have been overestimated by the apprehensive German burghers, but it would

have been equally wrong to underestimate the SPD's first important
electoral gains and the consequences of its being confronted with growing involvement in the parliamentary process. The schism, so characteristic of the Labor movement, would seem to have been overcome easily
by Bebel and Liebknecht (the leaders of the radical wing of the SPD),
as they induced the party to endorse Bismarck's social welfare measures.
Bismarck's Accident Insurance Bill of 1884 could not have counted on
strong Socialist support owing to the party's resentment of the repressive
treatment it was receiving at his hands.

Weber meanwhile had correctly seen an evolving pattern of change,
due partly to the party's changed self-image in the *Reichstag* following
its significant electoral gains in the fall of 1884. What Weber may have
had in mind too was the thriving local associations of skilled craftsmen
in the 1880's which gave the party added strength. While these *Fach-
vereine* were, at the outset, politically unaffiliated, ultimately they
entered the fold of the SPD. Hence during the 1880's, the Radicals got
started on a new course of assuming a positive parliamentary role on
behalf of the party. Seeking to preserve their feeling of distinctness as a
protest movement, they swung from a marginal role in politics to one
of parliamentarianism, especially in the State Diet of Saxony where the
Radicals outnumbered the Social Democrats.

Weber, however, would have responded uneasily to Karl Liebknecht's discovery: "Our party gradually puts away childish things and
emerges from its years of indiscretion,"[10] because he deplored the unwillingness of left-wing liberals and the socialists to give priority to
Germany's power-political interest, which he interpreted as a sign of
political immaturity. Actually the elections of 1884 materially weakened
the radicals within the party since most of the election gains benefited
the moderate wing. Nevertheless, the party leadership recognized that
a new phase had begun, during which the SPD ". . . was necessarily
becoming a modern parliamentary party which could not avoid involvement in all phases of the legislative process."[11]

Little vitality could be infused into the Party, however, because
". . . the three parties of the right (German Conservatives, Free Conservatives, and National Liberals) and the *Zentrum*, while not formally
combining in a cartel, jointly represented the dominant forces, economic,
political and social, in the new Germany, although it was not the *Reichstag* which made them dominant. The pull of this concentration of
power, combined with an economic prosperity which had been steadily
increasing since 1890 and the international nimbus and the growing
power of the Empire, was so powerful inside Germany that by the close
of the epoch even the two parties which had originally constituted the
opposition, the left-wing Liberals and the Social Democrats, had come

to accept the existing order, as August 4, 1914, and even November 9, 1918, were to prove beyond cavil."[12]

Since Weber wanted the parties to place all issues regarding the national power position of Germany above domestic strife, he particularly deplored the feuds between Bismarck and the *Freisinnige Partei* over the budget. He reproached the Party for confusing domestic issues with budgetary proposals affecting the vital national interest; he criticized Bismarck for repeatedly dissolving the *Reichstag* and for allowing controversies over the budget to create a domestic schism which ultimately could only be "greatly detrimental to the interests of the armed forces."[13]

At the same time, Weber held out little hope for a sound political program from the Liberals, whom he considered too doctrinaire.[14] As Mommsen states, Weber was to repeat this charge of ideological rigidity on the part of the Liberals on many later occasions. He saw an ideologically oriented conduct of policy resulting only in "lost opportunities."[15] In fact, Weber did not share his father's and Baumgarten's faith, widely held among Liberals, that upon the succession of another monarch, domestic policy would be liberalized. The fragmentation of the ranks of the Liberals appeared to preclude that possibility.[16] He expressed his contempt meanwhile for the "servile" speculation in which the *Freisinnigen* engaged regarding the change in monarchs on which they were staking their hopes for better times.[17]

Nor did Weber hold any brief for the National Liberals. As Mommsen reports, he had originally defended them against Baumgarten, who in the 1880's leaned increasingly toward the *Freisinnigen*.[18] However, when they lost some of their outstanding leaders in the seventies, notably Bennigsen, they seemed headed for a period of stagnation and Weber withdrew his support. He criticized especially the party's rejection of genuine liberal traditions and the complacency with which they confronted domestic social questions:[19] "In scathing tones he denounced the pressures brought to bear by the authorities during the workers' agitations, and he defended the workers' leagues as the 'only real centers of idealism in the whole Social Democratic Party'."[20]

Nevertheless, equating socialism with an intensification of the bureaucratization process, Weber opposed it as such. Deeply concerned with the discovery of suitable successors to Bismarck, Weber's intellectual stature and political wisdom led him on a lonely path of uncompromising principles at a time when few realized that the dilettantes and bureaucrats engaged in the Kaiser's game of foreign policy would ultimately bring diplomatic and military disaster to Germany.

Moving from an initial alignment with his father's party toward a rather more liberal position, Weber's principles and critical perspective made it impossible for him to be loyal to any party. Although the main drift was toward the Left, his political values retained a characteristic devotion to power politics and nationalism. As Stuart Hughes states, Weber started in politics to the right of his father, "as still more conservative and nationalist, and ended far to the left as a most eccentric sort of democrat. But he betrayed what he owed his father by the imperious—indeed, brutal—quality of his political utterances, and by the uncompromising fashion in which he insisted on Germany's national greatness right down to the day of his death."[21]

Ludwig Dehio similarly refers to the occasional slip of "some extremely sinister ideas" which stemmed from even the more clearsighted, as exemplified by Max Weber's words: "Let them hate us, as long as they fear us . . ."[22] And Dehio comments: "Words like these pointed to the future; but on the whole it is true to say that the daemonic nature of German aspirations to supremacy only reached its first stage in the first World War."[23] Moreover, Weber showed an unfortunate tendency to approach, even though somewhat more qualifiedly, the extreme Right's position as he castigated those who did not evince enthusiasm in shouldering the danger of war for the sake of German greatness. Looking back in 1916 he exclaimed: "Had we not been prepared to risk this war, then we should never have bothered to found the Reich."[24]

While Weber accepted the struggle for power as a fact of international as well as national politics, the goal of both the politicians and of their parties remained national self-interest. Yet, he was disdainful toward sectarian dogmatism and Machiavellianism. When the second piece of legislation dealing with the termination of the Kulturkampf was introduced in 1887, he chided the National Liberals for taking "utmost quietistic pleasure" in that which "is ours," and for their disinclination to burden themselves with any uncomfortable thoughts about the future.[25] He doubted that the National Liberals could long retain public confidence: "People's memories are short and no one recalls the party's previous accomplishments now."[26]

He also questioned the motives of the National Liberals, who advocated the humanization of the Kulturkampf merely for "political" reasons. This was really an admission that its cause had been unjustly fought: "If indeed it was not a matter of conscience but only one of opportunism, then certainly the Catholics are vindicated when they assert that we have violated the conscience of the Catholics for external reasons. . . . We will have acted without reference to conscience and will have thus suffered a moral defeat; and that is the worst part of this debacle since it prevents us from ever resuming the struggle and conducting it as it should be if it is to be successful."[27]

Weber thus anticipated the decline of National Liberalism, and saw that the split between them and the Freisinnigen threatened the movement's political effectiveness in the future. Without the collaboration of the *Freisinnigen,* the National Liberals could not maintain themselves in power. Deploring the "generally obtaining decadence" of the German parties, he feared that extremist parties on both the Right and the Left would ultimately ally themselves with the Catholic Center party and take hold of the reins of government.[28] As Mommsen observes, Weber was substantially correct in his appraisal.[29]

Toward the end of the 1890's Weber concluded that prospects for the future of German liberalism were dim. He concentrated his hopes and activities outside the liberal parties, both of which seemed doomed to political stagnation, at least in the immediate future, if not in the long run as well.[30] This realization that the Bismarckian legacy could not to be entrusted to any political party and that the era of Wilhelminian *Weltpolitik* promised to end abruptly in tragedy, "forced him to take as his special theme the analysis of power techniques, of politics as a vocation. Above all, his sociology is a theory of the politician class, the absence of which in Germany appeared to him to be the gravest menace of all to the future of the fatherland."[31]

In 1887, disillusioned with party politics, Weber became associated with the *Kathedersozialisten* (Socialists of the Academic Chair) who sought to maintain a critical and autonomous position vis-à-vis political and economic issues, particularly in the area of labor relations. This group sought to take the lead in promoting the intervention of the state when the "low level of comprehension" among political parties resulted in their failure to deal adequately with the economic problems arising from increasing industrialization. The state was envisaged as a means to ameliorate the class struggle. The quest for social justice was to be pursued, not in response to Marx's influence, but as a means of counteracting it. "Thus revolutionary Marxism found no room to develop in the authoritarian land of its conception. . . . The only element of Marxism that was to mature in Germany was the heritage of the Hegelian idea of power contained within it, and this took the form of visions of the total organization of state and economy."[32] Social reform in Germany was launched not as an assistance scheme for those in need; instead it was launched by and for the state.[33] "Unfortunately, most German Liberals were content to accept 'handouts' from 'Father State' and state guarantees of protection against foreign competition and social democracy."[34]

Max Scheler, one of Germany's foremost philosophers and a contemporary of Max Weber, insisted that as soon as the SPD found itself more closely involved in governmental functions, it would be less likely to criticize the state for its negativism toward political and social reforms.[35] Since the party's leaders would be quite willing to work inside the existing Imperial system, they no longer asked whether, after all, it is perhaps not their democratic duty to intervene when concentra-

tion of state authority in the executive branch reached the scale it did—
instead of leaving it to its own discretion. Richard Hunt shows persuasively how three variables: tendencies toward oligarchy, ossification,
and *embourgeoisement,* rendered the SPD incapable of seeing its own
responsibilities in coping with crises in the political system.[36]

The oligarchic tendency caused by the schism within the party
resulted ultimately in the left-wing minority's defection and the emergence of the party's conservatives as the controlling element in its
leadership. As the party began to participate more in the government,
it became ever more reluctant to jeopardize its newly gained powers.
What emerges from Wolfgang Abendroth's scrutiny is an illustration of
how the SPD succumbed, especially at the start of World War I, to the
wave of patriotism sweeping Germany. Seeking to trace how the Social
Democrats contributed to their own political impotence, he points to
the acquiescent attitude of its party leaders.[37] Nor did a majority of
intellectuals within the party, which by 1912 was the largest in Germany,
resist in August 1914 the temptation of enthusiastically endorsing the
the war. Even such poets as Richard Dehmel and Hugo von Hofmanns-
thal volunteered for duty in the armed forces. The "Manifesto of the
Intellectuals," underwriting the defense of the fatherland's just cause
against the enemy, contained the signatures of hundreds of intellectuals.
Max Weber was not alone later in honoring the war with meaningful
interpretations: the struggle of German culture against Western civilization and the values of German idealism as opposed to those of the
English shopkeeper mentality were constant themes in the writings of
many intellectuals. Only a small minority opposed the war openly and
consistently, the most notable including Hermann Hesse, Heinrich Mann,
and René Schickele.[38]

As a consequence, when one contemplates the German scene and
the disengagement of citizens from political affairs in both foreign and
domestic fields in the last two decades of the nineteenth century, and
extending to the very outbreak of World War I, Weber's preoccupation
with the creative manipulation of social problems for the sake of stimulating an intelligent reconstruction of Germany's foreign policy becomes
understandable. It is against this background that his association from
1886 on with the *Kathedersozialisten* and their younger version becomes
relevant. What makes his characterization of intellectuals of his own
generation particularly absorbing is the vividly descriptive manner in
which he described his contemporaries. Some he disparaged as "unpleasant types" of antisemites who, in his judgment, espoused such
views to achieve respectability. Many idealists whom Treitschke had
aroused to embrace a brand of mystical, national fanaticism were also
included. Finally, there were those who sported a pseudo-gentleman's

"jawing" habit, as well as a pseudo-realistic approach to the latest political fashion.

Yet, there emerged from his portrayal also an admiration for those among his colleagues who, in his view, were alone in their strength of conviction, who were also sufficiently forceful, and who were "therefore qualified to govern in future."[39] Despite the clouds on Germany's political horizon, Weber's mood was not entirely pessimistic. He conceived his colleagues' commitment as a salutary departure from the National Liberal platform of the 1870's.[40] Yet, Marianne Weber characterizes his mood even then as strangely resigned. He seemed to doubt whether his contemporaries were fully conscious of how heavily the curse of decadence weighed upon the nation, reaching from the lowest strata to the very top.[41] Nevertheless, he perceived creative forces at work to which productive scholarship could provide a link. In this light he saw the meaning of his membership in the *Verein fuer Sozialpolitik* (Association for Social Policy, founded in 1873).[42]

The historical school of economists represented in the *Verein* affirmed a reliance upon the state as the appointed guardian of the national welfare. Most of its members were "Nationalists, Monarchists, and Protectionists," but Schmoller and other moderates in the organization demanded that the state intervene on behalf of "trade unions, to promote factory legislation, to encourage collective bargaining and arbitration, and to enact such social reforms as national insurance . . ."[43] Both the historical school represented by the *Kathedersozialisten* and the Marxists agreed on certain points. Thus Schmoller, like Marx, acknowledged the coming of socialism. He attributed it, however, to an "alliance between socialism and the German 'bureaucratic and military monarchy,'" rather than to revolutionary action by an international proletariat. No defender of capitalism, Schmoller saw it as a stage of historical evolution. The program of the *Verein* sought to insure that the following stage would be "the outgrowth of peaceful evolution, rather than risk the dangers of foreign domination or military dictatorship," both being unavoidable risks accompanying revolution.[44] Schmoller, who more than any other individual brought his influence to bear upon the *Verein* between 1890 until his death in 1917, shared the views Weber was to express on the eve of the revolution, calling it "the most precarious of all games of chance."[45] Thus the *Kathedersozialisten*, while acknowledging the prevalence of class conflict, tried to find an evolutionary framework by enlisting "common heredity, language, morality, and religion as unifying agents."[46]

Mommsen calls Weber's vigorous participation in this association the single most important step in his emancipation from liberalism of the older vintage; it also represented his final dissociation from the political views of his father. Social and economic reforms having been sidestepped by liberalism previously, Weber now saw them as meriting a high priority. Germany having catapulted to the status of one of the most important industrial countries in Europe, antiquated economic dogma could no longer serve as a substitute for a progressive social policy in the legislative field.[47]

Meanwhile, his contact with the *Kathedersozialisten* pushed Weber, temporarily at least, closer to conservative views. His contacts in Berlin included the more conservative-minded circles. Although he wrote in 1888 that he was at odds with their views,[48] Wolfgang Mommsen reports that Weber was subsequently to accept them. Indeed, Alfred Weber personally related this information to Mommsen in Heidelberg.[49] In 1890 Weber's first vote was cast for the Conservatives, not for the National-Liberals. Possibly he hoped for more understanding from them of the need to cope with social problems, while simultaneously he was attracted to their stand on political power issues. Even then he did not really commit himself to any particular party. Later he referred to this first act of voting rather frequently without explaining, however, what motivated him.[50]

Essentially, Weber's identification with the Conservatives seems to have derived from his loyalty to the concept of the national power state as a guiding principle; this they shared most closely. While the National Liberals also professed this ideal, their antiquated economic views and policies, combined with their partiality toward certain interest groups, disqualified them, in Weber's judgment, for the role of national leadership.[51]

However, his evaluation of the parties following their response to Bismarck's resignation on March 18, 1890, also reveals Weber's ambivalence toward the Conservatives. The Center, the *Freisinnigen*, and the Social Democrats, whose ideals were opposed to Bismarck's policies and who had been stigmatized by him, could not have been expected to defend him. But the Prussian ministerial posts and high positions in the *Reich* were held by "*Conservative* creatures, whom he alone had raised up out of nothing. What did they do? They stayed on. 'A new chief?' that settled it. The presidential chairs of both the parliaments of the *Reich* and of Prussia were occupied by *Conservative* politicians."[52] The great Conservative parties thus allowed the chancellor to fall without any attempt to demand so much as an accounting for the reasons of his dismissal: "None of them stirred, but turned toward the new sun instead. This happening has no equal in the annals of any proud people."[53]

But the true measure of the failure of the Prussian Conservatives in the past fifty years, according to Weber, was their persistent inability to manifest political character in the service of the great affairs of the state. The only time they felt challenged was in cases involving their "pecuniary interests or their monopoly of civil service sinecures and bureaucratic patronage, or what is identical with it, their franchise privileges . . . The whole sorry apparatus of 'Christian,' 'Monarchical,' and 'National' phrases went and still goes into action: —the very same thing that causes those gentlemen now to approach the Anglo-Saxon politicians."[54]

Max Weber's negative assessment of the traditional governing classes was reinforced when he began to seek viable alternatives to the *status quo* by trying to mold Wilhelmian Germany into something closer to parliamentary democracy. The refusal of the Conservatives to develop realistic new domestic policies could only deepen the current crisis of German politics. The Conservatives surpassed even the Liberals in opposing the domestic economic and social policy Weber conceived to be of paramount national importance. Their even more pronounced subservience to lobbying groups proved an even greater impediment to issue-oriented politics.

Thus Weber's own Conservative period was no more than a brief interlude.[55] His change in perspective seems to have coincided with a turning point in his academic career from the field of jurisprudence to social science. He became increasingly immersed in economic and social problems and directed his attention toward an informed elite, the *Christlich-Soziale Bewegung* (Christian Social Movement), which opposed the traditional 'law and order' appeal, with its overtones of repression, as the remedy for socio-political ills. Certainly Weber was not attracted to the movement as a result of Pastor Stoecker's anti-semitic rhetoric. As his few references to Stoecker indicate, Weber rejected both the latter's conservative attitudes toward social questions and his qualities as a demagogue.[56]

The resulting lack of choice within the existing political system, which was simply incapable of producing the answers Weber wanted, caused him to isolate himself from political parties of either the Right or the Left. This left Weber in a dilemma. He displayed a cynical attitude toward the parliamentary politics of the ruling political parties which he saw entrapped in the muffling conformity of the political order of Imperial Germany. Their lack of sensible national priorities was illustrated by utter disregard for the structural changes of modern industrial society which made a sound domestic social policy for Germany mandatory. Yet, such a policy must never lose sight of the wider aims of the national power state operating in their service, and thus remain subordinate to them. Friedrich Naumann, in response to Weber's quest, wrote as follows: "We Germans must have something to regard as our own special task in the history of the world—some task that nobody else can fulfill as well as we. We need a national vocation within the household of universal humanity, so that we may be able to stand up for our national independence with all our heart and soul. Our faith in nationalism and our faith in humanity are for us two sides of the same question."[57]

Naumann also warned, agreeing with Weber, that even the best social policy would be of no avail if and when the Cossacks should arrive at the gates. National power goals required that national security be given top priority. Only a type of socialism capable of governing effectively, one which must be *deutsch-national*, was incontestable.[58] Naumann's dictum was: "To be anything at all, one must have an ambition to win something in the world."[59] Again, "What is nationalism? It is the urge of the German people to spread its influence over the globe."[60]

Toward the end of the nineties, Naumann's magazine *Die Hilfe* became an influential means for seeking a consensus on liberal imperialism among the German bourgeoisie. The intensification of contemporary imperialistic thinking is clear in the case of Hans Delbrueck. Until 1895, Delbrueck, editor of the *Preussische Jahrbuecher*, had not been greatly concerned with foreign policy. Now he wrote: "There is nothing more noble than for so great a power as Germany to set as her aims the maintenance of peace. But the policy of a great nation must not exhaust itself in that aim."[61] Referring to Weber's challenge, he continued: "What about German global policy? We have not yet entered into the real competition in the arena of world politics which grants satisfaction to a great nation, assuring future generations of a great future."[62] And again, "the unification of Germany would have been only a youthful prank, as Professor Weber whom I quoted previously stated impressively in his address, if it should have been the end and not the beginning of German power politics."[63] And Geiss concludes, ". . . the realization that the desired breakthrough to the status of World Power would be possible only by war was . . . widespread. . . . The implication of the new *Weltpolitik*—the great war—was thus clearly seen in Wilhelmine Germany, even before it was launched."[64]

Hans Delbrueck, who like Weber belonged to the small minority critical of the conduct of political affairs in contemporary Germany,[65] already in 1899 held out the ominous prospect of war:

We want to be a World Power and pursue colonial policy in the grand manner. That is certain. Here there can be no step backward. The entire future of our people among the great nations depends on it. We can pursue this policy with England or without England. With England means in peace; against England means—through war." [66]

Delbrueck, with Weber, favored a creative policy of political manipulation, in which England afforded Germany the opportunity of developing appropriate substantive policies. Both Weber's and Delbrueck's thinking moved outside the mainstream of German public ideology in counseling a policy of conciliation toward England, a policy especially inapposite to the Kaiser, most of his advisers, and the navy. In any event, the German government's lack of tactical ingenuity doomed this policy to certain failure. It is safe to argue, however, that both Weber and Delbrueck held consistently to the view that Germany's status as a world power called for a naval expansion program for the sake of *Weltpolitik*.

Both men, moreover, brought to the judgment of their society a liberal philosophy which at the same time provided imperialism with an "aura of respectability." [67] Weber and other liberals succeeded in creating a broadly based following, whereas the nationalists of the *Alldeutscherverband* (Pan-German Association) counted only a limited number, including Weber for a limited period, among their disciples. Some observers may find it difficult to avoid questioning Robert Nisbet's recent assertion: "He was politically liberal, not the conservative, much less the reactionary that some of the Left today in Germany is bent upon calling him." [68]

One wonders why the recent efforts made by German social scientists to recast Weber's political ideas may not be allowed to stand as a separation of his political persuasions from his scientific contributions. A significant minority of reputable scholars has felt obliged to acknowledge that Weber's greatness indeed rests in "the position his thought occupies in the contemporary social sciences" and his relevance to scientific study "which seems to become greater . . ." [69] But one cannot stop here. While Weber's scientific contributions have a life of their own, and while he was not the only adherent of the *Machtstaat* ideal, his very renown as a scholar cannot have failed to give it a greater breadth and bite. Moreover, a legitimate distinction can and must be drawn between his scientific approach to politics and his value judgments. The potential for agreement among scholars rests on the sufficiency of evidence, all apart from the narrative preferences of those involved, actually or allegedly on the Left, who are conducting the inquiries.

Mommsen is convincing when, in comparing Weber's position with that of some of his colleagues, he writes:

. . . his imperialistic thinking surpassed that of Delbrueck, Rohrbach, and Naumann by far in virulence and radicalism. Nor did he hesitate to draw the consequences such a policy entails at the domestic level. In his imperialistic arguments he occasionally engaged in an almost brutal manner of speech which corresponded to the type which one generally witnesses only from such geopoliticians as Ratzel and von Richthofen. His pronounced tendency to think in terms of power raised his appeal for a German imperialism to an extraordinary degree of radicalism.[70]

The imperialistic thrust of Weber's thought must indeed be considered a part of his political philosophy. He was certainly not alone in his outlook, but he stated it both forcefully and without attempting to disguise or ennoble it under a mantle of metaphysics.

When later Weber received an invitation to accompany the German peace delegation to Versailles, he accepted, though reluctantly, because his loyalty to his country bade him serve it in its hour of humiliation. Proposing that "designated war criminals" should offer themselves up to the enemy, he had written Ludendorff to this effect and received a negative answer. In a personal meeting with Ludendorff, Weber charged him and the general staff with having committed grave political errors. Ludendorff, in return, attributed to Weber co-responsibility for the mistakes of the new government and the revolution.

When Weber requested Ludendorff to give himself up to the enemy, the following memorable dialogue took place:

Ludendorff: How can you expect me to do anything of the sort?
Weber: The honor of the nation can be saved only if you give yourself up.
Ludendorff: The nation can go jump in the lake. Such ingratitude!
Weber: Nevertheless, you ought to render this last service.
Ludendorff: I hope to be able to render more important services to the nation.
Weber: In that case, your remark is not meant so seriously. For the rest, it is not only of concern to the German people, but a matter of restoring the honor of the *officer corps* and of the army.
Ludendorff: Why don't you go to see Hindenburg? After all, he was the "Generalfeldmarschall."
Weber: Hindenburg is seventy years of age, and besides, every child knows that at the time you were number one in Germany.
Ludendorff: Thank goodness.[71]

The conversation then turned to politics, focussing upon the causes of the collapse and interference in politics on the part of the German High Command. Ludendorff felt himself cornered and, anxious to change the subject, charged Weber and the *Frankfurter Zeitung* with responsibility for the "democracy":

Weber: Do you believe that I think this mess which we now have is *democracy?*
Ludendorff: If that is how you talk, we can perhaps come to understand each other.
Weber: However, the mess we had before was also no monarchy.
Ludendorff: What do you mean then by democracy?
Weber: In a democracy the people elect a leader whom they trust. Then the elected one says: "Now shut up and obey." People and parties must no longer interfere.

Ludendorff: Such a "democracy" is all right with me.

Weber: Afterwards the people may judge him. If the leader has made mistakes—to the gallows with him! [72]

This report by Marianne Weber of the conversation between her husband and Ludendorff must impress even the most detached reader. As Siegfried Kracauer states, Max Weber was quite able to foresee that the *leader* would send the people to the gallows first, before they had a chance to judge him! However, ". . . his intrinsic urges apparently interfered with his sociological judgment."[73]

From the human angle Ludendorff had profoundly disappointed Weber, who emerged from the interview with the following pragmatic conclusion:

Perhaps it is better for Germany that he does not give himself up. His personal impression would be unfavorable. Once again the enemy would find that 'the sacrifices of war which put this type out of commission, were worth while.' I now understand why the world defends itself against the attempts of men like him to place their heel upon its neck. If he should again engage in politics, he will have to be fought remorselessly.[74]

Even at that time Weber would have preferred a parliamentary monarchy: "However, recent events make it impossible to come out in its favor. 'A confession of loyalty' to the republic has thus been dictated to us."[75]

Wilhelm Ziegler recorded Weber's position on the issue of Germany's future structure, whether unitarian or federal, at the time the groundwork of the constitution was laid: "There must be as much unitarianism as possible in a federal constitution."[76]

As long as the German state had at its helm a monarch, Weber believed that its leaders should be selected by parliament. Now that the monarch no longer held the highest office, Weber demanded that the *Reichspraesident* be chosen directly by the people and that his authority be independent of parliament. He should be the supreme executive and in case of disagreement between government and parliament, he should be entitled to present his case directly to the people. Direct election of the president, according to Weber, limits party influence, especially upon the selection of ministers.[77] This provision, which became Article 41, aiming at a plebiscitarian president, coupled with Article 48, made the *Reichspraesident* sole guardian of the constitution which, as J. P. Mayer said in retrospect, was to have dire consequences as "the wolf was made to look after the sheep."[78]

Genuine parliamentarism presupposed two essentially equal highest organs of the state. In a parliamentary monarchy, the crown is positioned alongside parliament. In a parliamentary democracy, in which all political power emanates from the will of the people, the president is accorded equal status along with popularly elected representatives of the people only if he was not elected by them but by popular vote. . . .[79]

Johannes Winckelmann correctly draws attention to Weber's assertion that in view of the increasing limitations "of the purely *political* significance of parliament as such, what is absolutely required is a counterweight based on the democratic will of the people."[80] Subsequent historical developments have borne out Weber's estimate of the power status of the British prime minister: "not only has the British parliament lost its position as 'sovereign' but the Cabinet has also for some time ceased to be the center of power. All these changes have issued in the enormous increase in power of the Prime Minister." Johannes Winckelmann concludes that this development has caused the British scheme of government to move closer to the American presidential system.[81]

Article 48 of the Weimar Constitution provided that if public order and security were seriously endangered, the *Reichspraesident* might take all necessary steps for their restoration, intervening if need be, with the aid of the armed forces. . . .[82] As Hans Kelsen points out, in the presence of such exceptional circumstances most constitutions adhering to the principle of the separation of powers authorize the chief executive (in Germany, the chancellor) "to enact general norms in place of the legislative organ, without a special authorization emanating from this organ in the form of an 'authorizing statute' (*Ermaechtigungsgesetz*)."[83] While emergency powers of the chief executive are a fact, this does not imply

. . . that the ordinary legislative body is deprived of the possibility of regulating those same matters positively. Usually the head of the executive department is competent to regulate them as long as the legislative organ fails to do so. He loses his competence as soon as the legislative organ submits the matter to a regulation of its own.[84]

In this connection Herman Finer's comment is pertinent:

It [the power to take measures necessary to restore public security and order where these are seriously disturbed or endangered within the Federation] goes very far, permitting the authorities to abrogate either wholly or partly the fundamental laws laid down in the second part of the Constitution on the fundamental rights and duties of Germans. But the Constitution requires that the President of the Federation must, without delay, inform the Reichstag of any measures taken . . . and those measures must be withdrawn upon the demand of the Reichstag. It has been suggested that in the event of continued parliamentary deadlock the President could govern by virtue of this Article without Parliament. I cannot see how this can be done *within* the Constitution. For a cabinet would, by the Constitution, have to countersign and to accept responsibility; if it did not, then the Constitution would virtually be suspended. The justification for such a suggestion is the instability and internal weakness of German coalition Cabinets.[85]

Max Weber's influence upon the shaping of the Constitution made itself felt in his suggestion of *enquête* committees.[86] Weber had, as Mayer pointed out, the British parliamentary system in mind as a model. But this type of institution can only be expected to flourish

. . . within a political framework where the parties agree on the fundamental conception of the society in which they have their roots. Once this fundamental agreement is violated, or, as in the case of Germany in 1919, non-existent, even the best constitutional devices are doomed to failure.[87]

Such a "fundamental agreement" existed in England because at the time the modern constitution evolved those who formed the two political parties were members of a socially and economically homogeneous group. The unpropertied played no active role in politics and had only a minor part in the shaping of parliamentary institutions. The resulting consensus persisted until the rise of the Labour Party as a new force in British political life. The growth of this party, whose avowed aim has been to transform the economic system within the framework of the constitution, has subjected the British system to considerable strains; nevertheless, its institutions have remained firm. A time-honored tradition of compromise and moderation is shared by all parties, all of which have also been traditionally less doctrinaire and intransigent than their continental counterparts.

After the war, in 1919, general agreement existed on the need for greater centralization among the major political parties of the Reich. The Majority Socialists, the Independent Socialists, the Spartakists, the Democrats, and the Center Party were all persuaded that a greater degree of centralization was needed if they were to carry out their economic and social aspirations.[88] At the same time there was, outwardly at least, consensus on the desirability of a parliamentary system of government. Even the militarists found it expedient to acquiesce; indeed, Field Marshal Paul von Hindenburg allowed himself to become president of the Republic. The election results for the Constitutional Assembly in 1919 certainly showed a majority of all parties in favor of democratic government.

It is doubtful, however, whether all those who appeared to favor popular rights were genuine converts to the new system. Weber was probably not the only person who looked upon forms of government as mere techniques. Unlike the majority of the working class, who were made politically conscious through membership in the trade unions, large

portions of the bourgeoisie were politically numb. Without loyalty to
the institutions for which the Republic stood, they made no attempt to
defend them against the Nazis.[89]

In other contexts, Weber's political realism remained unimpaired.
When a parliamentary commission was formed for the purpose of inter-
rogating wartime leaders, Weber strictly disapproved of the fact that
a third of the commission, to which men like Hindenburg, Ludendorff,
Bethmann-Hollweg had to answer for their actions, consisted of Jewish
politicians. As Marianne Weber points out, Weber despised anti-
Semitism, but he regretted that the revolutionary leaders of the period
counted many Jews among them:

> Upon being asked if he had now also turned anti-Semitic, Weber angrily
> rejected the possibility: The historical situation of the Jews was in itself an
> explanation of the fact that these revolutionary-minded people should come
> from their ranks. But in view of prevailing attitudes, it was politically unwise
> that they should become conspicuous as leaders and that they should even be
> admitted as such. He thought in terms of *Realpolitik* as he saw the danger
> that thus desirable political talents would become discredited by public
> opinion.[90]

When Weber, at the recommendation of Prince Max, joined the
"Committee for Peace Negotiations," headed by Count Bernstoff: his
suspicions regarding the value of the Committee's conferences in Berlin
appeared justified. Nobody bore any appreciable responsibility. Weber
criticized the composition of the "experts," characterizing it as "purely
party-oriented . . . a severe mistake which will avenge itself; Stinnes, for
instance, would have belonged here but was refused."[91]

As seen earlier, only after some initial reluctance did Weber decide
to accompany the peace delegation to Versailles. When the Center
Party and the Social Democrats finally accepted the treaty terms, Weber
voted with the parties of the Right and with the Democrats against it.
In his opinion, instead of acceptance, people and government should
passively allow the occupation to take place. He believed the Allied
Powers would soon tire of policing Germany and renew negotiations.
The negation of the peace terms should not come as an outright rejection, but in the form of dissolution of all government in Germany and
the subsequent transfer of sovereignty to the League of Nations. This or
similar action would make all war settlements impossible.

For Weber the founding of the *Reich* had not represented the
climax but the starting point of a development which was crucial for
Germany's vital national interests. Germany's participation in the gigantic
expansion of capitalism in the West appeared mandatory to him if she
was not to sink to the level of a second-rate nation. A consistent foreign
policy on a grand scale and an effective performance of "world power

politics" Weber regarded as two sides of the same coin. In the long run foreign trade without the forceful political support of the national state was doomed to failure. A vigorous foreign policy backed by an effective global mobilization of Germany's economic markets and investment potential he also considered mandatory. In the process of fusing these ends, Max Weber's national power philosophy at times became identified with the harshest type of national imperialism.[92] One hesitates to designate Weber an advocate of economic nationalism in the more restrictive sense; perhaps more accurately, his economic nationalism might be said to involve "the notion of a country's seeking more 'autonomy' in its economic life than it would have sought in a well-knit system of economic internationalism."[93]

In effect, while all nations have national policies, they may be guided either by a nationalistic concept of national interest or by an internationally inspired concept.[94] Weber subscribed to the former criterion; nor was he alone in holding to it:

. . . there came about an intense crisis of conscience that overshadowed Troeltsch's last years and broke Meinecke's intellectual life in two. While the war was still in progress, both had argued that Germany's peculiar tradition of idealist and historically grounded values gave ethical justification to the national war effort: as opposed to the 'mechanistic' philosophies for which France and Britain stood, Germany fought for a deeper and more spiritual tradition. This line of argument, of which Thomas Mann was the most persuasive advocate, was common to German intellectuals in both the conservative and reforming camps. It helps explain why the latter, for all their opposition to annexation and their insistence on some version of democracy, remained steadfastly nationalist, and how they could still maintain that there was something ethical about Germany's war aims long after it had become evident that at home as on the front it was naked military force alone that mattered.[95]

When the war was over, however, both Troeltsch and Meinecke supported the Weimar Republic and its institutions. Both lived long enough to enable them to reflect upon World War I and its aftermath longer than Weber, who died in 1920. Troeltsch died in 1923 just before he was to deliver a series of lectures in England. These lectures, subsequently published under the title *Der Historismus und seine Ueberwindung*, suggest that Troeltsch had conquered the crisis in his historical thinking. Meinecke, who lived until 1954, confronted the Nazi destruction of the values of Western civilization, World War II and all its consequences. Decidedly anti-Nazi, he condemned the entire gamut of nationalism which Germany had run historically and which culminated in the Hitler regime. He pronounced judgment not only on Hitler but on Bismarck, too, whom he viewed as a "borderline case." In 1946 his reappraisal of the German situation, including World War II and a divided Germany, permitted Meinecke to see in it the spiritual victory of Weimar over Potsdam, and of Goethe over Bismarck.[96] Yet it must also be said that in his earlier work, published during the Nazi period,[97] he had, as Hughes suggests,

'sought refuge', like so many others of his more sensitive countrymen, in an ideal world of the spirit. Ultimately he had succumbed to his own vaporous brand of metaphysic. . . . As his personal response to the challenge of relativism, he followed Goethe in declaring his 'faith in final absolute values' for which he could offer no validation beyond the voice of his own 'soul.'
    In so doing, Meinecke retracted nothing of what he had written earlier. . . . The pragmatic separation between the sphere of ideas and the sphere of politics which had become increasingly explicit in his post-war writings he had now delineated even more sharply.[98]

From the foregoing, it becomes apparent that even those who had lived through World War II and who "had tried to go back to a time when the idealist tradition was still unencumbered by mystical abstractions and associations with the power-state,"[99] still failed to cope with Germany's political past, much less develop a clear-cut design of what would be desirable for her future. Weber's own inability to maintain a consistent party alignment suggests that he too shared this condition.

    Yet, as a political analyst of the major contemporary problems of his time, Weber can hardly be challenged. His vision anticipated changes which still lay in the future at the time of his death. He foretold the coming of the reaction against the Weimar Republic and the democratic system. Some of his wishes were to be fulfilled after World War II. The rigidly ideological element in German party programs was progressively reduced. The Christian Democratic Union, for example, was founded on a double compromise. On the one hand, progressive left-wing, trade-unionist groups, which subscribed to radical social reform and a measure of state control, joined forces with the more conservative elements, who in turn opposed socialist thinking and supported free enterprise. The result was a party without a rigid ideological line but with a practical political purpose, which expanded naturally as Adenauer's policies gained support among the voters. This fact alone would have compelled the Social Democrats to cast off the traditions and shibboleths of the past. In the fall of 1959 the new program adopted by the SPD at its Bad Godesberg Conference virtually renounced Marxism. The party was to be transformed from a proletarian apparatus into a people's party with a view toward gaining wide popular appeal. The need for national defense was accepted by the Left. These tactical changes by the two great contemporary political parties are notable, the Social Democrats increasingly practicing moderation while the CDU became a party with mass-based appeal.

In reviewing Weber's position vis-à-vis the German parties, one remarkable conclusion emerges. Despite his unsparing criticism of many of their policies, and his own inability to form a consistent attachment to any of them, he managed to enjoy the respect of those in opposite ideological camps: "Among democrats he ranks as a friend and mentor of an extreme and salutary tough-mindedness. The neo-Marxists honor him as the man who refused to hate or to outlaw his revolutionary adversaries, who consented to discuss his differences with them frankly and face to face." [100] As Fritz Ernst concludes, to understand Weber's views, one must trace the gradual crystallization of his line of thought ending ultimately in his qualified acceptance of parliamentarism.[101] Weber's final disenchantment with the consequences of the Bismarck era, is summed up in his own words: "The bureaucratic spirit ruled where another, namely the guiding spirit of the politician, should have ruled. . . . We are wearing an iron ring around our hearts." [102]

NOTES

[1] Edward A. Shils and Henry A. Finch, eds. and transl., *On the Methodology of the Social Sciences* (New York: The Free Press, 1948), p. 84.
[2] A. L. Lowell, *Governments and Parties in Continental Europe*, Vol. II, p. 42, cited in Enid Lakeman and James D. Lambert, "Voting in Democracies," in Harry Eckstein and David E. Apter, eds., *Comparative Politics: A Reader* (New York: The Free Press, 1967), p. 296.
[3] E. G. Passant, *A Short History of Germany 1815–1945* (Cambridge, Mass.: Cambridge University Press, 1966), pp. 94–95. Reprinted by permission of the publisher.
[4] *Ibid.*, p. 87.
[5] *Ibid.*
[6] *Ibid.*, pp. 87–88.
[7] *Ibid.*, p. 88.
[8] *Ibid.*, p. 92.
[9] Letter to Baumgarten of November 8, 1884 in *Jugendbriefe* (Tuebingen: J. C. B. Mohr [Paul Siebeck], 1936), p. 143. Quoted hereafter as *Jugendbriefe*.
[10] Vernon L. Lidtke, *The Outlawed Party: Social Democracy in Germany 1818–1890* (Princeton, N.J.: Princeton University Press, 1966), p. 237.
[11] *Ibid.*, p. 193.
[12] Fritz Fischer, *Germany's Aims in the First World War* (New York: W. W. Norton & Company, 1967), pp. 6–7.
[13] Cf. Special supplement to the *Allgemeine Zeitung*, 1898, Number 46, p. 4. Cited in W. J. Mommsen, *Max Weber und die Deutsche Politik, 1890–1920* (Tuebingen: J. C. B. Mohr [Paul Siebeck], 1959), p. 15.
[14] Cf. Letter of July 14, 1885, *Jugendbriefe*, p. 171.
[15] Mommsen, *op. cit.*, ftn. p. 15.
[16] Letter to Baumgarten of April 30, 1888, *Jugendbriefe*, p. 293.
[17] Cf. Letter to Baumgarten of June 29, 1887, *Jugendbriefe*, p. 249.
[18] Cf. Mommsen, *op. cit.*, p. 16 and also Weber's letter to his father of March 15, 1885, *Jugendbriefe*, p. 151f.

19 Cf. Mommsen, op. cit., p. 16.
20 Carlo Antoni, translated from the Italian by Hayden V. White, From History to Sociology: The Transition in German Historical Thinking (Detroit: Wayne State University Press, 1959), p. 122.
21 H. Stuart Hughes, Consciousness and Society: The Reorientation of European Social Thought 1890–1930 (New York: Alfred A. Knopf, 1958), p. 291.
22 Ludwig Dehio, Germany and World Politics in the Twentieth Century (New York: Alfred A. Knopf, 1965), p. 20. Reprinted by permission of Chatto and Windus Ltd.
23 Ibid.
24 Ibid., p. 83. The author refers to a lecture of October 22, 1916, printed in Weber's collected political writings (Politische Schriften, 2nd. ed.).
25 Letter to Baumgarten of April 25, 1887, Jugendbriefe, p. 234.
26 Letter to Baumgarten already on July 14, 1885, ibid., p. 170.
27 Letter to Baumgarten, April 25, 1887, ibid., p. 234.
28 Letter to Baumgarten of April 30, 1888, ibid., p. 297.
29 Mommsen, op. cit., p. 16.
30 Cf. Mommsen, ibid., p. 17.
31 Carlo Antoni, op. cit., p. 124.
32 Dehio, op. cit., p. 97.
33 Cf. Hans Rothfels, Die Deutsche Opposition Gegen Hitler (Frankfurt-Hamburg, 1957) [German Opposition to Hitler, Chicago, 1962], p. XLV cited in Ralf Dahrendorf, Society and Democracy in Germany (Garden City, N.Y.: Doubleday, 1967), p. 41.
34 Cf. John R. Staude, Max Scheler, 1874–1928. An Intellectual Portrait (New York: The Free Press, 1967), p. 49.
35 Cf. Max Scheler, Ressentiment, tr. William W. Holdheim, and ed. with introduction by Lewis A. Coser (New York: Free Press of Glencoe, 1961), p. 52 cited in ibid., p. 55.
36 Cf. Richard N. Hunt, German Social Democracy 1918–1933 (New Haven: Yale University Press, 1964), cf. also Carl Schorske, German Social Democracy 1905–1917 (Cambridge, Mass.: Harvard University Press, 1955), and cited in A. Joseph Berlau, The German Social Democratic Party 1914–1921 (New York, 1949).
37 Cf. Wolfgang Abendroth, Aufstieg und Krise der deutschen Sozialdemokratie (Frankfurt/Main: Stimme-Verlag, 1964).
38 Golo Mann, "Wer ist ein Intellektueller? Ueber das Auftreten des politischen Publizisten in der deutschen Geschichte," Die Zeit, Nr. 10, March 12, 1968, p. 8. Cf. also Anni Carlsson, ed., Hermann Hesse—Thomas Mann: "Briefwechsel" (Frankfurt: Suhrkamp Verlag/S. Fischer Verlag, 1968).
39 Letter to Baumgarten, July 20, 1888, Jugendbriefe, p. 298f. and Lebensbild, p. 131.
40 Letter to Baumgarten, July 20, 1888, Jugendbriefe, p. 298f.
41 Lebensbild, p. 138.
42 Ibid., p. 135.
43 Bernard Semmel, Imperialism and Social Reform: English Social-Imperial Thought 1885–1914 (Garden City: Doubleday, 1968), p. 196.
44 Ibid., p. 197.
45 Gustav Schmoller, Grundriss der Allgemeinen Volkswirtschaftslehre (Munich, 1923), Vol. II, pp. 562–647, cited in ibid.
46 Ibid., p. 199.
47 Cf. Mommsen, op. cit., p. 18.
48 Letter to Baumgarten of April 30, 1888, Jugendbriefe, p. 296.
49 Mommsen, op. cit., p. 18.
50 Lebensbild, p. 132
51 Cf. Mommsen, op. cit., p. 19.
52 P.S., 2nd. ed., p. 300.
53 Ibid.
54 Ibid., pp. 300–301.
55 Cf. Mommsen, op. cit., p. 19.
56 Cf. Letter to Baumgarten of March 13, 1888, Jugendbriefe, p. 294.
57 Naumann's formulation of Germany's Mission quoted by P. Rohrbach, Der deutsche Gedanke in der Welt. 1912 in Ludwig Dehio, op. cit., p. 89.
58 Die Hilfe, Vol. I, 1894/96, July 14, 1895.
59 R. Nuernberger on Naumann in Historische Zeitschrift, Vol. 170, p. 530, published the above quotation of 1895, cited in Dehio, op. cit., p. 82.

[60] Friedrich Naumann, *National-Sozialer Katechismus*, 1897, cited in *ibid.*, p. 72.
[61] Cf. A. Steger, *Deutsche Weltpolitik bei Hans Delbrueck* (Marburg University, unpublished Dr. Phil. dissertation, 1955), p. 36, cited in Dehio, *op. cit.*, p. 80.
[62] *Preussische Jahrbuecher*, Vol. 81, 1895, p. 388ff.
[63] *Ibid.*, p. 390.
[64] Imanuel Geiss, ed., *July 1914: The Outbreak of the First World War: Selected Documents* (New York: Charles Scribner's Sons, 1967), p. 23.
[65] Cf. Anneliese Thimme, *Hans Delbrueck als Kritiker der Wilhelminischen Epoche* (Duesseldorf: Droste Verlag, 1955), cited in Geiss, *op. cit.*, p. 23.
[66] J. Steinberg, "The Copenhagen Complex" in *Journal of Contemporary History*, Vol. I, No. 3, p. 27, cited in Geiss, *op. cit.*, p. 23.
[67] Weber's address as cited in *Preussische Jahrbuecher*, *op. cit.*, p. 390.
[68] Robert A. Nisbet, Book Review of Julien Freund, *The Sociology of Max Weber* (New York: Pantheon Books, 1968), in *New York Times Book Review*, *The New York Times*, Vol. CXVII, No. 40, 293, 1968, p. 6.
[69] *Ibid.*
[70] Mommsen, *op. cit.*, p. 80. See also Dirk Oncken, *Das Problem des Lebensraumes in der deutschen Politik* (Freiburg Universitaet, 1948), p. 98.
[71] *Lebensbild*, p. 664.
[72] *Ibid.*, p. 665.
[73] Siegfried Kracauer, *From Caligari to Hitler: A Psychological History of the German Film* (New York: Princeton University Press, 1947), p. 124, n.
[74] *Lebensbild*, p. 665.
[75] *Lebensbild*, p. 650.
[76] Wilhelm Ziegler, *Die Deutsche Nationalversammlung 1919–20 und Ihr Verfassungswerk* (Berlin: Zentralverlag G.m.B.H., 1932), p. 93; also see the historical jurist's who later joined the Nazi ranks, Carl Schmitt, *Verfassungslehre* (Munich: Duncker & Humblot, 1928), pp. 335–36. Weber himself, in "Deutschlands kuenftige Staatsform," written in November, 1918 (*P.S.*, p. 368), advocated that the new German state be based on a unitarian federal constitution. He did this because he believed that the socialization of sectors of the German economy would become inevitable as a result of Germany's economic situation and obligations to pay reparations. Weber conceded thus that some measure of socialization would be required for the rehabilitation of the German economy and that this by itself entailed a centralized administration. He was realistic enough to recognize the fact that due to the historical background it would not be feasible to discard federalist principles altogether.
[77] *Lebensbild*, pp. 650–51.
[78] J. P. Mayer, *Max Weber and German Politics: A Study in Political Sociology* (London: Faber & Faber, 1943), p. 78.
[79] *Entwurf der kuenftigen Reichsverfassung*, hrg. i. Auftrage des Reichsamts des Innern (Berlin [Anfang] 1919), Denkschrift (Amm. 29a) p. 24, parl. 1—cited in Max Weber, *Staatssoziologie: Soziologie der rationalen Staatsanstalt und der Modernen Politischen Parteien und Parlamente mit einer Einfuehrung und Erlaeuterungen*, ed. by Johannes Winckelmann (Berlin: Duncker & Humblot, 1966), p. 15.
[80] *P.S.*, 2nd. ed., p. 488 cited in Johannes Winckelmann, "Erlaeuterungen," p. 118. Professor Winckelmann also cites the objections raised to this Weberian point: cf. Karl Loewenstein, *Max Webers Staatspolitische Auffassungen in der Sicht unserer Zeit* (1965), p. 25 cited in *ibid.*
[81] *Ibid.*, p. 129, cf. also Karl Loewenstein, *Der britische Parlamentarismus, Entstehung und Gestalt*, RDE Bd. 208, (Hamburg, 1964), cited in *ibid.*
[82] J. P. Mayer, *op. cit.*, p. 78.
[83] Hans Kelsen, *General Theory of Law and State* (Cambridge: Harvard University Press, 1945), pp. 270–271.
[84] *Ibid.*, p. 271.
[85] Herman Finer, *The Theory and Practice of Modern Government* (London: Methuen & Co., Ltd., 1929–1932), II, 1152–53. Cf. Also Herman Finer, *The Future of Government* (London: Methuen and Co., Ltd., 1945), especially p. 50: "The acceptance, by Hindenburg, of a Chancellor whose Party had vowed to destroy the Constitution he had sworn an oath to defend, was in itself manifestly unconstitutional in spirit. More deadly for the German people and the Republic was the Decree of February 28, 1933, signed by the President. Ostensibly an answer to the Reichstag fire . . ., the Decree was issued in pursuance of the Constitution, Article 18, Section 2 . . . permitting the suspension of certain Constitutional guarantees in a state of high emergency. These

guarantees are the buttress of democracy; their abridgement the foundation of dictatorship.

86 Cf. Article 34 of the Weimar Constitution, which gives the Reichstag the right, and by the vote of one-fifth of its members, the obligation to establish committees of investigation. Cf. *Lebensbild*, p. 652.

87 Mayer, *op. cit.*, p. 76; also cf. Finer, *op. cit.*, II, pp. 1086ff.

88 See Finer, *op. cit.*, I, p. 352.

89 *Ibid.*

90 *Lebensbild*, p. 660.

91 *Ibid.*, p. 662. Cf. Fred H. Blum, "Max Weber: The Man of Politics and the Man Dedicated to Objectivity and Rationality," *Ethics*, (October, 1959, LXX, No. 1), p. 15: "In his political analysis Weber involved himself in contradictions which were out of tune with the depth of his analytical abilities and insight. He who stated repeatedly that economic and political power go hand-in-hand wanted to preserve the economic function of the 'gentlemen of heavy industry' while stripping them of their 'nefarious political influence.' He has been severely criticized for these views . . . such contradictions in thought indicate deep emotional undercurrents and conflicts which are not resolved. It may be argued that we are dealing here not with a real inconsistency but with a political compromise . . . there remains a great deal of evidence for contradictions and incompatibilities."

92 Mommsen, *op. cit.*, pp. 77–78. Cf. also Ludwig Dehio, "Gedanken ueber die deutsche Sendung, 1900–1918," *Historische Zeitschrift*, Vol. 174, 1952, p. 479 cited in Mommsen, *op. cit.*, p. 78.

93 Cf. Michael A. Heilperin, *Studies in Economic Nationalism* (Geneva and Paris: Publications De L'Institut Universitaire De Hautes Etudes Internationales—No. 35, 1960), p. 27.

94 *Ibid.*, p. 23.

95 Hughes, *op. cit.*, pp. 237–38.

96 Cf. Friedrich Meinecke, *Die Deutsche Katastrophe: Betrachtungen und Erinnerungen* (Wiesbaden und Zuerich: Brockhaus, 1946). Cited in Hughes, *op. cit.*, p. 245.

97 Meinecke, *Die Entstehung des Historismus* (Munich and Berlin: Leibniz, 1936), Vols. I, pp. 2, 4–5, II, pp. 626–7, cited in Hughes, *op. cit.*, p. 245.

98 Hughes, *op. cit.*, p. 244.

99 *Ibid.*, p. 246.

100 *Ibid.*, p. 333.

101 Cf. Fritz Ernst, *The Germans and Their Modern History* (New York: Columbia University Press, 1966), p. 145 fn.

102 *Lebensbild*, p. 596 cited in *ibid*.

IV

Max Weber's Prewar Political Views

Max Weber's inquiry into the relationship of values to power provides one of his most penetrating insights. As noted earlier, the main criterion for Weber's political views rested on his concept of the role which the German nation was to play.[1] His political philosophy was based essentially on the affirmation of national power as the noblest end toward which the striving of Germany must be directed. Weber's commitment to this position must be understood in terms of the fact that "liberty was identified with the freedom of the state from external restraints and not with the freedom of the individual from control by the state—or rather those acting in its name. The principal duty of all citizens was to serve the national community, and political structures intervening between its primary unit, the family, and its highest, the state, tended to be viewed as essentially unimportant, if not disruptive, elements in the task of preserving and expanding the unity and strength of the German people."[2]

Defining power as "the probability that one actor within a social relationship will be in a position to carry out his own will *despite resistance,* regardless of the basis on which this probability rests,"[3] Weber employed a conflict model in his definition of social relationships. "A social relationship will be referred to as 'conflict' insofar as action within it is oriented intentionally to carrying out the actor's own will against the resistance of the other party or parties."[4]

Weber apparently distinguished between two types of power, allowing both for situations marked by the absence of conflict and for others which contain conflict and require the triumph of one party over another. Yet, the latter conception of power received more emphasis. The *Machtstaat* alone could guarantee the expansion of German civilization, an end to be achieved by a deliberate use of appropriate economic and political weapons. "Since Weber is careful to distinguish power from other forms of social control in which cooperation is more crucial, his approach at least suggests that in the exercise of power, resistance and conflict in one degree or another are highly probable, and perhaps even expected. This idea of power, therefore, tends to imply a process of overpowering."[5] The power state, moreover, should preserve for each individual member his personality and freedom of thought while also bringing about the cooperation of classes, status groups, and parties.

The political training of the German people, teaching them to think and act rationally in the realm of politics, was an urgent corollary.[6] Indeed, Weber's personal dissatisfaction with the conduct of German politics seems to have been a powerful motivation for his analysis of political dilemmas, his search for prudent solutions to them, and his efforts to make these widely known. This may be seen in Weber's inaugural lecture given in the second semester in Freiburg on *Der Nationalstaat und die Volkswirtschaftspolitik* (The National State and Economic Policy), in 1895.[7]

His concern for national power manifested itself publicly for the first time in 1890–1891 when the *Verein fuer Sozialpolitik* commissioned Weber to make a report on the situation of the agrarian laborers in East-Elbian Germany.[8] Questionnaires were addressed to the landlords of estates and the study was completed within a year. In a long monograph deploring the fact that agrarian policy had been dominated by the parochial economic interests of the agricultural landlords, Weber advised a radical change providing for the promotion of the national interest. He raised the question: why is it that the Polish and Russian population is increasing in the rural parts of East Prussia while the German population is constantly decreasing? In Bismarck's time, Germany's eastern frontier was open for seasonal Slav labor, but closed to potential settlers.

Weber inquired into the danger of the new situation, the main cause of which seemed to be the dissolution of the old agrarian economy and its replacement by large estates. The East-Elbian agrarian workers, confronted as they were with patriarchal conditions of existence, were migrating to urban areas, hoping to receive regular wages and a free work contract. Both living and working conditions had become such that they lacked the incentive which might have induced them to stay. But the modern landlord, rather than providing the image of a paternal figure, was a businessman engaged only in profit-making, unencumbered by a genuine concern for his workers. Farm labor was now paid in money rather than in produce from the land, which weakened the bonds between the estate owner and his workers. They no longer shared the fruit of their labor in the accustomed manner; nor could the workers expect to purchase land of their own. All their continued stay on the estates held in store for them was a proletarian existence, but one in which the prospect of the kind of economic independence characterizing the urban industrial proletariat would have been dim. Weber found that the German workers' motivation for leaving the estates was not based upon the wish for higher wages; in fact, most of the workers who were leaving seemed to enjoy the highest earnings. However, both feelings of loyalty and conditions of vassalage no longer obtained, since the estate owner was no longer liable for the individual worker. As a consequence, Polish and Russian workers replaced German workers; their services were welcome to the landowners because they were cheap and the workers' status expectations were low.

Weber was particularly concerned that this trend had manifested itself in the East, where Germany was most vulnerable. Far from being only an economically significant trend, he thought that enterprises operating at the expense of the national interest deserved to be discontinued. More serious yet was the high rate of population losses in the most sparsely inhabited area of Germany, which facilitated the penetration of Slavs into German territory with attending debasement of German cultural and economic values. Noting that the departure of the German agricultural workers was inspired by their "grandiose illusion of freedom,"[9] rather than by aspirations to higher material standards, Weber urged that the current policy favoring the aristocracy, which had proved detrimental to the national interest, be abandoned. He proposed instead a national peasant policy in which the vital interests of the nation would be safeguarded, including the closing of the German frontier to the workers from the East so that the interests of German agricultural labor might be protected against the selfish practices of the estate owners. Weber strongly favored a systematic program of colonization of the German East with German workers, insisting however, that his was not a concern with the fate of the landworkers as such. The problem was to be tackled from the standpoint of *raison d'état* alone; neither criteria of social welfare benefiting the landworkers nor potential government subsidies designed to reduce expenses for the landed aristocracy governed his approach.

As Weber saw the problem, psychological rather than legal reasoning would have to be used to chain the peasants emotionally to German soil; consequently, their craving for land would have to be satisfied.[10] He argued, as he was to do throughout his career as a political writer, that the very foundation of the Reich could be vindicated only if it was recognized as the beginning rather than the end of German power politics. Hence the objective of social legislation should not be directed merely toward the attainment of the greatest good for the greatest number. Its central target should be the social cohesion of the nation which constitutes the source of its strength; the latter must be employed to augment Germany's position of power in the world. As Lewis Edinger writes:

> By integrating traditional beliefs with rising nationalist emotions and important social values, this political orientation effectively upheld the legitimacy of the established authorities in Hohenzollern Germany. For the most part the growing industrial middle class accepted and even embraced it with enthusiasm. In return for a form of state capitalism promoting their economic interests, the financial and industrial upper-middle class to the continuing rule of the traditional rural aristocracy which held key political positions in Imperial Germany. The rapidly expanding working class was 'negatively integrated' into the system, partly by becoming the beneficiary of the most advanced public social security system in the contemporary world, partly because its political and economic organizations developed largely into non-revolutionary interest associations whose members on the whole accepted passive roles in the system.[11] The peasantry, bound by traditionally strong, affective and economic ties to the ruling aristocracy—especially in protestant Prussia—and fearful of the changes caused by industrialization, provided the ruling groups with some of their most reliable soldiers and voters. Most of the intellectuals, deeply committed emotionally to national unity and integration, accepted the system and frequently employed their talents to propagate its conservation. . . . These political orientations which supported the Imperial regime obscured for almost fifty years the fundamental structural weaknesses which most of its citizens could not see or would not see until defeat in war brought about its collapse. . . . But the effort to fuse traditional Prussian conservatism with modern integral nationalism in the form of a thinly disguised autocracy was increasingly unequal to the demands placed upon the political system, particularly, but by no means exclusively, in international affairs.[12]

The theme of Weber's survey of agrarian conditions in East Prussia and the inferences he drew from it were employed even more forcefully in his subsequent inaugural address in Freiburg. Speaking again from the *raison d'état* point of view, Weber categorically declared the aim of life was not to make men happy, but rather the consideration of what kind of men there were going to be.[13] This maxim inspired Weber throughout his life. Not happiness but duty was the key concept. Thus Weber demanded that the state divide up the large estates and systematically colonize the area. And once again his primary concern was not with Prussian agrarian policy as such, but with the protection of German nationality. He conceived the duty of the state to rest in formulating its economic policy accordingly. Because Germany was a national state, the nation could not afford to evade this task.[14] The political lesson of linking economic policies with the national purpose would have to be learned. It was therefore time for economic policy lessons, which, he felt, had gone largely unrecognized. Weber contended that sparks tend to set fire to ready material: even though situations may have the appearance of being "peaceful," the outcome of international economic cooperation cannot always be mutually satisfactory. Hence the barriers to the latter should not be depreciated. His personal sense of responsibility for history caused him to see the world as one of conflict, as one in which one can never afford to mistake apparent peace for real peace. What engages Weber's almost compulsive interest is the effect obstacles to international cooperation have had on the policy of both the German government and military, and what this policy is ultimately doing to the character and prestige of German politics and to the German people.

Conflict being both unavoidable and universal in human existence, Weber, though a liberal, rejected the optimism of traditional liberal thought. He opposed any cult of consensus, warning that such illusions could not succeed in bestowing peace upon future generations. Past, present and future were read as a series of conflicts. The population problem alone could serve as one of the criteria for measuring the magnitude and intensity of conflict. Realism required that we rate peace and happiness even in terms of future goals as utopian and therefore unattainable. Political thought and action must recognize these facts and grant that living-space is predicated in the final analysis upon the human struggle for existence. Thus emphasis in foreign policy must rest on a continuous struggle for power. Weber was skeptical about lasting international agreements; although he granted that the relations between nations were neither always nor necessarily hostile, they did tend to organize themselves into hostile camps. From the perspective of the post-World War II era, Richard Pipes' verdict suggests that some of Weber's insights into the future of international relations were of necessity limited and need to be revised:

We have seen the West lose its global pre-eminence and almost simultaneously coalesce into a rudimentary supra-national bloc. In the postwar era the tendency everywhere has been for such large blocs to take shape, each united by political and economic interests and, to a lesser degree, by a common ideology. . . . It is too soon to tell whether such blocs will solidify and become prevailing forms of political and economic organization, or turn out to be merely a transitional phase leading toward a single world-wide community. . . .

The process of world integration has been initiated by imperialism, and although imperialism itself appears a phenomenon of the past, the forces it has launched are irreversible. Imperialism's one great achievement was to open up all parts of the world, writes William L. Langer, and to set all humanity on the high road to eventual association, and collaboration.

Whatever the future brings—many sovereign nations, several large supra-national blocs, or a United States of the World—it seems certain that the interdependence of the peoples of the world will continue to increase.

Self-sufficiency can be purchased only at the cost of prosperity and in the long run is untenable. Labor, goods, and capital are finding their way everywhere. The era of free trade after World War II promises to cement the world market even more solidly than did the first great wave of free trade in the nineteenth century.

This means that human beings will be increasingly wrenched out of the security and isolation of their communities and thrown together—often in competition—with people whose cultures are altogether different from their own. We are already witnessing an expansion of the labor market that would have appeared fantastic fifty years ago, with Turkish workers operating machines in German factories, German stewardesses staffing domestic airlines in the United States, American workers drilling for oil in Arabian deserts, and Arab waiters serving tables in Swiss mountain resorts. . . .

In such a thoroughly intermingled world the need for liberal values will be greater than ever. . . .[15]

While Ratzenhofer viewed international relations as inevitably hostile,[16] and while Carl Schmitt found himself largely agreeing with the latter,[17] Weber did not view all international relations as necessarily hostile. However, he did little to mitigate the effects of nationalism by embracing a philosophical approach to international politics that was to arouse in the minds of those with less integrity the temptation to exalt power in general and more especially in the role of military might. Moreover, as we shall have occasion to observe in the chapter on "Max Weber and the Republic," he shared at least, in part, the failure of understanding the dynamics of revolution with many of his and our contemporaries who view the turbulent social issues of politics and law merely in terms of order and discipline.

Weber is frequently associated with the school that equates political action with techniques employing violence; even though he did not originate the idea, his essay on "Science and Politics" contains a description of its development.[18] Religion, moreover, sanctioned this imperative. In fact, generally speaking, "Protestantism . . . absolutely legitimated the state as a divine institution and hence violence as a means. Protestantism legitimated the authoritarian state. Luther relieved the individual of the ethical responsibility for war and transferred it to the authorities."[19]

Since the distribution of economic power proceeded along lines which enabled one nation to benefit by the loss of another, and since economic pressure at times prescribed such a course of action, the prerequisites for an international body resembling, for example, the present United Nations, were lacking before such a scheme could be conceived. Since no state was likely to renounce its rights or possessions voluntarily, Weber believed all issues ultimately could be resolved only by force.

Politics and economics, moreover, were closely joined and subject to the same imperatives. Weber defined two kinds of functions for economics: one designed to serve as an explanatory and analyzing discipline, whereas the other operated in a sphere which necessarily evoked value judgments. The second context links economics with Germany's specific national character; in the area of economic policy a German theorist cannot do otherwise. This Weberian definition is based on a fundamental although restrictive assumption. His field of vision extended to the international scene only to the point at which the power-political interests of his nation were guaranteed. His basic premise embodied the principle that in the absence of such certainty, i.e., where the context specifies an activity for economics involving the necessity of making value judgments, at that level the national interest must receive priority.[20]

Because he discounted the possibilities of a permanent scheme of fruitful international cooperation, Weber regarded Germany's economic policy as a handmaiden of her politics. Political economy, as noted, was identified with political science. Carried to its logical conclusion, this notion comes to be a way of establishing the unlimited superordination of politics over economics. In Weber's terminology, however, the role of economics is not merely subject to the interests of those who happen to occupy positions of power at a given time, whether they are individuals or classes. He places all rights at the disposal of the permanent power-political interests of the nation. In Weber's calculus the ultimate value standard for both politics and economics was *raison d'état*.[21]

The tragedy of Germany's internal political situation was that neither the bourgeois entrepreneur nor labor was qualified to replace the decaying aristocracy. Under the last great Junker, the economic structure had already undergone a decisive change. The reason Bismarck's work ultimately failed lay in the fact that, although he had achieved Germany's unification, he had never achieved that inner social cohesion which makes for sound politics.[22]

The bourgeoisie, motivated by fear of the advancing proletariat, had succumbed to the authoritarian state. Whatever the catalytic agent might be, one thing seemed certain: it must come from within the bourgeoisie itself. Yet the sense of security of at least part of the bourgeoisie was so weak that it was notoriously searching for a new Caesar to protect it against challenges from the authorities which might curb its potential ascent in social status and in political expectation, a practice which had characterized German dynasties in the past.[23]

One of Bismarck's master strokes helping to perpetuate the authoritarian state had been his democratic gesture of granting universal and equal suffrage for the Reichstag, according to Weber, a "Caesarian gift of the Danaers" (the 'gift of the Greeks' of Bismarck's Caesarism).[24]

It will be remembered that the Prussian franchise remained as before, namely, a three-class system. Why was this important and how did Weber happen to speak of a "Caesarian gift of the Danaers?" The answer is found in his analysis of the position of the Prussian Landtag (Diet) in the German Empire. Prussia was undisputed master in the Bundesrat (Federal Council), for she had the right to veto any measure relating to the army and navy, tariffs, and indirect taxation. In the use of these wide powers the Prussian government was responsible only to the Landtag. The Landtag, thanks to the Prussian franchise, was conservative.[25]

This was not the only safeguard of Prussian dominance. The *Reichstag* could only complain to the chancellor who was normally also Prussian prime minister. Nominated by the emperor he was responsible to him alone. If it disapproved of any law passed by the Bundesrat, the Reichstag had no power to dismiss the chancellor and in the last resort could only refuse to grant the imperial revenues. Should this happen, moreover, the chancellor was able to dissolve the House.

Although severely critical of this state of affairs, Weber did not go as far as to suggest that Prussia abdicate her leadership. He did urge that the Prussian Landtag ought to reflect the opinions of the Prussian people. He was not concerned with Prussia's internal constitutional makeup, but regarded the matter from the point of view of the Landtag's influence upon the policy of the Bundesrat, that is, from the standpoint of national policy.

The main problem was: where was Germany to find potential leaders ready and able to take the place of the old declining aristocracy? The Prussian Junkers had indeed been the pillars of the Prussian dynasty. For centuries they had given the eastern provinces of Germany an admirable administration. However, although class domination was not inherently evil, the perpetuation of an economically dying class was untenable since it was bound to be unsympathetic toward emergent new forces in the structure of the national community. Weber paid homage, nevertheless, to the political style of the reigning establishment without which the state could not have previously conducted its power-political interests so successfully. He showed how this former power elite was destined to abdicate its leadership role since no economic public policy could conceivably restore the landed aristocracy to its former hegemony.[26]

The cardinal determinant of their decline, in Weber's view, had been the disappearance in modern society of the conditions required for the rule of a land-owning class. Speculating whether the bourgeoisie could be called on to assume responsibility for the conduct of German political affairs, Weber answered in the negative, placing the blame for its political immaturity upon its enforced political passivity in the past.[27]

A vicious circle persisted in which the complete lack of democratic government and the intensification of the class struggle in Germany reinforced the growing dread of democracy. This condition, rather than the German mentality, essentially underlay the preference for authoritarianism.

Weber's analysis was informed by a profound awareness of social change. Directing his attention to the possibilities offered by the restructuring of society, he pondered the prospects for the acquisition of new political qualities by the working class. German labor, in his view, emerged as petty bourgeois. Nevertheless, as he catalogued the advantages and disadvantages of each class, he attached great importance to the representation of the interests of labor. He conceded to it the right of employing economic warfare to achieve power. It would be wrong, moreover, to underestimate the degree of maturity reached by the upper echelons of the working class at both the political and the economic levels. On the other hand, he warned against the questionable claims for labor's political maturity voiced by a clique of journalists aspiring to monopolize its leadership; at the same time, he entertained misgivings about the selfishness of the propertied class which refused to admit to labor's considerably advanced level of economic maturity.[28]

The value of political parties lay, not in themselves, but only in their use as means to the ends of the German power state. The task of *Grosse Politik* is clearly to ground its assessment of situations upon the primacy of the great problems which are the real concern of political power from which everything else springs. Again and again in dramatically evocative statements, Weber referred to the unification of Germany as a youthful prank which she should have refrained from committing if she could not demonstrate that it marked the starting point for German world power politics rather than its consummation.[29]

Weber perceived as a gross anomaly the use and misuse of the German bourgeoisie by the traditional ruling class, the former having allowed itself to be systematically excluded from its rightful position as the entrepreneurial class in the modern state. In Ralf Dahrendorf's view, it was "neither the speed and lateness of industrialization as such, nor the inherited structures of the 'dynastic state'—of Prussia, of a long and painful process of national unification, of Lutheranism and the craving for authority, of Junkerdom and militarism—but the encounter and combination of these two strains of development in Imperial Germany that form the explosive core of a society in which the liberal principle could settle only haltingly and occasionally."[30]

Max Weber took the bourgeoisie to task for relinquishing its own aspirations to power leaving the field open to a feudalism with which leaders of big business and industry collaborate in return for aristocratic titles.[31] As a politically engaged intellectual exponent of that bourgeoisie, he employed his polemic powers hoping to give a judicious push at the right moment, in the right direction. From Weber's scholarly scrutiny there emerges a brilliant reconstruction of the total sweep of recent historical developments affecting the bourgeoisie. The outstanding immediate need for that class was to understand the causes and consequences of its abnegation of responsibility.

It was in the realm of foreign policy that Weber discovered a common platform for bourgeoisie and labor. Its true function was to be understood in the immense task of political education of the nation. He wanted to see a new dimension added to his countrymen's understanding of their past so as to project the necessity for a serious concern with political education. He addressed his challenge especially to those whose own qualifications equipped them to supply it, viewing this task as "the ultimate goal of our science."[32] Here already one can see that politics for him was not a profession, but a vocation. For him personally, it was not only a way of writing, but a way of living. The bourgeoisie having been too pressed by circumstances to reach the high level of this vocation, Weber concluded that the realization of Germany's political mission in the world depended upon the creation of a labor aristocracy that could demonstrate a superior competence and readiness to define policy goals, and then to carry out the policies to realize Germany's destiny as Weber envisaged it. Only given these conditions could responsibilities which proved too heavy for the bourgeoisie to shoulder be transferred to labor. But according to Weber's time-table, prospects for an early realization of this hope were dim.[33] If the desired results were to be attained, namely those aimed at the rethinking of Germany's historical mission, labor leaders would have to be taught to think in terms of the national welfare with an eye on the primary importance of Germany's role in foreign affairs.

Weber pleaded for collaboration among all groups to further the power-political education of the German people. Here he revealed again the basic political convictions which were to govern his later political writings.[34] His dictum, "we are a power state," was to remain the core of his thought. He regarded himself as an "economic nationalist" who placed the political-power interests of the state above all other values, as reflected in his inaugural lecture at the University of Freiburg:

In the main, the fruits of all economic, social, and political endeavors of the present will benefit not living but future generations. If our work can and will have meaning, it can only attempt to provide for the future, that is, for our successors. However, no economic policy is possible on the basis of optimistic hopes for happiness. *Lasciate ogni speranza* [Man, if you enter here, leave all hopes outside] stands written over the door to the unknown future of human history. It is not a dream of peace and human happiness. The question is not how men in the future will feel, but rather who they will be. That is the question which concerns us when we think beyond the graves of our own generation. And in truth, this question lies at the root of every economic and political work. We do not strive for man's future well-being; we are eager to breed in them those traits with which we link the feeling that they constitute what is humanly great and noble in our nature. . . . In the last analysis, the processes of economic development are struggles for power. Our ultimate yardstick of values is 'reasons of state,' and this is also the yardstick for our economic reflections. . . .[35]

Weber's Freiburg address evoked a warm response from Friedrich Naumann, who at that time was considered a "radical" because he declared himself in favor of some socialist ideas. He asked Weber to join him as coeditor of *Die Hilfe* (founded in 1894, a weekly periodical magazine), an invitation Weber accepted. He engaged Weber's *forte* in political analysis and oratorial power by deploying him as a speaker before various organizations, and in a series of evening lectures in Frankfurt.[36] There is no doubt that Weber welcomed this opportunity to urge the German public to save itself from political alienation and to cultivate an interest in foreign policy. Weber did not intend to neglect domestic affairs. Since his essential concern was the national power state, its internal stability and social regeneration remained for him essential preoccupations.

Meanwhile, the industrialist from the Saarland, von Stumm, like other builders of great industrial combines such as Krupp, Hugo Stinnes and August Thyssen, espoused a "patriotic" outlook by campaigning against *Die Hilfe*. In a speech before the Reichstag, of January 9, 1895, he declared Naumann and the "social pastors" to be more dangerous than the Social Democrats. Von Stumm had considerable influence on the Kaiser.[37] In fact, "the leading positions alike in heavy industry, in banking and in commerce came to be filled by men of essentially 'patriotic' outlook. This new class, which largely molded public opinion and exercized an increasing influence on governmental policy, was a characteristic phenomenon of the new Germany. The more it succeeded in introducing the principles of neo-mercantilism into German policy, the greater its influence became."[38]

Weber agreed that the stability of the political system and with it Germany's power-political role in the world depended upon steady economic growth, but he also believed that the politics of the economy is extremely important. It was his contention that political power in Germany had been inadequate to enforce economic measures designed to curb powerful economic groups.[39] Indeed, a group of entrepreneurs had emerged whose already powerful influence was increased by a virtual amalgamation with the traditional leading strata owing to the knighting procedure of many among the former. In addition to their personal influence on economic measures undertaken by the government, especially against organized labor, the German business elite

attained an overwhelming leadership role not only in German society
and its political institutions, but also in foreign policy:

A glance at the list of deputies in the Reichstag—even more, in the Prussian
House of Deputies—belonging to the Conservative, Free Conservative,
National Liberal and Zentrum parties will show how high a percentage of
them were so intimately connected by business interest with agriculture,
industry, commerce, etc., as to make a distinction between business and
politics almost unreal (the officers of the business associations . . ., nearly always sat in parliament, usually as National Liberals.) The link between
business and politics grew progressively closer in the opening years of the new
century, as the basic political outlook of the leading industrialists, bankers and
officers of the employers' associations came to conform more closely with that
of the intellectual bourgeoisie, the higher bureaucracy and army and navy
officers. The spiritual 'nationalization' of the German employer class, however,
tended to aggravate political crises. Furthermore, Germany began to measure
power by the yardstick of steel production, to regard Britain as an 'ageing
state', and to expect that the moulding of the future economic and political
shape of the world would lie with the U.S.A. and Germany alone.[40]

Weber now began to confront an extraordinary difficult task as he
reacted against certain effects of the Industrial Revolution, capitalism and
the aspirations of social democracy. Philosophically, Weber was profoundly conservative, a fact which his critical liberalism in practical
politics cannot obscure. His preoccupation with communal values, governmental traditions, and law and order attest to this conservative
outlook. Yet, in attacking Baron von Stumm's speech in the Reichstag
of January 9, 1895, and the landed interests in the Kreuz Zeitung, a
conservative newspaper which vascillated between acceptance and
rejection of his articles, Weber focused on the problems of economic
integration to be achieved by seeking consensus and contract, rather
than by coercion and force.[41] Weber's interest in social questions had
come about largely because of the dangers he anticipated to national
unity. Thus the search for solutions to the escalating conflicting interests
at the domestic level had led Weber to join the Christian-Social movement under Stoecker's leadership.[42] His mother's allegiance to the
socially aware Christian-Social program based on her profoundly
religious persuasion had also affected Weber's efforts to establish a
closer relationship with these circles. Ultimately it was through his
cousin and former fellow-student at Heidelberg, Otto Baumgarten, that
Weber first came into contact with them. Thus Weber attended the first
Evangelical-Social Congress convened by Stoecker in 1890 in which the
older Christian-Social members mingled with liberal theologians such
as von Harnack, as well as with leftist-oriented younger Christian-Social
members under Friedrich Naumann's leadership. The latter sought to

dissociate himself from Stoecker's conservatism and to find a common platform with all the participants at the Congress in the discovery of new forms of social and political endeavor based upon a Christian outlook.

These early contacts led Max Weber into a life-long friendship with Friedrich Naumann, culminating in a political partnership which was to become significant for both. Curiously, Weber's interest in Paul Goehre at first took precedence over his friendship with Naumann. Goehre had gained some attention with his essay, "Three Months as a Factory Worker"; this article gave added impetus to Weber's interest in social policy, leading to his literary cooperation with Goehre's *Die Christliche Welt*. In 1892 Goehre was subjected to extreme criticism by church authorities because of his championship of labor. The top echelons of the church hierarchy had succumbed to the intensified reactionary campaign led by von Stumm which resulted in anti-labor legislation. In an article in *Die Christliche Welt,* Weber attacked the simulation of the government's reactionary stand by the church authorities, charging them with entertaining petty bourgeois notions about dark and clandestine forces allegedly permeating the working classes.[43]

It is probably safe to argue that during this period Weber had consistently sought to awaken an understanding in protestant theologians for social problems, hoping to engage their efforts in support of the Christian-Social program, a fact also documented by his journalistic contributions to the *evangelischsoziale Zeitfragen,* a publication founded by his cousin Otto Baumgarten.[44] Weber perceived in such efforts a strategic value, namely that they would serve to modify Stoecker's orientation.[45]

While Weber continued to cooperate with both Goehre and Naumann, influencing especially the latter's political concerns, Weber's assumptions were based upon a clear assessment of the role of social and economic forces in both internal political stability and the power and prestige of Germany abroad. Contrary to Naumann, he did not subscribe to Christian-Social action rooted in deep religious concern for his fellowman. Nevertheless, during this prewar period, Weber prudently understood the necessity to work for greater social justice. But he was motivated primarily by neither Christian conviction nor social consciousness. While it is not my intention here to judge Weber as being less democratic than he is usually assumed to be, the characteristic feature of his basic political philosophy is his early acknowledgment that the structural changes inherent in modern industrial society demand changes in social policy. The foundation for this realistic appreciation remains the concept of the German power state.

In foreign relations, Weber accepted the struggle for power as a fact of international politics; he did not believe in a community of nations as an ideal worth pursuing because he did not think it feasible. The real question for him was: how does the German nation and its leaders deal with other nations and their leaders? The answer rests in the kind of desires issuing from men whose outlook is practical, realistic, and eminently rational. These men must be capable of making decisions in behalf of their countrymen who lack these qualifications, but with a broadly based educated public support as a foundation for their actions. Weber's conception of national self-interest played a central role in his attitude toward social issues, irrespective of changes in his political party affiliations.

One might wonder about the persistence of Weber's emphasis on power political considerations and his hostility to Naumann's motivations. The factor most responsible for this extraordinary phenomenon, according to Mommsen, was the general intellectual situation confronted by German liberalism. In 1848, in the face of lack of physical political force, liberalism was ordained to failure despite the high quality of its political ideas and ideals. Moreover, its sudden confrontation with Bismarck's achievement: the realization of the very goal of the liberal movement, namely the foundation of the German national state, even at the price of war with Austria, altered the bourgeoisie's attitude toward the realities of power. Their former idealist orientations were now replaced by the quest for *Realpolitik* which conceived domestic and foreign politics to involve intractable conflicts, for the most part not susceptible to amicable solution. Thus the priority which Max Weber accorded to the power concept might present itself in retrospect as not typically his own response to Bismarck's statesmanship. As Mommsen shows, the great power-political instincts of the Prussian Junker stratum, especially Bismarck's, were responsible for the reluctant yet pronounced admiration which Weber, the "class-conscious bourgeois," accorded to it.[46] What is compelling is that the ill-fated Revolution of 1848 ending in catastrophe for the Liberals, and the ambivalence of Weber's personal reaction to the traditionally negative relationship of liberalism to the phenomenon of power, sharply conditioned Weber's conception of power. Mommsen therefore takes issue with J. P. Mayer for having derived Weber's power concept from the "blood and iron-pattern" of Bismarck's politics.[47] As Lewis J. Edinger explains:

When unification grafted the authoritarian Prussian political system into German society in 1871 under the direction of Otto von Bismarck, the 'Iron Chancellor,' the quiescent and the activist orientations were largely fused by formal law and political practice. The relationship between the *Obrigkeit*, the authoritative organs of the political community, and the *Untertan*, the obedient subject, was deeply embedded in the political culture of the Hohenzollern Empire and retained its legitimacy for large sections of the public after the Empire's fall in 1918. The fusion was based on an orientation which identified the German state as the only organization that could safeguard the survival of the national community and provide for the welfare of its members in a world of enemies.[48]

Weber reiterated his conviction of the inescapable nature of the "conflict between man and man" for "elbowroom," applying the Darwinistic terminology of "struggle for existence" and the principle of "selection," biological concepts which in his later scholarly writings he condemned.[49] Weber's account shows the extent to which he thought the country badly served by Naumann's advice to treat the Polish question with moderation. He charged Naumann with letting social pity take precedence over the necessity of accepting the wisdom of social selection, undergirded by an appreciation of the requirements of power:

The new party must be a national party . . . it is only such a party which we lack: we lack a *national democracy*, to which we may entrust the conduct of government in Germany by means of the electoral process—a party of which we can be assured that it will safeguard the national and economic power interests. Accordingly, I am going to treat of a special subject, the treatment of which in your press has proved to me, that for the present you do not represent that party. It concerns the manner in which recently the so-called "Polish question" has been discussed in the *Zeit*. I am not concerned with isolated measures . . . but with the manner of treatment of these things in a German paper, as *Die Zeit* wishes to be. *Die Zeit* has attacked those who favored a forceful stand against the Poles, in as malicious a tone as Germans should never employ toward each other. There has been talk of a reduction of Poles to second-rate German citizens. The contrary holds true: we have transformed the Poles into human beings (in the first place.) In your conception of the 'Polish issue' ("Polenfrage") one is struck by that unpolitical trait of *Miserabilismus*. But politics is a hard transaction, and whoever wants to shoulder the responsibility to take hold of the spokes within the wheel of the political development of the fatherland, must have strong nerves and cannot afford to be sentimental in the conduct of temporal politics; whoever wants to conduct temporal politics must, above all, be free of illusions and acknowledge the one fundamental fact: namely the inevitable eternal struggle of man against man on earth as it actually occurs. If he does not do so, then he must refrain from founding a political party. In this Thueringian city, I would like to recall to you the old Thueringian *mot*: 'Landgrave, get hard!'[50]

Weber's early writings, nevertheless, call attention to the worst aspects of naive Bismarck adulation, based upon uncritical admiration of *Realpolitik* and linked to the supremacy of sheer force and the absence of conscience. While Weber searched for mainsprings of national revitalization, he knew how to distinguish spontaneous national sentiment from the imprint of negative tactical devices left by a successful use of great power politics. In this context the urgency of some current critics regarding Weber's own response to Bismarck is not entirely convincing, especially since Weber deplored the fact that Bismarck was not always appreciated for his truly great qualities, but rather for "the dash of arbitrary force and cunning characterizing the methods he employed in his statecraft in their apparent or actual brutal aspects."[51] Mommsen indeed rejects the portrayal of Weber as a disciple of *Realpolitik* in the negative sense of the term. The latter is guided by no other principle than *raison détat* and its own success; it is rooted neither in ultimate ethical nor in cultural values.[52] Mommsen rejects Mayer's verdict that "Weber was already thoroughly at home in the realm of German *Realpolitik*"[53] as a naive equation of *Realpolitik* with Machiavellian conduct.[54] While Weber surely made frequent references to this concept, he usually employed it to counter politics based on mere ideological principles. Power politics, in effect, were required for the realization of constructive politics.[55]

Weber also condemned as weakness any political course which sought escape from the unavoidable use of power. He even asserted that the ethics of the Sermon on the Mount was not only incompatible with political action but was, moreover, characterized by lack of dignity, except when applied by a saint.[56] J. P. Mayer, accordingly, deplores Weber's alleged questionable teachings, which bequeathed to the German people a "new Machiavellism of the steel age."[57] While conceding that some facets of Weber's thinking might seem reminiscent of Machiavelli, Mommsen points to the incidence of his value scheme external to the ethical sphere and to the profound sense of tragedy with which he viewed the conflicts arising between the two spheres. Much of Mommsen's analysis is rightly concerned with trying to show that contrary to Machievelli, emotionally as well as intellectually, the tragedy of these conflicts had clearly caught Weber in its grip. Perhaps the most remarkable aspect of Weber's interpretation of the paradox inherent in political action was his awareness of the jeopardy in which the "soul's salvation" was placed concomitantly. Machiavelli's peripheral allusions to such conflicts perhaps illustrate certain residues of Catholic beliefs. But the complete absence in Weber's writings of any trace of that aesthetic glorification of great power politics in which Machiavelli's writings abound points to one of the most significant differences between them.[58]

Ethics and politics, as reflected in Weber's writings, form a continuum of inner conflict; yet Weber is so honest that he frequently seems to stress the most negative implications inherent in politics, as if the aspiration to perfect politics as an art had to be balanced by periodic allusions to its dire consequences. Never accepting those parts of the established order which he considered wrong, Weber maintained to the end of his life what amounted to a treatment of politics as "a matter of faith."[59]

Nevertheless, many decisions necessarily involved a conflict between the political and ethical value spheres. While this single-minded rationality in its distorted forms could lead others to irrational and inhumane conclusions, in Weber's own thought the ethics of conviction prevailed over mere *Realpolitik*. As a man of almost excessive integrity, Weber considered the pursuit and assumption of power as both justified and compelling only in terms of criteria involving ultimate values. He rejected at face value any political claims based upon a peremptory policy aimed at mere tests of strength. In his judgment, such a course of action connoted a violation of the *ethos* of politics.[60]

Weber particularly cautioned against the danger which a professional politician might incur as he becomes imbued with an understandable sense of power, namely to "enjoy power for its own sake without subordinating that pursuit to a meaningful purpose."[61] His bitter acknowledgment of the prevalence of the mere "power politician," not least in Germany, was revealed in his stripping-down of that "cult busily engaged in our midst which seeks to glorify the mere 'power politician'," and which despite its strong impact actually culminates in a "vacuum and senselessness."[62] In considering what power politics is really about, he tried to point up the hollow ring it might produce. He thus divorced himself from mere power politics which remained a powerful tendency among the German bourgeoisie in the prewar period.

Weber's political judgments during this period are revealed by his association with his distinguished political and religiously oriented contemporary, Friedrich Naumann. After Naumann's own party did not materialize, he formed the *Nationalsoziale Verein* (National Social Association) in November 1896. At first its members could not agree whether more weight should be assigned to the "national" or the "social" regeneration of German society. Weber repeatedly criticized Naumann's program because he felt it stressed the latter at the expense of national interests. If Naumann based his appeal on the disparity in standards of life between the propertied and the unpropertied classes, he was bound to lose the support of both the middle classes, which he was anxious to win, and of the upper strata of the working classes. He would find himself with no definitive standard by which to judge what line he ought to take in any particular situation. In the end, the association would inevitably become a group animated by no recognizably consistent policy; it would find itself fighting against the landowners, the industrialists, the stock exchange, and the big commercial interests.

According to Weber only one course was open to Naumann: to support either the middle classes or the feudal aristocracy. He could not oscillate between them. The Social Democrats had lost the support of the middle class owing to their championship of the rights of the propertyless proletariat, and also because of their propaganda tactics which terrified the petty bourgeois. Weber again put forward the view that the true task facing a mature political party was not primarily the bettering of the lot of the lower strata in the nation, but the enhancement of the economic and political-power interests of the German state. The realization of this aim lay in the formation of a party, as yet unborn, which was national democratic and to which the electorate could confidently entrust its votes, knowing that the interests of the German state, as he envisaged them, would be paramount. Weber realized the meaning and extent of the consequences in the event this policy should be carried out consistently; yet he was prepared to sacrifice the social welfare of any class, be it East Prussian landowners or Ruhr proletarians, if Germany's status and prestige as a world power appeared to warrant it. This does not mean that Weber was against social reform.[63] It underscores again his tendency to judge any particular measure less from its desirability from the point of view of human welfare than by its consequences for the German state.

Several points of importance for subsequent German development are suggested here. Weber's insistence on the need to retain the support of the middle classes foreshadows the mode of thought and political strategy of the National Socialists in the twentieth century. The Nazis fully appreciated the importance of obtaining and retaining the full support of the bourgeoisie. Weber was among those who provided a clue on how to do this by dramatizing the overriding national interests of the state. This concept exerts a unifying influence, playing down the divisive sectional interests of the various substrata. The mistake of the *Verein* as well as the Social Democrats was to emphasize the factors making for disunity, such as economic inequities which could neither be eliminated nor resolved. Following Hobbes, Weber makes explicit the premise that the basic condition of men is one of conflict, and that whoever enters the arena of politics must realize as illusory any concept of the good society.[64] Accepting this principle of pervasive conflict in society, Weber sought to minimize its effects by diverting attention from group tensions which nourish dissent. He hoped to find a goal to which all members of the national community could subscribe. Thus his supreme aim, the strengthening of the German power state, could at the same time solve the problem of easing group tensions by means of such diversion. Unlike Naumann, Weber's political strategy stressed consensus rather than differences.

His interests did not include an exploration of the question of why liberalism did not accompany industrialization in Germany, even though he acknowledged that members of the industrial upper-middle-class tended to overrate their own political importance. As a class they were never absorbed by the Prussian aristocracy; they merely coexisted with it. The miscalculation inherent in the definition of their situation, however, caused them to dissociate themselves from men like Naumann who advocated liberal reforms, thus contributing further to the group tensions which he was trying to alleviate. The extent of Naumann's commitment to his ideals inspired Weber's respect. But the apparent divergence in the sources of their progressive stand on social policy is critical in assessing the viewpoints of the two men themselves:

Naumann believed that Bismarck's social policy had failed and he coupled this with an attack on Bismarck's conservatism for its restriction of political freedom. He looked, for his political ideals, to the 1848 revolution. In this way Naumann combined political liberalism with the social gospel. Yet he did not do this in the English or American manner, for there was a strong element of nationalism in the German tradition in Naumann's thought. His purpose was to reconcile the worker to the state and thus destroy that class consciousness which saw in the state one of the enemies of the working classes.[65]

Naumann's liberal persuasion and social program sprang from deeply held beliefs in Christian doctrine. However, his rearrangement of priorities was facilitated by the fact that, like Weber, he was rooted in German nationalist tradition.

Naumann, the Christian-Social pastor, had wrestled with the problems of capitalist expansion in Imperial Germany. More than most of his bourgeois contemporaries and certainly in a spirit superior to that of most of his colleagues in the Church, he attempted to mitigate the issues increasingly raised by Social Democracy. He countered the orientation of the latter with his championship of a "genuine practical social policy, a Christian workers' and people's party, and a 'Christian national renewal.'"[66] Naumann's assessment, seventy-five years ago, of Social-Democracy is interesting today. Writing in the *Christliche Welt*, he commented upon the "merit of Social-Democracy," which, in his view, consisted in the fact that "the big kettle had not exploded although the propertied classes . . . have certainly done enough in one life time to incite the people. In theory it (Social Democracy) is totally anti-capitalistic but in practice it does not hurt capitalism since its tenets proclaim that the capitalists dig their own graves."[67] While Social-Democracy today no longer adheres to its former article of faith, the relevance of Naumann's verdict, pronounced before the turn of the century, is illustrated by his statement: "Bourgeois society has found it convenient for a long time now to surround the word 'Social-Democracy' with an aura of fog connoting dread and defamation, but the fog will clear."[68] "What is impressive is that even Adenauer's election campaign witnessed the same fog; and the Social Democrats had to enter first

the 'school' of the Great Coalition to demonstrate their capacity to
govern and they are still in the process of doing so."[69]

Naumann's *Demokratie und Kaisertum* has been correctly criticized
as a testimony to "error and wishful thinking," whereas his deliberations
contained in his *Vom Kaiserreich Zur Republik* reflect the changes
which he underwent as the sincere liberal he was.[70] Before he had
glimpsed, however, the need for a shift in his orientation more adapted
to the requirements of the Republican era, and before he ultimately
came to terms with those persuasions, which still reflected the thinking
practiced in Imperial times, Friedrich Naumann had written: "Nothing
—but nothing will avail culture and morality in world history if they
are not protected and furthered by power! Whoever wants to live must
fight."[71] Naumann had clearly absorbed some of Weber's central ideas.

In the face of such ideas, the ideals of 1848, liberalism was bound to be
jeopardized in the name of national power. There is, therefore, a basic
contradiction in Naumann's thought which led him into a contradictory
political course. . . . All of his thought was advanced in the name of a
Christianity synonymous with freedom and justice . . . an ideology . . ., which
called for a liberal Germany that would dispense a Christian justice to the
working man, without, however, overthrowing society or abolishing property
relationships. Above all, his ideas reconciled many to the new-born German
Republic, and his death in 1919 deprived Germany of a man who might
have, had he lived, made a positive contribution to the new German Republic.[72]

Nevertheless, Max Weber and Friedrich Naumann disagreed basically on several points. Whereas Naumann hypothesized that the political
integration offered by the national power state would gradually lend
itself to social reforms, thus perceiving the latter as a means to an end,
Weber called for domestic, social and political collaboration, the *Leitmotif* being that an increased measure of social and political justice
would advance the interests of the national power state, employing the
former as a means of achieving goals and objectives of the latter. Weber
nevertheless joined the *Nationalsoziale Verein,* cooperating with
Naumann.[73]

Weber had been right; the paper ceased to exist within a year. The
Verein fused with some leftwingers of the bourgeoisie, the *Freisinnige
Vereinigung,* and with it formed the *Liberale Wahlverein,* thus making
common cause with the bourgeoisie as Weber had wished five years
earlier when the *Verein* was founded.

Although a liberal political group in the Saar had offered Weber
the candidature for the Reichstag in 1897, in appreciation of a speech
he had made in their territory, Weber turned down the offer since he
had just accepted a university appointment in Heidelberg.[74] Weber's

widow summarized her husband's attitude toward the political parties of that period as follows:

The *Nationalsozialen*—for the time being—cannot be seriously considered as having a public platform. With the left wing of the Liberals he shares the democratic ideals, but he misses in them the touch of a great national political pathos. . . . With the *Nationalliberalen* he shares their individualistic convictions, affirming with them also that industrial capitalism is an indispensable power for the national economy. Yet their lack of social and democratic convictions and socio-political empathy form a high wall. With the Conservatives and the Pan-Germans he has the national pathos in common; they, however, support the economic policy of the agrarians at the expense of German nationality and their fellow countrymen.[75]

Thus it is really difficult to point to any of the existing parties as corresponding closely to Weber's own political philosophy.

Weber had not shut the door completely to Naumann's plans, ostensibly hoping to influence the stand which Naumann and the *Verein* might ultimately adopt. In a letter to his wife, however, he expressed satisfaction that plans for founding a party were finally dropped, as he expressed doubt about the merits of founding even the *Verein*. Weber objected to Naumann's attempt, despite all his national considerations, to rally all "the weary and heavy-laden whose shoe was pinching them somewhere." Weber characterized them as people who although now without property aspired to its acquisition. By appealing to them, Naumann was destined to incur the hostility of those who had already acquired some property, including that of the rising income groups among labor.[76] Nevertheless, it seems that not least for personal reasons, Weber had little appetite for a really strong fight. While he regarded Naumann's early efforts as politically amateurish, he was undoubtedly aware that his own ideas had largely stimulated Naumann to think and act in terms of the national welfare. Moreover, Weber admired such courageous idealists whom he knew personally as men of integrity, although he did not conceal his impatience with their torments of conscience which, in his judgment, prevented them from coping with the realities of power.

In view of his close personal relationship with Naumann, as well as with Goehre, the historian Schulze-Gaevernitz, his cousin, Otto Baumgarten, and his brother, Alfred Weber (as well as his mother's identification with Naumann's concern with Christian social action), his own alienation from their position must have been depressing for him.[77] Not surprisingly, he protested at the manner in which the University of Heidelberg combined his appointment with the advice that Weber should disengage himself from Christian-Social efforts. The Kaiser reputedly had given vent to his mood at emerging democratic trends by referring to "Christian-Social" values as nonsense.[78] Weber's answer made clear that while he was nothing less than "Christian-Social," he could not comply with such a request involving Naumann's project. His respect for Naumann and his wish to disabuse the latter of his socialist notions precluded such a detachment particularly at that time.[79] Weber meanwhile entertained doubts whether he should accept a position in Heidelberg which would absorb him academically or whether he would prefer a more active political life.

Weber's association with the Pan-German League reveals further his emphasis upon the national interest as opposed to particularistic claims. The League was founded in 1890 initially to act as a patriotic group which objected to the proposed secession of the island of Heligoland to the British. Their broader objectives aimed at a German policy of expansionism. A belligerent anti-liberalism ran like a red thread through their policy, which embraced imperialistic aims on the continent of Europe as well as overseas. Their ideology combined a faith in the folk spirit with the demand for a genuine racial and cultural union "which would give the German *Geist* a vital role in culture, social organization and politics. . . . Moreover, they showed typical Volkish prejudices in selecting their areas of operation for example, rather than forging a strong link with industry, they preferred to devote themselves to agricultural issues. This position, however, was soon recognised as untenable in a Germany where a part of industry stood ready to contribute members and money to the Pan-Germans, largely because of their rapidly expansionist foreign policy." [80] The Pan-Germans succeeded in attracting as members of their organization such reputable men as Max Weber, Gustav Stresemann, (who at that time was president of the *Bund der Industriellen*), and Karl Lamprecht, the historian.[81]

In 1899, however, Weber withdrew his membership from the League, charging it with the betrayal of Germany's national interests for the sake of insuring the economic claims of the East-Elbian Junkers. The League had ignored Weber's proposal to close the frontiers to eastern settlers and "to chain the peasants psychologically to the soil" as a means of guaranteeing the security of Germany's eastern frontier as well as to protect the higher German culture of the region.

Believing the League did not have the national welfare at heart in this matter, Weber felt free to voice his view independently, thus fulfilling his own preference for the strong nation and the free individual. "To gain my freedom, to go on record publicly in this matter, I resign my membership."[82] As the foregoing discussion suggests, however, although Weber sought to fill both parts of this prescription, he was unable to equate them, since his ultimate yardstick was always the strong nation for which the interests of the individual might have to be sacrificed.

As will be remembered, Naumann, even though imbued with a spirit of national consciousness, saw the national power state primarily as a means to the end of domestic social reform. For Weber social policy remained a mere tool to consolidate national objectives. Mommsen characterizes his aversion to a policy derived from purely social considerations as reminiscent of Nietzsche's rejection of such sentiments.[83] Naumann's position on the agrarian issue after the turn of the century matched Weber's when he wrote that the German Reich must not be reduced to a "charitable institution for needy agrarians" if it wanted to "preserve its own spirit and historic character."[84] Weber's own strategy was quite straightforward; it was designed to place the onus of dividing Germany domestically on the Conservatives and to call upon the bourgeosie to close ranks and to face up to a contest of strength with the Conservatives. He opposed any policy in favor of the proletariat because it would compel the bourgeoisie to abdicate its potential role as a partner of the Conservatives and industrialists, who in turn would protect it against the rising ambitions of the working classes.

Especially central to a policy geared to social reform was the liquidation of rule by the big estate owners.[85] Weber had previously challenged Naumann "to decide which one of the opposing interests represented by the leading classes" he would prefer to support, whether it be the "bourgeois or the agrarian feudal ones. A policy that leaves this out of its consideration is utopian. Every ascending, new party confronts the decision to promote the development of the bourgeoisie or to unconsciously support feudal reaction."[86] As Weber had exhorted Naumann while he was still considering the formation of a new party: "If he had the future of the movement at heart," he should opt for the "bourgeois-capitalist evolution. Social Democracy has paved the paths to reaction because it opposed the bourgeoisie."[87]

The subsequent collapse of the *Verein*, reinforced by Weber's influence, led Naumann to adopt a more rightist outlook which embraced the policies of the *"Freisinnige Vereinigung."* During the ensuing personal internal struggle Naumann lost the support of Max Weber, whose own nervous illness had incapacitated him. Indeed, soon after Weber arrived in Heidelberg to occupy the chair of economics, he suffered a severe illness from which he never completely recovered and which brought several years of inactivity. From the fall of 1897 on, his life seemed to vary among nervous breakdowns, traveling, and intensive work. Weber's mental and physical health were decisively affected by the political conflicts of his time: "To deal with the political happenings which upset me to the innermost core of my being on a continuous basis now would mean that my constitution might bear up under that for a few months at most, and what is even more important: if one does not want to bungle a political cause, one needs to keep cool, and that I can hardly guarantee at the moment."[88]

By 1903 the worst of the illness appeared to be over, allowing Weber to embark upon a series of studies concerned with the methods of the social sciences.[89] During a visit to the United States in 1903, his interest centered chiefly around industrial relations, public administration, conditions in the Southern states, the Negro problem, and ethnic problems generally. His impressions of the religious sects and secular "voluntary associations," which occupied so prominent a place in American society, provided valuable material for *The Protestant Ethic and the Spirit of Capitalism.*

Max Weber's observations on the world scene, his understanding of the workings of man and society, as well as his journalistic writings, furnish an example of a recorder of historical events at his best.[90] His description of the struggle between opposites reflected his maxim that without conflict there can be no process of becoming and no development. It may be that Max Weber shared Hegel's conviction that the struggle, the courageous endurance, and the fighting out of opposites is indispensable for the development of one's consciousness of self, for one's status as a person, and for human dignity. He certainly gave a favorable portrayal of the sectarian spirit in America. "All that represents the given is simultaneously confronted with its opposite; for every position there exists a counter-position. . . . The plurality of interests, ideals and postulates leads men to devote themselves to them and subscribe to them, to engage in incessant conflict with each other."[91]

Despite his recovery, to enter the political arena was beyond Weber's physical capacity. Instead he now weighed the possibility of collaboration with his friend and younger colleague, Edgar Jaffé. Jaffé had approached Weber and Werner Sombart to join him as coeditors of the *Archiv fuer Sozialwissenschaft und Sozialpolitik,* an invitation which Weber accepted in 1904. The first issue featured his essay on *"die Objektivitaet Sozialwissenschaftlicher und Sozialpolitischer Erkenntnisse"* (the objectivity of social-scientific and sociopolitical insights).[92] It seems that Weber had some doubts concerning his participation even in that venture. At every move, as one comes closer to identifying Weber's intent, one confronts this unresolved paradox of his own conflicting values: the difficulty of his choice between his scholarly and his political allegiances, which found him emerging as a torn man. Some of the characteristically vehement expressions of his views undoubtedly stem from his agonized appraisal of Germany's fate, but this anxiety was aggravated by his constitutional susceptibility to irritation. Nevertheless, Marianne Weber insists that Weber's ultimate choice of the career of a scholar was made on stronger ground than commonly assumed. By this choice, he was both privileged and compelled to forego the obligation of bringing his sense of values to bear upon immediate political events—an obligation he would have had to confront as a politician. This type of direct experience and responsibility in the exercise of moral sensibility would have proved more taxing to his mental and physical health than the pursuits of scholarship. The latter activity permitted him, in effect, to remain outside the realm of "yes and no." Moreover, he did not have to bind his creative talent to a definite time schedule; he could progress as his condition allowed.[93]

As Mommsen notes, while Weber demanded from his associates[94] that they actively support the liberal cause, he himself withdrew increasingly to the purely scholarly area of concentration. Though the political dimension was of passionate concern to him, Weber did not encounter it single-mindedly. From this perspective, coupled with his illness, he may have purposely stopped short of plunging more deeply into politics by accepting the responsibilities of coeditorship with the *Archiv fuer Sozialwissenschaft und Sozialpolitik*.[95] Again Weber's ambivalence toward his own power-political drive may have prompted his renunciation of high political office. Friedrich Sell saw a symbolic analogy in the personality and fate of Max Weber to the greatness and failure of the German intellectual liberals around 1900. He noted their "penetrating insight, the earnest pursuit of the truth, and [their] inability to translate insight into action."[96]

While his passive role in politics cannot be understood in terms of his illness alone, clearly Weber had to bow to its pressure, which forced him at times to watch passively the mistakes committed by the German government. In 1915, however, he started entering the political arena again. From then on he no longer made his influence felt through Naumann as intermediary but addressed himself directly to his public:[97] "Nothing could be more misleading," concludes Johannes Winckelmann, "than the conception of Max Weber as having been 'first and foremost' the thinker and scholar. Such an interpretation would fall far short of reflecting the true meaning of his life because he combined at the same time within himself both the scientist and the politician and in the capacity of both he reflected the image of a truly philosophical being in our time."[98]

In his political writings at this time Weber tried to dispel the notion that the empire could take itself and Bismarck's masterstrokes for granted. The vision of Germany's unity at home and her political influence abroad was his governing principle for German policy. These indeed were the imperatives of all practical politics for the sake of the preservation of European culture. Weber deeply shared the thought of many of his countrymen who held, and still hold, that Germany must act as a buffer between Russian bureaucratization and Anglo-Saxon conventionalism.[99] The challenge extended to a nation organized as a power

state seemed inescapable. No doctrine could override the argument that
unless Germany recognized her responsibility to history by acting as a
custodian of European culture, the smaller nations and succeeding generations of Germans would condemn her for shirking her duty. Germany
must answer the question of how to cope with the prospect of future
world power, including ultimately the future of culture, "between the
'reglements' of Russian officials on one hand, and the conventions of
Anglo-Saxon 'society' on the other hand, with a dash of Latin 'raison'
thrown in."[100]

In Weber's thinking the task of saving posterity from such a fate
ranked uppermost. He dismissed the thought that either England or
France might constitute a permanent threat to Germany. Russia was
the haunting specter on the international horizon, which alone could
jeopardize the future existence of the Reich. Nor could a pacific policy
avert this threat. Any assumption that the German Reich could afford
to engage voluntarily in a pacific policy such as that conducted by
Switzerland is in error since "the mere existence of a world power . . .
represents an obstacle in the path of other states."[101] The greatest danger,
in his view, consisted in the "land hunger of Russian peasants conditioned by their lack of culture and the power interests entertained by
the Russian state church and the bureaucracy."[102] He could foresee no
alternative leading to a possible change in Russo-German relations. It
was on this balance sheet that Weber based his favorable attitude toward
an alliance with England in the prewar years. Fundamentally dissatisfied with imperial diplomacy, he prophesied the coming of the war
long in advance: " 'The politics of Europe is no longer made in Berlin.
It is only by a miracle that we are not yet confronted by a really serious
diplomatic situation.' (1892)"[103]

Bismarck's dismissal by the Kaiser brought a foreign policy based
on political dilettantism, staunchly upheld by the Conservative party in
the interest of self-protection. In 1906, when the dissolution of the
Reichstag occurred because the Center and Social Democratic parties,
in protest against colonial misadministration, had rejected an increase in
the budget for South Africa, Weber warned the Liberals against including a vote of confidence for the Kaiser in their platform. Instead they
should concentrate on campaigning against the Center party. His opposition was not based upon the latter's rejection of the colonial budget
but upon its character as a party of patronage instead of a champion
of an effective parliamentary system which might curb the Kaiser's
power.[104] Weber's reaction to the outcome of the elections for the
Reichstag in 1907 was one of disappointment since he had hoped
for stronger support for the liberal parties which would result in
diminishing returns for the Center. Hence the prospect of a bourgeois
consolidation of strength to oppose the Conservatives remained dim. Nor

did he regard as very promising the possibility of combining forces with the Social Democrats.[105]

Weber's sympathetic view of the cooperation between Liberals and Conservatives rested in his hope that in return for concessions in the area of finance affecting the Reich, the Liberals would receive a fair exchange in the form of concessions benefitting the Prussian franchise legislation. However, the results of Prussian parliamentary elections obviously precluded thoroughgoing electoral reforms, thus obviating the continued cooperation of the Liberals with the Conservatives. As a result, Weber reversed his position by asking Naumann not to close the door leading to "a jump to the Left." The *ratio* for a Liberal-Conservative bloc policy was, he stated in a letter to Naumann, no longer of interest to him. He questioned the usefulness of a merger between Naumann's *Freisinnige Vereinigung* and the *Freisinnige Volkspartei* because the latter would not allow itself to be significantly influenced by Naumann. In the former association the membership was composed of intellectuals, in the latter interest-groups and philistines predominated. Observing that the *Freisinnige Volkspartei* was veering increasingly to the Right, Weber wanted Naumann to prepare the way for himself to the point at which he could decently venture out in a Leftist direction.[106]

Since the Imperial establishment seemed resolved to boycott electoral reforms that could democratize Germany, Weber did not wish to see Naumann, the liberal, needlessly compromised by a seeming collusion with the forces of reaction who continued, against his hopes, to oppose intelligent reforms. He predicted that the cause of Liberalism was going to be arrested for several years to come; in four years there would be a clerical regime everywhere in the *Reich*. "After that comes the difficult task of preparing an 'alley for freedom.'"[107] With that future in view, he added, Naumann could not afford to be a "politically dead man." Behind Weber's prediction stood his pessimistic conviction that the anti-liberal forces would be able to maneuver the Liberal camp into a defensive position that robbed it of its potential to act in a politically meaningful sense.

Weber, meanwhile, attacked the policies of the Kaiser's administration. He had apparently hoped to infuse new life into potential dissidents by disparaging the political parties for allowing themselves to be manipulated by a regime whose continued existence presented a greater threat to Germany's international image than her colonial problems. He called for emancipation from the conception that the emperor's position and establishment was above and beyond criticism. Weber sought an informed public which would no longer subject itself unquestioningly to the dispensations of the governing powers. He continued to oppose "parliamentary patronage" behind the scenes as practiced by the Center party. Yet no opportunity to effect a radical change appeared.

A certain harmony, deriving its support from repression marked by orderliness, vitiated any potential opposition. Neither the Conservatives nor the National Liberals offered any alternative to the dominant Center party. Since they too had been incorporated into the prevailing "personal" regime of the Kaiser's version of constitutionalism, Weber hoped to awaken the establishment to its own shortcomings while exhorting the public to abandon its complacency about the stability of sham constitutionalism.[108]

Weber felt the Kaiser's highly advertised impulsiveness was not the only chronic ailment inhibiting the prospect of conducting "world politics." Instead neither in war nor in peace was anyone willing to assume responsibility. Self-preservation, whether on the part of the high command or civilian leadership, defeated any possible change in the situation, permitting the Kaiser's judgment to remain unassailable.[109]

In personal letters to important political figures, Weber protested against concrete incidents such as the crisis in "Morocco in 1905 (where the colonial ambitions of France and Germany clashed); in the Slav-Serb provinces of Bosnia and Herzegovina in 1908 (then annexed by Austria, thus infuriating Serbia and Russia); again in the Agadir incident in Morocco in 1911, in which Germany tried gunboat diplomacy, but was forced to back down. . . ."[110] Later, upon the announcement of unrestricted submarine warfare followed by America's entry into the war, Weber was reported to have stated that he experienced less suffering at that moment than during the previous two and a half decades which were marked by the "hysterical vanity of this monarch ruining everything I held dear and sacred. Now the consequences of human stupidity have become reality. And realities can be dealt with." [111]

This "human stupidity" could actually be traced back to the age of Bismarck, when certain indications pointed to Germany's impending isolation, marked first by her choice in 1879 of Austria-Hungary as her ally. The next decade brought Germany no closer to any other great power, even though a *modus vivendi* was achieved with Great Britain, despite latent conflicts concerning colonial issues. There was no chance for more cordial relations between Germany and Russia in any case, in Weber's view; the relations that existed, in fact, were not close, although a reinsurance treaty (1856–82) was concluded and extended again from 1882–1895. Russian public opinion became cumulatively antagonistic to Germany in the course of the Balkan crises. The 1890's brought new directions. Russia and England became further alienated from Germany. In 1893 Russia and France became partners in a military alliance. In 1897 Buelow assumed the office of foreign secretary for three years. In 1900 he remained in public office as chancellor for nine years. Admiral Alfred von Tirpitz had become secretary of the navy from 1897 on and a close confidante of the Kaiser. The world politics to

which Weber was initially not unsympathetic he now saw to have over-
played its hand, based mainly upon faulty estimates of Germany's
strength as well as upon the Kaiser's blunders. Imperial domestic as well
as foreign policy was dictated, as Weber put it, by "big talk" instead of
being guided by the logical pursuit of Germany's interests.[112]

In a letter to Naumann, Weber stated eloquently his conviction that
it was vital to let the country know that it must free itself from a structural arrangement which concentrated political power in the hands of
an incompetent monarch and the Conservative elements.[113] The Conservative party whose replacement he demanded was to blame for
choosing to defer to the "personal regime." "The truth is: A public
utterance of the monarch is immune from ruthless criticism at the domestic level. . . . But that does not deter foreign countries which take the
monarch at his word." [114] The Kaiser's ill-advised trip to Tangier, the
jeopardizing of peace to satisfy German prestige hunger in the Morocco
crisis, the Kaiser's Breslau speech containing the statement: "I do not
tolerate pessimists," and the creation of the *entente cordiale* in 1904—
all culminated in Germany's growing isolation and filled Max Weber
with anxiety.

In his Freiburg inaugural address, when referring to Germany's
colonial "power politics" in the 1880's, he characterized its spirit as
having been "sly and half-resistant which was not worthy of their
name."[115] Concerning the construction of the fleet, which Weber had
at one time heartily endorsed, he stated that the Kaiser's public statements had led the British to become apprehensive about the scope of the
German program. Actually, for purposes of defense, a fleet the size of
the French fleet would have proved adequate for Germany. For a
thorough blockade, even a navy as large as the British would not have
been adequate. Weber severely condemned Tirpitz' "would-be-great
politics,"[116] although in its early stages he favored it strongly because
it seemed a means to enhance Germany's image as a colonial world
power. Thus in 1898 when the first naval bills were introduced in the
Reichstag, he acknowledged their merit and found them to be rather
modest. Despite his critical attitude toward the Tirpitz naval program,
he had approved of it previously in a letter to Friedrich Naumann.[117]
On the other hand, Weber distinguished himself from most of his
associates in the liberal imperialistic camp, including Naumann, by
favoring a closer relationship with England in the prewar years, basing
his reasons on cultural as well as political motives.[118] Weber professed
disappointment, however, over the "non-generous conduct of English
politics" toward Germany's colonial aspirations.[119] Yet he was not prepared to concede that "Germany's acquisitions overseas constituted
grounds for serious conflict with England." [120]

In Weber's judgment, the supposed threat posed by the German navy was the major responsibility for the war with England. Even then, it was not so much the navy itself, as the propagandistic statements accompanying naval construction that aggravated the hostile sentiments which had long and unnecessarily characterized Anglo-German relations. Germany might have been able to find a way to overcome English misgivings had it not been for the Kaiser's repeated bombast regarding the naval construction project.[121]

In the prewar period there is no mention of specific interests or preferences on Weber's part regarding a colonial program for Germany. He appeared to favor what he judged to be Germany's own best interests, namely an "agreement on colonial spheres of interest in such uncivilized territories as Africa, abandoning, in exchange, the dispersed possessions" now held by Germany.[122] In seeking to bring some comfort to opponents of imperialist aims, Weber added that such colonial holdings were apt to prove a costly experience because they might alienate other powers, leading to an escalation of potential conflict.[123] "To take the place of our scattered possessions, we certainly do not require world conquest but should rather press for a regional sphere of interest such as other countries have without endangering anyone."[124] Unhappily, Weber never indicated what leverage Germany might have used which could have made their effort successful in getting this prescription accepted by other governments. On the one hand, concerning Germany's accession to *Weltpolitik* based on cooperation with England, his central thesis, correctly, was that the alienation and ultimate collapse of Anglo-German relations was due primarily to flaws in German diplomacy conducted by less than competent men. He was thus, however, offering far less room for an explanation of the incapacity of modern states to develop appropriate mechanisms for effectively dealing with international tensions.

In Weber's judgment, the dogmatic, repetitious pronouncements made by the Kaiser, replete with nationalistic clichés, constituted the main reason for the failure of German diplomacy. Especially since the monarch's telegram to the president of the Boer Republic in 1896, all hopes for keeping the conflict between Germany and England in low key were dashed.[125] The publication of the telegram had been a slap in the face to the British. With the honor of both countries involved, vital interests ordinarily subject to considerations of *Realpolitik* were subordinated: "As a consequence, subsequent attempts at an agreement, both before and during the Boer War, as well as any activities aimed at coming to an understanding over Africa or politics generally did not meet with the inner readiness for consensus of either nation; their sense of honor had come into play against each other, although both parties might have arrived at a negotiated settlement"[126] had they been able to approach each other without bias. As Bernadotte Schmitt argues, however: "A policy of naval expansion, the development of an African empire, commercial and financial penetration of the Near East could each be justified. But to pursue all three courses at the same time was the worst possible policy, for it kept alive the distrust and suspicion of the Entente powers, convinced them of the dangerous reality of German militarism and made them more anxious than ever to act together."[127] Perhaps, too, Weber tended to underestimate public sentiment in Britain:

Contemporary observers have commented on the militant patriotism, and even jingoism, which the Boer War had stimulated among all classes of Englishmen. The idea of 'empire building' had become popular. . . . By 1899 . . . Great Britain was in full possession of her imperial senses. . . . During the 'eighties and nineties' the great powers had been engaged in carving out empires and spheres of influence in Africa and Asia, and statesmen were relating these moves to the future prosperity of the nation.[128]

When the French proved hostile to Britain's efforts to pursue her interests in Africa and because of Russia's predatory posture in China, threatening the buffer states near the Indian border, there might have been one auspicious historical opportunity for an Anglo-German alliance as Weber wished. But Germany did not permit it to become a reality. As a result, as early as 1906, the British planned to merge with France in the event of a German attack: "German efforts to split the Entente at Algeciras in 1906 strengthened it instead. . . . The 'ententes' between Great Britain and both France and Russia turned into virtual alliances as a result of shifty German intrigues and—of greater significance—increasing British, French, and Russian fears of German strength. The diplomatic efforts of the Liberal-Imperialists to prepare for war with Germany were successful."[129]

Max Weber did not share the Anglophobia of a large segment of German intellectuals during the latter part of the nineteenth century.[130] Many German intellectuals in the period preceding the war, as well as during the war, engaged publicly in propaganda. One method of attack was the portrayal of Germany as the champion of "Western civilization against the barbaric East"[131]—an idea which Max Weber shared. The other argument urged glorification of the "German sense of duty and spirit of cooperation, which they contrasted with the selfishness and excessive individualism of the western democracies."[132] While Weber's own defense of German war aims was to concentrate on the first argument, he did not find the second argument very compelling. Yet both ideas were put forward by such members of the intelligentsia as Thomas Mann, Friedrich Meinecke, Werner Sombart, Max Scheler and Alfred Weber.[133]

In retrospect, Weber's analysis of the implications of certain prewar conditions and themes makes the coming of World War I seem almost inevitable. The German psychology of cultural imperialism, a widely held conception of social life as consisting of endless conflict, and a pervasive Russophobia, all of which Weber personally shared, aggravated by a provocative Imperial diplomacy, conditioned the German people for the tragic conflict which Weber had long forseen.

NOTES

1 Weber defines the "nation" as opposed to the state as "a community of sentiment which would adequately manifest itself in a state of its own. Hence a nation is a community which normally tends to produce a state of its own." Hans. H. Gerth and C. Wright Mills, *From Max Weber, Essays in Sociology* (New York: Oxford University Press, 1946), p. 176. "According to Weber the modern state is known to have the following characteristics: (a) it is marked by an administrative and legal order subject to change by legislation; (b) it claims binding authority over all action taking place in the area of its jurisdiction; (c) the use of force is regarded as legitimate only so far as it is either permitted or prescribed by the state." Talcott Parsons, *The Theory of Social and Economic Organization by Max Weber* (New York: Oxford University Press, 1947), p. 156.

2 Lewis J. Edinger, *Politics in Germany: Attitudes and Processes* (Boston: Little, Brown, 1968), p. 63.

3 Max Weber, *The Theory of Social and Economic Organization*, p. 152 (italics added)

4 *Ibid.*, p. 132 (italics added)

5 E. V. Walter "Power and Violence," *The American Political Science Review*, Vol. LVIII, No. 2, June 1964, p. 358.

6 Marcel Weinreich, *Max Weber: L'Homme et Le Savant: Etude sur ses idées directrices* (Paris: Les Presses Moderne, 1938), pp. 29ff.

7 *P.S.*, 1st. ed., 1921, p. 7ff. (The National State and Economic Policy).

8 Max Weber, "Die Verhaeltnisse der Landarbeiter im Ostelbischen Deutschland," *Schriften des Vereins fuer Sozialpolitik* (Leipzig, 1923), Vol. LV, Part 3.

9 *Ibid.*, p. 796ff.

10 *Lebensbild*, pp. 137–138.

11 Cf. Guenther Roth, *The Social Democrats in Imperial Germany* (Totowa, N.J.: Bedminster Press, 1963), *passim.*, and Carl Schorske, *German Social Democracy* (Cambridge, Mass.: Harvard University Press, 1955). *passim.*

12 Lewis J. Edinger, *op. cit.*, pp. 63–64.

13 *P.S.*, 1st. ed., p. 8ff.

14 *Ibid.*

15 Abridged from pp. 838–9 (as reprinted in Christian Century) by Richard Pipes in *Western Civilization: The Struggle for Empire to Europe in the Modern World*. Edited by William L. Langer, *et al.* (Harper & Row, 1968). Reprinted by permission of the publisher.

16 See Gustav Ratzenhofer, *Wesen und Zweck der Politik* (Leipzig, 1839).

17 See Carl Schmitt, *Der Begriff des Politischen* (Munich: Duncker & Humblot, 1932).

18 Cf. E. V. Walter, *op. cit.*, p. 159.

19 Gerth and Mills, *op. cit.*, p. 124.

20 *P.S.*, 1st. ed., pp. 19–20.

21 *Ibid.*, p. 20.

22 *Ibid.*, pp. 25–26.

23 *Ibid.*, p. 27.

24 *Lebensbild*, p. 125. This phrase, stemming from Greek mythology, refers to a gift calculated to harm the recipient.

25 *P.S.*, 1st. ed., p. 225.

26 *Ibid.*, p. 25.
27 *Ibid.*, pp. 27–28.
28 *Ibid.*, p. 28.
29 *Ibid.*, p. 29.
30 Ralf Dahrendorf, *Society and Democracy in Germany* (Garden City, New York: Doubleday & Co., 1967), p. 48.
31 *P.S.*, 1st. ed., p. 29.
32 *Ibid.*
33 *Ibid.*
34 Cf. *Ibid.*, "Deutschland unter den Europaeischen Weltmaechten" (Germany among the European World Powers), an address delivered on October 22, 1916, pp. 73–93.
35 Gerth and Mills, *op. cit.*, p. 35.
36 *Lebensbild*, p. 214.
37 Cf. *Lebensbild*, p. 231.
38 Fritz Fischer, *Germany's Aims in the First World War* (New York: W. W. Norton & Co., 1967), p.16.
39 Cf. *Lebensbild*, p. 231.
40 Fritz Fischer, *op. cit.*, p. 17. For interesting comparisons concerning the interrelationship of economic practice and the policy making in the Federal Republic of Germany see: Hans-Joachim Arndt, *West Germany: Politics of Non-Planning* (Syracuse: Syracuse University Press, 1966), and Werner Kaltefleiter, *Wirtschaft und Politik in Deutschland* (Cologne: Westdeutscher Verlag, 1966).
41 *Lebensbild*, pp. 231–232.
42 Cf. *Jugendbriefe*, letter to Baumgarten of March 13, 1888, p. 294 and pp. 298–300.
43 Cf. Mommsen, *op. cit.*, pp. 20–21 and *Die Christliche Welt*, 1892, pp. 1104ff, cited in *ibid.*
44 Cf. Mommsen, *op. cit.*, p. 22.
45 Cf. letter to Baumgarten of January 1, 1891 in *Jugendbriefe*, p. 325 cited in Mommsen, *op. cit.*, p. 22.
46 Mommsen, *op. cit.*, pp. 46–47. Cf. also *P.S.*, 2nd. ed., p. 19, Weber's inaugural address.
47 Cf. Mommsen, *op. cit.*, p. 47, who cites J. P. Mayer, *Max Weber in German Politics*, 2nd. ed. (London, 1956), p. 119.
48 Lewis J. Edinger, *op. cit.*, p. 62
49 *P.S.*, 2nd. ed., p. 9 ftn.
50 *Ibid.*, pp. 28–29, this excerpt is taken from a speech Max Weber delivered on November 23, 1896 at Erfurt during the deliberations by the delegates of the Christian Social movement concerning Friedrich Naumann's draft of a program for a prospective National-Social Party, according to Professor Johannes Winckelmann. After three days of deliberations, the National-Social Association (*National-Sozialer Verein*) was founded instead, which as Professor Johannes Winckelmann points out, Weber joined despite mental reservations concerning basic issues. See ftn. *P.S.*, 2nd. ed., p. 26. Cf. also Martin Wenck, *Die Geschichte der Nationalsozialen (1895–1903)* (Berlin: Buchverlag "Hilfe," 1905), p. 63f.
51 Mommsen, *op. cit.*, p. 47 and *P.S.*, 2nd. ed., p. 299, where Weber discusses Bismarck's legacy in an article on Parliament and Government in Reconstructed Germany ("Parlament und Regierung im Neugeordneten Deutschland,") which appeared in the summer of 1917 in the *Frankfurter Zeitung*.
52 Mommsen, *op. cit.*, pp. 47–48.
53 *Ibid.* p. 48 ftn.
54 *Ibid.*
55 *Ibid.*
56 *P.S.*, 2nd. ed., "Politik als Beruf," p. 538.
57 Mommsen, *op. cit.*, p. 51.
58 Cf. *ibid.*
59 *P.S.*, 2nd ed., p. 536.
60 *Ibid.*
61 *Ibid.* p. 535.
62 *Ibid.*
63 *Ibid.*, pp. 26–28.
64 *Ibid.*, p. 29.

148   *The Political Thought of Max Weber*

65 George L. Mosse, *The Culture of Western Europe: The Nineteenth and Twentieth Centuries* (Chicago: Rand McNally, 1961), p. 257.
66 Ansgar Skriver, "Wandlungen eines Liberalen: Friedrich Naumanns Gesammelte Werke—Lehrbuecher fuer Demokraten," Book Review of Friedrich Naumann, *Werke*, Vol. II: *Schriften Zur Verfassungspolitik*, edited by Wolfgang Mommsen; Vol. III: *Schriften zur Wirtschafts—und Sozialpolitik*, edited by Wolfgang Mommsen; Vol. IV: *Schriften zum Parteiwesen und zum Mitteleuropaproblem*, edited by Thomas Nipperdey and Wolfgang Schieder; Vol. V: *Schriften zur Tagespolitik*, edited by Alfred Milatz (Cologne/Opladen: Westdeutscher Verlag, 1964–1967) in *Die Zeit*, Nr. 44, November 5, 1968, p. 12.
67 Friedrich Naumann, *Schriften Zur Tagespolitik* (Vol. V) cited in *ibid.*
68 *Ibid.*
69 Ansgar Skriver, *op. cit.*, p. 12.
70 Cf. *ibid.*
71 Mosse, *op. cit.*, pp. 257–258.
72 *Ibid.*, p. 258.
73 *Lebensbild*, pp. 234–235.
74 *Ibid.*, pp. 234–235.
75 *Ibid.*, p. 237.
76 Cf. *ibid.*, p. 234.
77 Cf. Mommsen, *op. cit.*, p. 141.
78 *Ibid.*
79 *Ibid.*, p. 142.
80 George L. Mosse, *The Crisis of German Ideology: Intellectual Origins of the Third Reich* (New York: The Universal Library, Grosset and Dunlap, 1964), p. 219. Cf. also Alfred Kruck, *Geschichte des Alldeutschen Verbandes*, (Wiesbaden, 1954). Cited in Mosse, *ibid.*
81 *Ibid.*, pp. 219–220.
82 *Lebensbild*, p. 238.
83 Mommsen, *op. cit.*, p. 144.
84 Friedrich Naumann, *Demokratie und Kaisertum*, 1st. ed. (Berlin, 1900); 4th. ed. (Berlin, 1905), p. 155f.; cited in Mommsen, *op. cit.*, p. 151.
85 *P.S.*, 2nd. ed., p. 27.
86 *Ibid.*, pp. 27–28.
87 *Ibid.*, p. 28.
88 *Lebensbild*, p. 289.
89 *Ibid.*
90 Cf. Johannes Winckelmann, "Max Webers Verstaendnis von Mensch und Gesellschaft," in Karl Engisch, Bernhard Pfister, Johannes Winckelmann, *Max Weber: Gedaechtnisschrift der Ludwig-Maximilians-Universitaet Muenchen zur 100 Wiederkehr seines Geburtstages 1964* (Berlin: Duncker & Humblot, 1966), pp. 195–243. Reprinted by permission of the publisher.
91 *Ibid.*, pp. 240–241.
92 *Lebensbild*, pp. 289–291.
93 Interview with Marianne Weber in the summer of 1948; also cf. *Lebensbild*, p. 290.
94 Troeltsch indicated that Weber asked him for active participation in politics. He stated that he denied the request because he did not profess to be liberal despite being frequently sympathetic to liberalism. He based his reason for not being liberal on his Christian conviction (Christlichkeit) and its impact on political attitudes. (1904) Cf. Walter Koehler, *Ernst Troeltsch* (Tuebingen: J. C. B. Mohr [Paul Siebeck], 1941), p. 292, cited in Mommsen, *op. cit.*, p. 146.
95 *Ibid.*, pp. 146–147.
96 Cf. Friedrich Sell, *Die Tragoedie des deutschen Liberalismus* (Stuttgart: Deutsche Verlagsanstalt, 1953), p. 310. Cf. also Reinhard Ruerup, "Als die Liberalen regierten: Ein nahezu vergessenes Beispiel parlamentarischer Demokratie in Deutschland, *Die Zeit* Vol. 25, No. 14, April 3, 1970, p. 19.
97 Eduard Baumgarten, "Einleitung" in Johannes Winckelmann, editor, *Max Weber, Soziologie, Weltgeschichtliche, Analysen, Politik* (Stuttgart: Alfred Kroener Verlag, 1964), p. XXII.
98 Johannes Winckelmann, "Vorwort des Herausgebers," in *ibid.*, p. IX.
99 Cf. *P.S.*, 2nd. ed., p. 140 and *ibid.*, p. 171.
100 *P.S.*, 2nd. ed., p. 140.
101 *Ibid.*, p. 140.

102 *Ibid.*
103 Karl Jaspers, *Three Essays: Leonardo, Descartes, Max Weber* (New York: Harcourt, Brace & World, Inc., 1964), p. 197. Cf. also letter to Baumgarten of April 18, 1892 in *Jugendbriefe*, p. 345f. Reprinted by permission of the publisher.
104 Cf. Jaspers, *op. cit.*, p. 202.
105 Cf. letter of February 6, 1907 to Brentano in *Lebensbild:* He envisaged cooperation with the Social Democrats only on condition that they stop believing like 'braggarts' and begin to engage in practical politics. But Weber was dubious that they were ready to do so. Cf. *Lebensbild*, p. 405.
106 Letter to Friedrich Naumann of November 5, 1908 in *P.S.*, 1st. ed., p. 455.
107 *Ibid.*
108 *Ibid.*, pp. 451–452.
109 *Ibid.*, p. 456.
110 Hanson W. Baldwin, *World War I: An Outline History* (New York: Harper & Row, 1962), p. 16.
111 Karl Jaspers, *op. cit.*, p. 204.
112 *P.S.*, 2nd. ed., p. 484.
113 *P.S.*, 1st ed., pp. 456–457.
114 *P.S.*, 2nd. ed., p. 360.
115 *Ibid.*, p. 21.
116 *Ibid.*, p. 484.
117 Letter to Friedrich Naumann of November 12, 1908, p. 456 in *ibid.*, p. 456.
118 *P.S.*, 2nd. ed., p. 477.
119 *Ibid.*, p. 484.
120 *Ibid.*, p. 111.
121 *Ibid.*, p. 484.
122 Letter to Naumann of May 8, 1917 in *P.S.*, 1st. ed., p. 471.
123 *Ibid.*
124 *P.S.*, 2nd. ed., p. 161.
125 Cf. *Ibid.*, p. 360.
126 *Ibid.*, pp. 360–361.
127 Bernadotte E. Schmitt, *The Coming of the War, 1914* (New York: Scribner & Sons, 1930), Vol. II, p. 46.
128 Bernard Semmel, *Imperialism and Social Reform: English Social-Imperial Thought 1895–1914* (Garden City: Doubleday & Co., 1968), pp. 43–44.
129 *Ibid.*, p. 126.
130 Cf. Pauline Anderson, *The Background of Anti-English Feeling in Germany, 1890–1902* (Washington, D.C., 1939), cited in John R. Staude, *Max Scheler 1874–1928 An Intellectual Portrait* (New York: The Free Press, 1967), p. 72.
131 *Ibid.*, p. 65.
132 *Ibid.*
133 Cf. *ibid.*, pp. 65–66.

V

Max Weber and World War I

Having always conceived international relations, and indeed life itself, to be marked by pervasive conflict, the coming of the war in August 1914 did not take Weber by surprise. While several earlier crises had brought Europe to the brink of the abyss, especially between 1900 and 1914, in all previous cases catastrophy had been momentarily avoided. In every instance, Weber identified the threatening aspects of the situation very early. He foresaw that inevitably the great powers would some day engage in an enormous struggle for power. And yet most of what he saw pushing Germany toward this tragic fate he ascribed to the blindness of the Kaiser's personal regime and fatuous German diplomacy. The Kaiser's own *idées fixes* prevented him from gaining a proper perspective regarding strategy.

Weber's own tensions rose with every further distortion of perception emanating from the highest inner circles of the government. Germany's confrontation with a militarily and economically superior Entente he viewed with extreme pessimism. Utterly dismayed over Austria's running the risk of a break with Italy, believing that timely concessions might have prevented it, he wrote his wife in May 1915 that the entire diplomatic framework of the past twenty-five years had now collapsed and that he could hardly gain any satisfaction from the fact that he had always predicted such consequences.[1] Weber charged the Kaiser with the pursuit of mere prestige politics instead of realistic power politics, thus abdicating responsibility for the dire consequences of his actions.

Weber's conception is somewhat ambiguous in this respect and invites a fundamental question: Although historical evidence suggests that Wilhelminian *Weltpolitik* was largely responsible for creating the basic tensions which exploded into a major war, the personal guilt of the Kaiser may have been less than Weber's charges implied. Thus, as
150

will be seen subsequently, it is an open question whether the kind of policy Max Weber advocated would have prevented the outbreak of World War I. An expansionist policy, a larger military program, and a diplomacy which inculcated the possibility of a hot war would have constituted an equal threat to the other great powers. Even if the personal element in diplomacy had been absent, and considering the system of independent, sovereign national states, each pursuing its own welfare and power-political goals, could greater intelligence in diplomacy and more discrimination on Germany's part have led to the resolution of the conflicts by peaceful means?

Wolfgang Mommsen suggests that Weber's own imperialist power-political guide-lines for his nation, assigning the highest priority to it, are hardly defensible. Nor can one easily endorse the exclusiveness which he assigned to the employment of military and economic power as mere instruments of Germany's foreign policy.[2] Weber, however, never succumbed during World War I to the collective megalomania which took hold of other intellectuals in the shape of totally unrealistic war aims. "From the beginning of the war, he appraised the German military position soberly, even skeptically."[3] Unlike Weber, most men failed to retain a sense of proportion concerning Germany's actual power potential in the world. But, as Epstein writes: "Wilhelminian Germany—because of its size, population, geographical location, economic dynamism, cocky militarism, and autocracy under a neurotic emperor—was feared by all other powers as a threat to the European equilibrium; this was an objective fact which Germans should have recognized, irrespective of whether Germany . . . did or did not have intentionally aggressive designs (as affirmed by Fischer and denied by Ritter). Allied annexationist ambitions were . . . also in many cases morally outrageous, besides being undesirable because they precluded (equally with German annexationism) any negotiated peace, but their realization did *not* threaten the European equilibrium with the intolerable hegemony of a single Power, whereas the expansion of an already too powerful Germany did."[4]

Viewed in the perspective of our time, the principle operating here involved a mistaken notion of the relative positions of strength and "faulty brinkmanship." Accordingly Imanuel Geiss asserts, because "the world war developed out of a local war, then of continental war, the major share for causing it lies with that power which willed the local and/or continental war. That power was clearly Germany. She did not will the world war, as is borne out by her hopes of keeping out Britain, but she did urge Austria to make war on Serbia . . . Germany . . . was the only power which had no objection to the continental war. So long as Britain kept out, she was confident of winning a war against Russia and France. Germany did nothing to prevent continental war, even at the risk of a world war, a risk which her own government had seen from the beginning." [5]

The Allies saw the danger of a continental war becoming more and more imminent unless the original source of the infection could be controlled, namely the altercations between Austria and Serbia. Geiss states that inasmuch as the Allies' conception of priorities was the prevention of local war between those countries, their efforts were directed toward averting it. Nevertheless the responsibility for the coming of the war belongs to all the nations involved in it:

Russia by committing the technical blunder of providing the cue for German mobilization, instead of waiting until Germany had mobilized. The French attitude was almost entirely correct; her only fault was that she could not hold back her Russian ally from precipitating general mobilization. Britain might have made her stand clear beyond any doubt much earlier, since this might have been a way of restraining Germany.[6]

Yet, when all such arguments are through, peaceful coexistence based upon no more than merely mutual forebearance during a given crisis would have probably collapsed in any event sooner or later. Geiss judges the share of war guilt of the Entente to be considerably less than that of Germany because it reflected primarily a reaction to German rivalry. Germany's power drive brought her up short against the ultimate confrontation by her competitors whose claims had already been staked out. Weber's political instinct made him aware of the psychological repercussions provoked by the Kaiser's numerous blunders. But Weber himself failed to sense the likely reaction of Great Britain to certain aspects of German *Weltpolitik,* including her naval program. Britain regarded the latter as an immediate threat to her very status as a great power, and both Liberals and Tories agreed that she was entitled to protection of her national security, which in the absence of an Anglo-German naval agreement guaranteeing British supremacy might be threatened. Although Germany did not feel compelled to achieve equality with the British navy, the British were prone to view nervously any increase in German naval strength which might threaten Britain militarily.

Although favoring the naval buildup, Weber did acknowledge the necessity of coming to terms with England in this matter. Yet he thought it imperative to give priority to the threat confronting Germany because of her geographical situation; above all, Weber's fears of the "Russian colossus" caused him at times to lose some of his calm detachment. Viewing a rapprochement with France as all but out of the question, he advocated that German policy should aim at circumventing British hostility. Ludwig Dehio writes: "In 1914, confronted with the hatred of 'a whole world of enemies,' we experienced an intoxicating intensification of our whole being; but this sudden spiritual isolation, which was the result of our political isolation, contained the seeds of excess. This development, foreseen only by a few thoughtful men, was hastened by the accumulated emotions of the majority. . . . Encircled by hatred, the people replied with its own hatred. . . . Extremist and monomaniac ideas, which might have remained mere marginal phenomena in a calmer context began to spread. It is arresting to observe how the more clear-sighted tried to break this vicious circle by consulting the oracle of the *raison d'état* governing our internal policies; but the oracle's obscure replies only increased the confusion. . . . In spite of their admirable restraint, even those who favoured a negotiated peace could not tear one last veil from their eyes. Even they underestimated their island foe." [7]

Weber did not support the war for the sake of territorial aggrandizement, nor for economic advantage. In fact, he opposed noncombatants on the home front who advocated major annexations:

Every opportunity for attaining a peace restoring the status quo should be seized upon. Here, according to Weber, lay the real tragedy of the war. The great successes of the early period (which, when seen in retrospect, were nothing more than illusionary victories) merely befogged the political judgment of many Germans. . . . Big demands were being planned in anticipation of peace, which only strengthened the determination . . . of the adversaries to continue the war.[8]

Although chauvinism was alien to Weber, he welcomed the opportunity of sharing in the experiences of the war, the outbreak of which he had feared so much: "No matter what the outcome will be—this war is great and wonderful." [9] The war seemed to him a worthwhile experience because it evoked the supremely noble qualities of which men are capable when caught in a crisis situation, revealed in patriotism, in battle, in the spirit of fellowship, and in unity at home.

Also, when in contact with foreigners in the military hospitals of which he was in charge, Weber did not indulge in ethnocentrism. He insisted, for example, that equal care be granted to the wounded regardless of their nationality. Humane treatment of enemy soldiers was, in Weber's judgment, politically sound. If the word is passed on to the Allies that their nationals receive the same care granted to German citizens, the latter will be accorded similar consideration. In keeping with his personal philosophy, Weber granted an Alsatian professor who had a French wife permission to visit wounded Frenchmen for the purpose of cheering them with some gifts, whereupon the Alsatian was deemed suspect in some quarters. The military authorities were put under pressure as a result. Weber obtained clearance for his colleague by appealing to the military official's professional pride, telling him that it would be "unmanly" to bow to public opinion. A colleague of Weber's in charge of a military hospital arranged without Weber's knowledge to have guards escort the Alsatian professor in his hospital when he attempted to visit the French wounded. The Alsatian, deeply hurt by the incident, declined the visiting privileges under such conditions. Weber's inability to restrain his anger resulted in a break between him and his friend which continued for five years, although Weber apologized for having lost his temper in anticipation of eliciting from his friend an apology for his mistaken judgment.

Meanwhile, a Swiss professor found the atmosphere in Heidelberg no longer conducive to the continuation of his teaching appointment. He decided to resign and move to Switzerland. The difficulties he encountered when he applied at the local passport office caused Weber to intervene on his behalf. He criticized the war psychosis which poisoned the atmosphere with allegations directed against the Swiss professor. Stating that it reflected lack of political wisdom, Weber pointed out that negative reaction to this kind of procedure could be expected to come not only from Germany's enemies but from neutral countries as well. Moreover, he feared that such an incident might stir up unrest in Alsace itself. Although Weber acted protectively toward people of dual nationality whose position had become somewhat untenable in Germany, he had nothing but contempt for those who like the half-English Houston Stuart Chamberlain toppled over backwards to express pro-German sentiments. Nor did he appreciate half-Germans who while living abroad did not eschew negative statements about Germany.[10]

Weber enjoyed his administrative work in charge of forty military hospitals at the *Land* level, and nine new local ones in Heidelberg. His assignment during the war permitted him to exchange the isolation of the scholar for the very active life of a travelling hospital administrator. Since his duties required frequent visits to the various hospitals, his speeding car became known as the "yellow peril" or the "flying Dutchman." Above all, he enjoyed the performance of his tasks because they enabled him to see and feel most acutely the humanitarian ideal of brotherhood as he extended advice and active assistance to friend and foe alike among the wounded. Except for Sunday afternoons, his duties required his daily absence from home. On such afternoons, however, it was the gathering place for many friends who looked to Weber for an assessment of daily events and of the political as well as of the military situation generally. Among his guests were friends on leave from the battlefront. With them Weber agreed fully as they discounted the glowing reports of victories yet to be won. From the beginning, Weber regarded the war as being merely defensive rather than offensive in nature. Never underestimating the strength of the enemy and frequently designated as a pessimist, he felt that time was working against Germany. He opposed the constant ringing of church bells, the flag waving, and the continuous announcements of military victories; at no time did Weber lose sight of Germany's muddling into disaster.[11] At first, as will be recalled, he had viewed the war as "great and wonderful." He repeatedly paid homage to Germans as a great *Kulturvolk* who "could never-the-less be a match for the horrors of war away from home (which is no mean feat for a Senegal negro). . . . That is humanity at its best—and this must not be overlooked —in spite of the imposition of unpleasant activities. This experience remains—whatever the outcome may be." [12]

Weber's brother-in-law was killed during the battle of Tannenberg; his brothers were all in the service. On October 15, 1914 in a letter to Ferdinand Toennies, Weber wrote that while the experience of the war was uplifting, its value for him personally would have been enhanced if he could have actively participated in the fighting, but "unfortunately they cannot use me in the field as would have been possible, if it (the war) would have been waged in time—25 years ago." [13]

Yet, as early as 1914, Weber pondered the difficulties to be surmounted prior to the conclusion of a peace treaty:

What peace is conceivable? And when? Hundreds of thousands are dying as a result of our terrible diplomatic blundering—this, unfortunately, cannot be denied, and, therefore, I cannot see, even in the event of a successful ending, a really permanent peace for us. . . .[14]

Though the battle of Tannenberg held not only glory but the promise of victory for most Germans, Weber looked ahead. In a letter to his mother dated April 13, 1915, he again sounded somber, although he was moved simultaneously by the spirit which the war had inspired in his nation. Mourning his fate of having to witness the conflict behind a desk while the experience "passes me by," he had high praise for those who:

yet in spite of everything, can remain basically decent, as is the majority of our soldiers—this is genuinely human. . . . This experience will survive whatever the final outcome may be—it looks dark enough now particularly if Italy is not going to be calmed down.[15]

Weber's concerns included contemporary imperialist aspirations; in a letter to the *Frankfurter Zeitung* [16] he expressed his views on German war aims;

I am against any European annexations, even in the East. Instead, I favor, providing the military can enforce it, the creation of autonomous national states for Poland, Little Russia, Lithuania, and Latvia. We should reserve for ourselves the right to build and to occupy military bases (and to construct strategic railways) as far as Warsaw and north of there; the same terms for Austria from Warsaw on and to the south of it. Besides that only: customs union with Poland, Lithuania, and Latvia, otherwise full autonomy. No German settlement policy beyond our frontiers. In the West: military occupation: permanently of Luxemburg; of Liège and Namur for twenty years, pledging ourselves to evacuation after that. In return Belgium must fortify and defend Ostend and the southern frontier. Nothing else (in Europe). Thus only the militarily indispensable, no 'annexations' whatever.[17]

Weber seems to have differed from the mass of imperialists in Germany at that time, mainly by his attempts to confine current imperialist ambitions within bounds. On a visit to Brussels in the latter part of 1915, he wrote: "The liberally educated are opposed to the annexation (of Belgium). But such views have no influence at the present time. . . ." [18]

Time and again Weber challenged the government to state unequivocally that even should Germany regain the military initiative, she did not intend to extend the temporary military occupation of non-German territories in Europe indefinitely, intending thereby eventually to claim the right of annexation. Weber's desire to mute the offstage noises is certainly understandable. Annexationist programs were not supposed to circulate and were subject to censorship. Nevertheless, it seemed almost as if propagandistic speeches and publications were climbing a carefully planned peak: "Whether this propaganda was the result of a widespread popular demand, is difficult to determine. . . . Many observers testify, however, to the artificial character of German annexationist propaganda; and its origin among the annexationist pressure groups certainly lends credence to this view. . . ." [19]

The press exercized the greatest influence. The *Taegliche Rundschau, Leipziger Neueste Nachrichten, Rheinisch-Westphaelische Zeitung,* and *Post* demonstrated that Pan-German thinking did not merely represent the lunatic fringe.[20] Nor was this all: "Even the sophisticated *Zukunft* of Maximilian Harden temporarily was affected by the annexationist mania. As early as August 22, 1914, Harden defended Germany's 'right to extend her territory.' In September he reminded Belgium that she owed her culture, her colonies, and her independence to Germany, and that she had forfeited her privileges because of her cruel warfare against the invading Germans. A month later, Harden joined the most radical of the annexationists." [21] Although, as noted earlier, perhaps the most consistent and articulate critic of Wilhelm II, Harden recorded his own war aims as follows: "We shall remain in the Belgian Netherlands to which we shall add a thin coastal strip up to and beyond Calais. . . . From Calais to Antwerp, Flanders, Limburg, Brabant, and beyond the line of the Meuse: Prussia. . . ." [22]

In his classic work, Hans Gatzke demonstrates persuasively that the bulk of annexationist propaganda was actually disseminated quite openly, and, in fact, was reaching large segments of the German public. Moreover, he showed the "considerable" part played by university professors in propagandizing annexationist aims.[23] The list below represents only a small cross-section: "Colonial expansion, often in connection with annexations on the continent, was the subject of books or pamphlets by Professors Mirbt (Theology), von Liszt (Law) Backhaus (Agriculture) and even the well-known editor of the *Preussische Jahrbuecher*, Hans Delbrueck. . . ."[24] Weber's position, when compared to some imperialist pronouncements, appears eminently more moderate. Among general observations concerning annexationist propaganda during the early period of the war, the fact is that both the "large number and the early date of these publications indicate that, while to the average German the war was at first one of defense, to a small minority it was almost immediately converted into a struggle for territorial gains."[25] Public opinion generally favored an extension of the scope of German imperialism with an eye on Africa and certain parts of eastern France. Although consensus was lacking over what policy Germany should pursue concerning Belgium; ". . . most annexationists agreed that Germany should maintain some hold, direct or indirect, over Belgium's political and economic life."[26]

Max Weber's own style of imperialism, which at first glance appears formidable, seems rather less so considering that "to be a moderate or a *Flaumacher* (as the Pan-Germans called it), did not necessarily mean the rejection of any and all annexations."[27] Meanwhile, "German professors and other civil servants joined their voices to the general hue and cry for conquest of territory from Belgium, to the Baltic, to the Balkans. In May came the petition of the Six Associations and, in July, the petition of 1,347 professors, diplomats, and government servants. These remarkable documents conjured up visions of mountainous indemnities; long years of military occupation of Allied territories, a Germanized Belgium, Poland, and Baltic; possession of Belfort, Verdun, the coast of Flanders, Longwy, and Briey; as well as the destruction of England's power overseas. At times these terms were characterized as the prize of victory, compensation for losses; at other times as an insurance, required by strategy, against another war."[28]

Considering the prevailing climate of German public opinion, Hans Delbrueck seemed restrained indeed as he exhorted his countrymen not to indulge in a Napoleonic policy even if victory should be in sight: "Wars without end would be the result. However heavily we might chain other nations, we cannot keep them in fetters forever. Europe is agreed on this one point, never to submit to the hegemony of one single state. The aim of the war, he declared, should be that on land the balance of power must be maintained as it is, and that on the sea a similar balance must be attained." [29] Delbrueck's championship of a more moderate position caused a storm among the annexationists. In the *Taegliche Rundschau* his article was described as a "crime against the German cause" while the *Post* went so far as to charge him with "criminal subserviency to Germany's enemies." [30]

While admittedly Weber too appears as a moderate by comparison, one must agree with Gatzke's comment that "moderation among Germany's intellectuals and former diplomats . . . was by no means so great as the attacks of the pan-Germans may lead us to believe."[31] Nevertheless, it seems that total opposition to annexationist designs emanated only from some Social Democrats. Those who like Weber were credited with being anti-annexationist distinguished themselves only in degree from the more extreme annexationists. Hans Delbrueck was known as the leading intellectual within the moderate ranks. The closeness of his own and Weber's estimate of the relative threats Germany was facing from both England and Russia becomes apparent from Delbrueck's own evaluation: "The difference between the *Deutsche Tageszeitung* and myself lies in the fact that it considers England the most dangerous enemy of Germany's future, while I think Russia is." [32] Delbrueck and Rohrbach wanted to see Germany as the liberator of smaller peoples in Europe. Thus in 1926 Weber probably would have identified himself with Delbrueck's statement:

I often used to say openly: my annexationist aims are in no way smaller than those of others! They are only different. They are such that the others can accept them. . . . Both Rohrbach and I have always emphasized, the great idealistic aim of Germany must be the freedom and independence of small peoples. . . . This was at the same time in the interest of Germany's power.[33]

Chancellor Bethmann-Hollweg's exposure to annexationist pressure tactics from parliamentary as well as from extraparliamentary sources has been well documented:

The position and the task of the Chancellor had become more difficult with every month ever since the victorious advance of the German armies had come to a halt on the Marne in September 1914. Bethmann-Hollweg had comforted himself at the beginning of hostilities with the thought that a few powerful blows could bring the war to a quick end. As early as March 1915 he had written, in a confidential letter to von Valentini, the chief of the imperial civil cabinet: 'In the course of the last 25 years, the soul of our people has been poisoned by jingoism to such an extent that our people would probably become cowards if deprived of such arrogant self-praise.' [34]

Despite such evidence, it seems clear that the chancellor, far from being a reluctant captive of an aggressive militarist oligarchy, fully shared their expansionist views. This interpretation is put forward strongly in Fritz Fischer's remarkable book.[35] Accordingly, there was actually little difference in war aims between the civilian government and the military establishment. Bethmann-Hollweg was by no means merely tied to the latter in the formulation of policy. The most urgent problem for the chancellor also was to raise Germany towards equal standing with England and Russia. For the sake of this goal, the chancellor frankly proclaimed his imperialistic designs.[36] Herein lies the crux of his entire argument, skirted by German historians until recently and first brought to light in German by Fritz Fischer. It was Bethmann-Hollweg who drew up a systematic plan of German war aims, generally known as the program of September 9, 1914 which "remained the archetypal plan of all German policies till the end of the war." [37] Subsequent military reversals caused expectations of fulfillment of these dreams to have been temporarily scaled downward. To take one example, but an important one, when Germany was very interested in concluding a separate peace treaty with Russia in 1915, she was not willing to forego all her eastern territorial gains. Fischer claims that Bethmann-Hollweg must be understood to have "completely" agreed with the military leader that Germany's naval defenses needed building up. In fact, he wanted to concentrate on improving the fleet to be able to cope with England's potential ability "to deprive us of the fruits of victory over France and Russia." [38]

Golo Mann points out that even men endowed with such extraordinary intellectual equipment as Max Weber are "subject to the bewitchments of their age. The naval programme was enthusiastically received by most of the middle class; and also by that great scholar, professor Max Weber who agreed with Tirpitz that power, and yet more power, was needed in order to protect the German economy, and that in the dawning age of world politics this meant power at sea. . . . The socially minded democrat, which Max Weber claimed to be, surrendered as much to the cult of power as the imperial admiral, as the owners and managers of heavy industry, as the journalists of the newspapers financed by industry, as the clergymen, the teachers of gymnastics and those who spouted forth on the occasion of the Kaiser's birthday." [39]

Bethmann-Hollweg's September program concerning German war aims and the objectives of other groups such as the Pan-Germans represented an attempt to counteract some even more extreme proposals. Bethmann-Hollweg was not speaking only for himself when he devised his scheme of letting the "military . . . decide" whether demands for the amputation of certain French territories are justified such as "Belfort and western slopes of the Vosges . . . and coastal strip from Dunkirk to Boulogne." [40] Concerning Belgium, Bethmann-Hollweg envisaged the annexation of "Liège and Verviers to Prussia." Moreover, "Belgium, even if allowed to continue to exist as a state, must be reduced to a vassal state. . . . French Flanders with Dunkirk, Calais and Boulogne . . . can without danger be attached to this unaltered Belgium. . . ." [41] Luxemburg in Bethmann-Hollweg's program was to become a "German federal state and will receive a strip of the present Belgium province of Luxemburg and perhaps the corner of Longwy." [42] The destiny of Holland the chancellor had not yet worked out. In any case, that country would have to be "brought into closer relationship with the German Empire." [43] Furthermore, the chancellor envisaged an agreement effecting the economic dependence of France on Germany. [44]

The realization of this programme would have brought about a complete revolution in the political and economic power-relationships in Europe. After eliminating France as a great power, excluding British influence from the Continent and thrusting Russia back, Germany purposed to establish her own hegemony over Europe. If we concede that it is a statesman's duty, even in the midst of armed conflict, to conceive and to set before himself a dispassionate and imaginative picture of the world at peace, again, we cannot but ask ourselves uneasily whether Bethmann-Hollweg's picture could have provided an adequate foundation for an enduring peace in Europe. . . . [45]

Accordingly, German aims did not develop out of the war situation, according to Fischer. Instead they merely testified to Germany's will to power, which existed even prior to the war. Actually, Fischer portrays Germany's *engagement* as one of continuous struggle for power—"a struggle which far from being the result of an existing situation, was in fact the means by which events were to be shaped." [46]

It is now clear beyond serious doubt that powerful German interest groups accepted at least in outline the war aims set forth by the Pan-Germans, which were underwritten also by leading industrialists such as Alfred Hugenberg and Hugo Stinnes. There are indications that these groups sought to make as much political capital as they could out of German annexationist dreams. The plan called for Germany to retain Belgium, parts of Poland and the Baltic provinces. Germany was also to retain "Belgium, as well as the French coast as far as the mouth of the Somme . . . the belt of fortifications from Verdun to Belfort, and Toulon. . . . The possessions of France and Belgium in Africa must also fall to Germany. . . . Only the Russian fanatics wanted, like the German fanatics, substantially to change the position of their country in the world; the Germans . . . had . . . the more sweeping plans." [47]

Some of Bethmann-Hollweg's critics have portrayed him as an "annexationist in philosopher's attire" whereas others have characterized him as a "noble bureaucrat," simply not equal to the position he held and who only occasionally experienced "annexationist inclinations." [48]

Fritz Stern writes: "Perhaps Bethmann's most culpable act was to have seen and understood so much and to have said so little. His semi-silence, though understandable, facilitated the second and worse triumph of the very passions he deplored."[49] He was circumspect enough to anticipate possible consequences of his actions. Nevertheless he received the brunt of public criticism for the conduct of German foreign policy.

Questioning the validity of the parties' position on Bethmann-Hollweg, Weber censored them for their sustained air of disengagement from political responsibility. If the participation of the political parties meant anything at all, it must surely mean participating in the decision-making process, not merely in the discussion after the mistakes have occurred. Weber correctly pointed out that the parties concentrated their wrath upon the chancellor, seeking to demonstrate unequivocally that the government had committed Germany to a policy that insured the hostility of the rest of the world. Stating that the parties' refusal to underwrite the government's policy came only after it had been put into effect, Weber questioned their right to blame the chancellor for any resulting debacles. They criticized Bethmann-Hollweg on his alleged failure to shoulder responsibility for his own actions by passing it on to the Kaiser. Weber, moreover, pointed to an even more imperative question, namely what response the parties had made to criticism coming from the radical Left of government policy. Weber argued that the parties rose to the occasion by discrediting the Left, accusing it of being disloyal to the crown.[50]

Weber also castigated Admiral von Tirpitz' and his supporters' concept of how politics should be handled, especially in time of war. Tirpitz' sinister campaign, which he waged publicly against the chancellor, had all the earmarks of demagogy. Although Weber respected the admiral professionally, he felt alienated by his tactics. He deplored the dangerous attempts at indoctrination of the masses in which Tirpitz' supporters had engaged with the admiral's tacit approval, a fact which, as Weber mentioned, was properly noted in the Reichstag. Political dissent, moreover, could hardly be expected since certain interest groups collaborated with the admiral in misinforming the public. Together they were imposing upon an uninformed public their opinion on the issue of unlimited submarine warfare. Since the public lacked all knowledge of the risks involved, they were unqualified to make any judgments even when they were alone with their consciences.[51]

Bethmann-Hollweg's long-time secretary and associate in the Foreign Office, Kurt Rietzler, is reported to have characterized politics as "the art to employ evil and to achieve the good."[52] In Stern's judgment, Bethmann-Hollweg would have expressed the same idea. The fear of upsetting severely the international order, considering Germany's exposed position, prompted the chancellor to request and receive regular increases in appropriations for military purposes. In these efforts he acted in accordance with the Kaiser's wishes. Since his tenure of office depended solely upon the pleasure of the Kaiser, to whom he was directly responsible, he permitted personal considerations to enter into affairs of state: ". . . he defended his office more forcefully than his policy." [53] Consequently while the personal idiosyncrasies of the Kaiser caused him obstruction, they certainly functioned as direct and indirect pressures. Moreover, he was forced to make judgments which were unquestionably conditioned by differing ideological persuasions of the members of the Reichstag. Social mobility combined with the prospect that the politically privileged status of the upper classes was endangered because of their declining economic importance, had become a source of considerable disquiet to the conservative ranks.

This anxiety was frequently reflected in the sumptuary legislation whereby the upper classes guaranteed the external indices of their status.[54] An aging governmental system carries within itself the necessity of discarding all too much degenerative tissue. The inherent conditions, such as the implications of the distribution of political power after Bismarck's eclipse among several administrative heads, especially among the military, confronted the chancellor with insurmountable difficulties. Lines of responsibility were not clearly drawn. The bitter fight between the chancellor and the military leaders, who all too frequently received a sympathetic hearing at court, was due to the fact that not only did they lay claim to autonomy within their own departmental sphere, but they also sought to curtail the slender control of the chancellor over foreign policy.

To the intensity of the factional fighting were added the pressures emanating from interest groups and lobbies, as well as the intrigues of courtiers. Despite Germany's pretentions to great power status, the Reich possessed neither the necessary statesmanship nor the effective political system of some of its friends and competitors. Bethmann-Hollweg had hoped to conduct a conciliatory policy both at home and abroad, seeking to steer a middle course. The fact that a distinctly conservative policy would have proved inconceivable was certainly realized by its exponents themselves.[55] A liberal policy, including provisions for the extension of parliamentary powers, would also have been doomed to failure because "the Kaiser would not have tolerated it and the Reichstag could not have mustered a workable majority. Bethmann tried to employ half-measures which he also pursued only half-heartedly. . . ." [56] As Stern concludes, the chancellor was destined to fail in these efforts as he was destined to offend all sides: "He recognized—as did most of his more intelligent contemporaries—that the integration of the proletariat into the nation was the main requirement at the time, but he saw no way toward a solution of this problem. Instead the contrasts only increased before the war, and the feuding groups pushed themselves mutually into an ever more radical and unyielding position . . . as they did again during the war." [57]

The reconciliation of conflicts in German politics remained an unsolved problem, despite the considerable electoral gains of the SPD in 1912, for already in 1913 in connection with the Zabern incident, the military blatantly demonstrated its "contempt for the *Rechtsstaat*—and enjoyed the full backing by the chancellor." [58]

Max Weber's scathing remarks reflected his adverse reaction to the inept conduct of German affairs. Referring to the various diplomatic debacles, he drew attention to the response of what he contemptuously called "our Literati" vis-à-vis the persistent mishandling of Germany's foreign policy. Although all signs suggested that under prevailing conditions the diplomats were in a bind which prevented a genuinely constructive diplomacy, Weber pointed to the unwillingness of the "Literati," as they catered to the "most dreary philistine instincts" to inquire into the reasons for the weak links in German diplomacy. The endless chatter about the failure of the English version of the monarchical system to appeal to German tastes combined with the lip service paid in support of official policy constituted habits to which the "Literati" had formerly subscribed and which the right-wing press still continued to practice.[59]

In these circumstances, Bethmann-Hollweg was faced with difficult choices. Nevertheless, his ability and will to do what was necessary appear to have been stifled by an unwillingness to antagonize any of the principals in the government. Hence his cautious and unimaginative diplomacy suffers when measured against the high standards of Max Weber's distinction between the politician and the official characterized by a civil-service mentality.[60] The extremely complicated situation opened up few possibilities for independent action. The spirit of his diplomacy was marked by an unceasing sense of responsibility of a man who did not himself seek to engage in the wanton exercise of power although he did not want to abdicate power either. His well-considered efforts to conduct a cautious and realistic diplomacy redound to his credit. Nevertheless, he recognized that both the exercise of power and with it the responsibility for its results were divided. He calmed his conscience with the fact (in which there was much truth) that were he to resign, as Max Weber demanded of a political leader, his successor and his opponents would have pursued a less reasonable course.[61]

As Weber's distinction between an "official" and a "political leader" reminds us, the chancellor, being "formally a salaried official with pension rights" [62] was likely to be under a telling degree of strain, since unlike many other civil servants, he is subject to dismissal. As Weber writes: ". . . An official who receives a directive which he considers

wrong can and is supposed to object to it. If his superior insists on its
execution, it is his duty and even his honor to carry it out as if it corresponded to his innermost convictions. . . ." [63]

A political leader acting in this way would deserve contempt. He will often
be compelled to make compromises, that means, to sacrifice the less important to the more important. If he does not succeed in demanding of his
master, be he a monarch or the people: 'You either give me now the authorization I want from you, or I will resign,' he is a miserable *Kleber* (one who
sticks to his post)—as Bismarck called this type—and not a leader. 'To be
above parties'—in truth, to remain outside the realm of the struggle for
power—is the official's role, while this struggle for personal power, and the
resulting personal responsibility, is the lifeblood of the politician as well as
of the entrepreneur.[64]

None of the chancellors succeeding Bismarck, Caprivi, Hohenlohe,
Buelow, Bethmann-Hollweg were characterized by Bismarck's political
qualities; in fact, he did not tolerate men around him who were genuinely qualified politicians. All of the chancellors had a bureaucratic background. Weber had high words of praise, on the other hand, for Germany's

military and civilian bureaucracy (judging it to be) superior to all others in the
world in terms of integrity, education, conscientiousness and intelligence. The
military and, by and large, also the domestic performance during the war
has proven what can be achieved with these means. . . . It has become customary, for instance, to criticize German diplomacy, probably unjustifiably.
It appears likely that on the average it was about as good as that of other
countries. A confusion is involved here. What was lacking was the *direction*
of the state by a *politician*—not by a political genius, to be expected only
once every few centuries, not even by a great political talent, but simply by
a politician.[65]

As Fritz Stern has persuasively argued, Bethmann-Hollweg's image
presented itself as one that offered not only a departure from that of
other public figures in point of "style and character"; it had also been
assumed that his political objectives represented a divergence from the
objectives of official policy. Considering the high incidence of belief in
Germany's national destiny and the disinclination of the Kaiser to tolerate
divergent views, Fritz Stern's view appears to be justified in portraying
Bethmann-Hollweg as a man whose deep concern for Germany's future
proved clearsightedness but as one who had "no alternative to offer and
would not have had the power to enforce it."[66]

In a foreign policy address delivered to the Reichstag on April 5,
1916, Bethmann-Hollweg discussed its future course from the vantage
point of a victorious nation whose war aims would henceforth take
their cue from its future military successes. He indicated that whereas

Germany had initially viewed the war as a defensive one, following the turn of events, she had now shifted her position from the *status quo ante*. Weber's response was that the chancellor's position could be viewed as defensible only if he could be assured that there was absolutely no chance of serious peace negotiations in the near future. In Weber's view the facts seemed to support that assumption. Calling the speech far from politically judicious, he again emphasized that a great mistake had been made when it was not made clear at the outset that Belgium would not be retained permanently. There seemed to be no one capable of manifesting the perspective required for recognizing the dimensions of the "possible and useful." Above all, Weber contended, everything is judged by canons of purely domestic policy. The chancellor felt impelled to present an image of being possessed of as natural, decisive an aptitude for command as Tirpitz, otherwise he would be in difficulty with the Conservatives. Weber brilliantly traced the policy of the Conservatives and big industrialists as one based upon the reasoning that the longer the war, the more the Social Democrats would defect to the Left. This could only benefit the former, the "supporters of throne and altar." Weber made the politics of these groups seem realistic and practical; his detached analyses demonstrated their firm intention to prevent a negotiated peace based upon compromise. Their interest in forestalling such an eventuality was paramount, since they reasoned that otherwise they would be called upon to yield on the right-of-franchise issue.[67]

The sinking of the "Lusitania" Weber regarded as a grave tactical error and misfortune. Urging an early peace on the basis of the status quo, with no losses for Germany, but also no territorial gains, he wrote a memorandum regarding peace terms to the government and to the members of parliament. Public debate on war aims was still forbidden at this time; secretly, however, strong lobbies still continued to press for annexations in both east and west. Weber was convinced that the alternatives open to Germany consisted in either conducting world politics on the basis of alliances with other nations or in incurring through a European expansion scheme the risk of uniting all other powers in opposition to her designs: "He stated that Germany's interest would not be served if she were to enforce a peace resulting chiefly in a situation in which the heel of the German boot in Europe would stand upon everyone's toes." [68] Another danger in case Germany were to fail to resist the urge toward extravagant territorial claims in Europe was the almost certain fact of a long war. Any escalation of such claims would result in a vigorous counterpoise on the part of the Allies, protesting Germany's show of strength, and contribute to increasing the industrial supremacy of America and other countries overseas.

The conquest of Poland raised the vital problem of providing Germany with lasting protection against Russia. Could Poland, up to that time a part of Russia, be transformed into an independent state, thus forming a buffer between the Central Powers and the east? Weber saw the following difficult problems: (a) could Polish industry resist Anschluss to the Russian hinterland; (b) would Germany and Austria be able to come to an agreement regarding their respective rights of sovereignty and customs policies; and, most important, (c) what would be the attitude of the new state if Germany and Austria refused to give up Posen and Western Galicia?

Since final settlement with Poland had been postponed and Weber considered German military policy in Poland ill-conceived, he wished to use his command of the Polish language to seek contact with the Poles.[69] The undersecretary of state, however, refused him permission to visit Poland to talk with industrialists and to review official documents. Weber was refused even though he had acted through a deputy of the Center party. When in the fall of 1916 the new state of Poland was proclaimed, Weber deplored the act as having been premature. The German government's miscalculation soon became apparent when its call for Polish volunteers immediately following the proclamation received only a poor response. Germany had hoped to strengthen her forces by adding Polish soldiers to reinforce her troops at the Russian front. By the end of March 1916 Weber was disenchanted with "the whole Berlin atmosphere in which all talented people are disqualified by the resentful stupidity dominating the Reich offices."[70] Weber summarized the Berlin atmosphere as follows:

Politically everything here is not very confidence-inspiring. Nobody knows what will happen to Poland. The rather dubious hope for a separate peace with Russia still lingers on. Above all the situation in regard to America is really serious. . . . If only these crazy Pan-Germans and the Reich navy people will not get us into trouble with America. The immediate consequence would be that, first, half of our merchant marine, one quarter in American and one quarter in Italian ports (!) will be confiscated and used against us; thus at once the number of British ships will be increased—a factor which these asses have not counted on. Second, we shall have five hundred thousand American sportsmen as volunteers, brilliantly equipped against our tired troops, a fact which these asses do not believe. Third, forty billion in cash will be available to our enemies. Fourth, three more years of war,—thus certain ruin. Fifth, Rumania, Greece, etc., against us. And all this so that Herr von Tirpitz may show what he can do! Never has anything so stupid been thought of.[71]

Accordingly:

The state secretary of the navy, Admiral von Tirpitz, had hurled this apple of discord into the midst of the German people in conscious opposition to the wishes of the Chancellor. Behind Bethmann's back, in an interview granted to the American journalist Karl von Wiegand on November 21, 1914, Tirpitz spoke glowingly of submarine warfare as the certain way 'to force England to her knees.' [72]

He was perfectly aware that:

Bethmann as well as the Emperor opposed this idea, and he therefore took pains to have the interview published in America without the knowledge of the Chancellor, his superior. Bethmann, to be sure, was able to deal with this naval revolt: Tirpitz was dismissed on March 15, 1915. But no sooner had the Chancellor helped Hindenburg and Ludendorff into the Supreme Command (August 29, 1916) than he discovered that he had thereby created opponents who would recognize the prerogatives of the Chancellor even less than had Tirpitz—and who, moreover, were more powerful than himself. As early as the end of 1916 he felt obliged to complain about the obstructions that 'these two genial gentlemen continually place in the path of cooperation' and about their persistent efforts 'to militarize the whole of political life.' [73]

On the other hand, the evidence supports the view that unrestricted submarine warfare originated with the Center party, rather than with the military:

On October 2, 1916, the Centrist delegates adopted a resolution accepting in advance a declaration of unlimited submarine warfare in the event that the Supreme Command should wish to adopt such a policy.[74]

While the resolution did not affect the chancellor's authority granted him by the constitution, for all practical purposes the military now superseded the authority of the chancellor; ". . . this action strengthened Ludendorff's hand and weakened the position of the Chancellor, who could no longer count on a majority in the Reichstag." [75]

Although Weber had been thoroughly opposed to Admiral Tirpitz' naval policy, he now compared his enforced resignation to the effect of a lost battle:

Under whatever circumstances, the human nastiness of this monarch always remains the same in addition to the fact that the action was highly unwise. . . . Whatever His Majesty undertakes—it is certain to be wrong.[76]

It is an historical fact that

Bethmann and State Secretary Karl Helfferich had opposed with all their might the adventurous notion of an all-out submarine campaign because they were absolutely certain that such a step would be answered by an American declaration of war. To be sure, the admirals had solemnly promised to force England to sue for peace before the Americans would be able to join in the battle. But the ministers did not trust the admirals' calculations, calculations which Helfferich had painstakingly refuted. Count Bernstorff, the German ambassador in Washington, emphatically warned the Chancellor against a war with the United States.[77]

Even as Germany in the early stages of the war was gaining victories on the battlefield, she was losing ground in her diplomatic relations. Weber especially dreaded the deterioration of German-American relations. In March 1916 he submitted a critical statement on the subject of Germany's intensified submarine warfare to party leaders, to parliamentary deputies, the Foreign Office, and ultimately to the Reichs-Chancellor.

Weber, who frequently seemed at his best when he revealed pseudo-patriotic or pious abstractions as ruses and when he removed the halo surrounding such military heroes as Tirpitz and Ludendorff, nevertheless was to emerge as their champion after their fall. Weber himself had preferred a negotiated naval agreement with England and had advised against extensive territorial designs in Europe, yet he deplored Tirpitz' resignation even though the Admiral, anxious to pit his navy against the British fleet, went further than most in his annexationist claims, which included Antwerp and the Flanders coast in addition to sizeable colonial areas.[78]

Meanwhile, Weber continued to criticize the Kaiser's lack of diplomatic skill, particularly regarding foreign affairs and their impact upon the other great powers' perceptions of German objectives. Actually, as stated previously, historical evidence suggests that Weber overrated the Kaiser's share of responsibility for the deterioration of Germany's relations with other nations. The Morocco crisis in 1906 was not originally of the Kaiser's making. Weber, however, did not have complete access to secret documents and probably was not familiar with all the interior maneuvers within government circles. Consequently, he apparently based his judgment merely upon the public image presented by the emperor and its unfortunate effect. Later on, in fact, Weber did condemn leading German politicians for having foreclosed, by letting the Kaiser perform an essentially diplomatic mission, any possibility of coming to terms with England regarding Germany's interests in South Africa and with France regarding Germany's interests in North Africa.[79]

Weber's response to Pan-German aspirations remained unequivocal throughout the war. Any colonial *Weltpolitik* would have to be predicated upon an agreement with England. Any contemplated German annexations in the west would preclude the possibility of such an understanding; on the contrary, this would mean an increase in forces hostile to Germany. Above all, it would be most likely to accelerate what German policy should strive to reduce, namely the Russian menace. In case of war, Russia would not be backed by France only but by England as well.[80]

Weber introduced his lecture (in Munich, October 1916) on "Germany among the European World Powers" by stating that his remarks were not in support of any particular party's platform since both domestic and foreign policy, in his judgment, must be placed solely in the context of the vital national interest. Weber stressed again that his own party allegiance had undergone considerable change since he first cast his vote for the Conservative ballot. One of the most conspicuous features of Weber's political philosophy was shared by many other outstanding men of his own generation including, for example, Erzberger until 1917; namely "his nearly complete absorption in international affairs."[81] Contrary to Erzberger, however, Weber also manifested a concern for the increasing demands calling for an immediate reform of the Prussian franchise:

The controversy about war aims and the problem of political reform at home occupied Max Weber's thoughts continually. The fate of Germany depended upon the solution of such problems as much as on the military outcome of the war. The stage was being set for what was to come later—right down to the present day. . . .[82]

Stating once again that Germany was "a power state,"[83] Weber insisted that the very existence of neighboring power states presented an obstacle to any power-political decisions which Germany could make. Due consideration must always be accorded to neighboring powers such as France. Thus it was desirable for a power state to be surrounded either by weak smaller states or by a minimum of other power states. Fate had willed Germany to be in the singular position of having no natural frontiers, and to be located adjacent to three of the strongest land powers in Europe. No other country in the world was so situated. Obviously, Germany was in everybody's way. Consequently she would have to maintain a state of constant military preparedness. German politics, Weber reasoned, could not therefore afford to be guided by emotional factors devoid of any definite purpose; rather it must be inspired by an "objective policy" which rules out a "policy of hatred." He further insisted: "Objective politics signifies: no policy governed by vanity, agitatory speeches and boasts, but a policy of calm action."[84]

Weber attributed the war to two causes, (a) the power interests of bureaucracies and dynasties, and (b) Pan-Slavic ideology. He failed to allude to Pan-German aspirations as a possible factor.

But the Pan-German League was not just another expression of the imperialism of the time. Its peculiarity lay in its sharp domestic opposition to the black and red Internationals' (i.e., Catholics and Socialists) and in its demands for *Lebensraum* in Continental Europe itself. The hostility to Catholics and Socialists was sparked by the domestic coalition of pro-government parties and obviously designed to deny the fact that the Catholic Center party and the revisionists among the Social Democrats were moving toward the right. The demand for territory was based on the belief that, within her existing borders, Germany could not in the long run maintain her absolute sovereignty nor remain the foremost military power of the world. The lack of raw materials would lead to growing international complications; the country's limited territory made it appear more vulnerable than the other great powers. Therefore, the pamphlet that Heinrich Class, the president of the League, published pseudonymously in 1912, went beyond a general imperialistic program; it rejected universal suffrage, demanded a stricter law against the Socialists, sought to deprive Jews of full citizenship by giving them the status of resident aliens, and proposed to solve the social question by the conquest of new *Lebensraum*. This program expressed the hostility and aggressions of the ruling class of the empire in which the national-minded liberal middle class was by this time included; and if this ruling class persisted in its course it was bound to try to impose its will on Europe just as Bismarck's Prussia had done in Germany.[85]

Meanwhile, Weber continued to regard Russia as the paramount threat to Germany's long-run national interests. Although he did not consider his own forecasts infallible, perhaps "the voice of prophecy" can be detected in the following passage. Failing that, we might possibly find in it the German explanation of Germany's fear of Russia, a fear that today cannot be disregarded, particularly after the Soviet Union's occupation of Czechoslovakia in 1968, and the threatening position Russia has assumed at times vis-à-vis the Federal Republic of Germany:

The threat from the east will increase in the future as the population increases. This is not true of the west. And most of all: The Russian menace is the only one which is properly directed against our very existence as a national power state. England might paralyze our our maritime trade—our entire foreign trade only in the event of a coalition as it now exists. France might deprive us of a piece of land. A victorious Russia, however, is able to destroy our independence. . . . Russia not only threatens our position as a state, but also our entire culture, ultimately, civilization itself (*Weltkultur*), as long as she persists in being what she is now. This peculiar threat does not emanate from any other power. From the universal historical viewpoint, matters of conflict in the west, over Belgium, will appear like trifles as compared to developments in the east which will truly constitute decisions of world-wide importance.[86]

German relations with Poland revolved essentially around the question of Russia. In an article published in December 1915 in the *Frankfurter Zeitung* under the heading: "Bismarck's Foreign Policy and the Present," Weber concerned himself with the Triple Alliance and the

Western Powers; the second part appeared under the title "The Triple Alliance and Russia." In the latter Weber stated that the Polish problem was one of Bismarck's chief points of reference inasmuch as it controlled his eastern foreign policy almost entirely; it likewise shaped his internal policy with regard to the *Kulturkampf*. Elsewhere, Weber's fear of Russia is clearly evident:

. . . . While England is in the position to menace our trade and colonial possessions, while France might constitute a threat to the continental integrity of our soil, Russia is the only power which, should she be victorious, is capable of threatening the political independence of both Poland and Germany completely; in the future this situation is very likely to become acute.[87]

This attitude of Weber's did not spring from mere emotional antagonism:

Now only the future can tell us the further developments of Russian politics. Her imperialist ambitions and her intelligentsia's zeal to extend its blessings to foreign nations was and will remain a crying contrast to the tasks of culture (*Kulturaufgaben*) as yet unsolved in our country. . . .

Nobody who has studied the qualities inherent in the Russian nation will have reason to doubt that she will have a great future. But at present there are no paths leading in that direction. The Russian intelligentsia has tossed her old ideals overboard. Should the hatred of Germans, which existed already before the war, increase unchecked, as it has done during the war, beyond it—and this is, to judge from their attitude not impossible,—then we shall be compelled to draw the simple, practical consequences: we shall then try to really earn their hatred at least in contrast to our thus far apparently useless indifference.[88]

Bismarck's politics pre-supposed, if not in his words, nevertheless, in his actions, the ideals of the German national state. His policy concerning the Poles was an expression of this. . . . All culture today is and will remain absolutely nationality-bound, and this all the more, the more 'democratic' an appearance the external means of the spreading of culture takes on. But the state need not necessarily be a 'national state' in the sense that it seeks to direct its interest exclusively toward the interest of the one dominant nationality in it. It might well serve the cultural interest of several nationalities, this also in its own well-understood interest of the pre-dominant nationality. . . .[89]

Two points are germane here. First, according to Weber, Germany and Poland have common aims with reference to protection from Russian aggression. They must, as a result, recognize this as a fact by becoming allies. Secondly, Germany would not have to impose her cultural peculiarities or her language upon Poland just because she, Germany, was the more powerful. Marianne Weber related Weber's utter consternation when he learned of the clumsy methods which the German authorities employed in their relations with Poland and which threatened the rapprochement he sought.[90]

From this time until the end of the war, Weber's correspondence and journalistic writing concentrated on examining the roots of dissidence among Germany's top leaders. While acknowledging the increasingly coercive nature of the radical war demands which were undermining Bethmann-Hollweg's position, he realized the chancellor's setbacks at the foreign policy level were serious enough to warrant his removal. The chancellor had failed in his peace negotiations with Russia and in his dealings with Austria regarding the disposition of Poland. While Weber began to view him as a political liability, he took a dim view of the alternatives. In the event of Bethmann-Hollweg's departure, Hindenburg would be the only man in a sufficiently strong position to achieve national unity, although Weber complained that he too failed to measure up to the qualifications necessary for a statesman.[91]

Weber's impatience with the chancellor's inability to effectively silence his critics who in the fall of 1916 demanded increased submarine warfare is illustrated by his conclusion that if the chancellor could not enforce measures he considered appropriate to the situation he ought to resign.[92] Upon further reflection concerning a successor, he dissented from Professor von Schulze-Graevenitz' choice of Buelow. In his judgment, the latter did not enjoy sufficient confidence abroad. Hence, assuming that the war situation might not improve, and given the devisiveness at home, a peace which the entire nation would accept could be achieved only by Hindenburg. However, he would require the assistance of diplomatically trained advisers. Also, the latter's views appeared to Weber as rather changeable.[93]

Conversely, Weber soon realized that for a restive population split between those who wanted all-out victory and the Left, Hindenburg would hardly be the proper choice since he himself was in the radical annexationist camp. This led Weber to conclude that, if only by default, no matter how inadequate Bethmann-Hollweg might be, he would have to continue supporting him in his stand against the vindictive Right. After all, from the vantage point of Germany's image abroad, a less chauvinistic foreign policy seemed preferable to the intractability of the rightist forces. However, when Bethmann-Hollweg's peace offer in December 1916 met with no effective response from the Allies, Weber was forced to reconsider. The dismal situation resulting from the deterioration of the Western front and the fact of Rumania being added to enemy strength apparently gave substance to the argument by the powerful cliques and lobbies that without submarine warfare, Germany's military situation would remain critical. In a letter to Friedrich Naumann,[94] Weber criticized the lack of political imagination marking the diplomatic note Germany sent to the American government announcing the contemplated submarine warfare. Germany could have avoided antagonizing America unnecessarily if only she had chosen to provide adequate assurance that the new measure would be dropped as soon as a way to peace negotiations on the basis of equality could be found. Without such a clause, the German note was apt to complicate Wilson's stand, whereas it would have been a small price for Germany to pay. The very idea of America's potential entry into the war appalled Weber.

Soon, however, Weber moved against the prevailing tide of his own fatalism. Thus he wrote:

The hatred of the world against us is better than the cool contempt hitherto which will not return. . . . I am suffering less now than I did in all the 25 years during which I witnessed the hysterical vanity of this monarch spoiling everything that was sacred and precious to me. That which was previously faulted by human stupidity has now become 'fate.' And with fate one can manage to cope. It will still be worthwhile later too to be a German and nothing else, even if we should fare badly—which by the way, is rather questionable. The worst of it is the prolongation of the war, which is a probable consequence. But it has to be mastered, externally and therefore internally.[95]

Weber now hoped for an unprecedented effort to overcome the deadlock, especially since "England did not want peace by any means." [96] Hoping also that rational thought would now become a springboard for action, Weber continued to back Bethmann-Hollweg. He proceeded to censure sharply the intrigues engaged in by flag-waving rightists to displace Bethmann-Hollweg. (He recollected how traditionally Prussian ministers have been deposed by precisely such methods.) Erzberger (of the Center party) first met Stresemann (of the National Liberal party). Subsequently, another meeting was planned between Ludendorff, Erzberger, and Stresemann. Ludendorff together with Hindenburg requested an audience with the Kaiser, whose reaction to their agitation for Bethmann-Hollweg's enforced resignation was negative. Thus the meeting of Ludendorff with the deputies had to be cancelled. It has been suggested that Erzberger's interest in seeing the chancellorship go to Buelow was in all probability only 'tactical'. He hoped for a fair bargain; its substance was to be "Liberal support of the Peace Resolution, in return for Zentrum support in felling Bethmann." [97]

Stresemann's motivation for wanting to liquidate Bethmann-Hollweg was based upon his opposition to the chancellor's moderate stand on annexation and his lack of cooperation with the military establishment. The latter and Stresemann preferred Buelow because it was thought he would show more willingness to establish a working relationship between himself, the High Command and the annexationists. Erzberger also wanted to see Buelow replace Bethmann-Hollweg, but for opposite reasons, namely to oppose the aspirations of the annexationists more effectively and above all because he wanted National Liberal support for the Peace Resolution. As a target for elimination, the chancellor was primarily serving as a means to an end for Erzberger.[98]

Weber strongly disapproved of both Stresemann's and Erzberger's roles and insisted all the more upon the urgency of reforms of the franchise because otherwise, as he said, it escaped his imagination how the chancellor could conceive of political and economic reforms after the war considering that the Prussian parliament would then consist of those very people who profited from the war, with ministers occupying their posts by catering to such a parliament.[99] Weber was also upset about Stresemann's leading role in the agitation against the chancellor. Actually, in view of Stresemann's increasingly influential position in the National Liberal party, the party had:

become more favorable to parliamentary government and Prussian franchise reform than it had been before the war. Stresemann's primary desire was to eliminate Bethmann-Hollweg, whom he disliked as a weak and irresolute character. His candidate for the succession was also Prince Buelow, for whom he retained an inordinate admiration. . . . Erzberger knew of this common ground. He apparently wanted to utilize it in order to induce the National Liberals to support the Peace Resolution.[100]

Bethmann did not prove Weber wrong in his hope that he might yet achieve favorable action in behalf of democratization of the right of franchise for Prussia. He had procured the Crown Council's consent. His stand, furthermore, was upheld by the Kaiser when the latter rejected his offer of resignation on July 11. However:

On July 12 Ludendorff sent his ultimatum to the Emperor that Bethmann must go or else he would resign his post in the Supreme Command . . . Bethmann was not the man to fight for his position and the existing constitutional order against Ludendorff's arrogance. . . . He resigned as he had ruled, revealing impotence and lack of political flair. Erzberger had made the Chancellor's position difficult by creating the panic of July 6 and leading the Zentrum Party into opposition against Bethmann, but the primary responsibility for Bethmann's acquiescence in Ludendorff's ultimatum belongs to himself and cannot be blamed upon Erzberger.[101]

The Kaiser appointed as Bethmann's successor Georg Michaelis, which left the country encumbered with all the hazards to which an anachronistic and undemocratic franchise policy had subjected it since the foundation of the Reich. As Epstein notes, the Kaiser's choice illustrated even more than the military commander Ludendorff's ultimatum the farce of Imperial Germany's constitution:

Michaelis had played no previous political role. He had been a conscientious Prussian bureaucrat, who had won some public attention by a vigorous *Landtag* speech made in his role as wartime food administrator, in which he promised to crack down on chisellers. Ludendorff, who often thought firm language a substitute for wisdom, had been impressed and thought this an adequate qualification for the chancellorship. The Emperor had never met Michaelis personally prior to his selection.[102]

By 1917 relations between Germany and the United States had deteriorated to a point at which a declaration of war was imminent. Aware of his government's ineptitude through which all hopes of victory had miscarried, Weber devoted himself increasingly to the task of preparing the ground for inner reform. Thus he wrote:

Not a shot would I fire, not a penny war loan would I subscribe to, if this war were not a national war. If it were only for the preservation of our state structure, or for the sake of retaining this incapable dynasty and our unpolitical civil service, I would not support it. I do not give a hang (es ist mir voellig Wurst) about the form of state if only the politicians and not dilettante fools like William II would rule the country. . . . I see no other way than ruthless parliamentarization—*quand même*—to freeze these people out. The civil servants must be subordinated to Parliament. Altogether, without exception. They are technicians. . . . Forms of state are to me merely techniques like any other machinery. I would attack Parliament and defend the monarch if I were a politician or would promise to be one.[103]

In the summer of 1917, the *Frankfurter Zeitung* published a series of articles by Weber, which later appeared in pamphlet form under the title "Parliament and Government in the Reconstructed Germany." [104] Here he postulated that "one will hate or love the parliamentary system —however, one may not be able to remove it." [105] He hoped that the parliamentary struggle of one party against another would produce competent men endowed with powers of leadership. Essentially Weber sought to relate the political structure and the processes of power to the structure of German society in the Wilhelminian era. The parliamentary form of government provided a system in which the highest governmental positions could be filled by the leaders of parliament, instead of depending for appointment upon the whim of an incompetent monarch. However, Weber did not envisage true parliamentarianism, viewing it as an anachronism. For example, in a notable passage regarding parliamentary government, he mentions neither the role of the opposition as an alternative government, nor the part played by the rank and file of the majority party. Weber did not consider the leaders to be bound by their election mandate; instead, effective power should not be given to the people once the leaders are chosen: the electorate has had its say and must now defer to their leaders. In this context, consensus is achieved by the simple device of a politics of exclusion whereby the people may not engage in the political process until the new elections permit them to do so.

The numerous assembly in Parliament cannot rule or make a policy. No one claims that, not even the English. The whole mass of deputies functions merely as followers of the one, or several leaders who constitute the cabinet. They obey the leaders blindly as long as the latter are successful. That is as it should be.[106]

Meanwhile, with increasing economic complexity and rational administration, the bureaucratic apparatus had gained a tremendous influence:

This fundamental economic principle: the 'separation' of the worker from the means of production in the economic sphere from the means of waging war, from the means of administration in public service, from money in all spheres, from the means of research in the universities and laboratories—this is the common and valuable foundation of modern power—political and military state—and capitalistic enterprises. In both cases direction of power lies in the hands of that authority which the bureaucracy (judges, civil servants, officers, foremen, clerks, non-commissioned officers) either directly or indirectly obeys. It is the characteristic feature of all these institutions whose existence and functions, both in theory and practice, are inseparably bound up with this concentration of the means of production.[107]

Weber thus identified élitist politics with administrative reality everywhere.

For the purpose of forestalling any ruling clique, as had been the prevailing trend heretofore, Weber strove for a democratic selection of political leaders, accompanied by parliamentary control over the bureaucracy. He feared the trend within the parties, which were in his view legitimate organs of democratic control, toward bureaucratization. To this tendency he opposed his conception of charismatic leadership: wherever men gather in groups, a few people stand out because of their endowment, consisting of certain personal qualifications which induce one or more groups to accept them as leaders. The élite recognizes and also serves the aspirations and interests of the masses, and the nation.[108] This group is again divided into a "chief" (*Leiter*) in whom is vested the highest authority, and into the "administrative staff." These features obtain fundamentally in all groups, although Weber allowed for departures in exceptional circumstances. The most important exception pertained to the replacement of one individual as chief by a "collegial" body. In this case, "although there is an actually monocratic *primus inter pares*, his acts are normally subject to consultation with formally equal members, and disagreement in important matters may lead to breaking up the collegial body by resignation, thus endangering the position of the monocratic chief." [109]

The state "possesses an administrative and legal order subject to change by legislation, to which the organized corporate activity of the administrative staff, which is also regulated by legislation, is orientated." [110] Thus the ruling group must be legitimate. Weber held "legitimacy may be ascribed to an order by those acting subject to it in the following ways:

(a) By tradition; a belief in the legitimacy of what has always existed; (b) by virtue of the affectual attitudes, especially emotional, legitimizing the validity of what is newly revealed or a model to imitate; (c) by virtue of a rational belief in its absolute value (wertrational), thus lending it the validity of an absolute and final commitment; (d) because it has been established in a manner which is recognized to be *legal*. This legality may be treated as legitimate in either of two ways: on the one hand, it may derive from a voluntary agreement of the interested parties on the relevant terms. On the other hand, it may be imposed on the basis of what is held to be a legitimate authority over the relevant persons and a corresponding claim to their obedience. [111]

Weber notes emphatically that "the basis of every system of authority, and correspondingly of every kind of willingness to obey, is a belief . . . by virtue of which persons exercising authority are lent prestige." [112] His classification of the types of legitimacy became the basis for Weber's notable investigation of the nature of authority in contemporary civilization. He named three types of legitimate authority: rational-legal authority, traditional authority, and charismatic authority.

The first is said to rest on "a belief in the legality patterns of normative rules and the right of those elevated to authority under such rules to issue commands." [113]

Traditional authority is derived from "an established belief in the sanctity of immemorial traditions and the legitimacy of the status of those exercising authority under them." [114]

The third category, charismatic authority, rests "on devotion to the specific and exceptional sanctity, heroism or exemplary character of an individual person and of the normative patterns or order revealed or ordained by him." [115] Charisma (literally: gift of grace) in modern times, in order that it may become a permanent structure, would have to assimilate itself to modern institutions. All types of authority require an administrative staff characterized by efficiency and continuity:

There are two typical forms of charismatic provision with means-gifts and booty, that is, resources acquired by coercive methods, whether by force or not. But, once the position of authority becomes established, these must be transformed into regular sources of income which takes the form of acquiring segregated property granting benefices in the traditional form. According to circumstances, the authority structure of the charismatic movement may change in either a traditional or a rational-legal direction.[116]

As Weber makes obvious in *Politics as a Vocation,* the "chief" was not meant to change the course of world history alone; his "free will" depends upon the realm of objective possibilities. In Weber's own historical writings the "great man" was not granted an exclusive role in the moulding of social organization and ideas of modern civilization.[117] Observing that charisma may be reinterpreted in an anti-authoritarian direction, Weber pointed to the use of the plebiscite as a means of legitimizing leadership on a democratic basis. The "charismatic" leader may be said to reign in a democracy by virtue of the people's vote of confidence. His mandate would last as long as did their confidence.[118]

Weber saw that the demagogic party leader who might not allow other leaders to coexist with him, might turn dictatorial, in which case the plebiscite might be affected. He named both Napoleons as classic examples, even though legitimation by plebiscite had been carried out after seizure of power by force.[119]

On November 3, 1918, the sailors at Kiel mutinied. On November 4, Max Weber gave a political address in Munich on the subject of Germany's political reconstruction. He warned against separatist attempts to break away from Prussia as well as against the contemplated revolution:

> Revolution does not bring about peace. Bolshevism is a military dictatorship like any other and will collapse like any other. It is out of the question that the bourgeois society will be transformed into the socialist state of the future by means of a revolution. Its consequence would be occupation by the enemy and subsequent reactionary rule.[120]

Communists, including the Russian Bolshevist, M. Legien, interrupted Weber's speech with Communist slogans. For the first time, his widow reports, the masses appeared openly hostile toward him and he was unable to master the situation.[121] Almost immediately thereafter, Bavaria was declared a Free State, and a government of workers' and soldiers' councils in the Russian pattern was established. Weber now turned to the immediate problem of replacing the Kaiser's rule with new forms of political leadership and economic organization. His policies were characterized by a reluctant acceptance of a modified parliamentarianism and limited state control of Germany's capitalistic economic system. In both arenas, *Realpolitik* was to provide the guiding hand.

In October 1918, Weber, who had long been disgusted with the Hohenzollern dynasty, had defined his position as follows:

Just because I am a sincere believer in monarchical—though parliamentarily limited—institutions and in the Germany dynasty in particular, I feel that the present Kaiser must abdicate in the interest of the realm and dynasty. He can do this in a dignified manner by declaring that he thereby assumes to have acted according to what is right, thus following the command of his conscience as he perceived it to be his duty; fate had been against him and consequently he did not want to be a stumbling block to the new future of his people.[122]

In a letter to Friedrich Naumann, written the following day, Weber became even more intense.

Is there not one believer in monarchical institutions who is in a position to enlighten the monarch on what the hour requires of him? . . . I wish and demand from him an end of his regime; he should end it in a manner worthy of the dignity of a Kaiser in the interest of the nation, the dynasty, and history. . . .[123]

Weber showed signs of exasperation when the Kaiser failed to realize what the need of the hour demanded of him, namely his abdication. Instead, the latter came as if an afterthought on the very day the German Republic was proclaimed. The so-called revolution was characterized by Weber as "only a kind of narcotic for the people before the great misery sets." [124]

Weber publicly decried all the formulas and cliché's devised to rationalize the situation during the national emergency. These recitations and explanations had done nothing to answer the urgent problems of the day, much less to ease Weber's own persistent skepticism. Moreover, the conduct of "political masochists" who sought to unearth all sorts of evidence of Germany's war guilt in the hope of currying favor with the enemy, constituted, in his judgment, a divisive challenge to the national political purpose.[125] Here he reiterated his frequently voiced contempt for those who seemed to be "wallowing" in feelings of war guilt, "as if the outcome of a war were God's verdict . . ." whereas "the God of battles is with the more numerous battalions." [126] Yet if Germany had won the war, Weber would probably have seen the victory as a confirmation of Germany's historic mission.

Meanwhile, Weber evinced no confidence in a socialist future for Germany:

I agree with you that the free economic system we have had up to now probably (though in my estimation nothing can be said yet for certain) will not re-establish itself, except in a considerably modified form for reasons of currency and finance: not for any other reasons. I am not going to shed any tears if this should happen. But I—regard the plans for a "planned economy" as dilettante, objectively speaking, as totally irresponsible frivolity

which may discredit "socialism" for a hundred years and which may also
cast everything that might be possible now, into the abyss of a stupid reaction.
This reaction will unfortunately come and it is at this point that we differ.[127]

Two points are of interest here. Weber again takes his stand on
Realpolitik, when he points out that the "free economic system" will be
modified, "for reasons of currency and finance; not for any other
reasons." Here he had in mind the need for long-term credits from
abroad, and especially from the United States, for Germany's rehabilitation. "Nobody should deceive himself that foreign economic domination
can be avoided; a purely proletarian regime, even the best, will not
obtain credits from abroad." [128]

In a later chapter dealing in more detail with his attitude toward a
planned economy he characterizes such a system as "a totally irresponsible frivolity which may discredit 'socialism' for a hundred years." From
this it must not be deduced that Weber was really a friend of socialism
anxious to save it from present blunders so that its future success might
be assured. On the contrary, he was concerned lest the victory of the
planners endanger the foreign credits which Germany urgently needed.

Weber also believed that one of the main tasks of democracy consisted in silencing the titans of heavy industry politically.[129] However, he
believed that economically they were indispensable. He was playing
with fire when he recommended:

One has to use them in the proper places. One has to offer them the
unavoidable premium of profit, but one must not let them get the upper
hand. Only in that manner is progress in the direction of socialization possible.
Every educated socialist knows this; if he denies it, he is but a swindler.[130]

In the postwar period, Germany would have to relinquish all imperialistic dreams for some time and become a peaceful member of the
League of Nations. If she were deprived of any territory besides the
Alsace in either the east or the west or, if the victors should require in-
demnity payments beyond the compensation to Belgium, then

. . . the epoch of pacifism caused by fatigue will be followed by one in which
every one down to the last worker . . . will turn Chauvinist. Hatred among
nations will assume permanent characteristics and the German irredentist
movement will flame up using all the customary revolutionary means of self-
determination. Against foreign domination even the means of the Spartakists
are justified, and Germany's university students would have a task before
them. The League of Nations would be dead internally, no "guarantees" could
change that. English policy would have created a deadly enemy and President
Wilson would not be the universal peace-maker but the originator of an
increasing struggle.[131]

While Weber was opposed to the revolution, he was equally hostile toward the supporters of the old regime who blamed the revolution for having brought about national misfortune. The invention of the "stab in the back" legend infuriated him, especially when it was employed by his colleagues.[132] Marianne Weber reports that for decades Weber had been in sympathy with the aspirations of the proletariat for security and human dignity. He had even considered joining the socialist ranks as a party member. Still his own reasoning forced him to conclude,

... that one could only be an honest socialist as one could only be an honest Christian, if one were ready to share the way of life of the unpropertied, and, in any case, only if one were ready to forego a cultured existence, which he owed to their work. Since his illness this was impossible for Weber as his scholarship depended upon capital rent. Furthermore, in the essence of his being, he remained an individualist.[133]

Yet Max Weber's political philosophy did not always stress idealistic concern for civil or individual liberties. The concept of liberty, it appears was not always consonant with American or British connotations of democracy. However, he championed freedom in the academic sphere, attacking the Prussian system which supported religious and political discrimination in university appointments; he did so not only privately, but he made his views public in the *Frankfurter Zeitung*. Considering conditions in Germany, such an attitude spoke well for Weber's courage. He opposed anti-Semitism in German universities; he himself helped several Jewish scholars secure academic appointments. For instance, he sought to make his influence felt on behalf of his friend Georg Simmel. In his fight against bigotry he also tried to help Roberto Michels, whose appointment was resisted on the ground that his children were not baptized and because of his political beliefs which at that time were liberal, though he later became an apologist for fascism.[134]

As Meinecke correctly points out, it would be a grave mistake to assume that Weber had wanted to play the domestic Shylock by wishing to cash in on the demands of democracy in time of stress.[135] For that Weber was filled with too much anxiety for the future of Germany:

The protection of social and material privileges and interests handed down from the historical legitimacy of a monarch ruling 'by the grace of God' has ceased to exist. Thus the bourgeoisie has to depend upon its own strength and achievements as the laboring classes have long been compelled to do. . . . Certainly it is ominous for the development of national self-respect that democracy has not come to us after a successful struggle, as it did in Holland, England, America, and France, or, as we had hoped, in conjunction with an honorable peace;[136] instead it came upon the heels of defeat. The shameful bankruptcy of the old regime is an additional burden which contributes to lessen the prospects of political success. There will not be cheerful days in store for the nation in the immediate future. The Republic contains some seeds of hope; we will not know if they will all be fulfilled. The Republic must remain what it is now for all too many: a narcotic which serves as a measure of intoxication over against the terrible pressure of the collapse. Otherwise, all will soon be finished.[137]

Weber maintained that the German nation and its future position in the world towered sky-high above questions regarding forms of government.[138] In 1918, in an article published in the *Frankfurter Zeitung* on the subject of "The Domestic Situation and Foreign Policy," he wrote: "Only he who is capable of adapting domestic policy to foreign policy tasks can be called a politician in the national sense." [139]

As Otto Koellreutter correctly states:

To him the state is in the last alternative nothing but an "enterprise" (*Betrieb*) which like any other business concern, like every factory, for example, has to be managed by rational methods of organization. . . . The state thus becomes quite consciously . . . an object subservient to private politics made by individuals—an inescapable consequence resulting from Max Weber's position; this theory has proved to be correct in the experience of modern parliaments as a result of the disintegration of officialdom. From a purely economic interpretation Weber arrives at his conclusion and denies that the civil service has any capacity for political leadership. . . .[140]

Weber apparently nowhere made any attempt to try to rehabilitate the civil service which had been on the path to destruction ever since Bismarck's reign, owing to the latter's policies. Democratic thinking was entirely foreign to Weber, says Koellreutter, due to the fact that forms of government were but techniques to him, though at that particular moment the parliamentary form was advocated by him since it seemed to be the only conceivable and expedient alternative for the present. This "rational attitude," it seems, misled Weber insofar as he ignored certain historical conditions by comparing the entirely different tradition of the Anglo-Saxon political structure and that of the British Civil Service with German officialdom, from which almost all statesmen had been recruited, thus utilizing it as a political reserve.[141]

As seen earlier, Weber considered the reform of the Prussian franchise essential to strengthen the unity of the nation and to sustain its will to resist the enemy. For the same reason he advocated the parliamentary form of government, which moreover appeared to constitute the only means by which an incapable ruler could be removed. As Meinecke remarked, there is nothing particularly unique in Weber's design. What is significant, and perhaps symptomatic of later and increased utilitarian political reasoning, is the fact that

. . . the former simplicity in the relationship between *Weltanschauung* and political ideals has become dissolved. For the element of coercion inherent in expediency has ever more asserted itself in political action. . . . One can, for instance, decide upon democracy today without feeling the slightest inclination toward this form of government. One places one's actual wants determined by disposition and ideals into the background in the process of it, and decides for what is rational, that is, for that which seems to be the most expedient for the whole. This kind of thought and action is genuinely modern: however, any exaggerated rationalization of action reduces ideal values to a soulless substance.[142]

Meinecke thus deplored Weber's conceptualization of the state as a mechanical entity, forsaking nineteenth-century thought which regarded the state as a living moral being, whether from the legal, the romantic, or the historical point of view. Meinecke refers here to Weber's conception of the state, not the *Machtstaat*. He is correct when he says Weber reduced the state to a "machine-like entity," and such an enterprise cannot at the same time be a moral being. Weber considers that in the interest of efficiency all associations within the state must be subordinate: "The modern state is a compulsory association which organizes domination." [143] The *Machtstaat*, however, is characterized by an ideological function; in the case of Germany, the *Machtstaat* had the mission, according to Weber, of disseminating German *Kultur*. We in our generation have seen the *Machtstaat* spreading *Kultur* and have revolted against it, though in fairness to Weber it must be admitted that its bizarre manifestations would not have met with his approval.

In November 1918 Weber had diagnosed the potentialities of his countrymen as follows:

I am only glad about the humble matter-of-factness of the simple trade-union people, and also, that of many soldiers in the local "workers'—and soldiers' soviet" to which I am assigned. Without making a fuss about it, they have done a fine job; that is certain. The nation as a whole is one of *discipline*. But when that totters, well, then everything inmost in these people will also collapse.[144]

Perhaps less dangerous than the habit of discipline mentioned in this observation is the praise which Weber accorded it. He seemed to assume that the trade unions and the other voluntary associations had performed their task well but now they were no longer needed. He did not recognize that the German trade unions still had a vital task ahead of them, which, in fact, they did fulfill until 1933. He says:

The nation as such is capable of discipline. . . . The crucial problem is whether the mad Liebknecht gang can be put down. They will go through with their *Putsch*, that cannot be avoided. It will be of the utmost importance to counter it immediately and not to stage a wild reactionary game; rather we should conduct *"sachliche Politik"* (pertinent politics). All we can do is hope that this course can be taken—we cannot predict what will happen. If it should come to the worst, then we must let the Americans restore order, whether we want to or not. I hope we will be spared the shame of having the enemy direct our affairs.[145]

Acknowledging the shift in power politics, the scales having tipped in favor of the Anglo-Saxons, Weber and a number of his compatriots believed that Germany might yet come out on top as long as Russia could be kept down:

We will start from scratch once again as after 1648 and 1807. That is a simple fact. Only that today one lives and works more quickly and with more initiative. Not we but the next generation will see the beginning of a new rise. Naturally the self-discipline of sincerity forces us to admit: Germany's role in world politics is finished; the Anglo-Saxon domination is a fact —"ah, c'est nous qui l'avons faite" as Thiers said to Bismarck referring to our unification. This is very unpleasant; however, we have warded off much worse a fate: the Russian knout. This is our triumph.

America's world domination was as unavoidable as that of Rome after the Punic War. It is to be hoped that it will not be shared by Russia. This, to my mind, must be the aim of our future world policy, for the Russian danger is only banished for the present, not forever. For the moment the hysterical and disgusting hatred of the French is the main danger. . . .[146]

Weber's views here are somewhat similar to those of Nietzsche in *Beyond Good and Evil.* Both feared the territorial and cultural hegemony which they believed Russia would inevitably press for in the near future. Both agreed that the Russian menace would threaten the very existence of the cultural values and standards of Central and Western Europe. As Weber had pointed out, American world domination seemed inevitable, and though he did not think this desirable, he preferred it to that of Russia. In his view the former did not imply the same threat to European civilization, essentially because Americans had a greater degree of affinity with Europe as a result of their historical background and because of personal ties between Europeans and Americans. Both Nietzsche and Weber thought the Germans lacked a will to power; but to Weber this meant the will to increase and spread German culture by means of the *Machtstaat.* Nietzsche on the other hand regarded this condition, which he called the "disease of paralysis of will," as a *European* rather than a specifically German disease. He held that "it is worst and most varied where civilization has prevailed longest. . . ."[147] The two thus interpreted the phrase "will to power" differently: while Weber identified the absence of the "will to power" with the lack of political awareness characterizing the German people—that is, the will to bring

about the fulfillment of Germany's historic mission—Nietzsche's frame
of reference was Europe. He wanted to see Europe unified:

> . . . *to acquire one will*, by means of a new caste to rule over the continent,
> a persistent, dreadful will of its own, that can set its aims thousands of years
> ahead; so that the long spun-out comedy of its petty-statism, and its dynastic
> as well as its democratic many-willed-ness, might finally be brought to a close.
> The time for petty politics is past; the next century will bring the struggle
> for the dominion of the world—the *compulsion* to great politics.[148]

The last sentence of the above statement has a prophetic ring. On
this point Weber and Nietzsche would perhaps have found themselves
in agreement.

NOTES

[1] Cf. Letter to Marianne Weber, May 1915, *Lebensbild*, p. 562.
[2] Wolfgang J. Mommsen, *Max Weber und Die Deutsche Politik 1890–1920* (Tuebingen: J. C. B. Mohr [Paul Siebeck], 1959), p. 170.
[3] Fritz Ernst, *The Germans and Their Modern History* (New York: Columbia
University Press, 1966), p. 32.
[4] Klaus Epstein, "Gerhard Ritter and the First World War," in Walter Laqueur
and George L. Mosse, eds., *1914: The Coming of the First World War, Journal of
Contemporary History: 3* (New York: Harper and Row, 1966), p. 192. Cf.
also Gerhard Ritter, *Staatskunst und Kriegshandwerk: Das Problem des Mili-
tarismus in Deutschland*, Vol. iii. *Die Tragoedie der Staatskunst: Bethmann
Hollweg als Kriegskanzler (1914–17)* (Munich: Oldenburg Verlag, 1964).
[5] Imanuel Geiss, "The Outbreak of the First World War and German War Aims:
The Crisis of July 1914" in *ibid.*, p. 86.
[6] *Ibid.*, p. 87.
[7] Ludwig Dehio, *Germany and World Politics in the Twentieth Century* (New York:
Alfred A. Knopf, 1965), pp. 19–20.
[8] Fritz Ernst, *op. cit.*, p. 33.
[9] *Lebensbild*, p. 530.
[10] *Ibid.*, pp. 532–33.
[11] *Ibid.*, p. 534.
[12] *P.S.*, 1st. ed., p. 459, cited in Fritz Ernst, *op. cit.*, p. 33.
[13] *P.S.*, 1st. ed., p. 458.
[14] *Ibid.*
[15] *Ibid.*, pp. 458–59.
[16] This newspaper probably displayed more civic courage than any of its competitors. The exact date is missing (End of 1915).
[17] *P.S.*, 1st. ed., p. 459.
[18] *Lebensbild*, p. 544, cited in Fritz Ernst, *op. cit.*, p. 33.
[19] Hans. W. Gatzke, *Germany's Drive to the West (Drang nach Westen): A Study
of Germany's Western War Aims during the First World War* (Baltimore:
The Johns Hopkins Press, 1950), p. 47. Reprinted by permission of The Johns
Hopkins Press.
[20] *Ibid.*
[21] *Ibid.*, p. 50.
[22] Maximilian Harden, *Die Zukunft*, August 22, 1914, p. 251; August 29, 1914, p.
291; September 19, 1914, p. 379, October 17, 1914, p. 96; May 1, 1915 cited
in *ibid.*, p. 50.

23 *Ibid.*, Gatzke, *op. cit.*, p. 51.
24 *Ibid.*, p. 52.
25 *Ibid.*, p. 54.
26 *Ibid.*
27 *Ibid.*
28 John R. Staude, *Max Scheler: 1874–1928: An Intellectual Portrait* (New York: The Free Press, 1967), pp. 79–80. Even Theodor Wolff, ed., the liberal *Berliner Tageblatt*, manifested annexationist leanings (*Berliner Tageblatt*, August 10, 1914 cited in Gatzke, *op. cit.*, p. 57).
29 H. Delbrueck, "Der zukuenftige Friede," *Preussische Jahrbuecher*, Vol. 158, 1914, p. 191, cited in Gatzke, *op. cit.*, p. 58.
30 *Ibid.*
31 *Ibid.*
32 *Deutsche Tageszeitung*, April 5, 1916 cited in Gatzke, *op. cit.*, p. 135.
33 Nationalversammlung, *Das Werk des Untersuchungsausschusses*, "Die Ursachen des Deutschen Zusammenbruchs im Jahre 1918" (Berlin, 1925–29), U.A., 4, Reihe, XII (1) 51–52, notes 1 & 2 cited in Gatzke, *op. cit.*, p. 135.
34 Erich Eyck, *A History of the Weimar Republic* (Cambridge, Mass.: Harvard University Press, 1962), p. 1, and Bernard Schwertfeger, ed., *Rudolf von Valentini: Kaiser und Kabinettschef* (Oldenburg, 1941), p. 226 cited in Eyck, *op. cit.*, p. 1.
35 Fritz Fischer, *Griff nach der Weltmacht, Die Kriegszielpolitik des Kaiserlichen Deutschland* (Duesseldorf: Droste Verlag, 1961), published in the United States under the title *Germany's Aims in the First World War* (New York: W. W. Norton, 1967).
36 Hajo Holborn, "Introduction," to Fritz Fischer, *op. cit.*, p. XI.
37 *Ibid.*
38 Fritz Fischer, *op. cit.*, p. 99.
39 Golo Mann, *The History of Germany Since 1789* (New York: Frederick A. Praeger, 1968), p. 262.
40 Fritz Fischer, *Germany's Aims in the First World War* (New York: W. W. Norton & Company, 1967), pp. 104–105.
41 *Ibid.*
42 *Ibid.*
43 *Ibid.*, p. 105.
44 Cf. *ibid.*, p. 104.
45 *Ibid.*, p. 105.
46 Wolfgang J. Mommsen, "The Debate on German War Aims," in Walter Laqueur and George L. Mosse, *op. cit.*, p. 46.
47 Golo Mann, *The History of Germany Since 1789*, *op. cit.*, pp. 308–309.
48 Leonard Krieger and Fritz Stern, eds. *The Responsibility of Power* (New York: Doubleday, 1968), p. 271. Cf. also Fritz Stern, *Bethmann-Hollweg und der Krieg: Die Grenzen ver Verantwortung*, in *Recht und Staat in Geschichte und Gegenwart* (Tuebingen: J. C. B. Mohr [Paul Siebeck], 1968).
49 Krieger and Stern, *op. cit.*, p. 307.
50 Cf. Max Weber, "Parliament and Government in Germany" in *Economy and Society: An Outline of Interpretive Sociology* (Vol. 3, edited by Guenther Roth and Claus Wittich (New York: Bedminster Press, 1968), p. 1436.
51 Cf. *ibid.*, p. 1451.
52 Kurt Rietzler, *Tagebuch*, entry of March 4, 1916, in Fritz Stern, *Bethmann-Hollweg und der Krieg: Die Grenzen der Verantwortung*, *op. cit.*, p. 16.
53 Fritz Stern, *Bethmann-Hollweg und der Krieg: Die Grenzen der Verantwortung*, *op. cit.*, p. 17.
54 J. A. Schumpeter, *History of Economic Analysis*, ed. by E. B. Schumpeter (New York: Oxford University Press, 1954), p. 326.
55 Cf. Theobald von Bethmann-Hollweg, *Betrachtungen zum Weltkriege*, I (Berlin, 1919), p. 98, cited in Fritz Stern, *Bethmann-Hollweg und der Krieg: Die Grenzen der Verantwortung*, p. 10.
56 *Ibid.*, p. 10.
57 *Ibid.*, p. 11.
58 *Ibid.*, cf. also Hans-Ulrich Wehler, *Der Fall Zabern. Rueckblick auf eine Verfassungskrise des Wilhelminischen Kaiserreichs*, in *Die Welt als Geschichte*, XXIII, 1963, p. 27–46, cited in *ibid.*
59 Cf. Max Weber, "Parliament and Government in Germany" in *Economy and Society: An Outline of Interpretive Sociology*, *op. cit.*, p. 1437.
60 Cf. *ibid.*, p. 1403.

61 Cf. Fritz Stern, *op. cit.*, p. 17.
62 Max Weber, "Parliament and Government in Germany" in *Economy and Society: An Outline of Interpretive Sociology, op. cit.*, pp. 1403.
63 *Ibid.*, p. 1404.
64 *Ibid.*, p. 1404.
65 *Ibid.*, pp. 1404–1405.
66 Fritz Stern, *op. cit.*, p. 15.
67 Cf. *Lebensbild*, pp. 576–577.
68 *Ibid.*, p. 563.
69 *Ibid.*, p. 564.
70 *Ibid.*, pp. 566–577.
71 *Ibid.*, p. 571.
72 Karl von Wiegland, *Frankfurter Zeitung*, November 14, 1926, cited in Erich Eyck, *op. cit.*, pp. 7–8.
73 Bernhard Schwertfeger, ed., *Rudolf von Valentini: Kaiser und Kabinettschef* (Oldenburg, 1941), p. 245.
74 Theobald von Bethmann-Hollweg, *Betrachtungen zum Welkrieg*, 2 Vols. (Berlin, 1919–1921), II, 128, cited in Eyck, *op. cit.*, Vol. I, p. 8.
75 *Ibid.*, Vol. I, pp. 7–8.
76 *Lebensbild*, pp. 575–576.
77 Germany, Official Documents. *Untersuchungausschuss ueber die Weltkriegsverantwortlichkeit. Zweiter Unterausschuss des Untersuchungausschusses der Nationalversammlung* (Berlin, 1920). Enclosure 3, p. 186. English translation: *Official German Documents Relating to the World War: The Reports of the First and Second Subcommittees of the Committee Appointed by the National Constituent Assembly To Inquire into the Responsibility for the War, together with the Stenographic Minutes of the Second Subcommittee and Supplements Thereto*, 2 Vols. (New York-London, 1923). Cited in Erich Eyck, *op. cit.*, Vol. I, p. 8.
78 Cf. A. von Tirpitz, *Politische Dokumente* (Hamburg, 1926), Vol. II, pp. 58–59, 65, 144–145, 179.
79 Cf. *P.S.*, 2nd. ed., p. 364.
80 *Lebensbild*, p. 563.
81 Klaus Epstein, *Matthias Erzberger and the Dilemma of German Democracy* (Princeton: Princeton University Press, 1959), p. 117. Reprinted by permission of the publisher.
82 Fritz Ernst, *op. cit.*, p. 34.
83 *P.S.*, 1st. ed., p. 74.
84 *Ibid.*, p. 75.
85 Ernst Nolte, "Germany" in Hans Rogger and Eugen Weber, eds., *The European Right: A Historical Profile* (Berkeley and Los Angeles: University of California Press, 1965), p. 294.
86 *P.S.*, 1st. ed., pp. 84–85.
87 *Ibid.*, p. 42.
88 *Ibid.*, pp. 44–45.
89 *Ibid.*, p. 47.
90 *Lebensbild*, pp. 566–567.
91 Cf. letter to Marianne Weber of August 22, 1916 cited in *ibid.*, and cf. *Lebensbild*, p. 584.
92 Cf. letter to Friedrich Naumann of September 18, 1916, *P.S.*, 1st. ed., p. 465f.
93 Letter to the editors of the *Frankfurter Zeitung* of August 20, 1916, *ibid.*, p. 463.
94 Letter to Friedrich Naumann of February 3, 1917, *ibid.*, p. 466.
95 Letter to Karl Loewenstein of February 10, 1917, *ibid.*, pp. 467–468.
96 *Ibid.*, p. 467.
97 Klaus Epstein, *op. cit.*, pp. 194–195.
98 *Ibid.*, pp. 196–197.
99 Cf. *P.S.*, 2nd. ed., p. 189.
100 Klaus Epstein, *op. cit.*, p. 197.
101 *Ibid.*, pp. 199–200.
102 *Ibid.*, p. 201.
103 *P.S.*, 1st. ed., letter to Ehrenberg, pp. 469–470.
104 *Ibid.*, "Parlament und Regierung im neugeordneten Deutschland," pp. 126–260.
105 *Ibid.*, p. 159.
106 *Ibid.*, p. 167.
107 *Ibid.*, p. 167.
108 Here Weber furnishes us with the clue to his belief in the efficiency and bene-

ficence of charismatic leaders, but he fails to substantiate any reason for his belief that these leaders always know what is good for the masses. "As Weber treats charisma in the context of authority, its bearer is always an individual 'leader'. His charismatic quality has to be 'proved' by being recognized as genuine by his followers. This is not, however, as Weber is careful to point out, the ordinary case of leadership by 'consent' of the led, in the usual democratic meaning. The authority of the leader does not express the 'will' of the followers, but rather their duty or obligation. . . . And the leader does not compromise with his followers in a utilitarian sense. Recognition by them is interpreted as an expression of the moral legitimacy of his claim to authority." Talcott Parsons, *Essays in Sociological Theory Pure and Applied* (Glencoe, Illinois: The Free Press, 1949), p. 125.

109 Max Weber, *Wirtschaft und Gesellschaft*, partly translated and edited by A.M. Henderson, and Talcott Parsons, *The Theory of Social and Economic Organization by Max Weber* (New York: Oxford University Press), 1947, p. 393 (This is a translation of Part I of Wirtschaft und Gesellschaft, originally published as Vol. III of *Grundriss der Sozialoekonomie*).

110 T. Parsons, *The Theory of Social and Economic Organization by Max Weber* (New York: Oxford University Press, 1947), p. 156.

111 *Ibid.*, p. 130.

112 *Ibid.*, p. 382.

113 *Ibid.*, p. 328.

114 *Ibid.*

115 *Ibid.*

116 Talcott Parsons, "Max Weber's Sociological Analysis of Capitalism and Modern Institutions," *An Introduction to the History of Sociology*, ed. by Harry Elmer Barnes (Chicago: The University of Chicago Press), 1947, p. 306.

117 For a comparison of political leaders and followers, see James C. Davies, *Human Nature in Politics: the Dynamics of Political Behavior* (New York: John Wiley and Sons), 1963, pp. 274–330.

118 As has been pointed out, the people are in no position to interfere with the freedom of the leaders for whom they have voted. Weber's conclusion that the people, by voting for a certain man have to forego their right of participation in government until the next election, does not make for democracy. The leaders would under such a system arrogate to themselves a privileged position, for the electorate cannot know the qualities and contemplated actions of the leaders at the time of the election. So what looks like confidence is but deception. It is deception also because the leader is not personally known to the majority of the people and because much of what is attributed to the influence of the leader is in reality the influence of skillful emotional appeals such as impressive stage settings and martial music. But as Talcott Parsons points out, "there is ample empirical evidence of the susceptibility of our society to the type of movement which Weber describes, all the way from the prevalence of innumerable fads through the proliferation of many kinds of religious cults to the Communist and National Socialist movements themselves which are grand scale movements involving charismatic authority in the political field." Talcott Parsons, *Essays in Sociological Theory Pure and Applied* (Glencoe, Illinois: The Free Press), 1949, p. 132. Parsons quite rightly states that although Weber did not foresee the Nazi movement, he did realize that a movement of such a type might be the result of reaction against liberal institutions. See *ibid.*, p. 146.

119 *Wirtschaft und Gesellschaft* (Henderson and Parsons, *The Theory of Social and Economic Organization* by Max Weber), p. 387.

120 *Lebensbild*, p. 639.

121 *Ibid.*

122 *P.S.*, 1st. ed., letter to Professor Schulze-Gaevernitz, October 10, 1918, p. 477.

123 *Ibid.*, pp. 477–478 (Letter to Naumann).

124 *Ibid.*, letter to Helene Weber, November 18, 1918, p. 482.

125 *Ibid.*, letter to Professor Friedrich Crusius, November 24, 1918, p. 484.

126 *Ibid.*

127 *Ibid.*, letter to Dr. Otto Neurath, October 3, 1919, p. 488.

128 *Ibid.*, "Germany's Future Form of Government," published by the *Frankfurter Zeitung*, November, 1918, p. 351.

129 This is exactly what the Weimar Republic failed to do. Cf. Herman Finer, *The Future of Government* (London: Methuen & Co., Ltd., 1945), p. 45: "The democratic forces of Germany, that is to say the Social Democratic

Party and the Trade Unions, the Liberals and the Catholic Center, neglected to destroy the political power of the traditional groups when this might have been possible between 1918 and 1920. This was due to a division among themselves or within their parties. We consider the Social Democrats only. These were still in a state of mental and spiritual deference to the traditional governing classes. Terrified by the Soviet Revolution and by German left wing movements, they longed for order. Ebert, the first president of the German Republic, declared: 'I hate revolution like sin,' but he sought assistance from militarists who loved reaction like god."

130 *P.S.*, 1st. ed., p. 353.
131 *Ibid.*, pp. 348–349.
132 *Lebensbild*, p. 642.
133 *Ibid.*
134 For further reference regarding Weber's outlook concerning these matters, consult his widow's biography, *Lebensbild*, particularly p. 361.
135 Friedrich Meinecke, *Staat und Persoenlichkeit* (Berlin: Mittler & Sohn, 1933), p. 159.
136 It was not that Weber wanted the revolutionary spirit to be permanent. He only lamented the absence of public spirit and responsible citizenship evidenced in complete apathy in matters of politics on the part of the electorate. *P.S.*, 1st. ed., p. 347.
137 *Ibid.*
138 *Ibid.*, p. 256.
139 *Ibid.*, p. 256.
140 Otto Koellreutter, "Staatspolitische Anschauungen Max Webers und Oswald Spenglers," *Zeitschrift fuer Politik* (Berlin, 1925), p. 495.
141 *Ibid.*, cf. p. 496. By " 'rational' attitude" Koellreutter meant that Weber looked at the formal structure alone, not the spirit which animated it.
142 Friedrich Meinecke, *op. cit.*, pp. 159–160.
143 Max Weber, *Essays in Sociology*, translated and edited by Hans. H. Gerth and C. Wright Mills (New York: Oxford University Press), 1946, p. 82.
144 *P.S.*, 1st. ed., letter to Helene Weber, November 18, 1918, p. 482.
145 *Ibid.*, p. 482.
146 *Ibid.*
147 Friedrich Nietzsche, *Beyond Good and Evil* (1886), in *The Philosophy of Nietzsche* (New York: The Modern Library, n. d.), pp. 129–130.
148 *Ibid.*

VI

Max Weber:
From the Wilhelminian Period
to the Weimar Republic

Max Weber's concerns were not tied to a single grand political design for postwar Germany. He was frequently deeply immersed in schemes for partial political reform. Despite his depression over his country's misfortunes, the very act of devising standards for improvement signified an affirmative attitude. If disgust with the Kaiser's regime and distress over Germany's defeat were his immediate inspiration, in *Politics as a Vocation* he portrayed images of political leaders who were his answer to the question, "How do we rebuild?" If criticism and scathing denunciation were all so many of his contemporaries received from him both before and after the war, his was not a posture of resignation and withdrawal.

Weber, however, never permitted himself the illusion of painless social reform, nor did he envisage an effortless regenerative political education. Perhaps this is the main reason for the enduring relevance of his political thought. Although *Politics as a Vocation* was marked by scholarly detachment, it bears the stamp of Weber's personality. Max Rheinstein describes Weber at this time as "cool and objective, but behind this remoteness of the scholar we students could feel the fire of the passion which was burning in that extraordinary man and the iron will which kept it under control and which prevented the entry into his work as a scholar and teacher of those deep emotions and convictions for which he would plead so eloquently when he allowed himself to take a stand on the political problems of the day, always carefully announcing in such cases that he would now speak as a politician and not as a scientist." [1]

Max Weber's theoretical sociology of the state was never completed

190

because of his untimely death at the age of only 56. Johannes Winckelmann therefore took on the constructive task of combining parts of
Weber's *Economic History, Politics as a Vocation,* and "Parliament and
Government in Reconstructed Germany" in his work containing Weber's
sociology of the state. In omitting Weber's publicistic writings, Winckelmann judged the scholarly themes in Weber's sociology of the state as
the most compelling for our apprehension of the richness and complexity of that area of his concern.[2]

Contemporary American political scientists have rarely defined their
field of inquiry in application to Weber's reflections on the practical
aspects of politics. Politics being the object of the study of political
science, Weber viewed it as the "striving to share or striving to influence
the distribution of power, either among states or among groups within a
state."[3] By this definition, Weber's publicistic writings, though largely
dated, cover the ongoing political process in Imperial Germany, identifying both the political personalities and groupings and the political goals
they pursued. Here he pointed to possible alternatives and the means
which were or might have been employed in relation to given ends outlined by him. In his formal writings as well as in his correspondence,
he tried to ascertain the origin of given political issues as well as the
nature and extent of the struggle fought over them, always focusing
upon the factors determining the outcome.

Weber's political correspondence together with his formal political
writings constitute sources from which contemporary political science
can still distill useful information. His fluid description and analysis of
German politics is a political testament marked by an extraordinary and
continuous pitch of intellectual intensity. Perhaps the outstanding fact
about Weber's career as a political theorist is the powerful logical thrust
lying at the center of his work.

It has been said that Max Weber's inaugural address at the University of Freiburg constitutes the dividing line between historical periods.
On one side there is the age of Bismarck just concluded, on the other
appears the beginning of the new age, the prewar period: "Weber's
comprehension encompassed both the past and the future with equally
prophetic astuteness."[4] Apart from his academic treatises on politics,
many of the letters in Weber's extraordinary correspondence have a
scholarly validity of their own. While they are psychologically revealing
in a more personal sense, they contain, above all, a statement of characteristic themes and thus provide a comprehensive personal and political
biography because of the kind of continuity they give. These letters
reveal that the springs of Max Weber's political writings lay not only
in cool detachment but in deep anguish of spirit. They reflect his
emotional and political conflicts; in consequence, they may be seen as
a key to the strands of experience, personal and historical, which were

instrumental in shaping Weber's political writings; they also illustrate the pronounced inner restlessness that was to last to the end of his life. His letters may fail to render a full account of his personality, but they are a monument not only to his capacity for a keen understanding of the facts of political life but also to his need of imparting his knowledge to those on whom his insights not infrequently made an overwhelming impact. Indeed he often seemed to turn to his correspondence for much that pressed for release, which could not be incorporated in his scholarly work.

Max Weber's image of the existential struggle in which individuals and nations engage was an exceedingly harsh one. Political ideas and political value judgments always posed central questions concerning both reasons and purpose as well as the justification and aims of political domination. The formulation of this question derives from the traditional approach of political science.[5] For Max Weber the struggle for domination partly consisted in an unmerciful and unceasing contest "in which Germans and Slavs must engage each other for living space, like beasts of prey." Golo Mann comments that Weber's outlook contained both the truth and the error typical of his generation: "His assertion that Germany could live only as a world power with a great and bold global policy is eagerly seized upon by people who had best not become involved in that game." [6] It is striking how highly Weber valued the prestige factor in international relations, and one suspects that he overestimated its importance at times. Indications of this attribute are numerous. Toward the end of World War I Weber reacted angrily to the Peace Resolution proposed to the Reichstag by Erzberger, the deputy of the Center party. Precisely because Weber was pessimistic about the future he wanted his nation to appear strong and thus resolved to fight to the last to achieve an honorable peace. This reasoning also caused him to impress other nations with the image of Germany's internal unity whether real or, if necessary, imagined. Weber rightly saw political institutions of the past in a realistic unflattering light, damaging to both Germany's internal unity and her prestige abroad; hence his demand for democratization of Germany's political life. Political realism also prompted Weber, however, to reject even a majority resolution of the Reichstag, such as the Peace Resolution, if it could be interpreted by foreign governments as a sign of weakness which might encourage the latter to impose harsher peace terms.

Beyond this, yet another consideration induced Max Weber to his brusque rejection of the Peace Resolution, namely that democracy at home and hopes of peace abroad should be so closely linked. Weber reminded his countrymen that public indignation may prejudice the evolution of the democratic process of government. Yet the Reichstag crisis of July 1917 responsible for the Peace Resolution . . . "signalized the approaching end of the bureaucratic-authoritarian regime and the advance of the liberal-parliamentary system." [7] Erzberger's reason for introducing the Peace Resolution had been based largely upon the failure of German submarine warfare and the fact that Ludendorff, pessimistic about the prospects for naval successes, was preparing a winter campaign.

Colonel Bauer, Ludendorff's close associate, described Germany's military situation as disadvantaged vis à vis the superiority in armaments, the ratio being 4–1. Erzberger's answer was that the High Command had hoodwinked the German people, a fact Bauer admitted. Bauer and Erzberger then combined efforts to lay plans for a 'spiritual war food office,' designed to prepare the nation for a fourth winter of war: "The plan for the 'spiritual war food office' was accepted by Ludendorff but treated by Bethmann with habitual procrastination. This must have been one reason inducing Erzberger to use shock tactics in his July 6 speech to awaken the Reichstag to the urgency of the situation. Ludendorff's support and Bethmann's indifference helped to prepare the way for Erzberger's alliance with Ludendorff against Bethmann." [8] The Center party and the Left succeeded in obtaining the passage of a Peace Resolution in mid-July renouncing all annexations. The Left demanded the immediate introduction of the parliamentary system and Bethmann-Hollweg was forced to resign. While Weber learned to his satisfaction that his own essays had had a deep imprint upon the crisis, he rejected the fusion of domestic reforms with the Peace Resolution as most unfortunate. "One notices the upset created by the prospect of an endless war and financial ruin of the country, and the terribly unskillful manner in which Erzberger as well as the government are solving this crisis. First the sensation in the Reichstag, then the watchword: Parliamentarianism, that brings peace!—downright incredible, for who can know that?" [9]

Forecasting potential reaction at home and abroad, Weber recorded his fears: "Abroad the impression we give is that we are at the end of our strength and they will hope for more: Revolution—and that will extend the war. And at home, they will say now: these concessions were made under pressure from abroad." [10] Weber's criticisms did not lack a prophetic ring. He was afraid lest democracy be compromised by the charge that the future German constitution would be written under duress, its terms dictated by the enemy. Moreover, he did not necessarily correlate the end of the war with the introduction of democratization. In this context, Weber's penetrating analysis is as relevant today as it was then. He foresaw the stigma to be attached to the Weimar Republic which aimed at reducing its status to that of a creature of Germany's former enemies.

As will be recalled, in this war and postwar period the question of

Germany's future relation to the rest of the world dominated Weber's writings on politics. Another problem of constant concern was the backwardness of Germany's political institutions. Much preoccupied with questions of peace-making and constitutional reform, Weber urged both democratization and a negotiated peace. On the other hand, he feared the potential repercussions abroad which a favorable domestic response to peace proposals such as the one put forward by Erzberger might entail. Discretion should be exercized, he cautioned, so as not to furnish the Allies with renewed impetus to steer their course toward total victory. Thus public debates in the Reichstag should be avoided. The *Vaterlandspartei*, founded in the fall of 1917 and composed of Pan-Germans and Conservatives, being opposed to both peace resolution and domestic reform, demanded the permanent retention of Belgium and other occupied territories. In addition, these radical elements sought to influence the troops against both a negotiated peace and against government policy while at the same time presenting an image of that party's alleged superior patriotism.

To counteract the *Vaterlandspartei's* activities, the *Volksbund fuer Freiheit und Vaterland* began to campaign for a negotiated peace and domestic reform. At the end of December, Max Weber along with Troeltsch, Oncken, Naumann, Delbrueck, Gertrud Baeumer, and Brentano issued a public proclamation. As critical as Weber had been of the Peace Resolution for reasons noted earlier, he defended it against attacks by the *Vaterlandspartei*.[11] Weber was especially articulate in his criticism of military leaders who dabble in politics. To the Reichstag fell the obligation, Weber stated, to reassure not only Germany's allies, but also her armed forces, that the war would not be extended one day longer than Germany's honor and future required.[12] In December 1917, Weber publicly expressed his concern about the political indoctrination of the army and the infringement of the military establishment upon what is properly the sphere of the political parties lest it might be said later on: "Your good performance by means of the sword you have ruined again by means of the pen." The press reported this statement in distorted form and his opponents protested Weber's allegedly slanderous references in a telegram addressed to the Reichstag, charging that Weber had offended the honor of the army. In his defense Weber referred again to his own warning addressed to the officers to avoid the slippery ground of political party strife. If officers should attempt to move outside their own sphere of competence, the men under their jurisdiction as well as the nation might question their authority even in their own area of competence.[13]

Weber also feared that public confidence in the political and military leadership and institutions of the country could not be restored unless both took account of the legitimate demands of the disaffected.

The task was to be a difficult one, for satisfying some factions to gain their support tended to intensify the dissatisfaction and its articulation of others. He was most pessimistic about peace prospects for Germany in the absence of favorable conditions. Just at this time, when discussions about peace factors were reaching their peak, Germany was granted a respite. News of the Bolshevik Revolution reached Weber while he was on a visit to Vienna to discuss the possibility of a professorship in the Austrian capital. In mid-December the Bolsheviks declared their wish for an armistice and a negotiated peace based upon the principle of national self-determination, with a view especially to neighboring states. Weber's earlier article on Russia's transition to sham democracy had addressed itself particularly to German Social Democracy, which he was afraid might yet succumb to the temptation to join "in the swindle of the present Russian Duma-plutocracy, thereby morally stabbing our German army, which protects our country against uncivilized peoples, in the back." [14]

Weber's analysis of the Revolution was, in this instance, decidedly polemical. He had wanted to demonstrate to the Social Democrats that the peace talks were nothing but an exercise in diplomatic futility. His article had sought to demonstrate to the German workers that Russia did not represent a genuine democracy. Hoping to alert the Social Democrats against the danger of following the Russian example, Weber set out to prove that the real obstacle to the peace negotiations was the new regime. He maintained that its very existence required the continuation of the war.[15] Weber did not concede that lasting social and political changes could be expected from the Revolution. In fact, he refused to regard the overthrow of the Czarist regime as a "revolution," preferring to interpret events in Russia as having followed in the train of the removal of an inept monarch: "Not a 'revolution,' but a mere 'elimination' of an incapable monarch has occurred to date. At least half of the actual power is held by monarchically oriented circles who join in the current republican swindle only because the monarch has . . . not stayed within the objective limits of his power." [16]

Weber saw the attitude of the Russian leaders as one based on the expectation that "German Social Democracy, now when an army of Negroes, Ghurkas and all other barbaric riff-raff in the world is stationed at our borders, half crazy with rage, revenge, and greed to devastate our country,"[17] might yet be inclined to hinder the German war effort. Weber was convinced that neither anti-German feeling nor imperialist designs in the present hierarchy in the Russian government had changed. The rulers of Russia had a vested interest in the continuation of the war so as to consolidate their position. This goal necessitated the continued stay of the peasants in the trenches to prevent an uprising at home. Weber did not anticipate the survival of the regime at the expense of the bourgeoisie because no regime dependent upon credit could afford to exclude the bourgeoisie. He probably overestimated the role of the bourgeoisie by assuming that it constituted the only class that could command sufficient trust necessary for the extension of credit. Weber suggested that universally, recent experience confirmed his thesis that "revolutions are of no more than short-lived success if they are staged *either* by the bourgeoisie and the bourgeois intelligentsia alone *or* by the proletarian masses and the proletarian intelligentsia alone." [18]

Pointing out that all general strikes and insurrections had been doomed as soon as the bourgeoisie, especially the landowners among them, failed to cooperate, Weber challenged the Social Democrats to close ranks against the common danger. While he regarded the Revolution as a spent force which could not survive much longer, he still felt it essential that the German workers understood that behind all the "pious platitudes" concerning workers' rights, the Russian rulers saw fit to reconcile their socialist convictions with an imperialist policy. With the masses of the peasants being kept at the war front, those workers working in war industries at home could afford to opt in favor of continuation of the war. Nor did the leaders of Russia's Social Democrats and other social revolutionaries have any alternative in the current situation to playing the role of "fellow-travellers." Their ploy was well received because with their assistance the masses were deluded by the "revolutionary" image of the government.[19]

Weber prophesied the end of the Revolution once the bourgeois partners in the government such as Gutschkov, and Miljukov secured money from America or from the banks: *"then* the time will have come for the attempt to get rid completely of the socialist fellow-travellers with the help of commissioned officers and troops of the guard." [20] Even with all due consideration of the intentionally polemical nature of Weber's prognosis, it was nevertheless marked by a considerable misjudgment of the situation. Weber's analysis of the revolutionary process in Russia reflected a stubborn refusal to adapt to changing political conditions. While political problems do illustrate some elements of universality, in the Russian context of today Weber's assessment of the revolutionary events as representing no more than the removal of an incompetent monarch seems almost ludicrous. His political judgment appears to have collided with his emotions. Weber's references had been equally sweeping in regard to the "personal regime" of William II, whose significance he exaggerated at certain times. In his references to the Russian Revolution he did not grant that there were circumstances peculiar to Russia; when he reflected on the situation existing when the Czarist regime fell, he sought to establish a parallel to events in Germany when the Kaiser was forced to abdicate. Today, with the benefit of hindsight, one finds little in the literature dealing with the Russian Revolution to bear out Weber's predictions concerning the course it would take.

Weber's thesis also held that Russian nationalism and imperialism could be expected to continue under any regime. He therefore persisted in presenting his pleas to extend Germany's own sphere of influence in Eastern Europe, demanding an independent Polish state as previously guaranteed by Russia in 1815. Moreover, Weber pointedly demanded that Poland's eastern frontiers be determined by the Poles.[21] Demands such as these were not, as will become apparent later, conducive to the attainment of a separate peace with Russia. Nor did Weber believe the two Russian postrevolutionary regimes were ready to sign such a separate peace. Some of Weber's statements emphasizing the significance of the prestige factor, associating it intimately with national honor, prove disconcerting; they reflect his conception of German foreign policy dynamics as well as his sometimes intemperate attitude toward potential peace.

Meanwhile, at home, Weber demanded democratization to strengthen national unity. Accordingly, it seems that Weber would have welcomed, as a symptom of that process, the initiative seized by Center Party deputy Erzberger in the executive committee of the Reichstag for a Joint Peace Resolution to be sponsored by a majority in the Reichstag, consisting of Social Democrats, Progressives, and Center. The draft of the proposed peace resolution appeared to be almost identical with Weber's own demands as formulated in letters addressed to Naumann.[22] The irony of the resulting controversy is underscored further by the fact that Erzberger's estimate of the deteriorating situation in Austria bore a close resemblance to Weber's own.[23] Thus Weber's reaction to a step designed to secure a majority in the Reichstag on an important foreign policy issue was totally negative. He appeared to show little interest in its implementation, and his own position was one of dissent from the views of a majority of parliamentarians. Considering their feeble political heritage and the strain under which democratic forces were laboring, the very nature of Weber's disregard for them is disturbing. Referring to Erzberger as an "ass,"[24] Weber maintained that this "*type*" of "peace" propaganda was futile and could only be damaging to democracy: "Democratization must be demanded and enforced. But it will be harmed by fusing it with 'peace.' If peace should *nevertheless fail* to come, then democracy is *compromised.*"[25] Yet later on Weber was shocked by the conduct of Germany's peace negotiator, General Hoffmann who delivered a caustic speech at the Brest-Litovsk Peace Conference.[26] Weber would have been even more dismayed had he known that General Hoffmann deemed it necessary to take that hard line only in order to strengthen his own relationship with the High Command which had been impaired by his previously considerably less intransigent position.[27] Although Weber had been aware of the conflict between the High Command and the Foreign Office, he did not know about these complications which served to further aggravate the obstacles to the peace negotiations. Thus he wrote: ". . . The Hoffmann incident was a scandal. It could cost us the alliance."[28]

Meanwhile, even while peace negotiations were in progress, planning for a big offensive in the West was underway. Weber wrote unhappily about the projected casualty figures being "legendary and gruesome," even though all hopes were concentrated upon the outcome. He was skeptical about the justification of any grounds for optimism.[29] In fact, he referred to the military as having gone "completely mad."[30] "Should the franchise proposals miscarry and should the general strike follow," Weber writes, then "things may turn out badly—Rathenau is betting on three more years of war. That cannot be; there would be no way to get around a revolution. But everything is so unsure."[31] Weber's own mood was reflected in his assessment of his visit to Berlin in January: "politically everything is a mad-house, and sensible people are powerless. . . . What is being accomplished in the East, nobody knows; nor does anybody know how long Kuehlmann and even Hertling are able to stand up to the intrigues of the big industrialists and the Pan-Germans who always get through to the military. For in all non-military matters Ludendorff is completely blind."[32] Weber "complained about the publicized frictions concerning areas of competence between the military and political governmental agencies in relation to the peace negotiations in Brest: General Hoffmann's speech has spoiled everything in Vienna and also in Berlin. . . ."[33] Weber indicated that no one on the Left believed that electoral reforms would materialize, nor did Naumann believe in it; hence, he anticipated that Social Democracy would no longer be able to restrain the workers. Many of them were, in fact, deserting to join the Independents in response to the most recent events.[34]

Weber still did not abandon hope: "Russia, the most formidable enemy, is no longer able to continue in the war and must, as a consequence, accept a dictated peace at the end of March, which will place many parts of the country under German control."[35]

He attributed the deterioration of the domestic situation to the impasse of the peace negotiations at Brest-Litovsk created by the conduct of the German negotiating team and the agitation of the extreme Right, all of which was compounded by the war press office, its agents and other wire-pullers.[36] As soberly as Weber viewed the strike of the munitions workers, he feared that it might set off a chain of such strikes. Discussing the domestic situation in connection with foreign policy, he prophetically warned that "the role of any political party in Germany that would be guilty, directly or indirectly, of concluding a bad or irresponsible peace, thus stabbing the German negotiators in the back, would be finished. It would be haunted for decades. And this danger does exist." [37] He stated that Germany would accept peace only with those who would be able to guarantee compliance with the terms of the prospective treaty. He asserted that he had been informed on good authority (by radical socialists) that the Bolshevik regime could not survive longer than a few months. Weber further claimed that whether any succeeding government would honor the commitments entered into with that government was open to question. He viewed the government as representing "a very small minority," [38] supported by a high proportion of a war-weary army. Weber portrayed the nature of the government as a "purely *military dictatorship,* not one composed of generals, but rather of *corporals.*" [39] He branded as nonsense any notions that the government could count upon "'class-conscious' proletarian masses of the Western European type. What does stand behind it, is a *Soldatenproletariat.*" [40] Weber denied that either the Bolshevik government or the "well-paid soldiers" were interested in peace (the latter would lose their earnings), both pursuing imperialistic aims, as demonstrated by military invasions "under the pretext of 'liberation' in the Ukraine, Finland, and other territories. . . ." [41]

This particular observation, made fifty years before the Soviet troops invaded Czechoslovakia on August 21, 1968, has again a strongly prophetic ring. Weber referred to the regime as resting on foundations of "the purest militarism that existed anywhere at this time." [42] In his view, Russian bourgeois imperialism had been replaced merely by "Bolshevik soldiers' imperialism," which "as long as it exists, will threaten the security and self-determination of all neighboring nations. . . ." [43] Weber claimed, moreover, that "it is completely improbable that a government dependent upon these military mass instincts is even *able* to be sincere in its peace effort, even if it were so inclined. Everything follows from this." [44] While it would be possible, in his view, to maintain good neighborly relations with an honest, "pacifist, Russian federal republic," prospects for such a transformation appeared dim at that moment. Weber thus asserted ". . . whether Russian imperialist expansion was labelled as Czarist, cadet, or Bolshevik is naturally totally immaterial in effect." [45] His approach was obviously polemical. He stated openly that the demands for peace which the striking workers proclaimed testified to the fact that they absolutely had *no idea* of the true facts inherent in the situation. He argued that the Bolshevik government "did not want peace but force. All this will have to be explained to [German] labor by its leaders even though these facts may be ever so inconvenient—otherwise no serious debate is possible." [46]

It appears that Weber deliberately slanted his argument to serve his purpose, namely to combat the attraction which the peace propaganda coming from Russia held for the German Left. Indeed, Weber conceded that: "Concerning the Bolsheviks, I have described only *one* side (addressed as it was to Social Democracy!) The other being the pacifist tendency is also present." [47] As Mommsen rightly states, Weber knew very well that the exorbitant demands put forward by the German peace negotiators were responsible for Trotzky's refusal to sign such a peace. Thus he thought it politically imperative to defend Germany's actions at Brest-Litovsk. He would not go beyond criticizing the tone of General Hoffmann's speech;[48] pointing out that a nation at war requires a *united* front, at least before the *enemy*, Weber criticized its absence. Apparently against his own better judgment Weber was able to write: "What General Hoffmann said during the negotiations, was in political terms of its contents perfectly accurate and in terms of its contents it did not contradict the statements of the political agencies of the government." [49] Regarding both points, Weber did not mean what he said. As Mommsen stated, he held exactly opposite views and just because of that he believed that he had to state publicly an opinion contrary to his own personal views "on tactical grounds." [50]

Weber's position on the Russian Revolution reveals him as crossing the line between analyst of political trends and prophet of doom and ultimate collapse. In a similar vein, he portrayed the negotiations at Brest-Litovsk as hopeless from the start primarily because he believed the regime's chances of survival so limited; peace negotiations with a government whose demise was imminent seemed to hold little promise. This sort of overdramatization of only the negative aspects of the Russian Revolution may have proved persuasive, but it did not promote a sober assessment of the situation either then or now. As Mommsen emphasizes, Weber did not believe that spontaneous mass movements were behind these political phenomena; he believed only in historical constellations, which with the aid of great men at whose disposal was placed a solid administrative apparatus, would be endowed with aim and purpose.[51] Comparisons of Weber's ideas of the charismatic leader with those embracing the *Fuehrerprinzip* during the Third Reich have been bandied around too freely, but Weber's analysis of the processes underlying the Russian Revolution frequently also appears misleading. The latter was not to vanish as Weber and many others had hoped it would. Weber's insights into political developments in Russia, apart from the conclusions he drew from them, were sometimes extremely astute, but, apart from that, any complete assessment of the latter must take into account their intended effect. From his biased cultural perspective, he found it inconceivable that a lasting revolutionary recasting of society, regardless of how and where it occurred, was possible without the existence of the bourgeosie.[52]

Thus Mommsen writes: "So complete a destruction of the old organization of the state as Lenin consciously strove to bring about, did not lie within the realm of political possibilities envisaged by Weber's political-sociological horizon." [53] His views on revolution were shaped by his conviction that national interest prevails over any form of ideological cohesiveness and that ideological commitments were often of little relevance to governmental practices. Rather than revolutions of the old type, he expected *coups d'état* to occur.[54] Since Weber, seeing no chance of success for the Bolshevik Revolution, expected the early return of a thoroughly reactionary regime, he reasoned that *Realpolitik* demanded that Germany's interest in the Northeast required conditions designed to prevent neighboring peoples from fighting against Germany. Consequently Germany's objective should be to neutralize these states. He favored continued occupation of the territories already under Germany's jurisdiction since otherwise they would only benefit a new Miljukov government whose early return he anticipated.[55] The only explanation Weber could find for Trotsky's and Lenin's success was that their position was based upon a military dictatorship, and that their access to the governmental apparatus enabled them to maintain their power.[56]

In an address delivered to Austrian-Hungarian officers in June 1918 on "Socialism," Weber claimed that the "discussions in Brest-Litovsk had been conducted in a most sincere (!) manner *(in loyalster Weise* (!)). . . ." [57] He attributed the failure of the peace negotiations solely to Trotsky, asserting that it is not possible to conduct successful peace negotiations with "crusaders . . ., all one can do is to render them harmless, and that was the meaning behind the ultimatum and the command peace of Brest. Any socialist must see this and I know no one, regardless of orientation, who does not accept that—at least inwardly." [58] Weber tried repeatedly to justify the conduct of the German negotiations against his own better judgment for purely tactical reasons. Weber held fast to his negative criticism of the Russian experiment:

Any Russian, including Social Democratic intellectuals, who seizes power, will turn not only 'national,' but 'nationalistic' . . . great caution is needed! For when the peasants do return home, reaction will set in at first in very radical forms such as the demand for land expropriation and distribution. That is technically impossible, without entering into the sharpest conflicts of interest among the peasants . . . not to be solved without a dictatorship. In any case, since the proletariat is too weak and the propertied (the 'cadets' as well) are interested in it too, the outcome will be the return of monarchical power and with it the former situation, only resulting with a stronger Russia. Against that there is no remedy.[59]

As Mommsen correctly points out, Weber's interpretation of events ignored both the political *élan* of Lenin and his capacity for leadership. As will be shown subsequently, Weber indeed underestimated the latter's ingenuity. Political reasoning based on utility again interfered with Weber's sociological judgment concerning the true state of affairs in Russia.[60] Weber professed that in view of the readiness to enter into peace negotiations evinced by the Russians, "regardless of how much significance one may attach to that, and I do not value it very highly . . . the German government cannot possibly avoid a very obliging declaration directed toward Russia." [61] Weber feared that unless such a conciliatory stance were adopted by the German government, the mood in Russia would be one of defiance. While it was hard to predict how long this uneasy state of affairs would last, any encouragement of Russian enthusiasm for the war would be detrimental to Germany's national interest. Moreover, if Germany were to adopt a more belligerent attitude, neutral nations (especially Scandinavia) would become antagonistic toward her. Such a policy would also issue in a dangerous intensification of the ill-feeling already existing in Austria.[62] Weber, in fact, as mentioned previously, agreed with Erzberger in his pessimistic outlook of the situation in Austria. The deterioration of conditions there largely motivated Erzberger to press for an early negotiated peace for the Central Powers:

Czernin's flat statement in the April 12, 1917 memorandum that Austria must quit before the end of the year left an indelible impression upon Erzberger, especially since this was also the view of the Emperor Charles Erzberger . . . knew of Czernin's hope that the *Reichstag* would place a bridle upon the annexationism of Germany's military leaders. Czernin was later to claim credit for inspiring Erzberger's sponsorship of the Peace Resolution.[63] This became the basis of the subsequent charge that Erzberger had promoted defeatism as an Austrian agent. . . .[64]

Weber's convictions, which led him to urge the adoption of a conciliatory stance toward the Russians, were strengthened by his assessment of the mood prevailing among the Social Democrats, which he held to be adversely affected by the events in Russia and which was likely to become even more somber. Thus he had asserted as early as 1917 that it would be wise to enter negotiations with the Russians in any case on the basis of their declaration signifying readiness to do so. Whatever Russia's intentions, Germany should be willing to negotiate on the following terms: "no annexation, no compensation, mutual guarantees aimed at exclusion of all mutually threatening military measures, and a treaty providing for submission to arbitration." [65]

Winfried Baumgart's remarkable work on Germany's conduct of Eastern affairs in 1918 includes an illuminating account of the chief characteristics in the relations between the political and the military authorities in Germany as well as within the inner circles of each group.[66] Some of the historical facts which Baumgart unearthed from secret German archives and upon which Janssen's report focuses, are indeed startling. The fascination of his book lies primarily in the fact that it constitutes a revision of some of the problematic issues pertaining to both the war and the revolutions. It appears that "the imperialistic designs bordering on hallucinations which the Kaiser and Ludendorff shared with the leaders of heavy industry are *one* side of the story whereas the less transparent subterfuge of the Foreign Office is quite *another.*" [67]

The plans of the military leaders, backed also by some diplomats, saw the Caucasus as a " 'springboard for political activity in Persia, Central Asia, and in Russian territories between the Ural and the Ukraine'." [68] Prominent business and industrial leaders had a vested interest in the "economic and financial penetration of all of Russia." [69] Baumgart's thesis is that . . .

especially the plans of Germany's heavy industry . . . were built on quicksand. The policies of the Foreign Office and, above all, Lenin's action were to end all such plans. As a preventive measure, the Soviet government hurriedly established a state export monopoly and proceeded to nationalize the most important industrial concerns. And the German Foreign Office agreed that this nationalized private property need not be returned.

The Foreign Office and the High Command did not act in concert in matters of *Ostpolitik,* having been engaged in a bitter contest. Baumgart documents in detail the compromises achieved by the secretaries of state Kuehlmann and Hintze despite the dominant position of the military. . . .[70]

As early as July 29, 1918 Lenin is reported to have practically abandoned all hope and to have expressed the intention to leave Moscow.

The collapse of Bolshevist rule seemed imminent. On all sides enemy troops invaded Russia; counter-revolutionary governments mushroomed. In the North the British and the Americans had landed; the invasion fleet of the Japanese was positioned near Vladivostock; the Trans-Siberian Railroad was in the hands of the Czechoslovak Legion; in the South . . . the Cossack generals were pushing forward; in the Caucasus the Turks and the British were approaching the oil fields of Baku; in the small torso of Russia which the Soviet government still retained, one insurrection after another occurred; even the body guard, the Latvian regiments, became unreliable. And the German military, which had already subdued Finland, the Baltic, the Ukraine, and Southern Russia, stood ready to purge the spectre of the Revolution in Petersburg and Moscow.[71]

On July 29, at a secret meeting convened in the Kremlin, "Lenin was informed by his foreign minister Tschitscherin that the German government was ready to continue in its support of the Soviet Regime. Thereupon Lenin decided in response to the emergency on a most extraordinary step: . . . he asked the Germans for military support against the troops of the *Entente* in Northern Russia." [72] Ludendorff was favorably disposed toward the Russian offer, hoping to turn the tables upon the Russians at a later date. However, the initial conditions of German acceptance were to prove too costly for the Soviets. Their endorsement by the Soviet regime might have precipitated its overthrow since, in view of the anti-German sentiment, the march of German troops into Petersburg would have resulted in public outrage. German commanders in the field demanded drastic action, but the Foreign Office through its restraint actually saved Lenin's position. [73]

Both German envoys in Moscow, Mirbach and Helfferich, also had advocated a break with the Bolsheviks because they doubted their good faith. Despite the fact that German commanders stationed in the East were pleading that this opportunity not be allowed to pass, the Foreign Office, headed by an expert on Russian affairs, Admiral Hintze, protested the contemplated action, a move which saved Lenin's position. [74] Nevertheless, there are indications that Ludendorff and others of the military establishment recognized the maneuvers of the Bolsheviks for what they were sooner than some of the diplomats. Finally, the opportunity to march into Russia presented itself to Germany three times: "in the beginning of July following the assassination of Count Mirbach; in the beginning of August upon Lenin's own invitation; in the beginning of September after the attempted assassination of Lenin when the Red counter-terrorists were so fierce that the German consul general joined Allied representatives in protest." [75] The Kaiser's personal reaction was reported as having been extremely disparaging toward the audacity of the *"Proletenjanhagel"* with whom one would have to speak "in German." He reportedly interspersed his outbursts with excessive anti-Semitic remarks.

Janssen raises the question why both the Kaiser and Ludendorff allowed the Foreign Office to persist in its pro-Bolshevik policy and states that: "Baumgart's book contains a most surprising answer: To the Hohenzollern ruler, his newly-gained title as Duke of the Baltic meant more than the struggle against the much detested Bolsheviks. Almost all rightist Russian organizations, opposing governments and groups who wanted to make up to the Germans, were demanding a revision of the Peace Treaty of Brest-Litovsk; at the very least the Germans were supposed to return Estonia and Livonia, the very territories for which Germany had resumed the war in the East in 1918— over the objection of Kuehlmann." [76]

In view of Weber's appreciation of the Russian threat and his skeptical attitude concerning the survival chances of the Bolshevik Revolution, combined with the satisfaction he experienced because Germany had at least been able to avert the Russian "Knout," the following analysis is of interest: "Purely dynastic interests induced William II to sacrifice the opportunity to bring about the overthrow of the Bolshevik system. For the only government in Russia that was willing to let the Germans have Estonia and Livonia and to pay reparations was the Bolshevik government. Consequently, Berlin absolutely required the signature of the Soviet government under the so-called Supplementary Treaty; therefore at the request of the Foreign Office all disturbing actions on the part of the military were to cease as long as this treaty was not yet concluded. Lenin never intended to observe the treaty—he agreed only to gain a breathing spell in the struggle against the counter-revolutionaries." [77]

It is noteworthy that these German diplomats managed to succumb to their illusions. Moreover, Germany's foreign policy is shown as not yet aware of the new type of diplomacy inaugurated by the Soviet Union. Nevertheless, "it did not lack in logic and was closer to reality than the military dabbling in politics. . . . The former was originally designed by Richard von Kuehlmann. . . ." [78] Kuehlmann always considered the Treaty of Brest-Litovsk provisional in nature. In his judgment, in any future peace negotiations in which all her former enemies would be involved, Germany should be satisfied if she were allowed to retain her prewar boundaries. Hence, the Foreign Office reasoned that the Supplementary Treaty would serve well as judicious inducement to the other powers, inclining them toward concluding a reasonable peace. Kuehlmann continued his efforts to obtain such peace terms until the summer of 1918. Such a peace would have been ruled out altogether if Germany had sought to confiscate any more Russian territory. As Max Weber also said, Kuehlmann had to bow to many "senseless demands and accomplished facts of the military: Whoever today is surprised by the cynical tone of many diplomatic documents pertaining to those days should not forget that the arguments were often designed merely to convince the Kaiser and the military and to dissuade them from still more senseless experiments." [79]

It was only as a temporary measure that the Foreign Office conceived its objective of keeping Russia "paralyzed"; the duration of this policy was to be determined by the progress Germany would make in the struggle with the Western powers. All that was necessary, it was thought, was to let Russia stew in her own juice, namely to allow the Bolsheviks to carry on. As Admiral Hintze stated in a letter to Ludendorff:

'whoever works with the Bolsheviks in their capacity as *de facto* rulers and moans because of having to put up with bad company, is harmless;' however, 'if one should reject an advantage resulting from cooperation with the Bolsheviks, that's dangerous.' The Foreign Office was definitely prepared for the eventual fall of the Soviet Regime. In that event it intended to intervene militarily—in favor of the Soviets. For any succeeding government would have conducted itself more anti-German and more nationalistic.[80]

Besides, neither Kuehlmann nor Hintze believed that German military might itself was still capable of destroying Bolshevism. Yet Janssen stresses that both Fritz Fischer and Winfried Baumgart have demonstrated that German politics in the twentieth century is characterized not only by a

continuity of interests, aims and ideas but also by a continuity of conduct. After the first serious reversals in the West, Ludendorff first began to think in terms of a common German-Allied campaign against Bolshevism. As in April 1945 for Hitler and his followers, already then for Ludendorff too, the vision of an Atlantic-European crusade against the East had become the straw he was anxious to grasp before the fall. Just as after 1945, the German statesmen, following the collapse of 1918, were proficient at playing the tune of anti-Communism on the piano: On December 12, 1918, Ebert's administration was responsible for a suggestion made in a written communication to the Allies inviting them to join together in battle against Bolshevism in the East.[81]

So reads the account of German-Russian relations fifty years after Weber made his journalistic contributions to the *Frankfurter Zeitung*. The above chronicles the same era; using additional historical sources, however, and having the benefit of writing for a somewhat more detached public.

In *Politics as a Vocation*, Max Weber had illustrated the need for political science to become relevant to the vital issues of the political setting in which it functions even though it must abstain from value judgments. Weber's own moral and intellectual commitment, moreover, contrasts sharply with that of many contemporary political scientists and historians who have chosen to withdraw from the most crucial problems of the day, centering their attention upon methodological or less controversial concerns.

While Weber's personal political philosophy may be partly understood by the English-speaking reader from his essay *Politics as a Vocation*,[82] all of his political writings should be published in English as a collection. The impressive range of his scholarship coupled with an extraordinarily perceptive account of German political history is still relevant. A recent study, for example, in which the German historian Hans Raupach discusses the situation of the impoverished German East versus the more affluent Western parts of the country during the depression years, recalls Max Weber's own research more than half a century earlier. Raupach demonstrated, as Weber did before him, the delicate equilibrium of the Germans in the East vis à vis the growing Polish population.[83]

Another recent scholarly study, which draws upon Weber's earlier efforts, focuses upon the *Bund der Landwirte*, founded in 1893 to represent the interests of big estate owners, and probably the first modern pressure group in Central Europe. In this study cognizance was taken of the efforts of the German Junker aristocracy to preserve its privileges, which no professed aspirations on their part toward greater social justice could camouflage. Hans-Juergen Puhle shows how the *Bund*, while posing as the protector of large and small farmers generally, clearly spoke for the large estate owners in the eastern parts of the country. Their conservatism was total, economic, political, and spiritual. Bitterly opposing any concessions to the newly created conditions, they identified, when dealing with matters of vital national interest, with the Conservatives, thus insuring and promoting continued domination of that class. Agreeing with Weber's own conclusion, Puhle demonstrated how these agriculturists, engaged as they were in a life-and-death struggle, did all they could to preserve a social order threatened by the rise of industrialism. Paying homage to throne and altar, organizations such as the *Bund der Landwirte* unsuccessfully sought to counter the claims of an industrial society. Later, however, following the demise of the Empire, their nostalgia for the restoration of traditional class rule actually met with greater receptivity. Here Puhle continued Weber's theme, carrying it further by extending it into Republican times.[84]

Weber's pioneering study showing the implications of the policies of the big landowners represented one of the first really significant contributions to our understanding of conditions in Eastern Germany at that time.[85] As a countermeasure Weber strongly advocated extension of the powers of parliament, which, as he said, under conditions prevailing in Imperial Germany did little more than conduct "negative politics": "The entire structure of the German parliament today is designed merely to conduct negative politics: criticism, complaints, deliberation, modification and passage of government bills." [86] To the impotence of the Reichstag could be attributed also the weakness and fragmentation of the German political parties. Unlike Friedrich Naumann,[87] Max Weber discounted the potential initiation of the two-party system in which liberals and socialists would band together on one side, and conservatives and clergy along with right-oriented groups would join forces on the other. Max Weber has been proved correct that chances for a two-party system in Germany were precarious, primarily because of the Center and the socialists.[88] Unlike Naumann, who addressed his appeal to the working classes, Weber, as mentioned previously, designated himself as a bourgeois.[89] Although Naumann's independence of judgment cannot be questioned, he was nevertheless influenced by Weber's clear-cut political conceptualization and direction. Naumann had been able to breathe new life into the existing political party system, an attempt in which Weber supported him. Moreover, as stated earlier, it was due to Weber's influence that Naumann shifted his political persuasion from a "Christian-Social idealism of a primarily patriarchical stamp to one of a National Socialist type intended to combine a decisive domestic policy of social reform with national *Weltpolitik* abroad." [90] Max Weber's own framework for political analysis always gave priority to the field of international politics, although he recognized the reciprocal relationship of the domestic and foreign policy levels.

Naumann's new emphasis on the necessity to win the support of the working classes for the state and to launch them on a program of political education, training them to become the standard-bearers of the "national-imperialist idea," Weber saw as the real mission. Both men believed that ultimately Germany's future depended upon the success of this mission. Naumann wanted to lay the foundation for a new type of proletarian movement, one which would, unlike that of international Social Democracy, affirm the national power state.[91] However, Weber had strongly opposed the founding of a new party of the "weary and heavy-laden," demanding instead the formation of a consciously bourgeois national democratic movement. Under Weber's and Delbrueck's influence, the *Nationalsozialen* at the turn of the century campaigned strongly for an effective German foreign policy, including an impressive naval program. Liberalization of domestic policy, a program of social reform, and reduction of tariffs also became part of the National-Social Program. After the Reichstag elections of 1898 and 1903 spelled failure for the *Nationalsozialen,* Naumann dissolved the *Verein:* the majority of its members followed Naumann as he joined *Freisinnige Vereinigung,* which was formerly the left wing of the National Liberals and which subsequently merged with the *Fortschrittliche Volkspartei,* the precursor of the *Deutsche Demokratische Partei* of the Weimar Republic, the party which Max Weber also joined later. Although that party almost always managed to gain representation in the Weimar Republic's government. Naumann's death in 1919 soon after it was founded brought a distinct change. The National-Social element's influence receded into the background, while big business elements, including personalities like Hjalmar Schacht, exerted an increasing influence. As a result, the party lost much of its attractiveness for members of the younger generation. [It will be remembered that even before Max Weber's death the party endured heavy losses in membership.] The continued political influence of the DDP was due largely to the presence of highly respected persons within its ranks.[92]

The DDP was the first of the major political parties of the Weimar Republic to experience political collapse before the advent of Hitler:[93] "The end of the DDP marked clearly the end of the Democratic attempt, begun in November 1918, to reorient German liberal thinking and to build up a viable, democratic-liberal mass party in Germany."[94] Ironically enough, the DDP at its inception had been the party "committed most unequivocally to the basic principles of the Weimar Constitution."[95] Viewed by its supporters and opponents as the "champion and guardian of the new democratic state . . . its decline after 1919 and its ultimate dissolution in 1930 can be regarded as symptoms of the more general malaise of the Weimar Republic."[96] Its failure to defend its ideals anticipated the collapse of the Weimar experiment in democracy.[97] The founding of the DDP had virtually coincided with the end of the monarchy and the founding of the republic, namely with a national emergency. Nor were all founders of the party liberal by party background or conviction.

The founding of the DDP was announced by a manifesto, published in the *Berliner Tageblatt* on November 16, 1918.[98] Theodor Wolff, whose editorials in the *Berliner Tageblatt* reflected his civic courage and integrity, and a core of distinguished supporters were to leave their stamp on German politics. This group regarded it as sadly necessary that a merger between the two liberal parties, the Progressive People's Party (*Fortschrittliche Volkspartei*) and the National Liberal Party (*National-liberale Partei*) be prevented. Disavowing their past leadership, their philosophy and their policies during the war, they sought to counter Gustav Stresemann and other National Liberals who actively championed annexations and unrestricted submarine warfare and who generally demonstrated an unconscionable tolerance for the Kaiser's disastrous policies. The thesis was that the masses had lost faith in hypocritical liberals. The speed with which Wolff and his group founded the DDP was designed to forestall a coalition between the other two liberal parties; moreover, they also refused to endorse any move which would permit Stresemann and other National Liberals who had shared his views during the war to join the DDP. Wolff's strategy actually led to the prevention of a potential fusion between the two older parties, but the groups were joined by the majority of the FVP and a large part of the NLP: "Among the former members of these parties, there were many who conceived of the DDP as an all-embracing liberal *Sammelpartei* that would 'fulfill the historic task' of ending the traditional feud between the social-minded Progressives and the more nationalistic Right-wing liberals."[99] Attempts to unite liberals were made by leading figures among the liberals who were still continuing the good fight after the DDP had come into existence. What militated against the success of such a venture was the "irreconcilable nature of the conflict between the class-conscious Right-wing liberals and the Left-wing democratic liberals. . . ." [100]

Chanady argues that the plan to unite all liberals, including the FVP and the NLP, as well as the DDP and the *Deutsche Volkspartei*, expecting them to cooperate within a new democratic-republican party, was unrealistic and could only prove disruptive. He attributed the internal party strife to "inbred socio-economic prejudice and distrust, political and ideological differences, and personal feuds." [101] The party was undermined mostly by the individual members' fundamental outlook on the republic vis à vis the monarchy. Many of them professed their contempt for the former while inwardly remaining loyal to the latter. The minister of defense, Otto Gessler, for example, has been said to have referred to himself as a *Vernunftsrepublikaner:* this term, as noted earlier, referring to a person who rationally knows that there is no alternative to the Republic and thus supports it, but who concedes that his "'political passion was not for the Weimar Republic' and that his 'heart belonged to the past, to the Bismarck Reich'." [102] Weber in fact referred to his own critics concentrated within the left wing of the DDP as "doctrinaire pacifists and *literati* . . ." and the Republic appeared to him as a necessary evil which he could serve only with "the ethos of a public servant." [103]

Such ambivalence was common. Many prerevolutionary officials in high places in both the civilian and miltary parts of the establishment were retained by the Republican government. Although these men accepted the fall of the monarchy, they regarded themselves as no more than *verstandesmaessige Republikaner* who as civil servants had no alternative but to serve a new administration. The elected people's deputies were too overcome by the national political and economic collapse, and too impressed by the expertise of the bureaucracy and the military to restrain them in the exercise of power. Consequently their aim was primarily to establish order and a sense of national unity. Thus the people's deputies who were willing to sacrifice their socialist goals enabled the former Imperial civil servants and military leaders to claim a high degree of independence of action. As a result, the disaffected public servants took advantage of the opportunity to steer Germany on a course disloyal to the principles upon which the Republik was founded, essentially by keeping the vision of Bismarck's Reich alive.[104]

It was perhaps characteristic that Weber too should choose, as late as the collapse of the old Germany under monarchical rule, to advise against a radical break with Imperial traditions. Few political writers experienced the abyss of inner dualism so deeply as Max Weber, whose entire person was involved in the tragic meaning of life. What might have evolved into something viable in his political thinking was to be left fragmentary; he never really made political ends meet because he never really questioned his own first premises. While Weber's expositions stressed the significance of the emasculation of German liberalism by Bismarck, the fall of Bismarck, and the fateful compromise between the anachronism of an overly powerful landed aristocracy's interest and heavy industry, he still upheld his case for a monarchical system as late as after Germany's defeat of 1918 by advising against a radical break with its traditions.

Max Weber had grave doubts about Bismarck's merits as the political educator of his nation just as he lacked confidence in most of what the Kaiser stood for. Although his own hopes of attaining actual power had come to naught, now he was to have some influence on the development of the Weimar Republic. In company with many others, however, especially in scholarly circles, Weber never envisaged himself as a spokesman of the new Republic of Germany. Neither as a scholar nor as a political man of potential action could he really see Germany living up to its potential greatness under a republican regime.[105]

In his proposals for constitutional reform, his deep-seated conservatism remains clearly evident. Throughout the postwar period until his death in 1920, they reflected Weber's own special ideas on political criticism and its place in a wider life and culture. Even the strongest admirers of Weber's sociology are critical of some aspects of his political writings, and even his strongest opponents will acknowledge the rigor and contemporaneity of his criticism. To do Weber's political writings justice, admirers and critics alike must capture the atmosphere of a period of transition in all its ambiguous forms of expression relating to cooperation and conflict, of right and wrong beginnings, and of first trends of thought, because Weber's death had occurred in the early days of the Republic. Some of the attention Weber's political writings received was due largely to his courage in confronting some of the most controversial issues of political life. Weber's own life was subject to the tensions of his milieu. He anticipated the difficulties which the young republic would have to encounter, especially from conservative elements, if it were to abandon monarchical institutions altogether. Weber, in fact, knew that no complete ideological shift away from the monarchical system would occur since the pattern of responsiveness, even among more radical Social Democrats, and even before August 1914, had been favorable to a constitutional monarchy as the form of government most suitable for Germany.[106] Certainly the long-standing conflict between liberal and anti-liberal tendencies within both the nation and the political parties (in the latter case with the sole exception of the Independents who split from the Social Democrats), suggests why Weber emphasized the necessity for securing some *modus vivendi.* Believing that the validation of the Republican regime would be considerably weakened were it to ignore these tendencies, he publicly went on record opposing the Republican cause until the very outbreak of the Revolution.

Perhaps considering that Weber had given a very balanced account of the failure of the monarchy in Germany, it appeared all the more surprising that he should oppose the Republic for so long. Charging William II with inability to govern effectively himself, he further credited him with responsibility for the transfer of virtually all authority to the military establishment.[107] Weber, in fact, had recognized the bankruptcy of the monarchy in Germany much earlier than most of his compatriots. In trying to find a creative medium between the warring factions within German society, he conceived his own role to be a mediating one. Aware of the need for an elite in mass democracy which neither the past rulers of Germany nor any current ones appeared to be qualified to meet, his political writings became a medium for influencing the rehabilitation of the political life of his country at the very moment when the old centers of power were declining.

Yet Weber shared Nietzsche's insight into the mentality of the German people, especially their inclination toward unquestioning obedience and their lack of political imagination. Both of them saw earlier than most the signs of internal disintegration and the creation of deep and lasting schisms which no incompetent monarch could bridge. When World War I began, Weber's thoughts about the war were perhaps affected at least partly by the resultant unity of state and nation, a unity such as had not been experienced in peacetime. Whoever bore responsibility for starting the war, the fact remains that the vast majority of Germans did not question their own motives for entering it. The sense of unity was underscored by a lack of guilt feeling on the part of a nation that felt called upon to defend the fatherland against what was considered a malicious attack. As will be remembered from the chapter on Max Weber and the war, it was this oneness of the people which only a short time ago had been so divided, for which Weber had such high praise. He regarded the unity of the nation as a springboard to its rightful place in world politics. He was, of course, aware that the contribution to national unity and pride made by early military successes, still obtaining even after the setback at the Marne, constituted an important but unreliable index of the spirit of unity. He himself had criticized the indiscriminate submarine warfare which had been publicly portrayed as promising certain victory. After the great debacle at Verdun (1916), with the American entry into the war, the English blockade, and a last-ditch gigantic though ill-fated effort in 1918, the consequences were unavoidable. Essentially, neither a set of abstract rules nor a concrete code of behavior could now have stimulated the people's enthusiasm in support of any given political system.

Weber's lifelong concern had been with the question of emergence of political leadership in the modern bureaucratic state. His emphasis on charismatic leadership based upon his preference for strong executive leadership in a bureaucratic mass democracy marked an attempt to overcome the dualist dimensions of life for the sake of national unity and greatness which he cherished in the first part of the war. Yet, neither then nor in this postwar period did Weber lose the base for an abiding sense of parliamentary debate and respect for the rule of law. He was responsive to the need to serve the inalienable rights of the individual; however: "as a man of the nineteenth century he may have had a tendency to believe that these precarious conquests of political civilization were assured once and for all." [108]

Authoritarianism in Germany has been traditionally enlightened, demonstrating a genuine concern for the general social welfare. Weber himself saw social legislation as a means to augment the power of the state, a fact which does not obviate its humanitarian consequences. But the authoritarian state cannot be permissive in the transformation of subject into citizen with all that this conceptual change connotes. Dahrendorf rightly insists: "What is remarkable about Imperial Germany is that through-out the industrial revolution it managed to miss the road to modernity and instead consolidated itself as an industrial feudal society with an authoritarian welfare state. Even in the Weimar Republic, Germany did not embark on this road; the revolution to start the journey had not occurred." [109]

In addition, in both republics, Weimar and subsequently Bonn, and to some extent even in Imperial Germany, approximately half of the power elite consisted of lawyers. Of all aspirants to top positions, especially in government, they show the highest mobility as compared to other professional groups. This professional monopolization of the top positions might be conducive to a state of law (*Rechtsstaat*), but it does not necessarily insure a genuinely liberal society.[110] Conservatism and traditionalism coupled with a high degree of social and economic security have resulted essentially in an opportunism marked by moral indifference and a lack of political imagination. Ralf Dahrendorf only recently called for a drastic revision of Bonn's policy of staffing its most important embassies with men whose only professional equipment has been the study of law.[111]

In this historical context, Weber's own views become more intelligible. Weber's career began as a lawyer. He soon made bold use of his own seemingly inexhaustible scholarly talents while clinging stubbornly to some old values. Walter Weyrauch, a German lawyer who emigrated to the United States, appears to have had primarily German lawyers in mind when he writes:

Some of the personality features of lawyers even seem to encourage anti-democratic developments. Lawyers may cling to ultraconservative groups rather than to more permissive ones. . . . Lawyers will feel discomfort in situations in which power is unsettled or in flux. The resulting uncertainty is incompatible with the personality structure of many lawyers, and they may not feel secure until a dominating power center has been established.[112]

In his empirical studies Weber pushed into unexplored territory far beyond the confines of the pursuits of jurists. He was far too astute and cultivated for so limited a social profile. Yet, while he was firmly rooted in his own social background, and while his view of life included the urgent necessity for a far more imaginative political leadership, the determining forces in his thinking seem to have been essentially traditional and conservative, both attributes frequently ascribed to German holders of legal degrees. The particular social and political contours of the German scene to which he devoted himself undoubtedly differ from those of other cultures. Many German liberals besides Weber hoped that the establishment of the Empire would unify their socially divided and politically untutored nation; except for the Left, few had questioned the national quest for a great colonial empire supported by a strong navy. Few had refrained from opting for imperialism and naval armament. Many of Weber's colleagues had viewed the possibility of war with resignation rather than misgivings; some saw it as a means to bring the nation together. Max Weber and Friedrich Meinecke, though they modified their views subsequently too, wanted to procure for Germany a place in the sun. Although adopting a more restrained stance subsequently, it was too late to counteract some of the potential political influence of Weber's pre-war political writings and speeches: "Weber was a National Liberal but he was not a liberal in the American sense. He was not even, strictly speaking, a democrat. . . . He placed the glory of the nation and the power of the state above all else . . . but he believed neither in the general will nor in the right of peoples to self-determination nor in the democratic ideology." [113] Never accepting the primacy of the individual, he could not proceed from this basic premise to the alignment of ethical and social values. Collective values such as the sense of unity and comradeship in wartime might be viewed as social means to enhance individual contentment, prized for the sake of the individual. But Weber's ethnocentrism assumed the priority of the collective national interest: the individual as well as the social welfare measures from which he benefits exist ultimately for the sake of the nation and the state.

Herein perhaps lies the fundamental difference between Weber's concepts of liberalism and democracy and those of the western manner of thinking. But his views must be seen in the light of not only his own but of his country's alienation from certain patterns of attitudes and values which other western countries have traditionally embraced. Other German historians endow liberalism and democracy with both individual and collective meanings. After World War II the German historian, Gerhard Ritter, illustrates this fact poignantly: "Democracy in its original, strict sense not yet softened by liberal admixtures is not the safe-guarding of personal liberty against arbitrary rule and relentless force, but the immediate rule of the people."[114] There can be no question but that even after World War II the ideas of Gerhard Ritter and other reputable German scholars remained inapposite to prevailing western conceptions of the role of the individual in a liberal and democratic society.

Firmly grounded in the knowledge of Germany's own worth and conscious of her potential power, Weber refused to participate in any public debate of the causes of the German catastrophe or to stigmatize those responsible for it. He chastized as unmanly and immature any concentration on guilt feelings. Weber was critical of past errors in the conduct of policy, less because it reflected a policy that could only result in war, than because it was inept and frivolous. He defensively refused to define such policy as ethically objectionable.[115]

The way Weber himself described his reaction to the loss of the war affords an intriguing insight into this perspective. He had denounced his government's lack of foresight which caused it to overplay its hand when it engaged in unlimited submarine warfare and when it presented the Russians with the terms of the Treaty of Brest-Litovsk. Such pre-datory action was opposed to Germany's national interest.[116] Nevertheless, Weber resented being drawn into a morbid state of mind by what he saw as the nervous and cowardly attempt of those who tried to make judgments based on hindsight. His factualism represented a rational adjustment to the reality of a lost war which, in his opinion, demanded of himself and others an acceptance of a fate which "must be borne manfully and in silence."[117] As Weber explained to an English visitor, they could establish their contact either as "gentlemen" or as "old maids." They might discuss "guilt" and topics associated with that phenomenon, in which case neither he nor his guest could escape damage to their integrity. The other alternative would be simply to say: "We lost the match. . . . What is to be done to face the responsibility in history?"[118] Confused by obduracy on the part of British statesmen, he contended their attitude would have to give way to a more enlightened approach if all hope was not to be abandoned. He added that while an injury to Germany's interests could be sustained, an affront to her honor would not meet with forgiveness.[119]

Obviously, historical responsibility ultimately cannot be decided on the basis of national honor as a criterion. Weber was not alone in imposing upon this irrational argument a rationalistic method. Nor was his assumption acceptable that in the last analysis "the god of battles is on the side of the stronger batallions." [120] Meanwhile, many German historians distribute blame equally among the nations engaged in World War I. The tragic and sometimes pathetic attempt to come to terms with Germany's past gave rise to the notion that since most nations could not help sliding into it, no question of war guilt could conceivably be raised.

Weber's views are again apparent in his attitudes toward Ludendorff; he considered it shameful that the German press should have taken Ludendorff to task in October 1918. This great commander, he believed, should not be subjected to any evaluation other than that befitting his position. Even though Weber himself had criticized certain aspects of Ludendorff's conduct, he contended that a general must be permitted to believe in his star and to follow his venturous calling. His integrity must not be allowed to suffer. Granting the general's unfitness for politics, Weber's confidence in Ludendorff's heroic stature and aristocratic spirit remained unfailing. Marianne Weber relates that he not only believed in it but that, in fact, "he wanted to believe in it." [121] When confronted with criticisms of tactical decisions and military strategy that had extended the war, Weber publicly sided with Ludendorff and Hindenburg. He emphatically stated: "whoever reviles our commander in the field is a scoundrel." [122]

One of Weber's most remarkable traits, indeed, is exemplified by such unfailingly supporting reactions which reflect his own ethic of conviction as he defended those held up to public scorn. Honor and justice demanded such a course of action from him. Moreover, to preserve the dignity of the nation in its hour of defeat appeared to him more important than giving way to the ardor of despair or to any other high-pitched emotion. The tragic experience of the lost war, he argued, involved neither depression nor catharsis, but the maintenance of the dignity of the nation and the heightening of its vitality. This heightening comes in experiencing a community in existence to which he referred when speaking of the ordinary soldier in the field. However great his own critical awareness of the tradition in which he wrote and of his own place in it, he conceded nothing to it, even at considerable personal cost.

Weber had anticipated the coming of the Revolution for some time. He clearly recognized that the traditional lip service of public figures toward the working class was one of the main reasons for its increasingly extremist tone. The everlasting promises made to it underlay the sustained high emotional pitch evident within the movement.[123] Yet, the rule of some in the workers' and soldiers' councils he viewed critically. The public remarks of several of their representatives he regarded as mendacious. The new ethical precepts would stand the test of time no more than those practiced under the old regime which had become the target of their criticism.[124] Weber acknowledged that the Kaiser's delay in abdicating even after he must have realized that he could no longer hope to retain his throne added fuel to the already tenuous situation. Yet only a few days prior to the seizure of power by Eisner, Weber himself had sought to stem the tide of revolutionary trends, only to realize that his arguments went unheeded. While he was on friendly terms with Toller and had contact with a number of other revolutionary socialists, his suggestions inspired little response. During the reign of William II, the ground for misunderstanding has been Weber's persistent, challenging sharpness and the sheer weight of his critical faculties. Now on the eve of the Revolution he found himself confronted with the charge that he was not keeping in step with the times, that he was clinging to ideals which had become obsolete.[125]

Although Weber had prepared himself for the Revolution, he bitterly resented its timing. Coinciding as it did with the liquidation of the war under the most inauspicious circumstances, Weber charged it with responsibility for most of the nation's calamities. His characteristic historical sense of fairness failed him when he largely blamed the Social Democrats for accepting a policy that seemed to place the country and its future generations under the bondage of the victors. Marianne Weber stressed that while her husband had been unsympathetic to adherents of the former regime who originated the stab-in-the-back legend, he looked askance at the "unfaithful populace" which would not make a last stand. He was especially critical toward *obiter dicta* coming from colleagues who threw the academic mantle around their shoulders.[126]

Weber also deplored the lack of understanding in responsible circles for his own last hope, namely, that Wilson would realize that his role of arbiter between the great powers was contingent upon the maintenance of Germany's armed forces.[127] His restraining influence, Weber asserted, would be undermined in the event of Germany's disarmament. France, for example, could then afford to dispense with American military aid which they might well have required if they were to have been confronted with the possibility of having to continue the war. The unwillingness of Germany's new rulers to risk further combat against the external enemies filled him with deep resentment. Actually, Weber probably overestimated the influence that any appeal to communal values could exercise at this stage, considering that deep schisms had begun to develop despite all attempts aimed at inspiring national unity.

From the military point of view, when an attack by the Americans and the French on July 18, 1918 compelled the retreat of two German armies, the Germans were to abdicate the strategic initiative to the enemy for the remainder of the war. Ludendorff himself noted the seriousness of the failure of the German offensive, explaining that the thrust of the German army had not been adequate to administer the required decisive defeat to the enemy.[128] On September 2, 1918 William II wrote plaintively:

The campaign is lost. Now our troops have been running back without a stop since July 18. The fact is, we are exhausted. When the offensive was opened on the Marne on July 15, I was assured that the French had only 8 divisions left in reserve, and the British perhaps 13. Instead of this, the enemy assembles a crowd of divisions in the forest of Cotterêts, unnoticed by us, attacks our right flank and forces us to retreat. Since then we have received blow after blow. Our armies can simply do no more.[129]

Initially a difference of opinion had obtained among German military and civilian leaders regarding the capability of the nation to continue in the war. It will be recalled that Ludendorff and Hindenburg were responsible for initiating the move toward securing terms for an armistice. As negotiations between the German government and Woodrow Wilson wore on, however, the armistice terms appeared to be considerably more severe than the Germans had expected; only then did the military leaders start to retreat from their previous frantic efforts to convince the government of the need for an immediate end to hostilities. By now, however, the latter had become persuaded of Germany's inability to continue and they prevailed upon President Wilson to specify the terms which would satisfy the Allies. Ludendorff, meanwhile, resented the Allies' formidable demands sufficiently to urge continuation of the war. When the civilian government refused to take his advice, Ludendorff prepared the ground for the stab-in-the-back legend, namely, that the German army was not defeated on the battlefield but was betrayed by a collapse of the homefront. He thereby set the stage for the shibboleth that the civilian government rather than the High Command was responsible for Germany's misfortunes. That Ludendorff was eminently successful may be ascertained from the fact that Hitler later employed this argument most effectively to promote the rise of National Socialism and the demise of the Weimar Republic.

Accordingly, Weber's hope to hold out to the enemy the prospect of armed national resistance if the terms should prove unacceptable to Germany, would seem to be fanciful. He believed that both President Wilson's strength in the peace negotiations and Germany's bargaining position depended upon the retention of Germany's military might, insofar as she could not be forced into surrender without the use of

America's armed forces. Unless Germany's military potential power were preserved, Wilson's position would be completely undermined. Since America's allies could now write their own terms, Wilson would have to accept the fact that his efforts toward mediation would be rejected unless he were willing to risk going to war against his allies. Weber suggested that peace negotiations could be conducted without a prior armistice if the enemy should "insist on continuing the slaughter." [130]

The mediation of a compromise peace would indeed have been closer to the true national interests of the Allies because it would have been more likely to contribute to the preservation of a balance of power in Europe. Actually both Wilson and House should have received greater credit for having attempted persistently, as early as 1915 and 1916, to achieve that end. They failed principally because American military posture and isolationist traditions were such that the German government underestimated certain currents of American public opinion and how much weight would ultimately be brought against Germany.

Weber denigrated the Revolution because it would render Germany militarily defenseless and leave the vanquished at the mercy of the victors. The outspoken supporters of peace at any price, Weber could write, would effect an immediate dissolution of the army, thereby allowing no chance for a resumption of the war effort. Thus, Weber also takes up what was probably one of the most current themes in Germany: the German army was unbeaten in 1918 and surrender was brought about by domestic subversion. Some of Weber's public statements as well as his private utterances at that time dramatize his shortsightedness and his atypically uncritical attitude towards his nation's defeat. His estimate of the German will to fight on, as well as that of the armed forces, was too generous, and as a consequence his judgment of the revolution was misleading. He lacked both perspective and focus in this respect because he preferred not to admit the extent of Germany's military debacle and therefore either patently or unconsciously passed over the lack of military feasibility of continuing the war.

Yet, despite such highly debatable interpretation of the military situation and such vindictiveness toward the Revolution, Weber did not contribute to popular misapprehension by blaming social democracy as such for the Revolution, one of the main political myths Hitler later inserted so emphatically in his propaganda. One may nevertheless speculate upon the potential influence a man of Weber's stature might have had if, like Carl von Ossietzky and others, he would have seen fit to expose this aspect of official military propaganda instead of lending it substance by his professional competence and reputation.

Weber's letters at this juncture of German history serve as catalysts reflecting his philosophy in language unencumbered by the erudition of his formal writings. Genuinely human, these letters reveal not only his misgivings regarding Germany's immediate future, but they also reveal his personal feelings and the progress of his intellectual and political development. In a letter to Friedrich Naumann, Weber stressed the guilt of the German government for having committed Germany to a course of capitulation. As a result, Weber insisted, the German government and the party involved should give an accounting in public; all actions and transactions involved in the peace negotiations and the demobilization should be explained before the next elections. Weber demanded that this historical reckoning include determination of all the facts in detailed form, the evidence to encompass all manner of proofs and data relating to persons and dates relevant to a consideration of the vital decisions, down to the part played by each person involved and thus responsible for the situation.[131]

Looking in retrospect at Weber's accusations directed at the Social Democrats, Mommsen says that Weber came dangerously close to supporting the stab-in-the-back legend which arose subsequently, even though in a more vulgarized form, and which helped destroy the domestic policy of the Weimar Republic.[132] Weber, it seems, did not really consider other possibilities or alternatives in this context. The stab-in-the-back legend finds perhaps its closest approximation in Weber's article of January 2, 1919 in the *Fraenkischer Kurier*, "Innocent Social Democracy." If the characterization here is blunt, the words again illumine the emotional texture of Weber's pathos. We can ignore his rather dated remarks. In the light of events, what really matters are the far-ranging but interrelated considerations he uses to the political changes brought about by the Revolution.

Weber insisted it must ever be remembered that it was Social Democracy, including many Majority Socialists, to whom responsibility must be ascribed for charting a course which caused the German people to have "the knife pushed into its back" (*das Messer in den Ruecken gestossen*). Weber's account reaches its climax in his description of Germany's condition as one in which she had been rendered so powerless that she could not even have prevailed against the Poles or the Czechs. Ignoring the army leaders' previous frantic insistence on the urgent need, based on military considerations, for cessation of hostilities, Weber made it appear that the government, not the army leaders, was responsible for handing the nation over to her vindictive enemies.[133]

He apparently had not travelled far from the stand taken in 1893 when at the meeting of the Association for Social Policy he indicated that the presence of the Social Democrats was under no circumstances to signify an "agreement" with them, but that they were both welcome and indispensable as determined critics.[134] It is perhaps noteworthy that Eduard Baumgarten, whose sympathetic treatment of Weber's philosophy is well known, should have pointed to Weber as representative of a generation whose experiences and diverse forms of conduct were in part encompassed in the Hitler period. Baumgarten effectively demonstrates the necessity and the opportunity for restoring German priorities to their proper balance in the future.[135] Such analyses of the beliefs and ethical values bearing on World War I from the German point of view provide a valuable source of information.

Other observers have other points of view. Opposing Mommsen's criticism of Weber's recommendation for the direct election of the president of the Weimar republic and the effect of this constitutional provision on the legitimation of Hitler by the German people, Karl Loewenstein insists:

This hypothesis completely misreads the position of the president of the Weimar Republic. . . . What is more, Mommsen's thesis completely misunderstands Max Weber's political ethics. Such a distortion could not go unchided. . . . This perversion of Weber's thought would not be worth mentioning if Mommsen and others had not repeated the denigration . . . in addressing the Heidelberg congress of sociologists.[136]

It seems nevertheless that Loewenstein's somewhat uncritical analysis of Weber's attitude toward the Revolution and Social Democracy, overlooks some inapposite judgments. This is not altogether surprising, for a kind of provocative elusiveness is an essential part of Weber, and even of his own approach to his own role in practical politics. A man with no consecutive or binding political commitments to public life, Weber often presented the image of a solitary figure in German politics, standing at his lectern as an academician or sitting at his desk engaged in writing. This image represents one aspect of Weber the man and the political writer, but no more than one aspect. Weber had a penchant for all kinds of political actualities. With the mantle of a scholar's seclusion thrown around his shoulders, he constantly engaged in correspondence with numerous important public figures whose task was to deal with political dilemmas confronting the young republic. He somehow conveyed the impression that his political writings afforded him both a solace for not being in the position to exercise power himself and a medium of rehabilitating the political life of his country at a time when the old centers of power no longer existed and when he could not fully accept the new order either. There can be no absolute certainty as to how to summarize Weber's political role during this postwar transition; this ambiguity may be interpreted as part of his own ambivalance toward both scholarship and politics.

As one tries to orient Weber during this immediate postwar period, which also brought the end of his life, he emerges as poised between desperate affirmation and pervasive despair concerning his country's future. However ambivalent he may have been about the outcome of political events and however detached and meticulous his scholarship, it seems fair to conclude that Weber's one consistent, overriding political concern was the collective greatness of Germany as a nation state. As Raymond Avon concludes, ". . . the value which Max Weber, by free choice, placed above all others was . . . national greatness, not democracy or even the personal freedoms." [137]

NOTES

[1] Max Rheinstein, "Introduction" in *Max Weber on Law in Economy and Society*, ed. by Max Rheinstein (Cambridge: Harvard University Press, 1966), p. XLIV.
[2] Cf. *Max Weber, Staatssoziologie*, ed. Johannes Winckelmann, 2nd. rev. ed. (Berlin: Duncker and Humblot, 1966).
[3] Gerth and Mills, *op. cit.*, p. 78. Cf. also Vernon Van Dyke, *Political Science: A Philosophical Analysis* (Stanford: Stanford University Press, 1960), p. 134.
[4] Cf. Golo Mann, *Deutsche Geschichte des neunzehnten und zwanzigsten Jahrhunderts* (Frankfurt: Buechergilde Gutenberg, S. Fischer Verlag, 1964), p. 409.
[5] Cf. Manfred Haettich, *Lehrbuch der Politikwissenschaft: Grundlegung und Systematik*, Vol. I (Mainz: v. Hase und Koehler Verlag, 1967), p. 44.
[6] Golo Mann, *op. cit.*, p. 409.
[7] Klaus Epstein, *Matthias Erzberger and the Dilemma of German Democracy* (Princeton: Princeton University Press, 1959), p. 182.
[8] *Ibid.*, p. 187.
[9] *Lebensbild*, p. 601.
[10] *Ibid.*, pp. 601–602.
[11] Cf. *Lebensbild*, pp. 629–630 and *P.S.* 2nd. ed., article on "Vaterland und Vaterlandspartei," p. 217ff.
[12] *Ibid.*, p. 219.
[13] Cf. *Heidelberger Tagblatt* of December 10, 1917, cited in *ibid.*, p. 630.
[14] "Russlands Uebergang zur Scheindemokratie," in the *Hilfe*, April 26, 1917, *P.S.*, 2nd. ed., p. 210.
[15] *Ibid.*
[16] *Ibid.*, p. 205.
[17] *Ibid.*, pp. 209–210.
[18] *Ibid.*, pp. 193–194.
[19] *Ibid.*, p. 205.
[20] *Ibid.*, p. 206.
[21] Cf. *P.S.*, 2nd. ed., p. 207.
[22] Cf. W. J. Mommsen, *Max Weber und Die Deutsche Politik 1890–1920* (Tuebingen: J. C. B. Mohr [Paul Siebeck], 1959), p. 264.
[23] Cf. letter to the *Frankfurter Zeitung* of June 27, 1917 cited in *ibid.*, p. 264.
[24] Letter to Hohmann cited in *ibid.*
[25] Letter to Haussmann of September 7, 1917 cited in *ibid.*, p. 265.
[26] Cf. *Lebensbild*, p. 631.
[27] Cf. Richard von Kuehlmann, *Erinnerungen* (Heidelberg, 1948), p. 532, cited in Mommsen, *op. cit.*, p. 271.
[28] *Lebensbild*, p. 631.
[29] *Ibid.*
[30] Cf. *ibid.*
[31] Letter to Eulenburg of January 17, 1918, in *ibid.*
[32] Letter to Marianne Weber of January 13, 1918 (copy in Weber's estate) cited by Mommsen, *op. cit.*, p. 272.
[33] Letter to Oncken of February 1, 1918, *Lebensbild*, p. 632.
[34] *Ibid.*
[35] *Ibid.*
[36] *Ibid.*

37 *P.S.*, 2nd. ed., p. 280, "Innere Lage und Aussenpolitik," article in the *Frankfurter Zeitung* on February 3, 1918.
38 *Ibid.*
39 *Ibid.*
40 *Ibid.*
41 *Ibid.*
42 *Ibid.*, p. 281.
43 *Ibid.*
44 *Ibid.*
45 *Ibid.*, pp. 281–282.
46 *Ibid.*, p. 282.
47 Letter to Oncken of February 7, 1918, cited in Mommsen, *op. cit.*, p. 274.
48 Cf. Mommsen, *op. cit.*, p. 274.
49 *P.S.*, 2nd. ed., p. 284.
50 Mommsen, *op. cit.*, fn., pp. 274–275.
51 Cf. Mommsen, *op. cit.*, p. 275.
52 Cf. Mommsen, *op. cit.*, p. 275.
53 *Ibid.*
54 Cf. *Wirtschaft und Gesellschaft* cited in Mommsen, *op. cit.*, p. 275.
55 Cf. *P.S.*, 2nd. ed., *op. cit.*, p. 291.
56 Cf. Mommsen, *op. cit.*, pp. 275–276.
57 *Gesammelte Aufsaetze aur Soziologie und Sozialpolitik*, p. 515, and p. 517 cited in Mommsen, *op. cit.*, p. 276.
58 Mommsen, *op. cit.*, p. 276.
59 Letter to Friedrich Naumann of April 12, 1917 in *P.S.*, 1st. ed., p. 469.
60 Mommsen, *op. cit.*, p. 277.
61 Letter to Friedrich Naumann of May 8, 1917 in *P.S.*, 1st. ed., p. 470.
62 *Ibid.*
63 Ottokar Czernin, *Rede ueber die Politik waehrend des Weltkriegs* (Vienna, 1919), p. 16 also Czernin's *Im Weltkrieg* (Vienna, 1919), p. 211, cited in Klaus Epstein, *Matthias Erzberger and the Dilemma of German Democracy* (Princeton: Princeton University Press, 1959), pp. 187–188.
64 *Ibid.*, p. 188. Cf. also R. Fester, *Die Politik Kaiser Karls und der Wendepunkt des Weltkrieges* (Munich, 1925), cited in *ibid.*, p. 188.
65 Cf. letter to Friedrich Naumann of May 5, 1917, in *P.S.*, 1st. ed., p. 470.
66 Cf. Karl-Heinz Janssen, "Der Verhinderte Kreuzzug: Das aufregendste Kapitel des deutsch-sowjetischen Verhaeltnisses: Warum Kaiser Wilhelm die Bolshewiken nicht aus Moskau vertrieb: Deutschland brauchte Lenin's Siegel auf die Annexion des Baltikums," Book Review of Winfried Baumgart. *Deutsche Ostpolitik 1918: Von Brest-Litowsk bis zum Ende des Ersten Weltkrieges* (Vienna and Munich: R. Oldenburg Verlag, 1967), in *Die Zeit*, November 14, 1967, No. 45, p. 12. Reprinted by permission of the publisher.
67 *Ibid.*
68 *Ibid.*
69 *Ibid.*
70 *Ibid.*
71 *Ibid.*
72 *Ibid.*
73 Cf. *ibid.*
74 Cf. *ibid.*
75 *Ibid.*
76 *Ibid.*
77 *Ibid.*
78 *Ibid.*
79 *Ibid.*
80 *Ibid.*
81 *Ibid.*
82 Cf. H. H. Gerth and C. Wright Mills, *From Max Weber: Essays in Sociology* (New York: Oxford University Press, 1946), pp. 77–128.
83 Cf. Hans Raupach et al., edited by Werner Conze and Hans Raupach, *Die Staats—und Wirtschaftskrise des Deutschen Reichs*, 1929/33 Industrielle Welt: Schriftenreihe des Arbeitskreises fuer moderne Sozialgeschichte, Number 8 (Stuttgart: Ernst Klett Verlag, 1967).
84 Cf. Hans-Juergen Puhle, *Agrarische Interessenpolitik und Preussischer Konservatismus im Wilhelminischen Reich (1893–1914): Ein Beitrag zur Analyse des Nationalismus in Deutschland am Beispiel des Bundes der Landwirte und der*

Deutschkonservativen Partei, Schriftenreihe des Forschungsinstituts der Fried-rich-Ebert-Stiftung. Series B. Historisch-politische Schriften (Hanover: Verlag fuer Literatur und Zeitgeschehen, 1966).

85 Cf. "Die Verhaeltnisse der Landarbeiter im Ostelbischen Deutschland" (1892), *Schriften des Vereins fuer Sozialpolitik*, Vol. 55; "Privatenquêten ueber die Lage der Landarbeiter," 1892, *Mitteilungen des evangelisch-sozialen Kongresses.* "Die laendliche Arbeitsverfassung" (1893) *Schriften des Vereins fuer Sozialpolitik*, Vol. 58; "Entwicklungstendenzen in der Lage der ostelbischen Landarbeiter" (1894) *Archiv fuer soziale Gestzgebung*, Vol. 7.

86 "Parlament und Regierung im Neugeordneten Deutschland," in *P.S.*, 2nd. ed., pp. 294–431.

87 Cf. Friedrich Naumann, "Der Deutsche Reichstag," in *Die Deutsche Rundschau*, Vol. I, 1908, p. 326.

88 Cf. *P.S.*, 2nd ed., p. 372.

89 *Cf. Christliche Welt*, 1894, p. 477 cited in Mommsen, *op. cit.*, p. 139.

90 *Ibid.*, p. 140.

91 Cf. *ibid.*

92 Cf. Ludwig Bergstraesser, *Geschichte Der Politischen Parteien in Deutschland: Deutsches Handbuch Der Politik*, Vol. II, edited by Wilhelm Mommsen (Munich: Guenter Olzog Verlag, 1965), p. 209.

93 After its leadership voluntarily dissolved it, a large part of its membership continued its existence within the *Deutsche Staatspartei*, which had been founded on November 9, 1930 by liberals and leaders of the Democrats.

94 Attila Chanady, "The Dissolution of the German Democratic Party in 1930," *The American Historical Review*, Vol. LXXIII, No. 5, June 1968, p. 1433.

95 *Ibid.*

96 *Ibid.*

97 Cf. *ibid.* See also Erich Matthias and Rudolf Morsey, "Die Deutsche Staatspartei" in *Das Ende der Parteien 1933* (Duesseldorf, 1960), and Sigmund Neumann, *Die Parteien der Weimarer Republic* (Stuttgart, 1965), both cited in *ibid.*

98 Cf. Attila Chanady, *op. cit.*, p. 1434. Also see Otto Nuschke "Wie die Deutsche Demokratische Partei wurde, was sie leistete und was sie ist," in *Zehn Jahre Deutsche Republik*, edited by Anton Erkelenz (Berlin, 1928) and B. B. Frye, "The German Democratic Party 1918–1930," *Western Political Quarterly*, Vol. XVI, March 1963, p. 167 both cited in *ibid.*

99 Cf. Attila Chanady, *op. cit.*, p. 1434.

100 *Ibid.*, p. 1435.

101 *Ibid.*, p. 1437.

102 *Ibid.*, p. 1438.

103 *Ibid.*, cf. Otto Gessler, *Reichswehrpolitik in der Weimarer Zeit*, ed., Kurt Sendtner (Stuttgart, 1958), pp. 170–174, 336.

104 Cf. Wolfgang Elben, *Das Problem der Kontinuitaet in der Deutschen Revolution: Die Politik der Staatssekretaere und der Militaerischen Fuehrung vom November 1918 bis Februar 1919, Beitraege zur Geschichte des Parlamentarismus und der politischen Parteien*, Number 31 (Duesseldorf: Droste Verlag, 1965).

105 Cf. Wolfgang J. Mommsen, *Max Weber und die Deutsche Politik, 1890–1920*, p. 287.

106 *P.S.*, 2nd. ed., p. 324 and also Karl Loewenstein, *Max Weber's Political Ideas in the Perspective of Our Time* (The University of Massachusetts Press, 1966), pp. 13–15. See Loewenstein's discussion of Weber's case for the monarchical system in which Loewenstein seeks to support it by demonstrating its applicability when seen in the perspective of countries which have retained the monarchy as their form of government, herewith illustrating that ". . . Max Weber's opinion about monarchy as a socially and politically integrating institution was altogether correct." In this connection, Loewenstein cites seven West European countries in which the monarchy had, in fact, not only maintained itself but had also become more solidly based than many people of Weber's generation would have been willing to grant.

107 *P.S.*, 2nd. ed., p. 438.

108 Raymond Aron, *Main Currents in Sociological Thought, Vol. II: Durkheim/ Pareto/Weber*, translated by R. Howard and Helen Weaver (New York: Basic Books, Inc., 1967), p. 249.

109 Ralf Dahrendorf, *Society and Democracy in Germany* (Garden City, New York: Doubleday and Company, Inc., 1967), p. 64.

110 Cf. *ibid.*, p. 233.

111 Cf. *Allgemeine Zeitung*, Nr. 47, Saturday/Sunday—February 24/25, 1968, p. 1.

112 Walter E. Weyrauch, *The Personality of Lawyers* (New Haven-London, 1964), pp. 280f. Cited in Dahrendorf, *op. cit.*, p. 244.

113 Raymond Aron, *op. cit.*, p. 242.

114 Gerhard Ritter, *The German Problem: Basic Questions of German Political Life, Past and Present* (Columbus, Ohio, 1965), p. 45. Cited in Dahrendorf, *op. cit.*, p. 13.

115 Cf. *P.S.*, 2nd. ed., p. 476.

116 Reports in *Wiesbadener Tagblatt* of December 6, 1918 and in the *Heidelberger Tagblatt* of January 3, 1919, cited in W. J. Mommsen, *op. cit.*, p. 291.

117 Cf. *Lebensbild*, p. 658.

118 Letter to Oncken of February 29, 1919 in *Lebensbild*, p. 658.

119 Cf. *Lebensbild*, Letter to Oncken of February 19, 1919, pp. 658–59.

120 *P.S.*, 2nd. ed., p. 476.

121 Cf. *Lebensbild*, p. 663.

122 Weber expressed these sentiments at a meeting in Mannheim in November 1918. His remarks contained in his address were reported by Baumgarten, who had attended the meeting, and who subsequently permitted Mommsen to avail himself of the manuscript of a Weber lecture. Cf. Mommsen, *op. cit.*, p. 291. The foregoing may be seen to accord also with the general subject of a campaign speech delivered by Weber and reported by the *Heidelberger Tagblatt* of January 3, 1919, entitled: "Germany's Reconstruction":
    Pointing to Hindenburg's human stature, Weber commented that he stood "sky-high above it all." His worth had not proved itself solely to rest in his capacity as "the greatest commander in the field on earth but now also as an equally great German." Protective in his attitude toward Hindenburg, Weber referred to the charges brought against the High Command, as having been addressed not to him but to *Ludendorff.* To this observation Weber added an acknowledgement of the latter as one of the greatest contemporary commanders in the field whose role as a great commander, in Weber's judgment, warrants "A faith in his star. . . ."

123 Cf. letter to Helene Weber of November 18, 1918 in *P.S.*, 1st. ed., p. 481.

124 Cf. Max Weber, "Der Ort der Politik in der Ethik: Politische Schuld," address delivered in Munich, January 1919, printed in *P.S.*, 2nd. ed., p. 538 and from Eduard Baumgarten, *Max Weber: Werk und. Person* (Tuebingen: J. C. B. Mohr [Paul Siebeck], 1964), p. 540.

125 Cf. the letter G. W. Klein had written to Weber on November 6 and 7, 1918, *Lebensbild*, p. 640.

126 *Lebensbild*, p. 642, cf. also *P.S.*, 1st. ed., p. 484.

127 Cf. Weber's comments on armistice and peace, "Waffenstillstand und Frieden," *Frankfurter Zeitung*, October 27, 1918, *P.S.*, 2nd. ed., p. 435.

128 Erich Ludendorff, *Meine Kriegserinnerungen 1914–1918* (Berlin: E. S. Mittler und Sohn, 1919), p. 545.

129 Georg Alexander von Mueller, "Regierte der Kaiser?" *Tagebuchaufzeichnungen,* ed. Walter Goerlitz (Berlin and Frankfurt, 1959), p. 38 cited in Fritz Fischer, *op. cit.*, p. 625.

130 "Armistice and Peace," *Frankfurter Zeitung*, October 27, 1918, *P.S.*, 2nd. ed., p. 435.

131 Max Weber, letter to Friedrich Naumann, Heidelberg, October 11, 1918, *P.S.*, 1st. ed., p. 476.

132 Cf. Mommsen, *op. cit.*, p. 293.

133 Max Weber, "Die Unschuldige Sozialdemokratie," *Fraenkischer Kurier*, January 2, 1919. Cited in Mommsen, *op. cit.*, p. 293.

134 Cf. fn., in Eduard Baumgarten, *op. cit.*, p. 653.

135 *Ibid.*, p. VI.

136 Karl Loewenstein, *Max Weber's Political Ideas in the Perspective of Our Time* (Amherst: The University of Massachusetts Press, 1966), p. 70. Cf. also sources cited in Loewenstein. . . ; Wolfgang Mommsen, *op. cit.*, pp. 140, 143, 200f.; see Karl Loewenstein, "Max Weber als 'Ahnherr' des plebiszitaeren Fuehrerstaats," in *Koelner Zeitschrift fuer Soziologie und Sozialpolitik*, Vol. 13 (1961), pp. 275ff; see also Mommsen, *ibid.*, Vol. 15 (1963), pp. 295ff; see *Sueddeutsche Zeitung*, No. 107 of May 7, and *Frankfurter Allgemeine Zeitung*, No. 195 of May 8, 1964; all taken from Karl Loewenstein.

137 Raymond Aron, *op. cit.*, p. 248.

VII

Max Weber and the Republic

On December 1, 1918, Max Weber delivered a political speech in which he called upon the German nation to practice vigilance and discipline in the face of postwar dislocations. In his judgment the situation under a republican system of government entailed more risks than would have had to be faced had the Imperial regime survived. The old structure had provided the nation with cohesion and a sense of unity. The new German Republic would require leaders with great political skill and courage since the traditional ethos of the nation rested on very different foundations. Politically, the people were now at their lowest point of resistance after defeat. Since all too many had already divorced themselves from politics, their alienation would continue, aggravated by the broken hopes caused by a lost war. Nevertheless, Weber had only praise for the self-restraint practiced by the nation under these hard conditions.

Despite the collapse of the old regime, Weber's posture toward the Republic and its socialistic programme remained strangely ambivalent. Here again, his motives were essentially pragmatic. Although liberal in his views on routine political matters, Weber retained the profound conservatism that had been inherent all along in his political philosophy. Focusing upon typical conservative preoccupations with authority, order, community, and tradition, he challenged the premises upon which ideologically inspired progress was based, as well as the ongoing polemics against private enterprise. Yet addressing himself to "The New Germany," Weber confessed that his own position "approximated the convictions held by numerous economically trained members of Social Democracy, almost to the point of non-distinguishability." [1] He would, indeed, have joined the party, except that he would abandon his right to dissent even less from the authorities' official line than from the *demos.* He had been seriously alarmed by what the German experiment with revolution might do to the future economic structure of the country. While he paid homage to the effectiveness of the local workers'- and-soldiers' councils, and recognized the idealism within their leadership, he attacked the official policies emanating from Berlin and Munich.

Asserting that certain ideologues in Berlin and Munich would attempt to dismantle socialism, he still expressed the desire that Germany continue to push ahead along the road to planned socialization; in fact, he proclaimed time and again his fidelity to the new social order. Previously, however, Weber had made no secret of his hostility to socialism. His skepticism was clearly apparent: "A new order of things, which is the product of this terrible defeat and disgrace, will hardly take root." [2]

In attempting to draw up a balance sheet of his views, one is puzzled by the patent ambiguity of Weber's approach. In reality he rejected socialization of the economy in either the near or distant future. The economic strains caused by the war might temporarily require more intervention on the part of the government, yet he viewed this prospect with considerable pessimism. He especially feared increasing bureaucratization because it undercut the initiative of private enterprise. Unlike Schumpeter and Lukácz, he could not envisage socialism as a desirable direction of Germany's future economic development: "Weber was appalled at the thought that rationalization, which controls the sphere of the external relations among men, might enslave the soul to bureaucratization or purely technological utilitarianism. This fear he expressed in particular in the face of socialism, which tends toward a functionalization of the whole of human life, so that rationalization could become more burdensome to man than the situation which it purports to remedy." [3]

Under socialism, the competitive enterpreneurial spirit would become increasingly subject to regimentation at the hands of the state. Meanwhile he deplored the ambivalence of socialism, "which seeks to legitimize both the rights of the individual and those of the collectivity. All efforts tend toward the elimination of the exceptional, whether as the result of privileges of birth or of functions or of special jurisdictions, yet at the same time there is a definite trend toward greater docility to authority." [4] While a socialized economy might have certain short-run advantages, given the immediate consequences of the aftermath of war, in the long run socio-economic stagnation would inevitably result:

In a socialist community, direct mandatory and prohibitory decrees of a central economic control authority, in whichever way it may be conceived, would play a much greater role than such ordinations are playing today. In the event of disobedience, observance will be produced by means of some sort of "coercion" but not through struggle in the market. Which system would possess more real coercion and which one more real personal freedom cannot be decided, however, by the mere analysis of the actually existing or conceivable formal legal system. . . .

A (democratically) socialist order (in the sense current in present-day ideologies)° rejects coercion not only in the form in which it is exercised in the market through the possession of private property but also direct coercion to be exercised on the basis of purely personal claims to authority. It would recognize only the validity of agreed abstract laws, regardless of whether they are called by this name. Formally, the market community does not recognize formal coercion on the basis of personal authority. It produces in its stead a special kind of coercive situation which, as a general principle, applies without any discrimination to workers, enterprisers, producers and consumers, viz., in the impersonal form of the inevitability of adaptation to the purely economic 'laws' of the market. The sanctions consist in the loss or decrease of economic power and, under certain conditions, in the very loss of one's economic existence.

°(Weber here refers to the programs of the Social-Democratic parties, particularly those then operating in Germany.) [5]

He was obviously perturbed by the direction in which economic reform was moving. Although achievements of the Revolution should be retained "without mental reservation or ambiguity," he nevertheless deplored that these changes were the direct product of the Revolution, implemented by agencies conspicuously lacking in those administrative skills required for Germany's liberation from the present *cul-de-sac*.

If Weber, after having expressed himself so eloquently in opposition to socialism, nevertheless saw fit to accept it, he did so for two reasons. Though he answered the question as to the desirability of socialism in the negative, at times he doubted that its coming could be prevented permanently. Secondly, to establish some sort of working relationship with the Social Democrats, he appeared to consider an outwardly closer identification with leftist aims a propitious move within the context of a generally confused situation. Nevertheless, this merely tactical move did not signify a change in his convictions. In reality, at present he not only opposed the Independent Socialists and the Spartakists, but the Social Democrats as well. As seen earlier, he charged those in government positions with responsibility for having permitted the army to be disbanded and for allowing the officers' corps to be subjected to derision.[6] He felt that Ebert was under pressure by some deputies which left him without an organized army; such an army would be "on his side and that means: on the side of order." [7] Weber's assessment of Ebert was correct. Recently, numerous studies dealing with the November revolution of 1918 have challenged the myth that the policies pursued by Ebert were merely the result of situational factors, both domestic and foreign, lest Germany succumb to Bolshevist chaos.

Describing the danger of such an event as largely imaginary, they contradict the argument that the Weimar Republic was destroyed by the polarization of "Versailles and Moscow," leaving both the political parties and the government unable to forestall the event.[8] On the other hand, these sources also reveal Ebert's difficulties which explain why there was opposition to experiments such as workers'-and-soldiers' councils.[9] While he argued that the deputies had shown themselves to be irresolute toward the "Liebknecht gang," [10] in a letter to the editor of the *Frankfurter Zeitung* Weber exercized restraint in expressing his views concerning the workers'-and-soldiers' councils, saying that he had not yet drawn any final conclusions, and that above all he knew too little about their inner workings. However, he was certain that if successful, they would issue in the "dilettantization" of the economy. The economic measures endorsed by such a regime at a moment of greatest need for credit abroad could only be detrimental to the national interest.[11] Nevertheless, Weber sought for a time to assume a seemingly conciliatory stance toward socialization.

He may have reasoned that an intemperate note in his speech or any evidence of pressure in his conduct would have accentuated, or revived, the distrust and potential dislike within the ranks of even the moderate Left. At first, Weber's gesture might suggest an act of self-abnegation or at least that he had now publicly accepted a moderately socialist system, even though its realization might be long delayed. Although his personal preference lay elsewhere, Weber's public advocacy of socialism now conveyed an impression of total conviction. In part, while he had not dropped his cardinal political principles in the field of foreign policy, he had now come to recommend a conciliatory stance toward socialism with every outward sign of relish.

In point of fact, however, in advocating "planned socialization," [12] he could safely anticipate that its existence would be shortlived. His attitude is recorded in a letter to the effect that much of what had to be said now was designed in terms of "rebus sic stantibus," not "pour jamais," [13] and would go far in reassuring frightened middle-class citizens. On November 4, 1918, Weber publicly underscored his earlier contention by announcing that bourgeois intransigence precluded any chance that it might coalesce into any future state formed on a socialist basis.[14] He firmly believed that none of the then current experimentation must be allowed to threaten the permanent objective, Germany's adequacy as a power state.

Wolfgang Mommsen confirms that under no circumstances did Weber ever really accept the idea of socialization, for either the near or distant future. It is perhaps not too difficult to suggest Weber's true intent: behind the facade of a pro-socialist position, he intended by his criticism of the workings of the socialist system to work for its postponement in the future. In fact, in Mommsen's view, if Weber had not been convinced that in the long run this trend could not be reversed, he would have condemned all socialist leanings outright.[15] It would be suicidal, in Weber's judgment, to dismiss the sentiments of the governments of Germany's former adversaries, which were all purely bourgeois in character. Weber chronicled the forces which would widen the gap rather than promote equality of conditions with other nations confronting a growing trend toward imperialism. Thus Weber states that those subscribing to "radical illusions who in post-war Germany, like their counterparts under the old regime, would like to shoot every independent person telling them unpleasant truths cannot be told too often: we want to insure permanently the democratic achievements. But only in the form of a bourgeois-socialist government based upon parity."[16]

Weber further maintained that socialism had already been compromised by the obvious *"total inability* of the radical *literati."*[17] Weber's evidence in support of these conclusions is extensive. Germany's economic efficiency had worsened. However, the mistrust with which the radical Left regarded the cooperation between the Social Democrats and counterrevolutionary forces within both the military establishment and the bourgeoisie has also been vindicated.[18] Weber attacked vigorously the enormous wastefulness of the present administration, composed of what he referred to as "numerous babbling drones,"[19] and their absurd policy recommendations leading to the squandering of the remaining domestic means of production and of natural resources. The backwardness in production raised serious questions in his mind as to whether labor was capable of adjusting itself to meet even such basic needs as food requirements. He deplored the agitation against domestic private enterprise since the new formal organization of German society, viewed in terms of economic and social structure, could only strike the occupying powers as a failure to make an adaptive response to the needs of the hour. Thus the foreign military administration would, as a consequence, provide a protective cover for the domination of the German economy by foreign capital.[20] He had little doubt that the very presence of economic pressures would, at least in the immediate future, gravely darken the chances of anything but a line of bureaucratic command from the top to the bottom in the economic administration of the country. Weber foresaw a tremendous increase in government personnel occasioned by a more strongly socialized economy. In such circumstances, the private initiative obtaining under the reign of free enterprise would be severely limited. Weber, in effect, continued to subscribe to the principles of maximum voluntaristic organization of the economy.[21]

Conjuring up the vision of socialists as a collection of super-numerous wastrels, unlike other members of the intelligentsia among his contemporaries, including for example, Lukácz and Schumpeter, Weber could not bring himself to consider socialism an improvement over the present social order.[22] Mommsen notes his avowed readiness to maintain an open mind toward Social Democracy. He points to Weber's frequent references to several measures being indispensable for the success of socialism. These measures were usually close to his own heart, however, constituting a mere device directed at the ultimate defeat of socialist policies.[23] Weber appeared to equate socialism with publicly controlled syndicates and the process of socialization. In such a system, free enterprise and economic competition would have to give way to state regulation.

The most striking fact about Weber's conception of socialism is his rejection of the possibility that it might reduce the irrational elements inherent in capitalism. If there were any benefits to be gained from the basic features of socialist society, such as public ownership of the means of production or central planning, they would be short-lived. At best, they could only ease the nation's economic strains brought by the war. Socialism would contain the seeds of its destruction if the experiment got out of hand or were to continue indefinitely. The threat this posed Weber perceived to lie in the fact that under socialism any untoward effects of capitalism on human values would be magnified because of the central planner's monopoly over private initiative. Actually, Weber was left in a dilemma. He scorned those who live in perpetual hope of the coming crisis of capitalism while at the same time recognizing the problem of an undue influence of the big industrialists. Nor did Weber feel entrapped by socialism as did so many other members of the German middle class. Mommsen suggests that his fears of socialism were seldom spelled out because this would have involved an outright admission that socialism might yet establish itself in the future, in which case no amount of vigilance by intellectual dissenters like himself could prevent the infection from spreading.[24]

Never did Weber draw up a schematic outline of his views on socialism, nor did he ever ground his assessment of socialism upon a combination of historical method with political description and analysis. While he thought of socialists as utopians whom time would ultimately isolate from the mainstream, he appreciated the Marxist system of thought. He thought socialist critiques of capitalism had little relevance to the modern world, but he emphasized socialism's relevance and appeal in the realm of ethics. Yet, "to those who expect a socialist society of the future to create a major social transformation," Weber pointed out with some justification that central planning would tend to intensify the bureaucratic trend. "The division of labor and the use of special skills in administration would increase, and a 'dictatorship of the bureaucrats' rather than a 'dictatorship of the proletariat' would result."[25] Weber explicitly rejected the radical wing in the Social Democratic party with its dated revolutionary ideology and insistence, on pure class solidarity because he feared economic disaster and international discredit as a consequence. Yet he accepted responsible and dedicated trade unionists.[26]

Actually, during the 1880's, the left-wing radicals of the Social Democratic party had been quite willing to operate inside the existing system. This is but a fair comment on their successful attempt at combining the spirit of a protest movement with the exercise of modern parliamentary practices. In Saxony the radicals had dominated the Social Democratic delegation to the State Diet where they conducted themselves as genuine parliamentarians. As one of the radical leaders, Wilhelm Liebknecht, commented, "Our party gradually puts away childish things and emerges from its years of indiscretion."[27] Generally most election gains in 1884 had favored the moderates within the party; this was somewhat resented by Bebel, Bernstein, and Engels. All three of these men, but particularly Bernstein, displayed less and less reluctance about accepting recognition to the fact that the Social Democratic party ". . . was necessarily becoming a modern parliamentary party which could not avoid involvement in all phases of the legislative process."[28] The internecine factional struggles within the Social Democratic party in the Weimar Republic are particularly evident as one observes the reluctance of the Conservative leadership to change either the upper echelons of the party or the structure of its rank and file. In fact, the men at the top were extremely wary of risking past gains and regarded any criticism as an affront to their authority.[29] The paranoid anxiety characterizing the attitude of many Germans toward left-wing sentiments, especially within the top leadership, and elite hostility to the spirit of the young democratic republic were at least partly responsible for tipping the hand of the SPD. Hence, the left-wing opposition within the party was prevented from attaining adequate means of political expression.[30] Meanwhile, official hostility on the part of German elites helped create a rather permanent hiatus between radicals and bourgeois liberals, resulting in an ambivalent attitude toward the democratic process and parliamentary principles.[31] Weber himself typified the attitude of the elite; moreover, he failed to show all the reasons behind the debilitating effects which, he felt, were exercised by extremists within the party.

Weber was specifically concerned with establishing contact with leading political, diplomatic, and military figures of the day, including those among the Left, and his connections seemed labyrinthine indeed, as is apparent from his voluminous correspondence. At the outset he singled out the Spartakists and the extreme Left, the USPD (Independent Socialist Party of Germany), applying scathing criticism to their provincial view of the political universe; very soon, however, he began to devote sometimes cynical, and other times quixotic remarks to the elected representatives of the people while still maintaining liaisons with the political elites of the period.

Weber's attacks upon the new Weimar Republic have been brought out most patently in Mommsen's work. Writing after World War II, Mommsen had to hit hard to reveal Weber's political ambivalence.[32] It is indeed difficult not to feel at times that those whom Mommsen calls "the Weber orthodoxy" [33] want to convince us only of what we already know, namely, that Weber was not only the greatest social scientist of our age; he was both profoundly and inspiringly representative of it and most uniquely so. His political writings combined astute analysis with one of the most suggestive criticisms of the inner contradictions of the German social structure. Not their least merit was the blow-by-blow descriptions of events marking those fateful times.

Although since World War II some Germans have taken the opportunity of coming to grips with their past, analyses of both the Weimar Republic and the Third Reich as reflections upon German social structure have been somewhat neglected. And, for two decades West Germany has not often allowed itself to be reminded of the past performance, present role, and future prospects of rightist forces, while the Weimar Republic has frequently been an object of mockery if not hostility. Nevertheless, enough self-examination has occurred to indicate that historical tensions between the claims of the German state and those of individual morality remain central. Viewed in retrospect, Max Weber's own personality emerges as a decisive element in this Aeschylean tragedy of earlier times. Referring to the then current student revolts in West Germany, Kai Hermann writes:

. . . the rebels base their attitude not least upon the works of 'liberal critics' of the regime—even though they do not accept their premises or conclusions. . . . The anti-liberalism of the student left . . . is in the unbroken irrational and anti-democratic tradition of the German universities. The path from the 19th century *Burschenschaften,* the student fraternities of the *Wartburgfest,* to the recent Frankfurt Congress of the SDS is not all that indirect. It was the student fraternities that revolted against the spirit of the European Enlightenment. . . . They established the tradition of the gulf between 'morality' and 'reason') . . . ever since then German students have regarded political morality as merely a question of 'viewpoint.' [34]

Weber's personal tension as a member of his contemporary intelligentsia somehow anticipated the response of the German intelligentsia today as it is caught in a spiritual and political crisis of the first order. The synthesis of personal freedom and social justice has not been widely acknowledged, either in the Republic of Bonn or in that of Weimar, through the rational autonomy which Weber demanded.[35]

Following the war, Weber's thoughts about the new Social Democratic regime were profoundly affected by his pessimism concerning its ability to improve economy and society in Germany. He charged the new government with issuing propaganda of a kind indistinguishable from that of the previous regime. In this connection Weber predicted again the inglorious collapse of socialism.[36] While analogies are frequently seductive, Weber's distaste for his society, which was incapable of coping with the complexities of the situation may, at least in part, be viewed as a contribution to some of the young Left's anger, in Germany today, and for whom he also would have manifested little understanding:

> But will the young Left remain in the sectarian and nihilistic corner in which the authorities (and how stolid the German *Obrigkeit* can be!) have forced them. They must take time to think again. Then the student opposition may well become the radical reform movement which its first inspiration intended it to be, and perhaps—who knows?—emerge as a nucleus of a new Socialist European Left.[37]

It is difficult to agree with this optimistic view. By way of analogy, and in point of fact, at the close of 1918, the most brutal means of terror were employed in Germany in the attempt to counter opposition, beginning with Karl Liebknecht and Rosa Luxemburg. Contrary to Weber's charges against the Republic's alleged easygoing reaction to the Left, to be known as a spokesman for peace at times involved a risk to one's life, and frequently more so under the Republic than under the Kaiser's regime. It was, after all, the Republic which created the very army which ultimately failed the Republican regime. When German pacifists and Leftists sought to expose various schemes of secret rearmament their attempts were either thwarted or sometimes legally, sometimes administratively, punished.[38]

Uneasiness about the Revolution seemed to be almost universally part of the climate of the time. This uneasiness rested on an edge of fear, issuing in a self-paralyzing and self-destructive state. Thus, "Ebert's daily prayer read: 'How do we maintain the *Reich* and keep the economy in order?' No-one was able to foresee in what direction the Revolution would move in the several parts of Germany . . . Ebert was not the man to risk everything. . . . In its first proclamation the new government of the *Reich* promised its '*Volksgenossen*': 'Property must be protected against arbitrary intervention.' Certainly, that was a hard thing to take . . . for the radical Left. . . . Don't stand still, the left-wing socialist paper *Freiheit* warned. . . . 'We must press on . . .' Why not nationalize the mines, heavy industry, the chemical works, the large electrical manufacturing corporations? . . . Ebert and his colleagues, however, decided in favor of a watchword by means of which even forty years later elections could be won in Germany: 'Only no experiments!'"[39]

Actually the SPD itself dreaded any premature socialization, fearing the incidence of growing inflation and lack of capital reserves, as well as outmoded industrial plants and expectation of high demands for reparations from the enemy and the continuing naval blockade. The SPD itself bent over backwards to insure that Germany regain confidence abroad instead of "sowing seeds of further mistrust"; above all, it did not want to forfeit the prospect of American credits. Their reasoning was that no changes should be attempted until the conversion of production for peaceful purposes was completed and until the millions of soldiers were reintegrated into the economy. Only then might attempts at a new social order and a new economic system be investigated. Their thinking was based upon the hope that the proletariat would be so significantly enlarged upon by the influx of lower-class employees and impoverished middle-class people, that democratic elections would easily result in a majority of votes in its favor. This calculation turned out to be based upon an illusion: "The rude awakening occurred at the latest in the election to the National Assembly in January 1919: the SPD and USPD received less than half of the votes cast."[40]

Only recently, some younger historians and political scientists have suggested that "bolshevism" had not really been the only alternative to bourgeois democracy although both the SPD and the bourgeoisie liked to present it as the bogeyman. The other alternative might have been a "social democracy based upon soviets. During a pause between the mutiny at Kiel and the revolution in Berlin, the soldiers'-and-workers' councils had seized power; somehow the revolution had to be organized. In most of the workers' councils those occupying leading positions came from established cadres of the SPD and the trade unions. From the outset, the party executives, however, had regarded them as mere custodians of power. Ebert soon grew tired of them. . . . The trade unions, too, were not kindly disposed toward them; they rightly feared their competition since they strove for autonomy in industry which 'threatened to break down all barriers set up by trade union contracts,' as the trade union press indignantly protested."[41]

It has been said that the Revolution failed to inspire people to count their blessings, a symptom of the particular uneasiness it created. It was felt that it mirrored the shadow of Dr. Faust: "If the SPD had been so inclined, the soviets might have been extended into a system of democracy from the ground up, exemplified by co-determination in industry, in military barracks, in offices, and in trade-unions."[42] Whether such a system could have proved workable, especially in terms of eradicating the lines of demarcation between the legislative and the executive, is difficult to guess. In any case, no genuine attempts were ever made in that direction, although the champions of the soviet system struggled until the spring of 1919 to gain a hearing for it. The facts are, however, that the opportunities open to the proletariat in November 1918 were not seized. "Whatever followed in those weeks until the Spartakus-revolt in January 1919, the altercations between government and executive council, the dissension with the USPD, the 'counter-revolutions' from both the left and the right, ultimately served only to strengthen the position of Ebert and the SPD, and along with it: the cause of the bourgeois-capitalist social order, in league with the Free Corps and the Supreme Command and staunch monarchist officers." [43]

Weber meanwhile chose a lonely and a difficult path for himself. The new German government provided some hopes for an important post but these were frustrated largely by his own intransigence. The government could ill afford to sustain one of its most vigorous domestic critics. Mommsen, in fact, ascribed Weber's disdain of the government to his failure to receive a position of trust in it.

Since Germany had become a republic, the position of the government had been steadily eroded by rising voices of discontent. Weber's reaffirmation of his conservative heritage had reinforced the substantial remnants of opposition. In these circumstances his active political participation in the new government would have been of doubtful value. Moreover, the few prerequisites of a viable democracy existing in Germany at that time needed to be nurtured rather than challenged. The new government had, after all, taken control of a country devastated by war, of a people with no experience in government except imperial rule and little sense of loyalty or participation beyond the local level, and of a nation disorganized by the sudden collapse of the previous administration as a result of a lost war. Nevertheless, Friedrich Ebert considered Weber for the post of Secretary of State of the Interior. For reasons which remain unknown, this intention was dropped.[44] Mommsen concludes that in a government composed of Social Democrats and Independents, a man who had called the Revolution an irresponsible "carnival" could hardly have been tolerated, and particularly in view of Weber's eruptive temperament, which would have certainly induced him to clash with the Independent Socialists.[45] Ebert decided in favor of Hugo Preuss, partly because it was known that he had available a finished blueprint of both the constitutional reform of the Reich as well as of Prussia. In retrospect, since the Independent Socialists formed part of the government, Preuss was more qualified to conciliate between them and the Center party.[46]

Weber shared a characteristic feature of conservatives, their distrust of ideology, manifest in a preference for the existing order of society, despite its imperfections. Working policies exist, but these are hardly comprehensive man-made prescriptions for curing the ills of society. In the political arena Weber relied more heavily upon personal loyalty than upon shared convictions. This was a major difference between his own approach and that of the new government. The ruling parties *were* ideological; they advocated programs. Their hope of success rested in their ability to convince people that things could improve for them, and in securing support for their particular remedies. Hence they must change the whole existing basis of political support from the personal to the ideological. Weber thus seems to have abandoned his idea of closer cooperation with the government: "This government will never need me, and I will never serve in it." [47] Theodor Heuss wrote: "As serious as he had been in his opposition to the system under the Kaiser, as sharp, even scathing, was his scorn now against those who sought to get over the collapse and disintegration of authority by means of illusions and party phraseology." [48]

In reality, as mentioned previously, the Social Democratic party was in many ways more conservative than many Conservatives. Moreover, one of the great weaknesses of the SPD had been its traditional reluctance to take a firm position on military affairs. It had also been characterized by a grim determination not to be outdone in patriotism by parties to its right. That the SPD seemed always on the defensive during the days of the Weimar Republic did it great harm.

Weber correctly saw that the German November Revolution could not be expected to succeed unless it could enlist the full support of the middle classes. In theory Weber supported collaboration between liberal and socialist forces.

J. P. Mayer, on the other hand, wonders how Weber could be so sure that German heavy industry would be willing to embrace democracy:

Weber cannot conceive of an economic system which is not mainly based on the autonomous *entrepreneur*. He defines him as a bonus/wage-earner for organizational purposes (*Praemienlohnarbeiter fuer Organisationszwecke*). He works on his own responsibility in contrast to the official (*Beamte*) who works only for the pockets of the State. To regard the Stinnes, Rathenau, Krupp, and Borsig, etc., as 'bonuswage-earners' is indeed a surprising economic definition. Has Weber forgotten Marx' doctrine of the basic importance of *who* owns the means of production? Not quite. For he continues: 'We have indeed no cause to love the masters of heavy industry. It is one of the main tasks of democracy to break the dangerous *political* influence which they had on the old regime. Yet *economically* their achievements cannot be dispensed with. . . . The *Communist Manifesto* has rightly stressed the *economically*—not politically—*revolutionary* character of the work of the bourgeois capitalistic *entrepreneurs.* No trade union, still less no state socialist official, can replace the functions of the capitalists. One must apply them only at the right place; offer them the unavoidable premium of profit, but not allow them to become stronger than democracy. . . .' [49,50]

Mayer infers that:

The proclamation of the charismatic principle within the realm of the economic system must ultimately destroy democracy, once it concludes an alliance with the charismatic leader in the realm of politics. . . .

How could Weber assume that German heavy industry, not to mention the leaders of finance, would suddenly form one united bourgeois democratic front? Did not the history of German 'liberalism,' particularly after 1878, prove that the German *Grossbuergertum* preferred profits to democracy? If we look at the election statistics of the German *Reichstag* in 1919 and 1920 the answer to our question becomes evident: the *Deutsche Volkspartei,* the new political name of the National Liberal Party, sent in 1919 only nineteen members to the *Reichstag;* in 1920 already sixty-five. The Democratic Party . . . had in 1919 seventy-five deputies, in 1920 thirty-nine.[51]

Weber's ultimate aim even after the war remained the enhancement of Germany's power position in the world, for which domestic national unity was a prerequisite. Compromises with economic experiments under socialism, in his judgment, could but weaken Germany internally and reduce her chances to arrive at a working relationship with her former enemies.

Weber, along with other members of his party, the German Democratic party, could not bring himself to accept important parts of its program which caused serious internal discord. Some party members stood ready to compromise their economic convictions for the sake of preserving the Weimar coalition, composed of the Social Democratic party, the Center party, and the Democratic party, which lasted from January 1919 until June 1920. Others like Weber would not move from a fundamentally capitalist position. The party's vascillation between "free enterprise and a planned economy," and "nationalist truculence and compliance with the demands of the Allies," followed by the death of Friedrich Naumann in 1919 and the assassination of Walther Rathenau three years later, signalled the party's decline. By the latter part of the 1920's, the party had disintegrated.[52]

Fearful that any far-reaching socialization of private enterprise would ruin the Germany economy and reduce both the German working class and the German entrepreneur to servants of American capitalism, Weber saw Germany's economic recovery only against the background of an economically trained business class based upon free enterprise. Only with such representation would Germany be able to receive much-needed credits and loans from abroad. Hence the German bourgeoisie must live up to its responsibility of assuming political power and taking hold of the nation's reins.[53] To underscore his argument, Weber expressed his belief that the Western powers would not be inclined to negotiate a peace treaty unless the German government was at least partly composed of representatives of the bourgeoisie. Continuation of the revolution could only bring civil war and the national disgrace of prolonged occupation by the enemy. To the bourgeoisie he directed a passionate appeal to abandon their spirit of security-seeking and the preservation of a wide margin of safety vis-à-vis the authorities: The bourgeoisie must shed its fear of innovation and its impotence in the face of the challenge to responsible action. By now Weber was somewhat reconciled to the loss of the monarchical system if at least it encouraged the realization of the bourgeoisie's new role of "finally standing on its own feet politically." [54]

These arguments have led Herbert Marcuse to inquire whether Weber's conclusions may still be considered valid for the latest stages of the capitalistic system, a question he answered in the negative, citing Keynes as his authority. According to Weber, capitalistic rationality is rooted in free enterprise. In this context, Weber described the entrepreneur as a free agent responsible even for his own calculated risks. The entrepreneur is, of necessity, bourgeois in orientation, and his style of life typically finds representative expression in "inner-worldly asceticism." Implying that this conception would have to be revised, Marcuse asked whether the entrepreneur as the carrier of industrial evolution may still be regarded as the bearer of the late phase of the capitalist state; can, in effect, the rationality underlying the mature phase of capitalistic development still be said to be based upon reason emanating from inner-worldly asceticism? In Marcuse's view these questions must be answered in the negative. Instead, "inner-worldly asceticism" in this stage of capitalism is no longer a generating force but rather has become a factor impeding the successful operation of the system. As Keynes insists in the "affluent society" asceticism poses a threat whereever it serves to impede both production and consumption of surplus goods.[55] For Marcuse "not only is the working class written off as an agent of historical change but so is its bourgeois opponent. It is as if a " 'classless' society were emerging within a class society. . . ." [56] The previous antagonism between these two classes has been replaced by a uniting principle based upon an "overriding interest in the preservation and improvement of the institutional status quo." [57]

Marcuse is correct in asserting that Weber identified himself with the bourgeoisie: he precisely equated his own historical interpretation with the historical mission of the bourgeoisie. Consequently, in the name of this alleged mission, Weber accepted the alliance of representative strata of the German bourgeoisie with the organizers of reaction and repression. Marcuse, for example, accused Weber of having reserved for his political opponents in the ranks of the radical Left, the insane asylum and the zoological garden. Charging that the most intellectual of all sociologists had gone on a rampage against those intellectuals who sacrifice their lives for the revolution,[58] Marcuse concludes that, for Weber, "reason" ultimately remains *bourgeois* reason—or, more appropriately—*capitalistic* reason.[59] The reference to the fate which Weber held in store for the radical Left alluded especially to Rosa Luxemburg and Karl Liebknecht. A speech Weber gave in Karlsruhe had contained the statement: "Liebknecht belongs in an asylum for the insane and Rosa Luxemburg in the zoological garden." Weber took a dim view toward all that surrounded him now. Nevertheless, nothing could rob him of his faith in Germany's resurrection.[60] On the other hand, Marianne Weber reports that the murder of Karl Liebknecht and Rosa Luxemburg was censured by Weber.[61] In retrospect, Weber deplored the end which "the dictatorship in the street" had met, stating that, in his judgment, Liebknecht was an honorable man.[62]

On November 16, 1918 a group of people including Alfred Weber, Erich Koch-Weser, and Friedrich Naumann had met in Berlin to lay the foundation of the *Deutsche Demokratische Partei* as a political base for those members of the bourgeoisie whose general orientation was toward a democratic system. Although it was assumed Max Weber would certainly be among the founders, his political convictions prevented him initially from signing the charter because it subscribed to a republican form of government. Both publicly and privately Weber had only recently spoken out in favor of preserving the monarchy, and he felt that he could not reverse himself now even if it seemed politically opportune.

It should be remembered that Max Weber, in company with leading politicians, had anticipated long before that the monarchy would be placed in jeopardy in the event of either a long war or defeat. The Kaiser's "personal regime" had become tarnished already during the "Daily Telegraph" affair. At that time, in 1908, when Chancellor von Buelow compromised him before both the Reichstag and the press, the monarch's resignation had already been considered by the Bundesrat. Actually the Kaiser had ceased to rule long before 1918. To Falkenhayn and Ludendorff he left the conduct of the war, while he bequeathed to Hindenburg both his authority and representative functions. Karl-Heinz Janssen asserts that Hindenburg had become *Ersatz-Kaiser* already before 1925, namely in 1916.

The tree of the monarchy the external image of which seemed so powerful, had decayed long before President Wilson applied the axe to it in October. . . . Researchers even today have not been able to determine, whether Wilson wanted to merely deprive the Kaiser of his power or whether he wanted to dump him altogether. One would have to retain him perhaps, the U.S.-President commented occasionally, to prevent the triumph of bolshevism 'and to maintain at least a minimum of order.' But then followed immediately one of his ambiguous communications, which caused tempers in Germany to rise to a boiling-point. All the information reaching the Foreign Office from abroad appeared to confirm that Wilson aimed at abdication. Simultaneously, however (unintentionally), he aroused hopes in the German people and its leaders, that the sacrifice of the Kaiser and the Crown-Prince, would result in better peace terms.[63]

Consequently, a few days after Wilson's first note, public demands for the Kaiser's abdication became audible. From the perspective of the present, fifty years after the Revolution Janssen writes: "Social Democrats such as Scheidemann and Noske, liberal scholars like Hans Delbrueck and Max Weber stated 'if he goes without external pressure, he goes honorably; the chivalrous sympathy of the nation will then be with him. Above all: the position of the dynasty remains unharmed' and finally also representatives of high finance and heavy industry . . . drew the conclusion dictated by their interests, that since cooperation with the trade unions had become essential the Kaiser would be an inconvenience." [64]

Weber's own position favoring the abdication of the Kaiser to save the monarchy must be understood in the light of the climate of public opinion. It is interesting to note Janssen's observation which Golo Mann made in a recent essay namely that Max von Baden had wanted to prevent the abdication at all cost. This, in fact, is a generally accepted view. Yet the actions of the chancellor, Janssen writes, may also lead to the opposite conclusion, namely that because of his special relationship to the Kaiser, as relative and friend, his ability to act was circumscribed. He felt too inhibited to demand the Kaiser's abdication himself. However, he "did nothing to help him either; on the contrary he delayed action for several days despite the express wish of the royal couple to publish that famous edict with which the Kaiser had himself introduced parliamentary democracy in Germany." [65]

Ultimately the exigencies of the historical moment rather than a preference for the democratic form of government led Max Weber to join forces with the German Democratic Party, on whose behalf he made a successful speaking tour.[66] Weber seemed an appropriate candidate for the national assembly and Conrad Haussmann proposed his name for election to the executive committee.[67] He was actually elected to office during the following year. On his part, Weber did not try very hard to secure a seat in the national assembly on the Democratic ticket from the electoral district of Hessen-Nassau. It might have taken little effort to achieve this, since his closest political friends included

Friedrich Naumann and Conrad Haussmann, men who might have easily brought their considerable influence to bear on Weber's behalf.

In the end, his candidacy derived its impetus from outside the district. On December 19, 1918 Weber was nominated at a closed meeting of the Frankfurt German Democratic party over four other candidates to head the list for the Reichstag. Weber indeed received all but two votes. Weber regarded this vote as a spontaneous mandate from the several hundred members, and only this factor induced him to accept the nomination.[68] Yet, Mommsen states, it is almost incomprehensible that Weber could have been so optimistic as to assume that he ranked first also as a candidate for the Reichstag from the 19th district. His name had been placed first on the list at a closed membership meeting with the proviso that the final decision would be left to the Conference of Delegates of the province of Hessen-Nassau, which was to convene on December 29, 1918. Moreover, at this meeting the proposed list of the local party executive committee was virtually ignored with one exception, and competent men not necessarily related to the Frankfurt area ultimately received the nomination. Since few men have understood the power structure of modern mass parties as well as Max Weber, it seems strange that he failed to realize that the party leadership and membership in Hessen-Nassau, Wetzlar, and Waldeck might have different plans.[69]

With the help of numerous friends he could easily have secured the nomination. Instead, he paid no attention to the party organizers, nor did he prepare any speeches for his potential constituency. Having been "rather sure" he was going to win the nomination,[70] when he learned that the delegates at Wetzlar inserted his name in an inauspicious place on the party's list, he was both surprised and disappointed. His candidacy was liquidated and he withdrew resentfully.[71] All efforts to secure for Weber a place on some other electoral district's list failed. Reluctant to be known as a "patronized chaser after mandates," he wanted instead to be elected freely as a leader and as such to be sent to the National Assembly.[72] Thus, ironically, Weber did not seize power when it was offered to him; when his candidacy required him to campaign for it, he preferred not to seek office. Marianne Weber's explanation, supported by others, was that the subaltern character of political party organization prevented Weber from realizing his "talents as a statesman." [73] Weber's reaction suggests that instead of actively seeking office because he felt impelled to do so, he would have preferred to allow himself to be drafted.

Several questions may be raised about Marianne Weber's evaluation. First, there is the personal equation: how was it possible for such a man—scholarly in the highest degree, favored by politically influential friends, regarded by all who knew him as sensitive, transparently honest, passionately patriotic in his appraisal of the needs of his country, and endowed with a transcendant faith in his nation's historical mission—not to succeed in politics? Several answers suggest themselves. Most of Max Weber's contacts were restricted to academic circles and did not extend to all echelons of the party leadership. His critical spirit, his intellectual purity, his faith in his own beliefs were not infrequently and sometimes publicly counteracted by outbreaks of temperament. His social and economic views exposed him to the spurious criticism of lesser minds, and to those who discovered in him either radicalism, if they were to the right of him, or inconsistency, if they were left-oriented. The complexities of his personality were perhaps impenetrable by ordinary bureaucrats, whose numerical strength among the party leaders was considerable. His trenchant social and political criticism and his attacks against bureaucracy would normally have debarred any man for consideration for public office.

Secondly, there is the factual question; i.e., the contemporary social and political climate, especially within his own party. Chanady notes that for the three parties whose supporters and voters have been drawn from the Protestant upper and middle classes, their era of influence had approached the end long before the Nationalist Socialist party became a real force in German politics. The Social Democrats and the Catholic Center party owed much of their notable stability and continued popular support to the circumstances of their origin and to the reasons for which they were created. The SPD was the political expression of a class interest in German society, while the Center party was committed to a confessional world view and to a set of principles which stems from it.[74] Accordingly,

The Independent Socialists (7.6 per cent in 1919, 17.9 per cent in 1920) merged with the Social Democrats (some of them with the Communists) after the elections in 1920. The Communist party was founded in 1920. Although the combined vote of the Social Democrats and Communists decreased slightly by 1932, the absolute figure remained remarkably steady around the thirteen million mark. Much the same applies to the Catholic parties (Center and Bavarian Peoples' party), which managed to retain between five and six million votes in 1932–33. The Democrats' share of the total vote dropped from 18.6 per cent in 1919 to 8.3 per cent in 1920, 5.7 per cent in May 1924, and 4.9 per cent in 1930; the Peoples' Party from 13.9 per cent in 1920 to 8.7 per cent in 1928 and 4.5 per cent in 1930; and the German National Peoples' party from 20.5 per cent in 1924 to 14.2 per cent in 1928 and 7.0 per cent in 1930.[75]

Beyond such exogenous factors, Weber's fundamental personal ambivalence about political office is germane. On the one hand, he had great talent and he must have suffered considerable intellectual discomfort on that account when he confronted practical politics. The quality of his ideas, his personal involvement, the intensity of his voice made him appear as an irreverent intellectual. Refusing to suspend his deepest convictions, addressing Germans as members of a national community, imploring them in the morbid climate of defeat and revolution to think and act within the realm of objective possibilities, Weber called on them to shed juvenile illusions and to practice the art of the possible. He wanted Germans to recover the community of the past by allowing themselves to become engaged in its realization in their contemporary situation, even in the face of a perplexing and increasingly mass-industrial, bureaucratized world. *Yet he himself could not and would not make the necessary concessions to the rules of the game as practiced in modern political party life.* Professional politicians found his conduct, which alternated between the requirements of *Realpolitik* and rigorous practice of the ethic of conviction, hard to take. His inflexibility must have seemed to them an incalculable risk. He, in turn, found it difficult to stick to the 'party line' and this left him politically, as he himself noted, in a one-horse carriage.[76]

In her "Max Weber as Teacher and Politician," Kaethe Leichter explains this "political one-horse carriage," and his final "advances" toward the Republic and socialism, on the grounds of his deeply hurt national pride and his sadness at the lack of dignity evident in his own circles and among the bourgeoisie generally.[77] Yet, it was not in Imperial but in Republican Germany that an attempt was made to break through the net and find a place for Weber in which his political talents might have had notable practical consequences. These included the suggestion favoring a plebiscitary *Reichspraesident* and membership in Hugo Preuss' Constitutional Commission organized to draft the federal constitution. Most of Weber's suggestions concerning the presidential office were adopted, although his proposal for a centralized unitary state did not find its way into the final version of the constitution.

Meanwhile, his criticism of those who accepted Germany's war guilt inspired the government to seek his counsel as a member of the delegation to Versailles. There he wrote the memorandum concerning war guilt and from there too he returned full of resentment and despair, opposing the signing of the treaty, even at the cost of occupation of the entire country. Thus, in politics as in his life at the university, his leadership, his human stature, his pathos and his civic courage—all culminated ultimately in the status of an outsider. Equally removed from the reactionaries who could only look back and the Socialists who sought to fight for a better, though utopian, world, torn by Germany's defeat, alienated from the revolution, Max Weber was fated to remain outside the arena of political action which both attracted and repelled him.[78]

Weber tried, in effect, to wage a single-handed and endless war against what seemed to him the inane and corrupt political thinking of his times. It must have seemed to him that fate responded to his attacks against the Revolution by trying to condemn him to oblivion rather than allowing him any kind of political relevance. Kaethe Leichter concludes that the world had changed but the privilege of becoming instrumental in the shaping of the future was, despite his qualifications for leadership, not granted to Max Weber.[79]

It is, indeed, difficult to envisage any political initiative Weber might have taken which could have been of help to his party and his country, other than his efforts to convince both that great political errors can lead to monstrous tragedy, involving not only Germany but the whole world. His contact with the Democratic party while he was at the University of Munich was not a close one. Even though he was a member of the Democratic party's *Parteiausschuss*, a large national body whose impact on party policy was rather inconsequential, the attendance record shows that he was never present at its meetings.[80] Thus Max Weber, in whom a genuine passion for politics had always been a driving force and whose political analyses had never lost their incisiveness, began to cease to be effectual for all practical political purposes. He now withdrew from public life to devote himself to teaching and writing.

It may be assumed that the divergencies of opinion about Germany's future arose at least partly from a divergence of vantage point. Weber seems at times to have felt so alien to Germany's new postwar situation that he appeared to view his country as if from another planet; he seemed to reject lines of conduct which had to be pursued within the limits imposed by circumstances. And again, his ambivalence stemmed largely from his simultaneous engagement in the academic and the political arenas. Fully absorbed in the conflict inherent in two such inapposite pursuits, his sense of responsibility and his active sympathies involved him in emotional disaster. The academic environment appeared to represent to him a reassuring and uncontested stronghold, one in which he felt completely at home. Perhaps it became an indispensable necessity for him because he was not always capable of imposing limitations upon his actions. His mind seemed to be engaged in perpetual motion right up to the breaking point; the threat of breakdown under the strain of living at too intensive a pace hovered over him almost continuously as he trained himself to live at the highest pitch of his capacity.

On April 14, 1920, Max Weber wrote to Carl Petersen, then a member of the senate of Hamburg. The letter, written in answer to Petersen's invitation to reenter party political affairs actively, apparently never became generally known; yet, it is of considerable value for an understanding of Weber's hostility toward and disenchantment with the regime. Weber's last political act, his refusal of Petersen's invitation, coupled with the withdrawal of his membership from the *Parteiausschuss*, has received surprisingly little notice. In it he tried to inform Germany of the real issues, of how grave her danger was. Here, in a letter which illustrates the tragic personal and political compulsions of an intellectual self-consciously alienated from his society, he put his visions before any considerations of political compromise. Nurtured on yet more broken hopes regarding the potential effectiveness of his party, his alienation was reinforced by the low point which the Democratic party itself had reached by virtue of its political impotency. Early in 1920 large numbers of voters actually left it to join the German people's party led by Gustav Stresemann, thus giving a party competing for the backing of the middle class the leverage it needed to establish itself as a party with national appeal, transcending class and religious barriers.

In its first stage the party seemed to concentrate on bringing some unity of purpose to a war-weary and recalcitrant nation. But, as stated earlier, after Naumanns' death in August 1919 it failed to show the inspiration and leadership required to accomplish it. In its ranks

left-oriented democratic intellectuals who were among the founding fathers, social reformers of the National-Social Association, labor, employees and officials of the Hirsch-Duncker trade unions co-existed with the notables of the Progressives who failed to nominate two such outstanding though recent party members as Max Weber and Hugo Preuss, businessmen, bankers, middle-class industrialists who felt indifferent toward ideology but who needed the party for purposes of financing. Idealism and hard reality existed side by side in the DDP. The influence of the democratic left (who partly left the party again as early as 1919) and the National Social members soon subsided so that DDP became widely known as representative of capitalism.

Criticism of the Weimar coalition and the frequently obscure and vascillating attitude of the DDP—withdrawal from the government because of the Versailles Treaty only to return soon thereafter to the government—induced many voters to exchange it for the DVP or the DNVP.[81]

While Weber seemed keenly aware of the futility of renewing his efforts on the Democratic party's committee's behalf, he did not appear inclined to publicize his resignation from the *Parteiausschuss*. At the time of his death, his letter of resignation had not displaced the record of his active membership in that committee. He himself did not, it seems, intend to dissociate himself from the party. While the political system simply did not produce the answers he wanted, he apparently believed that no other party would have been capable of producing such answers. Weber's letter pointed up his attitude toward what he saw as the whole ethos against him; he demanded tough mandatory action, rejecting for himself any concessions to socialization.

Muenchen, April 14 (1920)

Esteemed Senator!

I am leaving the Committee of the Party and must also definitely decline your offer which is a *great honor* to me.

I have *not* broken with the party. But: I have in every meeting, *everywhere*, privately and publicly, declared that 'socialization' in its present meaning is 'nonsense': I have also declared it nonsense that we need employers such as Herr Stinnes and his type. With reference to the Factory Council Law (*Betriebsraetegesetz*) I have said '*Ecrasez l'infame*,' for it endangers the practicable future of socialism.

The politician shall and must make compromises. But I am a scholar by profession. The fact that I have remained a scholar was due to the party which—fortunately—kept me from a Parliament to which I did not aspire. To sit in Parliament *today* is neither an honor nor a joy, but I should have perhaps belonged to it while the constitution was debated. The *scholar dare* not make compromises nor cloak any nonsense. I definitely cannot do this. Those who have other views, such as Prof. Lederer and Dr. Vogelstein are unprofessional. If I acted as they have I would regard myself as a criminal to my profession.

I also did *not* agree with the choice of *members* and the *proceedings* in the Investigative Committee: gentlemen who are pacifists and who—regardless of how—are considered Jews should not have been seated. I do not think I could be suspected of being anti-Semitic; almost my whole circle of friends is Jewish and a cousin of mine was Felix Mendelssohn's wife. Indeed, I have been charged in a letter by an officer of being a 'Jew'. Although I value its leader, I do not agree with the local party which should not cloak reactionary machinations. But . . . is perhaps *vis major*.

I cannot become a Majority Socialist, because this party is compromising socialism against the convictions of its trained theoreticians. Naturally, I cannot join *Burschen* like Herr Stresemann who since his endorsement of the Mexican Dispatch in the *Reichstag* in 1917 should be, for all practical purposes, 'dead.' I shall *always* vote Democratic, and shall *always* emphasize the terrible *sacrifice* that today has to be made to govern. In this you can depend on my loyalty. Since our work together in the Constitutional Commission, where I learned to know you and respect you, I have developed the greatest esteem for you personally. Our party has been fortunate in *one* respect; in the choice of *this* leader.

But since your offer—the imposition of a duty on a party member—is not justifiable as long as I am a member, and since I *can* and *may* not accept it, I leave with deep respect and with the best wishes for the party.

This letter is not confidential. I will refer to it in my letter of resignation.

I cannot understand how the party can pass over Prof. *Alfred* Weber. He not only *understands* ten times more than I do about socialization and finance, but can also control Helfferich. Moreover, he is (possibly still!) in favor of socialization. I am in no position to give advice. But this advice I *may* give especially because my brother and I have very different views. This letter must remain confidential as far as he is concerned. Otherwise, he would abruptly decline it.[82]

Despite his disenchantment with party politics and the weakness of the Republic, Weber remained passionately nationalistic. He turned again to ways in which his defeated country might salvage something from the chaotic position in which it found itself following the war. His major concern was resistance to any demands for punitive reparations and the acquisition of German territory by the Allied powers.

In 1918, Weber's dictum had been that Germany must prepare for national resistance to any such claims by revolutionary means:

> If Poles should now march into Danzig and Thorn or Czechs into Reichenbach, the first thing to do is to train a German irredentist movement. I myself cannot do this, for reasons of health I am unsuitable. But every nationalist must do it and above all, the students must do it. Irredenta means: nationalism based upon revolutionary violent means.[83]

As Mommsen says of this and similar public appeals, all Weber's public speeches during the revolutionary period included the challenge to oppose the acquisition of German territory with guerilla warfare.[84] At a student convocation in Heidelberg Weber referred to this task as the great national objective which must be faced squarely by the young generation: "You know what it means to defy an enemy who comes to occupy the country and who can no longer be repulsed by an army . . . to believe in everything concerning the future, but to abandon all hope for oneself. The living may look forward only to imprisonment and court martial." Once the moment for action was at hand, without the benefit of rhetoric, he challenged the students to see to it quietly that "the first Polish official daring to enter Danzig would be hit by a bullet."[85]

Weber had hoped that the threat of widespread German irredentism would disabuse the Allies of any expectation that Germany would accept undue sacrifices of her eastern territories. In his articles in the *Frankfurter Zeitung*, he did not hesitate to virtually threaten the rise of a violent type of German nationalism; no predicament, however desperate, would dissuade Germans from using revolutionary means to attain national self-determination.

If Germany were to be forced to accept a peace prejudicial to her unity Weber predicted that within 10 years, all Germany would become chauvinist. He announced to the world the rise of a German irredentist movement if German brothers in the East or the West should be subjected to "political rape," as he called it. Referring to revolutionary means which would be employed, Weber differentiated them from those serving the Italians, Serbs, or Irish inasmuch, as in the German case, the action would be backed by the will of seventy million people. He indicated it was not merely his assumption but his full expectation that the students would stand ready to support it.[89]

Weber's pronouncements on the tasks of postwar Germany under the Weimar Republic raises more questions than they answer due to his early death. It will seem an inescapable conclusion that German irredentism supported by violence was, as Mommsen suggests, both program and forecast, subsequently realized in a much more horrible way than Weber ever envisaged.[87] While he considered charisma and bureaucracy as mutually exclusive, they merged in the regime of the Third Reich, which represented a state of "bureaucratized charisma" and by the same token a "state of permanent improvisation." [88] This emphasis upon "stability through movement" transcended the traditional institutional framework of German bureaucracy.[89]

As Guenther Roth correctly notes, because ". . . Weber had a highly articulate view of politics and took his stand on political issues that have remained controversial to this day, it is not always easy to distinguish specific critiques of Weber's politics and scholarship from their general implications for political sociology." [90] Viewing the ideological crticisms of Weber as deriving from three sources, namely Marxism, Nazism and Natural Law, Roth seeks to demonstrate the problem posed by the "interlocking system of the subjective intentions" subscribed to by the individual and the "complexity of historical reality" which any scholarly analysis must take into account. No political philosopher can effectively protect himself "against the misuse of ideas, against their deterioration into ideological coins and political weapons." [91] A special kind of truth emerges from this train of thought. Yet in spite of the author's detailed knowledge of Weber's work, a kind of aloof and donnish scorn colors his assessment when he suggests "ideas always have unintended consequences, and sociology largely lives off this fact." [92] Granted the scholar "must avoid a facile theory of antecedents, stepping stones and parallels, since it is in the nature of politics that differences of degree in belief and action are continued (the rule of the lesser evil)." [93] It is common knowledge, however, that German scholars, especially historians, have been quite instrumental in the channeling of public opinion. Here we must also admit frankly that German scholars bear a considerable share of responsibility for both anti-democratic and anti-Western attitudes. A clearer recognition of this factor might preclude relegating to the private sphere vital political concerns of a man as interesting as an individual, and as centrally located in the twentieth century, as Max Weber.

Roth concedes that Weber went through a "vociferously nationalist phase . . . at about the age of 30, but he quickly moved on to the liberal Left. . . ." [94] This argument is not altogether convincing in view of Weber's postwar political views when he was in his fifties. Despite the intellectual sagacity of American sociologists, it seems some of them have been reluctant to deal critically with Weber's political sociology, not altogether only in the perspective of our time, but also in terms of his own period. While Wolfgang Mommsen's painstaking critical study clearly places Max Weber in historical context, it hardly seems plausible, as Roth argues, that in his capacity as a "German historian, Mommsen is, of course, far removed from the interest of American sociologists in Weber, but his treatment becomes questionable to them the moment he interprets Weber's sociological analyses as political ideology." [95] Actually, the major result of Mommsen's work was a hard reappraisal of the total political man within the person of Max Weber. Undoubtedly, political critiques of Weber demonstrate the high cost exacted from a scholar when he enters practical politics, thus exposing himself to the "vehemence of political controversy." [96] All this and more may be granted regarding some of the conclusions from studies of Weber seeking to establish direct ideological linkages to Nazism, frequently presented in a condescending manner. Nevertheless, both Wolfgang Mommsen and J. P. Mayer have handled with refreshing detachment and balance Weber's role as a militant partisan who has probably given us the truest description of events in Germany in his own time.

Indeed, Weber himself was so honest that he seemed to lean over backwards in exposing his country's weaknesses, almost as if his titanic ethnocentrism had to be balanced by a continuing awareness of Germany's failings.

Weber himself, it will be recalled, was once briefly a member of the Pan-German Association, organized in 1890. Both Weber and Stresemann, whose own aims embraced "a strong imperialistic German foreign policy, soon left the organization—largely because they disagreed with the emphasis on agricultural issues. . . ." [97] The bitter currents during the revolution of 1918–1919 sent its political stock down because neither the reality of defeat nor the newly established order really gained acceptance. Probably Max Weber was too self-consciously alienated from German politics in the postwar period to succeed in creating an effective working relationship within the system. Here he was not alone. In fact, certain aspects of his bristling rebuff to the claims to political maturity made by the German political parties cannot be dismissed. The evidence of national vanity in his political speeches and articles, however, and his insistence upon the harsh facts implicit in defeat, he might well have deplored at a later date. Recent German history demonstrates that some charge of this kind is both true and important. The apparent need and readiness of many Germans, including Weber, to carry self-deception as far as they did suggests an inability to perceive the complexities and moral ambiguities of political existence.

If the Germans, including Weber, had understood fully the causes of the war and its political legacy, might not more than a minority have insisted upon an honest contemplation of the alternatives, however unsettling, and whatever the damage to traditional assumptions? A charge of national immaturity can be unjust, nor should it cover all people within a nation, and were it applied to Max Weber's political ideas summarily, it would caricature his role as a political analyst. Nevertheless, Max Weber cannot be analyzed outside the context of his whole generation and the tradition which he cherished. Especially recently there has been a revival of interest in Germany in the whole range of events connected with the November Revolution of 1918. It is no longer considered sound practice by the academic profession to sweep it under the carpet, to hold it up to ridicule, or malign it.[98]

The harsh ring of Weber's words concerning the need for German resistance by force to the potential loss of territory, especially in the East, revealed his assessment of Germany's failure to exploit whatever opportunities remained. In these circumstances, one may wonder what Weber's counsel might have been to West Germany today. Indications in his later writings, after the signing of the treaty, suggest he would have appreciated the wisdom of physical restraint, at any rate for the time being. We cannot know what conclusions he would have drawn ultimately. It is difficult to believe, however, that he would have hesitated to throw his support into whatever trends might develop to signify discontent over the lost territories. It seems unlikely he would have been ready to proclaim the intolerability of the status quo by calling upon West Germans to act unilaterally. But would he have agreed with Fritz Erler, Social Democratic member of the German parliament, when he wrote in 1956:

Germany's permanent borders can be fixed only in a peace treaty. For the moment reunification means simply the integration of the present four zones of occupation. The Oder-Neisse Line is not involved. No German government has a right today to make decisions about borders and thus prejudice the eventual peace treaty. . . . Every German knows that the eastern frontier cannot remain as temporarily defined. But he also knows that things will not be again as if Germany had not started the war and lost it. These matters have to be dealt with soberly; the time to do it will be at the peace conference with German representatives included.[99]

It would seem that while until Willy Brandt took office as Chancellor the Bonn government was officially adamant in its demands for unification on Western terms, current German reaction hardly corresponds to the attitude Weber demanded from his contemporaries. As Karl Loewenstein writes:

Reversing Clemenceau's famous dictum about Alsace-Lorraine, 'Toujours y penser, jamais en parler,' all Germans, even those favoring the rising nationalism, agree that unification on Western terms is an illusion . . . the

Germans themselves prefer the *status quo* . . . by probing deeper, one will easily discover that the desire for unification—if such there is—decreases proportionately with the distance from the eastern borders . . . in the Rhineland, West Germany's heartland, or in southern Germany, the people are wholly indifferent themselves to the fact that unification, desirable as it may be theoretically, is unattainable for a long time to come.[100]

Generally speaking, despite the controversies it raised, public reaction to the historical meeting between Brandt and Stoph in March 1970 at Erfurt, Weber's place of birth, supports this fact. From which vantage point would Weber view the partition of his country today, from the *Realpolitik* and European position, employing the *bon mot, rebus sic stantibus—toujours y penser,* or would he persist in the German nationalist position he held after World War I when he appealed to the nation to resist administration of German territory by the enemy? What would have been his verdict concerning the treaty signed between the Federal Republic and Poland signed on November 20, 1970 recognizing the SS Oder-Neisse Line as West Germany's eastern frontier? Especially in the East, Weber called for resistance which should include every means.[102] Regardless of what peace terms may ensue, "The East can and must resort to arms and refuse obedience to the government of the Reich: 'force us if you can'."[103]

Mommsen finds it doubtful indeed that such advice would have resulted in the retention of the Eastern territories. Any such manifestation of national heroism born of despair, even if it would have been executed as Weber wished, might have elicited some kind of reaction from the Allies. However, whether the Allies would have felt themselves sufficiently threatened by armed resistance to have offered more favorable peace terms is questionable. They would probably have countered by reinforcing their troops and tightening their control of the country. Certainly Weber magnified the potential effect this type of guerilla warfare would create. This last-ditch stand might have left to posterity an example of a national act of heroism beyond measure, symbolic of Weber's own personal courage. As a technique of political resistance employed by a nation which had experienced exhaustion and collapse, however, its relevance seems limited indeed.[104]

Weber was unsparing furthermore in his criticism of the radical Left because it agreed with the Allies on charging Germany with the sole responsibility for the outbreak of World War I. In fact, the Independent Socialists' reaction to the bill introduced into the Reichstag on July 13, 1918, calling for an additional sum of 13,000 million marks was negative, as was their vote. All other parties supported the government proposals.[105] The latter were censored by the other parties when Geyers, their spokesman, explained their action by saying: "This time again we shall vote against the war credits. The war has never been one of defense . . . in the west too Germany is seeking a peace of conquest and violence." [106] Fritz Fischer correctly notes the defaulting of all the political parties, which after having voted for the war credits were content to stay in the background. The Reichstag having recessed until the latter part of October, their range of options was small as was their impact on the formulation of German foreign policy.[107]

A last chance for Germany to extricate herself from the war without having the outcome determined on the battlefield had occurred on July 14, 1918. On that day President Wilson inquired about the terms on which Germany envisaged a settlement of the conflict. The essentially negative response is thought to have derived from the fact that Wilson's message reached the Germans shortly before they intended to launch the offensive on the Marne. Germany had previously extended peace feelers to the Allies separately in an attempt to divide them. Instead of giving a direct reply to Wilson, William II countered with a question regarding the terms on which America would agree on a peace treaty. Germany appeared not to want to contemplate an abrupt reversal of strategy. According to Fritz Fischer so long as one of the purposes of the German policy was to defeat Britain, no plan for a rearrangement of priorities was likely to appeal to the emperor. In fact, foreseeing a German victory over England, the Kaiser did not relish the prospect of a "way out" since he still anticipated Germany's hegemony in Europe.[108]

Germany's failure to try to negotiate her way out of the war when faced with the opportunity further complicated her situation after the decisive defeat following the Battle on the Marne. In an article "Zum Thema der Kriegsschuld" (Concerning the subject of war guilt), Weber hoped to counter the morally based charges with which the Allies had sought to substantiate the Treaty of Versailles. Strongly insisting that the system of Czarism alone was responsible for the war, Weber asserted that in 1914 no stratum in Russia opposed the war. Hence, war with Russia could have been avoided only temporarily following the deterioration of German-British relations. Weber rested his case on Russian imperialism; German Social Democracy on August 4, 1914, believed the war against Czarism in Russia was "a good war." [109] He praised Germany's military leadership for having accomplished its collapse, maintaining this feat would always redound to Germany's honor. Fritz Fischer has outlined the consequences of this view, to which so many Germans subscribed. Historical evidence suggests that after the war, the Germans tried to invoke both the stab-in-the-back legend and the proposition that Germany's decision to go to war were precipitated by purely defensive motivations. The gross overreaction of many Germans to defeat and the sustained high tension caused them to lunge out blindly in efforts to identify the Weimar republic as an insult to Germany's national honor which, accordingly, could be redeemed only if Germany once again became a power state.[110]

Weber's efforts to vindicate Germany's honor received additional support from the "Heidelberg Association for a Policy of Justice," founded by well-known public figures in February 1919 at the initiative of Prince Max von Baden. The object was to draw up as broadly based an appeal as possible, addressed to public opinion at home and abroad, to protest the peace terms and Germany's alleged war guilt. Weber suggested somewhat more extreme guide-lines than those adopted by other members of the association. His reasoning was that the distortions contained in the allegations of Germany's war guilt by the enemy needed to be rebutted. Referring to the "atrocity propaganda" of Germany's adversaries, he suggested the need for Germany to construct a case of her own by presenting in an "objective though impressive" manner the evidence in her possession regarding Allied atrocities. He also campaigned for the reconstruction of Germany's armed forces "on a democratic basis." [111]

Together with his brother Alfred, Delbrueck, Oncken, Brentano, Schuecking, Albrecht Mendelsohn-Bartholdy, Haussmann, and Graf Montgelas, Weber joined in the Heidelberg Association's first appeal on February 7, 1919 in the *Frankfurter Zeitung*. It demanded the establishment of a neutral, fact-finding commission charged with providing a disinterested account concerning the whole question of war guilt. The association argued that all the belligerent great powers of Europe shared in the war guilt.[112] Weber had previously charged Russia with the main responsibility, attacking her among other reasons for having mobilized her forces while still in the negotiating stages. He claimed that this move had not only made the coming of war in 1914 inevitable but that this act in itself constituted the outbreak of war. He furthermore accused France of having taken an ambiguous stand when war broke out because of her refusal to make her intentions clear as to whether or not she would maintain an attitude of neutrality. Weber felt that it ill-behooved France to assume the role of a nation that had sustained a surprise attack. Concerning Belgium, her neutrality differed in kind from that of Switzerland and Holland. In the latter case neutrality was invoked equally toward all countries. Belgium's political mistake was its failure to follow suit, inasmuch as she had protected her borders vis-à-vis Germany while neglecting to protect her coast or land border vis-à-vis France. Weber did nevertheless express sympathy for the reaction created by the German invasion of Belgium on the part of the Belgian people.[113]

While the Association did not catalogue the responsibilities of each country, it insisted that the Western powers, under the guise of meting out justice to Germany, had used this opportunity to realize their own "imperialist war aims" which they had "solemnly pledged" to abandon.[114] All protests remained unheeded, the Western powers remained intransigent. Consequently, the members of the Heidelberg association, no less than their countrymen, had to accept the conditions imposed at Versailles.

The success which the association enjoyed was tied primarily to the name of Max Weber, who at the initiative of Prince Max von Baden, issued an appeal to publicize German documents and to conduct hearings involving those concerned before a tribunal which was to be, in every respect, independent and impartial.[115] Actually, Weber himself was not too keen on the publication of German documents so long as the Allies did not signify their intention to publish their own documents. Any publication of "memoirs" characteristic of Ludendorff's and Tirpitz's type of writing came under his special fire.[116] The reason why Weber nevertheless backed publication was partly because, meanwhile, eight German delegates in Bern were in the process of publishing such an appeal which treated Germany's guilt as *res judicata,* and also because the British government had rejected the German proposal calling for a neutral commission to investigate the problem of war guilt. The Foreign Office, which had been given advance notice of Weber's projected appeal, appeared to favor such a move.[117] Weber's special request for an investigation of the "guilty parties" within the German government was based upon his theory of the ethic of responsibility which required that responsibility for conduct both before and during the war be established.

Since activity of the Heidelberg association was similar to that of the German peace delegation in Versailles, Count Brockdorff-Rantzau decided to ask Count Montgelas, Hans Delbrueck, and Albrecht Mendelsohn-Bartholdy to join his delegation. Their specific assignment was to draw up the response to the Allied war-guilt memorandum. Max Weber's own inclination was to turn his back on this "shameful treaty," to refuse to be involved in any aspect of it.[118] He reluctantly came to Versailles but almost immediately discounted any possibility of playing a positive role as he envisaged it:[119] "In any case, I shall not cooperate in any guilt-memorandum if any indignities should be either intended or allowed."[120] Ultimately Weber was commissioned to write the introduction to the memorandum regarding war guilt, which was passed on to the Allies and published later in the German White Paper concerning war guilt. Weber was extremely bitter because he felt he had not been properly consulted and in addition he was asked to compose the introduction to the draft.[121] He then added that he purposely wrote it in such a manner that he knew it would be rejected. However, it was due to his influence that Delbrueck's original draft was largely abandoned, in which the latter sought to defend the conduct of the Kaiser as well as the Austrian treatment of the Serbian issue.[122] His assignment to write the final formulation of the introduction to the document was confirmed only after his stand on the latter question became known. The final draft was accepted, although not without some ameliorating touches at the hands of Weber's collaborators.[123]

Weber's basic position on war guilt rejected the concept of moral guilt entirely, hence omitting the Austrian role in the Serbian question altogether. Admitting that mistakes had undoubtedly occurred in the formulation of German policy, he ruled out any errors in moral judgment. Nor was the problem of guilt to be dealt with on grounds of transgressions in the sphere of diplomacy. The question of guilt could be solved only if viewed both in terms of mistakes made at the diplomatic level and against the background of the total conduct of national policy at the political level on the part of each state. The criteria, in the main, should answer two crucial questions: "Which governments in the past have contributed most to the promotion of that condition containing a constant threat of war under which Europe had suffered for years before the war?"; and "Which governments have pursued political and economic interests which could have been realized only by means of war?" [124]

In Weber's opinion, only one government, Russia, could have achieved its purposes only through a war of aggression, supported by leading strata of Russian society imbued with an imperialist spirit. Repeatedly and squarely, Weber placed the blame for the war upon the Czarist system. The Central powers had no recourse other than to fight and were therefore honor-bound to do so. "Czarism—constitutes the most horrible system of enslavement of human beings and nations, which—up until the time of this proposed peace treaty—has ever been invented. Only a defensive war against Czarism" [125] induced the German people in 1914 to enter the battle. Mommsen points to the "characteristic one-sided-ness" of this judgment as one which corresponded closely with Weber's other views.[126]

Fifty years after Weber's death Fritz Fischer's latest contribution to the literature on World War I[127] has produced additional gnawing criticism of the avoidance by German scholars of a fair estimate of the distribution of World War I. To these Hans Rothfels replied that Fischer himself had employed a selective technique in his use of source materials. Rothfels argued that by limiting his review of the Entente's war aims in his earlier book, Griff nach der Weltmacht, to one page only Fischer had omitted certain crucial points relating to the origins and development of the war. When in the early months of the war Allied fortunes proved disappointing, the Allies sought to secure additional support which might tip the scales: as Holborn had said, "They brought—or one could almost say bought—Italy and Rumania into the war in 1915 and 1916. Dire military necessity seemed to make the price paid in the form of political promises inevitable." As a result, "in the secret treaties with the two states the Allies sacrificed liberal ideals on the altar of Mars and nationalism. . . . The British attempt to force the Turkish Straits in 1915 made it desirable to assure Russia that the Gallipoli expedition was not a design to establish western European domination over Turkey. . . . Consequently, Russia received a pledge that within certain limitations she could control Constantinople after the war."[128] Hans Rothfels criticizes Fritz Fischer for devoting exactly one line to the treaty affecting the Straits according to which Constantinople was virtually bequeathed to Russia and which granted England considerable advantages in Turkey. He charges that Fischer tended to minimize the role of Allied war aims. Rothfels charges that Fischer above all described the course of historical events as it supposedly developed as an age-old process inextricably involved with the aftermath of Bismarck and the evolution of German nationalist and imperialist aspirations.[129]

Fischer's *Krieg der Illusionen* was harking back to the theme of historical continuity tackled in *Griff nach der Weltmacht*, his earlier publication in which he had discussed the controversy over Germany's aims in World War I, namely whether the German war aims were to be viewed as a consequence of the situation or as a mere continuation of earlier expansionist tendencies. Fischer, in fact, applied the test of historical continuity as he saw it to Max Weber's famous Freiburg inaugural address statement concerning the unmistakable challenge and implications involved in the founding of the Reich[130] and to Weber's lecture, delivered in 1916, in which he stated in retrospect, that if Germany had not wanted to risk going to war, she might have done better to refrain from founding the Reich, in which event she might have continued her existence as a people living in *Kleinstaaten* (small states). This test was applied also to the diary of Kurt Riezler (personal adviser of Bethmann-Hollweg) to indicate a line of thought which, as Immanuel Geiss points out, parallels that of Max Weber; Riezler, like Weber, had viewed the founding of the Reich in 1871 as but a stage, a stepping-stone to subsequent *Weltpolitik*.[131]

Some of Fischer's assumptions may have been indirectly strengthened even by Gerhard Ritter (his critic), whose comments on Bethmann Hollweg's observation that Germany's invasion of Belgium should also be viewed as a consequence of the fact that "many if not most Germans considered the Belgian state founded as late as 1830 as a rather artificial creation (including its neutrality) devoid of any great historical dignity. . . ." Bethmann Hollwegg's efforts, when seen in this perspective, Ritter explains, " 'to render Belgium harmless' . . . do not appear incomprehensible. Almost the entire German intelligentsia, including such decided liberals and Friedrich Meinecke, had at first agreed with this attitude." [132] Nevertheless, Rothfels deplores Fischer's failure to cast specific characteristics and symptoms of German imperialism in terms of the international climate, if not the *Zeitgeist* itself. He feels that it might interest especially the younger readers today "to learn that the outbreak of war in 1914 very differently from that in 1939 was not only almost unanimously hailed in Berlin but also in Paris and London, and still in 1915 in Rome and in 1917 in Washington. . . ." [133] Rothfels scores Fischer's interpretation which, in both attitude and argumentation, despite its most impressive research accomplishment, appears to be characterized by certain features inherent in the procedure employed by a prosecutor.[134]

Wolfgang Schieder points out that Fischer portrayed Bethmann-Hollweg as a far more central figure than the author is inclined to admit today. It is not by accident that Bethmann's so-called *September-program* of 1914 constituted a cornerstone in Fischer's interpretation. "The really novel aspect of Fischer's portrayal is the interpretation of Bethmann as a systematic and resolute active power politician. . . . But in the traditional dualistic model of adherents of a peace based upon victory and a peace based upon common understanding, the first German wartime Chancellor had thus far been unanimously counted among the latter. . . ." [135] As Schieder points out, Fischer identified the chancellor with the former when war broke out, even though he could point only to a convergence rather than to an identity regarding war aims on the part of the government vis à vis the annexationists. Consequently, Schieder thinks that Fischer's "authenticity must be judged first of all in terms of his interpretation of Bethmann Hollweg's policy." [136]

In the absence of Bethmann's own testimony, the diaries authored by Kurt Riezler are especially noteworthy. Karl-Dietrich Erdmann, who is said to have been the only person privileged to use the Riezler diaries, has shown the internal schism and "basically pessimistic-fatalistic features" of Bethmann-Hollweg's political attitude. He showed convincingly that Bethmann was anything but an aggressive power politician. Unmistakably, however, he concluded that "from the outset Bethmann anticipated and accepted the risk of a general war as a 'leap into the darkness' and as a 'heavy duty' (Bethmann). Based upon this interpretation, Hillgruber deduced from Riezler's writings a political theory of a calculated risk, which during the July crisis in 1914 was binding for Bethmann. . . .Geiss, however, was the first to recognize the Darwinistic components in Riezler's thought." [137]

One of Fischer's chief complaints was that in the four decades from 1919 until 1969 nobody had employed the term "preventive war" to characterize the German government's policies during the July crisis.

Hence the success of the official agitation against the *Kriegsschuldluege* (war guilt lie).[138] Fischer regarded the propaganda proclaiming Germany's innocence as a means to achieve national rehabilitation. Significantly, the author recalled that at the conclusion of the war voices were raised who, for the sake of achieving an atmosphere conducive to a more favorable basis for peace negotiations, considered it vital that the German nation would acknowledge the responsibility of its government for both the outbreak of the war in 1914 and its four and a half year duration. Karl Kautsky, who had systematically examined German documents concerned with the July crisis, collected his insights in an essay explaining the origins of World War I, in which he ascribed the chief responsibility for its outbreak to the German government. The collection of these documents, however, was not to be published; instead it appeared as an official publication in the fall of 1919 only after the other authors such as Count Montgelas, Mendelsohn-Bartholdy, Walther Schuecking, Hans Delbrueck and Max Weber joined their efforts to publish the so-called *Professorendenkschrift* (professors' memorandum) "who as experts of the German delegation in Versailles argued against Article 231 and therewith inaugurated the official propaganda against the 'war guilt lie'." [139] Significantly, Fischer observes that thorough perusal of the German documents caused these experts "to be convinced that the German *Reich* had by no means been subject to a surprise attack, but on the contrary had played a decisive role in causing the war." [140] Basing his judgment upon a letter by Bethmann-Hollweg addressed to Gottlieb v. Jagow, who had been state secretary for external affairs in July 1914, the former chancellor expressed his fear that Schuecking might render an unfavorable judgment since he interpreted the German government's role as one of having favored a preventive war.[141] The true opinion of Montgelas also reflected the view that Germany, in fact, had waged a preventive war. Moreover, Fischer cited an essay published by Mendelsohn-Bartholdy in 1925 in which he acknowledged as indisputable the powerful influence the military exerted upon the formation of governmental policy, as well as cogency of the argument that for military reasons a preventive war had been contemplated.[142] Fischer reports that a member of the parliamentary fact-finding committee appointed to investigate the outbreak of war, the legal historian Hermann Kantorowicz, concluded "that Austria-Hungary with Germany's knowledge and consent aspired to fight a war of aggression against Serbia and that the German Reich had fought a preventive war against Russia and France, thereby recklessly causing the world war, that is a war involving England." [143] Fischer purports that in 1924 permission for publication of this testimony based upon compelling evidence was refused; subsequently, even after it had been twice revised and enlarged on the basis of newly available source material and investigations conducted in 1925 and 1927, this expert's verdict was suppressed. Not until forty years later did a German historian discover and publish this document.[144]

The tentative, groping spirit behind these inquiries reflects an awakening for those who have been troubled by the war and the militarization of Germany's national life. Because their convictions were engaged, they could not be silent. Because the German political system and political attitudes were not sufficiently responsive to pressures for change, they could not be heard. The point not to be lost, however, in discussing the inquiries into the causes and aims of World War I is that "the great conflict within Max Weber's soul involving the ethic of conviction and the ethic of responsibility was to remain unresolved for many genuine democrats. Aspiration to the ideal on one hand, and to hard reality on the other coexisted as though in a vacuum. Much honest striving and many profound ideas—one need only remember Max Weber and Ernst Toeltsch—could not be actively engaged." [145] As Neumann correctly asserts, this fact was highlighted by

the dramatic struggle between Richthofen and Friedrich Naumann during the first party rally of the German Democratic Party (DDP). . . . Reprimands referring to aversion to responsibility affected the party leader so strongly that it shattered his nerves. The withdrawal of the Democrats from the government on the occasion of the dictated peace, their opposition to the school compromise, leading almost to the rejection of the Weimar constitution itself and their hesitant and unstable attitude toward economic policy were understandable. But for the masses of the membership this state of suspension proved untenable. They turned away, not only in the period of general radicalization during the desperate months . . . in 1919/20; their exodus was final. . . . The greater part turned toward the right, the *Deutsche Volkspartei*.[146]

In Neumann's judgment, it was neither Naumann's early death nor really the reaction of the people's disappointment when confronted with democracy which doomed potentially positive consequences of the revolution to failure; rather it was the recovery from the first shock which had ensued from it and the gradual salvaging of the old positions by their former occupants. Thus it was possible for the former National Liberals to gather again under the new banner of the *Deutsche Volkspartei*.[147] The demise of the Democrats decisively affected Germany's political development. They had been able to bridge the gulf between the bourgeois parties and the Social Democrats. As Neumann correctly states,

building bridges between two worlds can be a strenuous task especially when the obligation to cope with the past and relativistic reasoning operate as weakening factors in that mission. The decline and demise of the DDP constituted the most shaking experience of the democracy in the days of the Weimar Republic. It points to the mental and political crisis of the German bourgeoisie, the full extent of which is illustrated by the road the *Deutsche Volkspartei* travelled.[148]

Clearly, Fischer's assessment caused considerable dismay also because it was viewed as support to the argument of Germany's adversaries today who insist that the Third Reich can be properly understood and evaluated only in terms of the continuing history of Germany "from Bismarck to Hitler." Most German historians of the post-World War II era had become committed to developing arguments against such theories which, in their view, could serve only to bedevil contemporary international relations. But, the suggestion that all the great powers had skidded into the war also is no longer acceptable. Schieder charges, however, that Fischer, apparently not satisfied with the momentum of his impact, compounded the distance separating him from some of his colleagues by intensifying his attack. Undoubtedly, Fischer's challenge has been taken seriously by his scholarly opponents, ranging from Gerhard Ritter to Egmont Zechlin, who have acknowledged the active part played by the German government in the July crisis, even though the consensus regarding its share of the blame is variable.[149] The tragedy of Germany, in fact, having been bound up with the undue influence of the military upon the civilian government, was that as the prospects for victory decreased, that influence increased even more. Most historians today will acknowledge this. Article 231, the War Guilt Clause, was the first article in the section on reparations of the treaty. This article was intended to state the theoretical obligation of Germany to pay the costs of the war. Thus the very introduction of Article 231 seemed to make the war guilt of Germany the only justification for reparations. Consequently, Germans were convinced that if it could be proved that Germany was not solely responsible for causing the war, there would be no justification for reparations. The importance of the War Guilt Clause in later years was heightened because of the use Hitler was to make of it and the sensitivity of German historians in the post-World War II era still. Weber, it seems, favored a rejection of the Versailles Treaty at any price, including such measures as outright refusal to ratify the treaty, dissolving the government, and transferring Germany's sovereignty to control by the League of Nations. As we have seen, he also hoped that occupation by the enemy would ultimately provoke armed resistance.[150]

Finally, Weber came to realize the potential consequences that might ensue from the rejection of the treaty, namely that radicalism might assert itself once more, placing the internal cohesion of the Reich in total jeopardy. He rightly feared, moreover, that should both the government and parliament reject the treaty, it might still gain acceptance through a plebiscite. Yet, on the other hand, he censured the German Democratic party for its inconsistent stand on the treaty because it had not opted for complete rejection.[151]

Once the treaty had become a *fait accompli,* Weber accepted the inevitable and called for the framing of a positive policy rather than wrangling over it in retrospect. However, his own mood was pessimistic. He rightly foresaw that France would exploit the provisions of the treaty to further her designs upon the Rhineland.[152] The intensity of his feelings is further illustrated by the fact that he broke with his own tradition of abstaining from value judgments in the lecture hall. Thus he opened one of his lectures with an explication of the current political situation. Saying that the national emergency created by the acceptance of the Treaty of Versailles provided the justification for this unusual step, he extended an emotional challenge to his students: "We can have only one common aim: to convert this peace treaty into a scrap of paper. The right to revolt against foreign occupation cannot conceivably be destroyed." [153]

As Mommsen observes, Weber's political values were not shaken in the slightest by the collapse of the German Empire. Indeed, the latter only strengthened his national consciousness. Passionately nationalistic as he stood by his values in the hour of defeat, he reaffirmed the principles of power politics (Germany's policy in the past) which he had always advocated. Thus at the very moment when public thinking began to undergo a transition away from power politics, Weber made a strong case for maintaining the criterion of power as the essence of and prerequisite for all political action, meanwhile denouncing pacifism in the most scathing terms.[154]

By the middle of 1919, one of his greatest concerns had become the resurrection of the German army officers' corps and how best to circumvent the Treaty of Versailles' prohibitions against the revival of the general staff. During a seminar in Munich in the spring of 1920, asked by a student about his own political plans, he answered: "I have no political plans save one, namely to concentrate all my intellectual faculties on the one question, namely by what means Germany may once again obtain a great general staff." [155] Mommsen referred to this project as the last one for which Weber fought after his withdrawal from the political sphere, on the grounds that "both from the right and the left lunatics were abroad in politics." [156]

When Fritz Fischer in 1961 in his spectacular "Griff nach der Weltmacht" charged Germany with responsibility for World War I as well as for World War II, his thesis proved to be a source of irritation to nationalistically oriented academic and political conservative circles. Nor did Fischer stop short of further implications. His research furnished the cue for the logical inference flowing from these new insights, namely an attack upon the problem of "continuity" in German history. In his latest article on this subject Immanuel Geiss in a recent review of three books dealing with the aspects of continuity marking Bismarck's *Reich*, the Weimar Republic, and the Third Reich, and even the Federal Republic of Germany points to the urgent need of continued scholarly research; it is the only way to counter false sentiments and cliches. In an extension of his inaugural lecture, the Freiburg historian charged that Bismarck's unconstitutional policies and the army bill in the early 1860s constituted the starting point for consolidating both the German social structure and the special constitutional development characterizing *"Preussen-Deutschland."* It was then also above all when Prussia's course in regard to her foreign policy which led to her attainment of the status as the leading world power in Central Europe was charted. The defeat of liberalism in Germany Hillgruber attributed to the defeat of constitutional freedom and the preservation of absolutism symbolized by the continuing defense of the army bills by the government though they proved unattractive to the parliamentary majority. Thus already in 1862 the most conservative and the least hopeful prospects for a sound political order won out.[157]

Geiss states that certainly from its inception in 1871, the newly founded Reich appeared to be unstable due to the conflicting positions between Liberals championing genuine parliamentary practices and those leading circles among ultra-conservatives "oriented toward the *coup d'etat.*" [158]

As Hajo Holborn states:

Outside of the socialist camp practically all these scholars thought of solutions within the framework of the existing constitutional order. Even those who like Max Weber were convinced of the necessity for a reform of the Bismarckian constitution did not see how it could be achieved in view of the great power of the monarchy, which, in the midst of an unexampled prosperity, enjoyed the full support of the upper and middle classes. This frustration generated political weariness and passivity among people who might have contributed to the conduct of politics or at least to political education.[159]

Similarly in its foreign policy, only three alternatives appeared to prove acceptable to those responsible for the conduct of governmental policy of the Reich, according to Hillgruber:

1. Germany and the other great powers should divide Europe between themselves into 'spheres of influence or areas of interests'; this was to be done at the expense of small and medium-sized states.
2. To guard against potential or actual rivals for power, purposefully designed preventive wars are to be waged.

3. The competing great powers should agree among themselves to establish a balance of power by concentrating their interests and by diverting resulting tensions overseas.[160]

German "world politics" ultimately led to German self-isolation, and as Hillgruber points out, there had been serious suggestions put to the government advocating the second alternative. Only a few weeks before the outbreak of World War I, the younger Moltke had urged a 'preventive war' against Russia, just as the older Moltke had requested such a war to be conducted against France.[161]

Defeat in 1918 and the Peace of Versailles served to destroy Germany's status as a great power only temporarily. She retained the potential ability to regain that status. Accordingly, the foreign policy of the Weimar Republic was generally aimed in that direction, or if this should fail, "force is to be applied, hence a new war (something about which there was agreement among statesmen and generals and clearly stated in top secret documents). Already on November 20, 1918 Seekt elaborated this new concept which Stresemann promoted and Hitler executed, a policy still in the phase of the '*Revisionspolitik*' until 1938—and one enthusiastically supported by nationalist conservative forces." [162]

Another author who occupied himself with the problem of continuity in German history, John C. G. Röhl stated that on the basis of recent documentary evidence very little had actually changed as one compares the Imperial and Republican objectives.[163]

Holborn states that "the activity and speeches of the belligerent German right added fuel all the time to the resistance in France against a generous policy with regard to Germany. Naturally the lack of appreciation of favors granted to Germany discouraged at times not only the French but also the British. But Stresemann wrested concessions from France and England." [164]

As Holborn correctly avers, no party was proud of the new constitution and the nonsocialist parties were concerned lest the break with the past would become too painful. Moreover, of the Democrats he said that

there were more "democrats by intellect" than "democrats by heart," which means that there were few Germans who believed in democracy as an absolute ideal. . . . All nonsocialist parties had cooperated to preserve the structure of German society. But they were also inclined to save as much as possible of the traditional political symbols. The new state was not named the German Republic, but the German Reich.[165]

Of Weber and the Republic it must be concluded that he remained essentially what he was during the time of William II, an advocate of national power politics, carrying his convictions with him into the era of the Weimar Republic. Weber, nevertheless, refused to become involved in any extreme right-wing activities and cannot therefore be considered as a spokesman for the forces of reaction which prepared the way for the Third Reich.

NOTES

1 *P.S.*, 2nd ed., p. 472.
2 *Lebensbild*, p. 642ff. cited in Fritz Ernst, *The Germans and Their Modern History* (New York: Columbia University Press, 1966), p. 74.
3 Julien Freund, *The Sociology of Max Weber* (New York: Pantheon Books, 1968), p. 148. Reprinted by permission of Random House, Inc.
4 *Ibid.*, p. 265.
5 Max Rheinstein, ed., *Max Weber on Law in Economy and Society*, translation from Max Weber, *Wirtschaft und Gesellschaft* (2nd ed., 1925) by Edward Shils and Max Rheinstein (New York: Simon and Schuster, 1967), p. 190.
6 Cf. letter to Crusius of November 24, 1918, *P.S.*, 1st. ed., p. 484.
7 *Ibid.*, letter to Crusius, December 26, 1918, p. 485.
8 Cf. Helmut Neubauer, ed., *Deutschland und die Russische Revolution* (Stuttgart: W. Kohlhammer, 1968).
9 Cf. Gerhard A. Ritter and Susanne Miller, *Die deutsche Revolution 1918–1919 —Dokumente* (Frankfurt: Fischer Buecherei, Buecher des Wissens Nr. 879, 1968).
10 *P.S.*, 1st. ed., p. 482. See letter to Crusius, of November 24, 1918.
11 *Ibid.*, p. 486. Letter to the editor of the *Frankfurter Zeitung*, April 14, 1919.
12 *P.S.*, 2nd. ed., p. 472.
13 Letter to Crusius of November 24, 1918, *ibid.*, p. 484.
14 *Muenchener Neueste Nachrichten*, November 5, 1918 cited in Mommsen, *op. cit.*, p. 295.
15 Mommsen, *op. cit.*, p. 295.
16 *P.S.*, 2nd. ed., p. 470.
17 *Ibid.*
18 Cf. Gerhard A. Ritter und Susanne Miller, *op. cit.*, also Cf. Waldemar Besson et al., *Jahr und Jahrgang 1918* (Hamburg: Hoffmann and Campe, 1968).
19 *P.S.*, 2nd. ed., p. 473.
20 *Ibid.*, p. 473.
21 *P.S.*, 1st ed., p. 488.
22 Mommsen, *op. cit.*, p. 295. Cf. also letter to Frau Else Jaffé-Richthofen, November 1918, *P.S.*, 1st. ed., p. 480f. Also cf. Theodor Heuss, "Max Weber in seiner Gegenwart," in: Max Weber, *P.S.*, 2nd. ed., p. XXVIIIf.
23 Mommsen, *op. cit.*, p. 294.
24 *Ibid.*, p. 296.
25 Reinhard Bendix, *Max Weber: An Intellectual Portrait* (New York: Doubleday, 1960), pp. 450–451. Bendix' quotations refer to phrases in Weber's lecture on socialism contained in Max Weber, *Gesammelte Aufsaetze zur Soziologie und Sozialpolitik* (Tuebingen: J. C. B. Mohr, 1924), p. 508, as reported by the author.
26 Cf. *P.S.*, 2nd. ed., p. 474. Also *Lebensbild*, pp. 653-54.
27 Vernon L. Lidtke, *The Outlawed Party: Social Democracy in Germany, 1878–1890* (Princeton: Princeton University Press, 1966), p. 237.
28 *Ibid.*, p. 193.
29 Cf. Richard N. Hunt, *German Social Democracy 1918–1933* (New Haven: Yale University Press, 1964).
30 *Ibid.*
31 Cf. Lidtke, *op. cit.*, p. 237.
32 Cf. Guenther Roth, "Political Critiques of Max Weber: Some Implications for Political Sociology" (Revised Version of a paper read at the annual meeting of the American Sociological Association, Montreal, 1964), *American Sociological Review*, April 1965, Vol. 30, No. 2, p. 220 fn., referred to subsequently in this chapter.

266   *The Political Thought of Max Weber*

33 *Ibid.*
34 Kai Hermann, "Germany's Young Left," *Encounter,* Vol. XXX, No. 4, April 1968, p. 69.
35 Cf. the notable studies by Karl Dietrich Bracher, *Die Aufloesung der Weimarer Republic: Eine Studie Zum Problem des Machtverfalls in der Demokratie* (Stuttgart and Duesseldorf, Germany: Ring Verlag, 1955), and Ralf Dahrendorf, *Society and Democracy in Germany* (Garden City, N.Y.: Doubleday, 1967).
36 *Vossische Zeitung,* No. 653, December 22, 1918. Cf. also *Wiesbadener Tagblatt,* report of Weber's address of December 5, evening edition, December 6, 1918. Weber charged that the Revolutionary government was engaged in a type of political agitation which could never have been conducted in a worse manner under the regime that preceded it. However, he predicted its collapse and along with it that of the faith in social democracy. Cf. Mommsen, *op. cit.,* p. 296.
37 Kai Hermann, *op. cit.,* p. 72.
38 Cf. Richard Barkeley, *Die Deutsche Friedensbewegung 1870–1933* (Hamburg: Hannerich Lesser, 1948).
39 Karl-Heinz Janssen, "November 1918: Die Revolution, die Keine War," *Die Zeit,* November 5, 1968, Nr. 44, p. 5. Reprinted by permission of the publisher.
40 *Ibid.*
41 *Ibid.*
42 *Ibid.*
43 *Ibid.*
44 Cf. Mommsen, *op. cit.,* p. 297 for an extremely interesting report covering the minutes of the meetings of the council of the deputies of the People's International Institute for Social History, Amsterdam (former SPD-Archives) Cabinet meeting of November 15, 1918, 10:30 A.M.: This report covers the appointment to be made to the position of a Secretary of State of the Interior. The discussion centered on the question whether Max Weber's qualifications, in addition, to Hugo Preuss, should not be considered with a view to a possible appointment to that position. The Cabinet did agree that President Ebert should keep the contact to Preuss open without obligation, however. In the afternoon meeting it was decided to nominate Preuss to the position. Appointment and explanation of the Council of People's Deputies in DZAI RKA 2, "Staatssekretaere Vol. 2, No. 1609. As Mommsen suggests, Weber probably never knew how close he had come to the greatest political opportunity of his life.
45 Mommsen, *op. cit.,* p. 297.
46 *Ibid.,* pp. 325–326.
47 *Ibid.,* and cf. Weber's letter to Marianne Weber of November 25, 1918, *Lebensbild,* p. 646. Whatever prospects there might have been for Weber to attain such a position they were probably obviated as a result of his utterances relative to the government under whom he would have had to serve. This assumption seems to find a corollary in a letter to Crusius of December 26, 1918 in which Weber acknowledged that because he had called the revolution a "bloody carnival" it had cost him the nomination to an important position. He praised Ebert but states that he has been frustrated in his efforts to rely on the troops. Cf. *P.S.,* 1st. ed., pp. 484–485.
48 Theodor Heuss, "Max Weber on the occasion of the 10th anniversary of his death," *8-Uhr-Abendblatt* of June 21, 1930 quoted in René Koenig and Johannes Winkelmann, eds., *Max Weber zum Gedaechtnis: Materialien und Dokumente zur Bewertung von Werk und Persoenlichkeit.* Special issue of *Koelner Zeitschrift fuer Soziologie und Sozialpsychologie* (Koeln and Opladen: Westdeutscher Verlag, 1963), pp. 158–59.
49 Max Weber, "Deutschland's Kuenftige Staatsform," in *P.S.,* 1st. ed., p. 353, cited in J. P. Mayer, *Max Weber and German Politics: A Study in Political Sociology* (London: Faber, 1944), p. 73.
50 J. P. Mayer, *op. cit.,* p. 73.
51 *Ibid.,* pp. 73–74.
52 H. Stuart Hughes, *op. cit.,* p. 373. Incidences of the fragmentation of the Democratic party may be ascertained from *Tagung des Hauptvorstandes,* February 4, 1919, roll 36/723; *ibid.,* April 12–13, 1919 roll 36/723. Five rolls of a collection of microfilmed documents reproduced by the Hoover Institution at the American Documents Center in Berlin stemming from the *NSDAP Hauptarchiv.* This material has been cited by Bruce B. Frye, "A Letter from Max Weber," *Journal of Modern History,* Vol. 39, No. 2, June

1967, pp. 122–124, secured and translated by the author and published with the permission of Dr. Edgar Petersen. Also by permission of The University of Chicago Press.
53 Cf. *P.S.*, 2nd. ed., pp. 472–475. A report in the *Frankfurter Zeitung* of December 2, 1918 on a political speech by Max Weber delivered on December 1, 1918 on "The New Germany."
54 *P.S.*, 2nd. ed., p. 441.
55 Herbert Marcuse, "Industrialisierung und Kapitalismus," Otto Stammer, ed., *Max Weber und die Soziologie heute: Verhandlungen des 15. Deutschen Soziologentages* (Tuebingen: J. C. B. Mohr [Paul Siebeck], 1965), p. 165.
56 Paul Mattick, "The Limits of Integration," Kurt H. Wolff and Barrington Moore, J., eds., *The Critical Spirit: Essays in Honor of Herbert Marcuse* (Boston: Beacon Press, 1967), p. 375.
57 Herbert Marcuse, *One Dimensional Man* (Boston: Beacon Press, 1964), p. xiii cited in Paul Mattick, *ibid.*
58 Herbert Marcuse, "Industrialisierung und Kapitalismus," Otto Stammer, ed., *Max Weber und die Soziologie heute: Verhandlungen des 15. Deutschen Soziologentages* (Tuebingen: J. C. B. Mohr [Paul Siebeck], 1965), p. 166.
59 *Ibid.*
60 *Ibid.*
61 *Lebensbild*, p. 653. Weber's speeches have been discussed also in detail by Wolfgang Mommsen, *op. cit.*, and see especially p. 300 for the address delivered in Karlsruhe. This speech was recorded in *Badische Landeszeitung* No. 7, *Mittagsblatt* of January 6, 1919, *Karlsruher Tagblatt*, 1st. edition of January 5, 1919, and *Badische Presse* No. 7, *Mittagsblatt*, January 6, 1919.
62 *Lebensbild*, p. 653.
63 Karl-Heinz Janssen, "Als der Kaiser ging: Der Sturz der deutschen Monarchien," *Die Zeit*, No. 43, October 29, 1968, p. 5. Reprinted by permission of the publisher.
64 *Ibid.*
65 *Ibid.*
66 Cf. Mommsen, *op. cit.*, pp. 299–300.
67 Cf. Haussmann's letter to Weber of November 24, 1918 (copy in Haussmann's estate) cited in Mommsen, *op. cit.*, p. 301.
68 Cf. Mommsen, *op. cit.*, p. 301. See also report in the *Frankfurter Zeitung* of December 20, 1918 cited by Mommsen.
69 Cf. Mommsen, *op. cit.*, p. 301.
70 Cf. Letter to Preuss of December 25, 1918 cited in Mommsen, *op. cit.*, pp. 301–302.
71 *Lebensbild*, p. 655.
72 *Ibid.*, p. 656.
73 *Ibid.*, cf. Mommsen, *op. cit.*, p. 302.
74 Attila Chanady, "The Disintegration of the German National Peoples' Party 1924–1930," *Journal of Modern History*, Vol. 39, No. 1, March 1967, p. 65.
75 *Ibid.*
76 Letter to Haussmann of May 1, 1917. The above discussion owes much to Mommsen's excellent analysis. Cf. Mommsen, *op. cit.*, pp. 302–303.
77 Kaethe Leichter, "Max Weber als Lehrer und Politiker," *Der Kampf Sozialdemokratische Monatsschrift* (Vol. 19, No. 9, 1926) reprinted in René Koenig and Johannes Winckelmann, *op. cit.*, p. 141.
78 *Ibid.*, pp. 141–142.
79 *Ibid.*, p. 142.
80 Cf. proceedings and the attending record contained in roll 36/746 of the party records cited in Bruce B. Frye, *cp. cit.*, pp. 122–124.
81 Walter Tormin, *Geschichte der Deutschen Parteien seit 1848* (Stuttgart: W. Kohlhammer Verlag, 1968), p. 145. Reprinted by permission of the publisher.
82 Bruce B. Frye, *op. cit.*, pp. 122–124.
83 Letter to Professor Goldstein of November 13, 1918 in *Lebensbild*, p. 615. Cf. Mommsen, *op. cit.*, p. 305.
84 *Ibid.*
85 This report was made by someone who had attended the meeting and was recorded in *Lebensbild*, p. 643 and discussed in Mommsen, *op. cit.*, p. 305.
86 Report of the *Vossische Zeitung* of March 11, 1919 cited in Mommsen, *op. cit.*, p. 306 fn., of an address by Max Weber delivered at a protest meeting of the faculty and students of the University of Heidelberg.
87 *Ibid.*, p. 306.

88 Frederic S. Burin, "Bureaucracy and National Socialism: A Reconsideration of Weberian Theory," p. 39 in Robert K. Merton, et al. (eds.), *Reader in Bureaucracy* (New York: The Free Press, 1952). Cf. Hans Gerth, "The Nazi Party, Its Leadership and Composition," *American Journal of Sociology*, XLV, January 1940, p. 537.

89 Wolfgang Sauer, in Karl Dietrich Bracher, Gerhard Schulz, and Wolfgang Sauer, *Die nationalsozialistische Machtergreifung* (Cologne and Opladen: West-Deutscher Verlag, 1960), p. 689.

90 Guenther Roth, "Political Critiques of Max Weber," *American Sociological Review*, Vol. 30, No. 2, April 1965, p. 214.

91 *Ibid.*, p. 221.

92 *Ibid.*

93 *Ibid.*

94 *Ibid.* fn.

95 *Ibid.*, p. 220 fn.

96 *Ibid.*, p. 222.

97 George L. Mosse, *The Crisis of German Ideology: Intellectual Origins of the Third Reich* (New York: The Universal Library, Grosset and Dunlap, 1964), p. 220.

98 Cf. Reinhard Ruerup, "Verunglueckte Revolution: Die democratische Massenbewegung vom November 1918," *Die Zeit*, April 30, 1968, Vol. 23, No. 17, p. 12. Cf. also Allan Mitchell: *Revolution in Bayern 1918/19, Die Eisner Regierung und die Raeterepublik* (translated from the earlier American edition) (Munich: BeckSche Verlagsbuchhandlung, 1968). Eric Waldman, *Spartakus: Der Aufstand von 1919 und die Krise der deutschen sozialistischen Bewegung*," translated from the American edition (Boppard a/Rhein: Harold Boldt Verlag, 1968 and Ernst Niekisch, *Die Legende von der Weimar Republik* (Koeln: Verlag Wissenschaft und Politik, 1968).

99 Fritz Erler, "The Struggle for German Reunification," *Foreign Affairs*, Vol. 34, No. 3, April 1956, p. 393.

100 Karl Loewenstein, "Berlin Revisited," *Current History: A Monthly Magazine of World Affairs*, Vol. 50, No. 297, May 1966, p. 268.

101 *P.S.*, 2nd. ed., p. 444 and Mommsen, *op. cit.*, p. 306.

102 See report of January 4, 1919 in both the *Karlsruher Tagblatt* and the *Badische Landeszeitung* of January 4, 1919. Cited in Mommsen, *op. cit.*, p. 307.

103 *Ibid.*, p. 307.

104 *Ibid.*

105 Fritz Fischer, *Germany's Aims in the First World War* (New York: W. W. Norton, 1967), pp. 623–624.

106 *Ibid.*

107 *Ibid.*

108 Cf. *Ibid.*

109 *P.S.*, 2nd. ed., pp. 479–480.

110 Fritz Fischer, *op. cit.*, p. 638.

111 Letter to the *Frankfurter Zeitung* of February 9, 1919. *P.S.*, 1st. ed., p. 485–486.

112 Letter to the *Frankfurter Zeitung* 1st. Morning Edition of February 13, 1919, cited in Mommsen, *op. cit.*, p. 308.

113 *P.S.*, 2nd. ed., pp. 481–482.

114 *Frankfurter Zeitung*, 1st. Morning Edition of February 13, 1919, cited in Mommsen, *op. cit.*, p. 308.

115 Letter to *Frankfurter Zeitung* of March 20, 1919, *P.S.*, 2nd. ed., p. 491. See also Mommsen, *op. cit.*, p. 308–309.

116 Cf. letter to Delbrueck, October 8, 1919, cited in Mommsen, *op. cit.*, p. 309.

117 Letter to Oncken, March 21, 1919, cited in Mommsen, *op. cit.*, p. 309.

118 *Lebensbild*, p. 663. Cf. also Mommsen, *op. cit.*, p. 310.

119 *Lebensbild*, p. 663. Cf. also Mommsen, *op. cit.*, p. 310.

120 *Lebensbild*, p. 666.

121 *Lebensbild*, pp. 667–668.

122 Delbrueck's draft is contained in Delbrueck's estate, cited in Mommsen, *op. cit.*, p. 310.

123 Cf. Mommsen, *op. cit.*, p. 311. Cf. also *P.S.*, 2nd. ed., p. 560ff. "VI. Rueckblickende Betrachtungen" (Appendix) "Bemerkungen zum Bericht der Kommission der Alliierten und Assoziierten Regierungen ueber die Verantwortlichkeit der Urheber des Krieges." Vol. 27. May 1919 signed by Hans Delbrueck, Max Graf Montgelas, Max Weber, Albrecht Mendelssohn Bartholdy. In:

Das Deutsche Weissbuch ueber die Schuld am Kriege (Mit der sog. Professoren-denkschrift), 1st ed., Berlin 1919, p. 64 and in *P.S.*, 2nd. ed., pp. 560–61.
124 *Ibid.*
125 *Kriegsschuldgedenkschrift*, p. 68. Cf. *P.S.*, 2nd ed., p. 479, and see Mommsen, *op. cit.*, p. 311.
126 *Ibid.*
127 Fritz Fischer, *Krieg der Illusionen: Die deutsche Politik von 1911 bis 1914* (Duesseldorf: Droste Verlag, 1969).
128 Hajo Holborn, *The Political Collapse of Europe* (New York: Alfred A. Knopf, 1966), pp. 85–86.
129 Hans Rothfels, "Fritz Fischers Anklage gegen das Wilhelminische Deutschland: Das zweite Buch des Hamburger Historikers ueber die deutsche Politik von 1911 bis 1914," Book Review: Fritz Fischer, *Krieg der Illusionen: Die deutsche Politik von 1911 bis 1914* (Düesseldorf: Droste Verlag, 1969). *Frankfurter Allgemeine Zeitung*, No. 65, March 18, 1970, p. 10.
130 Fritz Fischer, *Krieg der Illusionen*, pp. 69–70; cf. Max Weber, *P.S.*, 2nd. ed., p. 23.
131 Immanuel Geiss, "Zur Beurteilung der deutschen Reichspolitik im Ersten Weltkrieg: Kritische Bemerkungen zur Interpretation des Riezler—Tagebuchs" in Wolfgang Schieder, ed., *Erster Weltkrieg: Ursachen, Entstehung und Kriegsziele* (Koeln-Berlin: Kiepenheuer & Witsch, 1969), p. 228.
132 Gerhard Ritter, "Der Kanzler und die Machttraeume deutscher Patrioten 1914," in *ibid.*, p. 134.
133 Hans Rothfels, *op. cit.*, p. 10.
134 *Ibid.*
135 Wolfgang Schieder, *op cit.*, p. 16.
136 *Ibid.*
137 *Ibid.*
138 Fritz Fischer, *Krieg der Illusionen*, p. 671.
139 *Ibid.*, p. 668.
140 *Ibid.*, p. 669.
141 *Ibid.*
142 *Ibid.*
143 *Ibid.*
144 Cf. *ibid.*
145 Sigmund Neumann, *Die Parteien der Weimarer Republik* (Stuttgart: W. Kohlhammer Verlag, 1965), p. 49.
146 *Ibid.*, p. 50.
147 Cf. *ibid.*
148 *Ibid.*, p. 54.
149 Schieder, *op. cit.*, p. 12.
150 Cf. Letter to Marianne Weber, June 20, 1919, *Lebensbild*, p. 668.
151 Letter to Marianne Weber of June 28, 1919, *Lebensbild*, pp. 669–670. Mommsen, *op. cit.*, pp. 312–313.
152 Cf. Mommsen, *op. cit.*, p. 313.
153 *Ibid.*
154 Speech delivered to the students of the University in Munich. "Politik als Beruf," *P.S.*, 2nd. ed., p. 493ff.
155 Gustav Stolper, *This Age of Fable* (New York, 1942), p. 318. The author had been a student attending Weber's seminar.
156 For explanation of the related Count Arco case, see *Lebensbild*, p. 684 and previous discussion in this book.
157 Immanuel Geiss, "Die Kontinuität der Tradition," Book Review *Die Zeit*, Nr. 46, November 13, 1970, p. 14. Cf. Andreas Hillgruber. *Kontinuität und Diskontinuität in der deutschen Aussenpolitik von Bismarck bis Hitler.* Düsseldorf: Droste Verlag, 1969.
158 Geiss, *op. cit.*, p. 14.
159 Hajo Holborn. *A History of Modern Germany 1840–1945.* Vol. III. (New York: Alfred A. Knopf, 1969), p. 411.
160 Hillgruber, *op. cit.*, quoted in Geiss, *op. cit.*, p. 14.
161 *Ibid.*
162 *Ibid.*
163 John C. G. Röhl. *From Bismarck to Hitler. The Problem of Continuity in German History.* London: Longman, 1970, quoted in Geiss, *op. cit.*, p. 14.
164 Holborn, *op. cit.*, p. 629.
165 *Ibid.*, p. 557.

VIII

Max Weber on Political Theory
and Practice

An examination of Max Weber's political writings confronts
one simultaneously with Weber, the renowned and respected scholar
and Weber, the political analyst engaged in raising current political
events to the level of public consciousness. This implies the need for
establishing the nexus between a researcher's moral guide-lines and the
kind of theoretical framework within which he places his research
findings. Few areas of academic inquiry are more important. And, few
areas have inspired more controversy and ambivalence than the role
of value judgments in social science. The significance of the issue,
moreover, is underscored by the fact that Max Weber was primarily
responsible for perhaps its most sophisticated analysis. Here, as in so
many instances, his political thought and action remain relevant to our
own time.

In his address to the German Sociological Association at its annual
meeting in Heidelberg in 1964, Raymond Aron stressed this aspect of
Weber's influence. Weber, he said, must be regarded as "belonging to a
past which cannot even now be considered finally closed." Evidence of
this could be seen in "the controversies created by Wolfgang Mommsen's
book, *Max Weber und die Deutsche Politik*, which were not of a purely
scientific character." [1] Accordingly, in Aron's view, the interest stirred
by Mommsen's book and by the proceedings of the German Sociological
Society's convention of 1964, themselves derived from the following
topics:

1. the current interest in Wilhelminian Germany.
2. World War I, its causes and consequences.

270

3. the Weimar Republic.
4. Hitler and World War II.

Insofar as he was a most articulate architect of the power theory, Weber must be seen as a representative of a past whose interpretation is, of necessity influenced by our awareness of the present.[2] Some of Weber's writings, moreover, are of particular interest because of their relevance to contemporary France. Aron points to the affinity between Weber's proposals for a constitution for post-World War I Germany and the actual constitution of the Fifth Republic of France.[3] He notes too the contemporary emphasis on the European community which binds Frenchmen and Germans together; citizens, and especially sociologists, of Europe should engage in the study of nationalism, both past and present, and more especially, in that of power politics. Aron is careful to refer to Weber's distinction between science and politics, while at the same time exploring the occasions on which Weber failed to follow his own example.

In defining the term *Machtpolitik,* Aron distinguished between a narrower and a broader conceptualization. The political relationships *between* states, existing as they do in competition for power, remain ungoverned by supranational legal authority and international adjudication. In that sense, Aron states that all foreign policy, including its contemporary practice, in all ages, qualifies for the term "power politics." The second definition of *Machtpolitik* is more inclusive. Here all politics becomes equated with power politics, including domestic politics if the goal and/or the principal means employed involve the stress on the use of power as a means. The more an analysis stresses authority and power, the more it emerges as power politics.[4]

Aron considers Weber qualified as a typical power politician in both senses. His orientation was fathered by Machiavelli, while Nietzsche might be considered his spiritual brother. In his view, serious discussion should not be concerned with the ancient preoccupation as to which form of government is preferable. The significance of this question pales before what to him seemed the essence and perennial condition of political life, namely the struggle between nations, classes, and individuals for positions of power and authority. Yet, Weber made it clear that the true force of liberal and parliamentary institutions lay for him in their ability to guarantee Germany the prerequisites necessary for her to attain her aim as a great nation. The thrust and tenor of Weber's reasoning are directed to making them relevant and appropriate as instrumental proof that Germany is capable of taking her place among the world's great powers.[5] Weber, in a remarkable passage, said: "Only *Herrenvoelker* (master nations) may feel called upon to manipulate the spokes of international developments. If nations not

endowed with this *tiefe Qualitaet* (deep quality) should try their hand
at it, then not only will the sure instinct of other nations rebel against
it, but they themselves will fail internally as well." [6]

Some of Weber's critics, even those inclined to sympathize with his
basic view of life, have been repelled by this element of harshness in
his thought. Weber, on the other hand, had sought to advance the
creation of viable political institutions which would ensure the political
participation of a nation of *"citizens"* rather than the mere passive acceptance of bureaucracy by a nation of *"subjects."* No adherent to
liberalism can deprecate Weber's record of profound commitment to
the parliamentary form of government. Yet he also spelled out what
Aron calls: "the synthesis of liberalism and imperialism in Weber's
value system meant: the justification of the parliamentary system based
upon the power interests of the nation was to accord to spontaneous
inclinations or perhaps to, more yet, to strong antipathies an instrumental character." [7]

As Aron notes, Weber never provided a body of thought which
used sociological categories to describe and analyze the struggles of
states, nations, and peoples. Little attention was paid, except in passing,
to the ways in which culture and power relate to each other. His discussion of what might be called a sociology of international relations in
one chapter of *Wirtschaft und Gesellschaft,* had, unfortunately, to remain
unfinished.[8] Given the chance, Weber probably would have engaged
further in theoretical modes of political analysis, supported by a body
of substantive data and backed by his profound knowledge of history,
especially in this area of his keenest interest. Aron argues that Weber's
nationalism preceded or at least paralleled his sociological investigations
and his scientific accomplishments:

He has met it in all its living reality during his years of study in the heart
of Wilhelmine Germany and has, apparently without reluctance, absorbed it
without much reflection. In some points, Weber has followed the teachings
of the celebrated lectures on politics of Treitschke, even though his own
philosophy is much more pessimistic, and one might say, more tragic. He had
decided once and for all that the highest value, to which he would subordinate all else in politics, is the God (or demon) to whom he had sworn
loyalty, namely Germany's greatness.[9]

Even though Weber deplored Treitschke's virulent polemics, his
own civic courage and violence wielded with the pen outside the classroom present a temptation to apply to him what he had previously
applied to the authors of the *Communist Manifesto:*

In theory, if not in practice, they always refrained from moralizing. It never
entered their minds (at least, so they claim) to lament the evil and infamy

of the world. Yet, in reality, they were extremely passionate men who did not follow this rule at all.[10]

Carlo Antoni observed that Weber's main weakness must be sought in "his insistence upon the purely technical aspects of political power. Other intellectuals of that period, such as Troeltsch and Meinecke, who pointed out the urgent need for democratic reforms, avoided any appeal to natural law ideologies, but they sought to revive the Kantian tradition of the autonomy of the will and responsible liberty, the ideas of the 'reform epoch,' of Stein, Gneisenau and Boyen." [11] Weber's skepticism toward a parliamentary system in the ideal meaning of the term prompted him to concede that true parliamentarianism would be possible only where there were local governments and aristocratic parties. Predictably in France, and in some other Latin countries parliamentarianism might still be able to bestow certain blessings which however generally belong to the past. England, the erstwhile paragon of a parliamentary nation, had outgrown this phase already, in Weber's view.[12]

J. H. Hexter and Peter Laslett have recently warned against predating and assigning too much weight to "the rise of the middle classes" in England. Laslett especially stressed the late duration of aristocratic rule in *The World We Have Lost* (1955). The late beginnings of middle-class rule were also underscored by Hexter:

. . . the so-called middle classes never in fact displaced the (aristocratic) ruling segment. . . .

(Moreover) the ruling (aristocratic) segment exercised a (governmental) function as much as it occupied a position. And it went on exercising this function . . . until the beginning of class politics in 1900. The middle class never rose, at least it never rose to the top: and it never ruled.[13]

Hence, in the recent development of the Labor party, its political leadership inside and outside parliament is constituted nearly equally of working-class and middle-class people. At the same time, Labor's rank-and-file support is drawn mostly from the working class. British sociologists characterize two-thirds of Labor's electorate as working-class. In an election of great Labor success, nearly 65% of working-class people vote for Labor: "What is crucially distinctive is Labor's small middle-class support. It is unlikely that Labor today receives much more than 15% of the vote of the third of the population identified as middle-class." [14] The scarcity of the latter in the Labor party's rank and file reflects the failure of Labor's political values to capture the imagination of the middle classes, indicating that the ideological approach to political issues has not yet been abandoned in British politics. The malaise of the Labor party is compounded by the almost complete lack of interest and sympathy of middle-class youth.[15] Nor are the British trade-unions serving as a political training ground: "British workers do not accept the guidance even of their own elected trade-union officials: between 90 and 95% of all working-time lost in British strikes is chargeable to 'unofficial' stoppages which the trade-union organization has not approved . . . Britons are not easily ruled: it is their distinction." [16]

Aron particularly stressed the almost total absence of ideological justification in Weber's thinking. His originality lies less in his identification with nationalist sentiment, fairly representative of the late nineteenth century, than in the passion with which he proclaims the necessity of conducting *Weltpolitik* as an inevitable consequence and ultimate justification of Bismarck's work. Another original factor distinguishing Weber from his contemporaries was his recognition of the diabolical character of power and the sacrifices demanded by a power state. While Treitschke held small states and their particularism up to ridicule, Weber rejoiced that German nationality groups existed outside the borders of the national power state. His feeling was that the simple virtues of the citizen and genuine democracy could not be realized in any great power state. Such more intimate and perennial values could be nurtured only in political communities which renounce aspirations to political power. Thus, in Weber's view, so genuine a German as Gottfried Keller might never have achieved such uniqueness, "had he lived in such an 'armed camp' as this state, of necessity must be." [17]

Concerning the relationship between nation and state on the one hand, and between nationalism and imperialism on the other, Aron considered Weber a product of his age. Recognizing the legitimacy of other nations' aspirations toward autonomy, he nevertheless categorically rejected any thought of a compromise with France concerning Lorraine. As for a plebiscite in Alsace, the very thought struck him as ludicrous.[18] Scheidemann's declaration of April 1917, that the annexation of Alsace-Lorraine had been a "mistake," thoroughly enraged him.[19] Conversely, Weber was keenly aware of the errors in German policy in that area. The Alsace had been denied equal rights and privileges along with other provinces within the Reich so that when Allied war aims anticipated the return of Alsace-Lorraine to France, Weber was anxious to see the old 'wound' closed.[20] German officialdom governed the Alsatians autocratically, while the conduct of the German military establishment there invited criticism. Meanwhile, the Alsatians' affection for France increased in direct proportion to their negative reactions to German provocations.

Weber did not press for the inclusion of non-German or foreign population elements within the Reich. Yet he certainly did not subscribe to the principle of nationality *per se*. The partition of Central Europe into so-called national states inevitably encompassing national minority groups seemed neither desirable nor capable of effective realization. In retrospect, one is inclined to agree with Aron's marginal note stating that perhaps Weber was right.[21] Weber's primary interest then was directed to see that Germany's power interest achieved relative compatibility with certain demands put forth by other nations.

A study of Max Weber's views on foreign affairs reveals no single pattern of thought. The quintessence of his thinking included the image of Russia as Germany's arch enemy, the only power he considered capable of threatening Germany's very existence. These feelings of antagonism prompted him to campaign for a German policy of friendly relations with Poland; not that his sympathies for Polish demands had increased since his inaugural address at the University of Freiburg, but writing during the war of 1914–18, his concern for Germany's national interest increased as the military tide turned increasingly against her. Urging greater public awareness of the impending disaster, he advocated the creation of autonomous states under military protection of the Reich, tied to it with economic strings which, he believed, would provide a maximum of security against Russian imperialism.

In Aron's estimation Weber did not go far enough, not being ready to concede to Poland complete independence any more than he was ready to sacrifice Germany's military security or political advantage to the manifest preferences of the population.[22] As in the case of the territorial dispute with France over Alsace-Lorraine, in the case of Poland's sovereignty Weber remained unconcerned with ideological frameworks and moral principles. He certainly was unwilling to grant the right of national self-determination unless forced to do so by circumstance. His interest focussed upon the relative strength of and any qualitative or quantitative changes in national feelings on which he based his indisputably realistic assessments. These assessments concerned threats to Germany's national security in the form of possible annexations in Europe, coupled with suggestions for ways to mobilize the national feelings of Eastern Europe to accord favorably with German aims against Russia.[23]

In dealing with Aron's charges against Weber on the first count, namely that his thinking was dominated by the spirit of the times, which prevented him from granting Poland complete independence in the same way he ignored the possibility of free elections in Alsace-Lorraine, we may question why Aron relegates Weber's premises and conclusions to a bygone age? Weber's political strategy has a contemporary ring in Germany today and elsewhere too.

For example, in defense of his opposition to official American policy in Vietnam, Hans Morgenthau notes American misconceptions about the nature and conduct of foreign policy. He attributes United States involvement in Vietnam with all its disastrous consequences to the personal motives of those who have conceived it or whose legacy it has become. He says that the honor and prestige of the United States has been risked, not over a controversial issue of foreign policy or strategic considerations of a military nature, but over a psychopathological phenomenon. Morgenthau has the gravest reservations concerning the lack of political maturity underlying the personalization of the anxiety with which potential loss of face is met, which, in his view, underscores the ambivalence of American foreign policy. Neither America's vital national interest nor America's prestige is at stake; what is at stake is the position of those responsible for the promulgation of these policies. The wish of the policy-makers to retain power and to assure themselves of a place in history is crucial in the current conduct of American policy in South-East Asia.[24] Like Weber, Morgenthau stresses the fateful significance of power in all its aspects and ramifications but, also like Weber, Morgenthau opposes the equation of national with military power and the increasingly improvident use of this type of power.

He identifies the psychological mechanism operative in the Bay of Pigs invasion as being the same one which increased the commitment of the United States in Vietnam. While the former was shortlived, in Vietnam the magnitude of the risks and the potential long-range commitments in view of increasing escalation is far more insidious. In his posthumously published book, Robert Kennedy explains that during the Cuban Missile Crisis, President Kennedy had been reading Barbara Tuchman's book, The Guns of August, recalling the events leading to the First World War. Robert Kennedy relates the shock his brother felt over the manner in which both sides had skidded into that war and his wish to avoid the same mistake of stumbling into war with the Soviet Union over the issue of the missile sites in Cuba. It was this resolve on Kennedy's part which caused friction between him and the military establishment throughout much of the missile crisis. Morgenthau suggests that the risks involved in such confrontations are not only of a political or military nature. What may be impaired in his judgment, is the very identity of Americans; their very status as a great nation may be placed in jeopardy and with it their mission in the world.[25]

So far as the manifest preferences of the population are concerned, which Weber in his time was willing to ignore, this inclination, too, appears to be characteristic of our own age. The secretary of defense of the United States stated on February 15, 1965, that "the choice is not simply whether to continue our efforts to keep South Vietnam free and independent but, rather, whether to continue our struggle to halt Communist expansion in Asia." [26] There appears to be an affinity here between Weber's use of Poland as a pawn in confrontation with Russia and the United States' role in Vietnam to stop Communist China's influence. Neither can lay claim to ethical neutrality or purity, unless one considers the anti-Communist crusade as both the moral principle and the rationale of a global foreign policy.[27]

In the service of the cause which is to stop Communist expansion: "We thought we could deprive the Viet Cong of popular support by herding unwilling peasants into strategic hamlets, and it did not occur to us that . . . by uprooting the peasants we helped the Viet Cong recruit them."[28] Arguing against bombing North Vietnam "because we don't know what else to do," Morgenthau refers to seizing the chance of bending the situation in Southeast Asia to rationally defined interests, if only the president had at his disposal advisers such "as a Richelieu, a Talleyrand, a Bismarck or—why go abroad—a Hamilton!"[29] Thus while Max Weber's attitude toward Alsace-Lorraine and Poland may resemble official American policy toward the population's wishes in Vietnam, his criticism of the conduct of German foreign policy under the Kaiser was not too far removed from Hans Morgenthau's role as a critic of United States policy in Vietnam. What Morgenthau has been deploring is the absence of coherence and well-thought-out purpose in foreign policy which in his view, has characterized the American climate.

International relations in our period of history are by their very nature controversial. They require decisions concerning the purposes of the nation and affecting its chances for physical survival. By dealing with the subject matter but not with the issues underlying these decisions, a theory can appear to contribute to the rationality of these decisions without actually doing so.[30]

Still, Max Weber's negative response to governmental actions, which in his judgment were grossly out of proportion with Germany's actual power position, is reflected in Morgenthau's own view on the foreign policy of the United States in Vietnam:

. . . the United States is incapable of liquidating the war because of its faulty perception of reality and its unattainable goals. It acts upon the assumption that it is defending South Vietnam against aggression. If only North Vietnam left its neighbor alone, to quote Mr. Rusk's celebrated phrase, there would be no trouble in South Vietnam. For this reason, we are bombing North Vietnam, we plan to construct a barrier which is supposed to seal the South off from the North, we are willing only to negotiate with the government in Hanoi, and we might even invade the North. However, fruitful negotiations with the government in Hanoi are impossible not because we refuse to cease unconditionally the bombing of the North . . . but because we seek to gain at the conference table what we have been unable to achieve on the battlefield: the destruction of the Viet Cong as an organized political force.[31]

Consequently, facts must be properly understood; illusions and grand designs for changing them are unwarranted:

. . . a contemporary theory of international relations must put current notions about international relations, such as beliefs in world-wide conspiracies, naturally evil nations, and revolutions at the service of such conspiracies and nations, to the test of empirical verification. The contemporary theories of international relations are irrelevant to that task. They laboriously evade it.

For these beliefs, which serve the psychological needs of the believers rather than the quest for truth, a theory of international relations worthy of the name must substitute the empirical examination of the historic data that may prove or disprove, as the case may be, the assumptions upon which governments act, and the unexamined beliefs by which the man in the street forms his judgments.[32]

However, what is clearly characteristic of an otherwise so complex age is

that this moral foundation upon which the legitimacy of democratic government has rested in the past is no longer as firm as it used to be. A government armed with nuclear, biological and chemical weapons of mass destruction still intends to protect the life of its citizens against a government similarly armed. But in truth it cannot defend its citizens, it can only deter the prospective enemy from attacking them. If deterrence fails and he attacks, the citizens are doomed. Such a government, then bears the two faces of Janus: insofar as it is able to deter, it is still its citizens' protector; if it fails to deter, it becomes the source of their destruction.[33]

The distance between Morgenthau's pronouncements within the province of the political relations among men, and Weber's profoundly prophetic reflections encompassing the whole human condition, is not so great. It can be readily understood as Weber concludes:

Nobody knows yet who will live in this cage of the future . . . whether at the end of this tremendous development entirely new prophets will arise . . . whether there will be a great rebirth of old ideas and ideals or, if neither, mechanized petrification embellished with a sort of convulsive self-importance. For that last stage of cultural development it might well be said . . . 'Specialists without spirit, sensualists without heart, this nullity imagines that it has attained a level of civilization never before achieved.'[34]

Yet, if one were to compare the position of Max Weber with a critic such as C. Wright Mills, one would have to point out that Mills had no strong national affections or commitments because he "did not 'believe' in America, nor did he 'love' America."[35] While Weber's highest value was always Germany's national interest, Mills' criticism of his country's foreign policy was not motivated by a feeling for the nation-state, including his own; he could not grant allegiance to it. "I cannot," he wrote in *Listen, Yankee,* "give unconditional loyalties to any institution, man, state, movement, or nation. My loyalties are conditional upon my own convictions and my own values;" and these, he confessed, "lie more with the Cuban revolution than with the official United States reaction to it."[36] Weber's response to Germany, in contrast, critical as he could be of his own country, placed his nation above all other values:

The Germans, he was convinced, were a disciplined people: their weaknesses were known, but also their competence and their sensitiveness to the beauty of everyday life, in contrast to other peoples, who looked for beauty in emotional transports or gestures. One hundred and ten years ago, Germans showed the world that they—and they alone—were able, in spite of foreign rule, to become a great civilized nation. Let us do it again now. 'I believe,' he wrote, 'that this Germany is indestructible, and I have never felt the fact of being a German to be a gift of fortune so much as in these dark hours of Germany's shame.' Looking back over the years, he said: Germany is the only nation to which history twice, after the total collapse of 1648 and 1806, granted a renewal. It will have a third renewal after the icy night through which it is now condemned to pass.[37]

POLITICS AS A VOCATION

The state, in Weber's conception, belongs to those categories of human interaction to be analyzed in terms of understandable actions of participating individuals. The individual is the fundamental unit of society. All social institutions, moreover, can be reduced to thought constructs which may be employed as tools in the analysis of social facts:

Interpretative sociology considers the individual and his action as the basic unit, as its 'atom' . . . if the disputable comparison for once may be permitted. . . . In general, for sociology, such concepts as 'state,' 'association,' 'feudalism' and the like, designate certain categories of human interaction. Hence it is the task of sociology to reduce these concepts to 'understandable' action, that is, without exception to the actions of participating individual men.[38]

Max Weber's lecture delivered at Munich University in 1918, entitled *Politics as a Vocation,* is indispensable for a discussion of the practical aspects of his political philosophy.[39] Here Weber defines the state as "a human community that (successfully) claims the *monopoly of the legitimate use of physical force* within a given territory. The state is considered the sole source of the 'right' to use violence."[40] Thus

" 'politics' for us means striving to share power or striving to influence the distribution of power, either among states or among groups within a state."[41]

According to Weber, public functionaries in the modern state are divided into two categories: administrative officials and political officials. The civil servant should not engage in politics. Indeed, Weber considered the fact that Germany had been ruled by a bureaucracy a basic reason for its irresponsible politics under the Kaiser.[42]

In contrasting the civil servant with the politician, Weber stated that the former was under obligation to carry out the orders given by his superiors to the letter, regardless of his own convictions. Without this "moral discipline" and "self-denial" the whole apparatus would collapse. The political leader's responsibility was of a different order. His is a personal responsibility and he must therefore take a stand on issues confronting him. Formerly, in the old party organization, "circles of notables and . . . members of parliament" had ruled. Modern forms of party organization, however, "are the children of democracy, of mass franchise, of the necessity to woo and organize the masses, and develop the utmost unity of direction . . ."[43]

Professional politicians perform organizational functions: "They do so either as 'entrepreneurs'—the American boss and the English election agent are, in fact, such entrepreneurs—or as officials with a fixed salary. Formally, a far-going democratization takes place."[44] Initially, Weber argued, society evolved from a nonspecialized mass. In the earlier type of society, conditions for genuine leaders to come to the fore were more favorable. Subsequently, the quest for a stable foundation for the exercise of authority brought about the gradual development of more routinized and systematic organizational forms. Weber pointed to the importance of the modern political "machine" with its function of maintaining internal unity, agreement on objectives, and loyalty to its leaders. Those who control the machine also are able to control the will of others, and to influence the choice of the party leaders. The man who has been endorsed as the head of the machine and who is assured of its support can become the leader, even with the parliamentary party staying in the background. The manner in which such machines operate suggests the advent of plebiscitarian democracy.

Followers would have to be educated to recognize their need for such a leader:

. . . it has to be clearly realized that the plebiscitarian leadership of parties entails the 'soullessness' of the following, their intellectual proletarianization. . . . In order to be a useful apparatus, a machine in the American sense— undisturbed either by the vanity of notables or pretensions to independent views—the following of such a leader must obey him blindly. . . . This is simply the price paid for guidance by leaders.[45]

Weber concluded that

. . . there is only the choice between leadership democracy with a 'machine' and leaderless democracy, namely, the rule of professional politicians without a calling, without the inner charismatic qualities that make a leader, and this means what the party insurgents in the situation usually designate as 'the rule of the clique.' [46]

Undoubtedly, party machines are bureaucratic in character.[47] But national elections in the United States should have gone a long way toward proving the worth of the democratic process. Millions of American voters who are the listening, viewing, and reading public of the radio, television and the press, all designed to help conduct election campaigns (with the press not infrequently supporting the Republican candidate), have shown that they can do some independent thinking. They have not drifted down the path of "intellectual proletarianization." Nevertheless, Roscoe Drummond is correct when he asserts that Americans must institute electoral reforms because they do not really participate adequately in the selection of their president:

The times require and demand reforms now: They have already been too-long delayed, not because of the public's indifference, but because of congressional unresponsiveness.

How can it be said that the American people democratically elect their President unless they also have the opportunity to democratically nominate their presidential nominees?

Three reforms are needed to open wide the democratic process to fuller and more accessible voter participation:

Take the time bomb of the Electoral College out of the Constitution and provide that the President and Vice President be chosen by direct popular vote. This requires a constitutional amendment.

Provide for a national preconvention advisory primary so that the voters of each party shall have the right and the means of authoritatively telling each party convention which candidates they most want to see nominated. This can be done by congressional action.

The political parties themselves should take further steps to make certain that the voters in each state have a far better opportunity to choose the delegates to the conventions.

The overriding and urgent objective of all these reforms is not merely to tidy up the mechanism of the presidential election. That's incidental. The real objective is to open the whole elective process so that more voters more readily, more visibly and more influentially can participate in decisions which affect their government and their lives.[48]

In Max Weber's philosophy of history, as developed in all his works, the process of "rationalization" was central. "Rationalization" denotes the elimination of magic, of intuition. This elimination of supernatural forces has resulted in an affirmation of work-a-day life (*Die Bejahung des Alltags*) which distinguishes our culture from the Christian and the medieval views of life. Man's role has been affected fundamentally by the consequences of rationalization in a rationally ordered society. This society may be characterized by anomie, by a lack of direction as regards the ends and purpose of life, but according to Weber this isolation does not alienate the individual from society. On the contrary, it compels the individual to stand on his own feet and endows him with a sense of responsibility.

As the scientific attitude has become prevalent, the fear of the supernatural has decreased. Man no longer believes in a divinely ordered society, but in one he himself can direct to an ever-increasing degree because of his constantly growing knowledge. The position of the individual has become problematic in the face of the numerous institutions of government and industry, of systems and corporations which have resulted from the process of rationalization. In his struggle with these powerful institutions man becomes aware of his freedom, according to Weber. He regards the responsibility of the individual not merely as a product of rationalization, but also as its most outstanding blessing.

Rationalization refers essentially to the adequate adaptation of means to ends. It issues in the compartmentalization of all of life as well as areas of human knowledge. It leads to the removal of traditionalism from virtually all aspects of human existence. It generates the adoption of a pragmatic outlook on life caused by the "disenchantment of the universe." Finally, it results in the full development of bureaucracy, which gives rise to a unique form of social life. On the one hand, according to Weber, individual freedom increases as a result of rationalization; on the other, rationalization brings with it bureaucracy which limits individual liberty.[49] Therefore he urged the individual to keep a constant watch to prevent bureaucracy from increasing more than absolutely necessary to the efficient functioning of the social mechanism.

In posing the question of how to salvage some remnants of individuality, Weber arrived at the same conclusion as Carlyle. He sought to differentiate the concept of charisma [50] from the concept of bureaucracy:

> In contrast to any kind of bureaucratic organization of offices, the charismatic structure knows nothing of a form or of an ordered procedure of appointment or dismissal. It knows no regulated 'career,' 'advancement,' or regulated and expert training of the holder of charisma or of his aids. It knows no agency of control or appeal, no local bailiwicks or exclusive functional jurisdictions; nor does it embrace permanent institutions like our bureaucratic 'departments' which are independent of persons and of purely personal charisma. Charisma knows only inner determination and inner restraint. The holder of charisma seizes the task that is adequate for him and

demands obedience and a following by virtue of his mission. . . . His charismatic claim breaks down if his mission is not recognized by those to whom he feels he has been sent. If they recognize him, he is their master—so long as he knows how to maintain recognition through 'proving' himself. But he does not derive his 'right' from their will, in the manner of an election. Rather, the reverse holds: it is the *duty* of those to whom he addresses his mission to recognize him as their charismatically qualified leader.[51]

Gerth cogently notes that Weber did not intend to give a one-sided view of the "sovereignty of the charismatic man" to minimize the mechanics of institutions:

> . . . on the contrary, by tracing out the routinization of charisma, Weber is able to assign a heavy causal weight to institutional routines. Thus he retains a social determinism by emphasizing charisma's routinization. His handling of the problem testifies to his constant endeavor to maintain a causal pluralism and to bring the economic order into the balance.[52]

Similarly, the

> 'philosophical' element in Weber's construction of history is this antinomic balance of charismatic movements (leaders and ideas) with rational routinization (enduring institutions and material interests). Man's spontaneity and freedom are placed on the side of heroic enthusiasm, and thus there is an aristocratic emphasis upon elites ('virtuosos'!). The emphasis is intimately associated with Weber's attitude towards modern democracy.[53]

Directing his attention to the inner satisfaction which the politician derives from his career and to the requirements which the aspiring politician has to meet, Weber found that the politician's supreme enjoyment is awareness of his power over his fellow men. Three qualifications are considered necessary for a responsible politician: *passion, responsibility,* and a *sense of proportion.* He must always conquer the mortal enemy of all rational devotion to a cause: vanity. Since politics implies a struggle for power, it is normal for the politician to be imbued with the "power instinct." Personal vanity, however, might cause the politician to fall victim to two kinds of deadly sin, the one, lack of objectivity, the other, irresponsibility. Thus the craving for personal aggrandizement induces the careerist to place himself in the foreground:

> Although, or rather just because, power is the unavoidable means, and striving for power is one of the driving forces of all politics, there is no more harmful distortion of political force than the parvenue-like braggart with power, and the vain self-reflection in the feeling of power, and in general every worship of power *per se.* The mere 'power politician' may get strong effects, but actually his work leads nowhere and is senseless. (Among us,

too, an ardently promoted cult seeks to glorify him.) . . . From the sudden inner collapse of typical representatives of this mentality, we can see what inner weakness and impotence hides behind this boastful but entirely empty gesture. It is a product of a shoddy and superficially blasé attitude towards the meaning of human conduct; and it has no relation whatsoever to the knowledge of tragedy with which all action, but especially political action, is truly interwoven.[54]

Weber here alluded to the Kaiser's attempts to solve some of the most crucial political problems from an emotional point of view, thereby destroying the desired political effect, particularly in the case of the *Daily Telegraph* affair.[55] He failed, however, to draw attention to the fact that in a democratic apparatus personal vanity has a chance of being more effectively controlled than in any other system.

Weber frequently referred to the element of tragedy inherent in human experience, especially in decisive moments, and in particular in politics. While he would certainly have condemned Hitler's boastful and imprudent conduct, the question has been raised as to whether he might not have given the German people a clean bill of health today on the ground of their "tragic" involvement which, though he would have deplored it, might yet have met with understanding and sympathy on his part.

The answer to this question, which is almost impossible to give, would have provided a more profound insight into the conflict between Weber's unquestionable personal integrity and his brand of national honor. As noted elsewhere, Marianne Weber's retort in this connection was *"Jeder Mensch ist ein Geheimnis"* (Every man is a secret in himself).[56]

Weber held that political planning required the politician to subject himself to self-discipline and to familiarize himself thoroughly with the realm of "objective possibility" which must, indeed, be his sole frame of reference. He failed to point out that these objectives are often best achieved when the politician works in close collaboration with colleagues.

The professional politician must also have faith. It is immaterial whether he serves national, ethical, cultural, secular, or religious causes, as long as he believes in something:

> However, some kind of faith must always exist. Otherwise, it is absolutely true that the curse of the creature's worthlessness overshadows even the externally strongest political successes.[57]

For Max Weber, however, faith was not pipe dreams but a confidence based on the power of Germany and on the role she had to play. Mention was made previously that Weber rejected vulgar chauvinism as much as he did the advocacy of remorseful appeasement. In *Politics as a Vocation,* as well as elsewhere, his hope was that the reconstruction of Germany would result in the restoration of her former position and status among the nations. For the realization of this purpose Weber, one suspects, would have made a pact with anyone, even with the devil himself. It was not offenses against ethical principles which Weber feared most, but rather the planless stupidity of some of the would-be politicians among his compatriots.[58]

Inquiring into the relationship between ethics and politics, Weber confronted the import of his distinction between absolute ethics and politics. The interpretation he gave it illustrates how literally he applied both concepts. "The absolute ethic of the Gospel was not a cab to be taken at will; it was all or nothing." Weber further underlined his position by relating the parable of the wealthy young man of whom it was said that "he went away sorrowful because he had great possessions." Weber supported his thesis by pointing to the evangelist's commandment as being both unconditional and unambiguous as the young man was asked to surrender *all* his possessions. Considering the characteristics of the contemporary international power-structure, it must be viewed as one in which the concept of ethics may cast its spell but with an air of fantasy considering the imperatives of political and other spheres of life.

The command "turn the other cheek" is equally absolute in its requirement. This ethic, which demands acceptance of humiliation, can be met only by a saint. Universal love means that evil should not be employed to combat another evil; force constitutes an evil. The politician, however, may have to decide in favor of force; if he tries to avoid this path, he may become guilty of having allowed another, possibly even a greater, evil to win out. Anyone wishing to practice the unconditional ethic cannot employ political weapons such as strikes.[59] Since political action must at times avail itself of whatever means of violence may be at its disposal, if the occasion demands the political leader must stand ready to use force. He cannot afford to let moral scruples interfere with what he considers sound judgment. Nor can he permit his actions to conform to precepts of the absolute ethic. A responsible leader must anticipate the foreseeable consequences of his actions and respond accordingly. In effect, the political leader must address himself to tasks confronting him in *this* world; hence he must reckon with *all* the forces operative in *this* world:

No ethics in the world can dodge the fact that in numerous instances the attainment of 'good' ends is bound to the fact that one must be willing to pay the price of using morally dubious means or at least dangerous ones—and facing the possibility or even the probability of evil ramifications. . . . It is of course utterly ridiculous if the power politicians of the old regime are morally denounced for their use of the same means (to face 'some more years of war') however justified the rejection of their *aims* may be.

The ethic of the ultimate ends must apparently go to pieces on the problem of the justification of means by ends.[60]

Thus Weber insisted:

Whoever wants to engage in politics at all, and especially in politics as a vocation, has to realize these ethical paradoxes. He must know that he is responsible for what may become of himself under the impact of these paradoxes. I repeat, he lets himself in for the diabolic forces lurking in all violence.[61]

Yet the political leader still did not escape moral responsibility. Weber did not wish to see the use of force covered by the mantle of Christianity, regardless whether the motive was held to be adequate in terms of the end justifying the means. Ultimately the politician's actions must be judged by the relevance of means to ends. He must estimate in advance the price that may have to be paid for the attainment of a given goal. His calculation must also include the indirect cost which paying that price might entail, namely the infringement of other values. Nor does the end itself solely determine the means to be employed. The end itself may partly depend upon the means which the politician can command. It is precisely this contingent atmosphere in which the politician may assess the means to achieve his potential ends which reveals that the process of rationalization contains a liberating element: the multiplicity of choice open to the politician. This element constitutes his freedom to act in accordance with the dictates of reason. Meanwhile, the fact that he cannot escape the consequences of his actions in the light of ultimate values, causes his action to be a responsible one. Thus the freedom of the individual becomes equated with the possibility of choosing "in the light of his own conscience and his personal outlook among the values at stake." [62]

Weber next proceeds to differentiate and examine two types of ethic: the "ethic of responsibility" as opposed to the "ethic of conviction." Essentially, all ethically oriented conduct must confront two inherently different and irrevocably contradictory guide-lines, i.e., all human behavior may be geared to "an ethic of ultimate ends" or to an "ethic of responsibility." Weber cautioned against the assumption that the ethic of conviction is to be equated with absolution from responsibility; nor is the ethic of responsibility to cushion acts of sheer opportunism. He did stress the gulf that exists between the directive of the "ethic of conviction," namely that according to which, religiously speaking, "the Christian does rightly and leaves the results with the Lord," and conduct which is judged on the basis of its rational chances of success in a given situation.[63]

One might wonder here whether Weber underestimated the potential political force manifest in the creed of nonviolence. For example, the American civil rights leader, Dr. Martin Luther King, and his organization, the Southern Christian Leadership Conference, were successful in engaging many in the cause of civil rights; until his death, he and his organization served as a conduit for social and political activism. Because of its nonviolent and integrated character, some political analysts deemed the movement crucial. The threefold nature of its cause—the battle for equal rights, the campaign for economic opportunity, and the crusade against what King called the "unjust and immoral" involvement in Vietnam—was political in content. His has been a movement of militant nonviolence rather than of mere passive resistance. It has employed civil disobedience as a means against unjust segregation legislation. He chose thereby to confront the authorities directly in an effort to abolish these inequities. Mass marches as well as peaceful demonstrations were vested with heavy political pressure. Nevertheless, while in 1964 Congress passed the most far-reaching civil rights bill and while in 1965 the Voting Rights Act became law, the benefits of these legal measures have yet to be translated into social reality. King's commitment to nonviolence as the answer to some of the most crucial contemporary problems at both the moral and political levels, addressing itself as it did to peace at home and abroad, deserves to be considered as an alternative to the power-oriented types of political action usually espoused by Max Weber.

Weber noted, without questioning the vision, that life may contain moments when a man must act in accordance with a principle:

'Here I stand; I can do no other.' . . . In so far as this is true, an ethic of ultimate ends and an ethic of responsibility are not absolute contrasts but rather supplements, which only in unison constitute a genuine man—a man who can have the 'calling for politics.' [64]

Weber insisted more characteristically, however, that the politician must base his appraisals of people and situations on concrete firsthand information rather than on wishful thinking. Hence, subscribing to the ethic of responsibility means including in one's calculations sociopolitical as well as personal human instabilities. If the politician fails to provide recipes for action and formulas for prediction, others should not have to pay the price for his failure; rather he must, in Weber's view, be held accountable. The ethic of conviction is typically carried out on the basis of its ethical or religious consideration, based upon purity of intention rather than on the effect it might create. To this category Weber would have assigned Martin Luther King's mission. "To rekindle the flame ever anew is the purpose of his quite irrational deeds, judged in view of their possible success. They are acts that can and shall have only exemplary value." [65]

To secure the realization of the "good" end, the means employed are not always morally defensible and might not even conform to the standards of commonly accepted respectability. Weber disclaimed any ethic which could settle the problem of ". . . when and to what extent the ethically good purpose justifies the ethically dangerous means and ramifications." [66]

His view of the world conceived it as an arena in which conflict was everywhere in evidence. Social science could not be expected to set up a scale of values because of the fact that different values often conflict; particularly where ultimate values are concerned, the evidence points to irreconcilable conflict. The process of rationalization underscored this basic conflict of values all the more. The irreconcilable conflict of the "struggling gods" led him to state:

> He who seeks the salvation of the soul, of his own and of others, should not seek it along the avenue of politics, for the quite different tasks of politics can only be solved by violence. The genius or demon of politics lives in an inner tension with the god of love, as well as with the Christian God as expressed by the church. This tension can at any time lead to an irreconcilable conflict. [67]

Weber emphasized that

> . . . the early Christians knew full well the world is governed by demons and that he who lets himself in for politics, that is, for power and force as means, contracts with diabolical powers and for his action it is *not* true that good can follow only from good and evil only from evil, but that often the opposite is true. Anyone who fails to see this is, indeed, a political infant. [68]

The possibility of adverse consequences or even total failure resulting from political action might have to be met. This is the potential price which has to be paid. No objective criteria could exist which might be helpful in the consideration of the price; social science, too, could supply the data concerning its fairness. [69]

Weber insisted moreover that all politicians must be fully prepared to suffer the consequences of their actions. As pointed out previously, Weber's charismatic leaders were distinct from Fascist leaders inasmuch as they were, at least in theory, responsible to the masses who could depose them. [70] Even democratic governments could not altogether escape such practices as Weber described. Accomplishment of absolute justice as a goal to be realized on earth is predicated upon a following, a human "machine." To sustain such a "machine" becomes feasible only by means of offering it the required "internal and external premiums," whether these be "heavenly or worldly rewards." Weber noted that the modern class struggle itself may prescribe as built-in premiums the selection of means to satisfy hatred and the satisfaction of the craving for revenge. Complying with the need of meeting resentment and catering to the need of "pseudo-ethical self-righteousness," the opposition may have to be scorned and charged with heresy.[71]

Under external political rewards Weber listed "adventure, victory, booty, power, and spoils." The leader's good luck depends largely upon the smooth "functioning of his machine and . . . not on his own motives." His success is also contingent upon his capacity to maintain payment of premiums to his followers on a permanent basis. Actually accomplished ends, instead of resting upon the political leader's own discretion, become cognitive data that are relevant in relation to the conditions under which he labors, as they are prescribed to him by his follower's motives; from an ethical point of view, these "are predominantly base." His entourage itself can be controlled only as long as he can inspire an authentic trust in his person. His cause, moreover, will be espoused by only part of his party; to hope for the support of the majority would not be in keeping with realistic expectations.[72]

The following commentary, which diagnoses social action magnificently, again mirrors Weber's fearless and yet pessimistic view of the "brave new world":

This belief, even when subjectively sincere, is in a very great number of cases really no more than an ethical 'legitimation' of cravings for revenge, power, booty, and spoils. We shall not be deceived about this by verbiage; the materialistic interpretation of history is no cab to be taken at will; it does not stop short of the promoters of revolutions. Emotional revolutionism is followed by the traditionalist routine of everyday life; the crusading leader and the faith itself fade away, or, what is even more effective, the faith becomes part of the conventional phraseology of political Philistines and banausic technicians. This development is especially rapid with struggles of faith because they are usually led or inspired by genuine leaders, that is, prophets of revolution. For here, as with every leader's machine, one of the conditions for success is the depersonalization and routinization, in short, the psychic proletarianization, in the interests of discipline. After coming to power the following of a crusader usually degenerates very easily into a quite common stratum of spoilsmen.[73]

For Weber the crumbling base of Germany's political situation was dramatically clear. He feared that within ten years from the time he delivered this address, Germany would be thoroughly under the sway of reaction. At present she had to make do with the minimum certainties of leadership and workaday administration. Foreseeing not "summer's bloom but rather a polar night of icy darkness and hardness, no matter which group may triumph externally now," as his country's fate, he wondered who among the enthusiasts for the "revolution" would still be alive. Noting the then current void of ideas, he wanted to see a new and firmer stability established. At this point he addressed himself particularly to his student audience:

Will you be bitter or banausic? Will you simply and dully accept world and occupation? Or will the third and by no means the least frequent possibility be your lot: mystic flight from reality for those who are gifted for it, or—as is both frequent and unpleasant—for those who belabor themselves to follow this fashion?
. . . Politics is a strong and slow boring of hard boards. It takes both passion and perspective. Certainly all historical experience confirms the truth —that man would not have attained the possible unless time and again he had reached out for the impossible. . . . Only he has the calling for politics who is sure that he shall not crumble when the world from his point of view is too stupid or too base for what he wants to offer. Only he who in the face of all this can say, "In spite of all!" has the calling for politics.[74]

NOTES

1 Cf. Raymond Aron, "Max Weber und die Machtpolitik," in Otto Stammer, editor, *Max Weber und die Soziologie heute: Verhandlungen des 15. Deutschen Soziologentages* (Tuebingen: J. C. B. Mohr [Paul Siebeck], 1965), p. 103.
2 *Ibid.*
3 *Ibid.*, p. 104. Cf. also Mommsen, *op. cit.*, p. 202f. and more especially pp. 330–386 on the election and functions of the *Reichspraesident*.
4 Aron, *op. cit.*, p. 104.
5 *Ibid.*, pp. 104–105.
6 *P.S.*, 1st. ed., p. 259 cited in *ibid.* p. 105.
7 *Ibid.*, p. 106.
8 Max Weber, *Wirtschaft und Gesellschaft* (3rd. ed., 1947, Part II, Chapter III), pp. 619–630. Cited in Aron, *op. cit.*, p. 106.
9 *Ibid.*, p. 107.
10 Max Weber, *Der Sozialismus* (Vienna, 1918), reprinted in *Gesammelte Aufsaetze zur Soziologie und Sozialpolitik* (Tuebingen, 1924).
11 Carlo Antoni, *From History to Sociology: The Transition in German Historical Thinking* (Detroit: Wayne State University Press, 1959), p. 132.
12 Cf. *ibid.*, p. 132.
13 J. H. Hexter, *Reappraisals in History* (New York: Harper & Co., 1963), p. xii.
14 Oscar Gass, "Britain under Socialism," *Commentary*, Vol. 41, No. 2, February 1966, p. 65.
15 Cf. Mark Abrams, *Must Labour Lose?* (London: Penguin, 1960) and Richard Rose, *Politics in England* (Boston: Little, Brown & Co., 1964).
16 Oscar Gass, *op. cit.*, pp. 67–68.
17 Max Weber, *Gesammelte Politische Schriften*, 2nd. ed. (Munich: Drei Masken Verlag, 1921), p. 60. Cf. also, Aron, *op. cit.*, p. 108.
18 Cf. letter written by Weber to Robert Michels dated June 20, 1916, in Weber's

estate and quoted in Mommsen: "Such 'Kitsch' (trash) coming from the political nursery as a plebiscite in Alsace-Lorraine, you had better keep to yourself in my estimation. An uninfluenced plebiscite in Rome would yield papal rule, while an uninfluenced plebiscite in Sicily might result in expelling the Piemontese. In any case, given the necessary means I would be prepared to stage one myself." Mommsen, *op. cit.*, p. 258.

19 Cf. letter to Naumann dated April 12, 1917, *Gesammelte Politische Schriften*, p. 468.

20 *Ibid.* Literally Weber said: "Equal status of the Alsatians with the *Reich*— but for God's sake, nothing more than that!"

21 Cf. Aron, *op. cit.*, p. 109.

22 *Ibid.*

23 Max Weber, *Wirtschaft und Gesellschaft* (3rd. ed., Part III, Chapter II, 1947), pp. 227–229. Cf. also Aron, *op. cit.*, p. 109.

24 Cf. Hans J. Morgenthau, *Vietnam and the United States* (Washington D.C.: Public Affairs Press, 1965), pp. 18–19.

25 *Ibid.*, p. 19.

26 *Ibid.*, p. 53.

27 *Ibid.*, p. 82.

28 *Ibid.*, p. 14.

29 *Ibid.*, p. 56.

30 Hans. J. Morgenthau, "Common Sense and Theories of International Relations," *Journal of International Affairs*, Vol. XXI, No. 2, 1967, p. 213.

31 Hans J. Morgenthau, "What Ails America," *The New Republic*, Vol. 157, issue 2761, No. 18, October 28, 1967, p. 19.

32 Hans J. Morgenthau, "Common Sense and Theories of International Relations," *op. cit.*, p. 212.

33 Hans J. Morgenthau, "What Ails America?" *op. cit.*, p. 18.

34 Max Weber, *Die Protestantische Ethik und der Geist des Kapitalismus* (Tuebingen, 1934), p. 204, quoted in Fred H. Blum, "Max Weber: the Man of Politics and the Man Dedicated to Objectivity and Rationality," *Ethics*, LXX, October 1959, p. 13.

35 Ralph Miliband, "Mills and Politics," ed. Irving L. Horowitz, *New Sociology: Essays in Social Science and Social Theory, in Honor of C. Wright Mills* (New York: Oxford University Press, 1969), p. 79.

36 C. Wright Mills, *Listen Yankee: The Revolution in Cuba* (New York: 1960), cited in *ibid.*, p. 79.

37 Max Weber cited in Karl Jaspers, *Three Essays: Leonardo, Descartes, Max Weber*, translated by Ralph Manheim (New York: Harcourt, Brace & World, Inc., 1964), pp. 205–206.

38 Max Weber, *Gesammelte Aufsaetze zur Wissenschaftslehre* (Tuebingen: J. C. B. Mohr [P. Siebeck], 1922), p. 415; also see *Wirtschaft und Gesellschaft*, Part III of *Grundriss der Sozialoekonomie*, 2nd. ed. (Tuebingen: J. C. B. Mohr [P. Siebeck], 1926), I, 6.

39 Max Weber, "Politik als Beruf," *Gesammelte Politische Schriften* trans. in Hans H. Gerth and C. Wright Mills, *From Max Weber: Essays in Sociology* (New York: Oxford University Press, 1946), pp. 77–128.

40 Weber, "Politik als Beruf," *ibid.*, p. 78.

41 *Ibid.*

42 For a vivid account of the character of bureaucracy in the nineteenth century in Germany, see Herman Finer, *The Theory and Practice of Modern Government* (London: Methuen & Co., Ltd., 1929–1932), II, p. 1212ff.

43 Gerth and Mills, *op. cit.*, p. 102.

44 *Ibid.*

45 *Ibid.*, p. 113.

46 *Ibid.*

47 For a penetrating analysis of the anti-individualistic consequences of modern bureaucracy, see Robert Presthus, *The Organizational Society: An Analysis and a Theory* (New York: Vintage Books, 1965).

48 Roscoe Drummond, "It's time now to change procedure for elections," *Staten Island Sunday Advance*, Vol. 83, No 15, 693, November 24, 1968, p. E2. Reprinted by permission of the publisher.

49 On Weber's examination of the relationship between democracy and bureaucracy see Peter M. Blau, "Critical Remarks on Weber's Theory of Authority," *The American Political Science Review*, LVII, No. 2, June 1963.

50 The Greek word "charisma" denotes a divine gift of grace, repeatedly used by Weber to describe a magical, non-rational type of leadership.

51 Gerth and Mills, op. cit., pp. 246–247 (Wirtschaft und Gesellschaft, II, 753).

52 Ibid., p. 54.

53 Ibid., p. 55.

54 Gerth and Mills, ibid., pp. 116–117.

55 Cf. Finer, The Theory and Practice of Modern Government, II, 1080. Reference is made here to the Kaiser as an "irresponsible dabbler in foreign policy." The kaiser's draft of the Daily Telegraph interview here mentioned, which was a gross insult to England's honor, had not been read by any official responsible for censoring such documents, and illustrates the above characterization.

56 Conversation of the writer with Marianne Weber. See also Marianne Weber, Erfuelltes Leben (Heidelberg: Lambert Schneider, 1946), p. 350.

57 Gerth and Mills, op. cit., p. 117.

58 Cf. Karl Jaspers, Max Weber, Deutsches Wesen im Politischen Denken, im Forschen, und Philosophieren (Oldenburg: Gerhard Stalling, 1932. Bremen: Storm Verlag, 1946), p. 35.

59 Cf. Gerth and Mills, op. cit., pp. 119–120.

60 Ibid., pp. 121–122.

61 Ibid., pp. 125–26.

62 Wissenschaftslehre, p. 150. Also see Loewith, "Max Weber und Karl Marx," Archiv fuer Sozialwissenschaft und Sozialpolitik, Vol. LXVII, 1932, particularly p. 83. Cf. also Siegfried Marck, "Max Webers Politisches Vermaechtnis," Die Neue Zeit, Vol. I, Stuttgart, 1923, pp. 312–18. See also Fred H. Blum, "Max Weber: The Man of Politics and the Man Dedicated to Objectivity and Rationality," Ethics, LXX, No. 1, 1959, pp. 1–17.

63 Cf. Gerth and Mills, op. cit., p. 120.

64 Ibid., p. 127.

65 Cf. ibid., p. 121.

66 Ibid.

67 Gerth and Mills, op. cit., p. 126.

68 Ibid., p. 123.

69 Cf. Lowell L. Bennion, Max Weber's Methodology (Paris: Les Presses Modernes, 1933), pp. 29–30: "Weber also presupposes fundamentally and uncritically a radical, worldly conception of man, rejecting every theory which aims to reduce the idea of man from a hierarchy of values or concepts. . . . He (Weber) distinguishes between social science and social politics, demanding from every investigator that he make it plain where the thinking scientist stops and the willing man begins. One is never left in doubt as to whether Weber, the scholar, is writing or Weber, the political propagandist, is speaking, although in both instances his work is outstanding because of its logical and convincing style." See also Paul Honigsheim, "Max Weber: His Religious and Ethical Development," Church History, XIX, No. 4, December 1950, pp. 210–239.

70 The only machinery provided for the check upon the Weberian leaders, as will be remembered from earlier discussion, was that of periodic elections at definite intervals at which the electorate could make its will known.

71 Cf. Gerth and Mills, op. cit., p. 125.

72 Cf. ibid.

73 Ibid.

74 Ibid., p. 128 (The word "banausic" equals the word "philistine").

IX

Max Weber on Capitalism
and Bureaucracy

The history of ideas, particularly of Marxist ideas, reveals the "ambiguous legacy" of Marxism, tellingly displayed in many areas of subsequent research. While the study of bureaucracy was not one of Marx's central concerns, his assessment of its position within the power structure provided useful formulations for Max Weber, Robert Michels, and other scholars. Both Marx and Weber were concerned with the effect of bureaucratization on the political life of individuals and groups in modern society, including the United States. Even specialists in organizational theory have usually neglected Marx's ideas in analyzing Weber's writings on bureaucracy. American sociologists have tended to overlook certain major themes involving power, individual freedom, and alienation contained in the writings of both men. An historical and cross-cultural preoccupation with these concepts underlay the studies of each of them, whereas organizational theory today frequently tends to be nonhistorical and more culture-bound.[1]

Although Marxist doctrine has been criticized for its historical materialism, its ontology is not exclusively materialist. Adam Ulam notes that Marxism appeals most to semi-proletarianized or uprooted peasants who long for the "good old days" when their actions were governed by "natural elements"—the village elders, the family patriarch, and the religious authorities—instead of the less appealing state or industrial overlords. The fulfillment the uprooted peasant sees in Marxism consists of the utopian vision in which state and factory, both symbols of coercion, have "withered away."[2] Marx, of course, viewed bureaucracy within the context of the class struggle, the ultimate collapse of capitalism, and the ultimate triumph of the communist system. Bureaucracy represented the tool of the ruling classes: ". . . bureaucracy, as the state itself, is an instrument by which the dominant class exercises its domination over the other social classes."[3]

Both Marx and Weber concerned themselves with the tremendous impact of economic organization upon other social institutions, including the political, religious, and familial phases of social life.[4] However, for Marx, bureaucracy was essentially "transient and parasitic" because its *raison d'être* rested in its role of guarding the status quo and privileged position of the ruling classes, in whose interest it reinforced social conditions fostering social injustice. Therefore, Marx believed that ". . . bureaucracy and further bureaucratization become unavoidable and indispensible in a society divided into classes."[5]

With the appearance of the classless society following the historical phase during which, according to Marx, the dictatorship of the proletariat prevails, the need for bureaucracy to serve as the tool of the dominant class no longer exists since it no longer exists. Consequently, the "withering away" of the state with the establishment of the classless society, will be accompanied by the "withering away" of bureaucracy. The term "class," according to Weber, applies to people who are in the same economic situation, a class being a category of persons who have similar life chances of receiving which are valued in a society and which are to be obtained only by income or property. Marx believed that inequalities in the latter inevitably culminate in the formation of classes as parties whose objective is the struggle for control of the political and economic order. Weber, disagreeing with Marx, advanced the idea that classes, representing economic categories, do not necessarily organize themselves politically to gain power. "Politics," Max Weber wrote, "means striving to share power or striving to influence the distribution of power, either among states or among groups within a state."[6] While this definition applies equally to politics everywhere, the manner in which the struggle for power is carried on and the people who participate in it differ from one country to another. Although status may be closely allied with functions of a position, including its power and economic rewards, class, status, and party, as Weber indicated, do not always converge.[7] In Marx's scheme, the establishment of the classless society will result in the "gradual absorption of bureaucracy into the society as a whole. Thus instead of having an oppressive structure which is separated from and antagonistic to the rest of society, in the communist state those functions of bureaucracy which are not parasitic will be performed by all social members. The administrative tasks, losing their exploitative character, will consist in the administration of things and not of people, as was the case with bureaucracy."[8]

Marx viewed bureaucracy as but one aspect of the generally prevailing conditions of alienation. Alienation, in his view, exists both inside and outside the bureaucracy so long as capitalism has not been replaced. The bureaucrat, Marx viewed as being steeped in "self-aggrandizement," "sordid materialism," and "the struggle for promotion, careerism, the infantile attachment to trivial symbols, status, and prestige."[9] Marx's thoughts on alienation, his description of the loss of intrinsic meaning and pride in workmanship, and the loss of intrinsically meaningful satisfactions are of continuing interest. His analysis of some bureaucratic features was incisive and proved seminal for subsequent analyses. It is when "he tries to explain . . . characteristics by linking them to the structure of society as a whole, one feels that his observations are forced and distorted . . . to fit within his general theoretical framework." [10]

Conversely, for Max Weber capitalism and bureaucracy were just one aspect of rationalization. Both Max and his brother Alfred Weber believed that on "all social levels, men were being forced to submerge their private identities in the service of huge organizational machines. The original objective of social policy, to assure a minimum of security in the face of a totally uncontrolled and often brutal form of capitalism, was now fulfilled. The difficulty was that especially in Germany, too little of this progress had been achieved through the independent action of the workers' own associations, so that the cost in subservience to the state had run too high." [11] Both Max and Alfred Weber were apprehensive of the "cultural consequences of the general regimentation and advised individuals to protect the privacy of their personal life against their employers and their government alike." [12] Both favored labor union's political education and collective bargaining, hoping thereby to curtail the state's paternalism in its administration of social policy. Just as Marx had viewed the effects of bureaucratization as but one aspect of capitalism, Weber argued that the separation of the worker from the means of production is but one aspect of the process of rationalization marking modern society, viewing it as its most pervasive and complex problem. Just as the soldier is separated from the means of violence, so in bureaucracy the civil servant does not own the means of administration, nor does he possess political power. Max Weber clearly distinguished between the civil servant and the politician:

. . . the civil servant is honor-bound to carry out conscientiously the order of higher authorities, perfectly as if the order corresponded with his own convictions. This applies even if the order is opposed to his own views and if, over his remonstrances, the authorities persist in wanting it carried out. Without this moral discipline and self-abnegation, in the highest sense, the whole apparatus would fall apart. The honor of the political leader, by contrast, rests precisely in an unshared personal responsibility for his actions, one of which he cannot and must not rid himself or transfer.[13]

While Marx identified bureaucracy with public administration of the state, Weber's interest focused upon its incidence in business and industry, in labor unions, in educational institutions, as well as in government. Everywhere he perceived the impersonal, cold, and abstract rationality of bureaucratic claims which to him could only increase rather than disappear, if capitalism were to be replaced by socialism or communism. Since this trend toward rationalization could only be anticipated to assert itself more and more, it would have to be accepted as a *fait accompli*. Specifically the characteristics of bureaucracy are:

I. There is the principle of fixed and official jurisdictional areas, which are generally ordered by rules, that is, by laws, or administrative regulations.
    A. The regular activities required for the purposes of the bureaucratically governed structure are distributed in a fixed way as official duties.
    B. The authority to give the commands required for the discharge of these duties is distributed in a stable way and is strictly delimited by rules concerning the coercive means, physical, or otherwise, which may be placed at the disposal of officials.
    C. Methodical provision is made for the regular and continuous fulfillment of these duties and for the execution of the corresponding rights; only persons who have the generally regulated qualifications to serve are employed.
II. The principles of office hierarchy and of levels of graded authority mean a firmly ordered system of super—and subordination in which there is a supervision of the lower offices by the higher ones.
III. The management of the modern office is based on written documents . . .
IV. Office management, at least all specialized office management . . . usually presupposes thorough and expert training.
V. When the office is fully developed, official activity demands the full working capacity of the official . . .
VI. The management of the office follows general rules, which are more or less stable. . . .[14]

In Weber's judgment, then, from the social organizational standpoint, life had generally become routinized because capitalism requires a type of social organization capable of meeting large-scale administrative objectives on a rational-legal basis rather than on a traditional basis. Bureaucracy in urbanized mass society is directed toward the achievement of efficiency. Weber believed that the really creative human spirit manifests itself only in charismatic forms. Yet capitalism reflects the destruction of the charismatic component in society because all human activity has to adjust itself to the needs of the "system." Thus:

The capitalistic economy of the present day is an immense cosmos into which the individual is born, and which presents itself to him, at least as an individual, as an unalterable order of things in which he must live.

It forces the individual, insofar as he is involved in the system of market relationship, to conform to capitalistic rules of action. The manufacturer who in the long run acts counter to these norms, will just as inevitably be eliminated from the economic scene as the worker who cannot or will not adapt himself to them will be thrown into the streets without a job.[15]

As Weber conceived of bureaucracy, it prevails in all areas of social life requiring large-scale administration. Whereas it was known to have existed in ancient Egypt and Rome, as well as in China, in modern Western civilization the acquisitive nature of capitalism gave an even greater role to bureaucracy because capitalism had to rely on methods designed to obtain an optimum of formal rationality of capital accounting in productive enterprise. Weber saw no way by which any society operating under conditions of modern technology could avoid bureaucracy. Its prime objective, *efficiency,* derived from the necessity to bring an optimum of knowledge and experience to bear upon any task. Specialization of functions and appointment were the essential tools for the procurement of qualified personnel. To rule out favoritism and the possibility of following personal rather than organizational goals, the formulation of policy was divorced from the administrative decision-making process. Rights, duties, and privileges were stipulated, with social relations being of necessity impersonal. Authority was characterized by a hierarchichal order and there were set rules for standardized tasks. Thus socialism, Weber stated, far from offering an escape, would only tend to increase bureaucratization. In fact, Weber considered socialism but an intensification of this trend since it would entail acceleration in the size and scope of government. Inevitably, government would require an increase in bureaucracy as it took over government-operated enterprise from private enterprise. Thus socialism would inhibit the dynamic and creative role that private enterprise, regardless of its defects, plays under capitalism.

Marx had considered centralized means of production as the first basis of the socialist order followed by "socialized labor" which implies, according to Bukharin, principally the relations within the working class and the production bond among all workers. Explaining Marx's position, Bukharin stated: "It is upon this production relation of co-operation in general, that the temple of the future will rest." [16]

Albert Salomon saw the difference between Marx and Weber as one of political perspective. Rejecting Marx's dictum of the class-determined character of science and its ultimate revolutionary goals, Weber viewed the function of science as one of providing man with opportunities which would enable him to deal with all historical reality objectively. He viewed reality as a chain of causes leading "at times from technical to economic and political fields and at times from political to religious and then economic fields. There is no point of equilibrium at any place. And that not infrequent version of historical materialism whereby the 'economic' factor represents something 'final' in the series of causes, this view is to my mind scientifically completely discredited." [17] Economic factors, in effect cannot be considered in isolation from other factors. Weber sought to demonstrate their connection with religious, political, geographic, and cultural factors and to supply the links between them. For Weber the yardstick with which reality must be measured was "what human types received the chance to become representative groups both from the viewpoint of the development of classes of political leaders and also from the viewpoint of 'old and eternal human ideals'." [18] While Weber's views in practical politics were essentially liberal, his political philosophy had a rather conservative orientation. Albert Salomon comments:

> His scientific insight showed him what would be the economic costs in the sense of technical rationalization, of an ethically oriented socialism and how, therefore, the desired goals of higher standard of living and higher cultural levels might easily become converted into the opposite. Even these facts would perhaps not have prevented him from becoming a socialist had he only recognized the binding character of its ideals. This, however, he found impossible. Like no one in his epoch, he foresaw what human consequences a socialist community would entail and what the concomitant human types in such a society would be. [19]

On the other hand, Joseph Schumpeter argues that the

> economic interpretation of history does *not* mean that men are, consciously or unconsciously, wholly or primarily, actuated by economic motives. On the contrary, the explanation of the role and mechanism of non-economic motives and the analysis of the way in which social reality mirrors itself in the individual psyches is an essential element of the theory and one of its most significant contributions. Marx did not hold that religions, metaphysics, schools of art, ethical ideas and political volitions were either reducible to economic *motives* or of no importance. He only tried to unveil the economic *conditions* which shape them and which account for their rise and fall. The whole of Max Weber's facts and arguments fits perfectly into Marx's system. Social groups and classes and the ways in which these groups or classes explain to themselves their own existence, location and behavior were of course what interested him most. . . . But if ideas or values were not for him the prime movers of the social process, neither were they mere smoke. [20]

Weber was again similar to Marx in being convinced that: "Interests (material and ideal), not ideas, dominate directly the actions of men. Yet the 'images of the world' created by these ideals have very often served as switches determining the tracks on which the dynamics of interests kept actions moving." [21]

Marx perceived the essence of man's alienation to lie in his separation from the fruits of his labor; Weber feared that alienation might grow more acute in an era of mass democracy and technocracy.

To administer their complex technology and labor markets men developed elaborate social structures or bureaucracies which are no less impersonal in their effects than machines. Indeed, that is their aim; and the attempt further to 'rationalize' the conduct of human affairs by subjecting it to rules, regularity and a hierarchy of command—the distinguishing characteristics of bureaucracy as described by Max Weber—has enormously increased the power of alien forces over men. . . . As Weber wrote, bureaucracy became particularly appropriate for capitalism because 'the more bureaucracy depersonalizes' itself, the more completely it succeeds in achieving the exclusion of love, hatred, and every purely personal, especially irrational and incalculable, feeling from the execution of official tasks. . . . Weber extended the concept of alienated labor to all organized or institutionalized work situations and he described a universal bureaucratic trend in which soldiers, scientists, civil servants—all were 'separated' or alienated from their respective means of production or administration 'in the same way as capitalist enterprise has separated the workers from theirs.' [22]

Under capitalism, in Marx's view, with accelerated industrialization, the worker becomes alienated because he finds he cannot relate meaningfully to his work. Marx viewed the modern economy as essentially irrational because of the paradox inherent in the rational technological progress of the forces of production and the fetters of private property. As Marx saw it:

The object produced by labor, its product, now stands opposed to it as an *alien being,* as a *power independent* of the producer. The product of labor is labor which has been embodied in a thing, and turned into a physical thing; this product is an objectification of labor. The performance of work is at the same time its objectification. This performance appears, in the sphere of political economy, as a *vitiation* of the worker, objectification as a *loss* and as *servitude to the object,* and appropriation as alienation.[23]

Modern capitalism and its institutions impressed Weber as eminently rational. For Marx the class struggle operated as the historical mechanism. To this idea Weber opposed the concept of rationality as embodied in bureaucracy and capitalism. Socialization, rather than obviating the need for bureaucracy, would intensify alienation, alienation being based upon the loss of personal and communal values. For Marx history was a linear social process. He was convinced that

as the economic foundations of society changed, so also did the property relationships, the political ideas, and institutions, even the religion and the culture. Thus the whole range of man's social activities was raised to a higher and more complex level. This . . . did not mean that capitalist society was either stable or enduring, though Marx continually insisted that it was the most advanced form of social organization that was possible for a long period in history. There would come a point . . . at which capitalism would . . . be obsolete and bar the progress of humanity towards a wider and more prosperous society. Technical and economic development . . . would open new perspectives to man, would awaken hopes which capitalism would be unable to satisfy without destroying the very methods of production and exchange on which it rested.[24]

Although managerial transactions often do not correspond to the rational and impersonal processes Weber portrayed, and although numerous informal and seemingly deviant practices tend to counterbalance some of the adverse consequences of the bureaucratic trend, Weber sees the latter both as a necessary instrument of large-scale enterprise and as an unmitigated threat, one which threatens to be irreversible. With Marx self-alienation has been superimposed by external forces. The reintegration of the self Marx foresaw with the establishment of the classless society, whereas Weber feared that modern man might voluntarily forego his aspiration to freedom, abdicating also his pursuit of noble purposes, especially political ones, and therewith his intellectual detachment and moral integrity.

With intensified technical rationalization occurring in any organizational society, alienation would, according to Weber, be certain to continue under socialism. For Marx emancipation from alienation begins with the overthrow of the bourgeoisie by the proletariat. Marx seems far more optimistic than Weber when he writes: "Political emancipation certainly represents a great progress. . . . It is not indeed the final form of human emancipation, but it is the final form of emancipation within the framework of the existing order. It goes without saying that we are speaking here of real, practical emancipation." [25] Nevertheless, revolution marks only the beginning of the end of alienation. It is, however, a prerequisite for the attainment of emancipation from the oppression responsible for alienation. Thus Marx foresees the

dictatorship of the proletariat which will effectively prevent a counter-revolution and pave the way for the classless society in which there will no longer be any need for the state as an instrument of class rule. Men, for the first time in history, will then be really free. . . . The only limits on production will be the scarcity of the earth's resources and the degree to which man is able to harness them to his own ends. Both Marx and Engels were convinced that limitless opportunities of advance lay before mankind once its energy was no more squandered in social struggles and was devoted to the proper and extended use of its great technical discoveries. For them the victory of socialism marked the day on which the childhood of the human race would end and, conscious of the laws of science and society, men would begin to work together in a creative unity for their common prosperity and fulfillment.[26]

Because of the significant role played by the *locus* of political power in world affairs, its study has attracted a great body of scholars and produced a sizeable amount of academic analysis. This literature consists largely of historical treatments of the concept of power by specific political theorists and in specific epochs. Few subjects comprise such a variety and complexity of phenomena, and Weber's emphasis, taking its departure from Marx, distinguishes between political power, economic class, and social status. He dissociated himself sharply from Marx's conception of the intimate link between power and the role played by the class structure. Modern mass society causes the role of political parties to appear "in sharp contrast to this idyllic state in which circles of notables and, above all, members of Parliament rule. These modern forms are the children of democracy, of mass franchise, of the necessity to woo and organize the masses, and develop the utmost unity of direction and the strictest discipline. The rule of notables and guidance by members of parliament ceases. 'Professional' politicians *outside* the parliaments take the organization in hand." [27]

In Weber's scheme the concept of class is linked closely to the economic realm. Weber and other liberals considered government and social institutions to be tied to narrowest conceptions of self-interest:

But unlike the earlier effort to root the pure ideal of freedom in an amoral reality, the new version of dualism attempted to balance realistic and ethical motifs within the ideal itself. From the industrial facts of the society they derived a social ethic and from the power conflicts of the national states they derived the ethic of democratic community. These moral impulses they attached to the older ideal of individual freedom for the purpose of intensi-fying its ethical validity and its practical effectiveness simultaneously. . . . Thus the ideal became a national, socially minded democracy with a realistic orientation. Freedom would be realized by a people's state, unified by the Emperor, equalizing economic benefits at home and asserting the national interest powerfully abroad.[28]

As noted earlier, the main reason for Weber's rejection of socialist aspirations was his conviction that "any rational socialism" would have to appropriate the bureaucratic practices of capitalist societies and, in fact, add to them. A socialist system would surpass a capitalist system in requirements of a pervasive apparatus with established formal rules and regulations. Weber, moreover, rejected the idea that the emancipa-tion of the workers could be achieved only following the destruction of capitalism. Indeed, he envisaged any rise in their living standards as possible only under the capitalistic system. Any socialist experiment could only arrest this process. He saw no chance for the working classes to realize even a fraction of their aims.[29] This sentiment was underscored in a letter of 1907 to Robert Michels: "Political democracy is the only thing that might be achieved in the foreseeable future perhaps, and that is not a minor accomplishment. I cannot prevent you from believing in more than that, any more than I can force myself to believe in more than that."[30] The political emancipation of the working classes in a democratized Germany, he hoped, would result in dissolving the "reactionary" alliance between industry and the conservatives, which alone obviated a progressive social policy.

As noted, to Max Weber, who believed that labor could function only within the capitalistic system, the prospect that the Social Democrats would continue to subscribe to the idea of the class struggle did not seem to be a major obstacle. Instead, he viewed most of the party's leadership with some contempt, especially after he had attended the Mannheim Party Convention of the Social Democrats in 1906. Its petty bourgeois officials, combined with a fanatical clique of journalists, hardly justified the fears of the German bourgeoisie and should have appalled the Russian revolutionary Social Democrats present at the convention, in his judgment. Wolfgang Mommsen comments that Weber's own position, which again rested on the defense of the power state, could hardly enhance his understanding of the current situation of the Social Democrats. Since the convention had to concern itself with the question of a general strike and the methods to be employed in it, he could only conclude that the party leaders lacked all power instincts, a quality which he judged to be essential for every competent politician. Personally, he respected a radical orientation, as exemplified by the Anarchists, which did not count the cost of a hopeless struggle, more than the attitudes of the Marxists. The contrast between revolutionary agitation and the party's reluctant timidity in confrontation with revolutionary action, while simultaneously rejecting an outright revisionist policy, repelled him to the utmost.[31]

As noted earlier, Weber's rejection of the Social Democrats and their program of socialist economic planning reflected his conclusion that such would only enhance the historical trend toward bureaucratization and hence the alienation of the individual. Socialism in effect would serve neither human nor economic ends, since increased bureaucracy characterized both systems:

The drift of all society . . . was towards the creation of largescale organization, hierarchically organized and centrally directed, in which the individual counted for naught. Marx's emphasis on the wage worker as being 'separated' from the means of production became, in Weber's perspective, as Gerth and Mills succinctly put it, 'merely one special case of a universal trend.' The modern soldier is equally 'separated' from the means of violence, the scientist from the means of enquiry and iron, said Weber, is that, from one perspective, capitalism and socialism were simply two different faces of the same, inexorable trend.[32]

The bipolar character inherent in the forces of charisma and rationalization pervading the historical process lead Weber to conclude that the odds favored the ultimate victory of bureaucracy, in which the "technical man" may well prevail over the "man of culture." His pessimistic outlook is, at least in part, predicated on the concepts of "legality" and "legitimacy" which even today are not easily distinguishable. Max Weber's insights are both telling and relevant to our own day:

Weber had noticed that most modern societies, and more particularly the State, are 'legal' societies, societies where 'commands are given in the name of an impersonal norm rather than an arbitrary decision, a favour, or a privilege.' Hence Weber concluded that 'rational legitimacy,' which he identified with legality, was the only type of legitimacy to survive in the modern world. In it 'every single bearer of power of command is legitimated by the system of rational norms,' and his power is legitimate so far as it corresponds with the norms. Obedience is thus given to the norms rather than to the person.[33]

The success of the bureaucratic organization lies precisely in its technical superiority over every other form:

Precision, speed, consistency, availability of record, continuity, possibility of secrecy, unity, rigorous coordination, and minimization of friction and of expense for materials and personnel are achieved in a strictly bureaucratized, especially in a monocratically organized, administration conducted by trained officials to an extent incomparably greater than any collegial form of administration or in any conducted by 'honoratiores' or part-time administrators.[34]

Weber credited the Prussian administrative system with success because it met the criteria of this bureaucratic principle, illustrating in fact the need for bureaucratic norms and governmental organization in the administration of a modern capitalistic economy. Recalling the processes which adjudication underwent throughout history, Weber wrote:

Bureaucracy provides the administration of justice with a foundation for the realization of a conceptually systematized rational body of law on the basis of 'laws', as it was achieved for the first time to a high degree of technical perfection in the late Roman Empire. In the Middle Ages the reception of this law proceeded hand in hand with the bureaucratization of the administration of justice. Adjudication by rationally trained specialists had to take the place of the older type of adjudication on the basis of traditional or irrational presuppositions.[35]

With adjudication based upon rationality, Weber contrasts those types which are guided by primarily sacred traditions—charismatic, khadi, and empirical principles of justice: "Charismatic justice derives its authority from the 'revelations' of an oracle, a prophet's doom, or an ordeal. Khadi-justice is in accordance with concrete ethical or other practical value judgments. Empirical justice makes use of 'analogies' and reference to 'precedents'." [36] Charisma, which provided the only hope for overcoming the negative aspects of bureaucracy, Weber defined as:

. . . an *extraordinary* quality of a person, regardless of whether this quality is actual, alleged, or presumed. 'Charismatic authority,' hence, shall refer to a rule over men, whether predominantly external or predominantly internal, to which the governed submit because of their belief in the extraordinary quality of the specific *person* . . . the legitimacy of their rule rests upon the belief in magical powers, revelations and hero worship. The source of these beliefs is the 'proving' of the charismatic quality through miracles, through victories and other successes, that is, through the welfare of the governed. Such beliefs and the claimed authority resting on them therefore disappears, or threaten to disappear, as soon as proof is lacking and as soon as the charismatically qualified person appears to be devoid of his magical power or forsaken by his god. Charismatic rule is not managed according to concrete revelations and inspirations, and in this sense, charismatic authority is 'irrational.' It is 'revolutionary' in the sense of not being bound to the existing order: 'It is written—but I say unto you. . . .' [37]

The very conditions of modern industrialized society tend to inhibit or vitiate charisma. Technological progress, increases in population, and intensification of the bureaucratic trend in combination bring rationalization to bear upon almost all aspects of life, reducing the survival chances of the private sphere and, above all, of charisma. Wolfgang Mommsen noted Weber's sense of resignation when he perceived "the charismatic glorification of reason" as "the ultimate form" which "charisma had assumed in its fluctuating course."[38] Weber pointed to a future which held in store the possibility of a new type of bondage in the form of American " 'benevolent feudalism', German so-called 'Welfare institutions', in the Russian factory-made constitution—everywhere the new House of Bondage is ready and waiting to be occupied." [39]

Weber's theory of bureaucracy in contrast to Marx's thus illustrates his conviction that social change would occur in the direction of ever-increasing rationality in social arrangements. Capitalistic forms of social organization flowing from the rational conduct of individuals and the creativity of entrepreneurs would ultimately be replaced by bureaucratic society in which collective rather than individual rationality would obtain. In fact, "modern 'bureaucracy'—is seen by Max Weber as an incident in the development of 'modern capitalism' which, in turn, is characterized by a prevalence of purposive rationality in social action unparalleled at any other time and place in the memory of man." [40]

Weber's analysis of the authority structure in modern bureaucracy has been especially influential in the United States. For Weber, "all administration means domination." [41] Authority, *Herrschaft*, the essence of bureaucratic relationships. Weber classified primarily in terms of the grounds on which the quest for obedience is made and obeyed. He described three modes of authority. (1) The "traditional" form, in which loyalty is attached to the person of a leader because he serves and is guided by tradition:

A system of imperative co-ordination will be called 'traditional' if legitimacy is claimed for it and believed in on the basis of the sanctity of the order and the attendant powers of control as they have been handed down from the past, 'have always existed. The person or persons exercizing authority are designated according to traditionally transmitted rules. The object of obedience is the personal authority of the individual which he enjoys by virtue of his traditional status. The organized group exercizing authority is, in the simplest case, primarily based on relations of personal loyalty, cultivated through a common process of education.[42]

(2) The "rational-legal" form in which loyalty is attached to formal rules, but not to persons, on the ground that they are legally enacted, and expedient or rational. This form of domination obtains when "a system of rules that is applied judicially and administratively in accordance with ascertainable principles is valid for all members of the corporate groups." [43] (3) The "charismatic" form in which loyalty is attached to the person of a leader because he possesses unusual personal qualities.

Weber regarded traditional authority as deriving from historically based rules, according to which a certain individual or group of individuals are empowered to exercise authority. Thus the recognition of such rules presupposes an extrarational motivation. Legal authority on the other hand derives its impetus from the recognition of norms setting down the rights and privileges of individuals holding positions in the hierarchical order to engage in the making of rules and regulation. In this scheme legal authority constitutes the legitimate source for the hierarchical structure of authority. Weber's critics have pointed out that contacts occurring within horizontal relationships received relatively little attention from Weber and that a minimum of allowance is made also for the possibility of less rigidity in the relations among colleagues through channels of communications and reciprocal influence. Moreover, by implication it seems that in the lower echelons of the bureaucracy where individual competence is lower, persons occupying such positions in the bureaucracy appear to place less reliance upon horizontal relationships than upon directives from above. Yet, charismatic authority signifies an emotional bond between leaders and followers. In this form of authority the symbolic connotation relating to the authority figures is highly significant.

Systems characterized by either traditional or rational-legal authority strengthen the exercise of legal authority. Under the legal authority system, however, recognition of statuses and rules is based upon their inherent rationality in integrating organizational means with clearly delimited objectives. Organization theory and research have since raised some critical substantive and methodological questions concerning this facet of Weber's theory of bureaucracy. Alvin Gouldner, for example, in attempting ". . . to clarify some of the social processes leading to different degrees of bureaucratization, to identify some of the crucial variables, and to formulate tentative propositions (hypotheses) concerning their interconnections," [44] found that legal authority systems do not universally contain prescriptions for the establishment of relationships, whether based upon equality or authority. One of the variations from bureaucratic practices that may occur is to be found in "informally" constituted organizational bodies, for example. In terms of influence, the importance of the hierarchical order may be overshadowed by professional competence and individual initiative, especially in the scientific sector where specialized knowledge and skill frequently supercede the stress on rank within the hierarchy. Reliance upon cooperation within committees and work groups frequently leads to the reduction of emphasis on differences in rank in order to establish a more collegial climate conducive to carrying on activities largely based on exchange of communication between professionals. Weber did not foresee such relatively "self-directed" units of bureaucracy in which: "the informal group and its norms . . . constitute a functional equivalent for bureaucratic rules to the degree, at least, that is served to allocate concrete work responsibilities and to specify individual duties." [45]

Loewenstein's suggestion that Weber's fear of the ascendancy of an unrestrained bureaucracy might have been linked to his own outlook and values is well taken, even though Weber had cautioned against it:

. . . we shall have to ask ourselves whether Max Weber, from his germano-centric viewpoint, did not overestimate the dangers of uncontrolled bureaucracy. . . . Nowhere in his writings . . . do we find any discussion on the institution of administrative courts as possible recourse against administrative abuses and arbitrariness. . . .[46]

Loewenstein concludes that . . . "the lance that Max Weber hurled against bureaucratic omnipotence missed its mark." [47]

And yet, while Weber knew that entering this "house of bondage" might be costly, resulting in the "disenchantment of the universe" and loss of the heroic greatness that might be possible under the leadership of an "ideal politician," he also placed a high value upon the efficient operation of bureaucracy. The bureaucrat's situation, in contrast to that of the politician is marked by the absence of personal involvement. Whereas the politician must adopt a political course of action the risks of which he must face and for which he must be responsible, the bureaucrat is responsible only for the execution of the task assigned to him. Even though he must be judicious and have an aptitude for his specific tasks, his responsibility ends at that point. Reinhard Bendix describes the ideal of the latter to be one of "impartiality and expertise in the service of decisions made by others" while the politician is oriented toward "partisanship and a powerful drive to make decisions for the community as a whole." [48] Weber intended his scheme of political analysis to be applicable to political processes and institutions across the whole range of human societies, although initially his comparison of politician and bureaucrat was stimulated by his anxiety over the political future of Germany.

Reinhard Bendix argues with some justification that Weber failed to foresee the contingency that attempts might be made to "*simulate* publicly all aspects of charismatic leadership—the manifestations of the leader's extraordinary gift, the unconditional devotion of his disciples, and the awed veneration of his large following—saturating all channels of communication so that no one could escape the message. Modern dictatorships have used such centrally organized public hagiology extensively. . . ." [49] Bendix refers to the prospect of the operation of the "great lie" and the "will to believe," which could inspire a broadly based faith in charisma, given the proper public climate. On the other hand, he points to "built-in limitations" of "charisma by publicity." [50] While people might in time grow weary of having to listen to stories glorifying spectacular acts on the part of their leaders, Bendix wisely cautions against any assumptions leading to the conclusion that this would necessarily militate against charismatic leadership since ". . . central manipulation of news is still compatible with credibility." [51] Totalitarian regimes tend to seek expressions of support for their leader from persons enjoying public esteem based on their "reputation for probity and independent judgment." [52] These public affirmations of trust may be solicited with or without pressure; they will still serve their intended purpose, if only in the short run. The media may be utilized by the leader himself to proclaim his utmost faith in his mission. In fact, a "sense of personal mission will justify the manipulative enhancement of the charismatic appeal," [53] provided that it does not become inimical to the appeal as such. Moreover, the fact that the leader inclines toward media manipulation need not tend to counteract the people's trust in him. Naming Mao Tse-tung as a case in point, Bendix correctly infers that, on the contrary, "a people's recognition of that charisma—born of 'the will to believe' and manifest in their devotion to duty—may endure long after they have begun to discount the credibility of the leader's entourage and of the whole apparatus of media manipulation." [54]

As noted earlier, although Weber maintained a pessimistic attitude toward the ultimate consequences of bureaucratization, he did not go so far as to state categorically that bureaucracy would prevail in the end: ". . . Weber repeatedly stresses that inherent in the bureaucratic type of organization are tendencies which both favour and discourage bureaucratic domination. Thus, whether bureaucracy will remain a simple tool at the service of its legitimate masters or whether it will replace them depends on the external forces operating upon it within a specific social structure." [55]

Weber's ideal type of bureaucracy has shaped much of organizational theory. Since his studies of bureaucracy were first published, the intervening years have served to reinforce several of their underlying arguments; but meanwhile, new perspectives have been added. Weber's work invites us to discover in it the satisfactions and tribulations of "social prophecy." Social scientists since Weber's time have shared with him the conviction that bureaucracy is highly repressive to individual freedom, and that the advantages inherent in a system of social control designed to regulate modern societies from the vantage point of maximum efficiency and advanced technology are bought at the expense of specific types of deprivation.[56] Weber sought to find the hidden costs of this type of social organization, even when he approved of its necessary functions; this factor is partly responsible for the persuasiveness of his arguments, suggesting the high cost in personal freedom that would have to be paid with increasing bureaucratization of all social life.

Recently, Michel Crozier has offered another alternative to Weber's vision of the future, based upon two factors affecting emerging social structures which Weber did not anticipate; these factors concern the means employed by organizations to achieve conformity involving

(1) the constant progress in the techniques of prediction and organization; and (2) the growing sophistication of the individual in an increasingly complex culture. Organizational progress has made it possible to be more tolerant of the personal needs and idiosyncracies of individual members: one can obtain the wanted results from them without having to control their behavior so narrowly as before. Cultural sophistication . . . has increased the individual's capacity for accommodation . . . and his possibilities of independence. . . . Participation is much less dangerous for them, since they have learned to be more flexible and since they can participate without committing themselves quite so much. The cost of quitting and finding a

substitute participation is . . . both psychically and materially much less heavy than before. The more tolerant modern organizations demand much less from their members, and the latter's freedom and flexibility allow them also to demand much less in return.[57]

With a reduction in rigid attitudes on the part of organizations and their members as pressures on both diminish, the demands upon the 'organization man' may also decrease as will their overall rigidity.[58] Despite the multiplication of the "number and complexity of the rules . . . modern organizational patterns will be more flexible, much less 'bureaucratic' than before. Organizations will be content with a more temporary loyalty from their members, even at the highest echelons, and individuals will not press the organization to protect them by using the rules in the most binding way." [59]

Without denying the trend toward increasing rationalization, Crozier concludes that this phenomenon need not issue in a more "bureaucratic" way of life in the dysfunctional sense which Weber and subsequent writers envisaged. Benefiting from additional research that has become available in recent years, Crozier suggests that it is "only when large-scale organizations become more flexible and can eliminate some of their bureaucratic vicious circles that they can overstep significant stages of growth." [60] Looking at the historical process in this light, Crozier states that the forebodings entertained by many concerning the rise of a 'technocracy' have not yet been substantiated:

When progress accelerates, the power of the expert is diminished and managerial power becomes more and more a political and judicial power rather than a technical one. Managers' success depends on their human qualities as leaders and not on their scientific know-how. As science invades the domain of the experts, those aspects of their roles which it affects decrease in importance.[61]

Nevertheless, fearing the "incubus of a Parkinsonian bureaucracy . . . Weber arrived by another route at what Troeltsch referred to as the characteristically German idea of freedom, where freedom depended on the exercise of the state's authority." [62] Weber made no claim for his theory of bureaucracy as an empirical model since he was primarily interested in the formal rational aspects of administrative behavior. However, while Weber "conceived the ideal bureaucrat as a mere administrative tool," some post-Weberian research focusing its analysis upon the "organisation as a whole," views the bureaucrat in a multidimensional way: "The bureaucrat is . . . seen as a whole human being with emotions, beliefs, and goals of his own; goals which do not always coincide with the general goals of the organisation." [63] Thus Crozier points out that, in fact, "bureaucratic forms in the dysfunctional sense correspond to the impossibility of eliminating all elements of charismatic power from the functioning of large-scale organizations. Bureaucratic privileges and vicious circles follow from the necessity of resorting to charismatic-like power in an otherwise ever more rationalized world." [64]

It should be remembered, on the other hand, that Weber's concern was not primarily with the general question of social-personal development. His concern was to analyze structural changes in historical processes, seeking to ascertain the evolution and persistence of historical trends. He intended to assess the structural strains in political organization and social structure, pointing out how certain characteristics could place limits upon potential changes arising from them. Weber did not accept Marx's dictum that social systems were transformed by their own inner dialectical processes. What Weber demonstrated, on the contrary, was that when various strands of historical experience exist in combination, unpredictable results may ensue. While "essentially all historical governments have been based upon mixtures of the several types of legitimacy . . .," Weber suggested that ". . . new injections of the charismatic element could occur at various points in the evolution of the political system. This, indeed, is the most fascinating aspect of the whole argument. One has the impression that Weber's charisma was the initiating force in the machinery of the historical process. It stood for the original source of renovation and vitality in history. The institutional apparatus, which was designed to channel and to perpetuate it, also reduced its substance, so that new infusions were necessary from time to time." [65]

In Weber's analysis we find the combination of a historical explanation with a sociological analysis of the emergence of one type of system from another. In tracing the trend of increasing rationalization of administration, Weber sought to establish links between these changes and major changes in economies, especially with the emergence of impersonal market situations, the introduction of money and rational calculation, and the severance of economic relations from traditional obligations. Unlike Marx he "directed attention away from the economic contradictions and social injustices of the capitalist system. He made that system a part rather than the essential cause of the modern dilemma. This shift of emphasis implied a predominant concern with the cultural shortcomings of modernity. . . ." [66]

As noted previously, critics of Weber's treatment of bureaucracy have chided him for neglecting the impact of informal, personal relationships in bureaucracy. While this may be an omission on Weber's part, it does not detract from his central theme. His insights seemed to induce Weber "above all . . . to realize that the cameralist line in social policy implied a degree of bureaucratization that transformed even the radical politics of labor organizations." [67]

Weber thus underscored the social impact of the growing burden of democracy not only for his own time, but he extended it to emerging systems of socialism, mixed economies, and totalitarian societies. Bureaucracy is the ultimate response to the quest for a stable foundation for the exercise of authority designed to achieve more routine and systematic forms of organization, organizations which tend toward being increasingly routinized, legalistic and technically structured. As Merton and Nisbet point out, with the spread of the technological revolution and its accompanying demands for specialization, ". . . rules and regulations, intended to increase the efficiency and justice of government ministrations to the citizen-clientele, become a new source of estrangement, of Kafka-like labyrinths in which the needs of the citizens are distorted and disregarded rather than served." [68]

Weber, although not always explicitly, showed modern societies to be characterized not only by certain structural characteristics such as growing differentiation and specialization, which necessarily lead to specialization of bureaucratization, but also by far-reaching changes in the structure of the social centers, in the pattern of participation in them, and of access to them. He sensed . . . that, while in the first stages of modernity most social tensions and conflicts evolved around the broadening of the scope of participation and channels of access to the centers," [69] subsequent periods may produce quite different problems, such as the manifestation of "growing apathy toward the very central values, symbols, and centers, not because of the lack of possibility of access to them but because of, in a sense, overaccess to them." [70] Consequently, the disenchantment of the universe may become traceable to the fact that "attainment of participation in many centers may indeed be meaningless, that the centers may lose their mystery. . . ." [71] Increasing bureaucratization and specialization may serve to reinforce this trend. Yet these trends cannot be held solely accountable for giving rise to such problems: "Rather it is the combination of these trends to bureaucratization with the changing structure of participation in the centers that may account for . . . demystification and . . . routinization of the charismatic in modern settings." [72]

Weber's critics, as noted, frequently ignore the ideal-typical intent supporting his concept of bureaucracy; his aim was to contrast the rational type of bureaucracy characterizing capitalistic societies with its counterpart in precapitalistic feudal societies; both were viewed in ideal-typical terms. It was never Weber's intention to deviate from the task he set himself, which was to conduct a comparative analysis of social structures applied to particular sociocultural settings in their historical contexts. This orientation may well become crucial to current assessments of contemporary political and social trends, for example those involving student revolts and minority groups' protests.

Max Weber's treatment of bureaucracy was not without ambiguity insofar as the role of bureaucracy in confrontation with political change, especially in Germany, is concerned. Essentially, the problem is that bureaucracies tend to have more influence upon policy than Weber's rational model of officialdom would suggest.

According to Weber, a rational bureaucracy is typified by both a sense of obedience to and protection by impersonal law on the part of government employees. The loss of these things led many civil servants to become followers of Hitler: "Their loyalty, in turn, facilitated the Nazi chiefs' conduct of public administration by individual measures ('from case to case') instead of rational norms. All this was most pronounced at the policy-making level." [73] The elimination of rational norms did not always become a matter of conscious knowledge in the case of the lower civil servant who was conscious of himself as merely following instructions from above. If he did become aware of the implications of these orders, his response was likely to be an even stricter observance of procedural rules to enable him to preserve his own sense of security. Consequently, ideological mysticism and arbitrary discretion replaced the rule of law. The rise of the police state was based upon the submergence of the legal state in irrationality and rule by force: "Although it is true that most of that machinery (traditional state machinery) retained its outward identity until the end, the acceleration and intensification of these encroachments and permeations after 1942 preclude the application of Weber's rule of bureaucratic stability to Nazi Germany." [74]

In effect, Weber's conception of the civil servant as merely an animate instrument does not fit actual conditions. His greatest contribution to organizational theory is that he provided a framework for a systematic theory of formal organization. He emphasized the interdependence of the various structural attributes of complex organizations. Weber, however, was concerned primarily with the formal, manifest functions of bureaucracy, paying little attention to their unanticipated consequences, both functional and dysfunctional.[75] It would seem that Weber himself was more conscious of the hypothetical character of his findings than some of his less critical admirers. Alvin Gouldner points out that Weber's reasons for concentrating on the functional aspects are to be found in the premises on which his analysis of bureaucracy is based. An illustration of these may be seen in "Weber's functional analysis of bureaucratic rules as securing predictability of performance and eliminating 'friction'." [76] This "conflict-free" assumption is challenged, however, as Robert Presthus shows, by the tension between authority based upon the hierarchical order and that based upon the know-how of the specialists found throughout large-scale organizations.[77]

The neutral position of the civil service requires the unconditional loyalty of the official to the state and to the government. The German civil service has developed traditions which have survived imperial Germany, the Weimar republic, the Nazi period, and which remain viable today. Notable among them are the caste feeling of the bureaucracy, its recruitment from the upper classes, its strongly authoritarian pattern, and its tradition of unquestioning obedience. A federal law of 1953 regulating the civil service in the Federal Republic requires officials to accept unreservedly the constitutional order as established in the Basic Law; their conduct must be oriented toward its preservation. The civil servant is exhorted to counter all tendencies opposed to this order. Having always been extremely conservative by virtue of both its historical background and its recruitment, the official German apparatus was unlikely to experience doubts concerning its loyalty to either the imperial state or to the Hitler regime. Loyalty to democratic governments presents quite different problems. As mentioned previously, the Weimar republic found itself confronted with the necessity of having to retain the services of highly professionalized officials of the Empire. Replacements for such officials could not be found easily. It is difficult to ascertain exactly how much the democratic process was undermined by the civil service, but it is widely believed that official opposition helped considerably in destroying the republic.

The same problem for democracy exists today in Germany, and its magnitude is even more difficult to assess. The problem arises from the fact that following the collapse of the Nazi regime, the bureaucracy had to be reestablished on the basis of the existing reservoir of civil servants, a large proportion of whom were Nazis or persons affiliated with the party or one of its branches. One of the most serious omissions involving the replacement of authoritarianism with democracy in German public life has been the failure to reform the civil service. The resistance to reform is again due largely to the need for a competent civil service. The special circumstances of the immediate period following World War II relegated the problem of democratic government to second place, giving priority to the practical urgency of rebuilding Germany politically, economically, and militarily. This fact coupled with some recent election results underscores the elements of instability that continue to pervade all levels of German life.

Today the main threat which the German bureaucracy presents still lies in the rather authoritarian attitudes of officialdom toward both the public and the legislatures, rather than in Nazi persuasions. Loyalty to the *Rechtsstaat* is still pronounced. At the outset, the Allies insisted upon the removal of officials from electoral struggles and from being seated in the legislatures. In the British zone, civil servants were required to follow the English pattern, namely to abstain from political activity. The American and other military government authorities sponsored the provision in the Election Law of 1949 "that *federal* officials must give up office if elected, but they were still allowed to campaign for election . . . still nearly 15 per cent of the *Bundestag* of 1949 were or had been officials." [78]

While Weber was fully aware of the entrenched position of German officialdom, he must have underestimated the resistance of the civil service to a potential diminution of its own role in the German political arena: "The Allied pressure to open the higher jobs to outsiders and promotion from below rather than keep the traditional exclusive regular entrance at specified education levels, was resisted by German tradition, for after 1945 the civil servants were themselves in high authority during the remaking of the German state, and they still are." [79]

NOTES

[1] Cf. Nicos P. Mouzelis, *Organisations and Bureaucracy: An Analysis of Modern Theories* (London: Routledge & Kegan Paul, 1967).

[2] Adam Ulam, "The Historical Role of Marxism and the Soviet System," *World Politics*, Vol. VIII, No. 1, pp. 20–45, cited in Mary Matossian, "Ideologies of Delayed Industrialisation," in Claude E. Welch, Jr., ed., *Political Modernization: A Reader in Comparative Political Change* (Belmont, California: Wadsworth, 1967), p. 330.

[3] Mouzelis, *op. cit.*, p. 9.

[4] Cf. Karl Marx, *Capital: A Critique of Political Economy* (New York: Modern Library, 1936), pp. 11–13; Henderson and Parsons, *op. cit.*

[5] Mouzelis, *op. cit.*, p. 9.

[6] H. H. Gerth and C. Wright Mills, *op. cit.*, p. 78.

[7] *Ibid.*, pp. 180–195.

[8] Mouzelis, *op. cit.*, p. 11.

[9] Cf. *ibid.*, p. 10 and Karl Marx, "Critique de la philosophie de l'état de Hegel," in *Oeuvres philosophiques*, Vol. 4, Paris 1947, p. 102, cited in *ibid.*

[10] *Ibid.*, p. 15.

[11] Fritz K. Ringer, *The Decline of the German Mandarins: The German Academic Community 1890–1933*, (Cambridge, Mass.: Harvard University Press, 1969), p. 160.

[12] *Ibid.*

[13] Max Weber, *P.S.*, 1st. ed., p. 415.

[14] Cf. Gerth and Mills, *op. cit.*, pp. 196–198.

[15] Max Weber, *The Protestant Ethic and the Spirit of Capitalism*, translated by Talcott Parsons (London: George Allen & Unwin, Ltd., 1930), pp. 54–55.

[16] Nicolai Bukharin, *Historical Materialism* (New York: International Publishers, 1934), p. 253.

[17] Max Weber, *Aufsaetze zur Soziologie und Sozialpolitik* (Tuebingen, 1924), p. 456, cited in Albert Salomon, "Max Weber's Political Ideas," in *Social Research*, Vol. 2, No. 3, August 1935, p. 373.

[18] Albert Salomon, "Max Weber's Political Ideas," *ibid.*, p. 377.

[19] *Ibid.*, p. 378.

[20] Joseph A. Schumpeter, *Capitalism, Socialism, and Democracy* (New York: Harper, 1950), pp. 10–11.

[21] *Lebensbild*, pp. 347–8, cited in Hans J. Morgenthau, *Politics Among Nations: The Struggle for Power and Peace* (New York: Alfred A. Knopf, 1967), p. 8.

[22] Eric and Mary Josephson, "Introduction," in Eric and Mary Josephson, *Man Alone: Alienation in Modern Society* (New York: Dell Publishing Co., 1967), pp. 22–23.

[23] T. B. Bottomore, and M. Rubel, eds., *Selected Writings in Sociology and Social Philosophy*, translated by T. B. Bottomore (New York: McGraw-Hill, 1956), p. 171.

[24] Norman Mackenzie, *Socialism: A Short History* (London: Hutchinson's University Library, 1949), p. 47.

[25] T. B. Bottomore, trans. ed., *Karl Marx: Early Writings* (New York: McGraw-Hill, 1964), p. 15.

[26] Mackenzie, *op. cit.*, pp. 51–52.

[27] Gerth and Mills, *op. cit.*, p. 102.

[28] Leonard Krieger, *The German Idea of Freedom: History of a Political Tradition* (Boston: Beacon Press, 1957), pp. 463–64.

[29] See Mommsen, *Max Weber und die Deutsche Politik 1890–1920*, p. 120.

[30] *Ibid.*, citing letter of November 6, 1907, written to Robert Michels in answer to the latter's defense of his socialist persuasion.

[31] Cf. *ibid.*, pp. 121–122, and especially *P.S.*, 2nd. ed., p. 22.

[32] Daniel Bell, "In Search of Marxist Humanism: The Debate on Alienation," in *Political Thought since World War II* (New York: The Free Press of Glencoe, 1964), pp. 153–154.

[33] Alexander Passerin d'Entrèves, *The Notion of the State: An Introduction to Political Theory* (Oxford: Clarendon Press, 1967), p. 143.

[34] Max Rheinstein, *Max Weber on Law in Economy and Society* (New York: Simon and Schuster, 1967), p. 349.

[35] *Ibid.*, p. 351.

[36] *Ibid.*

[37] Gerth and Mills, *op. cit.*, pp. 295–296.

[38] Wolfgang J. Mommsen, "Max Weber's Political Sociology," p. 38, quoting from *Wirtschaft und Gesellschaft*, p. 734.

[39] *Ibid.* Cf. "Zur Lage der Buergerlichen Demokratie in Russland" (1906), in *P.S.*, 2nd. ed., p. 60.

[40] Werner J. Cahnman, "Max Weber and the Methodological Controversy in the Social Sciences," in Werner J. Cahnman and Alvin Boskoff, *Sociology and History: Theory and Research* (New York: The Free Press of Glencoe, 1964), p. 119.

[41] Cf. Max Weber, "On Law in Economy and Society," cited in Robert Presthus, Book Review of Bertram M. Gross, *The Managing of Organizations* (New York: The Free Press, 1964), *The American Political Science Review*, Vol. LXI, No. 4, December 1967, p. 1107.

[42] Henderson and Parsons, *The Theory of Social and Economic Organization*, *op. cit.*, p. 341.

[43] *Ibid.*, p. 333.

[44] Alvin W. Gouldner, *Patterns of Industrial Bureaucracy* (Glencoe, Illinois: The Free Press, 1954), p. 27.

[45] *Ibid.*, p. 164.

[46] Karl Loewenstein, *Max Weber's Political Ideas in the Perspective of Our Time* (Amherst, Massachusetts: The University of Massachusetts Press, 1966), p. 39.

[47] *Ibid.*, p. 39.

[48] Reinhard Bendix, "Structure of Authority: Introduction," in Reinhard Bendix et al., eds., *State and Society: A Reader In Comparative Political Sociology* (Boston: Little, Brown & Co., 1968), p. 295.

[49] Reinhard Bendix, "Reflections on Charismatic Leadership," *ibid.*, p. 626.

[50] Cf. *ibid.*, also see Erich Feldmann, *Theorie der Massenmedien: Presse, Film, Funk, Fernsehen* (Munich: Ernst Reinhard Verlag, 1962), p. 39.

[51] Bendix, *op. cit.*, p. 626.

[52] *Ibid.*

[53] *Ibid.*

[54] *Ibid.*

[55] Mouzelis, *op. cit.*, p. 26.

[56] Cf. Robert Presthus, *The Organizational Society* (New York: Vintage Books, 1965).

[57] Michel Crozier, *The Bureaucratic Phenomenon* (Chicago: The University of Chicago Press, 1967), pp. 296–97.

[58] William H. Whyte, Jr., *The Organization Man* (New York: Simon & Schuster, 1956).

[59] Crozier, *op. cit.*, p. 297.

[60] *Ibid.*, p. 299.

[61] *Ibid.*, p. 300.

[62] W. M. Simon, "Power and Responsibility: Otto Hintze's Place in German Historiography," in Leonard Krieger and Fritz Stern, eds., *The Responsibility of Power: Historical Essays in Honor of Hajo Holborn* (Garden City: Doubleday, 1969), p. 232.

[63] Mouzelis, *op. cit.*, p. 57.

[64] Crozier, *op. cit.*, p. 300.

[65] Ringer, *op. cit.*, p. 177.

[66] *Ibid.*, pp. 157–58.

[67] *Ibid.*, p. 159.

[68] Robert K. Merton and Robert A. Nisbet, *Contemporary Social Problems* (New York: Harcourt, Brace and World, Inc., 1966), p. 723.

[69] S. N. Eisenstadt, "Introduction: Charisma and Institution Building: Max Weber and Modern Sociology," in S. N. Eisenstadt, ed., *Max Weber on Charisma and Institution Building: Selected Papers* (Chicago: The University of Chicago Press, 1968), pp. liv–lv.

[70] *Ibid.*, p. lv.

[71] *Ibid.*

[72] *Ibid.*

[73] Frederic S. Burin, "Bureaucracy and National Socialism; A Reconsideration of Weberian Theory," Robert K. Merton, et al., *Reader in Bureaucracy* (New York: The Free Press, 1952), p. 43.

[74] *Ibid.*, p. 43.

[75] Cf. Robert Presthus, *op. cit.*, p. 6ff.

[76] Alvin W. Gouldner, "On Weber's Analysis of Bureaucratic Rules," Robert K. Merton et al., *op. cit.*, p. 49.

[77] Robert Presthus, *op. cit.*, p. 57.

[78] Herman Finer, *op. cit.*, p. 710.

[79] *Ibid.*, p. 710.

X

Max Weber's Political Legacy

Max Weber's political legacy cannot be said to rest on any formally elaborated theoretical base. Instead it is, at root, an attitude toward national and international problems, such as power, politics, domination, and the concept of the state which implies a certain method of action. Max Weber's political thought, however, does rest on three solid bases: the German *Machtstaat* whose solidity, prestige, and status must be assured; its historical mission, a common, determined effort to secure for Germany a role of conducting *Weltpolitik;* and a conviction that strong, charismatic political leadership was the critical requirement for creative party politics.

To these basic principles Max Weber adhered throughout his life. In the next century, political scientists and sociologists will perhaps be able to evaluate Weber's guiding principles in all serenity; today indifference is rare, impartiality difficult. Moreover, since Max Weber was a very complex personality, and his political writings strongly support this fact, it is easy for readers to reject certain of their aspects and to admire others. As Reinhard Bendix concludes, "Despite their polemical note, his occasional political writings contain important considerations, especially with regard to the problem of leadership and bureaucracy which give an insight into his political analysis of legal domination." [1] While interest in Weber's political writings has been overshadowed by interest in his sociological and economic analyses, contemporary political problems were of passionate concern to Max Weber. [2]

Nevertheless, Weber frequently lacked something in human relationships, especially toward party politicians and toward the younger generation. Little given to compromise, he permitted himself to force issues more than those whom he addressed were prepared to sustain. Theodor Heuss, in the second edition of Max Weber's *Gesammelte*

317

Politische Schriften (edited by Johannes Winckelmann, 1958) entitled "Max Weber in Seiner Gegenwart," mentions one occasion especially on which Weber spoke out so vehemently against William II that he shocked many of his listeners. In the summer of 1917 under the sponsorship of the publisher, Eugen Diederichs, a gathering of poets, scholars, and politicians convened at Burg Lauenstein in Thuringia. Heuss suggests that Weber's own reason for attending was motivated by his fear that some of the *literati's* discourses marked by a folkish brand of romantic nationalism would entail unaffordable public risks. At the same time he vowed that after the war he would resume his attacks upon the Kaiser with such intensity and persistence that the latter would have to press charges against him on the grounds of *lèse-majesty*. And then Buelow, Tirpitz, Bethmann, Jagow, Falkenhayn, Hindenburg, Ludendorff, and others would also have to testify under oath so that the sins committed against the German people might be determined before the courts.[3]

As a political writer, Weber sometimes placed himself in the position of an observer who himself acts as a disturbing element in the behavior he observes. In the long run, he was and felt himself to be isolated. His attitude of clinical detachment concerning the forces which condition human existence sometimes gave an impression of an intellectual game, conducted by someone standing outside and above it. Actually, he was far too human not to be affected by the experiences he described (for instance during the war), experiences that penetrated every fiber of his being. Weber was too deeply involved in the political life of his nation to portray political events with exactly the same impartiality, tracing them with the same icy precision he employed when dealing with his strictly academic subject matter.

Theodor Heuss, who following World War I became the first president of the Federal Republic of Germany and who wrote a most notable biography of Weber's close associate, Friedrich Naumann, recalls an anecdote which lived on in his memory. On a Sunday afternoon, at the halfway juncture of World War I, he and his wife were guests at the Weber home across from the castle in Heidelberg. By that time, Germany's military position had deteriorated after initial successes; Germany's domestic situation, too, had become increasingly disturbing. In his commentary before his circle of friends, he became so deeply immersed in his own thoughts and shaken by his own analysis that he rose from his seat, causing Mrs. Heuss to record her impression of Max Weber on that day in a revealing statement to Marianne Weber: "he is like an emperor whose scepter has been stolen." [4]

Weber's legacy as a political analyst and commentator must be viewed continuously within the context of the general political climate in Germany. As previously noted, an examination of historical events in prewar Germany, as well as the various socio-political and economic responses to these events during and after World War I, provide ample evidence that Weber grew up in a country with a consistent and self-renewing pattern of conservative and frequently reactionary thinking. Weber's ideas, moreover, took shape in a political atmosphere essentially unfriendly to both social and political criticism; he was bound to become controversial as he analyzed the trend from an essentially liberal political climate to one favoring nationalistic ideologies, conservative both socially and politically, with political norms often bordering on reactionary thought.

From the time Weber first began to think in political terms, he foresaw the decline of liberalism apparent after the defeat of France in 1871. He criticized the selfish interests of the big industrialists and of the East Elbian landed aristocracy. While he accepted the necessary consequences demanded by capitalism and the industrialization of his country, he deplored the prerogatives reserved for those who, under the benevolent protection of Wilhelminian Germany, were allowed to disregard the rights of the working classes. He criticized the consequences arising out of the economy's organization into cartels, trusts, and monopolies at a time when such views could only separate him from many members of his own class. Yet he wanted to see German society firmly established upon a bourgeois foundation. It was with all the more regret that he discovered the German bourgeoisie had allowed itself to be co-opted as defenders of the social and political status quo instead of rallying behind the cause of its own cultural and political ideals. Weber, moreover, was opposed to the class system practiced in Prussian diet elections:

In Prussia . . . before the republic a class election system was practised in the elections to the chamber of deputies of the diet which was highly favourable to the moneyed population groups. For the elections, which were direct, the electors were divided into three classes: the largest tax-payers, paying one third of the total taxes in the electoral district, formed one class, those next in order, paying another third of the total of the taxes, formed a second, and all the remaining electors a third class; each class separately elected the same number of representatives to the electoral assembly by which the deputies were appointed. As an illustration of the effects of this classification it may be mentioned that in the election of 1903 3.4 per cent of the electors belonged to the first class, 12 per cent to the second, and 84.6 per cent to the third class. No figures are available for the participation of different occupational groups under this system. But the voting frequency within each of the three electoral classes was established for each election, and as these classes to a certain extent represent different social groups, the figures are not without interest. It is only natural [as the following table shows] that they should demonstrate a relatively high level of participation in the highest electoral class, and a decline from one class to another.

Electoral participation in Prussia, 1893–1913.

Electoral classes	1893	1898	1903	1908	1913
I	48.1	46.2	49.2	53.5	51.4
II	32.1	30.7	34.3	42.9	41.9
III	15.2	15.7	21.2	30.2	29.9
Average participation	18.4	18.4	23.6	32.8	32.7 [5]

Weber had argued that the universal process of bureaucratization brought fundamental changes in the operation of parliamentary democratic procedures. No longer characterized by free debates on major issues, parliament became a place where the power struggle of modern political parties was carried on. The masses of citizens became divided into a few political actives and a preponderant passive majority.[6] Without the benefit of mass organization and the requisite financial means, and in the absence of personal influence, the individual citizen was incapable of articulating his will and making his opinion count: the party apparatus provided the necessary voice of the people.

In this connection, Mommsen comments on the "radical conclusions" which Weber derived from his own diagnosis of modern mass democracy, and which caused him to persist in his demand for leaders with "a distinctly personal-plebiscitarian orientation." [7] The party machine was thus not a means to its own ends but rather found its real meaning in the hands of the great political leader. Its object was to secure for him a mandate from the people in support of his political aims. Since Weber conceived of the "castration of charisma" as a potential threat to which the politician was exposed by the party bureaucracy, Mommsen stressed Weber's conviction that the more like a machine a party is organized, the greater its need for a great leader. The party itself stands ready to accommodate the leader with its following, for it is his charisma which will capture the vote of the masses at election time. Rule by a leader backed by a machine was, according to Mommsen, Weber's last word on the development of modern mass democracy.[8]

Consequently, Weber placed few limitations upon his concept of the plebiscitarian leader. Not content to merely suggest that the masses are "politically passive," and that therefore they required a political leader who would outline the goals to be followed, Weber intentionally reduced the participation of the masses to a minimum, expecting them to follow the leader on the basis of their trust in his intrinsic qualities. What binds the people to the leader is to be found first and foremost in his charismatic qualifications themselves. The people tend to assume rather than test the validity of certain objective aims he may pursue. Ultimately they will not concentrate on making a judgment whether objectively his political actions are right or wrong; instead his actions will be measured with the yardstick of success.[9]

The plebiscitarian-democratic type of authority has become compromised, however, by its transformation into the charismatic-authoritarian type. Mommsen suspects that Weber was aware of the fact that the plebiscitarian leadership-democracy could cause parliamentary government in a traditional state which defers to a constitution to abdicate its *raison d'être* in favor of the charismatic-authoritarian type, even though nominally it may survive in its old guise.[10]

Regarding Weber's own attitude toward the realization of the plebiscitarian-charismatic leadership form, not in a rational-legal type of democracy but under the totalitarian system of a fascist dictatorship, Mommsen as stated earlier had no doubt that Weber would have fought passionately against it. He was opposed to any policy which would stoop to employing "the low instincts of the masses and nationalistic emotions." [11] The "ethic of responsibility" to which he subjected the political leader "would have been diametrically opposed to the delusions of grandeur and the brutal narrow-mindedness of fascist domination." [12]

It takes little effort to caricature some of Weber's ideas into a vulgarized version of ideas foreshadowing the Third Reich, but this would entail a failure to review them and other dominant voices among his contemporaries in proper historical perspective. It is the merit of Mommsen's thoughtful book that he avoided this pitfall. The thrust of Mommsen's argument is that Weber underemphasized the role of parliament by assigning to it the function of a training ground for potential leaders among politicians, reducing it further by allowing it to serve as a control organ of the administration. Given the historical role Weber attributed to charismatic talents, he sought to ensure opportunities for the great demagogue to supplant the obtaining impasse.[13] Mommsen points out that the Nazi political philosopher Carl Schmitt took this road in building upon Weber's own theories:

Such an endeavor was made all the easier since for Weber the fundamental values of democracy had to take the backseat to national power interests. Weber's democratic elite theory which recommended the 'rejection of the party state' and the "ennoblement of the 'egalitarian' democracy" through its transformation into a 'leader oligarchy' as a way out of the mass democratic reality of the state under the Weimar Republic, lent itself to development in that direction, however little this would have met with his own intentions.[14]

Mommsen's verdict is noteworthy:

The year 1933 ushered in the charismatic-plebiscitarian type of leadership domination backed up by 'the machine,' although this occurred in a form incomparably different from that which Weber had in mind. Nevertheless, one will have to admit in all honesty that Weber's teachings concerning charismatic leadership domination coupled with the radical formulation of the meaning of democratic institutions, have contributed their share to making the German people inwardly ready to acclaim the leadership position of Adolf Hitler.[15]

While Marcel Weinreich looked upon Max Weber as a political instructor of his people, Mettler rejected this conception of Weber's role in the political life of his country.

Weber once spoke of the 'profoundly unhappy age' of which the prophets of that time were conscious. An 'unhappy' age has also 'burdened him.' . . . His mission has been to meet with dignity the strenuous task of seeing the final stage of a period with 'its burden' and in its significance to its very end. To speak of Weber, the educator, is something one had better avoid. His person does not connote a mythos for us. What we respect in him is his manly courage and his incorruptible integrity.[16]

Why has Weber played but the part of Cassandra, one might ask. Moreover, would he have been a desirable molder of the character of German politics?

Weinreich has tried to answer the question why this man who was so passionately interested in public affairs remained condemned to political impotence.[17] He considered external factors, such as short-sightedness and cowardice on the part of Germany's rulers, partly responsible. Another factor of major significance, he thought, was the fact that Weber did not have the general public behind him.

Weber failed to try to gain the support of "the man in the street" because he had never wanted to flatter the masses and had always stressed the importance of his continued independence from the *demos* as emphatically as his unwillingness to surrender his freedom of thought and speech to the authorities. His crushing honesty could not permit a procedure aimed at a pleasing presentation of his program, giving it the appearance of enticement. In his lecture on *Politics as a Vocation,* Weber had named three qualities with which a politician should be endowed: passion, a sense of responsibility, and perspective. In the true leader all three qualifications are combined. Jaspers and Weinreich both concluded that Weber's own shortcoming resided in the defective state of one of these indispensable qualities. While Weber had been passionately concerned about his country's fate, expressing his thoughts eloquently and unreservedly, he decidedly lacked what he himself had referred to as the *"Machtpragma."* Since he did not strive for power, he never obtained it. He apparently expected political power to fall into his lap on the strength of his reputation as a scholar and political theorist. When this did not happen, he refused to use influence for his own advantage, for he deemed it unethical.

In theory, then, Weber recognized that a politician has to be more politic than just, but he believed himself to be above such contrivances.[18] An episode in Marianne Weber's biography reveals that, particularly in November 1918, Weber would have been willing to place himself at the helm of the ship of state. However, he lacked the necessary support. The younger generation admired Weber as the able teacher and penetrating scholar, but failed him too.

Marianne Weber asserts that it was not surprising that the pacifist and Communist elements among the youth rejected Weber's national ethos; that, however, even the youth brought up in the "traditions of Germany," chose to turn its back on Weber, struck her as a symptom of the utter moral exhaustion wrought by the war. Thus she quoted a friend's report of a gathering at which Weber spoke:

Weber explained the hopelessness of the political situation with which the present generation was faced in straightforward language and without mercy; he did so for the express purpose of drawing the consequences which were then not understood but which his national creed dictated to him: 'You know the methods employed in the Russian Revolution of 1905.' The watchword was then: to place all faith in the future but to give up all hope for oneself. All that the living generations could expect was incarceration and court martial. When that time comes, if you are resolved not to make big speeches but to see to it that the first Polish official entering Danzig will be struck by a bullet—if you are resolved to go the way which will then be unavoidable—then I shall be at your disposal, then come to me.[19]

Considering that some of these youths of whom Weber demanded such a course of action, which he himself was not prepared to undertake, had just returned from a four-year ordeal, one finds it difficult to share Marianne Weber's consternation, nor can their reaction be ascribed to battle fatigue only.

It is true that the German soldier was tired of fighting, particularly since he did not really know, at least toward the end after Ludendorff had declared the war lost, what he was fighting for. For the same reason, perhaps, did the youth reject Weber's offer which is reminiscent, even if in tone only, of Churchill's role during World War II in which he held out as a reward no more than continued sacrifice. Churchill, however, had made his appeal at the beginning of the struggle, and it was well understood by the English people.

Apart from the moral implications in Weber's plan, it would appear that the young generation professed no desire to follow "German traditions" so soon after the silencing of the guns. Thus one reads:

These words which were accompanied by a beckoning movement of the arm, as if he wanted to pull his comrades to himself, were followed by an icy, non-comprehending silence. This silence might have had some other meaning; however, further developments show that this was not so. Weber continued in his suggestions of possible actions to be taken; he talked about the honor of the students and expressed the hope that Germany, who in Treitschke's words had been the only nation among the European peoples who had been blessed with a second youth, may now have its third.[20]

The Nazis, however, were to employ quite different means to insure the support of the German youth than Weber did:

'A swine is he who wears *couleur*[21] as long as Germany lies on the ground.' The silence continued but at this stage the lack of understanding turned into anger. Students later ostentatiously walked up and down in front of Weber's home. Subsequent to this incident Weber returned his own ribbon to his fraternity. Never again was he to speak about the will of this moment to resist the enemy even in the knowledge of certain defeat.[22]

Weber, of course, had always held that the "vital interests of the nation are above democracy and parliamentary procedure." [23] In his first lecture in 1919 at the University of Munich, he began with a resumé of the political situation. Stating that it was to be his first and last word on politics, which did not belong in either the classroom or in science generally, he stressed that Germans could only have one common aim: to make the peace treaty null and void.[24]

In view of this, is it not conceivable that Weber might have endorsed any regime willing and able to rid itself of the treaty obligation? It is on the one hand significant that in the Third Reich in 1934, von Schelting defended Weber against the charge that he had been an opponent of liberalism.[25] Yet Jaspers, in dealing with the alleged potential role Weber might have played in anticipating Nazi ideology through his own political thought, counters such suppositions by stating that totalitarian domination would have spelled the end of the kind of politics Weber envisaged. To the charge that Weber's sociological concepts of charismatic leadership and domination and his political motives approached Nazi precepts, though its phraseology might have furnished them with a better appearance, he answered that Weber's realistic insights into the significance of power and violence did not mean that to see the devil, recognizing him for what he is, is tantamount to identifying with him. Nor, in Jaspers' view, does the separation between the ethics of responsibility and the ethics of conviction entail unprincipled action in the arena of power politics. While the Nazis glamorized the state, Weber conceived it as a puzzling monster, though a necessary one. Summing up, Jaspers concedes that Max Weber's concept of "charismatic leadership" might have confused those who equate insight with will. It would seem that Jaspers is not free from ambiguity himself:

When in 1918, Max Weber conceived of a democracy with a strong leader, he saw that there were no leaders. Leaders can develop only on a political proving ground, which today is provided only by a genuine democracy. They cannot appear spontaneously when the need for them arises. Max Weber might have said with Nietzsche: 'The necessity for such leaders, the dreadful danger that they may not appear, or that they may warp or degenerate—these are our real anxieties and grounds for gloom.' [26]

To the question whether Weber by reason of his nationalistic stand would have pledged loyalty to *any* German state, Jaspers replies affirmatively. For Weber, neither the constitution nor the ruling class of the moment was of any consequence, but rather whether the political system permits men of the highest political caliber to rise to the top, "and whether it makes possible social justice and freedom." [27] Actually, Weber himself never subscribed to the belief that any form of government, including democracy, would be capable of appreciably reducing the cost of social conflict. He thought conflict an inescapable fact of life.

However, Jaspers, J. P. Mayer, as well as Gerth and Mills, disagree with those who view Weber as a forerunner of the Nazis:

To be sure, his philosophy of charisma—his scepticism and his pragmatic view of democratic sentiment—might have given him such affinities. But his humanism, his love for the underdog, his hatred of racism and anti-Semitic demagoguery would have made him at least as sharp a 'critic,' if not a sharper one, of Hitler than his brother Alfred has been.[28]

Although some of Weber's concepts bordered on unprincipled opportunism, his personal political record is consistent with the judgment of Gerth and Mills. In fact, Weber's political orientation shifted from the Right (the Conservatives) toward the left of center (the Democratic party). Nor is this all. It will be recalled that on December 1, 1918, Weber expressed his almost complete agreement with the Social Democrats. The fact that he was not a party member, he maintained was due to his determination to retain his freedom of expression toward the *demos*. Because the enemy's forms of government were mostly bourgeois, he considered the Revolution especially unfortunate because it reduced even further Germany's bargaining position.[29]

Weber also attacked the Social Democrats for their internationalistic sentiments, which he thought to characterize the German labor movement more than the French or English. He saw the weaknesses inherent in German Social Democracy, which were to be largely responsible for its subsequent extinction in the days of the Weimar Republic. As early as 1907, he had made the following observations:

The one question is, which . . . has most to fear *in the long run*, bourgeois society or Social Democracy? I, personally, think the latter, at least so

far as concerns those elements in it that are exponents of *revolutionary
ideology*. That there are by now certain conflicts within the Social Democratic bureaucracy it is plain to view, and if, on the one hand, the material
interests of professional politicians, and, on the other, the revolutionary
ideology, could develop unhindered, and if, further, the Social Democrats
were no longer, as now, excluded from the *Kriegervereine,* and were allowed
to enter the ecclesiastical administration at present closed to them, *then* serious
internal problems would indeed be in grave danger. Then we should see
that Social Democracy would never permanently conquer the towns or the
State, but that on the contrary the State would conquer the Social Democratic
party. I cannot understand why *bourgeois* society should regard it as a danger.
. . . I think that no prince would continue to fear this party which has no
real source of power, whose political impotence is manifest even today to all
who choose to see. If the party seeks political power and yet fails to get
control of the one effective means of power, military power, in order to overthrow the State, its dominance in the community and in public corporations
and associations would only show its political impotence still more distinctly,
and the more it sought to rule simply as a political party and not objectively,
the quicker it would be discredited.[30]

But Weber's estimate was only partly correct. As noted earlier, the
Social Democrats lost revolutionary ardor when they began to subscribe
to conciliatory revisionism. So it was not merely exclusion from the
Kriegervereine and the ecclesiastical administration which brought about
the decline in revolutionary spirit that Weber foresaw. The fate that
was to overwhelm the German revolution lay in the general political
backwardness and in the internal dissension of German labor. Germany
did not have, at that time—as Great Britain had after World War II—
one large democratic Labor Party which could carry out its policies
within the framework of the middle-class state, presenting a carefully
planned socialization program. To these handicaps were added serious
economic and international difficulties after the war. The combination
of these elements contributed largely to the weakness of the Social
Democrats when in office.

Pessimism and even despair characterized Weber's efforts towards
an equation of democracy, the charismatic leadership principle, and
imperialism within the framework of a conceptual scheme. Democracy
as a form of government did not hold for him the possibility of reducing
the cost of social conflict, for he thought conflict inevitable, no matter
what the form of government. Had he lived to see the Third Reich,
Weber's personal moral integrity and his human compassion would
probably have been suicidal, as was true in the case of other Germans
who tried to help victims of Nazi oppression. He could not have defended men like Ernst Toller on the ground that they had acted unwise-
ly, politically, but in full accordance with their "ethics of conviction."[31]

A comparison of Weber with another eminent German, reveals certain similarities between the novelist Thomas Mann and Max Weber. In November 1914, Mann had published an essay called *"Gedanken im Kriege"* ("Thoughts in War"). In it he saw the war as "purification," "liberation," and an "enormous hope"; he also wrote that German victories "filled our eyes with tears and gave us such happiness that we could not sleep at night." The closing lines of "Thoughts in War" contained the assertion that "only Germany's victory guarantees Europe's peace" and that undoubtedly the Germans, "the most important people in Europe, would win the war, as history does not crown ignorance and error with victory." [32]

In January 1915, Mann published an essay on "Frederick and the Coalition" with the subtitle: "A Sketch for the Day and the Hour." Inquiring into the justification of Frederick the Great's right to attack other nations, he wrote as follows:

His right was the right of a rising power, a problematical, still illegitimate, still untested right, which had to be fought for, which had to be created. If he were beaten, he would be the most miserable adventurer, 'un fou,' as Louis of France had said. Only if success proved that he was commissioned by fate, only then could he claim to have been in the right, always in the right.[33]

Certainly Mann's aversion to democracy, asserted clearly in his *Betrachtungen eines Unpolitischen* (Reflections of a Non-political Man),[34] cannot be denied. While his brother Heinrich Mann had always fought the militarist mentality, Thomas Mann experienced his own remarkable conversion very late. Since Mann was in his early forties in World War I, when he might have been expected to have reached maturity. Thus he wrote in 1938:

I must regretfully own that in my younger years I shared that dangerous habit of thought which regards life and intellect, art and politics, as totally separate worlds. In those days we were all of us inclined to view political and social matters as non-essentials, that might well be entrusted to politicians. And we were foolish enough to rely on the ability of these specialists to protect our highest interests.[35]

In December 1945, Thomas Mann wrote in answer to Walter von Molo, a German writer who, in the name of other German intellectuals, asked him to return to Germany. The following are excerpts from Mann's letter:

I have become somewhat estranged from Germany through all these years. Germany, you will have to admit, is a disquieting country. I confess that I am afraid of the German wreckage—the human wreckage as well as the rubble of stone and iron. . . . Sometimes it is books that come to me. Shall I confess that I did not care to see them and soon put them away? It may be superstition, but in my eyes, books that could be printed in Germany from 1933 to 1945 are less than worthless and had better not be touched. There is a smell of blood and shame about them; they should all be ground into pulp.[36]

And again, complaining about the misfortunes of exile, Thomas Mann wrote to his fellow Germans in the homeland: "None of this did you have to bear and suffer, all those of you who swore allegiance to the 'charismatic Fuehrer' (horrible, horrible, this intoxicated erudition!) and carried on 'culture' under Goebbels." [37]

Marianne Weber, referring to the now famous conversation between Weber and Ludendorff and to some of Weber's speeches, told this writer that one could not accord the spoken word the same weight that one might be inclined to give the written word. In the writer's opinion, however, this distinction does not absolve a man, for his spoken word may, as would be true in Weber's case, have an even greater effect upon his audience, particularly if this audience is composed partly of youth who saw in him their teacher.

In a letter addressed to Theodor Heuss, Emil Praetorius recalled on April 9, 1958 how he together with Kurt Riezler were virtually spellbound as they listened to Max Weber in Munich, although the latter appeared extremely nervous and upset. His passionate address, delivered on the eve of the Revolution in a crowded hall at the Wagner-braeu, created a lasting impression upon his listeners.[38]

However, this much is certain: Max Weber was not alone in his glorification of German *Kultur*. The fact that writers of the stature of Thomas Mann, and of the popularity of Emil Ludwig, who once shared Weber's conception of the war as being "great and wonderful" became emigrants, does not justify their conduct during World War I and immediately afterwards. Such "liberals" were numerous and therefore should not be singled out individually, yet they aided in shaping the outlook of the generation which was to degrade German *Kultur*. It is perhaps not fitting that these writers and other intellectuals should now pour out their wrath upon this "disquieting country" without reserving a share of its guilt for themselves.

To the question of how Weber would have reacted had he lived to see National Socialist Germany, Jaspers replied that "His despair of the Germans would have certainly reached unprecedented depths." [39] Jaspers is somewhat equivocal as he inquires into what Weber's political thought and action during that period might have been: "A state which did not hold its authority in tenure from the nation was not a state to which, as a German, he could give allegiance. For this state destroyed the nation step by step and prepared for its end." [40] Although Weber might have joined the resistance movement to eliminate Hitler to obtain the best possible terms for Germany (during the latter part of World War I, as noted previously, he had urged the Kaiser to abdicate voluntarily to obtain a better settlement for Germany), prospects that he might have joined in efforts designed to counter the Nazi regime, seem uncertain:

Would Max Weber have allowed himself to be destroyed as a sacrifice for what is German? I do not believe so. We cannot know. Perhaps he would have remained silent. But of one thing I feel sure: to despair of the Germans altogether, totally and forever, would not have been possible for Max Weber.
. . .
When politics, understood as the politics of free people reacting to the course of their destiny, comes to an end, what then? Then the individual, deprived of his political dignity, may still be allowed, within the existential sphere left to him, to realize what is exposed at any moment to ruin from without: the intimacy of private existence in human relationships between individuals, the knowledge of things, inner truthfulness, fortitude amid destruction. Politics is destiny, and continues to be so even when this destiny signifies the end of politics, but politics is not the ultimate end for man as man.[41]

In his preface Jaspers pointed out that in any consideration of Max Weber's political thought, "one has to go back to a past as dead as if centuries separated it from today." [42] In retrospect, can we really afford to do this? I think not. It is true that the astuteness of Weber's political analysis escaped most of his own contemporaries and probably remains misunderstood by most of ours. When Jaspers states, however, that "one has to be willing to set aside all prejudice caused by the evil of Hitlerism and the crimes committed by Germans in the name of Germany," and that "one must not allow our present knowledge of the presuppositions to totalitarianism and of analogies of meaning to cast its shadow backwards on all that preceded the totalitarian state in Germany," [43] the hard facts of contemporary Germany militate against this approach. The need for the reconstruction of a democratic political culture in post-World War II Germany attests to the vital significance of building up a heritage of political culture, which in addition to beliefs, values, cognitions, and symbols, also encompasses the techniques of socialization, recruitment, political institutions, and political history.[44] Against the background of these factors must be considered the constants and variables in the composition of politically relevant elites.

Moreover, when Jaspers states that Max Weber's political thinking cannot be linked with nationalistic thought both before and during World War I, Weber's form of nationalism being "uniquely Max Weber's own," this claim again seems to violate the fact. Unquestionably, his quest for political freedom and human dignity were utterly foreign to adherents of Nazi ideology. But to say that these considerations "trans-

cend all passing political situations" is equivalent to saying that all
remaining components of Weber's political thought and action are obviated by his personal integrity and his genuine liberalism in other areas
of his work and thought.

Weber's contribution as a political figure was his clearsightedness
which made him refrain from pursuing "power for power's sake," if it
was incompatible with Realpolitik.

> Everywhere the framework of a new bondage is ready, waiting only for
> the slowing down of technical "progress" and for the victory of "interest"
> over "profit," in combination with exhaustion of as yet "free" territory and
> "free" markets, to make the masses tractable to its compulsion. At the same
> time the increasing complexity of the economic system, its partial nationaliza-
> tion of "municipalization" and the territorial magnitude of national organisms
> is creating ever more clerical work, and increasing specialization of labor,
> and professional training in administration—and this means the creation of a
> bureaucratic caste. . . . Whatever spheres of "inalienable" personality and
> freedom are still unwon by the common people in the course of the next few
> generations and while the economic and intellectual "revolution," the much-
> maligned "anarchy" of production, and the equally maligned "subjectivism"
> (by which and which alone, the individual has been made self-dependent)
> still remain unbroken, may perhaps—once the world has become economically
> "full" and intellectually "sated"—remain unachieved by them, for as far as
> our weak eyes can pierce the impenetrable mists of the future of mankind.[46]

What relevance does Max Weber's political thought have for contemporary politics generally, and the conduct of American politics, in
particular?

Perhaps the first great question surrounding the person of Max
Weber has been whether his powers of political vision really also
reflected his political ability.

Secondly, unquestionably Weber's political talent, seen in his
grasp of situations and their resolution prior to anyone else's assessment,
is sorely required by those on whom the "guilt" of power inevitably
devolves.

Thirdly, the tension between the practical politician and the
scholar personified in Weber illustrates how the former must engage
in compromises which the latter cannot justifiably sustain.

Fourth, Weber masterfully exemplified the tension between man
practicing mere politics and man practicing statecraft. In establishing
the image of the great statesman whose caliber and moral fortitude
permit him to defend his cause against the opposition, Weber has
rendered a valuable service to all interested in statecraft. He has shown
the qualifications necessary "to bore through hard boards with passionate
patience and a sure eye." He opposes this task to that self-perpetuating
business which usually accompanies routine performance.

Fifth, Max Weber furnished his contemporaries as well as posterity with an image of what Jaspers has called "magnificent tactlessness." Especially in a time characterized by the Great Debate, as applied to Vietnam, China, and Latin America, this trait, although often eminently offensive, must be seen as a legitimate force, especially in a democratic society.

Sixth, Weber's failure is demonstrated by his lack of social emphasis on postwar international relations, with the exception of Poland and Alsace-Lorraine (of which the United States also has been guilty), a fact which must occupy us as we confront the intensification of the Vietnam buildup with its novel nuclear possibilities, as well as cold war tensions elsewhere.

Seventh, Weber's assessment of conceptions and misconceptions of the national interest could be seen as a guide applied to American interest in South-East Asia, and elsewhere.

Eighth, Weber has pointed up the unmet obligations to focus upon great issues, or small ones, and to provide the opportunity for qualified youth to play its part.

Ninth, even though perhaps negatively, Weber has portrayed the conflict between the forces of nationalism and internationalism. While placing no faith in the latter, his appraisal of the origins of World War I and of Germany's place in the post-World War era are indicative of certain trends in contemporary Germany.

Tenth, debates on major matters of foreign relations have often been relegated to the initiative of private bodies, not always disinterested. It is to the credit of American democracy that the United States has never established a pseudo-elite of scientists working in full collusion with the government as Germany has known, evading an anxious public. In Germany, Weber was a pioneer in permitting his scholarly fund of knowledge to benefit the public. His example in this area belongs to social scientists of the world, not only to those of his own country.

Writing from a contemporary perspective, Mommsen views the task of creating a democratic order, which does not entail "leaderlessness" and a lack of genuine authority, as one of the most urgent items on the post-World War II German agenda. The real challenge he sees is fitting this pattern into the basic values of liberal self-determination in the midst of a society dominated by a bureaucratic order and various interest groups. The dimensions of the challenge are illustrated by current political developments which carry within them tendencies inherent in modern industrial mass societies toward authoritarian forms of domination shrouded by a more or less democratic disguise. Mixed forms of authoritarian-charismatic and constitutional rule have not been abundant only within younger nations, they may also be observed in parliamentary democracies founded on great traditions.

Mommsen points out the fate of the fourth French republic which has, in fact, born out Max Weber's contention that a parliamentary democracy without a leader, without some strong center of authority, cannot survive. It should be recalled, especially now after de Gaulle's death, that almost prophetically Mommsen wrote in 1959:

But the dangers of a transformation from a legal constitutional rule into total forms of domination have manifested themselves here too. Even though de Gaulle's regime has shown some wise moderation and has not gone very far in pushing the parliamentary system aside . . . there are, nevertheless, some disquieting signs on the horizon for the future of western democracy as such. No one will be able to predict today, whether the governmental system under de Gaulle will have a greater future than did its predecessors. What is discernible, however, are the problematic aspects of Max Weber's charismatic leadership democracy as they arise anew. For the new French Constitution in many respects strongly resembles Weber's suggestions for the draft of the Weimar Constitution in 1918–1919. The quasi-plebiscitarian leadership position of de Gaulle . . . corresponds to Weber's conception of the office of the *Reichspraesident*.[47]

Mommsen is quick to add, however, that the power position of the parliamentary bodies within the present French constitutional system, thanks to numerous restrictions on their activity as well as their influence, is considerably weaker than Weber had envisaged. Moreover, de Gaulle ended the practice of holding an administrative position while holding membership in one of the legislative bodies. Weber had fought passionately against this rule in the German constitution under Bismarck, to make it possible for leaders of political parties to rise to power in this capacity and to center responsibility for governmental policy in the parties themselves. Hence, Mommsen had warned against pursuing the comparison of Max Weber's proposals with the current French constitution too far. The resemblance between them, striking as it may be, is largely a formal one.

Hermann Hesse, a German writer who moved to Switzerland shortly before World War I, wrote significantly: "I do not distrust the present state because it is new and republican, but because it is too little of both." [48] Unlike Weber, Hesse had welcomed the Revolution of 1918, but had come to relinquish all earnest hopes for "a German Republic which deserves to be taken seriously. . . . Among 1,000 Germans there are even today 999 who do not acknowledge any war guilt. . . . In brief, I find myself as far away from the mentality which dominates Germany, as in the years 1914–1918." [49] He concluded that instead of the tiny step toward the left which the people have taken, he had been "driven many miles to the left." [50]

Possibly the view could be taken that had the Weimar constitution followed the pattern of the current French constitution, perhaps following more closely the more democratic form Weber had proposed, Germany might never have seen the rise of the Nazi regime. Mommsen, however, states that "considering Max Weber's plans for the *Reichspraesident* we have come to the opposite conclusion." [51] He supports this far-reaching assertion by stating:

For Weber's constitutional proposals, their basic democratic features notwithstanding, were marked by unmistakably authoritarian features and were thus not immune to a totalitarian reformulation. Political charisma, in its pure essence, devoid of value content cannot furnish the firm foundation, upon which alone a genuinely democratic system of government can be built.[52]

Somewhat nostalgically, Mommsen continues:

In the essential points, therefore, we will have to take different paths than Max Weber. The appeal to charisma and the great demagogic talent of the political leader will not be valid for us as a genuine way out of the dilemma. . . . We will have to seek new ways of rational value-oriented forms of political community life, which may be counted on to oppose the bureaucratic tendencies as well as those fostered by political interest groups typical of modern society.[53]

Mommsen emphasizes the need to protect the rights of the individual citizen as guaranteed by the constitution and the principles of the *Rechtsstaat* far more than Weber considered either possible or necessary.

Max Weber's political ideas seemed innovative and liberal as opposed to those of the "Literati" whom he attacked as the defenders of social privilege. He attacked the antiparliamentary talk of ideologically backward-leaning colleagues who, as he said, "feared for the prestige of their own social grouping: that of the diploma-holder".[54] As Bramsted observes:

The spirit of the authoritarian vigour of the ruling class is most strongly embodied in the figure of a government official (Regierungsassessor) who later becomes a county squire. He belongs to a very rich industrialist family and wishes to make up for his upstart ennoblement by out-Junkering the Junker. His family seeks to win greater esteem by purchasing an estate in its home county. This squire (Landrat) is a typical representative of that socially ambitious Assessorismus which, together with its connection with the student-corps and official patronage, Max Weber has described as one of the most characteristic features of the second empire.[55]

Weber championed responsible government for which constitutional changes were indispensable. Yet, since the issue of the merits of domestic reform was intimately bound up with the question of the value of the best reform "if the Cossacks are coming," we are confronted with "the almost insufferable placidity with which Max Weber treated the problem of violence in domestic politics." By the same token, "Weber regarded . . . the struggle between nations and their values as a built-in factor of a dynamic world order." [56] Yet, as Simon argues, Weber must be credited with ranking among the small minority who could "point without self-contradiction at the hollowness of the 'ideas of 1914'." [57]

In Germany and on the part of a few scholars in the United States, a more critical attitude seems to have replaced the earlier rather bland treatment of Weber's political views. From the following exchange of letters emerges the question: How far are social scientists in America prepared to go in their assessment of Weber's political viewpoint? The controversy treated in the two following letters sheds some light upon the answer. Benjamin Nelson here defends the credentials of Max Weber, the distinguished scholar.[58] Herbert Marcuse, on the other hand, perceived Weber's analysis politically ineffectual because of his unwillingness to advocate a radical transformation.[59]

To the Editor:

In his letter "Storm over Weber" (January 3), Benjamin Nelson enthusiastically quotes Brand Blanshard for reminding us that Max Weber "fought a hopeless battle against German *Kaisertum.* . . ." The fact is that Max Weber was a convinced monarchist. When he fought against William II and demanded his abdication he did so because this Kaiser, by his stupid policies, compromised the Kaisertum and the dynasty. As late as October, 1918, less than one month before Germany became a republic, Max Weber wrote: "The Kaiser cannot with dignity remain on the throne and he damages the dynasty which we wish to preserve." And one day later: "No reasonable human being in Germany will expect anything to come of revolutionary and republican experiments; it is therefore absolutely vital that the dynasty be preserved . . . at the cost of (letting go) its representatives who have become impossible."

Mr. Nelson continues his letter with a report which misrepresents the commemorative meeting of the German Sociological Society in 1964. I ask the following questions: (1) Who characterized Max Weber's objective sociology as a "total failure"? (2) Who denounced Max Weber as a "main inspiration of the Hitler event of 1933 and its aftermath"? (3) Who was the "enraged detractor" who charged Weber with a "major part of the blame" for the adoption and success of the "Final Solution"? (4) And finally, who asked the rhetorical question whether the concentration camps "were not the ultimate fruit of Weber's endorsement of 'scientific value neutrality' and bureaucratic-legal rationality"?

I attended the meeting of the German Sociological Society from beginning to end and I did not hear any of Max Weber's "countrymen" say the things Mr. Nelson imputes to them. If Mr. Nelson derives his charges from a misreading of the paper which I (at most an excountryman of Max Weber's) delivered at the German Sociological Society meeting, he should say so and quote his text. Mr. Nelson owes it to your readers and to the academic profession to substantiate his charges by presenting his evidence.

Herbert Marcuse

Newton, Mass.[60]

Benjamin Nelson's reply to Herbert Marcuse's letter appears below:

To the Editor:

The following bits of evidence should suffice to give a foretaste of the perplexing documents which readers will soon be able to examine for themselves in the official text of the Heidelberg Proceedings. . . .

First, I recall the seemingly innocent remark by Prof. Juergen Habermas, that Carl Schmitt was a "legitimate pupil" of Max Weber. Was that not an endorsement of the view propounded in the sensational German book, "The Destruction of Reason" (1951, expanded edition 1960) by the famed Hungarian-Marxist-Leninist intellectual, George Lukács? Weber's views, Lukács insists, found their logical fruition in Schmitt, the immensely influential political publicist who helped pave the way for Hitler.

This instance should alert readers to a fact they might miss from the ingenuous look of Professor Marcuse's questions. Interpreting the esoteric dialectics in which Professor Marcuse and his friends chose to express themselves necessarily requires finding mundane equivalents for their aesopic idiom in the public language of everyday speech. The only matter cited in Professor Marcuse's letter which I placed in quotes are two eerie euphemisms of current vintage—"Hitler Event of 1933" and "Final Solution," which I refrained from assigning to any speaker.

Now to Professor Marcuse's own words—the responsibility for the unauthorized translation and italics are mine: To what *was* he referring in Heidelberg when he spoke of capitalist society's "release of pent-up aggression in the form of the legitimation of medieval cruelty (torture) and the scientifically managed annihilation of human lives"? Not to Auschwitz, as I had implied in my letter? To Hiroshima? To both? To neither? . . . To something which had indeed not yet happened, but which was now on the drawing board, above all in "affluent" America?

Did no one emphasize Weber's share in the responsibility for these developments? No one imply that Weber's objective sociology was a total failure? Explained Professor Marcuse? Weber's critique of capitalist rationality suddenly stops short and ". . . accepts the allegedly inevitable and becomes apologetic—worse, it becomes a *denunciation of a possible alternative: a qualitatively different historical rationality.*" Must not a self-contradictory sociology which has such noxious consequences as those ascribed to Weber—and his American admirers at Heidelberg—be called a *total* failure?

The applause for Professor Marcuse's dialectics by the enthusiastic partisans who swarmed into Heidelberg to take part in the proceedings against Weber was tumultuous. Why? One hopes Professor Marcuse will explain one day.

Benjamin Nelson

Stony Brook, N. Y.[61]

It seems likely that Max Weber's political writings will now become subject to an evaluation in our own contemporary setting; aided by the benefit of hindsight, frequently lacking in compassion, the debate will probably continue for some time.

Even though Weber's suggestions for Germany's future may prove unacceptable, his evaluation of "the attitude of the normal German toward government bureaucracy" which he characterized as holding a "superpersonal spell," traceable to orthodox Lutheranism,[62] may point the way toward a change. As Mommsen points out, Weber severely criticized Lutheranism for having invested Germans with a lack of critical faculty toward the position of officialdom, which could only strengthen the latter's hold on the ship of state under the cloak of monarchical legitimation.[63] It was because Weber despaired over the political impotence abounding in Germany that he felt himself compelled to write:

As sky-high as Luther towers over all the others, *Lutheranism* is for me, I cannot deny that fact, in its *historical* forms of development the most horrible of all the horrors. Even in its ideal form, in which you portray it in hopes of future developments, it is for me, *for us Germans,* a configuration of which I am not sure—how much strength can be derived for the penetration of life.[64]

Weber's preference was for puritanism, which espouses a more rational attitude toward state and bureaucracy. In contrast to the pseudoreligious mysterious cult of officialdom as seen through German lenses, puritanism perceives its role as nothing other than business like everything else.[65]

Following World War II, the climate of public opinion in Germany today has been reflected in an uneasy concern with the past. The 1964 Convention of the German Sociological Society at Heidelberg, together with other signs on the horizon, indicate the possibility of a breakthrough beyond something more than a safe, enameled, and pedestrian vision. Yet Germany's political future depends upon her potential for assimilating and coming to terms with the facts and meaning of her past. The German public's frequently uncritical reliance upon their officials and the rigid priority it assigns to the values of law and order reflect its alienation from the prerequisites for political democracy:

Quite naturally perhaps, but nevertheless with great danger to the developing democratic process, the Germans relied too much on their trained officials to help them decide questions of policy. The position of the trained civil servant too was unassailable. . . . The *Ministerialrat* Dr.—was glorified. The representative of the people was less important than the bureaucrat, and the bureaucrat always seemed to be interested in short circuiting or trammeling the elected official who "smelled of the people." Moreover, the training of civil servants under the Republic did not inculcate proper respect for the people, and the large number of relatively low-voltage parliamentarians who became ministers did not give the trained civil servants much competition in the struggle for power.[66]

Considering the traditionally low incidence of mass political interest and involvement of the German population, the appearance of current stability despite the absence of genuine political integration may in fact prove highly vulnerable and deceptive: "For a democracy in which substantial numbers of persons—both voting and non-voting—are, politically speaking, totally uninterested and uninvolved may be one in which democratic political consensus and commitment are relatively low. Skepticism, cynicism and hostility may not be far removed from apathy and ignorance, especially under potential conditions of external and internal crisis." [67] In the Federal Republic right-wing and revisionist trends have been in evidence. Yet, among various politically relevant characteristics, even political conservatives tend to profess generally accepted standards of political expression. Conversely, this accommodation to current official norms of political habits and conduct probably does not represent an accurate reflection of their own true political preferences. In fact, this accommodation often serves as a screen, camouflaging their actual alienation from the current political climate, and based upon an uninformed and frequently hostile frame of mind.[68]

In a democracy, communication between the social sciences and the citizenry must be expanded or we may well head for a situation "where the most important political questions will be settled in a discussion only between the experts and the ruling politicians, while the sovereign people must make do with a kind of illusory publicity with politically insignificant sensations as its themes. Then no true and well-considered public opinion could be formed any longer on the really important questions: and if this happens a state will have been reached that can no longer be called a democracy." [69] Max Weber's informing concept as applied to his public did credit to him, the social scientist. The passive role he assigned to the 'sovereign people,' however, together with his conception of authoritarianism in combination with democracy in principle, deny him the place in the active political arena which he rightfully occupies as a philosopher and social scientist.

Max Weber's political thought derived from his conception of a basic historical antagonism between the ideal of individual responsibility and the products of rationalization, especially as reflected in modern workaday life and its concomitant bureaucracies. He believed that lasting freedom is not attainable by substituting the rule of law for personal authority; instead emphasis should be placed on maximum "enhancement of personal authority under conditions which guarantee the necessity for the political leader constantly to prove his worth while excluding the decline of his dominance into sterile tyranny." [70] Weber's emphasis on the influence of great men in history led him to assume that only if great statesmen are able to attain positions of power will freedom retain its meaningful content.[71]

The practical implications of Max Weber's political philosophy have become a subject of heated controversy in recent years, especially since the hundredth anniversary of his birth in 1964. The *International Social Science Journal*, with the assistance of the *Deutsche Gesellschaft fuer Soziologie*, featured in its first issue in 1965 four significant articles on Weber's contribution, ". . . placing it in perspective in the light of developments since his death in 1920." [72] In his address commemorating Max Weber's centenary at the Free University of Berlin, Reinhard Bendix significantly referred to Weber as:

. . . an extremely awkward authority, for his work excels neither in simplicity of ideas nor in clarity of exposition. It can so easily be spoken of at many different levels, and offers points of departure for the most varied interpretations. This is borne out by the fact that, in recent years, not only Weber's political ideas but also his concepts such as charisma, economic rationality, bureaucracy, etc., have been cited both in support of, and in opposition to, the tendencies of modern society towards democracy and towards dictatorship. . . . Of relevance . . . are the striking dissimilar reactions in post-war Germany and America, which were revealed recently at the fifteenth meeting of the *Deutsche Gesellschaft fuer Soziologie*. Repeatedly, German sociologists exposed the political dangers latent in Weber's thinking, whereas American sociologists manifested greater interest in the substantive core of his work. It should be added that some colleagues objected to this very distinction. . . .[73]

Considering the position taken by American sociologists, there is much truth in Bendix' characterization. Perhaps, too, this is why many social scientists heretofore have, with few exceptions, stopped short of penetrating Weber's political writings but instead have continued to draw on and deepen their explorations of "the substantive core of his work." This orientation may be responsible for the notable absence of reassessments of the relationship between Max Weber's immense intellectual scope and the tragic ambivalence of some of his private equations in politics. Particularly in Germany, members of the academic profession, some of whom maintained an all too passive position in the Third Reich, might be justified in being painfully aware of Weber's "noble nihilism" and its potential practical implications in the context of recent German political history.[74] Perhaps the uneasiness toward Weber's insistence on the facts of power, as well as his emphasis on the absoluteness of the national principle is further intensified, at least in some German academic circles, by recent themes employed by ultraconservative and

Neo-Nazi movements, however insignificant they may appear to be. Given their past performance, their ideological-propagandistic commitments and the constellation of forces supporting them, within and without the radical movements, it may be assumed that this thwarted avenging spirit can rouse itself. As Norman Macrae writes:

It is undoubtedly true that a lot of the people who had it most comfortable under Hitler are now—after a brief hell period—in 1945–48—having it most comfortable again. To move from class-ridden top business and civil service circles in Britain to similar class-ridden circles in Germany is to move from one revealing set of complexes to another; it suddenly dawns on one that while in Britain the whole governing machine is too often playing Hamlet, in Germany it has often within its lifetime played at least Seyton in Macbeth. . . . The main point to stress is that the English form of self-delusion, both about ourselves and about Germany, has become economically the more misleading and therefore the more dangerous.[75]

Wolfgang Mommsen has characterized Weber's position as being marked by what would appear to be an internal contradiction: "The utmost possible freedom through the utmost possible dominance."[76] Weber, in domestic as well as foreign policy, was much in favor of coming down "strongly on the side of the 'will to power'."[77]

It is here . . . that we find the real reason for the almost insufferable placidity with which Max Weber treated the problem of violence in domestic politics. He took over in its entirety the traditional doctrine of 'reasons of State,' and described the constitutional State as the typical modern form of power dominance but without much attention to its basis of rational values.[78]

The political synthesis of nationalism and the concomitant prerogatives of the power state were defended by classifying them as residing within the realm of faith. Performing the function of two component parts of a complementary relationship, the legitimacy of their claim was established:[79]

. . . he postulated the primacy of national interest, as opposed to the entire complex of political and legal institutions. . . .[80]

The tracing of any ideological lineages is further complicated by the complexities of German politics in Weber's own time and also by his subjective intentions.[81] Nevertheless, Mommsen notes a certain link between the apparent inconsistency characterizing Weber's stress upon the need for democracy and individualism on the one hand, and the absolute claim of the nation state on the other. Weber conceived of the struggle for power among nations as one which they must pursue as bearers of "autonomous cultural ideals and the extension of their influence throughout the world." [82]

The compelling element for Weber is his vision of the nation-state as furnishing the last court of appeal and moral formulation. Carl J. Friedrich criticizes Weber's position: "The close relation between the psychological and the nominalist misinterpretation of phenomena like authority is strikingly illustrated in the approach of Max Weber, who, confusing authority with legitimacy, misses one of the key aspects of authority, by minimizing its rational aspect." [83] Weber stressed that "the great nation states were called upon to defend, if necessary by force of arms, the validity and prestige of their cultures and, if necessary, also to expand them . . . the struggle between nations and their values as a built-in factor of a dynamic world order," [84] Weber regarded as inevitable.

As a writer capable of understanding the real impasses of Western civilization and the movements of thought and feeling that rack our time, Weber envisaged the updating of traditional foreign policy options. He deplored that so few of his contemporaries appreciated the increasing insularity and regression of the notion that all original thought at the political level must be ignored because it is not welcome to established thinkers, or because it may be "subversive." Weber feared lest Germans turn themselves into people in flight from their own mediocrity, which might only aggravate the fate that is certain to overtake any nation in the international arena in which, as he believed, demonic forces engage each other in a life-and-death struggle. Thus Weber was able to write in 1916 that Germany should have done without the founding of the German Empire if she were too faint-hearted to fight this war. Paul Sethe comments that while he led the fight against the regime of Kaiser William II, it occurred neither to him nor to his contemporaries that the policy of the Kaiser could find no more convincing vindication than Weber himself offered through such phrases. [85]

Subscribing to the idea of a powerful nation state, the concepts of "nation" and "power state" signified for Weber two sides of the same coin. Both national and cultural worth, accordingly, can be demonstrated convincingly only if the nation's foreign policy is conducted from a position of strength. Hence, Weber's merciless criticism of the bourgeoisie. The image of the "nation" and the "nation state" as representing the greatest historical achievement was widely accepted by many other liberals of that period. The nation possessed for Weber the highest ethical value; national power politics was not to be circumscribed by ethical precepts. Consequently, genuinely political action could be measured only with the yardstick of the rational chances of success. [86]

Max Weber's political essays must be viewed as impressive testimony to the passion he himself demanded of the politician, and with which he presented his political convictions, frequently against those in authority as well as against prevailing public opinion. Nevertheless:

Max Weber has not made any attempt to draw the consequences of his methodological position, namely to establish empirical evidence: (1) for his personal convictions within the framework of his own scientific writings; (2) for the claim of its general application and absolute validity; nor, does he seek to 'prove' them on the basis of the material yielded by his sociological and historical research. The capacity for distancing himself from his own value judgments in the act of dealing with scientific questions and insights is probably the most fascinating element in the personality of this great scholar, which is sometimes confusing at the same time.[87]

Abramowski comes close in this assessment of Weber, the political writer, to Mommsen's conclusion, which ultimately presents itself as the dilemma between the absolute national principle and the advocacy of democratic and individualistic principles: "As a political thinker, Weber affirmed the German national state as Bismarck had created it. In his sense of belonging to the German people and its culture and in the greatness and power of his own nation he saw an indisputable high 'value', though even until today it is considered extremely controversial whether for him this value was an absolute, highest value, or whether the personal liberty of the human individual and the political freedom of the citizen did not rank higher for him." [88]

On this last point, I can only refer again to the conversation which I had with Marianne Weber, whose answer to the question as to what course her husband would have pursued in the Third Reich was, "Jeder Mensch ist ein Geheimnis," ultimately every man is a secret. It has been established that Weber did entertain limited imperialistic aspirations. To him these seemed an inevitable consequence of the founding of the Reich. He likewise favored a strong navy to augment Germany's position as a colonial power. But his work on imperialism in *Wirtschaft und Gesellschaft (Economy and Society)* is a paragon of objective analysis marked by ascetic restraint in relation to his own ideals. It was typical of Max Weber to investigate mercilessly that which touched him most deeply and engaged him most passionately, applying to it the coldest objectivity in the process.[89] This is probably one of Max Weber's most impressive and enigmatic achievements as a political writer; it marks him as one of those lonely and intense writers whose experience seems to epitomize as it illuminates the problems of his time. In fact, his relevance may become greater in the next century, for his work inevitably reminds us how and where the journey of the twentieth century began.

Yet, according to J. P. Mayer a proper perspective on Weber's relevance for recent German political history also demands taking cognizance of Weber's "inability to see through his own prejudices, as his

acceptance of the power-state idea and his Russophobia prove." [90] Mayer
points to this fact as being "all the more surprising, if one considers
Weber's longing for objectivity. He despised, yes indeed he *hated* the
interference of one's own valuations . . . when scientific objectivity
alone was demanded." [91] Mayer implies that Weber's quest for freedom
from value judgment in the social sciences was made especially difficult
by the "overwhelming strength of his own passions." [92] Scholarly detachment conflicted with political commitment, despite his heroically honest
efforts at suppressing his own sentiments: "Since Weber predicated on
the one hand the irrational world of values and on the other the world
of rational instruments, the unitary substantive, rational universe of the
nineteenth century world was split asunder and the realm of the rational
was reduced to the stature of the mere instrumental and functional. This
notion harbored the dangerous implication that, in the last analysis,
what counted most was the development of the most efficient means for
the realization of ends, since there can be no rational choice of ends in
terms of their intrinsic value." [93] Wolfgang Mommsen's point that a
comprehensive view of Weber's intellectual attitudes is difficult to
establish is well supported by his hypothesis that Weber's thinking
". . . so apparently pragmatic and neutral in its value judgments, is
[actually] predicated on a definite historico-philosophical theory. . . ." [94]

A number of studies have created Max Weber's political philosophy
in its current context. Among the first and most relevant in English is
J. P. Mayer's *Max Weber in German Politics*, (1944, 2nd. ed., 1956). It
deals with Max Weber's role in practical politics which looks now like
a kind of watershed between one period—the exploration of Weber's
relationship with political science during his own time—and that of a
critical judgment of his political insights in the perspective of our own
time. Until very recently, however, analyses of Max Weber's scholarly
writings have been dominated by either a turning away from this aspect,
assigning to these writings a lesser significance, or else they have been
treated somewhat apologetically. The last ten years have seen a revival
of interest in a critical revaluation of Weber's tremendous intellectual
power and his insights into history and practical politics, initiated by
Wolfgang Mommsen's *Max Weber und die Deutsche Politik 1890–1920*
(1959). Mommsen's book has opened paths that are as yet followed only
timidly. This intricately detailed and structurally well-balanced account
has enjoyed rather wide acceptance in Germany, yet his position on the
relationship between Weber's political philosophy and German political
history since his time has been received with some disdain, if not
hostility, by American critics. Conversely, in this area too, members of
the academic profession in Germany and elsewhere in Europe have
exhibited a certain dualism in their treatment of Weber, distinguishing
between the eminence of his sociological research on the one hand,

and his political commentaries on the other. Such writings are exemplified by Raymond Aron's memorable address, recorded in the Heidelberg Symposium of the fifteenth convention of the German Sociological Society, *Max Weber und die Soziologie heute* (1965). Max Weber's devotion to political commentary would suggest that, were he alive today, he might declare that by neglecting this aspect of his work, we are rejecting the critical task of a comprehensive review and evaluation of the total man and his work.

Max Weber's main interests included the creation of conditioned ways of life, serving to insure circumstances conducive to the rise of "charismatic" leaders. To some extent, in his fear of bureaucratic suffocation and his struggle against traditional authority, Weber himself symbolizes the charismatic man. Christoph Steding asserts that Weber himself was bound up in a constant process of self-emancipation; in other words, he underwent a continuous process of reaccommodation in the face of particular political situations: "He is completely indifferent as to whether his conduct is judged against the background of the old 'Obrigkeitsstaat' (magisterial state) of the Kaiser, or that of the post-revolutionary 'Volksstaat' (people's state)." [95]

When Weber spoke of the solution implied in the "mystic flight from reality," he probably was referring to the followers of the Stefan George school whose primary interest was to find a faith by which to live. Weber had not intended to formulate any *"Weltanschauung."* He dreaded the prospect of a resulting stereotyped outlook on life. An ideological battle had ensued between disciples of the poet Stefan George and the older generation of academicians over the meaning assigned to history and literature. The issue under discussion went beyond a dispute concerned with the pragmatic view of history. It also transcended mere methodological differences. While the "old" group believed that history could be viewed objectively, the "young" took the view that not objectivity but inspiration derived from history was the goal. In their view history was to be viewed as a legend with a lesson or a moral to teach.

Weber's lecture on "Science as a Vocation" contained his argument against the principles and value system of the *George-Kreis.*[96] Erich von Kahler's rejoinder, though he did not represent the *George-Kreis* in every detail, formally contrasted Weber's views with those of the *Kreis.*[97] He describes the function of science as one of prescribing certain orientations, a view which has now been generally accepted. He differs from Weber's interpretation of science, which asserted that science did not and could not enable man to know all, to pass value judgments, or to set goals.

What man could accomplish through science was a formulation of general rules and the prediction of possible consequences ensuing from a given course of action. Science might also shed light upon the means to be employed for the realization of the goal, furnishing the technical "know how."

Weber stated that though science could supply man with abundant intellectual ammunition in the struggle for a better social and political order, it was not its task to judge the values inherent in the goal. That decision rested with one's religion or patriotism, which constitute attitudes based on emotion. Weber especially refused to be regarded as a prophet, although some writers have tried to attribute the gift of prophecy to him. Not only did he say that "politics is out of place in the lecture room," [98] he condemned professors who acted as prophets, Modern science was vocational in nature, composed of several subject-matter areas for the furtherance of explanation and the increase of pertinent knowledge.

It is not the gift of grace of seers and prophets dispensing sacred values and revelations, nor does it partake of the contemplation of sages and philosophers about the meaning of the universe. This, to be sure, is the inescapable condition of our historical situation. We cannot evade it so long as we remain true to ourselves.[99]

Weber would have found it difficult to submit to an adaptation of science to political expediency as practiced by the Nazis. He thoroughly opposed indoctrination, even of his own views; he did not wish to see them added to the labyrinth of already existing dogma:

What is hard for modern man, and especially for the younger generation, is to measure up to *workaday* existence. The ubiquitous chase for 'experience' stems from this weakness; for it is weakness not to be able to countenance the stern seriousness of our fateful times. . . . Those of our youth are in error who react to all this by saying, 'Yes, but we happen to come to lectures in order to experience something more than mere analyses and statements of fact.' The error is that they seek in the professor something different than what stands before them. They crave a leader and not a teacher. But we are placed upon the platform solely as teachers. And these are two different things, as one can readily see.[100]

The *George-Kreis* was interested in rules of conduct rather than in a specialized study of history. Both Weber and the *Kreis* regarded it as the duty of science to provide understanding and meaningful interpretation. Weber treated science as a separate unit, however, governed by laws of its own and applicable only to its own sphere. He also penetrated to the core of the crisis in which modern science finds itself by his criticism of those German youth "whose feelings are attuned to religion or who crave religious experiences," [101] and who supposed that "redemption from the rationalism and intellectualism of science is the fundamental presupposition of living in union with the divine." [102]

According to Weber, the meaning of science is determined by the fact that it had furnished both the justification and impetus for the process of "disenchantment of the universe" that has uniquely dominated Western civilization.

Scientific progress is a fraction, the most important fraction, of the process of intellectualization which we have been undergoing for thousands of years and which nowadays is usually judged in such an extremely negative way.[103]

Weber held that life as an entity and a vessel of values was outside science's jurisdiction; intellectualization meant solely the procurement of technical means and the calculation of actions. He unreservedly rejected "the modern intellectualist form of romantic irrationalism." [104] To the youth contending that "the intellectual constructions of science constitute an unreal realm of artificial abstractions, which their bony hands seek to grasp the blood-and-the-sap of life without ever catching up with it," [105] Weber replied that the two important instruments of scientific knowledge were the concept of the "abstract" as realized significantly for the first time by Socrates, and "the rational experiment," the means of "reliably controlling experience" without which modern empirical science would be unthinkable.[106]

Weber's conviction was sardonically expressed in his reference to those who were not prepared to face up to present-day demands "like a man." To them Weber extended the invitation to

. . . return silently, without the usual publicity build-up of renegades, but simply and plainly. The arms of the old churches are opened widely and compassionately for him. After all they do not make it hard for him. One way or another he has to bring his "intellectual sacrifice" — ' — that is inevitable. . . . In my eyes, such religious return stands higher than the academic prophecy, which does not clearly realize that in the lecture-rooms of the university no other virtue holds but plain intellectual integrity. . . . We want to draw the lesson that nothing is gained by yearning and tarrying . . . [for new prophets and saviors]. We shall set to work and meet the "demands of the day," in human relations as well as in our vocation. This, however, is plain and simple. . . .[107]

Here we find one of Weber's fundamental themes running through the practical aspects of his philosophy: "each finds and obeys the demon who holds the fibers of his very life." [108]

Mettler has inquired into Weber's conception of the "practical." Apart from the obvious aspects of science, Weber understood the "practical" to connote all that falls under the heading of human interaction, which would include moral and political action. This leads Mettler to ask what remains after one has recognized the disharmony of faith and science. He does not see that the "faith problem" should have been solved by the fact that the sphere of "science" was confronted by Weber with an irrational sphere. Objecting, Mettler states that faith has to be considered on an entirely different basis from that on which scientific theory rests; yet, in his opinion, it is not admissible to permit the individual to find and obey the demon of his own life.

Mettler also points out that in politics Weber could not carry his pluralist stand through consistently. Weber's separation of theory and practice is in grave danger even when formulated clearly:

Although scientific theory remains unaffected by the demands of the market, political practice has been left to its own devices (as a field within its own rights) and lacks leadership from above. The "demon" to which Weber refers so often is least of all qualified to replace a political ethic; for it cannot cope with excesses. In politics it does not operate with a clear view; instead, it imports the well-known and unavoidable back and forth of demonisms from left to right. "Practice" thus conceived allows the persistence of primitive political attitudes to exist side by side with differentiated ethical attitudes; if the political attitude is not primitive to start with, the danger exists that it might develop in that direction.[109]

Sell brings up the question how it was possible for one as broad-minded as Max Weber to adhere to such a "rigorous and one-sided view, which particularly in the United States, may be disputed after the educational experiences of the last few years."[110] He answers by saying that Weber must have realized how "once the doors were opened to unlimited subjectivity," knowledge and teaching would fall victim to political radicalism:

This would not only imperil civilization, but also violate a principle which was sacred to him: the idea of truth. In analyzing the complex personality of Max Weber, we find that truth and the search for truth were the harbor to which he retreated from the conflicts of life. He had, however, to prove to a sceptical world that objective truth could be found and that absolute standards of cognition could be acquired.[111]

This Max Weber tried to do particularly in his comparative study of religions. He ascertained that there existed great differences in the types of social structure, motives, and leadership applicable to various areas of human life, especially in the fields of politics and economics. Since each set of historical data had a uniqueness of its own, the social scientist was in no position to discover concepts valid for all occurrences. These certain concepts which Weber called "ideal types" [112] can only be obtained by ruthlessly simplifying the complexity of historical data; thus behavior may be studied in terms of the degree to which it approaches to or deviates from this ideal type, despite the danger that this may result in exaggerating social uniformities. Nevertheless, the value of Weber's method of ideal constructs and of his method of causal explanation as well, was proved by the fact that he employed them in the course of his own investigations, thus giving a practical demonstration of their utility.

Since Weber purposely failed to give young people an outline of how they should conduct their lives, they could not "follow" his example. Stefan George, to whom a sizeable portion of the German youth movements looked as their spiritual leader, strove toward the transfer of responsibility to a "chief," thereby freeing his followers from accountability. Weber, however, maintained that the competence of a "Fuehrer" could not do away with the responsibility of each person for the consequences of the task he assumed. Weber defended the postulate of the moral autonomy of the individual; man's very spiritual existence is based on this premise. If man claimed moral autonomy, it followed that he would have to take the full share of responsibility for the tasks he set himself. This was a duty as fundamental as the right of self-determination and its logical corollary. [113]

George's mission as founder of *Bund und Staat* had proved utopian largely because he sought to create his Reich without regard for the realities of life and the complexities involved. His new abstract order ignored all cultural and biological factors which condition the human race. These he endeavored to conquer through the ties which the *Bund* was to provide. His own objectives became crystallized in a discussion with Max Weber in which George rejected for himself and his circle social and economic factors as fundamental facts upon which the life of the citizen, in society in general and the state in particular, is based. Weber referred to this fact especially in *Wirtschaft und Gesellschaft* when he conceded that artistic, charismatic youths are often inclined to accept a *Weltanschauung* which underemphasizes the facts of economic conflict. This was also a rather widespread phenomenon among *rentiers*. An illustration of Weber's thesis is the so-called *Geist*-books, a scientific series of publications of the *Kreis* in which Wolters, Gundolf, Friedemann, Vallentin, Kantorowicz, Bertram, and Hildebrand, under George's sponsorship, attempt to interpret history as legend and heroic deed engaged in by individuals whose excellence forms the historical process of becoming. Franz Schonauer considers the *Kreis* members successors to Plutarch and descendants of Carlyle who on their part anticipate the new Reich's return to the golden age of heroism. [114]

Kahler had occupied himself not with the problematic nature of science as a calling but with an inquiry into its meaning and *élan vital*. He analyzed correctly the essential features of Weber's conception of science as consisting in the freedom and value of science and in its ethical neutrality, which failed to orient itself toward any particular goal outside its own sphere. He further recognized Weber's methodological presuppositions, including: (a) causal analysis as over against Ranke's conception of history as a mere record of *"wie es eigentlich gewesen ist"*; (b) the analytical device of heuristic rationalism which aids the social scientist in ascribing with greater accuracy causation in the historical process to such irrational factors as the role of charisma; and (c) the ideal-type as an abstract concept.[115]

In stating the position of the *George-Kreis*, Kahler opposed Weber's evaluation of science with the pragmatic outlook:

. . . we are asking as follows: this is our life. It demands the satisfaction of some noble requirements. Is that which is called science qualified to meet these needs, and if so, to what degree? On the answer depends the justification of its existence or at least the meaning which it holds for us.[116]

Weber had also asked whether science was entitled to pronounce judgment upon the political *Weltanschauung*. He denied it by his separation of the academic sphere from that of practical political leadership. Thus Weber's "science as a calling" did not share the *Kreis'* conception which assigned to science the task of prescribing directives. The only certainties the *Kreis* knew were "life" and its law of becoming. In other words, it believed in a definite basic philosophy of life which would make it possible to construct a scale of values as well as permit the solution of the value problems inherent in science.[117] Knowledge and understanding were accordingly bound up with a cosmic and at the same time subjective *Gestalt* law. In it the meaning of science finds its realization.[118] This fundamental bond which the *Kreis* saw between science and the *Gestalt* idea makes it apparent that the former depended for its very existence upon the latter.

George himself lived withdrawn from the public and the contemporary literary scene. His friends thought of themselves as a new élite whose influence was entitled to reach into all areas of human life. George, in his *Der Stern des Bundes* (1914), and *Das Neue Reich* (1928), gave his followers instruction, hope, dogma, and rites of pagan character. Personally out of touch with reality, he took no notice of social and political tensions. Human relations interested him only in regard to the requirements of his "élite." The politically thickening atmosphere of the postwar era caused him to propagate his ideals of aristocratic selection and rebirth with even greater conviction.

George's ideology took the shape of a mystical nationalism. He saw in himself the leader (Fuehrer) and in his élite the young leaders. They were to become masters of the world, setting an example to the people, yet without the obligation to consider the individual needs of those who were outside the circle of the elect. In George's terminology *"Volkheit"* represents past, present, and future generations compressed into an ideal unit made up of the most excellent of national traditions and achievements.

It is not altogether surprising that a Nazi writer should have written as follows:

The central problem was: On which general spiritual and value-judging foundations of science, from the standpoint of Weltanschauung, did the *Kreis* stand? The more this conception of science, with its foundations and goals, approximates our own, the more decisive is for us a further examination of its foundations and value concepts in relation to their validity of limitations. . . . Any spiritual reconstruction must, in view of the most extreme of George's conclusions, press toward uncompromising decisions in our day.[119]

At first the Nazis sought to spread George's ideas among the educated classes by means of their propaganda techniques. George initially had some illusions about them which, however, soon vanished. Shocked by the events in Germany in 1933, he was not tempted by Nazi offers but went to Switzerland instead, where he died soon afterwards.

In spite of the gulf separating Weber from George and his circle, Weber's personal courage and intellectual integrity won him the admiration and respect of the younger generation and the friendship of Stefan George. Weber's opposition to romantic myths in practical affairs was reflected at the previously mentioned meeting of the Congress of Culture at the Thuringian Castle of Lauenstein in 1916. Among the participants had been scholars, social reformers, political writers, artists, and representatives of various other professions. Prominent figures included the pan-German and social reformer Max Maurenbrecher; a large number of professors attended, including Friedrich Meinecke, Werner Sombart, and Ferdinand Toennies; among the literary representatives were Richard Dehmel, Walter von Molo, Karl Broeger, and Ernst Toller. This occasion gave proof, as others had done before and were to do afterwards, of the current trend of intellectual remoteness from the stark reality of the trenches. Young veterans like Ernst Toller looked askance at their nebulous phrases, the dominant feature of which was an aggregation of utopian state-romanticism. Some of the ideas expressed called for the founding of a German religion, others sought salvation in the supposed existence of a specifically German spirit. Again, others wished for the birth of a new German state symbolizing the realization of the absolute on earth.[120]

Denouncing all such mystical phrases, Weber repeated his demands for realistic parliamentary reform. While he distinguished himself from many of his colleagues by coming forward with a definite program which brought him the respect of the younger generation, he failed again to win the country's youth to his position, for instead of mere governmental reform, many among them wished to see the emergence of a new social order.[121] Since, however, Weber's ultimate norm was still the German state, his plans aimed merely at technical changes in forms of government and bureaucracy, not at the profound changes in the social system which some of the German youth demanded.[122] As Reinhard Bendix writes:

In stating his case Weber deliberately rejected the idea that youth could find leadership and authentic experience in the universities.

Leadership cannot be found in the academy, and those academicians who want to assume this role should engage in it where they can be challenged politically. Nor can the university teacher provide experience in the sense the churches offer it to the believer. Let those who search for authenticity learn that the individual who simply fulfills the exacting demands of the day, if he has found himself, expresses the creative spark that is within him. Weber addressed these remarks to a generation which rejected his skeptical commitment to the Enlightenment tradition. The young men of the 1920's, like their age-mates in the years before World War I and today, demanded experience and action rather than words. Their drive had culminated in the enthusiasm with which they greeted the outbreak of war in 1914, and with which they were joining extremist movements of the Right or Left in 1918 to 1920.[123]

NOTES

[1] Reinhard Bendix, Max Weber: An Intellectual Portrait (New York: Doubleday & Company, Inc., 1960), p. 432.
[2] Wolfgang J. Mommsen, Max Weber und die Deutsche Politik 1890–1920 (Tuebingen: J. C. B. Mohr [Paul Siebeck], 1959), p. 1.
[3] Theodor Heuss, "Max Weber in Seiner Gegenwart," in P.S., 2nd. ed., cited in Bernhard Zeller and Eberhard Pikart, eds., Theodor Heuss: Der Mann, das Werk, die Zeit: Eine Ausstellung (Tuebingen: Rainer Wunderlich Verlag; und Munich: Koesel Verlag, 1967) (Theodor Heuss Archiv—Stuttgart), 1967, p. 386. In his introduction to Weber's Politische Schriften, Heuss vividly describes his meetings with Max Weber.
[4] Bernhard Zeller and Eberhard Pikart, eds., op. cit., p. 386. For a very interesting and entertaining account of the groupings and private circles around Heidelberg University professors see Erich Rothacker, Heitere Erinnerungen (Frankfurt: Athenaeum Verlag, 1963), especially p. 60f.
[5] Herbert Tingsten, Political Behavior: Studies in Election Statistics (Totowa, N.J.: The Bedminster Press, 1963), p. 136.
[6] Max Weber, Gesammelte Politische Schriften (Munich: Drei Masken Verlag, 1921), p. 389. See also Mommsen, op. cit., pp. 387–396.

[7] Mommsen, *op. cit.*, p. 397.

[8] *Ibid.*

[9] *Ibid.*, p. 400.

[10] *Ibid.*, pp. 400–401.

[11] *Ibid.*, p. 410.

[12] *Ibid.*

[13] *Ibid.*

[14] *Ibid.*

[15] *Ibid.*

[16] Artur Mettler, *Max Weber und die Philosophische Problematik in Unserer Zeit* (Leipzig: S. Hirzel, 1934), p. 93.

[17] Marcel Weinreich, *Max Weber: L'Homme et le Savant:* (Etude sur ses Idées Directrices, Paris: Les Presses Modernes, 1938), pp. 30–32.

[18] It should be remembered that party discipline and party organization were much stricter in Germany than in most West European countries. Party programs were of a more binding character on the individual members and the national organization, parliamentary deputies, and the cabinet members. Thus it may be said that political individualism did not play so great a role in Germany as in most other democracies. Outstanding political personalities were not numerous in Germany anyway, and the few that existed found it very difficult to assert themselves against the party machine. Cf. Fritz Morstein-Marx (ed.), *Foreign Governments. The Dynamics of Politics Abroad* (New York: Prentice Hall, Inc., 1949), especially Chapt. xvi, "German Empire and the Weimar Republic," by John Mason Brown, p. 326.

[19] *Lebensbild*, p. 643.

[20] *Ibid.*, pp. 643–44.

[21] Colored ribbons and special clothes were worn in German student fraternities to signify membership.

[22] *Lebensbild*, p. 644.

[23] Max Weber, *op. cit.*, p. 129.

[24] *Lebensbild*, pp. 673–74.

[25] Alexander von Schelting, *Max Webers Wissenschaftslehre: Das Logische Problem der historischen Kulturerkenntnis. Die Grenzen der Soziologie des Wissens* (Tuebingen: J. C. B. Mohr [P. Siebeck], 1934), pp. 343–52.

[26] Karl Jaspers, "Max Weber as Politician, Scientist, Philosopher," *op. cit.*, p. 227. For a detailed discussion of Weber's political contributions, see Jaspers' entire section on Weber "The Politician," *ibid.*, pp. 196–229.

[27] *Ibid.*, pp. 227–228.

[28] Max Weber, *Essays in Sociology*, translated and edited by Hans H. Gerth and C. Wright Mills (New York: Oxford University Press, 1946), p. 43. Weber's position was analogous to that of Niemoeller, who criticized some of the Nazi measures (especially those with regard to the position of the Church), and who was therefore interned. Yet when war was declared he was ready to forgive and forget and volunteered as a submarine commander.

[29] Cf. Max Weber, *Politische Schriften*, p. 377.

[30] Max Weber, *Gesammelte Aufsaetze auf Soziologie und Sozialpolitik* (Tuebingen: J. C. B. Mohr [P. Siebeck], 1924), pp. 409ff.; in (trans.) J. P. Mayer et al., *Political Thought, The European Tradition* (London: J. M. Dent & Sons, Ltd., 1939), p. 321. Reprinted by permission of Faber and Faber Ltd.

[31] Toller was accused of high treason and brought to trial before a Munich "Standgericht." See *Lebensbild*, p. 673, for reference to the part played by Max Weber in this trial.

[32] Thomas Mann, "Gedanken im Kriege," *Die Neue Rundschau*, XXV, 1914, p. 1484.

[33] Cited by William Ebenstein, *The German Record, A Political Portrait* (New York: Farrar & Rinehart, 1945), p. 39.

[34] Thomas Mann, *Betrachtungen eines Unpolitischen* (Berlin: S. Fischer, 1929), especially p. 16.

[35] Thomas Mann, *The Coming Victory of Democracy* (New York: A. A. Knopf, 1938), p. 65. Mann was in his forties in World War I, when he might have been expected to have reached maturity.

[36] Thomas Mann, "Letter to Germany," *Prevent World War II* (New York: Society for the Prevention of World War II, 1945), p. 26. In the first three years of the Nazi regime Mann's books were still printed and sold in Germany, including the first two volumes of the Joseph tetralogy. For further reference, cf. Ebenstein, *op. cit.*, p. 44. Cf. also Hermann Hesse—Thomas Mann:

"Briefwechsel," edited by Anni Carlsson (Frankfurt Suhr Kamp Verlag/s. Fischer Verlag, 1968).

37 Thomas Mann, "Letter to Germany," *op. cit.*, p. 26.

38 Bernhard Zeller and Eberhard Pikart, *op. cit.*, letter of Emil Preatorius, April 9, 1958, p. 387.

39 Karl Jaspers, "Max Weber as Politician, Scientist, Philosopher," *op. cit.*, p. 229.

40 *Ibid.*

41 *Ibid.*

42 *Ibid.*, p. 190.

43 *Ibid.*

44 Cf. Lucian W. Pye and Sidney Verba, eds., *Political Culture and Political Development Studies in Political Development* (Princeton: Princeton University Press, 1965).

45 Cf. Jaspers, *op. cit.*, pp. 190–191.

46 Max Weber, "Zur Lage der Buergerlichen Demokratie in Russland," *Archiv fuer Sozialwissenschaft und Sozialpolitik*, XXII, 347ff. In (Also translated) by J. P. Mayer, *Political Thought The European Tradition*, pp. 322–23.

47 Mommsen, *op. cit.*, p. 211.

48 *Hermann Hesse—Thomas Mann,* "Briefwechsel," ed. and trans. by Anni Carlsson; Suhrkamp Verlag/S. (Frankfurt: Fischer Verlag, 1968), letter of February 20, 1931, p. 12.

49 *Ibid.*, letter written December 1931, pp. 16–17.

50 *Ibid.*, p. 18.

51 Mommsen, *op. cit.*, p. 412.

52 *Ibid.*

53 *Ibid.*, pp. 412–413.

54 *P.S.*, 2nd. ed., p. 429.

55 Ernest K. Bramsted, *Aristocracy and the Middle–Classes in Germany: Social Types in German Literature 1830–1900* (Chicago: University of Chicago Press, 1967), p. 239. Cf. also Max Weber, "Wahlrecht und Demokratie in Deutschland," *P.S.*, 2nd. ed., pp. 34–40.

56 W. Mommsen, "Max Weber's Political Sociology and His Philosophy of World History," *International Social Science Review*, Vol. XVII, No. 1, 1965, pp. 41–42. Reprinted by permission of the publisher.

57 W. M. Simon, "Power and Responsibility: Otto Hintze's Place in German Historiography," in Leonard Krieger and Fritz Stern, eds., *The Responsibility of Power: Historical Essays in Honor of Hajo Holborn* (Garden City: Doubleday, 1969), p. 232.

58 Benjamin Nelson, "A Reply," *The New York Times Book Review*, February 28, 1965, Section 7, pp. 34–36. c 1965 by The New York Times Company. Reprinted by permission. Also by permission of the author.

59 Herbert Marcuse, "Comment," *The New York Times Book Review*, February 28, 1965, Section 7, pp. 34–36. c 1965 by The New York Times Company. Reprinted by permission. Also by permission of the author.

60 *Ibid.*

61 Benjamin Nelson, *op. cit.*, 34–36.

62 Max Weber, *Wirtschaft und Gesellschaft*, Part III of *Grundriss der Sozialoekonomik*, 2 Vols., 2nd. ed. (Tuebingen: J. C. B. Mohr [P. Siebeck], 1925), p. 683.

63 Mommsen, *op. cit.*, pp. 182–183.

64 Weber's letter to Adolf von Harnack, letter of February 5, 1906, cited in Mommsen, *op. cit.*, p. 183.

65 Mommsen, *op. cit.*, p. 183.

66 James K. Pollock, "Foreign Government and Politics: The Role of the Public in a New Germany," *The American Political Science Review*, Vol. XXXIX, No. 3, 1945, p. 467.

67 Rodney P. Stiefbold, "The Significance of Void Ballots in West German Elections," *The American Political Science Review*, Vol. LIX, No. 2, 1965, p. 406.

68 Cf. *ibid.*, p. 404. Also J. Habermas, et al., *Student und Politik: Eine Soziologische Untersuchung zum Politischen Bewusstsein Frankfurter Studenten* (Neuwied: Hermann Luchterhand Verlag, 1961), partly summarized by Kurt Tauber in "Nationalism and Social Restoration in Post-War Germany," *Political Science Quarterly*, Vol. 78, March 1963, pp. 83–85.

69 Hans Paul Bahrdt, "Gelehrte Muessen Sich Verstaendlich Machen: Wo Spezialisten ihre eigene Sprache haben versagt die Demokratie" (Scientists Must Make Themselves Understood: Democracy Fails Where Specialists Develop Their

Own Language) *Die Zeit: Wochenzeitung fuer Politik, Wirtschaft, Handel und Kultur* (No. 11, March 13, 1964, editorial).

70 Mommsen, "Max Weber's political sociology and his philosophy of world history," pp. 40–41.

71 *Ibid.*

72 Editorial, *ibid.*, p. 7. Cf. also Reinhard Bendix, "Max Weber's Sociology Today," *ibid.*, pp. 9–22; Wolfgang Mommsen, "Max Weber's Political Sociology and his Philosophy of World History," *ibid.*, pp. 23–45; Talcott Parsons, "Evaluation and Objectivity in Social Science: An Interpretation of Max Weber's Contribution," *ibid.*, pp. 46–63; and Pietro Rossi, "Scientific Objectivity and Value Hypotheses," *ibid.*, pp. 64–70.

73 Reinhard Bendix, "Max Weber's Sociology Today," *op. cit.*, p. 7.

74 See Leo Strauss, *Natural Right and History* (Chicago: University of Chicago Press), p. 2.

75 Norman Macrae, "The German Lesson: In Search of the Stone," *The Economist,* Vol. CCXXI, No. 6425, October 15, 1966, pp. iv, vii.

76 Mommsen, "Max Weber's Political Sociology and his Philosophy of World History," *op. cit.*, p. 41.

77 *Ibid.*

78 Cited in Mommsen, *ibid.*, cf. *Wirtschaft und Gesellschaft*, pp. 361 et seq.

79 See Mommsen, *op. cit.*, p. 41. In support of his own statement Mommsen cites *Wissenschaftslehre*, p. 501.

80 Cited in Mommsen, *op. cit.*, p. 41. Cf. for an indirect justification of this see *Wissenschaftslehre*, p. 501.

81 See Ernst Nolte, "Max Weber vor dem Faschismus," *Der Staat* (2, 1963); also Ernst Topitsch, "Max Weber und die Soziologie heute," Otto Stammer, ed., *Max Weber und die Soziologie heute* (Verhandlungen, 1965), pp. 19–38.

82 Mommsen, "Max Weber's Political Sociology and his Philosophy of World History," *op. cit.*, p. 42.

83 Carl J. Friedrich, "Authority, Reason, and Discretion," in Carl J. Friedrich, ed., *Authority* (Cambridge, Mass.: Harvard University Press, 1958), p. 32, fn., cf. *Politische Schriften*, p. 124.

84 Mommsen, "Max Weber's Political Sociology and his Philosophy of World History," *op. cit.*, p. 42.

85 Cf. Paul Sethe, *Deutsche Geschichte im Letzten Jahrhundert* (Frankfurt/Main: Verlag Heinrich Scheffler, 1960), p. 187.

86 Cf. Helga Grebing, *Geschichte der Deutschen Parteien* (Wiesbaden: Franz Steiner Verlag, 1962), pp. 34–35.

87 Guenter Abramowski, *Das Geschichtsbild Max Webers: Universalgeschichte am Leitfaden des okzidentalen Rationalisierungsprozesses*, Kieler Historische Studien, edited by Horst Braunert et al., Vol. 1 (Stuttgart: Ernst Klett Verlag, 1966), p. 180.

88 *Ibid.*, pp. 180–181.

89 *Ibid.*, p. 281.

90 J. P. Mayer, *op. cit.*, p. 27.

91 *Ibid.*

92 *Ibid.*

93 William J. Bossenbrook, *The German Mind* (Detroit: Wayne State University Press, 1961), p. 388.

94 Mommsen, "Max Weber's Political Sociology and his Philosophy of World History," *op. cit.*, p. 25.

95 Christoph Steding, *Politik und Wissenschaft bei Max Weber* (Marburg, 1932), p. 16.

96 Max Weber, "Wissenschaft als Beruf," *Gesammelte Aufsaetze zur Wissenschaftslehre*, originally an address delivered at Munich University in 1918, translated by Hans H. Gerth (New York: Oxford University Press, 1946), pp. 129–56.

97 Cf. Erich von Kahler, *Der Beruf der Wissenschaft* (Berlin 1920), particularly p. 5.

98 Gerth and Mills, *From Max Weber: Essays in Sociology* (New York: Oxford University Press, 1946), p. 145.

99 *Ibid.*, p. 152.

100 *Ibid.*, p. 149. Cf. also Lowell L. Bennion *Max Weber's Methodology*, Dissertation, University of Strasbourg (Paris: Les Presses Modernes, 1933), pp. 47–48.

101 Gerth and Mills, *op. cit.*, p. 143.

102 *Ibid.*, p. 142.

103 *Ibid.*, pp. 138–139.
104 *Ibid.*, p. 143.
105 *Ibid.*, pp. 140–141.
106 Cf. *ibid.*, p. 141.
107 *Ibid.*, pp. 155–56.
108 *Ibid.*, p. 156.
109 Artur Mettler, *Max Weber und die Philosophische Problematik in Unserer Zeit* (Leipzig: S. Hirzel, 1934), pp. 91–92.
110 Friedrich Carl Sell, "Intellectual Liberalism in Germany About 1900," *Journal of Modern History*, XV (1943), 227.
111 *Ibid.*, p. 227.
112 Cf. Max Weber, *Gesammelte Aufsaetze zur Wissenschaftslehre* (Tuebingen: J. C. B. Mohr [P. Siebeck], 1922), p. 270. "Ideal types serve to establish 'historical causality' which is concerned with the imputation of concrete effects to concrete causes and not with the ascertainment of abstract laws."
113 Weinreich, *op. cit.*, pp. 36–37.
114 Franz Schonauer, *Stefan George in Selbstzeugnissen und Bilddokumenten* (Reinbeck bei Hamburg: Rowohlt Taschenbuch Verlag, GmbH., 1964), pp. 152–153. Cf. also the chapter on "Max Weber's prognosis of plebiscitarian mass democracy and Caesarism" in relation to the various types of leadership distinctions in Karl Loewenstein, *Max Weber's staatspolitische Auffassungen in der Sicht unserer Zeit* (Frankfurt am Main und Bonn: Athenaeum Verlag, 1965), pp. 65–74.
115 Kahler, *op. cit.*, p. 22.
116 *Ibid.*, p. 10.
117 *Ibid.*, p. 32.
118 Cf. *Ibid.*, pp. 41, 61.
119 Hans Roessner, *Georgekreis und Literaturwissenschaft: Zur Wuerdigung und Kritik der geistigen Bewegung Stefan Georges* (Frankfurt: Moritz Diesterweg, 1938), p. 115.
120 Ernst Toller, *Eine Jugend in Deutschland* (Amsterdam: Querido Verlag N.V., 1935), pp. 84–85.
121 Fritz Droop, *Ernst Toller und seine Buehnenwerke* (Berlin: Franz Schneider, 1922), pp. 8–9.
        The relationship of Weber to the younger generation, notably the followers of Stefan George, has been subjected to examination by Albert Salomon, "Max Weber's Political Ideas," *Social Research*, II, No. 2, 1935, especially p. 282.
        ". . . he (Weber) had much in common with the poet Stefan George in his criticism of the age. The cult of personality, negative self-reflection, uprooted thought without foundation, which destroys the deepest basis of human existence and runs its course in a vacuum—all these phenomena seemed also to Weber symptoms of disease and elements of spiritual and psychic decomposition. But he could not see any genuine salvation in the 'Maximin cult' of the poet now in the religious veneration accorded to George by his pupils.
        "To him as to his Puritans, every attempt to deify the earthly straying man was 'idolatry' and a cowardly flight from individual responsibility in favor of absolutist authority. For his stern and heroic attitude such a personal surrender of freedom and individual will for inner decision seemed a flight from the terrifying aspect of life. He always affirmed a personal attachment to a charismatic leadership, but this was never to bring about a *sacrificium intellectus*. Therefore to Weber the harshness and severity of George's curse upon the entire age seemed merciless and unjust, quite apart from his criticism of George's romantic misunderstanding of both history and reality."
122 Cf. Fritz Fischer, *Germany's Aims in the First World War* (New York: W. W. Norton, 1967), p. 330.
123 Reinhard Bendix. "Sociology and the Distrust of Reason." *American Sociological Review*, October 1970, Vol. 35, No. 5, p. 835.

XI

Max Weber:
The Tragic Ambivalence

In his evaluation of Weber's contributions to contemporary political science in Germany, Hans Maier suggests that, essentially, apart from the enormously stimulating effect of his scholarly works, his political influence did not transcend the period of the Weimar Republic. World War II and its aftermath had caused traditional concepts such as the national state and power-political considerations to lose the sharpness of their outline, at least on the surface. Hence Weber's monumental work, while towering over the accomplishments of most political writers, still bears the stamp of a bygone age.

Many observers have noted that Weber never laid claim to the prestige of science insofar as his own political views were concerned. Even though his views were formulated with all the precision at his command and supported by his immense fund of knowledge, he himself considered his political writings strictly separate from his scientific work. Because Max Weber developed his own normative approach in his political writings, they can stand alone without laying claim to a systematic theory of politics. Notable exceptions may be found in his earlier works, particularly in his inaugural address delivered at Freiburg[1] in which he tried to coordinate his scientific and political aspirations. Even here, as Maier indicates, a closer examination points up some discrepancies apparent in his later work. An example is Weber's discussion of agrarian conditions in West Prussia which focuses on the role played by the physical and psychological differences among discreet nationality groups in their economic struggle for existence.[2] In later writings his ultimate value, the national power state, appeared "no longer as rational and scientific, but rather as an irrevocably determining, although not comprehensible factor, reaching in from the outside—the sphere of demonic fate—into the bright world of scientific analysis."[3]

Maier sees a pervasive dualism: on the one hand, an extreme and sustained subjectivization still rejecting any claim to science. On the other, there is constantly in evidence a passionate undertone, a volcanic emotion in his treatment of German affairs, which culminates in a strong drive to communicate his own ideas, to stimulate activity, and above all, an often quixotic, intractable national political pedagogy. The ethos which Weber had banished from rational "disenchanting" science thus returns in the form of that very "Kathederprophetie" which Weber had so emphatically rejected.[4]

Maier characterizes Weber's political orientation as a *"compositum mixtum"* reflecting the *Weltanschauungen* of his own time. Following Raymond Aron,[5] he finds Weber's political philosophy resting essentially on the Darwinian component underlying man's struggle for existence. Visible too is the Nietzschean component, especially in Weber's social politics, according to which emphasis is not placed upon the intrinsic value of the welfare of the people, nor upon the assistance the state can render through its service, nor even upon the happiness of the individual; what matters is the quality of the human being. Moreover, there is the economic component, namely, the scarcity of goods, the resultant conditions of poverty and the allied Marxist conception of the class struggle, in which even the interests of the ruling classes cannot always be expected to be compatible with those of the national interest. Finally, there is the national component, which stresses the community interest, to which all others must be subordinated.

In the years between 1917–1919, when Weber hoped to build a new political science on sociological foundations, in Maier's opinion, his efforts miscarried. Since he insisted upon freedom from value judgments, he capitulated, as Maier put it, before scientism, which had depoliticized the individual political disciplines and descientized politics. His conception of politics as a struggle for power, his scepticism toward the possibility that the politically appropriate act might also qualify as ethically right, was typical of that "ambivalent political ideational formation" which has characterized German political thinking since the foundation of the Reich. Finally, Maier insists, the separation of science from political conviction, the position which Weber consistently stressed as an obligation to which the pursuit of science bound him, deprived Weber's research of much of its educational influence.[6]

Weber's power-politics point of view is no longer as strongly represented in political science in Germany today. While the present generation of students admires Weber's achievements, for them he has nevertheless taken his place in history; certain aspects of his political significance are viewed as dated, a fact even more apparent when seen in the latest contemporary perspective. This change of perspective was brought about primarily by the events of the Nazi period. "It is no accident that experiences under totalitarianism pointed up the limitations of the Weberian work especially poignantly. Hence his unconditional pluralism and relativism, his pessimistic conception of the eternal struggle of values strikes us as an expression of weakness in view of the ideological threat confronting us in our time." [7]

Arnold Bergstraesser stresses that Weber personally would have resisted the political direction and means characterizing a totalitarian state, "whose advent was a reaction he had feared. But we find in his sociology of the state no norm-supplying support against the dehumanization of the political realm which we have experienced and still experience." [8] Yet, it is also true that the image of Max Weber is not merely a memory upon which we reflect as one does upon an antiquated relic. He stands out as a great teacher whose soberness inspires unsentimental, disillusioned observations of reality; a thinker of supreme intellectual integrity; a foe of phrases and false pathos. Future generations may well overlook any mistakes and time-boundness of Max Weber's political theory, and look instead to his human qualities. "For it is here where the lasting effect of his being lies: Purity and strength, a sense of responsibility which answers for that which has been recognized as correct, and finally the unconditional devotion to truth and knowledge, from which the university still derives its meaning today as a community of those who teach and those who study." [9]

To the younger generation Weber bequeathed three maxims: First, to bore through hard boards; anybody can drill through thin ones. Secondly, to fulfill the commonplace duties of workaday life; interesting and exciting tasks are easier to perform, but the neverending chores to which all are subject are the hardest to do. Thirdly, to be able to keep silent. As Loewenstein points out, the latter task seemed to give Weber himself the greatest difficulty: "During the eight years in which I knew him, he was constantly involved in scientific or political feuds which he carried on with unmerciful hardness and during which he frequently overstepped his bounds." [10] In focusing on Weber's patriotism and his continued allegiance to the idea of the power state, Loewenstein inquires:

What else could he be?! Today he is being reproached that he subscribed to the *Machtstaat*. He did subscribe to the *Machtstaat*. No other choice existed for him at that time. Neither in Germany nor elsewhere in Europe was there any incidence of noble pacifists or internationalists during the period from 1914 until the end of the war. He had to subscribe to the idea of the *Machtstaat* because he believed that the German people and the German culture were worthy of being protected against the onrushing Slavic flood. He wanted to provide an opportunity for the German cultural mission in the world. His feeling for the *Machtstaat* was not reserved for any one privileged class. He hated the satiated bourgeoisie. He hated the Junkers, and

he had very little understanding for the embourgeoisement and bureaucratization of the proletarian leaders. But Germany as a whole constituted a value
for him. Whoever charges him today with having been a disciple of the
Machtstaat, that he was, as it were, a precursor of the horror of yesterday,
misinterprets him completely.[11]

Contrary to some of Weber's more critical admirers, Loewenstein
fails to suggest any alternatives which Weber might have found open
to him or which he himself might have opened up. Nor does he see
any reason for being skeptical of some of the criteria by which Weber
was guided.

No discussion of Weber's astuteness, however, would be complete
without reference to the question, What would have become of Germany
if Weber had attained the position of leadership for which his political
acumen seemed to qualify him? Sharing at one time the conviction of
some of Weber's friends and collaborators that his exclusion from the
political scene was "the greatest misfortune that could have befallen
Germany," [12] in retrospect Loewenstein now sees this fact in a different
light. While admitting that Weber's human stature and political wisdom
would have entitled him to ranking among the great, he would nevertheless "have made only enemies." [13] Weber had a talent for creating
and becoming a focus of controversy; not even his friends would claim
that his judgment was always equal to his ingenuity, nor that it was
certain that time would always uphold it. Loewenstein's conclusion that
Weber would not have been able in any way to stem the tragic tide
of events under the Weimar regime is surely justified.

Following Germany's defeat in 1918, Max Weber's aim had been
to point the way to potential factors which might release the Germans
from their "arrogant eccentricities" and set the nation on a more progressive political course.[14] What Weber was unable to anticipate, and
what only hindsight enables us to appreciate, as Loewenstein states, is
the fact that World War I in reality represented essentially an overture
to world revolution. At present we find ourselves exposed to it; indeed,
we are experiencing its full impact without being able to anticipate its
outcome. What this world revolution means for us is "the devaluation
of parliament as the articulation of the people's will; the ascendancy
of a strong executive at the expense of parliament; the increase and
spreading of naked despotism whether in civilian or military disguise;
the total political party and the total state; the gigantic influence of
the mass media as a means to dominate the formation of public opinion
and where the welfare state itself has not been established, at the very
minimum the extension into everyday life of state control resembling
that of the welfare state." [15]

This entire course of events could only have been predicted by a prophet. Viewed from a contemporary perspective, we can still discover "enough and more than enough" of Weber's talent for anticipating the future correctly.[16] Democracy, constituting nothing but parliamentarization, remained for him the sole alternative to the *"deutschen Obrigkeits-staat"* (authoritarian state). Similarly, his sober attitude, devoid of all illusions, accords a place to freedom devoid of all idealization and ideological content. His attitude toward freedom is *zweckrational* (rational-purposeful). For him, both freedom and political self-determination for the citizen meant essentially the absence of authoritarian tutelage, particularly at the hands of the bureaucracy. He did not place his trust in a freedom vested in the minds and convictions of men, a judgment derived from his own funded knowledge of history. To it he also owed his reliance upon certain institutions and techniques of self-government.[17]

Just as Weber found alien any ascription of ideological content to freedom, he was indifferent toward all other ideologies. All ideologies, whether conservative or liberal, capitalist or socialist, were merely "infrastructures," situationally conditioned by factors of history and milieu. He emphatically denied to ideologies any justification as on absolute value. Loewenstein considers this one of Weber's most significant contributions to the history of ideas, one for which Weber himself never took much credit, perhaps because he largely overcame the ideological in his own scholarly system of thought.

Loewenstein sees present realities concurring with Weber's political judgment at still another point. The changed significance of the two-chamber structure within the parliamentary system had engaged Weber's attention. An upper chamber which enhanced the technical improvement of the legislative program and which employed the experience of inactive elder statesmen appeared advisable to him. However, he did not envisage that it would occupy the same status as the lower chamber in the law-making process. The almost universal rejection of the two-chamber system by the newly founded national states has tended to confirm Weber's political judgment. Only in a federated state does an upper chamber appear to be justified, inasmuch as it seems indispensable in ensuring sustained governance. Weber's projection for Germany included the traditional assembly of government representatives adopted by the Weimar constitution and which again gained acceptance in 1945. As a result, the function of the *Bundesrat* (Federal Council) as a central organ, begun under Bismarck, could be retained.

Loewenstein further questions whether the cause of federalism is served if all important decisions are made at the national level, even under the Basic Law of Western Germany, following time-honored national tradition. This query, however, lends itself to contradiction :

In 1950 the German Federal Government and Parliament drew up the Federal Youth Plan as its programme for the support of youth and independent youth work. Each year since then, the Plan has been carried through as a Government measure, with the approval of the Bundestag and the Bundesrat and with the collaboration of the Laender youth authorities and independent youth associations. The fact that the programme has such a broad basis of sponsorship is in itself sufficient to show that there is no question of State interference with the freedom of youth or youth work, but that the State is working in partnership with society to perform a service.

The first basic element of the Federal Youth Plan follows from the constitution of the German Federal Republic, known as the Basic Law. According to this, the *Laender* are autonomous, particularly in the field of education. The Federal Government cannot therefore extend its support to all aspects of youth work, but it must restrict its action—in agreement with the *Laender* —to those matters which are of outstanding importance to the Federal Republic as a whole or which can only be effectively and legally dealt with at the Federal level. This presupposes that initiative will be taken and work done for the welfare of youth by the smaller groups in community, district and Land, and calls for the cooperation of the Federal Government with them.[18]

That this avowed purpose has been met in large part is corroborated by Peter Merkl who notes that, following World War II, reestablishment of state governments and constitutions occurred long before a national government was entrusted with the responsibility for future democracy in Germany: "Thus the new German democracy was based from the start upon a federal system whose *Laender* (state) politics was as democratically sound and about as stable as the Bonn government has turned out to be. In fact, looking back upon the sound political record of each of the West German *Laender* today, one cannot help noting the number of *Land* Minister Presidents, other important ministers, and legislative and party leaders who have held office there almost continuously since the early days of the Occupation. The democratic *Laender*, of course, also constitute a training ground and reservoir of new democratic leadership for the national government." [19]

There has been a surprising consensus among political parties on the desirability of Germany's return to federalism.[20] Merkl points to the viability and usefulness of the present *Laender* governments, attributes which even the party then in opposition had recognized: "Even the SPD (Social Democratic Party), which gave federalism only lukewarm support in the beginning, has discovered its great virtues: the presence of *Laender* governments offers the party out of power at the federal level a splendid opportunity to exercise authority and to take on the governmental responsibility denied to it for so long in Bonn." [21] SPD opposition had been based on the fact that it did not want to support American ideas, which favored the CDU (Christian Democratic Union) position that a weak federal authority was preferable. The SPD feared too weak a central government: "The Allied Powers were sensible enough to recede on this issue, especially touching the respective financial powers of *Laender* and Bonn."[22]

Reviewing Max Weber's contribution to political science, Loewenstein states that his political writings presage subsequent developments such as universal democratization, the inexorable ascension of bureaucracy in all spheres of life, and the plebiscitarian type of mass society with its implicit leanings toward Caesarism. Weber's gift as a seer he conceives all the more remarkable considering that most of these political developments were embryonic in his own time. What Weber failed to take into account and could not have predicted was the enormous influence of the mass media serving the manipulation of public opinion. For the rest, it behooves us to regard our own political insights, which in the light of experience we take for granted, also as an important part of the legacy of Max Weber.[23]

As mentioned at the Heidelberg Convention of 1964, various scholars attempted to demonstrate the contemporary validity of Weber in present-day sociology and political science. The charge has been made that the compartmentalized analyses of the potential consequences of several of Weber's works masked his true intellectual stature. Skillful links between disciplines were missing, making an adequate appreciation of Weber's accomplishments more difficult. Alois Dempf considers this shortcoming as all the more serious since certain of Weber's basic attitudes were criticized at the meetings, some of which it was felt, needed correction, particularly his postulate of freedom from value judgments because the interpretation accorded to this Weberian concept tended to give him the appearance of a positivist and neutralist.[24]

Admittedly, this concept may have lent itself—indeed, it must have lent itself—to caricature; although there have been many constructive results stemming from the postulate of *Wertfreiheit*, there have also been practical consequences which are deplorable. One shares with other critics of Weber what one might call the image of his nobly depressing rectitude. Rectitude, however, is not enough, and depressing rectitude, however noble, is rather less than enough.

Weber, in effect, occupied himself with the practical aspects of political culture in various parts of his writings. In the balance, cultural prestige and power prestige are intimately related.[25] Consider, for example, Weber's view of rivalry among nationalities and national cultures in Eastern Europe.[26] Next to military security and economic interests, Weber judged the "national cultural community" as one of the "three rational components for the marking of political boundaries."[27] As we have seen, Weber's postulate of freedom from value judgment does not operate in this sphere. Cultural achievements are suitable not only for the creation of a basis upon which national policy may be legitimately conducted, but culture itself ranks higher than power and, hence, may serve as its ideological justification. Applying this perspective, Weber distinguished power states from "externally small nations." [28] He refers to the cultural mission incumbent upon a power state in contrast to the lesser role which small nations may play.[29] The configuration of culture in the world must remain the responsibility of the great powers.[30] Small nations have other cultural outlets, and the cultural properties they possess and which are left to their care are presumably of a different nature.

Emmerich Francis reasons that it would be difficult not to conclude that Weber was largely bound by the bourgeois values of his own age, in which the concept of the *Kulturnation* was central. Indeed, the bourgeoisie conceived national culture as the ultimate value.[31] While this conception of culture frequently occurs in Weber's publicistic writings, it did not receive the same emphasis in his theoretical research. Weber, for example, could not have applied the same meaning when he explained that the problem of the essence of politics occupies a prominent place in the "region of general problems of culture." [32]

A real bridge between history and sociology, meanwhile, was built by Max Weber, who released sociology from extratheoretical aims and value orientations. He enriched sociology immeasurably by giving it the historical substance with which to work. As a child of bourgeois revolutions, and thus subject to the limitations of his own age, he began by looking to the past to diagnose his own time. He was thus able to counter the conceptualization of history as a product of automatic social and historical processes.

In seeking to explain how Max Weber conceived of man and society, Johannes Winckelmann characterizes Weber's conception as an *"agonal"* one, at the head of which appears the inscription "pólemos," the origin and principle of which is the idea that conflict underlies all social relations. The plurality of interests, ideals, and postulates leads those who subscribe to them into perpetual conflict.[33] Looking back over the centuries, perhaps as far back as the dawn of mankind, relations between men, when fully explored, indicated to Weber that we live in a world of scarce resources whose allocation, whether social, political, or economic, can never be "ideal." Weber was acutely aware of the magnitude of the resulting struggle as the critical phenomenon, however formal or peaceable, pervading the social process. Conflict determines progress, not accommodation or assimilation. ". . . Power and influence require struggle; organization and colleagiality require struggle; a profession requires competition and struggle, and especially mankind's highest good, freedom, can be granted us only at the price of a never slacking, undaunted readiness for combat." [34]

Power and struggle thus remain, in Weber's view, the tragedy of man's fate. Intellectual integrity prevented him from attempting to disguise this state of affairs by seeking to harmonize antagonisms. Nor did he engage in a scientific quest aimed at locating extenuating reasons which might provide a theoretical framework for accommodation. Indeed, his opposition to any such attempts was unbending. "Seldom did Max Weber find more sarcastic formulations than when he opposed the concept and maxim of 'accommodation.' Whoever merely seeks adjustment has surrendered as an effective participant in his culture and society, forfeiting his birthright to exercise his freedom to reason, denying himself the privilege to examine, select, and then decide." [35] It is hard to imagine a proposition more at odds with current democratic assumptions wherein politics is the art of the possible and accommodation the norm.

Wrestling with the angel, as it were, for its own future is the task of mankind. It is not only interests which are at stake; instead, the highest ideals and postulates of mankind must serve as criteria to ensure that choices are made wisely. Weber applied this conceptual framework to both material and nonmaterial spheres of life, for which appropriate priorities for investment purposes must be established. Education, for instance, is a form of investment whereby people acquire knowledge, skills, and attitudes employable and hence valuable in later life. Like any other form of investment, it entails a current cost and the expectation of future benefits. Educated people may thus be thought of as constituting a stock of capital—in this case, human capital. As with other forms of capital, it is subject to depreciation; knowledge and skills become obsolete, and people die.

To view education as investment and its outcome as the formation of human capital need not in itself imply a narrow, utilitarian approach to its purposes. Investment in human knowledge and skills, derived from education, is undoubtedly an important determinant of economic growth for any nation. Hence society also has a stake in decisions relating to educational investment. For while individual initiative might be relied upon to secure private benefits, education in general and political education in particular generate benefits of a collective nature as well. Certainly, these social benefits provide the fundamental justification for governmental encouragement of educational activities. Society at large benefits both from mass education and especially from the contribution of highly educated élites.

Nisbet rightly points to Max Weber's pessimistic view of the "self-sterilizing" effects of education. Ultimately Weber feared the advent of a new, educated élite which would be as opposed to liberty and equality as the aristocracies founded on religion, property, and war had been in his day: "He thought that the rationalization of education, the increasing dependence of government and society on the technical skills and knowledge vouchsafed by education, would make for a new stratum of privilege and power with the diploma succeeding the coat of arms." [36] Here again, Weber anticipated the modern thrust toward professionalization. But the types of élites Weber foresaw had a direct negative relationship to administrative meritocracy and universal education:

The development of the diploma from universities, and business and engineering colleges, and the universal clamor for the creation of educational certificates in all fields make for the formation of a privileged stratum in bureaus and offices. Such certificates support their holders' claims for intermarriages with notable families (in business offices people naturally hope for preferment with regard to the chief's daughter), claims to be admitted into the circles that adhere to 'codes of honor,' claims for a 'respectable' remuneration rather than remuneration for work well done, claims for assured advancement and old-age insurance, and, above all, claims to monopolize social and economically advantageous positions. When we hear from all sides the demand for an introduction of regular curricula and special examinations, the reason behind it is, of course, not a suddenly awakened 'thirst for education' but the desire for restricting the supply for these positions and their monopolization by the owners of educational certificates. Today the 'examination' is the universal means of this monopolization, and therefore examinations irresistibly advance.[37]

Although Weber's work did not include a systematic treatment of either educational institutions or higher learning generally, his observations in this field are scattered throughout his writings. Both his sociology of religion and his sociology of authority contain significant references to education. Higher learning is conceived by Weber as playing a decisive role in the establishment of qualifications for authority, and a rational, organized society based on office-holding secures its power position through education-based authority containing residues of mystery.[38]

Weber sought to penetrate with all the force of his being the ethically problematic aspects of power, even though, as Johannes Winckelmann writes, he was convinced of the impossibility of man resisting the abysmal "demon of power." [39] He therefore believed that priority had to be accorded to responsible action within the political realm in order to counter the inevitably competing entanglements. This tragic aspect of history as a fact of life characterized both Weber and his brother Alfred.[40] In discussing Raymond Aron's address at the Heidelberg Convention honoring the 100th anniversary of Weber's birth, Hans Paul Bahrdt states that we cannot today speak on the same level of "power," "nation," and "world politics," as Weber did. Even under the Kaiser the Germans might have fared better had they been more moderate in their estimation of Germany's power potential, "even more so than a Max Weber was inclined to believe."

On the other hand, though we have to admit Weber overestimated the political and military power of Germany, even in the second half of World War I, we can do him justice only by stressing also how very far he separated himself from the Pan-Germans and, subsequently, the annexationist elements who lacked that sense of perspective which Weber considered one of the most important virtues of the politician.[41] In an address at the Ludwig-Maximilians-Universitaet in Munich, again on the occasion of the 100th anniversary of Max Weber's birth, Bernhard Pfister noted Weber's contention that Germany, being a national state, must reserve for itself the right to protect German interests in the East, especially in East Prussia, West Prussia and Posen. The state, moreover, should select its own means to insure an effective economic policy. Pfister asserts that Weber himself was prone to make both economic and socio-political value judgments, always stipulating, however, that it should be clearly stated that one speaks from this perspective, and also that one should be aware that not the scientist but the politician has the floor.[42] Weber's journalistic-political writing as well as his public political position, especially from 1915 to his untimely death in June 1920, Pfister sums up in one sentence: "As a German democrat he felt the call to shoulder responsibility, to commit himself publicly on questions of domestic and foreign policy both before and after the collapse."[43]

The uneasiness over the tension between Weber's ardent convictions regarding the priorities he had established as given values and his postulate of freedom from value judgment at the analytical level is reflected in Max Horkheimer's discussion of value judgments and objectivity. As a student in Munich in 1919, he had experienced Weber's application of this postulate. Horkheimer relates how he, like many of his fellow students were profoundly interested in understanding the Russian Revolution. Most of all they wanted to gain insight into its significance for the rest of the world, as well as for the West, and to learn how the West, and especially Germany, should respond to this event. Could the positive aspects of the revolution be strengthened and the negative ones be limited, thereby avoiding Russian isolation and regression into a new and dangerous nationalism? Horkheimer indicated that the first signs of a totalitarian development in Russia in the direction of Stalinism and in Germany in the direction of National Socialism were already on the horizon.

In this atmosphere Max Weber delivered a lecture on the Soviet System. The lecture hall was apparently overflowing, yet the disappointment that followed was extreme. Instead of theoretical explication and analysis oriented toward a step-by-step discussion of the scope of the event and the alternatives for a reasonable approach to it as a future policy, Weber engaged in finely balanced definitions of the Russian system and clearly formulated ideal types through which the Soviet system might find expression. Everything was so precise, so strictly scientific, so free from value judgment that the students went home rather sadly. As they left the lecture hall, many thought Weber merely ultraconservative; later on, that judgment had to be revised. Shortly afterwards, in another lecture, Weber debated with students, many of whom were members of certain conservative fraternities. In this instance, however, his deliberations were reported to have included value judgments. Hence, as Horkheimer concludes, from where we stand today, following a period of world revolution marked by charisma and more, Max Weber might have agreed after all with the view that political analysis cannot be divorced so completely from normative preferences.[44]

Weber's work as a publicist seeking to influence popular opinion was astoundingly articulate whenever he protested against those expressions of government authority designed to prevent creative charisma from seizing the initiative. His writings were marked by a sense of inevitability and urgency, inspired by the tragic events occurring in his time. The years between the turn of the century and Weber's death in 1920 had been years of revolutionary change and a search for meaning and objectives. Living at a moment in history in which the old world, the German Empire, had died and a new order (the Weimar Republic) was too powerless to be born, his own political orientation remained firmly grounded in the moral autonomy of the power state. The extent of his commitment to the idea of the power state is to be measured by his basic article of faith which, in his judgment, must remain inviolate, namely that the necessary justification of the power state was its own preservation and aggrandizement. Weber's reasoning, before and after World War I, was based on the overriding assumption that any other policy would be prejudicial to Germany's interest since the primary aim of her foreign policy must be the protection of national security from the "Russian menace." During the war he had argued that not only must Germany's eastern frontiers adjoining Russian territory be made secure, but that she must fortify herself against other eastern neighbors. In one sense his fear of Russia was nothing more than an example of familiar reaction to the imbalance of power between the large and small states. Weber feared most the potential magnitude of her national power; he was more apprehensive of what she might become and do rather than of what she was and did then. Today we can only speculate how Weber would have reacted to the agreement between West Germany and Poland that the line of the Oder and Neisse Rivers will mark the Western border of Poland which was signed on December 7, 1970 in Warsaw.

Weber's philosophic outlook on the future of mankind was essentially pessimistic. Yet his commentary on contemporary society and the direction in which it was heading did contain some hope that man might be able to anticipate his fate and take positive measures to alter it; accordingly he visualized the possibility of transcendance of even a firmly established social structure, provided new social values were given an opportunity to materialize.

Max Weber presented an eloquent plea for man to retain control over his values and goals and to resist becoming the captive of a social order that subverts humanism for the sake of bureaucratic efficiency: "No one knows who will live in this cage of the future, or whether at the end of this tremendous development entirely new prophets will arise, or there will be a great rebirth of old ideas and ideals." [45] Thus the grim future Weber had foretold, in which the genuinely human element must give way to rationalized efficiency, might yet be averted. The process of depersonalization encountered on the march toward progress in which traditional values are bent and twisted might yet be counterbalanced by the dialogue into which man could enter "the world of judgments of value and of faith." [46]

Political scientists as well as sociologists have been spurred by Weber's writings on the relationship of faith in the realm of human affairs to values in the realm of ideals and ideas. Political issues today more than ever compel us to deal with values. Our attention is continuously engaged by such vital issues as the conflict between the Soviet Union and the United States, and possibly China; the revolutionary developments in Asia and Africa; and progress in research on nuclear energy and accomplishments in space. Major political and ethical problems are raised by each individual issue, which together emphasize the contemporary experience of crisis. Whatever decisions may be forthcoming in confrontation with these issues, they will affect people on a global scale. Since our contemporary crisis involves our lives politically, we find ourselves compelled to make judgments concerning political conduct, our own as well as of that of our adversaries, concerning available means and preferred ends. The conception of the hiatus between science and values has caused some areas of inquiry to be neglected in the quest for answers concerning the desirable consequences of political action. Political science, consequently, has not been expected to provide vital information concerning possible courses of political action likely to reflect political wisdom. Yet, it has become imperative that all the intelligence available to us be applied in dealing with the critical problems confronting us. Lacking the conviction that the democratic system is preferable to any alternative system of political values, one will not be apt to examine policy issues from the perspective of human welfare unless one accepts the premises that values of a political nature may justify objective support. Furthermore, lacking that conviction, policy issues might then be viewed only on the basis of opinions, cross-pressures and prejudices. Since the principle of adherence to policies centering on the cause of human freedom is thus undermined, political advisers are likely to emerge who will be concerned primarily with implementing the will of those who happen to be in power.

The "Weberian controversy" has become an important concern for many social scientists engaged in central problems of contemporary Western civilization.[47] Weber's own investigations into the origin of and changes in values, and the ways in which they affect human behavior may be said to have charted the course for both political sociologists and political scientists. Today prime importance is ascribed to the relationship of a social system's present operation to predisposing factors in its history, as linked through the key values of that social system.[48] This vantage point is rooted in Weber's theories on comparative method and analysis of values in which the development of different systems in different nations was based first upon the different incidents in their respective histories and, second, upon the recurrence of those incidents, with modifications.[49]

Weber's own discourses on social and political policy have furnished today's political scientists with a more complete vision of the role played by values in modern political life. A central problem of political science today is that the advances within the fields of political theory and political research have not yet been matched by an equivalent advancement toward the integration of the two into a science of politics. As Bertrand de Jouvenel stated in his address before the International Political Science Association in Geneva in 1964: "It seems a most urgent preoccupation for people committed to political forecasting to see what can be done for the progress of liberty in a materially progressing society, the features of which could not be imagined in the seventeenth and eighteenth centuries." [50]

While posterity has tended to stress the elements of pessimism toward the future in his political thought, Max Weber's lasting contribution to political science lies in his profound grasp of "the role of the political scientist as a detector of problems, a role that breathes life into his role as a student and designer of institutions." [51]

Weber's sociology generally reflects a decidedly political perspective, as shown in this chapter's brief summary of some of the major themes contained in his political sociology which may be brought to bear upon political science. His sociology of the state presents a new challenge to both political sociologists and political scientists. As few others have done, Max Weber made practical politics in Germany a prime object of sociological attention. Austere and difficult as Weber's vision may strike us, its liberating effect may be that his political writings reveal him not only as a man with the concerns of the political theorist, but also as a man whose intense identification with his nation motivated him as a political analyst to press for action.

Ultimately, Weber was not capable of abdicating all political activity. Although he had accepted his teaching appointment at the University in Vienna with the idea that he would now withdraw from politics, from his perspective in 1918, he could not evade his political responsibility. His students numbered more than 300; no lecture hall was sufficiently large to seat all of them. Yet irrespective of the success of his teaching, he relinquished it in the hope of contributing to the political education of his country as a political journalist. At the end of his life, Max Weber felt impelled to state: "No—I was born for the pen and for the speaker's platform, and not for the lectern. This confession is somewhat painful for me, but absolutely unequivocal." [52]

From where Max Weber stood, it would seem that although he espoused liberal views, he did not hold out much hope for the survival of liberal democracy. His pessimism was again based on his concept of history reflecting the struggle between nations and institutions. Since an enlightened form of autocracy appeared to function more effectively, Weber maintained a skeptical attitude toward democracy:

Max Weber saw the struggle for existence, of the individual as well as of nations, in very grim terms. For him life was a permanent, relentless war, and Germans and Slavs must fight like wild beasts for space in which to live. His views show where his generation was right and where it was wrong. His claim that Germany could only exist as a world-power with a daring grand-scale policy was all too quickly taken up by people who would have done better to leave well alone.[53]

Nisbet points to the tension in Weber "between the values of political liberalism and the values of a humanistic or cultural conservatism, however reluctant this conservatism might be." [54]

The danger of paralysis through the spread of bureaucracy within modern mass society Weber saw as the ultimate threat. This explains his quest for the plebiscitarian-charismatic authority of the great demagogue, endowed with the capacity to offset through the revolutionary character of charisma the ever-increasing trend toward bureaucracy. Weber postulated the mechanisms and circumstances under which the emergence of charismatic leadership and its integration with routine may be expected to occur and what factors could be expected to enable it to coexist dynamically with traditional and bureaucratic authority: "The charismatic quality of an individual as perceived by others, or himself, lies in what is thought to be his connection with (including possession by or embodiment of) some *very central* feature of man's existence and the cosmos in which he lives. The centrality, coupled with intensity, makes it extraordinary." [55]

Edward Shils points out that in modern societies belief in both the charisma of the populace and that of the highest authority is not uncommon; nor are the tensions of populism and constitutionalism uncommon. Within democratic societies, we are confronted with "both a legitimacy conferred on rulers by the acknowledgment of the charisma-bearing populace, and the legitimacy drawn simply from the charisma of very powerful (and effective) authority as such." [56] Wolfgang Mommsen admits that there are grounds for applauding Weber for seeking to replace the authoritarian tradition in Germany with the person of the democratic demagogue by whose greatness it may be expected that demagogy will once again attain the positive value which characterized it in antiquity. As Mommsen also argues, however, Weber's failure to consider the ultimate consequences raises serious questions. Perhaps Weber went too far in his despair over our civilization so that the question arises whether he would have needed to commit himself quite so singlemindedly to this concept, without at least considering the fundamental problem of limitations regarding the means involved in mass demagogy. Weber's theory that the masses should acclaim the leader on the sole ground of his qualifications of leadership has, in Mommsen's view, opened the way to an objectification of the formulation of policy, even though this might not have been Weber's intention. Mommsen supports his view with Weber's own admission that irrational and emotional factors may very well gain in importance within a plebiscitarian "Fuehrerdemokratie." [57]

Since Weber conceded this possibility, Mommsen finds it all the more surprising that he did not probe more deeply the question whether a plebiscitarian-charismatic leadership system such as he demanded would not lead to an emotionally charged political life which might culminate in charismatic rule by force, reducing the will of the people to the mere function of acclaiming the actions of the leader, and the system of legitimation of the democratic constitution to no more than formal legalisms. Insofar as charisma demands that the people follow the leader as long as his career is marked by success, no effective brakes could be applied to his actions which might have distinguished the rule of the "dictator of the electoral battlefield" from the plebiscitarian rule of a totalitarian dictator. Unfortunately, Weber's conceptual framework with its radical value-neutrality often permitted political phenomena to be regarded from a purely formal viewpoint. This fact prevented him from distinguishing between genuine democratic charisma which places itself at the service and disposal of the collectivity and that type of charisma which directs its appeal to the meanest instincts and emotional drives of the masses, employing any means to accomplish its objectives regardless of ethical considerations. [58]

While Weber feared that the bureaucratization of the political apparatus would prevent both the selection and the rise of charismatic leaders, he was not, it seems, apprehensive about the possibility that a leadership democracy might be transformed into a charismatic dictatorship. Nisbet suggests that if Weber had lived to experience the coming of the Third Reich, he would have arrived at a different conclusion: "For despite (and perhaps because of) the heavy layer of bureaucracy over German society, it was all too possible for an individual who combined in his person the charismatic traits of the prophet, shaman, and berserker to achieve the power to shake a society as few charismatic individuals in history have been privileged to do." [59] Weber, however, believed that rationally and bureaucratically organized mass parties would furnish a sufficiently effective counterpoise to any potential emotional excesses which might manifest themselves on the domestic front in the struggle for power.[60] Overestimating, as he did, both the inevitability and the potency of bureaucratization,[61] Weber neglected to inquire into the problem of the limits and misuse of charisma. Concerning his own attitude toward the fascist style of charismatic rule, there can be no doubt: any policy which avails itself of base mass instincts and ultra-nationalistic emotions, he would have fought with the utmost passion. His insistence upon the ethic of responsibility, which demanded that the politician give a rational account to himself of the consequences of his actions, seems diametrically opposed to the megalomania and brutal narrowness of fascist rule.[62]

Georges Friedmann points out that the rationalization process, in Weber's view, applies similarly to industry, administration, agriculture, trade and finance. While all of workaday life is affected by it, so also is the development of technical means of mass communications which take their cue from media of information which have undergone the same process. Hence Weber was caught in a dilemma whereby increasing rationalization in the service of economic ends would culminate in rigidities penetratable only by the charismatic hero:

We may be permitted the assumption that Max Weber's reactions to the greatest personalities among the 'charismatic demagogues' in the West since the second world war would have been favorable if not enthusiastic. One might dream for a moment concerning Max Weber's attitude toward a 'charismatic demagogue' who to us Frenchmen is especially close today. But Max Weber was too closely directed at rationalization to have been able to anticipate what it implied in terms of irrationality.[63]

Ernst Topitsch, who had rejected all charges raised against Weber at the Heidelberg meetings, therein joining his American colleagues, points out that critics do not seem to consider that totalitarian regimes without exception have found Weber's thought hostile to their own purposes because a science free from value judgment would have to deny these regimes that higher legitimation which they so categorically require and for which they employed other schools of thought, such as Carl Schmitt's.[64] In this connection Topitsch cites S. D. Stirk, who maintained that a science free from value judgment in Max Weber's sense would, in fact, have offered a guaranty against National Socialism, had it been employed.[65] Loewenstein notes that since his death in Germany Weber's "demands for the end of administrative secrecy and impartial control of the administrative services" have been essentially satisfied because under the republican systems of both Weimar and Bonn, "the system of judicial review of administrative acts" has been enhanced. Moreover, "truly independent courts for constitutional questions have been created to deal with any infringement of the rule of law by the highest organs of the government." [66]

In spite of their democratic orientations, Mommsen considers Weber's constitutional projects to include certain authoritarian traits which could not be expected to remain immune to a totalitarian reformulation. Political charisma without the benefit of value content to give it direction cannot provide a firm foundation upon which to build a genuinely democratic order. Hence, Mommsen argues, we must choose different paths than Max Weber selected for himself. The appeal to charisma and the great demagogic talent of the leader no longer constitute for us a workable way out of the dilemma. Instead, new forms of value-oriented structuring of the political community must serve as potential counteragents against the bureaucratic trends and selfish types of political action by interest groups characterizing modern society. The rights guaranteeed to citizens by their constitution will have to receive greater attention than Max Weber accorded them in his own time. Nor can the nation any longer be the ultimate yardstick of political action. The inclination to regard the power position of one's own state as the ultimate value will yet have to be overcome.

It may still be stated that Max Weber's intellectual honesty, which was never satisfied with comfortable ideological schemes nor intellectual shortcuts, challenges us who live in the contemporary world to emulate the urgent personal dedication with which he explored the unhappy facets of political life.[67] One may wonder, however, if the experiences sustained in our epoch do not press us to consider them and try to "place" them somewhat more fully than Weber did.

Viewed in current perspective, Max Weber did not express himself in the terms of our time even though he anticipated many of its problems. Yet, even though he joined the Right in the area of foreign policy, he ranked far above its exponents in sobriety and rational perspective. However emotionally involved he had become in his national consciousness in the hour of defeat, he maintained his distance from the reactionary nationalistic forces then sweeping Germany. It should be remembered that when the nationalists began to agitate, not only against the extreme Left but also against the democratic factions he countered their activities sharply. As early as November 1918, he rejected the notion of counterrevolution.[68] He publicly opposed rightist activities, the spreading of which he foresaw. Because of his open acknowledgement of where he stood, his own colleagues and students scorned him.[69] The anti-Semitic antics of the Munich students Weber opposed unequivocally, in spite of the fact that Weber himself had characterized Eisner, a Jew, as a mere demagogue. The amnesty granted Eisner's murderer, and the nationalistic demonstrations conducted by the students in connection with this case brought Weber's intense disapproval, which he again was not afraid to express in public.[70] The demonstrations by the fraternities in front of Weber's home occurred in response to a civic courage which did not shirk the risk of losing the affection of students. For the colleagues of his time and ours, both in Germany and in the United States, he furnished an example worth emulating.

In answer to the great question which was asked then and which is still asked today, namely, whether Weber really had the calling to lead his nation in its hour of defeat, one must conclude that he was temperamentally unsuited. Although Weber's own friends at Heidelberg certainly strongly hoped for it,[71] Weber's prospects for realizing his talents in the field of practical politics remained dim. In addition to personal considerations, including his ill-health, he was too much the scholar and, ironically, too much politically committed, to endure the compromise and the intellectual backing-and-filling required of the active political role. His fundamental political ideals belonged to an era which had ended beyond recall; to that extent, he was perhaps too much a captive of the past to provide leadership under the new conditions facing postwar Germany. "As a politician Max Weber has never been able to dissociate himself from 'Germany in its old glory' which he might have wanted to rebuild following its collapse." [72]

The scholarly yet lively biography of Max Weber by Arthur Mitzman [73] portrays Weber's personal life as interesting, turbulent and anything but dull and plodding, though scarred by strongly antagonistic feelings against his father. There emerges from Mitzman's work a general theory of personal socialization as he traces the influences stemming from Weber's family and friends upon Weber's ideas and values in practical politics. Mitzman's thesis in the first part of his book holds that Weber's outlook before 1897 was moulded by "his struggle to escape from and finally challenge the dominance in the Weber household of his father, a dominance which he identified subconsciously with the political hegemony of the Junkers over the landworkers in particular and the German people in general." [74] The second part of his book was designed to demonstrate that Weber's *Weltan-schauung* "after 1902 was structured by the lessons he drew . . . from the agonizing collapse which resulted from this struggle." [75] Robert A. Nisbet suggests that Mitzman's analysis "reduces itself to what Mitzman, borrowing from Freud, calls the 'primitive city' of Weber's mind: 'composed of conscious and unconscious attitudes toward his family, his society, and himself.' From agonized response to an authoritarian father and to a deeply religious mother is drawn much of that whole aspect of Weber that forms the subject of 'The Iron Cage'." [76]

The intensity of Weber's rejection of his father, his compulsion to act toward him as he did and his seeming lack of remorse after the final clash between father and son, with the death of the father to follow soon thereafter, reflect Weber's image of his father as a despot, particularly as Weber saw his father's disposition toward his mother. Yet Max Weber "*Never Did* succeed in totally eradicating his father's nature from his own spirit. The twin dangers of succumbing to a ruthless egotism . . ., or to the servile comfort of an easy bureaucratic routine . . ., haunted him all his life; his inability to shake loose from these ghosts was a most important factor in his breakdown." [77]

Weber in his private and public sphere at times may have resembled *Prometheus Bound* of Aeschylus, appearing as an almost superhuman symbol of human rebellion, courage, strength, vitality, and quixotic sympathy. Yet, in reading Mitzman's interpretation, despite his engagingly poignant analogies, one might have some doubts concerning this biographer's preoccupation with psycho-analytic concepts. Nisbet trenchantly criticizes the approach for failing to "distinguish clearly between the actual sources of a set of ideas and the psychological contexts of Weber's acceptance, his internalization of these ideas. . . . There is also the obvious fact that Weber read, reflected, and learned—as well as merely responded to psychological torments." [78] Mitzman points to

. . . a certain constancy in his [Weber's] personal commitment to what he conceived to be the interests of the German nation. But these are only the forms, the flasks, inside which the intoxicating spirits of defiant, late-liberal hope have degenerated into the gall and vinegar of twentieth-century pessimism. . . . With the exception of a brief period after the outbreak of World War I, he no longer views the German people . . . as capable of being inspired by the 'breath of the powerful national passion' that permeated the Jacobean Convention. The *Leitmotiv* of Western history has changed from progress through self-liberation to enslavement through rationalization.[79]

Mitzman points to the "political corollary" reflecting at least a "partical internalization" of his father's attitudes and values, namely his predeliction for the German power state:

This ideal, however, if left unmodified, tended to incorporate both of the demons Weber fought against: the cynical ruthlessness represented by Treitschke (and by Weber Sr. in his despotism over his family) and the comfortable servility of the *Untertan* (the face his father showed to his superiors.) To ward off the demons, Weber put two conditions on his sanction of the *Machtstaat* . . . which alone gave legitimacy to it. Its components of ruthlessness and bureaucratic servility were jointly subordinated to the ideals represented by his mother and uncle. . . .[80]

In consequence, his mother's social consciousness and his uncle's intellectual integrity and lack of commitment to ideologically based political programs influenced Weber's own trend of thought. In an effort to reconstruct Germany's political past, Hajo Holborn probed deeply into the preoccupation with power in which individual German political writers engaged themselves, concentrating especially on its "daemonic qualities, its seductiveness, its ability to corrupt and destroy. Holborn was always fascinated by power and always felt that the Germans had an unsure instinct for it, largely because, in contrast to *other* nations, they were long deprived of it and so came to desire it more strongly. . . . Many Germans of liberal persuasion became more anxious to correct that situation than to win the kind of political liberties enjoyed in Western countries. . . ."[81]

To this should be added that much of the failure of the system in Germany was rooted in the failure of the middle classes to assess fairly the needs of the lower classes. Also, the twin phenomena of ever-increasing rationalization and rapid technological changes which Weber foresaw alone did not carry the risks implicit in rationalization and the "take-over by machines"; instead, part of the problem was also the persisting incompetence, timidity, and disintegration of the "political public" living with an outdated conceptual apparatus and the parallel ossification of the socio-political and economic apparatus of the German state. In the light of these circumstances the German bourgeoisie never really sought to attain a democratic form of government. Craig succinctly sums up Holborn's main findings as they relate to the origins and development of certain trends prevailing in nineteenth-century Germany, the implications of which for the future promised to be tremendous, were any power vacuum to eventuate: "an excessive and uncritical admiration of material progress; the tendency of leading historians to emphasize the role of the state at the expense of the society it was meant to serve and the prevalence of the philosophy of law . . ." implying that the law's ultimate objective is and should be the "preservation of the conditions in which the state could live and grow; the decline of political criticism (let alone activism) in the universities; and the general disdain in which intellectuals held political activity, which struck them as a distraction from matters of the spirit."[82] Holborn

himself sought to steer a path between the extreme polemical interpretations of the causes of World War I, namely the charge of German
militarism and imperialism on the one hand, and the equal distribution
of guilt among all belligerents on the other. For him it was both
the high readiness level observable in German thinking to respect power
and to let the government utilize it at its discretion, even an irresponsible government, which accounted for the "half-jubilant, half-fatalistic
mood" with which Germany entered World War I.[83] Moreover, the naive
adherence to the mere categories of "Bildung und Sparen" (education
and savings) resulted plainly in an abdication even within the labor
movement from its own political responsibilities. In 1918, while the
German kings departed, the generals stayed. Ultimately, the inability
of the Social Democrats to press for and to firmly carry through with a
definite program to realize social aims established in their own minds
was to result in persisting dissatisfaction of especially the younger
generation within the working class for essentially the status quo continued within Germany's social structure.[84]

Finally, as stated elsewhere in this book, the preponderance of the
legal profession in top public and private administrative positions permitted this conservatively oriented occupational group more influence
in both the formulation and application of legal policy than any other
in the population. Viewed in historical perspective, personal psychological considerations are doubtless important but could hardly be said
to serve as the chief explanation of Max Weber's own political sentiments. As Wolfgang Kaupen's [85] revealing study shows, the strong and
relatively enduring influence exercized by the family, primary and
secondary education, and subsequent professional training generally
serve to incline German lawyers to favor strict adherence to a hierarchical order. Interestingly enough, already as students enrolled in
law school they appear to be more judgmental and less permissive than
students pursuing other fields of study. Thus Weber's home influence
was certainly not unique; moreover, he was involved in the same type
of schooling as other students aspiring to a law degree, which must
have affected him similarly in his political and social views of the world.

Weber's own emphasis upon Germany's historical mission and his
concern with the qualitative improvement of the German people, in
which individual happiness cannot be a major consideration, correlates
with conceptions traditionally cherished by both Germany's historical
and legal professions. Finally, many university professors who like
Weber were too old to fight in World War I sought to support the
cause of patriotism by supplying psychological weapons. In this as well
as in their preoccupation with power most of them were guided by a
psychological *Leitmotif* (guiding principle) which transcended the individual's family situation and academic background, motivated as they

were by the widely felt psychological *Nachholbedarf* (previously suppressed demand to make good on Germany's power political claims in
relation to other nations).

While Weber favored a democratic and socially progressive constitution, any such democratization was to him but a means to an end,
namely to create conditions in which new leaders could carry on Bismarck's original work. His internal social reforms, even though he
toyed with socialist ideas, in which he could not bring himself to
believe, remained vague in their outline. In any case, domestic issues
were at all times subordinated to the German power state's role in
the realm of international politics. He was oblivious to and viewed
negatively any attempts which might have extricated Germany from
the vicious circle which the age of imperialism had bequeathed to the
European nations. As his strictures against the Kaiser's diplomacy and
the passive political role of the bourgeoisie suggest, he was less alienated
by the imperial system than by the failures of its leaders. It is doubtful
whether he would have been inclined to play Gustav Stresemann's conciliatory role, regardless of his own ability to adapt himself. On the
contrary, especially in defeat and failure, honor demanded that one
remain true to one's own political convictions and not to bow to the
pressure of circumstance. Otherwise one must wait and—remain silent![86]

NOTES

[1] Max Weber, "Der Nationalstaat und die Volkswirtschaftspolitik," *Gesammelte Politische Schriften* (Munich: Drei Masken Verlag, 1921), p. 163.
[2] Hans Maier, "Max Weber und die deutsche politische Wissenschaft," in Karl Engisch, Bernard Pfister, Johannes Winckelmann, eds., *Max Weber: Gedaecht-nisschrift der Ludwig-Maximilians-Universitaet Muenchen zur 100. Wiederkehr seines Geburtstages 1964* (Berlin: Duncker & Humblot, 1966), pp. 172–73.
[3] *Ibid.*, p. 174.
[4] *Ibid.*, pp. 174–75.
[5] Cf. Raymond Aron, "Max Weber und die Machtpolitik," in Otto Stammer, ed., *Max Weber und die Soziologie heute*, Verhandlungen des 15. Deutschen Soziologentages (Tuebingen: J. C. B. Mohr [Paul Siebeck], 1965), pp. 103–120.
[6] Maier, *op. cit.*, pp. 180–181.
[7] *Ibid.*, p. 182.
[8] Arnold Bergstraesser, "Max Weber, der Nationalstaat und die Politik," *Politik in Wissenschaft und Bildung*, 1961, p. 72, Cited in Maier, *op. cit.*, p. 182.
[9] Maier, *op. cit.*, p. 183.
[10] Karl Loewenstein, "Persoenliche Erinnerungen an Max Weber," in Engisch et al., *op. cit.*, p. 35.
[11] *Ibid.*, pp. 35–36.
[12] *Ibid.*, p. 36.
[13] *Ibid.*
[14] Karl Loewenstein, "Max Weber's Beitrag zur Staatslehre in der Sicht unserer Zeit," in Engisch et al., *op. cit.*

15 *Ibid.*, p. 133.
16 *Ibid.*
17 *Ibid.*, p. 134.
18 Heinrich Voggenreiter, ed., *Der Deutsche Bundesjugendplan: Jugend in Freiheit Verantwortung* (Bad Godesberg: Voggenreiter Verlag, 1961), pp. 32–33.
19 Peter H. Merkl, *Germany: Yesterday and Tomorrow* (New York: Oxford University Press, 1965), p. 207.
20 *Ibid.*, p. 215.
21 *Ibid.*, p. 224.
22 Herman Finer, *Governments of Greater European Powers: A Comparative Study of the Governments and Political Culture of Great Britain, France, Germany, and the Soviet Union* (New York: Henry Holt and Company, 1956), p. 690.
23 Loewenstein, "Max Weber's Beitrag zur Staatslehre in der Sicht unserer Zeit," in Engisch et al., *op. cit.*, pp. 145–46.
24 Alois Dempf, "Max Weber als Kultursoziologe," *op. cit.*, p. 57.
25 Max Weber, *Wirtschaft und Gesellschaft*, p. 530.
26 *P.S.*, 2nd. ed., p. 120.
27 *Ibid.*, p. 169.
28 *Ibid.*, p. 170.
29 *Ibid.*, p. 213.
30 *Ibid.*, p. 121.
31 Emmerich Francis, "Kultur und Gesellschaft in der Soziologie Max Webers," in Engisch, et al., *op. cit.*, pp. 97–98.
32 *Ibid.*, p. 98. Cf. also Max Weber, *Gesammelte Aufsaetze zur Wissenschaftslehre* (Tuebingen, 1951), p. 153. See also p. 163.
33 Johannes Winckelmann, "Max Webers Verstaendnis von Mensch und Gesellschaft," in Engisch et al., *op. cit.*, pp. 240–241.
34 *Ibid.*
35 *Ibid.*
36 Robert A. Nisbet, *The Sociological Tradition* (New York: Basic Books, Inc., Publ., 1966), p. 298.
37 *From Max Weber: Essays in Sociology*, H. H. Gerth and C. Wright Mills, trans. and eds. (New York: Oxford University Press, 1946), p. 241f, cited in Nisbet, *op. cit.*, p. 298–299.
38 Cf. also Thorstein Veblen, *The Theory of the Leisure Class* (New York: Mentor, 1953), p. 236f.
39 Johannes Winckelmann, "Max Webers Verstaendnis von Mensch und Gesellschaft," in Engisch et al., *op. cit.*, p. 242.
40 *Ibid.*, p. 242. See also Alfred Weber, *Das Tragische und die Geschichte*, 1959, and Kurt Lenk, "Das tragische Bewusstsein in der deutschen Soziologie," *Koelner Zeitschriften fuer Soziologie*, Vol. 16, 1964, pp. 257–287.
41 Hans Paul Bahrdt, "Discussion" of Raymond Aron's address "Max Weber und die Machtpolitik," Otto Stammer, ed., *Max Weber und die Soziologie heute* (Tuebingen: J. C. B. Mohr [Paul Siebeck], 1965), p. 124.
42 Bernhard Pfister, "Max Weber, Persoenlichkeit, und Werk," in Karl Engisch, et al., *op. cit.*, pp. 20–21.
43 *Ibid.*, p. 25.
44 Max Horkheimer, "Diskussion Zum Thema: Wertfreiheit und Objektivitaet; Einleitung zur Diskussion," Otto Stammer, ed., *op. cit.*, pp. 65–67.
45 Talcott Parsons, trans., *The Protestant Ethic and the Spirit of Capitalism* (London: George Allen & Unwin, 1930), pp. 182–183.
46 *Ibid.*
47 Cf. Gerhard Lenski, *The Religious Factor* (New York: Doubleday, 1961), p. 6.
48 Seymour Martin Lipset, "The Value Patterns of Democracy: A Case Study in Comparative Analysis," *American Journal of Sociology*, Vol. 2i, No. 4, August 28, 1963, pp. 530–531.
49 Cf. Max Weber, *The Methodology of the Social Sciences* (New York: The Free Press, 1949), pp. 182–185.
50 Bertrand de Jouvenel, "Political Science and Prevision," *American Political Science Review*, Vol. LIX, No. 1, March 1965, p. 38.
51 *Ibid.*
52 *Lebensbild*, p. 625.
53 Golo Mann, *The History of Germany Since 1789* (New York: Frederick A. Praeger, 1968), p. 209.
54 Robert A. Nisbet, *op. cit.*, p. 17.

55 Edward Shils, "Charisma, Order and Status," *American Sociological Review*, Vol. 30, No. 2, April 1965, p. 201.
56 *Ibid.*, pp. 205–206.
57 Mommsen, *Max Weber und die Deutsche Politik 1890–1920*, p. 407. Cf. also, *P.S.*, 2nd. ed., p. 391 where he refers to the dangers of the strong possibility that such an order may be characterized by the preponderance of emotional elements in the conduct of politics.
58 Mommsen, *Max Weber und die Deutsche Politik 1890–1920*, pp. 407–408.
59 R. Nisbet, *op. cit.*, p. 256.
60 *P.S.*, 2nd. ed., p. 392, and Mommsen, *Max Weber und die Deutsche Politik 1890–1920*, p. 409.
61 *Ibid.*, cf. also *Wirtschaft und Gesellschaft*, p. 695.
62 Mommsen, *op. cit.*, pp. 409–410.
63 Georges Friedmann, "Discussion of 'Industrialisation and Capitalism' " in Otto Stammer, ed., *op. cit.*, pp. 203–204. The discussion referred to the address by Herbert Marcuse concerning this topic.
64 Ernst Topitsch, "Max Weber und die Soziologie heute," *ibid.*, p. 31.
65 Cf. S. D. Stirk, *German Universities through English Eyes* (London, 1946).
66 Karl Loewenstein, *Max Weber's Political Ideas in the Perspective of Our Time* (Amherts, Massachusetts; The University of Massachusetts Press, 1966), p. 40.
67 Mommsen, *op. cit.*, pp. 412–413.
68 *Ibid.*, pp. 319–320.
69 *Ibid.*, p. 320.
70 Cf. Mommsen, *op. cit.*, p. 320, see letter of January 9, 1920 to V. Lukàcz (father of Georg Lukàcz): . . . "The academic mood has become extremely reactionary and besides radically antisemitic."
71 *Lebensbild*, p. 633, 640ff., 655. Cf. also Arthur Liebert, "Max Weber" *Preussische Jahrbuecher*, Vol. 210, 1927, p. 304ff., Gertrud Baeumer, "Nachruf auf Max Weber," *Die Hilfe* (1920), p. 386. Ernst Toeltsch, *Deutscher Geist und Westeuropa* (Berlin, 1925), p. 250.
72 Robert Wilbrandt, "Max Weber" and also "Ein Deutsches Vermaechtnis," *Die Neue Rundschau*, Vol. 39, May 1928, p. 450.
73 Arthur Mitzman, *The Iron Cage: An Historical Interpretation of Max Weber* (New York. Alfred A. Knopf, 1970).
74 *Ibid.*, p. 6.
75 *Ibid.*, pp. 6–7.
76 Robert A. Nisbet, *Book Review* of "The Iron Cage: An Historical Interpretation of Max Weber, by Arthur Mitzman (New York: Alfred A. Knopf, 1970): *The New York Times Book Review*, Section 7, February 15, 1970, Vol. CXIX, No. 40, 930, p. 12.
77 Arthur Mitzman, *op. cit.*, p. 50.
78 Robert A. Nisbet, *op. cit.*, p. 12.
79 Arthur Mitzman, *op. cit.*, pp. 167–168.
80 *Ibid.*, p. 51.
81 Gordon A. Craig, Book Review of Hajo Holborn, *A History of Modern Germany 1840–1945* (New York: Alfred A. Knopf, 1969), *The New York Times Book Review*, August 24, 1969, Vol. CXVIII, No. 40, 755, p. 3.
82 *Ibid.*
83 Cf. *ibid.*
84 Cf. Richard M. Watt, *The Kings Depart* (London: Weidenfeld and Nicolson, 1969).
85 Cf. Wolfgang Kaupen. *Die Hueter von Recht und Ordnung. Die soziale Herkunft, Erziehung und Ausbildung der deutschen Juristen—Eine soziologische Analyse; Soziologische Texte.* Vol. 65, Neuwied: Hermann Luchterhand, 1969. Cf. also Ludwig Bendix, *Zur Psychologie der Urteilsfaehigkeit des Berufsrichters und andere Schriften; Soziologische Texte,* Vol. 43. Neuwied: Hermann Luchterhand, 1968, and Thilo Vogel. *Zur Praxis und Theorie der richterlichen Bindung an das Gesetz im gewaltenteilenden Staat.* Berlin: Duncker & Humblot, 1969.
86 Cf. Mommsen, *op. cit.*, pp. 322–23. Also see Weber's letter to Crusius of November 24, 1918 in *Politische Schriften*, p. 484. previously referred to in these pages: "What one now says publicly is naturally always 'rebus sic stantibus, not *pour jamais!*' 'Toujours y penser. . . .' "

XII

Max Weber and the Present

As the subtitle of this book, "In Quest of Statesmanship," suggests, Max Weber moved beyond historical analysis to a philosophical comprehension of the past in quest of statesmanship for the future. The focus in this book has been on Max Weber, the political man. He cast his first ballot for the Conservative party in Imperial Germany and his last vote for the Democratic party in the early days of the Weimar Republic. This book represents an attempt to retrace the process of the development of his political thought, spanning this crucial period in German history. A number of themes run through his account of German politics, only a few of which can be noted in this brief review, an attempt having been made throughout the book to illuminate them more fully in both their historical and current context.

Max Weber, German statesman and scholar, died in 1920, just fifty years ago. Although he has long been known as one of the most renowned sociologists, the scholarly task he performed in fusing the political dynamics of German society with its sociological facets has not been fully explored. Meanwhile, although Weber's thought was motivated essentially by his political concerns, the fact that few of his major scholarly writings are exclusively and explicitly concerned with political questions has contributed to the failure of contemporary political scientists to pay him due attention.

In his stimulating account of "Weimar culture," [1] Peter Gay recently portrayed political science as a casualty of Imperial Germany. While he points to some notable German achievements in the fields of comparative government and public administration in the 1850's and 1860's, political scientists and historians were preoccupied with less conspicuous areas of concentration. With the notable exception of Max Weber, rather than dealing with contemporary politics and contemporary history, they

380

focused upon the past. Commenting on the lack of awareness of social and political reality among German academicians generally, Franz Neumann paid homage to Weber's theoretical knowledge supported by his "mastery of a tremendous number of data, and a full awareness of the political responsibility of the scholar." [2]

While Weber himself conceived his ultimate role to be that of mentor, political adviser, commentator, and intellectual critic rather than as a man of actively creative leadership in practical affairs of state, his policy aims were frequently negated by those in authority. Perhaps today, a half-century after his death, as the demands of foreign policy continue to require political wisdom of the highest order, Weber's quest for statesmanship and his strong personal convictions regarding the need to develop institutions that could provide leadership may again be invoked. Nevertheless, it "is characteristic of German social science that it virtually destroyed Weber by an almost exclusive concentration upon the discussion of his methodology. Neither his demand for empirical studies nor his insistence upon the responsibility of the scholar were heeded." Indeed, Weber "really came to life" [3] in the United States, where his sociological works have received a more comprehensive response.

Weber's political thought was characterized throughout by a deep pessimism encompassing not only the hard fate of contemporary Germany but his appreciation of increasing bureaucratization and disenchantment of Western society. Perhaps, too, his inability to affect the course of German political events underlay his mood. He has demonstrated that in Wilhelmian Germany there was little chance for genuine statesmen and master politicians to rise to the top. It would require many decades for the pattern established then to be broken. As Paul Honigsheim comments sympathetically: "One can imagine what the man suffered when obliged by his love for Germany, he climbed down into the political arena only to get covered with mud there—he knew this was unavoidable if one were involved with politics." [4] Honigsheim captures the essence of Weber's response to the first two decades of the twentieth century:

. . . dark clouds overshadowed everything. They were not caused by Max Weber's illness. . . . Something else oppressed him much more. . . . Weber really loved Germany and felt ethically obliged to work for his country to the extent of risking his life for it. But he saw it taking a course that would lead to destruction. [5]

His political philosophy provides insights into Weber's personality and into the spirit of his time. His was the reaction of an intellectual giant who lived through an era and who today is still able to restore our understanding of the contemporary relevance of history. Weber did not claim that his approach to the formulation of foreign policy was designed to emphasize the moral quality of the ends being sought; he was concerned instead with the importance of a realistic assessment of the adequacy of means. Yet Weber's writings reveal a manifest need to define and redefine publicly the principles of conduct that governed the German people. They also articulate a strong concern with the mission of his nation, and with the peculiar experience of being a German. They reveal the anguish that lies behind Weber's judgments concerning the hiatus between Germany's social and psychological characteristics and her publicly proclaimed creed and aspirations. Quoting Alexander Herzen, who applied this dictum to Russia, Weber argued that the German fatherland neither is nor should be the land of its fathers; it instead ought to be the land of its children.[6]

At a time of many new urgencies, Max Weber's political writings remind us to look again at the past to obtain a clearer view of the future. Yet, in identifying and reconstructing statements that would seem to bear, directly or indirectly, on Weber's socio-political ideas, there is a danger of forcing upon the material an unwarranted cohesion and consistency. Perhaps the principal issue here turns on the relationship between Weber's earlier political values and his later ones. Some American sociologists have argued that Weber's political orientation changed substantially after his famous inaugural address at the University of Freiburg in 1895, and that any attempt to treat the essence of his political thought as a self-consistent entity would be misleading. As one of Germany's leading political analysts, Weber had begun his political career by rendering a most extensive, yet closely coordinated account of national policy. This included his first attempt as a trained economist and jurist, and practising specialist in political economy to make sense out of the complex changes in the relations between private and public economic power. The quality of the German character and population, the structure of German society, and the meaning of Germany's historical experience—all had important implications for Max Weber's political thought. As his understanding of the German character and its values changed, especially as manifested by his studies of agrarian conditions in East Elbian Germany, so did his evaluation of German society and its political problems. Thus he wrote: "When the bases of the acquisition and distribution of goods are relatively stable, stratification by status is favored. Every technological repercussion and economic transformation threatens stratification by status and pushes the class situation into the foreground." [7]

As Weber probed the essential meaning underlying the social cleavages, he concentrated his political attacks upon the disproportionately high representation of rural areas in the Prussian legislature and in the entire German government and the tax and tariff concessions enjoyed by the landed estate owners. Like other leading personalities in the non-Marxist social reform movement, Weber was displeased that the Conservative party "habitually used patriotic phrases to justify repressive policies, while never losing sight of its agrarian clients' own particular interests." [8] Thus Weber's subsequent changes in party affiliation did not reflect any significant shift in his political outlook, but rather his permanent conviction that a "great struggle was coming and that such a struggle was necessary to assure Germany's position as a world power," and "he advocated a transition to democracy . . . because the democratic process would improve the selection of political leadership necessary for Germany to embark on world politics. The thinking of Weber was dominated by the notion of world power." [9] Hence, the "institutions of society, the life of the people, must be fitted into the purposes of power politics." [10]

Weber's political behavior may be explained primarily as that of a man who agreed that the Conservatives would " 'tear us apart instead of uniting us' " and so turned to the National Liberal party hoping that it would support social reform. When the National Liberals persisted in their opposition to concrete proposals for reform, caught up as they were in the struggle of economic interest groups, it became obvious that the

mandarin reformers were never completely at home in the bourgeois liberal camp. They were always trying to transform the liberal parties, to direct attention away from entrepreneurial interest politics, to guide them toward moderate social reform, and to interest them in progressively cultural and educational programs. The ordinary channels of Wilhelminian politics could never really satisfy the accommodationists. . . .[11]

Ringer suggests that the accommodationists, among whom he ranked Weber, could easily qualify as "enlightened conservatives." He rightly concludes that this would almost rule out locating any liberals among German professors.[12] His chief argument is that "mandarin politics" did not find a political home in the existing party framework. Thus ultimately Weber, like Meinecke and Troeltsch later, became a *Vernunftsrepublikaner*, who chose to support the Weimar Republic for rational reasons, which failed to replace his emotional attachment to the monarchy, although he had opposed the person of William II. However, earlier than most, Weber recognized that "only a strong parliamentary democracy was capable of a strong foreign policy under the conditions of modern industrial society, and Weber was one of the few who could point without self-contradiction at the hollowness of the 'ideas of 1914' and at the failure of the imperial regime to carry out a successful foreign policy even while giving it priority. In contrast to the tradition

of the 'primacy of foreign policy' from Ranke to Hintze, Weber attached
that principle to the interests of the nation as a whole and not only
to those of the monarchy." [13] Finally, as Simon correctly explains:
"Weber had cause to change his political opinions very little, because
his ideas on domestic reform, radical and extreme at the turn of the
century, were by and large realized in the first year of the Weimar
Republic, and because he died prematurely." [14]

In Germany the separation of ethics from history propelled "most
German historians into a passive acceptance of things as they were,
and the segregation of history from other disciplines alienated most
German historians from the social sciences. Despite all his vast historical
erudition, most historians dismissed Max Weber as an 'outsider'." [15]
Georg von Below expressed the sentiments of his colleagues when he
insisted that historians did not need sociology.[16]

Max Weber clearly perceived the "ethical irrationality" of the world
as he acknowledged the impossibility of resolving ethical conflicts scientifically. He remained faithful to his belief in the possibility of objective
inquiry in history and in traditional political attitudes. While acknowledging the ethical irrationality of the world, he retained his own value
commitment to the vital national interests of the German power state.
The crisis of German liberal thought was no isolated phenomenon:
". . . if the course of events demonstrated the intellectual inadequacy
of the philosophy of value of German historicism, it showed equally
the inadequacy of this philosophy of value for a liberal theory of politics.
Closely related to the crisis of German historicism was the crisis of
German liberal thought . . . many of the German liberal and democratic thinkers from the Wars of Liberation to the Weimar Republic—
Humboldt, the 'classical liberal historians' of the Vormaerz, the men
around Friedrich Naumann such as Max Weber, Hugo Preuss, Ernst
Troeltsch, and Friedrich Meinecke, who formed an important part of
the non-socialist liberal opposition of the Wilhelminian period and were
among the intellectual god-parents of the Weimar Republic—stood in
this tradition." [17] Thus, the "Weimar spirit . . . was born before the
Weimar Republic; so was its nemesis." [18]

With the coming of World War I, distinguished historians such
as Troeltsch, Meinecke, and Hintze called attention to "Germany's
special mission to preserve, and spread Kultur, a product in which
Germans apparently excelled, and which they thought they must defend
against the barbarous mass society of Russia, the effete decadence of
France, the mechanical nightmare of the United States, and the un-
heroic commercialism of England." [19] In this connection it must be said
that some of Weber's own statements leave it far from clear that he
escaped the contagion of his society altogether. However, unlike Max
Lenz, Otto Hintze, Erick Marks, and Hans Delbrueck, before World

War I, Weber did not subscribe to Ranke's mystical faith in the nation state. The state was not an object of exaltation in his view. He conceived of it essentially as an *Anstalt* (institution) without a social sensorium, or *Betrieb* (enterprise). However, he fully accepted Ranke's other dictum, that the nation state is engaged in an unrelenting struggle for power. Weber manifested greater faith than some of his colleagues in the possibility of an accommodation with England. Nevertheless, it seems clear that Weber was never able to connect German foreign policy to world peace through international law. The age of imperialism demanded that Germany "must arm and, if necessary, fight to secure its proper place among the great powers." [20]

The argument upon which historicism based its case was that the state was endowed with a metaphysical reality. Other lesser institutions were also characterized by this phenomenon. As Iggers observes:

The classical German historians assumed rightly that freedom is meaningful only within an institutional framework. They prided themselves on possessing a much more realistic understanding of the role of power in society than did their Western colleagues closer to natural-law traditions. Nevertheless, they showed themselves relatively incapable of the empirical, value-free analysis of power and political behavior that Max Weber demanded. Their metaphysical conception of the state as a group person prevented them from developing a truly political concept of the state. [21]

Both defeat in war and revolution brought some modification in German historical thinking. However, "the myth-making mentality . . . went underground and emerged in disguised form, more inaccessible than ever to unmasking or self-criticism." [22] Within the province of his scholarly political analyses, however, Weber held such intellectual themes under firm control. His power of historical judgment, the cohesion of his theories, coupled with his historical perspective and sociological insights, are unassailable. The lost war and the events of the revolution, if anything, strengthened his faith in traditional political attitudes. Apparent inconsistencies in his public speeches may be explained in terms of the specific purposes and audiences to which he addressed himself.

Weber was obviously not a liberal in the sense of mid-twentieth century liberalism. In many respects he shared the type of liberalism espoused by many of his fellow social scientists. The role of pride in his nation is perhaps much more important than has been recognized. Defeat and the consequent settlement at Versailles were a personal humiliation which demanded redress to restore Germany's self-esteem. While many of Weber's statements of personal creed and rational ideas both before and during the war make him sound like a rational voice in the wilderness, his effort after the war to convince his countrymen that an Allied move to deprive Germany of her Eastern territories might be thwarted by a last stand of armed resistance to the enforcement of the Versailles treaty could be read as an ominous portent. His intransigence, while it did not appeal to a war-weary German people, was based, at least in part, upon the hope that such a demonstration of national solidarity would be likely to elicit respect from the enemy. Furthermore, Weber anticipated that the Bolshevik Revolution and the Western response to it would cause the Allies to ease their animosity to Germany sooner than some of the public statements made by their statesmen might suggest. Thus a major and remarkably prescient theme which preoccupied Weber was the common objective of the Allies and of Germany to destroy or at least contain the Bolshevik regime.

Weber's brilliance is again manifested in his treatises on the course which mankind would have to chart to equip itself to deal with the new challenges of a universe characterized by an "increasingly scientific, rational, mechanical and economically logical society" producing " 'disenchantment'—a tension between the emotional desires of the heart in love with mystery, affection and tradition and the dominant rationalistic interpretation of the world of nature and the world of man. From this tension could come wild revolt—emotional, brutal and sentimental orgies like the Nazi movement in Germany. More usually it would be felt as a constant ache of dissatisfaction." [23]

With characteristic detachment, Max Weber assembled the complex historical events into a penetrating record, marked by all the interpretative skill that makes him one of the most perceptive political thinkers of our time. Pointing to the imbalances in the German social structure, Weber wove together those strands of German political history he deemed relevant to the development of the process of mass political education. Weber spoke frankly, neither despairing nor wishing to console, about changes in the conditions of life and the potentially terrifying possibilities ensuing from them. His legacy was not a blueprint containing ultimate answers. Weber, in fact, offered the least dramatic and most rational course to posterity conceivable to him. His convictions on foreign policy, for example, remained sharply defined throughout his life. He threw his full scholarly and political weight behind the maintenance of the balance of power concept. He was willing to explore any possibilities open to the great powers to engage in a bargaining process among themselves. The interests of the smaller nations suffered accordingly. Together with other nationalistic liberals Weber had patriotically supported the war effort. Yet he strongly opposed the presumptuous "parvenue features" of the German countenance abroad, just as he recognized the need for democratic reforms at home, pointing out that the "Anglo-Saxon conventions also mold personalities down into the lower strata." [24]

While his attitudes toward political and social change were cautious and restrained, Weber's authoritative account of pressing social problems involving the national interest reflected a very intense personal involvement. Even his ultimate support of the Republic following the demise of the monarchy was an attempt to satisfy a profound need which penetrated every aspect of his being. His very health—physical, emotional, and mental—was contingent upon his finding the answer to the ultimate problem: How could Germany's national interest best be served? Weber's earlier expressions on the subject of a possible change to the republican form of government certainly revealed his mixed feelings. His ultimate acceptance of it involved a reappraisal of Germany's postwar situation rather than an endorsement of liberal democracy. Nevertheless, when Weber took up his vocation as a political writer, he especially criticized the social injustices resulting from industrialization. One of the most dangerous pitfalls Weber saw in the tendency to retain an undemocratic constitution was the inevitable retention of an undue amount of influence by the landed aristocracy. Weber's aim was not the construction or discovery of some changeless political order. His aim was rather to find paths to reforms within the existing social and political apparatus. He seems always to have felt that the power-political concerns of the state demanded the amelioration of the class struggle. Although he denied the existence of any abstract moral "nature of things," thereby eliminating the possibility of any set of moral ideals existing apart from certain, ethically responsible human beings, he did not imply that there were no objective moral standards. Nor did he view morality as a purely private, subjective matter in which the selfish interests of a class or the caprices of a ruler may be accepted as a valid standard of human conduct. On the contrary, Weber had a high regard for the nobility of the human spirit, as expressed in his ethic of conviction.

Beneath the social and technological crisis of the modern period Weber traced the outlines of a deepening spiritual crisis—a tendency to turn away from faith in an overarching sense of unity, exploring human responsibilities. Essentially, in spite of World War I and the disillusionment that followed it, Weber had hoped to play a catalytic and constructive political role, not only accelerating the development of political consciousness in the younger generation, but awakening and fostering a politically creative impulse in them. From the vantage point of Western democracies, then, Weber diagnosed at the heart of the German political malaise the absence of democratization of her political life. Denying the viability of authoritarian rule, he suggested that Germany could achieve her national goal only as a state that derived its authority from broad popular support. However, he did not share the emphasis prevalent in Western democracies upon parliamentary responsibility. History had attested to the vulnerability of Germany's geographic exposure; hence the circumstances required her to be governed by a strong central authority.

Weber's political thought was not, however, meant to be substantively final and fully authoritative for future political thinkers. Instead, his political writings furnish seminal points of departure and an invitation for dealing with political realities. As a result, political thinkers today can confront their own time and experience in more adequate ways, informed by particular Weberian insights and hypotheses. To be a student of Max Weber means the discovery of high intelligibility in a context of ever-increasing political vicissitudes, involving *Verstehen* of political thought, emotion, and action.

In many respects, Weber's line of thought was shaped by and entered into much of the thought, emotion and action of his time—and with scholarly fruitful results. He foresaw the fate of Western civilization as one in which the dominant trends were increasing bureaucratization of society, emphasizing the importance of science and reason. Socially and politically, Weber demonstrated the man-made nature of different social structures, challenging posterity to design its social and political organization along rationally tested lines. Insisting that the process of rationalization brings demythologization as it supersedes illusory conceptions of the social and political scene, Weber extended a hard challenge to those wearing blinders, those with a closed mentality. Despite the enigmatic quality of his own personality, in his search for creative thought and language we find a deepening preoccupation with the open-ended, imaginative examination of many alternatives in public policy.

Weber's influence is legitimately to be sought where human engagement deepens our perception of specific concrete political experience. In their interpretation of political history, political thinkers today genuinely acknowledge Weber if they can demonstrate a profound awareness of the unique features of the individual historical datum in all its manifestations and a true understanding of social and political interaction between individual and society, and between various segments of society.

Efforts to distinguish historical periods have led to the division of German history into those of Imperial Germany, the Weimar Republic, the Third Reich, and the Federal Republic of Germany. The breaks in this historical scheme suggest an element of discontinuity in historical thinking, permitting limited meanings to emerge in a limited context. The phenomenon of National Socialism, for example, has been dissociated from previous German history as a combination of apparently disparate ideas, having no significant roots in German political attitudes and values. The connections between historical periods and historical conceptualizations emerges when one magnifies them by scrutinizing such issues as parliamentary responsibility, the role of political parties in a democracy, war guilt, the stab-in-the-back legend, and the response made to the Treaty of Versailles. But to attempt to trace various perceptions emerging from recent German history to Max Weber's *direct* influence would be an exercise in mental acrobatics. Tracing specific ways of political reasoning back to Weber would involve precisely the type of travesty in scholarship which Weber sought to combat. Nor could an ideological critique of his failures and inadequacies detract from his versatility, depth, and political genius. Weber's analysis of German politics was original, thorough, and scholarly, albeit polemical. Some recent criticisms tend to overemphasize the differences between his "Machiavellian" conception of politics and that of other politicians. At the same time, they undervalue Weber's shrewdness as a tactician, as well as the political realism to which his writings on organization, bureaucracy, mastery of the political machine, and above all, his discourses on statesmanship, bear testimony. His views on charisma similarly illustrate the subtleties and tensions in his thought,[25] and have become the subject of a growing body of literature.

The question of linkage between Weber's thoughts on the role of strong charismatic leadership and recent Germany history raises a perplexing issue. Nevertheless, and despite a pessimistic realism, Max Weber was profoundly conscious of the dire consequences of a coercive political order, militating against the very internal unity and solidarity so essential for the continuity of the power state's mission abroad. Admittedly, like that of Naumann and Troeltsch, Weber's response to Western European imperialism was a view of history based essentially on the interaction of the great powers. The supremacy of the state to promote the general welfare remained uncontested; even economics was the "handmaiden" of power-political considerations.

Naumann, Troeltsch, and many others shared Weber's conception of the role of the German *Machtstaat* which, in their judgment, was the "primary solution for the domestic social and economic problems of an industrial society in an expansive foreign policy. They championed democratization as a means of strengthening the nation in the international power struggle." [26] They believed that individual rights and personal freedom were attainable within the existing order, suggesting that the "Hohenzollern monarchy, with its aristocratic and authoritarian aspects and its unique bureaucratic ethos, guaranteed a better bulwark for the defense of individual liberties and juridical security than a democracy in which policy would be more responsive to the whims of public opinion than to considerations of reasons of state." [27] Any inherent contradictions seemed to be capable of resolution:

. . . the aristocracy in Germany remained, on the one hand, a country-nobility of struggling agriculturists whose members could be called true aristocrats only with an effort,[28] and on the other hand, a military, court and diplomatic nobility that was the exclusive representative of the German military monarchy.

Despite this there was . . . a certain amount of contact and amalgamation between upper middle-class and aristocracy. Practically every section of the middle-class acknowledged for the most part the deeply-rooted political privileges of the Junkers, ensuring for themselves thereby, in return, the assistance of the state-machinery against the newly organized proletariat and against foreign competition.[29]

A powerful state may thus protect individual freedoms. Moreover, it is in the *Rechtsstaat* that protection of such rights and freedoms is said to be best achieved, "in a constitutional monarchy which provided organs of popular representation but maintained important prerogatives of executive rule, especially regarding foreign affairs and a military free of parliamentary control. This position was held even by such early twentieth-century critics of the Wilhelminian state as Friedrich Meinecke, Ernst Troeltsch, Max Weber, Hans Delbrueck, and Friedrich Naumann." [30]

In his eminently incisive analysis of the evolution of German Conservatism, Klaus Epstein distinguishes three main types of Conservatives: Defenders of the *Status Quo*, Reactionaries, and Reform Conservatives.[31] The Reform Conservative is confronted with the necessity to defend himself against attacks from Conservative quarters, where he is frequently regarded as a traitor, as well as against those mounted by Progressives, who chide him for his "backward" ideas. Since Max Weber's conceptual *Weltanschauung* probably corresponded most closely with the Reform Conservative position, the substance of later criticism of Weber's political attitudes may be viewed in this light. He had witnessed the risks involved in constructing a policy based upon the chauvinism of the Pan-Germans, deeming it irresponsible. Not only, he believed, must the politician in a policy-formulating position anticipate and bear responsibility for the consequences of his political acts, but the national interest must constitute the touchstone of his policy. Domestic discipline and devotion to national goals were attainable only if the demands for democratization were met, social stability being fundamental to national security. He envisaged a forward-looking dialogue with the working class, not because of any commitment to social planning, but because of the implicit challenge to Germany's power-political interests.[32]

Max Weber's legacy is manifest in the writings and viewpoints of many individual scholars. One suspects that his influence will become even more significant as his tenets undergo the test of time and as they are applied by succeeding generations to their own social and political experience. Certainly, Weber's crucial importance as a political scientist is clear in the perspective of our own time when the failure to assess accurately the consequences of a given course of action can threaten national survival. Weber's political discourses thus supply both an indispensable retrospect and prospect of German policies, foreign and domestic, while presenting a model and a challenge to all those engaged in political decision-making.

In the final analysis, Max Weber's thought and writing symbolize political wisdom. His detached appraisal of contingencies; his careful analysis of rational policy alternatives (and his attending rage and despair at the Kaiser's dilettantism); and his heroic confrontation of the inherent moral dilemma raised by all political action—all reaffirm for contemporary political leaders and for those of us who must follow them the tragic fact that politics is indeed the art of the possible.

NOTES

[1] Peter Gay, *Weimar Culture: The Outsider as Insider* (New York: Harper & Row, 1968), see esp. pp. 37–38.

[2] Franz L. Neumann, "The Social Sciences," in *The Cultural Migration: The European Scholar in America* (1953), pp. 21–22, cited in *ibid.*, p. 38.

[3] *Ibid.*

[4] Paul Honigsheim, *On Max Weber* (New York: The Free Press, 1968), p. 7.

[5] *Ibid.*, p. 3.

[6] Cf. Max Weber, "The Prussian Junkers," in *From Max Weber: Essays in Sociology*, edited and translated by H. H. Gerth and C. Wright Mills (New York: Oxford University Press, 1946), cited in S. N. Eisenstadt, ed., *Max Weber On Charisma and Institution Building* (Chicago: The University of Chicago Press, 1968), pp. 218–219.

[7] Max Weber, in Gerth and Mills, *op. cit.*, pp. 193–194.

[8] Fritz K. Ringer, *The Decline of the German Mandarins: The German Academic Community 1890–1933* (Cambridge, Massachusetts: Harvard University Press, 1969), p. 132.

[9] Felix Gilbert, "Political Power and Academic Responsibility: Reflections on Friedrich Meinecke's Drei Generationen Deutscher Gelehrtenpolitik," in Leonard Krieger and Fritz Stern, eds., *The Responsibility of Power: Historical Essays in Honor of Hajo Holborn* (Garden City, New York: Anchor Books: Doubleday & Company, Inc., 1969), p. 444.

[10] *Ibid.* Cf. also Dirk Stegmann. Die Ehben Bismarcks: Parteien und Verbände in der Spätphase des Wilhelministren Deutschlands: Sammlungs politik 1897–1918 Köln-Berlin; Kiepenheuer, Witsch, 1970, pp. 11–112.

[11] Fritz K. Ringer, *op. cit.*, p. 133.

[12] Cf. Ringer, *op. cit.*, p. 134.

[13] W. M. Simon, in Leonard Krieger and Fritz Stern, *op. cit.*, pp. 232–33; also see Gustav Schmidt, *Deutscher Historismus und der Uebergang zur parlamentarischen Demokratie: Untersuchungen zu den politischen Gedanken von Meinecke, Troeltsch, Max Weber* (Luebeck and Hamburg, 1964), pp. 13–15, cited in *ibid.*

[14] *Ibid.*, pp. 235–36.

[15] Peter Gay, *op. cit.*, p. 89. Cf., also Hans Mommsen, "Zum Verhaeltnis von politischer Wissenschaft und Geschichtswissenschaft in Deutschland," *Vierteljahrshefte fuer Zeitgeschichte*, X, 1962, pp. 346–347, cited in *ibid.*

[16] *Ibid.*
[17] Georg Iggers, *The German Conception of History: The National Tradition of Historical Thought From Herder To The Present* (Middletown, Conn.: Wesleyan University Press, 1968), pp. 271–272.
[18] Peter Gay, *op. cit.*, p. 91.
[19] *Ibid.*
[20] *Ibid.*, p. 90.
[21] Georg Iggers, *op. cit.*, pp. 272–273.
[22] Peter Gay, *op. cit.*, p. 91.
[23] Donald G. MacRae, *Iedology and Society, Papers in Sociology and Politics* (New York: The Free Press of Glencoe, 1961), p. 83.
[24] Max Weber, "The Prussian Junkers" in S. N. Eisenstadt, *op. cit.*, p. 216.
[25] Cf. Wolfgang J. Mommsen, "Universalgeschichtliches und politisches Denken bei Max Weber," *Historische Zeitschrift*, CCI, 1965, pp. 557–612.
[26] George Iggers, *op. cit.*, p. 12.
[26] Georg Iggers, *op. cit.*, p. 12.
[28] For the analysis of the situation of the Junkers, see Max Weber, *Wahlrecht und Demokratie in Deutschland* (Berlin, 1918), p. 33, cited in Ernest K. Bramsted, *Aristocracy and the Middle-Classes in Germany: Social Types in German Literature 1830–1900* (Chicago: The University of Chicago Press, 1967).
[29] Ernest K. Bramsted, *op. cit.*, pp. 229–300.
[30] Georg Iggers, *op. cit.*, p. 15.
[31] Cf. Klaus Epstein, *The Genesis of German Conservatism* (Princeton: Princeton University Press, 1966). Supporters of the *status quo* subscribe to "ahistorical" views whereas reactionaries engage in romancing the past, sacrificing "historical accuracy." The Reform Conservative, by contrast, emphasizes the elements of historical experience, seeking to gain an "understanding of historical development and sees the inevitability of certain changes"; consequently, he endeavors to maximize continuity by effecting adjustments within the existing order to "modern needs." *Ibid.*, p. 7f. Cf. also Martin Greiffenhagen, "Konservativ heisst defensiv: Klaus Epsteins unvollendete Geschichte des deutschen Konservatismus." *Die Zeit*, No. 17, Vol. 24, April 29, 1969, p. 14.
[32] Cf. Dirk Stegmann, *op cit.*, pp. 335–336.

Appendix A

Max Weber:
A Biographical Sketch

Max Weber's life and political writings punctuate his deep concern with the preservation of Germany's role in world politics. Spurred on by his studies of socio-political pressures, economic inadequacies, and occupational status differences, he endeavored to discover ways to establish a domestic equilibrium and to give foreign policy the primacy it occupied in his thinking.

The fact that Max Weber's personality and political writings reflected the characteristic features of German politics between 1885 and 1920 inspired the present study, which has sought to provide a fairly detailed analysis of the impact of German political events upon Max Weber, the political analyst and commentator, as well as to find a rationale for his own political ideas and behavior.

The convolutions of German political life are woven throughout his writings; therefore an acquaintance with the psychological climate of German politics is desirable for gaining a better understanding of Weber's deepest concerns. Although Weber's political philosophy was essentially pragmatic, it can by no means be considered a mere congeries of his opinions. Nor can it be assessed as simply a result of the historical circumstances which either produced it, or at the least, provided its impetus. Weber himself had a strong affinity for politics as a vocation. He sought to incorporate his scientific findings in this conception of politics in an existentially meaningful sense. His intense *engagement* in the political life of his country did not, nor could it, lead to any definite systematic theory construction. Nor did he emulate Marx by setting up a utopian formula aimed at the establishment of an ideal state. Since Weber never had an opportunity to become a professional politician, it is difficult to estimate the greatness of his political stature by pointing to concrete examples of his behavior in the public arena.

It remains an enigma whether circumstances, including his own disposition, his extended illness and the apprehension it produced in him concerning his ability to endure the strain accompanying the role of practical politician, were responsible for his inactive role. Since his ideas regarding practical politics were never systematized and translated into a conceptual plan aimed at an ideally suited (for Germany) form of government, he was not always understood by the public at large. The more inaccessible to the lay public his ideas appeared, the more it beheld him as speaking from some Olympian height.

Max Weber's mystique stems from the extraordinarily complex nature of his being and from the monumental quality of his intellectual effort. To his friends and some of his students he opened up new vistas of thought, according to which every political act required consideration in the context of its relevance to both time and place. Certainly Weber did not perceive the mainspring of political behavior to reside in popular sovereignty; nor did he believe its locus rested in monarchical rule. In Weber's judgment, politics demanded an essentially matter-of-fact approach to the conduct of human affairs—one that must remain utterly devoid of sentimentality.

Raymond Aron writes: "Weber did not harbor more or less vague sympathetic attitudes toward this or that orientation nor did he wish for a less rational civilization based upon sentiment or dream of overcoming real conflicts by means of an intellectual revolution; his politics originated in his thinking as an historian who is at the same time a man of action rather than in the thinking of a literateur or a moralist; it constructs no system and gives no binding answers, but renders judgment. Acting means making one's decision in a given unique situation which one did not want to occur, to accommodate oneself to the circumstances, and then to pursue a goal." [1]

Tracing the ebb and flow of human history, political philosphy meant no more and no less to Weber than an intensification of the idea of action at a given moment; from the point of view of permanent influence to be conscious of the conditions compelling us to act; and ultimately, an analysis of political decisions in the context of their implications for the reciprocal relationship between ideals and reality. Max Weber remained true to this conception of political philosophy all his life, throughout which he showed, by illustrating his judgments with examples based upon history, when human will and the moment could effectively coincide: "On the basis of existing facts and his valuations, Weber judged every action suitable for every moment. He was always prepared to ask the question which silences political literateurs: 'what would you do if you were secretary of state,' and to give an answer." [2]

Essentially political sociology connoted for him *Herrschaftssozi-*

ologie (sociology of domination). Domination, in turn, is related to power in that it is both its empirical and practical articulation. Whereas power is "the probability that one actor within a social relationship will be in a position to carry out his own will despite resistance," domination is "the probability that a command with a given specific content will be obeyed by a given group of persons." [3] Accordingly, "domination (*Herrschaft*) is central to the political phenomenon and . . . the political group is essentially a group exercising domination. Political action may consequently be defined as the activity which claims the right of domination on behalf of the authority established in a territory with the possibility of using force in case of need. . . ." [4]

Concerning Weber's conception of the state, Don Martindale states:

Sociologically, Weber believed, a state cannot be defined in terms of its ends, for there is scarcely any task which some political association has not undertaken somewhere, at some time. On the other hand, no one can say for all times and places what task is exclusively the property of the political association. Hence, in the end one can only define the political association in terms of its means above all, in its use of physical coercion. The relation between the state and use of force is especially intimate today, though in the past many other institutions, beginning with the family, have had normal and frequent recourse to it. Today, however, we have to say that a state is a human community that (successfully) claims the *monopoly of the legitimate use of physical force* within a given territory.[5]

It would be unrewarding to attempt in this brief biography a detailed analysis of Max Weber's antecedents and of hypothetical formative influences upon him. But it seems appropriate to give a brief outline of his life and work. He was born at Erfurt, Thuringia, on April 21, 1864, into a German bourgeois family which took great interest in the cultural and political life of the nation. The historical developments accompanied by the tense emotions of those years before World War I were to serve as first-hand stimuli to him. Brought up in a Germany which had been established as a Reich, there could be no question of an inner conflict between the attractions of adherence to the pre-Bismarck era of German society and the new national consciousness. His father was a municipal councillor in Berlin. His interests were vested in his activities as an active politician and member of the National Liberal party; he was a member of the German parliament and a deputy of the Prussian diet. Young Weber's political inspiration, as a consequence, never had occasion to dry up while he was still in his parental home, which was frequented by such outstanding members of the political and academic world as the leader of his father's party, Bennigsen, Rickert, Julian Schmidt, Dilthey, Julius Goldschmidt, Sybel, Miquel, and Mommsen. While his own political talent took some time to mature, he came to recognize at an early point in his life that the problems besetting the new national state were more complex than many of his contemporaries seemed either prepared or willing to admit. Particularly in the political sphere (where ceaseless and often fruitful controversy was carried on between highly disparate factions) he could catch a glimpse of the practical aspects of this fact in his own home environment. Insatiably curious, open-minded, and endowed with an enormous appetite for intellectual activity, he found these early contacts enriching to himself as a person, and subsequently as a scholar as well. Certainly they must have proved exciting, and an inspiration and active assistance as he climbed the academic ladder at an unusually fast pace.

His mother, active in social work and in the struggle for the emancipation of women, was a potent influence upon Weber. She appeared to him as a rock-like symbol of integrity and human generosity. Although she was not a member of the state-church, her religious convictions nevertheless formed the core of her life. She relied heavily upon religion as a source of strength partly, perhaps, to compensate for the fact that her marriage to Weber's father was an agonizing experience for her. Each of Weber's parents seemed profoundly detached from the other's life. His father differed sharply from his wife in temperament and was otherwise absorbed by his own interests. Max Weber felt a deep affection for his mother, whom he credited with having helped him by her example to grow in human stature. By the same token, he resented his father who, in his estimation, resented his mother's personality. In fact, several times the son had encouraged Helene Weber to leave her husband. The gulf between the two men grew after Weber left home and was never to be bridged. During his student days, Weber's cousin, Fritz Baumgarten, had occasion to be in close contact with the Weber family; he wrote home to his own mother that, in his opinion Helene Weber was blameless in the situation since her husband acted like a bully at home. On the other hand, Helene Weber regretfully told her nephew about her disappointment over Weber's lack of religious conviction which he had shown during the period of instruction preceding his religious confirmation in 1879. In fact, Helene Weber suffered keenly from the fact that a state of alienation existed between herself and all her children in an area so important to her as religion was.[6]

In 1869 Max joined his parents, who had taken up residence in Berlin-Charlottenburg, a comfortable residential area in Berlin. The year before he had suffered a case of meningitis, severe enough for the doctors to entertain doubts concerning his chances to retain his sanity. Although he made a remarkable recovery, his physical condition remained weakened for some time. Later young Max accompanied his father on several trips through Germany, but Marianne Weber noted that his formal education interested her husband rather less. From his travels he wrote numerous interesting letters to his mother which reflected a clear hard imagery and a search for means of expressing himself on complicated subjects, revealing, moreover, an early acute sensitivity. His letters draw attention to his processes of thinking and perceiving and are a valuable source for studying his process of becoming from his youth. Attesting to his interest in the classroom, is the fact that Weber proceeded to read Cotta's forty-volume edition of Goethe. When he was between fifteen and sixteen years of age, he became a most avid reader of various types of literature in a number of fields, but especially in history. His reading interests encompassed Curtius' *History of the Greeks*, works by Mommsen and Treitschke, a history of the United States, and Hehn's *Cultured Plants and Domestic Animals*. In his letters to Fritz Baumgarten, six years his senior, he commented on Homer, Herodotus, Virgil, Livy, and, as previously mentioned, Cicero.[7]

In 1882, when young Weber passed the university entrance examination (*Abitur*), his high-school teachers were astounded by the extent of his knowledge. His irreverent spirit, especially his lack of deference toward his teachers, caused some to question Weber's sense of moral responsibility. His first year as a student Weber spent at the University of Heidelberg, where he studied economics under Professor Knies, whose lectures, however, seemed uninteresting to him. He also attended Professor Kuno Fischer's lectures in philosophy and Professor Immanuel Bekker's lectures on Roman institutions and legal history. He studied historiography under the historian, Erdmannsdoerffer.

At the start of his first semester in Heidelberg, his reading habits again covered a vast range of literature. While his interests were primarily intellectual, he could not resist the many invitations which he received from fraternities, so that, although somewhat reluctantly, he finally joined the *Alemannen*.[8] Nor was he without family contacts there, since his mother's sister lived in the town of Heidelberg with her husband, the church historian, Adolf Hausrath. It seems that Weber generally preferred to spend his leisure time with his cousin, Otto Baumgarten, with whom he had bonds of common intellectual interest; in fact, while he was in military training in Strassburg, he attended a seminar offered by Otto's father, Hermann Baumgarten. Weber's visits at his uncle's home caused him to throw himself into intense intellectual dialogues which were to become instrumental in shaping his own thinking processes. Baumgarten helped his nephew gain a new understanding of himself and his own central concerns. What began to crystallize for Weber was the feeling that each individual is surrounded by contradictions. Hence it is up to him to discover the existential dichotomies within himself as well as externally. He began to view man as under obligation to himself to determine from his own individual capacities the meaning-giving values of his life. Upon completion of his year of military service, Weber transferred to Berlin to continue his studies in 1884. It appears that the sojourn in Strassburg, as well as his previous commitments in Heidelberg while he was a member of a fraternity, had constituted too heavy a financial burden for his father to allow him to continue there. In Berlin, Weber chose as his field of concentration the study of jurisprudence. In law school he attended lectures by Beseler, Brunner, Gierke, Aegedy, and Gneist. Concerning the latter's lectures, Weber called them "true masterpieces," devoid of propaganda à la Treitschke; the teaching area of Gneist covered German and Prussian administrative law. Weber's disdainful remarks concerning Treitschke's tirades in the lecture hall suggest that he found them repugnant because he misused his teaching in the lecture hall to indoctrinate his students politically.[9]

Weber's attitude toward military service then was comparable to the intellectual regimentation he saw Treitschke practice in relation to his students. His letters from Strassburg had contained a vivid portrayal of "the extremely dull army routine," which tends to shrink the faculties of the brain.[10] He protested the attending waste of time which, as military routine is wont to do, served to transform men into robots.[11]

In 1885 Weber enrolled in the University of Goettingen, which marked his final year of actual class attendance. He subsequently returned to Berlin as *Referendar* (Junior Barrister) at the *Landesgericht* (County Court) in Berlin. The year 1889 saw the successful completion of his doctoral thesis with Professor Goldschmidt acting as his thesis supervisor on the subject *Zur Geschichte der Handelsgesellschaften im Mittelalter* (The History of Trading Companies in the Middle Ages).[12] In 1891 Weber was graduated with honors. When he defended his thesis before a faculty committee Mommsen pointed out that even though he remained unconvinced of the correctness of Weber's argument his defense had been conducted so brilliantly that he did not wish to stand in his way. He honored Weber with this compliment: "When I go to my grave, I can think of no one to whom I would rather say: 'Son, the spear is too heavy for my arm, take over, highly respected Max Weber'." [13]

By 1891 Weber had established himself as a jurist. Now he began to publish a series of studies of Roman agrarian history under the title: *Die Roemische Agrargeschichte in ihrer Bedeutung fuer das Staats und Privatrecht*. In the following year, under the sponsorship of the *Verein fuer Sozialpolitik* (Association for Social Policy), Weber conducted the studies discussed in detail in this book on the situation of farm workers in East Elbian Germany: "Die Lage der Landarbeiter im Ostelbischen Deutschland." [14] As previously mentioned, this organization, of which Weber was a life-long member, had been founded in 1873 by some of Germany's most renowned economists such as Adolf Wagner, Schmoller, Brentano, and Knapp, although subsequently an effort was made to make it more inter-disciplinary.

In the spring of 1892 Weber was asked to substitute for his *Doktor-vater* Professor Goldschmidt, then fatally ill. In 1893 the University of Berlin appointed him as assistant professor of commercial law. A change in his personal life occurred at that time also when he decided to marry a distant relative, Marianne Schnitger.[15]

One basic inner conflict that remained unresolved for Max Weber lay in the necessity to choose between two different careers, that of scholar and that of practical politician. Although his uncle, Hermann Baumgarten, had helped greatly by encouraging him in the direction of selecting the former, the decision in its favor seemed to appear to Weber at certain junctures of his life an artificial attempt to bring balance into his life. Because the attempted solution was indeed somewhat artificial, sufficiently so for posterity to inquire into the course of events if Weber had walked the road of a politician, his conjecture was interrupted by or at least interspersed with recurrent conflicts, although Weber was able to persuade himself periodically that it was non-existent. Weber had hoped to settle the issue once and for all rather than remain indecisive about it, thereby giving himself, in fact, a double-barrelled protection of being free from doubt. Although it remains questionable whether he would have emerged as a successful politician, even in his own estimate, his response seemed to himself one of arbitrary rightness. His profound involvement in practical politics itself confronted him periodically with a re-creating of the conflict, however. To understand this fact about Weber is to understand a part of what motivated his political philosophy.[16]

Weber's political writings themselves, throughout his life, were marked by one fundamental trait, namely the relative ease to move seemingly effortlessly from politically publicistic to politically academic themes, and often to combine them in a single work. Refreshing in approach, this mobility was frequently also eminently innovative. Significantly, he remarked in a letter to his wife, in which he had asked her to marry him: "I will walk the way which I must walk and which you now know." [17] But even after that, it seemed that his mind continued intermittently to speak with two voices; one was the voice of enjoyment of, or at least commitment to, academic life; the other was the voice of inner despair which told him that he stood merely at the periphery of political happenings while he could take no direct influence since he was not himself at the center of where policy was made. But even if the despairing voice seemed to him at certain intervals as the true one, abandoning the role of the scholar for which he had opted was unthinkable, insurmountable, in fact, on both mental and physical grounds. Nor did the career of scholar lack in tempting attractiveness.

Geheimrat Althoff, commissioner for Prussian educational affairs, was vastly impressed by Weber's reputation as a successful lecturer and wanted him to succeed his former teacher, Goldschmidt, permanently. Since Weber's youth appeared to militate against his endorsement by his prospective colleagues for so high a position, Althoff sought to insure the appointment on all sides. To bind Weber morally, he had held out the prospect of fulfillment of various wishes Weber had expressed. On the other hand, when the commissioner learned of an offer Weber had received before his own and that thus far the position had been kept open for him, he informed his counterpart, the commissioner for educational affairs for Baden, that the University of Berlin was certain to have more to offer and that, at best, Weber would be inclined to regard the University of Freiburg as but a stepping stone. Weber's reaction was sharp and immediate. Previously Althoff had agreed to propose Weber's appointment to the faculty at Berlin, but in the last analysis to allow Weber to reserve the right for himself to accept or reject the offer. Thus when the contract appointing him to the University of Berlin reached Weber, he was dismayed to discover a clause obligating him to turn down other teaching offers at other universities. He took exception to the violation of the agreement. Althoff sought to create an alibi for himself by stating that the letter of contract had been written prior to his discussion with Weber. Weber did not regard the explanation as given in good faith, finding Althoff's whole conduct suspect. Preferring to avoid any future contact with that official, Weber proceeded to accept the appointment in Freiburg in preference to the one in Berlin, in spite of the attractions the latter must have had for him. Thus Weber began his teaching career in 1894 as a full professor by teaching in the area of economics rather than jurisprudence and by occupying a professional chair at the University of Freiburg rather than at the University of Berlin. The disadvantage that decision entailed was both personal and professional. He had to forego frequent contact with his mother, who was living in Berlin, and also his association with the hub of political activity to be found only in the capital.[18] Nevertheless, the personal and professional contacts he made while he was teaching in Freiburg were significant for him at both levels. The most notable among them were probably Wilhelm Rickert, Hugo Muensterberg, and most important for the later dissemination of Weber's own political views, Friedrich Naumann, who was both his friend and political partner for whom Weber had served as mentor as well. Nor is it so surprising that Weber changed teaching fields since he had been accustomed to deal with jurisprudence historically, focusing especially upon the link between the socio-economic structure of various societies throughout history and legal practices. Even while still working on his thesis on medieval trading companies, he oriented himself increasingly toward the field of history itself. Upon the resignation of another of his former professors, Karl Knies, from his chair of economics at the University of Heidelberg, Weber was appointed to that position. He was to meet his former professors again, now as a colleague, among them Kuno Fischer, Immanuel Bekker, and Erdmannsdoerffer. He was associated also with Georg Jellinek, Paul Hensel, and Karl Neumann. Weber was also in contact with sociologists, such as the subsequently leading Marxist critic of the Weimar Republic, George Lukácz.[19]

A close personal friendship developed between Max Weber and Ernst Troeltsch (Troeltsch lived for some time in Weber's home in Heidelberg) that was to become academically fruitful for both. It was Troeltsch who was to see in Germany's military defeat a parallel to the weakening of her moral fiber.[20] Georg Simmel and Robert Michels were also known to Weber during that period.

Early in the summer of 1897 Max Weber's mother had planned a visit to Heidelberg. The events to follow were to leave Max Weber with a sense of catastrophe, not unrelated to his subsequent illness. Helene Weber's intention to come to Heidelberg unaccompanied by her husband were to be frustrated by the protest voiced by Max Weber, Senior. He wanted to be included in her plans; otherwise he sought to prevent her from making the journey alone. In the end, and after considerable altercation which was to be continued in Heidelberg, both parents arrived at Max and Marianne Weber's home there. His father's habit of mind had always created a barrier between father and son, which now asserted itself all the more in that tense situation.[21] The climax of the occasion presented itself when Max Weber defended his mother's prerogative to pay an annual visit to him and his wife without the benefit of his father's company. He went so far, in the context of an emotionally highly charged moment, to threaten to break off relations with his father altogether unless the latter agreed on principle to let his mother spend between four to five weeks annually alone at his home. Failing the older Weber's consent to that proposition, no purpose would be served to maintain the contact between father and son. No agreement was reached and the breach between the two men was never healed. The true state of his parents' marriage unfolded in front of Weber's eyes on this occasion, although the violence of the argument extending from Weber's father to both his son and his wife merely underscored the deterioration of the relationship as it had existed for many years. The feeling of guilt that the subsequent death of his father from hemorrhage evoked, and at a time when his restricted life had become intolerable for him, shook Weber more than is generally realized, although the shock itself may have been compounded by a delicate state of health probably reflecting other traumatic events in his life.

Soon after his father's death, Weber underwent the worst of a succession of illnesses. The following summer, upon returning from a trip to Spain, he suffered an attack of illness the cause of which appeared to be emotional. His health improved until the end of the fall semester. By then his psychological condition could no longer sustain the additional strain under which his lecturing placed him. The medical diagnosis pointed to the incidence of a psychiatric illness, which was worsened by Weber's sleeplessness due to tension. Not being able to lecture regularly, Weber handed in his resignation. His request was not heeded; instead he was awarded a leave of absence.

Upon medical advice he sought exercise, and spent much time in traveling to Spain, Italy, France, Switzerland, Holland and Belgium; these trips resulted in temporary improvements of his health, but above all, in research where fruitfulness is attested by his prolific writings. In October 1903, when it became apparent that recovery was to be but temporary, he was appointed *"Honorarprofessor"* (professor emeritus).

After he had visited several European countries, Weber received an invitation to come to the United States to address the Scientific World Congress held in 1904 in St. Louis, Missouri; he accepted and travelled to America with his wife and his colleagues Troeltsch and Hensel.[22] During this period Weber collected data for his scholarly treatise, *The Protestant Ethic and the Spirit of Capitalism* (1904–1905), and other works forming part of his sociology of religion.[23]

Weber's interest centered around American society as a whole, and American institutions, social, political, and religious in particular; city life impressed him profoundly, especially the busy spirit of Chicago where the chain-belt system and the meatpacking plants inspired both awe and horror in him.

In Haverford Weber systematically attended religious services to extend his knowledge of American religious communities. In St. Louis, where he had met a Westphalian immigrant, he was impressed by the fact that this man, once poor in his own country, had now attained wealth and social status without having been requested to testify to his own worth by producing various documents such as graduation certificates and family records.

The Webers visited Oklahoma and also went to see relatives in Mount Airy, N. C. Back in New York, they visited the Jewish quarter and attended the Yiddish theater as well as religious functions of various sects. The Negro problem caught Weber's interest also. He frequented Columbia University to gather additional material for *The Protestant Ethic and the Spirit of Capitalism*.

Weber visited Columbia, Harvard and the University of Chicago. Almost amusing, though Weber himself did not intend to be, is his account of the Chapel services, especially his comment on the announcements referring to football, baseball, and cricket games made at the close of the service.[24]

His return to Europe marked the completion of the *Protestant Ethic.* His sociology of religion was contained in his posthumously published major work "*Gesammelte Aufsaetze zur Religionssoziologie,*" 1922–1923 (Collected Essays on the Sociology of Religion). The also posthumously published *Wirtschaft und Gesellschaft,* 1925 (Economics and Society), constitutes an investigation of different cultures viewed from the socio-economic perspective. Concerned with essentially sociological problems, he aimed at an interpretation of cultural and historical phenomena. The comprehension of contemporary western civilization could be achieved only by a precise conceptual formulation relating to a body of facts which should be comprehended in a systematic conceptual scheme.

Max Weber's writings are characterized by an unbalanced external framework; this fact may be attributed to his changing interest in special topics, which he studied and set forth within the widest possible context of meaning. His work also reflects a concern with the theoretical aspects of science and with logic and formalism based upon precise historical investigations of a strictly scholarly character. Nevertheless, his writings are difficult to classify because they represent a series of wide-ranging intellectual analyses whose scholarly character frequently does not entirely exclude day-to-day political problems.[25]

The indisputable importance of Max Weber's scholarly writings has resulted in continuous efforts toward making them accessible to the academic profession in Germany and abroad. When he died in 1920 at the age of only fifty-six, many of his articles, which had meanwhile secured for him an international reputation, were dispersed in numerous periodical magazines and archives. These were subsequently collected and published under his widow's direction. Other manuscripts had not yet been published and were barely readable. Max Weber himself lived long enough to publish only the first part of his main work, *Wirtschaft und Gesellschaft,* and the first volume of the *Gesammelte Aufsaetze zur Religionssoziologie*—and those works he had submitted to the publisher immediately preceding his death. Several of Weber's letters are incomplete and numerous others cited in Marianne Weber's biography, *Max Weber, Ein Lebensbild* (Tuebingen, 1926, second edition, Heidelberg, 1950) require correction because several unwarranted liberties had been taken in them. Unfortunately some letters were totally lost, partly as a result of World War II and the ensuing confusion. Nevertheless, Marianne Weber's impressive biography together with Max Weber's own *Gesammelte Politische Schriften* still constitute the main sources for an understanding of Max Weber's political philosophy. Quantitatively, Max Weber's political writings are considerably fewer in number than those of other political writers of his stature, as well as in comparison to his own scholarly work in other fields. Hence intensive use had to be made of those sources which were available and others which might shed additional light upon Max Weber's political ideas and their practical application. Recently, research efforts directed toward Weber's historical and political writings have become more concentrated and cumulative.[26] *Wirtschaft und Gesellschaft* remained fragmentary during his lifetime except for the first section, and the editors' task of arranging the material was made difficult since there was no table of contents. *Wirtschaftsgeschichte*[27] (*General Economic History*), also posthumously published, represents a collection of students' notes of the last series of lectures Weber gave. His essays on methodology did not appear in book form until after his death, under the title *Gesammelte Aufsaetze zur Wissenschaftslehre*, in 1922.

Weber's prolific original research and writing was augmented further by another important role. In 1903 he, Werner Sombart, and Edgar Jaffe established the *Archiv fuer Sozialwissenschaft und Sozialpolitik* (Archives for Social Science and Social Policy), and he also contributed to the *Archiv fuer soziale Gesetzgebung und Statistik* (Archives for Social Legislation and Statistics). For the German Sociological Society, founded in 1909, Weber administered sociographic investigations, all these activities attesting to his organizational involvement in research.

In 1918, after a long enforced absence from the classroom owing to his illness, Weber accepted the chair of sociology, especially created for him, at the University of Vienna. In 1919 at the University of Munich he succeeded the renowned economist Lujo Brentano. He remained in that position until his death the following year.

Weber was among the members of the German delegation sent to Versailles with the memorandum on German war guilt. However, as his widow reported, he left the scene of the Peace Conference suddenly so that he would not have to underwrite Germany's "*mea culpa.*" He also served as a member of the commission responsible for the first draft of the Weimar constitution.

As close as he was to politics, Max Weber was never to realize his aspirations to active participation in politics. In 1919 his name appeared on the Democratic party list of potential candidates standing election for the National Assembly. Through "a political accident," Weber did not receive the nomination.[28]

At the age of fifty-six, then in the second semester of his teaching at the University of Munich, Max Weber was stricken with pneumonia and died on June 14, 1920. Only after his death could the general public know the extent of his scholarly achievements. After the scattered material of earlier years was collected and published in systematic form, Weber became more widely acclaimed. Probably it was due chiefly to his illness that Weber never completed the systematic development and methodological clarification of his theory of society. He left to his colleagues and students (among whom his widow probably ranks first) the task of editing and publishing his treatises.

Max Weber's political writings must be considered with two perspectives in mind; those dealing with theoretical aspects investigating perennial as well as contemporary problems based upon his analysis of political action; and those representing Weber's personal verdicts regarding historical events set against the background peculiar to them. His political legacy represents a multi-layered and most complex work—continuing research into which can yield no final answers which would not seem presumptuous. Weber's writings generally provide hard reading, partly due to the extreme fluctuations typical of his style, which may swing like a pendulum from a pedantic legalistic phraseology to concisely formulated pronouncements, with an undercurrent of scarcely disguised passion permeating them. The juxtaposition of isolated statements, illustrations, and explications is frequently followed by a carefully constructed conceptual framework, characterized by a self-contained entity with a definite beginning and end.

As a systematic thinker, Weber sought to come to grips with reality in its totality and within its historical context, seeking to ascend to ever-higher peaks of rational formulation in his scientific investigations as well as in his political commentaries. At times Weber succeeded in so objectifying himself while objectifying his subject-matter that his own personality remained virtually hidden. In his political writings, however, he often passionately and forcefully sought to provoke serious reevaluation of how a particular situation should be understood and put into a general frame of reference. Writing with a rare blending of scholarly objectivity and profound patriotic concern, it is here that Max Weber frequently reveals his own position. Johannes Winckelmann cogently points to the difficulty presented by the fact that Max Weber's personality encompassed the image of both the scientist and the politician. There is always the risk, accordingly, that too little is selected from too much material: "Yet, nothing would be further from the truth than that Max Weber was 'above all' a scientist and a scholar. That is absolutely incorrect and would not at all correspond to the existential meaning he accorded to his life. He embodied both the scientist and the politician, uniting in both roles the configuration of a truly philosophical existence in our time." [29]

Max Weber defined, asked, and answered questions of the highest relevance to the German situation, Western civilization, and ultimately to the world situation. His political writings have touched the imaginations or permeated the lives of his contemporaries (they were meant to); above all, they were designed to stir thought, to provoke reflection—

activities which were never really widespread in Germany. There is little, however, of sweetness and light in them. Marianne Weber, in her book, *Max Weber, Ein Lebensbild*, presents a brilliantly written and calmly rational account of Weber's thought processes. Nevertheless, she has contributed inadvertently to the fragmentary nature of her husband's publications in the process of sometimes arbitrarily ordering and collecting his writings, done mostly posthumously. As a result, the added subdivisions of his work bear an artificial character yielding the impression of compartmentalization. Moreover, a certain bias was introduced into some crucial interpretations; nor was all available material included in Marianne's Weber's biography. Weber's monumental work, viewed from a total perspective, while it is held together by an essentially marked cohesion, nevertheless not infrequently suffers from having been detached from the context. As a consequence, the rather accidental arrangement of the titles sometimes clouds the actual sequence and nomenclature of Weber's process of thought.[30]

Recent researchers have indicated that for the sake of focusing more sharply on Weber's research findings, greater use should be made of historiographic methods, the objective of which must be a careful examination of all source materials. The data should be presented in the context of their own content and method of presentation; this done, the postulated value commitments, if any, should be examined so as to deduce from these Weber's own political philosophy. Only if all the evidence is accounted for may some of the questions be raised again, now with added justification because of new slants, new insights, newly discovered cohesion and coherence, and finally because of their fundamental relevance.[31]

Wolfgang Mommsen argues that even the best available studies provided by those students of Weber's who intended to render an interpretation of his writings viewed in terms of universal history, were undertaken from particular points of view. In this connection, Mommsen mentions Reinhard Bendix; *Max Weber—An Intellectual Portrait*, in which Weber's sociology of religion has admittedly received particular emphasis.[32] As Mommsen indicates: "It would seem that some time must still pass before a comprehensive analysis of this nature can be attempted, although almost half a century has elapsed since the publication of his principal sociological work." [33]

The universality and enormous variety of Weberian fragments, the lack of familiarity with his diverse levels of analysis, when viewed in combination with his synthesizing methodology, do not make his work easily accessible to the historian or the political scientist. Consequently, both have not infrequently demonstrated an ambiguous reaction poised, as it were, between "respectful lack of understanding and an understanding based upon certain reservations." [34] Exceptions were Otto Hintze and Friedrich Meinecke.[35]

Weber's own scholarship was characterized by an undogmatic stand towards causal relationships in the social sciences. Weber was concerned not only with research in the content of social and economic life, he also tried to clarify the terms in which problems must be stated and analyzed. The first part of Weber's main theoretical work, *Wirtschaft und Gesellschaft*, presents the main sociological definitions which emerged from his historical studies. He did not merely state the terms, however, he also defined and analyzed the methods he used and wished to see used in order to achieve more objectivity in the social sciences.

His early interest in social history was responsible for his subsequent interest in the Protestant ethic and its influence on the evolution of capitalism. This, in turn, moved him to inquire into the relationship between Protestantism and capitalist business methods. Meanwhile, his quest to obtain a fuller understanding of the effects of religion upon social life led him far beyond the study of the evolution of Protestantism in Western Europe. He traced the influence of religion on the social life of the Chinese, the Indians, and the Hebrews. His study of the relationship between Protestantism and capitalism, intended as a critique of Marx's interpretation of history, aimed at determining the link between a purely spiritual conception, the Lutheran concept of the "calling," and the Calvinistic idea of "justification by merit" on the one hand and economic and social life on the other. He studied other civilizations to compare and contrast them with Western rationalistic capitalism.

Rejecting a monocausal interpretation of history, Weber never pretended not to be conscious of the fact that he was devoting his own efforts toward only one aspect of the rise of capitalism which he considered highly significant although, in his judgment, it has been largely overlooked. In his *Gesammelte Aufsaetze zur Wissenschaftslehre* he pointed to history as an analytic tool which must be employed to ascertain multicausal connections, so as to establish the origin, nature, and process of a certain event and situation.[36]

Weber's methodological formulations have practical as well as theoretical limits. These cannot be transcended even within his own system. Yet this fact does not detract from the indelible imprint his work left upon the epistemology of the social sciences. Weber envisaged the social sciences of the future as attaining the status of a reliable source for the social engineer from which he could confidently draw his desired supply of reliable data. Conversely, the social scientist is committed to freedom from value judgment, thus making certain that his own work is as objectively based as possible. This does not make the social science valueless in the determination of goals. Though themselves unable and unauthorized to pronounce judgment as to "the best goals," they may fulfill the function of demonstrating to an individual what he must do to attain a given goal. Moreover, they may also serve to demonstrate how the achievement of one value may or will affect other values. As Julien Freund explains:

In a sense, every human science deals . . . with the social phenomenon. The questions with which sociology deals constitute merely one aspect of the possible forms of social analysis, alongside those raised by political science, economics legal science or ethnology. More precisely, as a discipline using both the causal and the interpretative methods, it attempts to explain certain social relationships and to understand the meaningful approach adopted by men in the face of the historical and empirical developments of various sequences and given correlations of factors.[37]

While the function of science did not include the privilege of pronouncing value judgments, even Christianity could not take its place in this area since by its very nature it was inapplicable to an important sphere of human relations, namely politics. To illustrate that Christianity provided an unsuitable measuring rod for the ethical desirability of a given course of action, Weber chose the maxim "Resist not Evil." He pointed out that no responsible person, and particularly no politician, could follow this rule consistently, unless he were a saint. Weber developed this theme particularly in Politics as a Vocation, where he insisted that two systems of ethics exist, one called an "ethics of responsibility," the other an "ethics of conviction."

The first, he held, operated in the sphere of politics where the moral element could not be a matter of genuine concern, whereas in the second system moral principles have primacy irrespective of the consequences. Weber demanded of the politician that he be held responsible for the consequences of his acts, especially acts of violence; he did not, however, deny him the moral right to "contract with the diabolic powers of violence." Indeed, Weber maintained that a politician is compelled to do so. Thus he did not free the politician from moral responsibility. The criterion by which the politician is to be judged is whether his acts were justifiable within the province of "objective possibility"; that is, he must measure his actions rationally by their chances of success. Weber demanded that the politician follow that course of action which seemed to reduce evil consequences to a minimum. Nevertheless, "Politics is the process which ceaselessly aims at forming, developing, obstructing, shifting or overturning the relationships of domination."[38]

The notion that one must discriminate between the moral codes applicable to states and those applicable to private individuals, is not new. Weber merely reaffirmed the Machiavellian doctrine that princes and states cannot be required to act according to the ordinary rules of morality, but only according to "reasons of state." The statesman may not become totally amoral, but the existence of the double standard must be assumed because of the very nature of politics, with which the struggle for power is identical. The politician must not attempt to circumvent the code of ethics applicable to politics; on the contrary, he must adhere to it unequivocally.

In spite of the fragmentary character and unbalanced external framework of Weber's writings, it is possible to reconstruct a fairly complete outline of his ideas.

The internal unity of his philosophy of history is based upon the unity of the problem which was consciously circumscribed in regard to time and space, but one which dominated all other questions. . . . Why has a specifically 'rational' culture of universal historical significance developed only in the occident, and above all in Western Europe? Why was it only here that we can see the rise of a rational science and technology, a rational industrial capitalism, and a rational work routine, a specifically bourgeois economic society and a bourgeois entrepreneurial class, a rational bureaucratic organization of the state, and a rational legal code? What are the historical origins and developmental trends of this particular form and of the behavioral norms? How do they differ from corresponding non-rational or prerational structures? Why did not a similar 'rationalization process' occur outside of Europe, especially in Asia in the course of which some of the attributes of modern Western culture might have made their impact? Consequently, in the context of world history European rationality, Weber reasoned, represented a unique case, the key concept being the occidental rationalization process.[39]

Central also to Weber's research was the discovery of the link between the characteristics and prerequisites of modern capitalism and the Western European middle classes on the one hand, and the modern rational forms of domination on the other. Abramowski points out that while at the heart of Weber's work in this area lay an explanation of the peculiar rationality of our world, his universal historical investigations generally contributed simultaneously to our historical and human understanding of ourselves: "Underlying the scientific problem concerning the European cultural rationality Weber was guided by a deep concern for the more fundamental existential question, namely that of the significance of the forces of a rational capitalism, a rational science, rational equipment of all kinds and bureaucracies for us as human beings. Considering the conditions produced by the progressive 'bureaucratization' and the scientific 'Entzauberung' (disenchantment) of the universe, what meaning may be salvaged for human freedom and responsible action; and what possibilities might still obtain for a meaningful style of life?"[40] As Abramowski notes, ultimately the answer to this question may be found in Max Weber's conception of the human personality whose roots are grown in the ethics of responsibility; when viewed from this perspective, Weber's research into the various aspects of the rationalization process gains a special significance and points to the profound pathos of his search for answers. Thus H. Stuart Hughes writes:

> The problematic character of rationality in the Western world came to torment him ever more profoundly. Here also we may be led to suspect a kind of world weariness: Weber's intellectual struggle had become intolerably intense. The value-spheres that he had delineated he had eventually found irreconcilable. As the individual, Weber argued, must make a clear choice between a career in scholarship and a career in politics, so he was obliged to opt for one or another ethical system. If he chose the 'ethic of ultimate ends' of the Sermon on the Mount, then he could not participate in the life of the world. This was an ethic fitted only to sainthood; it did not pose the question of the practical consequences of actions. But if a man chose to become an active participant in public affairs, then he was condemned to an 'ethic of responsibility' that might well violate his personal standards of morality. To serve the public good, he would be obliged to commit acts at which his soul recoiled. . . .[41]

Hughes sees Weber's efforts directed at pushing "all the contradictions to their point of maximum lucidity," as "a kind of perverse vocation for self-torment."[42]

As stated several times and reaffirmed by Freund, Weber's ideas have always been controversial, "even as he wished. . . . Weber was and remains a source of inspiration; he never wanted to be a master. . . ."[43] Freund asserts that at various times Weber

> found himself completely isolated, abandoned by those who had called themselves his best friends. This isolation was no doubt due to his political attitude. . . . But he was similarly isolated even on the purely scientific terrain of the discussion of the concept of ethical neutrality . . . at certain memorable meetings of the Association for Social Policy. Some of his positions on public affairs aroused the fury of nationalist students, who went so far as to invade his class-room to prevent him from lecturing. A perusal of the pious biography written by his wife, Marianne Weber, affords but the merest inkling of the outbursts, revolts and scandals he provoked. Those who knew him say that he was like a volcano in constant eruption, at the same time retaining an inward calm which added to the confusion of those who argued with him.[44]

It has been said that, "almost twenty years after the end of World War II and more than forty years after his death, Weber symbolically had to stand trial before a sort of intellectual denazification court at the Heidelberg meetings of the German Sociological Association, supposedly dedicated to honoring the centenary of his birth."[45] Comparing some of the German with the American contributions at this Convention, one realizes how divergent, though not necessarily absolutely irreconcilable, the paths to a meaningful interpretation of Weber's political philosophy can be, and more especially when viewed from the vantage point of contemporary political sociology. As stated previously, some fundamental differences were apparent in the views of Herbert Marcuse on one hand and Raymond Aron and Wolfgang J. Mommsen on the other. The greatest difference, however, existed between Marcuse on one side and Reinhard Bendix and Benjamin Nelson on the other. Nevertheless, a consensus appears to have been achieved concerning *certain* aspects of Weber's conceptualizations, including his beliefs, cognitions, values, and symbols relevant to the political situation of contemporary Germany. There is much less agreement however, on the precise linkage of these to the latter.[46] Weber's emphasis upon the need for charismatic leadership to counter the effects of increasing bureaucratization, it has been suggested, may even have steered some of his own students toward Hitler and the Nazi movement. The question has been raised:

whether there was not too much *furor teutonicus* in him? Well, yes, perhaps there was. But Weber, who had more of the Lutheran than the Calvinist in him, answered these questions himself when he appealed at one time to the Lutheran 'Here I stand, I can do no other,' in defining the limits of man's responsibilities for the consequences of his actions. For us, then, Max Weber is a sort of hero fit for modern intellectuals because he exemplifies the way in which the moral stamina to live with some of the major existential dilemmas of an age can enrich a scholar's work and ennoble his life far more than shallower attempts to 'resolve' what can only be resolved by sacrificing a considerable part of the complexity of experience.[47]

It seemed that at the Heidelberg Convention of the German Sociological Society, a major impulse was not simply to canonize Max Weber nor to denounce him, but to gain a genuine understanding of a most complex personality who can neither be forgotten nor followed. While Benjamin Nelson conceded that "Weber could and did become crude and gauche in some of his forays into *Machtpolitik*," he also pleaded: "Surely we have not been gathered here in his beloved Heidelberg to hear this one side of the story. Nor is this in any profound sense how his life and work demand to be understood." [48]

Herbert Marcuse's recurring theme regarding Weber's political philosophy reflected a comment on Weber's dedication to capitalism which led him to engage in "malicious combat against the socialist attempts of 1918." [49] Accordingly, Marcuse argued, socialism was held to be opposed to both the idea of occidental reason and the idea of the national state; hence socialism is a universally historical error, if not a universally historical crime. Marcuse asked what conclusions Weber would have come to had he lived to see "how it was not the West but the East that has developed the rationality of the West in its most extreme form?"[50] Apparently, the issues which divided the speakers at the convention were pervaded by a spirit of protectiveness on the part of those on Weber's side—mostly the American visitors to the convention—directed against Marcuse and some of his German colleagues, who in reappraising German political culture in Nazi- and postwar Germany focused on those of Weber's political attitudes which seemed relevant to this enterprise. Marcuse suggests that Weber was enraged by the Revolution for three reasons:

(1) In his view, the Revolution would have destroyed any hope of a reasonable and bearable peace treaty for Germany. (In this argument he came close to the 'stab-in-the-back legend', Mommsen conceded).
(2) He believed that any socialization would endanger the future of the German economy.
(3) In his view any temporary dilettante regime of the extreme left would of necessity provoke an equally dilettante regime of the extreme Right.[51]

Max Weber, states Mommsen, was an aristocratic liberal in his basic outlook, even though he sometimes employed means which could not be considered liberal in actual fact. Nevertheless, as Mommsen insists, at no time did Weber envisage a direct alliance with the Right. On the contrary, all his life he fought *against* an alliance of the German bourgeoisie with the Junkers and *for* a closer relationship with a socialist Left on a moderate basis.[52] Mommsen protested emphatically[53] against the parallel drawn by Marcuse implying a direct line to the planned destruction of millions of people through rationally contemplated acts of violence culminating in genocide.[54] The appraisal made by Mommsen closely approximates the author's.

Weber never formulated a definitive conceptual framework for his philosophy. Instead of systematizing his political ideas, especially in the area of foreign relations, he focused on problem-solving, concentrating on the immediate requirements as he saw them. *The ultimate yardstick of his views was always the national interest of Germany.* What was formidable perhaps was the degree to which he remained convinced that all problems could be made to yield to his methods. Nevertheless, friends and foes frequently found themselves taken aback by Weber's rigorous judgments and often forceful prescriptions, only to learn subsequently how astute some of his insights and solutions proved to be.

The sustained as well as revived interest in the life work of Max Weber, though essential, is by no means a sufficient response to a changed world and the changed role of Germany in the world. No mere accumulation of facts, no matter how complete, is capable itself of advancing our understanding of Weber in relation to his country's history and its part in international politics. Neither political science nor sociology may claim a monopoly of insight in the ordering and inter-relating of the data arising from Weber's own work and those derived from studies concerned with it. Nevertheless, these two fields provided analyses aimed at making explicit Weber's concepts, the criteria of their relevance, the techniques of ordering the relevant data in the light of recent German history, prewar as well as postwar, and the ways fellow scholars integrate and systematize their own findings.

As Raymond Aron correctly states, the contradictions to be found in Max Weber's political attitudes do not detract from his human stature:

This 'nationalist' cared above all for the value of the individual, defending the claims of labor and supporting all who were victims of collective institutions. He accepted the war between the gods, nations, and men, but he despised a world in which everyone cheats. May everyone select his ideal. . . . The scruples of an intellectual consist in having to differentiate between that which one knows and that which one believes—that which one wants and that which is—without these scruples Weber could not have sustained himself in life, but with them he could not enter the field of action.[55]

It is the concept of rationalization which establishes the method-ological link between Max Weber's scholarly writings and his philoso-phy. The modern world has undergone the process of disenchantment, having had to divest itself of magic phenomena and mystical forces. Since the process of rationalization has penetrated into economics, religion, and all other forms of human existence, the human individual continuously faces the danger of himself becoming rationalized. The sole means of salvation from such an existence, in which man himself be-comes the victim of rationalization, Weber saw in the kind of intrinsic freedom he indicated, which nevertheless would not infringe upon those areas of human existence which have a just claim to rationalization. In the area of politics, it will be recalled, Weber demanded that free-dom oppose itself to the "castration by bureaucracy," while in the field of ethics freedom manifests itself in the decision-making process, pro-ducing crises of conscience whose resolution occurs through the selection of the highest values.

Max Weber did not place his faith in social and political move-ments which promised to deliver man from walking the road to serf-dom and thus lead the way toward freedom. The concept of the "charis-matic leader" appealed to Weber as containing the chance for a genuine opportunity for man to develop his human faculties. Aron's assessment of the outcome of Weber's inner struggle is somewhat more optimistic than Hughes': "Ultimately Weber viewed mankind's worthy objective to be the struggle of man against the blind determinism of the world and the resolution of conflicting requirements." [56] Raymond Aron correctly views Weber as a "clearsighted nationally oriented German" [57] who already in the prewar years anticipated the disaster. However, Aron also points to him as one whom we should not seek to understand on the basis of his attitude to his country only, but as a man of the twentieth century "who combines courage with clearsightedness and who intensely shares our fate fearing that the individual would lose his identity in the bureaucratic organization, that freedom would give way to a rationalized economy, and that the person would disappear under the domination by the masses." [58] Hence the essence of Max Weber's life and work transcend the fate of Germany coexistent merely with his own lifetime.

NOTES

[1] Raymond Aron, *Die Deutsche Soziologie Der Gegenwart: Systematische Einfuehrung In Das Soziologische Denken,* translated by Iring Fetscher (Stuttgart: Alfred Kroener Verlag, 1965), pp. 119–120. *La Sociologie Allemande Contemporaine,* by Raymond Aron, P.U.F., 1935. Reprinted by permission of Presses Universitaires de France.

[2] *Ibid.,* p. 120.

[3] Max Weber, *The Theory of Social and Economic Organization* (New York: Free Press), p. 152, cited in Julien Freund, *The Sociology of Max Weber* (New York: Pantheon Books, Random House, 1968), pp. 218–221.

[4] Julien Freund, *op. cit.,* p. 221.

[5] Don Martindale, *Institutions Organizations, and Mass Society* (Boston: Houghton Mifflin, 1966), p. 295.

[6] For a background of Weber's personal history his widow's biography is the only extensive account. Unless stated otherwise, all references to this topic are based on Marianne Weber: *Max Weber: Ein Lebensbild* (Tuebingen: J. C. B. Mohr, 1926).

[7] Max Weber, *Jugendbriefe,* edited by Marianne Weber, letters written in the years 1876–1893 (Tuebingen: J. C. B. Mohr, 1936), p. 3.

[8] German university students were accustomed to attach considerable significance to membership in the fraternities because they were thought to invest the individual with social status during their student days. Professional appointments were often determined by membership in these *"Studentenverbindungen"* (student associations).

[9] *Lebensbild,* p. 126.

[10] *Ibid.,* p. 77.

[11] *Ibid.*

[12] *Ibid.,* p. 120.

[13] *Ibid.,* p. 121.

[14] *Ibid.,* p. 136.

[15] In view of the part which Weber later played in German politics, it is doubtful whether he could ever have become a successful politician.

[16] *Lebensbild,* p. 122.

[17] *Ibid.,* p. 90.

[18] For a more detailed account see: *Lebensbild,* pp. 210–13.

[19] Cf. Georg Lukácz, *Geschichte und Klassenbewusstsein* (Berlin: Der Malik-Verlag 1923), and Victor Zitta, *George Lukácz' Marxism: Alienation, Dialectics, Revolution—A Study in Utopia and Ideology* (The Hague: Martinus Nijhoff, 1964).

[20] Cf. Ernst Troeltsch, "Die Revolution in der Wissenschaft," *Gesammelte Aufsaetze*

zur Geistesgeschichte und Religionssoziologie, ed. Hans Baron (Tuebingen: J. C. B. Mohr, 1925), p. 653.

21 Cf. *Lebensbild,* p. 393.

22 *The Rural Community 'Deutsche Agrarverhaeltnisse in Vergangenheit und Gegenwart'. Vortrag fuer den internationalen Kongress in St. Louis, 1904 (Congress of Arts and Science),* edited by H. J. Rober (Boston, 1906), Vol. VII, cited in *Lebensbild,* p. 716.

23 Cf. *Lebensbild,* pp. 243–92.

24 The entire account of the couple's travel experiences can be found in *Lebensbild,* pp. 292–317.

25 The only recent comprehensive study of Max Weber's political philosophy is the outstanding work by Wolfgang J. Mommsen to which this present study is greatly indebted. Cf. Wolfgang J. Mommsen, *Max Weber und Die Deutsche Politik 1890–1920* (Tuebingen: J. C. B. Mohr [Paul Siebeck] 1959). During World War II, a competent little book filled the gap, authored by J. P. Mayer, entitled: *Max Weber in German Politics* (London: Faber & Faber, 1943; 2nd. edition, London, 1956). Karl Loewenstein's book *Max Weber's staatspolitische Auffassungen in der Sicht unserer Zeit* (Frankfurt am Main: Athenaeum Verlag, 1965) also treated Weber's political thought, but unfortunately in a rather uncritical vein and without documentation. On the other hand the more controversial aspects of Weber's political themes are subjected to excellent and thought-provoking discussions in *Max Weber und die Soziologie heute,* Verhandlungen des 15. deutschen Soziologentages, edited by Otto Stammer (Tuebingen: J. C. B. Mohr [Paul Siebeck] 1965). Three good recent summaries of the political thought of Max Weber are contained in H. Stuart Hughes, *Consciousness and Society: The Reorientation of European Social Thought 1890–1930,* 2nd. ed. (New York: Alfred A. Knopf, 1961), Karl Jaspers, *Three Essays: Leonardo, Descartes, Max Weber,* translated by Ralph Manheim (New York: Harcourt, Brace & World, Inc., 1964), pp. 187–274, and Raymond Aron, *Main Currents in Sociological Thought* (Vol. II, Durkheim/Pareto, Weber. New York: Basic Books, 1967). An invaluable service has been rendered to the English-speaking reader of Weber's works by Guenther Roth's and Claus Wittich's translation of Weber's *Economy and Society,* the first complete English edition (The appendix contains one of Weber's major political essays, "Parliament and Government in Reconstructed Germany" (A Contribution to the Political Critique of Officialdom and Party Politics)) (New York: Bedminster Press, 1968); an introduction by Guenther Roth precedes the excellent translation of Weber's work. Also, a vital contribution to an understanding of Weber's sociology of the state is Johannes Winckelmann, ed., *Max Weber—Staatssoziologie,* 2nd. rev. ed. (Berlin: Duncker & Humblot, 1966).

26 Two studies making an indispenable contribution are Johannes Winckelmann, ed., *Max Weber—Soziologie-Weltgeschichtliche Analysen—Politik,* with an introduction by Eduard Baumgarten (Stuttgart: Alfred Kroener Verlag, 1964), and Raymond Aron, *Deutsche Soziologie der Gegenwart: Systematische Einfuehrung in das soziologische Denken,* translated by Iring Fetscher (Stuttgart: Alfred Kroener Verlag, 1965). Cf. especially "Die Synthese Von Systematischer und Historischer Soziologie im Werke Max Webers," pp. 92–148.

Among other notable appraisals of Max Weber's political historical thought to be included are the eminently astute introduction by Hans. H. Gerth and C. Wright Mills, *From Max Weber: Essays in Sociology* (New York: Oxford University Press, 1946), and the excellent summary of Weber's historical theories and political thought by Gerhard Schulz, "Geschichtliche Theorie und politisches Denken bei Max Weber," *Vierteljahrshefte fuer Zeitgeschichte,* Vol. 12, No. 4, 1964, pp. 325–350. Reinhard Bendix, *Max Weber—An Intellectual Portrait* (Garden City: Doubleday & Co., Inc., 1960) and Eduard Baumgarten, ed., *Max Weber—Werk und Person* (Tuebingen: J. C. B. Mohr [Paul Siebeck], 1964), must also be considered important reference works. The latter contains selected writings of Max Weber, including heretofore unpublished letters and less publicized materials; unhappily they were not edited in a completely unbiased manner.

First-rate portrayals of Weber's historico-sociological theory are Robert A. Nesbit, *The Sociological Tradition* (New York: Basic Books, Inc., 1966), Guenter Abramowski, *Das Geschichtsbild Max Webers,* Kieler Historische Studien (Stuttgart: Ernst Klett Verlag, 1966), and Ernst Topitsch, "Max Webers Geschichtsauffassung", *Wissenschaft und Weltbild,* Vol. 3, 1950, pp.

252–270. Cf. also Don Martindale, "Max Webers Beitrag zur Kultursoziologie und zur Theorie der Zivilisation," in special issue No. 7, "Max Weber zum Gedaechtnis," of the *Koelner Zeitschrift fuer Soziologie* und Sozialpsychologie," Vol. 15, 1963, pp. 294ff. An interesting presentation also is Julien Freund, *The Sociology of Max Weber* (New York: Random House, 1968). Also Reinhard Bendix, "Max Weber's Sociology Today," *International Social Science Journal*, Vol. XVII, No. 1, 1965, pp. 9–22, and Wolfgang Mommsen, "Max Weber's Political Sociology and His Philosophy of World History," *ibid.*, pp. 23–45. Weber's historical sociology has been discussed extensively by Karl Bosl, "Der 'Soziologische Aspect' in der Geschichte," in Karl Engisch, Bernard Pfister, and Johannes Winckelmann, eds., *Max Weber: Gedaechtnisschrift der Ludwig-Maximilians Universitaet Muenchen zur 100. Wiederkehr seines Geburtstages 1964* (Berlin: Duncker & Humblot, 1966), pp. 41–56, Alois Dempf, "Max Weber als Kultursoziologe," *ibid.*, pp. 55–66, and Friedrich Luetge, "Max Weber als Wirtschafts-und Gesellschaftshistoriker," *ibid.*, pp. 147–162. A penetrating study relevant to Weber's philosophy of history is Carlo Antoni's, "Max Weber" in *From History to Sociology: The Transition in German Historical Thinking*, translated by Hayden V. White (Detroit: Wayne State University Press, 1959), pp. 119–84. Cf. Benedetto Croce, "Soziologie und Geschichte," in *Theorie und Geschichte der Historiographie: Gesammelte Politische Schriften in Deutscher Uebertragung*, Part I, Vol. 4, Tuebingen, 1930, p. 299ff. and Theodor Schieder's comparison between Burckhardt and Weber in *Staat und Gesellschaft im Wandel unserer Zeit, Studien zur Geschichte* des 19 and 20. Jahrhunderts (Munich, 1958), p. 176ff., cited in Gerhard Schulz, *op. cit.*, p. 329.

27 *Wirtschaftsgeschichte, Abriss der Universalen Sozial-und Wirtschaftsgeschichte*, edited by S. Hellmann and N. Palyi, 2nd. ed. (Munich, 1924); English Translation by Frank H. Knight (London: George Allen & Unwin, Ltd., 1930).

28 Talcott Parsons, "Max Weber's Sociological Analysis of Capitalism and Modern Institutions," *An Introduction to the History of Sociology*, edited by Harry Elmer Barnes (Chicago: The University of Chicago Press, 1947), XIII, 288. Cf. also pp. 115ff., *infra*.

29 Johannes Winckelmann, "Vorwort des Herausgebers", *Max Weber-Soziologie— Weltgeschichtliche Analysen-Politik*, edited by Johannes Winckelmann (Stuttgart: Alfred Kroener Verlag, 1964), pp. VIII–IX.

30 Cf. list of Weber's writings in the bibliography.

31 This line of thought has been perceptively and convincingly explored by Wolfgang J. Mommsen, *Max Weber und die deutsche Politik 1890–1920*. For an indication of the diversity of opinion and level of open debate, which exists among Weber scholars, particularly as applied to Mommsen's study, see Ernst Nolte, "Max Weber vor dem Faschismus," in *Der Staat: Zeitschrift fuer Staatslehre, Oeffentliches Recht und Verfassungsgeschichte* (Berlin: Duncker & Humblot, Vol. 2, No. 1, 1963), pp. 1–24. Nolte's analysis also represents a complementary interpretation adding a new dimension to an understanding of Weber's role and significance as viewed from the perspective of our own time.

32 Wolfgang J. Mommsen, "Max Weber's political sociology and his philosophy of world history," *International Social Science Journal*, Vol. XVII, No. 1, 1965, p. 24. Mommsen refers here to Bendix' own statement contained in pp. 64ff.

33 *Ibid.*, p. 25.

34 Gerhard Schulz, "Geschichtliche Theorie und politisches Denken bei Max Weber," *Vierteljahrshefte fuer Zeitgeschichte*, Vol. XII, No. 4 (Stuttgart: Deutsche Verlags-Anstalt, 1964), p. 328.

35 Cf. Otto Hintze's review of Weber's *Gesammelte Aufsaetze zur Religionssoziologie*, in Schmoller's *Jahrbuch*, Vol. 46, 1922, pp. 251–58, and of *Wirtschaft und Gesellschaft*, *ibid.*, Vol. 50, 1926, pp. 83–95. Meinecke's review of Weber's *Gesammelte Politische Schriften* even appeared in the *Historische Zeitschrift*, Vol. 125, 1922, p. 272ff., under the title "Drei Generationen deutscher Gelehrtenpolitik." However, Meinecke, while he respected Weber as a scholar and while his political views did not differ significantly from Weber's own, never arrived at a conclusive evaluation of Weber's historical importance as a political scientist or as a historian.

36 Significant contributions to the study of this aspect of Weber's work are: Dieter Henrich, *Die Einheit der Wissenschaftslehre Max Webers* (Tuebingen: J. C. B. Mohr, 1952); Ernst Topitsch and Wilhelm Weber, "Das Werturteilsproblem seit Max Weber," *Zeitschrift fuer Nationaloekonomie*, Vol. 13, 1952, pp. 158–201; Walter Wegener, *Die Quellen der Wissenschaftsauffassung Max Webers und*

die *Problematik der Werturteilsfreiheit der Nationaloekonomie* (Berlin, 1962); C. von Ferber, "Der Werturteilsstreit 1909–1959; Versuch einer wissenschaftsgeschichtlichen Interpretation," *Koelner Zeitschrift fuer Soziologie und Sozialpsychologie*, Vol. 11, 1959, pp. 21–37; Alexander von Schelting, *Max Webers Wissenschaftslehre* (Tuebingen, 1934); Talcott Parsons, *The Structure of Social Action* (New York and London, 1937, second edition Glencoe, Ill., 1949), Chapter XVI; Raymond Aron, *La philsophie critique de l'histoire*, 2nd ed. (Paris, 1950), Part IV; the role of values and their relationship to the social sciences in the context of Max Weber's methodology is taken up in R. Dahrendorf, *Gesellschaft und Freiheit* (Munich, 1961), especially pp. 26–48 and G. Myrdal, *Value in Social Theory* (London, 1958); there are also two brief but notable contributions, one entitled, "Scientific Objectivity and Value Hypotheses," was delivered by Pietro Rossi to the Fifteenth German Sociological Congress, Heidelberg, April, 1964, and published in *International Social Science Journal*, Vol. XVII, No. 1, 1965, pp. 65–70, the other being Edward A. Shils, "Social Science and Social Policy," *Philosophy of Science*, Vol. 16, 1949, pp. 219–42. For his formulation of ideal types see especially Alfred Karsten, *Das Problem der Legitimitaet in Max Webers Idealtypus der rationalen Herrschaft* (Hamburg, 1960), and Friedrich H. Tenbruck, "Die Genesis der Methlogie Max Webers," *Koelner Zeitschrift fuer Soziologie und Sozialpsychologie*, Vol. 11, 1959, pp. 573–630; for his concept of *Verstehen* see especially Johannes Winckelmann, *Gesellschaft und Staat in der verstehenden Soziologie Max Webers* (Berlin, 1957). Julien Freund, *The Sociology of Max Weber* (New York: Pantheon Books, Random House, 1968). R. Dahrendorff, *Society and Democracy in Germany* (Garden City, N.Y.: Doubleday and Co., Inc., 1967), published in Germany under the title *Gesellschaft und Demokratie in Deutschland* in 1965. Copyright by R. Piper and Co., Verlag, Muenchen, 1965. Also J. P. Mayer, *Max Weber and German Politics* (2nd ed., London, 1956). W. J. Mommsen, *Max Weber und die deutsche Politik* (Tuebingen, 1959). Max Weber, *Gesammelte Aufsaetze zur Wissenschaftslehre* (Tuebingen, 1951).

37 Julien Freund, *The Sociology of Max Weber* (New York: Pantheon Books, Random House, 1968), pp. 286–87.

38 *Ibid.*, p. 221.

39 Guenter Abramowski, *Das Geschichtsbild Max Weber*, Kieler Historische Studien (Stuttgart: Ernst Klett Verlag, 1966), pp. 13–14.

40 *Ibid.*, p. 14.

41 H. Stuart Hughes, *Consciousness and Society: The Reorientation of European Social Thought 1890–1930* (New York: Alfred A. Knopf, 1958), pp. 329–330.

42 *Ibid.*, p. 330.

43 Julien Freund, *op. cit.*, p. 32.

44 *Ibid.*, pp. 32–33.

45 Guenther Roth and Bennett M. Berger, "Max Weber and the Organized Society," *The New York Times Book Review*, (April 3, 1966), p. 45.

46 Otto Stammer, ed., *Max Weber und die Soziologie heute; Verhandlugen des 15. Deutschen Soziologentages* (Tuebingen: J. C. B. Mohr [Paul Siebeck], 1965). Cf. especially Herbert Marcuse, "Industrialisierung und Kapitalismus," pp. 161–180; Raymond Aron, "Max Weber und die Machtpolitik," pp. 103–120; Wolfgang J. Mommsen, "Diskussion ueber: 'Max Weber und die Machtpolitik'," pp. 130–138, and "Diskussion ueber 'Industrialisierung und Kapitalismus'," pp. 215–216; Reinhard Bendix, "Diskussion ueber: 'Industrialisierung und Kapitalismus'," pp. 184–191: and Benjamin Nelson, "Diskussion ueber: 'Industrialisierung und Kapitalismus'," pp. 192–201.

47 Guenther Roth and Bennett M. Berger, *op. cit.*, p. 45.

48 Benjamin Nelson, *op. cit.*, p. 198.

49 Herbert Marcuse, *op. cit.*, p. 161.

50 *Ibid.*

51 Wolfgang J. Mommsen, "Diskussion ueber: 'Industrialisieurung und Kapitalismus'," *op. cit.*, pp. 215–216.

52 See *ibid.*, p. 216.

53 See *ibid.*, p. 215.

54 See Herbert Marcuse, *op. cit.*, p. 176.

55 Raymond Aron, *Deutsche Soziologie der Gegenwart: Systematische Einfuehrung in das soziologische Denken, op. cit.*, pp. 128–219.

56 *Ibid.*, p. 150.

57 *Ibid.*

58 *Ibid.*

Appendix B

A Note on Max Weber's Methodology

An abundant crop of students concerned with the philosophy of history, or more generally with the methodology and epistemology of the social sciences, emerged in Germany during the last quarter of the nineteenth century. Ranke, with his limitation of history to fact-finding, had stifled rather than encouraged this trend, although he was not to remain uninfluenced by certain ideas of "Historismus." However, the emergence of sociology as a separate discipline as well as the strong German philosophical tradition of ideology provided an impetus to historians to concentrate upon the perennial problem of a meaningful interpretation of the process of history. Marxism, both as a challenge and as an actual influence, had greatly contributed to the reestablishment of history as philosophy. Conversely, "scientism," that is the application of quantitative and statistical analysis to social phenomena in the fashion of Solvay and Buecher, came into vogue as a result of the impact of the advances of natural science. Psychology also claimed a hearing in the interpretation of society past and present. A *pot pourri* of confusing theories in turn called for epistemological clarification and the delimitation of the proper fields of inquiry assigned to the historian as against the natural scientist or sociologist. In grappling with this problem, the work of three men most impressed itself on the minds of their contemporaries: Windelband, Rickert, and Dilthey. In his own treatment of the same phenomenon, Max Weber partly drew from them, partly repudiated their theories.

A principal question occupying these men was the logical distinction between natural science and that whole field of knowledge applied to the study of man, including history, political science, economics, and social psychology, and which came to be known as the social sciences. For Weber the question had special significance because it involved,

418

as we shall see, a number of his fundamental methodological propositions. Dilthey divided these two fields of inquiry in terms of the nature of the material with which they deal, assigning to the scientist, broadly speaking, all phenomena of matter, and to the social investigator those of the human mind. Man with his "soul" and "will" was thus set apart in a neat corner, since these attributes, according to Dilthey, were inaccessible to positive knowledge, and accessible only to "understanding" based on *Einfuehlungsvermoegen*, that is the ability of the investigator to put himself into the place of the subjects investigated.[1]

Weber, on the other hand, perceived no logical difference in the character of the material, regarding both historical and scientific data as empirical knowledge in exactly the same qualitative sense.[2] In his judgment, and that of Rickert, the real difference derived from the point of view (*Betrachtungsweise*) from which the material is ordered. Weber's rejection of the idea that history (as well as other social sciences) is "logically unique" because it deals with so-called irrational phenomena like "free will" is the cornerstone of his thesis, anticipating the possibility of objective historical knowledge. Reduced to its simplest terms, his estimate of the correct relationship between scientific and historical knowledge proceeds along the following lines: both historian and scientist are confronted with the task of ordering a vast amount of empirical knowledge into a system designed to do a maximum degree of justice to the peculiar significance of the material on hand. Both deal with data showing certain regularities in the order of their occurrence, regularities which we call laws in those cases in which cause and effect appear fixed. Actually, however, empirical data merely furnish us with rules of probability with varying degrees of mathematical accuracy. Whether this probability be greater or smaller, or whether it can be expressed quantitatively at all, is logically irrelevant, as shown by the exact sciences like physiology, biology, etc., which also have to operate with data of lesser certainty than, for instance, physics.[3] Turning to human behavior, we observe that men generally react in a certain manner to a defined set of circumstances, and that changes in their behavior are always related to changes in those circumstances. Purely formally, this observation suffices for the general definition of causality, quite regardless of our knowledge of the psychological content of this process. Thus there exists a chance for predictable human behavior which we may call its rationality. Rational human actions, then, are such as can be fitted into the pattern of our experience in its widest sense.[4] Like any other set of observations making up empirical knowledge, they are subject to scientific investigation.

Against those who see in the unpredictability of the historical process, and in the interference of the autonomous will of the "hero," proof that history is a sphere of accident, not of law, and of freedom, not of necessity, Weber strikes out in two directions.[5] First, he addresses himself to what seems to him the true relationship between rationality and freedom, and secondly, to the matter of causality and predictability. According to his definition of rationality as a chance for predictable behavior, there can be no antagonism between rationality and freedom. On the contrary, the freer the will, the greater the rational component of man's actions, because absence of pressure results in the highest possible degree of purposefulness. And it is, after all, exactly the habit of men to act with regard to a definite purpose which constitutes the reason for rational behavior. Whether these purposes are dictated by "interests" or by "values" will depend on the circumstances. In any case, however, even if the values sought are irrational, the actions of men must be called rational as long as they bear an understandable relation to any system of values accepted by them. Weber is convinced that this principle is applicable even to the highest complexities of emotional phenomena: only the insane behave entirely irrational.[6]

What follows from this? Principally that human behavior is understandable in the light of our knowledge of human purpose, and that the two are causally related. But what of the question of predictability? Would not the assumption of history as a causal process imply, at least in principle, that it must also be a predictable one? Not necessarily, as suggested by the following analogy: If a rock falls to the ground, it will break into many parts. The scientist observing this event will be able to explain it afterward according to his empirical knowledge as a "true-to-law" process in which the number of particles as well as the direction of each were causally determined. Yet no amount of precise observation will enable him to predict either number, direction, or speed with accuracy. This, in Weber's thesis, is exactly analagous to the logical structure of historical events.[7]

It may seem that the preceding argument tends to establish the case for a close affinity of the methods of history and of science. For this reason it is important to mark well the dialectical turn which enables Weber to arrive at the opposite conclusion. So far we have been concerned with the logic of the material: viewed from this angle the fall of the Roman Empire is, so to speak, comparable to our falling rock. But what is not at all comparable is the *goal of our inquiry* in the two cases. To the scientist, the individual event as such has no interest whatever because his search is directed at those measureable quantitative relationships which are formulated as "natural laws." To the historian, on the other hand, it is the individual event which counts. His interest is centered on the qualitative uniqueness adhering to historical processes by virtue of their significance for our own culture values. Therefore the methodology of history calls conversely for the formation of concepts "of ever greater actual content, hence ever smaller extent." [8] To establish general "laws" of historical evolution may be entirely possible, but it would be a useless pursuit, tending to deprive history of its living meaning which is contingent upon individual rather than upon generalization.[9]

Closely related is the question of the objectivity of historical judgments. Since this question lends itself to discussion on many different levels, it might be profitable to define first what it meant in the discussion which Weber entered with his article on the "Objectivity of our Knowledge of Society." [10] Breaking down the logical content of any historical work, one finds it made up of three kinds of judgments: 1) judgments as to facts, 2) causal judgments, that is the correlation of concrete causes to concrete effects in any particular or general historical situation; and 3) explicit or implicit value judgments, in which the behavior of historical groups or individuals is measured by some ethical norm. With few exceptions, social philosophers have generally conceded the possibility of valid statements in the first category, subject only to the epistemological limitations of all knowledge. Thus the greatest methodological problem of historical research in its narrower technical sense does not enter here. Weber's discussion proceeds on the basis of the assumption that facts are at least theoretically ascertainable. His concern is with the problems presented by judgments in the last two categories.

Starting with his concept of the rationality of human behavior, causal analysis necessarily appeared to Weber as the very core of the labors of the historian. Although he recognized the need for detailed research, he had little patience with those who followed too literally Ranke's prescription that history is merely the record of *wie es eigentlich gewesen ist*. The important thing to him was why things have been as they were and not otherwise. The obvious difficulty of objective causal analysis lies in the fact that causal relations in history are not verifiable by the test of the experiment, as they are in the sciences. Each constellation in the process of the evolution of mankind, though it may contain elements which are frequently repeated, also contains elements which are unique. Furthermore, the number of facts which may go into the interpretation of any portion of history is theoretically infinite, hence it is impossible to assemble complete data. These theoretical difficulties have led many historians to deny altogether the possibility of objective causal judgments in history. According to their reasoning, whatever degree of plausibility and general acceptance it might attain, the interpretive work of the historian in terms of cause and effect could never attain the rank of positive empirical knowledge. Causal judgments then would appear as mere surmises or opinions, always open to challenge from some other point of view. Carried to its logical conclusion the argument would culminate in the thesis of the absolute subjectivity of historical knowledge, most consistently stated by Croce in his doctrine of the contemporaneity of all history.

In his polemic against this school of thought, Weber pointed out that the complexity of data is only a limiting factor, not one which in any sense vitiates objectivity. The same condition prevails in many of the so-called exact sciences, biology for instance. The point, in his opinion, was that in spite of the infinite number of historical facts, the number of facts relevant to any particular problem could be limited without arbitrariness. Causal analysis, though admittedly difficult, can attain a high degree of objective validity by utilizing to the full the methods of analogy and comparative interpretation. While the historian is deprived of the benefit of experimental verification, he must think in terms of verification of his conclusions by intellectual processes. In order to establish the causal significance of any one factor in a chain of events, he must eliminate all other possible factors by "thinking them away," and by drawing into comparison a large number of situations, otherwise as closely analogous as possible, in which this particular factor was absent. By abstraction he might be able to trace the course of history under modified conditions, always checking the flight of his imagination by solid factual information. The "if" question, usually looked upon by historians as idle speculation, thus became in Weber's theory one of the cornerstones of historical thinking. It lies at the very heart of the process which Weber calls "causal imputation" (*Kausalzurechnung*), consisting in the steps just described. Evidently, it is based on the assumption that the number of possible developments in any particular situation is small enough to allow such a procedure. For if "anything could have happened" in the absense of any one factor, the social scientist trying to follow this method would obviously be engaging in the labors of Sisyphus. Actually, this idea is central to Weber's methodology and further developed in the concept of "objective possibility," which signifies a concrete chance for a certain outcome of a defined historical situation. It is in terms of probability then that we can determine the "adequacy" of the causal correlation which we seek.[11]

Weber has given us a classical example of this method in the "Protestant Ethic," where many pages are devoted to a comparative analysis of economic systems in different civilizations in order to establish the decisive causal significance of the religious factor in the rise of modern capitalism. If posterity has not regarded his conclusions as "objectively valid" in the sense of his methodology, this does not necessarily constitute an argument against it. For in principle the theory, or epistemology, of historical knowledge has nothing to do with the success of any one investigator.

There are, however, logical difficulties in the thesis of "causal imputation." The weakest link in Weber's whole chain of reasoning seems to be that the rational intent of individuals appears as the determining element of their social behavior thus becoming the pivot of all causal correlation in history. Weber rejects the "Zeitgeist" theories in which the "spirit" of a period, or of a people, attains the dignity of a supra-individual reality, acting as "historical force." "Historismus" in this sense is to him—and rightly so—pure metaphysics. Yet in his own solution he refuses to go all the way in the opposite direction, which would reduce his position to mere "psychologismus." On the contrary, with equal vigor he rejects the idea that the final answers to the riddle of society lie with the science of psychology.

Without psychological foundation, however, the whole concept of the rationality of human actions remains hopelessly vague if applied to the individual.[12] If accepted on Weber's own terms simply as a "chance" or "probability" based on experience only (and entirely without psychological content), the objection arises that it seems logically impossible to use statistical concepts which have meaning only as tools of quantitative measurement without quantitative implications. The word "chance" has no scientific significance whatever unless it means a chance of a certain magnitude. Deprived of quantitative content it is little more than just a way of speaking, and certainly not capable of conferring upon any conclusions derived from it the sanction of scientific validity.

In his later work, especially in the posthumously published *Wirtschaft und Gesellschaft*, there are strong indications that Weber at least partially abandoned his earlier theories on the objectivity of causal judgments, and tended ever more to accept the distinction made by Dilthey between positive knowledge in science and "understanding" in the social field. Thus he approached more closely the position taken by the theorists of the so-called *"Verstehende Soziologie"* which was fundamentally at odds with his whole view of the relationship between science and history, without, however, formally repudiating any of his previous statements.[13]

In any case, the search for causes always remained for Weber a highly legitimate concern, and indeed, the foremost task of the social scientist and historian. Evaluative judgments of any kind, on the other hand, were to him anathema. Inasmuch as history could claim scientific value, the historian must cease to be a moralist and stop thinking of himself as sitting in judgment over past generations. Not only must he be *sine ira et studio* in the generally accepted sense of an obligation to give both sides a fair hearing, he must also declare himself incompetent to decide between them. In other words, he must be more than merely free from any particular moral bias: he must free himself from the bias of morality altogether, at least as far as his work is concerned.

History is, to use the term coined by Weber, *wertfrei:* "It can never be the task of an empirical science to search for valid norms and ideals in order to derive from them rules for practical conduct." [14] The apparent simplicity of this argument should not deceive us about the tremendous complexity of the logical and philosophical problem involved. Ever since Plato identified true knowledge and virtue, men have striven to attain, on one level or another, a rational synthesis of the two. Both ethical absolutism and ethical relativism in their various forms take issue with Weber's thesis of *Wertfreiheit,* though on opposite grounds. So it is not surprising that he found himself under considerable fire on this point, his critics insisting that *Wertfreiheit* in the last analysis is impossible because any interpretation of values—without which history is unthinkable—requires in turn orientation within a certain framework of values. Since all significant historical data are in some way related to values, and since it is this relation which gives them meaning and interest, the requirement of *Wertfreiheit* would reduce the historian to a mere compiler of statistics. Weber himself realized that evaluative judgments necessarily enter into the primary work of the historian, namely into the selection of the material, and that there can be no objective measure of what is, and what is not, worthwhile subject matter. Furthermore, subjectivity enters in yet another sense, inasmuch as the pursuit of historical knowledge itself is based on the objectively undemonstrable assumption that culture is valuable.[15] It may be that this concession partially vitiated the principles of *Wertfreiheit* because there is in practice no logical hiatus between the process of selection and that of analysis. In fact, the former is probably more often determined by the latter than vice versa. Thus it would seem that Weber throws evaluative judgments out the front door, only to let them creep in surreptitiously by the back door. It is, for example, difficult to read Weber's essays on the sociology of religion without feeling that their author actually regarded the "irrational," otherworldly values of oriental society as ethically on a higher plane than those of our rational capitalistic order.[16] It would also be possible to cite any number of statements from Weber's work which patently contradict the requirement of *Wertfreiheit.*[17] As Mommsen points out, Weber was convinced that the ideal types could be developed on a purely empirical basis. He believed that he had discovered a method of operation which would permit the analysis of human action through the centuries independent of value judgments. Viewed from this vantage point, values merely constitute material for empirical analysis. However, as Mommsen states: "There appears to be no doubt today but this grandiose undertaking could not have succeeded completely. Weber's vast sociology was by no means free from value judgment." [18]

The broader aspects of this question are clarified by analysis of the position of some of the most important schools of thought regarding "values." *Historismus* generally had resulted in a wide acceptance of the "historicity" or relativity of ethical or other ideals, leading to the conception that the real task of the historian lies in the continual reinterpretation of the values of the past in terms of those of the present, a trend which might be said to have culminated in Croce. Hegelian dialectics with its long-run identification of the "real" and the "desirable," expressed in the formula: *alles was ist soll sein,* pointed toward another solution, in which the validity of ethical norms is simply demonstrated by their practice. Marxism, too, derives the objective measures of values from the process of history itself by its equation between progress and necessity, although its relativistic approach to value systems seen as ideologies was perhaps more conspicuous. Building upon the Hegelian-Marxian foundation, Troeltsch and Mannheim tried to show that the sanction of history is the true test of the validity of ethics; hence the "absolute validity."

It is especially against all such attempts to equate the actuality of history with that of morals that Weber fought. The principle of *Wertfreiheit* stemmed precisely from his conviction that no such equation was possible, and that neither the accomplished nor the impending triumph of any set of values has the least significance with regard to their validity.[19] On the other side of the philosophical fence were the adherents of the phenomenologist school, led by Husserl and Scheler, who rejected both Weber's ethical agnosticism and form of ethical relativism on the ground that an objectively valid hierarchy of values can be shown to be "given" in the same sense as time and space are "given" in physics.[20]

While Weber's methodological propositions include practical as well as theoretical limits which cannot be consistently overcome within his own system,[21] the importance of his contribution to the epistemology of the historical sciences should not be underestimated. His criticism of what may be called historical agnosticisms is basically sound, even though his demonstration of the possibility of positive knowledge of causal correlation in history may fail to bridge the gap between individual motivation (rational intent) and social causation. Although it cannot be carried into the sphere of the absolute, the principle of *Wertfreiheit* remains a valuable practical approach to historical writing, and a true measure of the degree of the historian's emancipation from the "ideologue." Thus Arnold Brecht writes:

As Max Weber's name has become a trademark for 'value-free science' it is important to stress that the emphasis of his article was rather on the methods by which science *can* deal with value judgments than on full abstention. 'What is the implication of this proposition?' he asked after the statement just quoted. And he answered: '*It is certainly not that value judgments are to be withdrawn from scientific discussion in general. . . .* Practical action and the aims of our journal would always reject such a proposition.' This was followed by the fundamental statement that '*criticism is not to be suspended in the presence of value judgments.* The problem is rather: what is the meaning and purpose of the scientific criticism of ideals and value judgments?' It is this question to which the main part of his analysis addressed itself.[22]

The theory of ideal types, moreover, has been of great importance for the development of sociology, especially in its application to structural analysis of socio-economic organization along the lines of *Wirtschaft und Gesellschaft* and the *General Economic History*. While Weber found few contemporary disciples in the strict sense of the word, his methodological concepts have nevertheless profoundly influenced a whole generation of students in the field of social science.

NOTES

[1] Reinhard Bendix, *Max Weber: An Intellectual Portrait* (Garden City: Doubleday & Co., 1960), p. 274 ff.

[2] For a comparison of Weber and Rickert see Alexander von Schelting, *Max Webers Wissenschaftslehre: Das logische Problem der historischen Kulturerkenntnis. Die Grenzen der Soziologie des Wissens* (Tuebingen: J. C. B. Mohr [P. Siebeck], 1954), pp. 220–222, p. 232 ff. Also: Marcel Weinreich, *Max Weber: L'Homme et Le Savant* (Paris: Les Presses Modernes, 1938), pp. 45–66.

[3] Max Weber, *Gesammelte Aufsaetze zur Wissenschaftslehre* (Tuebingen: J. C. B. Mohr [P. Siebeck], 1922), p. 224.

[4] Andreas Walther, "Max Weber als Soziologe," *Jahrbuch fuer Soziologie*, Vol. 2 (Karlsruhe: G. Braun, 1926), p. 42. For the formal definition of rational behavior see Max Weber, *op. cit.*, pp. 227–229. For an excellent discussion of Weber's thesis see Walther Wegener, *Die Quellen der Wissenschaftsauffassung Max Webers und die Problematik der Werturteilsfreiheit der Nationaloekonomie* (Berlin: Duncker & Humblot, 1962), p. 163.

[5] Weber attacked these problems especially in his critique of Eduard Meyer, a well-known German historian of the period; Weber's answer to the thesis of historical subjectivism based on the uniqueness of the psychological material is incorporated in this polemic. Weber, *op. cit.*, pp. 274–277. See also Schelting's very extensive discussion of Weber's critique of Eduard Meyer in Schelting, *op. cit.*, p. 269 ff.

[6] Max Weber, *op. cit.*, p. 226. Cf. also Schelting, *op. cit.*, p. 186.

[7] Max Weber, *op. cit.*, p. 65.

[8] Max Weber, "Roscher und Knies und die logischen Probleme der historischen Nationaloekonomie. I: Roschers historische Methoden. II and III: Knies und das Irrationalitaetsproblem" (*Schmollers Jahrbuch*, 1903–1906). Cf. also Wegener, *op. cit.*, pp. 123–225.

[9] Compare A. Salomon, "Max Weber's Methodology," *Social Research*, Vol. I, 1934, p. 159 ff. A. Schelting, *op. cit.*, pp. 123–225.

[10] Max Weber, "Die Objektivitaet Sozialwissenschaftlicher und Sozialpolitischer Erkenntnis," *Archiv fuer Sozialwissenschaft und Sozialpolitik*, Vol. 19, 1904. Cf. also Wolfgang Mommsen, *Max Weber und die Deutsche Politik 1890–1920* (Tuebingen: J. C. B. Mohr, 1959), p. 69 f.

[11] Max Weber, *Gesammelte Aufsaetze zur Wissenschaftslehre*, pp. 274–276. Cf. Wegener, *op. cit.*, pp. 141–143.

[12] Cf. Walther Wegener, *op. cit.*, pp. 39–42.

13 See Schelting, *op. cit.*, p. 370 ff. Cf. Walther, *op. cit.*, p. 32. In this connection see also Talcott Parsons, "Max Weber 1864–1964," *American Sociological Review*, Vol. 30, No. 2, April 1965, pp. 171–175.

14 Max Weber, *Gesammelte Aufsaetze zur Wissenschaftslehre*, p. 149; also Talcott Parsons, "Wertgebundenheit und Objektivitaet in den Sozialwissenschaften: Eine Interpretation der Beitraege Max Webers," *Max Weber und die Soziologie heute* (Verhandlungen des 15. Deutschen Soziologentages (Tuebingen: J. C. B. Mohr [P. Siebeck], 1965), pp. 45–64.

15 Max Weber, *Gesammelte Aufsaetze zur Wissenschaftslehre*, pp. 174–175.

16 For a discussion of this question see Hermann J. Grab, *Der Begriff des Rationalen in der Soziologie Max Webers: Ein Beitrag zu den philosophischen Grundlegung der Sozialwissenschaft)*, (Karlsruhe: G. Braun, 1927), p. 36 ff.

17 See Max Weber, *General Economic History*, translated by F. H. Knight (London: George Allen & Unwin, Ltd., 1927), p. 84: "The mismanagement of the Northern victors (in the American Civil War) who even gave the Negroes a privileged position, resulting in a universal exclusion of the negroes from the suffrage and in the establishment of a strong caste distinction." And p. 86: "From the end of the 16th century the Czars placed their entire power and that of their entire administration at the service of the nobility. The peasant had no more rights than a Roman slave and the right of knouting was expressly granted to the lords." Both of these statements may be entirely acceptable by standards of objectivity generally, but not by that of Wertfreiheit, because they do appear to carry evaluative weight. It is hardly possible to regard the reference to conditions in Russia without sensing the implication of a condemnation of the system. However, in fairness to Weber it should be mentioned that he did not personally supervise the publication of *General Economic History*, which was compiled from his lectures posthumously. Possibly he would have eliminated such passages.

18 Mommsen, *op. cit.*, pp. 69–71. Other examples of incongruity are cited in this work.

19 Max Weber, *Gesammelte Politische Schriften* (Munich: Drei Masken Verlag, 1921), p. 23, p. 154; and Schelting's discussion of the principle "Wertirrationalitaet" in Weber, *op. cit.*, pp. 32 ff.

20 See Grab, *op. cit.*, p. 13 ff. for criticism of Weber from this point of view.

21 Max Horkheimer, "Diskussion zum Thema: Wertfreiheit und Objektivitaet," *Max Weber und die Soziologie heute* (Verhandlungen des 15. Deutschen Soziologentages (Tuebingen: J. C. B. Mohr [P. Siebeck], 1965), pp. 65–67.

22 Arnold Brecht, *Political Theory: The Foundations of Twentieth-Century Political Thought* (Princeton: Princeton University Press, 1967), p. 223.

INDEX